Preparation Processes of Nonfinancial KPIs for Management Reports

MÜNSTERANER SCHRIFTEN ZUR INTERNATIONALEN UNTERNEHMENSRECHNUNG

Herausgegeben von Peter Kajüter

Band 18

Zu Qualitätssicherung und Peer Review der vorliegenden Publikation

Die Qualität der in dieser Reihe erscheinenden Arbeiten wird vor der Publikation durch den Herausgeber der Reihe geprüft.

Notes on the quality assurance and peer review of this publication

Prior to publication, the quality of the work published in this series is reviewed by the editor of the series.

Matthias Nienaber

Preparation Processes of Nonfinancial KPIs for Management Reports

Empirical Evidence on Process Design and Determinants

PETER LANG

Bibliographic Information published by the Deutsche Nationalbibliothek
The Deutsche Nationalbibliothek lists this publication in the Deutsche Nationalbibliografie; detailed bibliographic data is available in the internet at http://dnb.d-nb.de.

Library of Congress Cataloging-in-Publication Data
A CIP catalog record for this book has been applied for at the Library of Congress.

Zugl.: Münster (Westfalen), Univ., Diss., 2019

D 6
ISSN 1868-7687
ISBN 978-3-631-80279-3
E-ISBN 978-3-631-80434-6 (E-PDF)
E-ISBN 978-3-631-80435-3 (EPUB)
E-ISBN 978-3-631-80436-0 (MOBI)
DOI 10.3726/b16237

Peter Lang – Berlin · Bern · Bruxelles · New York · Oxford · Warszawa · Wien

This publication has been peer reviewed.

www.peterlang.com

Preface

Due to their ability to convey additional information regarding a firm's economic, ecologic and social performance, the importance of nonfinancial key performance indicators (nfKPIs) in corporate reporting has steadily been increasing in recent years. This importance is reflected in the growing supply of nfKPI disclosures by companies and the demand for nfKPIs from stakeholders such as capital market participants or the general public. To support this trend, regulators have strengthened the requirements for nfKPI reporting through for example the CSR directive in Europe. Furthermore, several standard setters such as the Global Reporting Initiative (GRI) or the International Integrated Reporting Council (IIRC) provide frameworks for the preparation of nfKPIs for corporate reporting.

Nonetheless, nfKPI disclosures vary strongly between firms with regard to the scope and extent of their disclosure. As one reason for potential differences between disclosures, Matthias Nienaber looks at the preparation process of nfKPIs for the management report, which until now has been considered a "black box". On the basis of interviews with experts from different areas and hierarchical levels in three publicly listed and four privately held German companies, the study examines the preparation process using two research questions. First, the study determines the design of the preparation process, which consists of the phases and participants of the process. Second, the study examines factors influencing the design of preparation processes. These research questions are addressed by individually analyzing the processes of the case firms through within-case analyses and by comparing and contrasting these findings in cross-case analyses. In the course of the analyses, the study discusses the findings in the light of a theoretical framework of organizational theories, namely institutional theory, behavioral decision theory and the promotor model.

Regarding the preparation process design, the process phases are determined on the basis of a conceptual process model developed in accordance with practitioner guidelines and reporting frameworks. While the study finds similarities regarding the general process phases such as the materiality analysis or the composition of the report draft, firms can differ strongly with regard to, for example, the formality of the process or the sources used to collect nfKPIs for the management report draft. On the basis of the promotor model the study identifies the roles of the process participants and examines their communication with other participants and internal or external stakeholders. Although the promotor structures within the firms appear to be effective when preparing nfKPIs for the management report, the study finds that promotor roles are distributed differently across firms. On the one hand, multiple participants in large firms seem to share individual roles. On the other hand, smaller firms with fewer participants tend to combine roles due to limited resources, fewer preparation tasks or the participants' overview over the internal information environment. Finally, the study uses the integrated theoretical framework and the findings of the previous analyses to determine factors influencing the design of the preparation process. These internal and external factors vary in their influence on the process design and are regularly interlinked depending on the particular context of the firm. While the study confirms organizational size and listing as important influencing factors, other factors such as an integrated reporting format or regulatory requirements can also influence the process design to a considerable degree. Overall, the theoretical framework supports an understanding of how the process design can be affected from within or outside of the firm.

The study contributes to an understanding of the preparation process of nfKPIs for management reports in multiple ways. The foundations of this study aim to clarify the associated terminology regarding nfKPIs and the preparation process. Furthermore, this explorative study extends the literature on preparing mandatory nonfinancial information in corporate reporting. Through its solid research design and theoretical framework, the study enables in-depth insights into the preparation process from several organizational perspectives. Similarly, the process model and empirical findings provide valuable contributions for process stakeholders such as preparers, statutory auditors, management report users, regulators and standard setters.

In the light of these contributions and the growing relevance of nfKPIs in management reporting, I strongly wish that this thesis will attract attention of both academics and practitioners alike.

Münster, June 2019 Prof. Dr. Peter Kajüter

Acknowledgement

"Never allow your knowledge to stand in the way of truth." (Ajahn Brahm)

I have conducted this study during my time as a PhD student at the Chair of International Accounting at the University of Münster. The Münster School of Business and Economics accepted this thesis as a dissertation in May 2019.

In this acknowledgement, I am expressing my deep gratitude to everyone who has supported me throughout this exciting phase of my life. First, I wish to thank my academic teacher and supervisor Prof. Dr. Peter Kajüter. Ever since my bachelor studies, he has supported and encouraged me to pursue my goals in academia and practice. Through his high demand on quality, his constructive feedback and helpful guidance he contributed greatly to the success of this study. Moreover, his trust and confidence allowed me to grow as a researcher, teacher and colleague. I would also like to thank Prof. Dr. Hans-Jürgen Kirsch and Prof. Dr. Bernd Kempa as the members of the review committee.

Likewise, I want to express my gratitude to my current and former colleagues at the Chair of International Accounting. Ever since our time as student assistants, Prof. Dr. Martin Nienhaus has taken on an important role as a mentor and friend. I am very thankful for his guidance, feedback and inexhaustible positivity. I will never forget the countless Currywurst dinners with him and his wonderful family. Many of these have also been accompanied by Martin Vogelpohl, with whom I had the pleasure to share an office for two years. In addition to the laughs we shared over our favorite shows and jokes, I am very thankful for his sincerity and support throughout the years. Similar to him, my fellow qualitative research colleague Henrik Schirmacher provided valuable support from the early beginnings to the final review stages of my dissertation. In addition to his motivating and uplifting words, I thank him and Martin Vogelpohl for their comedic talent in cheering up my busy days. Moreover, I owe my gratitude to Kai Schaumann and Daniel Gayk, with whom I spent countless hours preparing and coaching students for case study competitions. I thank both of them for these highly educational experiences and for their relentless motivation and spirit to advance case study teaching in Münster. Not to forget, I dearly remember our athletic successes in tower running, relay marathons and triathlons.

I am also very thankful to Dr. Stefan Hannen, who has trained me in the art of preparing our chair's annual report and other press-related tasks. In addition to our time creating amusing "art pieces", I cherish his feedback and guidance with regard to my research and my doctoral studies. Similarly, I thank Manuel Herkenhoff for his patience and motivation to acquire these tasks from me. Not only am I absolutely sure that his Photoshop skills will exceed mine by far in the near future, I am also amazed at his natural talent in swimming. I thank Stephanie Eckerth for always being open for my questions and for encouraging me to pursue my goals. She has always inspired me to help others even in the busiest times. I am grateful for many enjoyable table soccer matches with Friedrich Kalden, who amongst all the "trash talk" surrounding these matches always found the time for helpful advice. With my office neighbor Max Meinhövel I share fond and amusing memories of our flat at Monash, our Master studies and our mutual graduation ceremony. He always lent me a helping hand when I needed one.

To Marcel Baki, I want to express my gratitude for his gladly received supply of chocolate, pastry and relentless humor. Similarly, I would like to thank my younger team colleagues Tobias Gerwing, Niklas Kerkhoff, Florian Kooke, Arne Lessenich, Christoph Mauritz, Jonas Pöhler, Christian Rave, Moritz Steffien and Maximilian Wirth for their support and countless contributions to the team spirit. Furthermore, I will always keep fond memories of the unforgettable times I had with my former colleagues Dr. Gregor Hagemann, Dr. Florian Klassmann, Dr. Daniela Peters, Dr. Maximilian Saucke, Dr. Moritz Schröder and Dr. Alexander Schulz. I am always looking forward to meeting them again on the Chair's Christmas parties. In addition, I owe great thanks to our Chair's student assistants for their support. I particularly want to thank Paul Bruns, Katharina Högemann, Christopher Oehler, Philip Unrein and Saskia Warm for their efforts in various phases of my thesis. Finally, I sincerely thank our Chair's secretary Tobias Langehaneberg for assisting me in terms of administrative challenges and for being a wonderful companion for tea breaks.

Additionally, I am very thankful to my friends and club colleagues for taking my mind off work. In particular, I owe gratitude to Sven and Sabrina Tietz and Miriam Varón Romero for making my time in Münster a wonderful and memorable experience. I am looking forward to creating numerous new memories with them in the future. Similarly, I am grateful for my friends from school and university with whom I love to share memories of the "good old days" and who are also always up for creating new ones. I always enjoy reconnecting with them throughout my time in Münster and beyond.

This thesis would not have been possible without the support of my family. Numerous family meetings with aunts, uncles and cousins took my mind off the challenges ahead and helped me to reconnect with those things in life that are truly important. I am also incredibly lucky to welcome my mother-in-law Isabella Chodura and her relatives into my family. I thank her and all of my new and old relatives for being there for me in good and tough times. Particularly, I thank my sister Julia Nienaber and my brother Felix Nienaber for the fun trips, enjoyable conversations and their humor which always lift me up when I am in need. Moreover, I drew a lot of my inspiration and strength from the values my grandparents have taught me. I will never forget your love, dedication and encouragement.

From the bottom of my heart, I want to thank my wife Astrid Nienaber. Ever since we met, we have trusted and supported one another. Whenever I was challenged, you knew exactly how to lift me up. Whenever I could, I lent you a hand and cheered you up with one of my jokes. I could not have dreamt of a better wife, partner and friend as you. Together with you, I am excited to begin this new phase of life that lies ahead of us.

Finally, I am especially grateful to my parents Maria and Klaus Nienaber, without whom this thesis would not have seen the light of day. In all these years in Bocholt, Tucson, Dortmund, Münster, Melbourne and Essen you have always been at my side. I am unimaginably lucky to know that you are always there for me with your unconditional love and support. For everything you have given, I thank you with my whole heart. I am looking forward to the countless opportunities to be there for you as well.

Münster, June 2019 Matthias Nienaber

Overview of contents

Table of contents

Index of figures

Index of tables

Index of abbreviations

AA1000AS	AccountAbility 1000 Accounting Standard
AKEU	Arbeitskreis Externe Unternehmensrechnung der Schmalenbach-Gesellschaft für Betriebswirtschaft e.V.
AktG	Aktiengesetz (German Stock Corporation Act)
ASCG	Accounting Standards Committee of Germany
BGBlt.	Bundesgesetzblatt (Federal Law Gazette)
BilReG	Bilanzrechtsreformgesetz (German Accounting Law Reform Act)
BiRiLiG	Bilanzrichtlinien-Gesetz (Accounting Directives Act)
BMJV	Bundesministerium der Justiz und für Verbraucherschutz (Federal Ministry of Justice and Consumer Protection)
BT-Drucksache	Bundestagsdrucksache (Bundestag printed matter)
CEO	Chief Executive Officer
CFO	Chief Financial Officer
CFOA	Assistant to the Chief Financial Officer
CMO	Chief Marketing Officer
CO_2	Carbon dioxide
Col.	Column(s)
COO	Chief Operating Officer
CPO	Chief People Officer
CSR	Corporate social responsibility
CSR-RUG	CSR-Richtlinie-Umsetzungsgesetz (CSR Directive Implementation Act)
DBM	Database manager
DNK	Deutscher Nachhaltigkeitskodex (German Sustainability Code)
Dr.	Doctor
DRÄS	Deutscher Rechnungslegungs Änderungsstandard (German Amendment Accounting Standard)
DVFA	Deutsche Vereinigung für Finanzanalyse und Asset Management (Society of Investment Professionals in Germany)
Ed.	Editor
Eds.	Editors
EFFAS	European Federation of Financial Analysts Societies
e.g.	Exempli gratia (for example)

ESCP-EAP	ESCP Europe Wirtschaftshochschule Berlin (formerly: École Supérieur de Commerce de Paris – École des Affaires de Paris)
Et al.	Et alia (and others)
Etc.	Et cetera (and so forth)
e.V.	Eingetragener Verein (registered association)
EU	European Union
EY	Ernst & Young (accounting network)
FASB	Financial Accounting Standards Board
FEE	Fédération des Experts-comptables Européens (Federation of European Accountants)
FMJ	German Federal Ministry of Justice
FTSE100	Financial Times Stock Exchange 100
GAAS	German Amendment Accounting Standard
GAS	German Accounting Standard
GRI	Global Reporting Initiative
HA	Head of accounting
HDAX	German stock index consisting of the 110 largest corporations
HDBM	Head of database management
HEIR	Head of external and internal reporting
HER	Head of external reporting
HGB	Handelsgesetzbuch (German Commercial Code)
HLEG	High-level expert group on sustainable finance
HMQR	Head of management and quarterly reporting
HR	Human resources
HRM	Human resources manager
HRS	Human resources strategy manager
HSC	Head of safety controlling
HSE	Health, safety and environment
http	Hypertext Transfer Protocol
IAASB	International Auditing and Assurance Standards Board
IAS	International Accounting Standard(s)
IASB	International Accounting Standards Board
i.e.	Id est (that is)
IDW	Institut der Wirtschaftsprüfer in Deutschland e.V.
IDW EPS	Entwurf eines Institut der Wirtschaftsprüfer in Deutschland e.V. Prüfungsstandards

IDW PS	Institut der Wirtschaftsprüfer in Deutschland e.V. Prüfungsstandard
IEEE	Institute of Electrical and Electronics Engineers
IFAC	International Federation of Accountants
IFRS	International Financial Reporting Standards
IIRC	International Integrated Reporting Council
IR	Investor relations
IRM(s)	Investor relations manager(s)
ISAE	International Standard on Assurance Engagements
ISO	International Organization for Standardization
IT	Information technology
KPI(s)	Key performance indicator(s)
KPMG	KPMG International (accounting network) (formerly "Klynveld, Peat, Marwick and Goerdeler")
KSFs	Key success factors
MD&A	Management's Discussion and Analysis of Financial Condition and Results of Operations
MEIR	Manager for external and internal reporting
MQR	Manager for management and quarterly reporting
MSc	Master of Science
MSD	Manager of the sustainability department
MSP	Manager sustainable procurement
n.F.	neue Fassung (revised version)
nfKPI(s)	Nonfinancial key performance indicator(s)
NGO(s)	Nongovernmental organization(s)
No.	Number(s)
Nr.	Nummer (number)
OFR	Operating Financial Review
p.	Page
Par.	Paragraph
pp.	Pages
PRM	Public relations manager
Prof.	Professor
QDA	Qualitative data analysis
QEHS	Quality, environment, health and safety

R&D	Research and development
Rec.	Recital
RGBl.	Reichsgesetzblatt (National law gazette)
RNE	German Council for Sustainable Development
SAP	Database software provided by SAP SE (formerly "Systemanalyse und Programmentwicklung" – Systems, Applications & Products in Data Processing)
SASB	Sustainability Accounting Standards Board
SC(s)	Safety controller(s)
SEC	Securities and Exchange Commission
Sent.	Sentence
SME(s)	Small and medium-sized enterprise(s)
StB	Steuerberater (tax consultant)
UK	United Kingdom
UN	United Nations
UNEP	United Nations Environment Programme
URL	Uniform Resource Locator
US	United States
USA	United States of America
Vol.	Volume
Vs.	Versus
WCED	World Commission on Environment and Development
www	World Wide Web

Index of symbols

&	And
€	Euro
n	Number of observations
§	Paragraph
§§	Paragraphs
%	Percent
✓	Permitted (according to GAS 20)
✗	Not permitted (according to GAS 20)

1 Introduction

1.1 Motivation and research questions

In recent years, the growing importance of nonfinancial reporting in general and **nonfinancial key performance indicators (nfKPIs)** in particular has substantially changed the landscape of corporate reporting. As both stakeholders and reporting firms highlight the relevance of nfKPIs and their reporting (*EY* (2015); *Dong* (2017); *Smith/van der Heijden* (2017); *Givoly et al.* (2019)), the demand and supply of this information has steadily been increasing. In addition, this growing trend has been supported by regulators, particularly in the European Union (EU), who have strengthened nfKPI reporting through the modernization directive (2003/51/EC) and the corporate social responsibility (CSR) directive (2014/95/EU). Moreover, voluntary reporting frameworks such as the Global Reporting Initiative (GRI) Standards or the International Integrated Reporting Framework of the International Integrated Reporting Council (IIRC) provide guidance on nfKPI reporting.[1]

While the importance of nfKPIs in corporate reporting is growing, studies find significant **differences and inconsistencies** in terms of nfKPI reporting across firms (*Mio et al.* (2015); *Schaefer/Schröder* (2015); *Fisch/Mujkanovic* (2015)). Besides external factors such as firm visibility or industry (*Hahn/Kühnen* (2013), p. 12), researchers also examine internal factors such as decision-making processes to explain differences in reporting. Common explanations with regard to firm-internal decision processes are the firms' use of discretion (*Osann* (2010), p. 3; *Bouten/Everaert* (2015), pp. 26-28), the noncompliance with regulation (*Day/Woodward* (2004), p. 55) or differences in understanding of the term nfKPIs itself (*Haller et al.* (2017); *Stolowy/Paugam* (2018)). Moreover, prior research suggests that the **internal organization** of the preparation process affects the disclosure decisions of nfKPIs (*Solomon/Edgley* (2008), p. 337).

In the context of decision-making processes for nfKPI disclosures, preparers face several **challenges**. Firms are commonly challenged by identifying material nfKPIs (*Arena/Azzone* (2012), p. 671; *Calabrese et al.* (2015), pp. 314-315), measuring and standardizing such indicators (*Luft* (2009), p. 310; *Ittner/Larcker* (2009), pp. 1237-1240) and managing the complexity of the phases and participants of the preparation processes (*Tarca et al.* (2011), pp. 47-48; *Osann* (2010), p. 259). Thus, to ensure a successful preparation process of nfKPIs, "management must know the people and processes involved in putting it together" (*Rouse* (2013), p. 91).

While extensive research exists on the characteristics, determinants and consequences of nfKPI reporting (*Hahn/Kühnen* (2013), pp. 10-14; *AKEU* (2015), pp. 240-244; *Grewal et al.* (2015)), few studies have analyzed the **preparation of nfKPIs** from an internal perspective:[2]

> *"There has been little prior research work into the internal processes of corporate ethical, social and environmental reporting or attitudes which influence decision-making. [...]*

---

1 For an overview of the regulation and guidance on nfKPI reporting see section 2.2.

2 For an overview of the literature on preparation processes nfKPIs and corporate reporting see chapter 3.

[A]cademic research has been lagging behind developments in practice in this respect." (Adams (2002), p. 228)

For this reason, many researchers have called for more **research on the design of the preparation process of nfKPIs** and on how internal and external factors influence this process (e.g., *Belkaoui/Karpik* (1989) p. 47; *Larrinaga-González/Bebbington* (2001), pp. 287-288; *Gray* (2005), p. 16; *Adams/Frost* (2008), p. 288; *Hahn/Kühnen* (2013) p. 15). Such research could support an understanding of the phases of the preparation processes, the roles of process participants and major challenges of the process (*Searcy/Buslovich* (2014), p. 150). Moreover, findings could provide insights into how internal and external factors influence the phases and roles comprising the preparation process of nfKPI reporting (*DiMaggio/Powell* (1983), pp. 157-158; *Thomson/Bebbington* (2005), pp. 529-530). In the face of the growing importance of nfKPIs and their reporting, this study aims to address this gap in the literature.

This lack of research regarding the preparation process of nfKPIs calls for an **explorative research approach**. Moreover, heterogeneous preparation processes and organizational contexts obstruct standardized quantitative research approaches. Thus, this study uses semi-structured expert interviews to inductively determine the preparation process of nfKPIs for management reports. This reactive and interpretative approach enables to determine both the process phases and the relationships and communication between the participants. Through a multiple case study approach with firms of different industries, sizes and ownership structures, the process and participant structures can be contrasted and interpreted on the basis of their particular contexts. In addition, factors can be derived which influence preparation processes. Overall, this approach is in line with calls for more qualitative research on the preparation processes of nonfinancial reporting (*Adams/Frost* (2008), p. 300; *Osann* (2010), pp. 261-264; *Searcy/Buslovich* (2014), pp. 167-168).

Following calls for research on mandatory nfKPI reporting (*Hahn/Kühnen* (2013), p. 15; *Searcy/Buslovich* (2014), p. 168; *Erkens et al.* (2015), p. 46), this study focuses on preparation processes of nfKPIs for management reports[3] in **German firms**. For this study, the German regulatory environment is suitable for several reasons. First, by transforming the European modernization directive and CSR directive into national law, German lawmakers have established and strengthened mandatory nfKPI reporting by requiring firms to include relevant nfKPIs in their management reports or in separate nonfinancial reports, respectively. Therefore, German management reports should provide a minimum mandatory acceptable level of nfKPI reporting (*Cohen et al.* (2012), pp. 68–69). Second, management reporting regulation in Germany has a long tradition characterized by continuous improvements (*Fink et al.* (2013), p. 7). Third, German management report regulation plays a leading role in Europe in requiring particular formats and contents of the report through national reporting standards such as the German Accounting Standard No. 20 "Group Management Report" (GAS 20). Fourth, preparing and publishing management reports is required for all listed and almost all medium-sized and large non-listed German firms. Thus, German firms are very experienced in preparing such documents. Fifth, German firms are

3 Due to the largely analogous requirements and for simplification reasons, the term "management report" refers to both management and group management reports in this study, unless stated otherwise.

required to have their management reports audited by a statutory auditor with reasonable assurance.[4] This circumstance points to an already existing instrument for auditing the reliability and credibility of nfKPIs in management reports (*Fink et al.* (2013), p. 287). In summary, German management reporting is particularly suitable for this study due to extensive regulation and considerable experience of reporting firms regarding the mandatory preparation of nfKPIs.

Based on the high relevance for research and practice, this study focuses on the preparation processes of nfKPIs in management reports of German firms. The overall goal of this study is to reveal and analyze the phases and participants constituting this process and to shed light on the factors influencing the preparation process. Therefore, the following **research questions** are pursued:

1) How is the preparation process of nfKPIs for management reports designed?
2) What influences the design of the preparation process of nfKPIs for management reports?

To analyze these research questions, this study uses within-case and cross-case analyses of the nfKPI preparation processes of three publicly listed and four private German firms. The first research question is separated into analyses of the phases and participants of the preparation process of nfKPIs for management reports. The second research question draws from the results of the analyses to identify factors which influence the preparation processes.

This study provides several **contributions.** First, preparers of nfKPIs for management reports or nonfinancial reports can learn about the steps and challenges related to the preparation process. These insights could help them benchmark and optimize their own reporting processes. Second, auditors can learn from differences and challenges related to the preparation processes of nfKPIs to prepare themselves for or improve their own audit processes of nfKPIs. Third, the results of this study can inform management report users about the preparation of management reports to help them analyze the credibility and trustworthiness of nfKPIs in management reports. Fourth, it can help other researchers understand processes and influencing factors of preparing nfKPIs, which could support analyses regarding the determinants and consequences of nfKPI reporting. Finally, this study can help standard setters and regulators understand how requirements regarding nfKPIs are applied within reporting firms and which reasons could exist for differences in nfKPI reporting.

1.2 Scientific positioning

As a foundation for approaching the research questions at hand, this section sets out the scientific objectives, approach and strategy underlying this study. Overall, the term "science" refers to a process of systematically gaining knowledge (*Raffée* (1974), p. 13; *Fülbier* (2004), p. 267). Such scientific knowledge requires reasoning, which differentiates this type of knowledge from intuition and beliefs (*Kornmeier* (2007), p. 4). In addition to discussing the definition of science, the **philosophy of science** – as a so-called meta-science – provides

[4] This requirement exceeds the demands of European audit regulation (*Kajüter et al.* (2017), p. 803).

guidance to researchers on how to attain scientific objectives (*Kornmeier* (2007), p. 8; *Frank* (2007), col. 2010).

Schweitzer differentiates four **objectives of science** (*Schweitzer* (1978), pp. 3-9). According to the descriptive objective, science precisely documents and defines the characteristics of a research object. Exceeding these descriptions, the explanative objective explains causal relationships. The pragmatic objective of science uses these relations as a basis for projections and decision-making. Finally, the normative objective of science uses theoretical knowledge to conduct value judgements and to provide recommendations. By providing rich and in-depth descriptions of real-life processes, the study at hand follows the descriptive objective of science. On this basis, the study examines the commonalities, differences and contexts of the cases to provide explanations for the design and influencing factors of the preparation processes. Subsequently, this study derives implications for preparers, users, auditors and assurance providers of management reports and informs both standard setters and regulators. While these implications support the pragmatic objective of science, this study does not provide normative recommendations with regard to the preparation process of nfKPIs for management reports.

Research in the science of business administration today is mostly shaped by two scientific approaches: constructivism and critical rationalism (*Fülbier* (2004), p. 268). **Constructivism** assumes that knowledge is derived from arguments using deductive reasoning (*Fülbier* (2004), p. 269; *Kornmeier* (2007), p. 40). While arguments can in the best case be mutually accepted, constructivists believe that theories regarding human behavior can be revoked (*Lorenzen* (1974), pp. 113-118). This is justified by the assumptions that human actions are not deterministic and that arguments are fallible (*Kornmeier* (2007), p. 40).

Similar to constructivism, **critical rationalism** assumes that human reasoning is fallible (*Fülbier* (2004), p. 268; *Popper* (2005), pp. 16-17). As a consequence of this assumption, absolute and verifiable proof can never be achieved through reasoning (*Lingnau* (1995), p. 124; *Popper* (2005), pp. 16-17). Nonetheless, reasoning can be perceived as valid until it is determined to be incorrect (*Bartel* (1990), p. 58). To advance scientific knowledge, researchers attempt to falsify and readjust positions and arguments in the form of hypotheses (*Popper* (2005), pp. XXXIII-XXXIV, 16-19; *Kornmeier* (2007), p. 42).

To date, the majority of research studies in business administration follows the critical rationalism approach (*Fülbier* (2004), p. 269). Considering the constraints of critical rationalism in the context of complex and multi-perspective phenomena, solely relying on this research approach would limit the possibility for scientific advancement and innovation (*Brühl* (2017), pp. 3-9). Hence, allowing for a **variety of scientific approaches** enables researchers to examine complex phenomena from different angles and perspectives.

This study follows the constructivist approach. Building on the insights and perspectives of various organizational participants, the researcher reconstructs and analyzes preparation processes of nfKPIs for management reports. Through contrasting these processes and combining the results with extant theory and literature, the study inductively determines the design and influencing factors of the preparation processes.

In conjunction with selecting a scientific research approach, researchers need to decide on a **research strategy**. In the science of business administration, three major research strategies prevail (*Grochla* (1978), p. 71):[5] conceptual, analytical and empirical.

The **conceptual** research strategy aims at reconstructing complex relationships through reasoning to develop plausible recommendations (*Grochla* (1978), pp. 72-78). This research strategy typically yields descriptive deductions which are not tested empirically.

In contrast to this strategy, the **analytical** research strategy uses abstract models to analyze specific phenomena (*Grochla* (1978), pp. 85-93). Researchers test different methods on these models to find optimal solutions for a research problem. In this approach, researchers knowingly abstract the models from reality to a certain extent to arrive at a basis for decision-making.

The **empirical** research strategy investigates whether theories can be transferred to real-life phenomena or if they should be rejected (*Grochla* (1978), pp. 78-85). Such investigations can be carried out by contrasting the real-life phenomena to theoretical descriptions. Another mode of investigation can be to test causal relationships suggested by the theories.

After analyzing the preparation process of nfKPIs and deriving a conceptual framework, **this study** uses an empirical research strategy. On the basis of in-depth descriptions of real-life preparation processes, these phenomena are compared and contrasted to provide explanations for the design and influencing factors of preparation processes of nfKPIs for management reports. This serves to advance extant theories and to provide stakeholders of these processes with relevant implications.

1.3 Outline of the study

The outline of the study is displayed in Figure 1-1. Based on the motivation, research questions and contribution of the study at hand, **chapter one** presents the scientific research strategy followed by this study. This step provides reasons for the selection of the research approach applied.

Chapter two presents the conceptual foundation of the study. The first part of the chapter lays out the terminology of the study by differentiating nonfinancial information from financial information. This serves as a foundation for developing the term nfKPIs. Subsequently, the term management reporting is discussed. The second part of the chapter presents the requirements and guidelines of relevant for management reporting on nfKPIs in Germany. Subsequently, the third part of the chapter develops a conceptual framework for the preparation process of nfKPIs.

Chapter three reviews the two separate research streams of the preparation of nfKPIs and the preparation process of corporate reports. Subsequently, the chapter summarizes the shortcomings and gaps in the literature and derives how they are addressed in this study.

---

5 While researchers generally focus on one research strategy, they typically apply the other strategies as well, albeit to a lesser extent (*Grochla* (1978), p. 68).

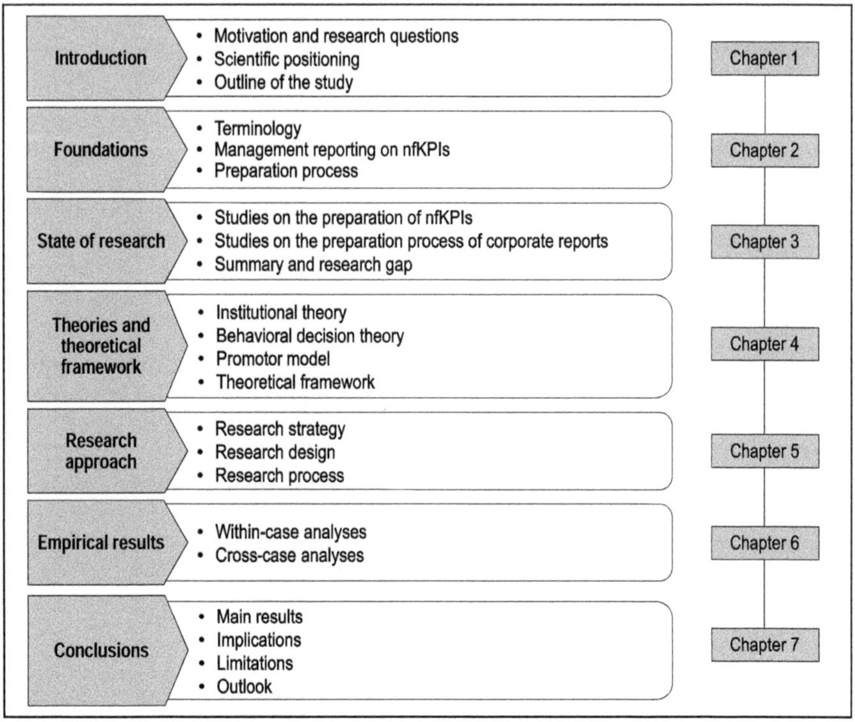

Figure 1-1: Outline of the study

The theoretical foundation of this study is presented in **chapter four**. The chapter discusses the institutional theory, behavioral decision theory and the promotor model. Each theory is then linked to the preparation process of nfKPIs in management reports. Building on this, the chapter presents an integrated theoretical framework for the study. This framework combines the perspectives of all three theories to form a suitable model for examining the design and influencing factors of the preparation process of nfKPIs.

Chapter five discloses the research approach of this study in three successive sections. First, the suitability of the qualitative research strategy of this study is discussed. Subsequently, principles of qualitative research are identified. Second, the chapter discusses the selection and implementation of case study research as the fundamental research design of the study. The final section discloses the research process of this study by presenting the methods applied to select, collect and analyze the data and by discussing the quality criteria applied.

Chapter six presents the empirical results of this study. The first section of chapter six provides within-case analyses of the case studies. This section describes the organizational profile of each case firm and analyzes the phases and participants of their preparation process. In the cross-case analysis, the results from the case studies are compared and contrasted with regard to the phases, participants and influencing factors of the preparation processes.

Moreover, the results are discussed in the light of extant literature and the theoretical framework of this study.

The study closes with **chapter seven**, which highlights the main results and implications of this study. After discussing the limitation of the present research, the study ends with an outlook for future research and regulatory developments.

2 Foundations

2.1 Terminology

In contrast to financial information, the terms **nonfinancial information and nfKPIs** embrace a wider range of concepts, indicators and areas of corporate performance (*Haller et al.* (2017), pp. 407-408; *Stolowy/Paugam* (2018), pp. 528-531). However, only few researchers provide criteria and definitions to differentiate these types of information from financial information or KPIs (*Eccles/Krzus* (2010), pp. 81-84; *Erkens et al.* (2015), pp. 20-26). Thus, this section sheds light on the rather elusive concepts of nonfinancial information and nfKPIs. To do so, section 2.1.1 delineates financial from nonfinancial information and discusses the dimensions of nonfinancial information. Building on this, section 2.1.2 develops nfKPIs as a subcategory of nonfinancial information. Subsequently, section 2.1.3 discusses the term management reporting to identify media for internal and external nfKPI reporting.

2.1.1 Definition and dimensions of nonfinancial information

The **distinction between nonfinancial and financial data** is addressed differently within the literature. Instead of defining nonfinancial information, researchers commonly contrast it to financial information.[6] Nonfinancial information is typically distinguished from financial information with regard to the location, nature and units of measurement of the information (*Luft* (2009), pp. 311-312; *Orens/Lybaert* (2010), p. 40; *Erkens et al.* (2015), pp. 24-25).

First, nonfinancial information differs from financial information regarding the **location** of disclosure. The Financial Accounting Standards Board (FASB) defines nonfinancial information as "disclosures and metrics [which] include index scores, ratios, counts and other information not presented in the basic financial statements" (*FASB* (2001), p. 5). Therefore, a distinguishing feature of nonfinancial information is their presentation outside of the financial statements (*Robb et al.* (2001), p. 72). This definition could for example refer to information in the management report or sustainability report as nonfinancial information.

According to the second criterion, financial and nonfinancial information can be differentiated by the **nature** of the information. Based on the assumption that nonfinancial information is neither derived from financial accounting nor from financial statements, it is defined by some authors as "non-accounting information" (*Amir/Lev* (1996), p. 28; *Barker/Imam* (2008), p. 320). Hence, nonfinancial information is not calculated on the basis of an accounting standard and does not refer directly to financial statement information (*Admiraal et al.* (2009), p. 15; *Eccles/Krzus* (2010), p. 83). In this context, earnings forecasts are considered as financial information because they reflect financial statements measures (*nature*), although they are published outside of the financial statements (*location*) (*Orens/Lybaert* (2010), p. 40).

6 For a review of the literature on the definition of nonfinancial information see *Erkens et al.* (2015).

The third differentiation criterion focuses on the **units of measurement** of the information. Some authors suggest that currency denominated information should be defined as financial information, in turn defining nonfinancial information as non-currency denominated information (*Nagar/Rajan* (2001), p. 496; *Cinquini et al.* (2012), p. 560). Hence, warranty costs would be considered financial information while the amount of warranty claims is regarded as nonfinancial information.

To distinguish nonfinancial from financial information, **this study** draws from the first two differentiation criteria. Figure 2-1 summarizes the deduction of this definition. With regard to the location, disclosures provided outside of the financial statements are considered to be nonfinancial information. However, as financial statement information such as revenues or assets can also be disclosed outside of the financial statements – for example in the management report – this study further differentiates the information by its nature. Although measures such as customer profitability or quality costs can be derived from accounting information (*Luft* (2009), p. 308), they are not calculated on the basis of an accounting standard and are therefore considered to be nonfinancial information. The same holds true for compound measures such as warranty costs or CO_2 emissions per € 1 million of revenue, as these neither refer to financial statement information nor are they calculated according to an accounting standard. Evidently, these first two methods allow for currency denominated nonfinancial information (*Flöstrand/Ström* (2006), p. 581). To preserve a broad definition of nonfinancial information, the third differentiation criterion is not used in this study.

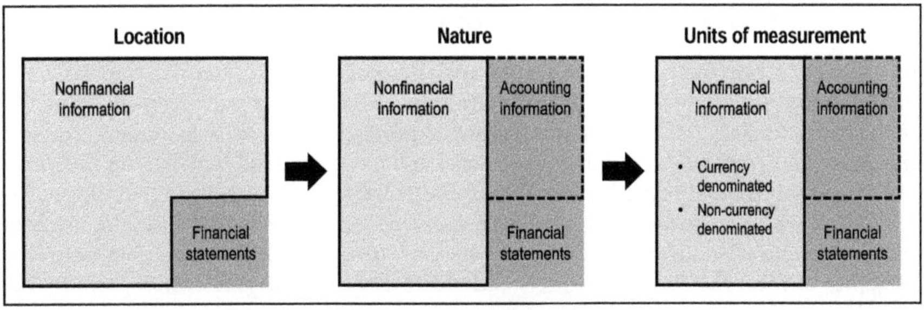

Figure 2-1: Deduction of the definition of nonfinancial information

In summary, this study applies the following **definition** of nonfinancial information:

> *Nonfinancial information is currency and non-currency denominated information which is disclosed outside the financial statements, is not calculated on the basis of an accounting standard and does not refer directly to financial statement information.*

Research highlights the **broad scope of nonfinancial information**. Studies on nonfinancial information examine corporate reporting with respect to economic (*Amir/Lev* (1996); *Nagar/Rajan* (2001); *Wyatt* (2008)), environmental (*Cormier/Magnan* (2003); *Holland/Foo* (2003); *Guidry/Patten* (2012)) or social performance (*Spicer* (1978); *Gray* (2002); *Fifka*

(2012)).[7] In the corporate reporting literature, various concepts join these three dimensions of nonfinancial information to explain the construct of **sustainability**.[8] Two major concepts that have emerged are *CSR* and *corporate sustainability* (*Loew et al.* (2004), pp. 70-74; *Labbé/Stein* (2007), p. 2661; *Hahn/Kühnen* (2013), p. 6.). Figure 2-2 illustrates the relationship between the sustainability concepts and the dimensions of nonfinancial information, which are explained in the following.

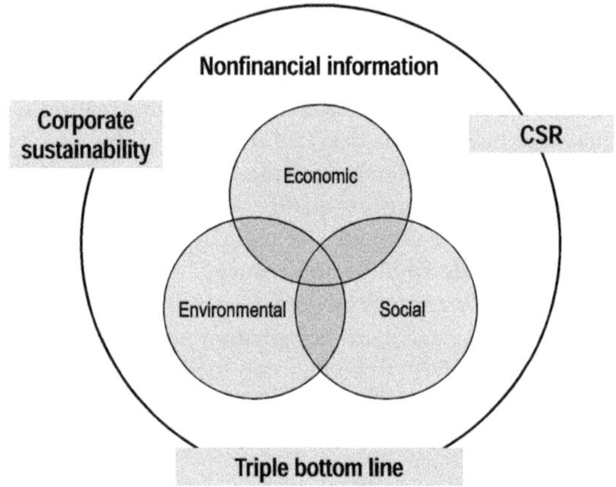

Figure 2-2: Dimensions of nonfinancial information and sustainability concepts

Initially, the **CSR** concept focused on the social responsibility of companies towards the public (*Loew et al.* (2004), pp. 7-11). Environmental issues have later been added to this concept after ongoing debates on environmental protection. Today, it is seen as a concept which supports companies in integrating social and environmental matters into their economic and stakeholder-related actions (*Loew et al.* (2004), p. 73; *Horrigan* (2010), pp. 34-35). The **corporate sustainability** concept mandates that firms should meet the needs of current direct and indirect stakeholders (*intragenerational justice*) "without compromising its ability to meet the needs of future stakeholders as well" (*intergenerational justice*) (*Dyllick/Hockerts* (2002), pp. 131-132).[9] To do so, firms need to "maintain and grow their economic, social and environmental capital base" (*Dyllick/Hockerts* (2002), p. 132). As both the CSR concept and the corporate sustainability concept have gradually converged over time, they largely overlap and are seen as consistent (*Loew et al.* (2004), p. 74; *Hahn/Kühnen* (2013), p. 6).

---

7 While some researchers focus on individual dimensions, many others analyze them in combination. Moreover, some authors combine general nonfinancial dimensions with specific areas of nonfinancial information such as governance (*Eccles et al.* (2011); *Cohen et al.* (2015); *Brooks/Oikonomou* (2018)).

8 For a discussion of the most important concepts see *Blaesing* (2013), pp. 12-17.

9 This definition transfers the general definition of sustainability from the United Nations World Commission on Environment and Development (the so-called Brundtland Report) to the sustainable development of companies (*WCED* (1987); *Hahn/Kühnen* (2013), p. 6).

Both concepts strongly build on the three dimensions of sustainability in connection with the so-called "**triple-bottom-line**" (*Elkington* (1997), pp. 70-74). This triple-bottom-line concept highlights that the long-term overall success and sustainability of a firm is likely not based on economic success alone (*Gladwin et al.* (1995), p. 879). Proponents of the triple-bottom-line argue that a company needs to balance its success in the economic, environmental and social dimensions to sustain its position in the market in the long run (*Elkington* (1997), pp. 73-74; *Crane/Matten* (2016), pp. 32-37).

In the light of these sustainability concepts, the three dimensions of nonfinancial information shed light on the effects of a firm's actions. The **economic** dimension reflects the dimension most widely equated with corporate success. It is commonly assumed that the economic purpose of companies is to preserve and expand capabilities to create profits while remaining competitive in the market (*Ramanathan* (1976), p. 516; *Labbé/Stein* (2007), p. 2661; *Boms* (2008), pp. 89-91). From a nonfinancial perspective, the economic success of a firm can be evaluated by the firm's ability to accumulate tangible and intangible assets such as market share, innovations or procedural knowledge (*Roos et al.* (1998), pp. 15-18; *Ashton* (2005), pp. 57-58; *White* (2010) p. 31). However, this traditional view typically disregards potential effects of economic actions in terms of the environmental and social dimensions (*Boms* (2008), pp. 89-91). Such effects are indicated by the intersections between the dimensions in the figure above.

Following the idea of the triple-bottom line, the scope of corporate goals is broadened through the environmental and social dimension (*Dyllick/Hockerts* (2002), p. 133). The **environmental** dimension builds on the circumstance that natural resources are limited and companies are an integral part of the ecosystem (*Crane/Matten* (2016), pp. 33-34). To preserve this ecologic capital, companies need to effectively manage their consumption of natural resources (*Lovins et al.* (1999), p. 146). This resource consumption can for example be measured by the amount of waste or green-house gas emissions generated for the production of a firm's products. The **social** dimension reflects how an organization's actions affect both its employees and society as a whole with respect to social stability, justice and equal opportunity (*Blaesing* (2013), p. 17). Information on social performance could for example comprise injury rates of workers or the engagement in local community development programs.

Companies often perceive **a conflict of objectives** between the economic and the other two dimensions (*Clausen et al.* (2001), p. 37; *Gray/Milne* (2004), pp. 74-75). Thus, firms try to avoid interferences with economic goals by limiting environmental and social goals to tight budgets (*Walley/Whitehead* (1994), p. 50; *Gray/Milne* (2004), p. 75). Moreover, environmental and social goals are only preferred when they do not collide with financial goals or when they are financially profitable. However, focusing heavily on the economic dimension neglects **interlinkages** between all three dimensions. Researchers argue that interactions between the dimensions lead to a long-term integration of environmental and social goals into economic goals (*Dyllick/Hockerts* (2002), p. 136; *Schaltegger et al.* (2006), pp. 7-12; *Lozano/Huisingh* (2011), p. 106).

On the basis of these dimensions and of the sustainability concepts, this study takes on a **broad understanding** of nonfinancial information. While, for example, a particular information could stem from one individual dimension (e.g., market share as an economic information), it is also possible for nonfinancial information to reflect an overlap of two or three dimensions (e.g., resource consumption as both an economic and environmental information).

To offer a holistic view of their sustainable development, companies should **report** their performance in all three dimensions (*Gray/Milne* (2004), p. 75; *Hahn/Kühnen* (2013) p. 7). In addition to traditional financial reporting, such holistic reporting enables companies to present their stewardship with respect to their usage of common resources and their impacts on the environment and society (*Benston* (1982), pp. 95-100; *Gray/Milne* (2004), pp. 75-76).[10] Therefore, reporting on nonfinancial information should address the economic, environmental and social dimension. Suitable reporting media for such disclosures are discussed in section 2.1.3.

2.1.2 Nonfinancial KPIs

In this section, a definition of nfKPIs is derived by identifying the individual elements of this term. Building on the definition of indicators, KPIs are identified as a subcategory of this type of information. Subsequently, the characteristics of indicators and KPIs are combined with those of nonfinancial information to derive a definition of nfKPIs.

Indicators

The accounting literature differentiates indicators from key figures (*Küpper et al.* (2013), pp. 476-477; *Weber/Schäffer* (2016), p. 177). **Key figures** are reported in quantitative form and reflect certain relevant economic realities in a condensed way (*Schaltegger et al.* (2007), p. 119; *Küpper et al.* (2013), p. 471).[11] By reducing complex economic realities to insightful and actionable data in the form of key figures, decision-making processes can be simplified and accelerated (*Lachnit* (1979), pp. 15-19; *Weber/Schäffer* (2016), pp. 177). Moreover, interrelated key figures can be used to construct key figure systems as a basis for analyses or developing goals (*Küpper et al.* (2013), pp. 472-473).

Similar to key figures, **indicators** can also condense complex economic issues to quantitative figures (*Bossel* (1999), p. 9; *Weber/Schäffer* (2016), p. 177). However, key figures typically form a subset of indicators (*Franceschini et al.* (2007), p. 60; *Küpper et al.* (2013), p. 477). The scope of indicators is commonly broader in comparison to key figures, as indicators can include qualitative information (e.g., employee training or community engagement programs) and can also be used to approximate indirectly measurable items (e.g., employee satisfaction) (*Gallopín* (1997), p. 17; *Schaltegger et al.* (2007), p. 119; *Küpper et al.* (2013), p. 477). In the latter case, inferences can be drawn only to a certain extent, as the underlying

---

[10] The benefits and challenges of this type of reporting are critically discussed in the literature (*Hahn/Kühnen* (2013); *Brooks/Oikonomou* (2018)).

[11] Key figures can be classified as absolute measures (e.g., total assets or profit) or ratios (e.g., return on equity) (*Küpper et al.* (2013), pp. 471-472).

relationship between the indicator and the issue of interest is typically unclear or difficult to determine (*Küpper et al.* (2013), p. 477). Nonetheless, these indicators can be used as a reference for interpreting or forecasting particular issues (*Gladen* (2014), p. 9).

Indicators can be **classified** with regard to their object of observation and their objectivity (*Picot* (1977), pp. 210-211; *Wysocki* (1981), pp. 119-122; *Weber* (1983), pp. 98-100; *Kaplan/Norton* (1996), pp. 31-32). Figure 2-3 illustrates these classifications.

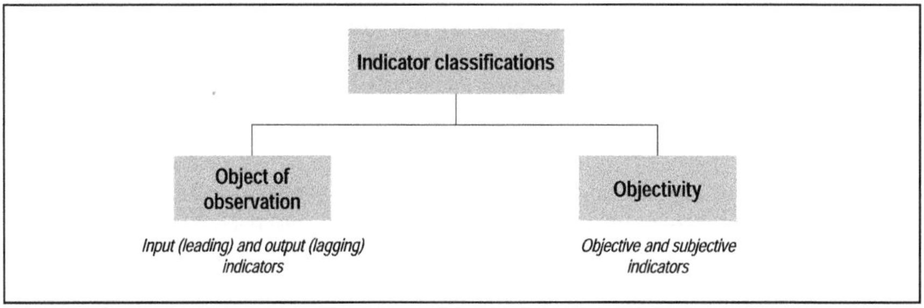

Figure 2-3: Indicator classifications

On the one hand, the **object of observation** of indicators describes the input factors (*input indicators*) applied to achieve certain goals (*Jäger* (1974), p. 124). In this context, input indicators are often referred to as *leading indicators*, as they provide guidance and early signals for the attainment of the targeted goals (*Kaplan/Norton* (1996), pp. 31-32). Input indicators could for example be the ratio of trained sales assistants or percentage of electric cars in a delivery fleet. On the other hand, an indicator could also examine the output factors (*output indicators*) (*Jäger* (1974), p. 124). In this context, indicators form *lagging indicators* relating to specific financial or nonfinancial goals (e.g., a 10% increase in sales revenues or a 10% reduction in CO_2 emissions) (*Kaplan/Norton* (1996), pp. 31-32). With these indicators, firms can assess whether or not their goals have been achieved (*Figge et al.* (2002), p. 271). In connection to sales assistant trainings, an output indicator could be the sales revenues or service quality perceived by customers.

Measuring input factors is often more straightforward than measuring output factors (*Weber* (1983), p. 98). However, output factors typically have a higher correspondence with the goals that are evaluated. Moreover, relationships between input and output indicators can be visualized in a **cause-and-effect network**, in which input indicators can also act as outcome indicators for preceding performance drivers (*Kaplan/Norton* (1996), pp. 30-31; *Epstein/Roy* (2001), p. 595; *Figge et al.* (2002), p. 271).

In terms of their **objectivity**, indicators may reflect measures that can be validated objectively (*objective indicators*) such as the number of patents submitted. Contrarily to objective indicators, indicators could also be based on subjective perceptions (*subjective indicators*) such as customer satisfaction scores (*Kaplan/Norton* (1996), p. 10; *Luft* (2009), p. 312).[12]

[12] While some authors support the use of objective performance measures (*Ittner et al.* (2003)), others emphasize the importance of subjective measures (*Bushman et al.* (1996); *Moers* (2005)).

Due to their limited focus on specific, measurable aspects of reality, indicators face particular **caveats.** Potential risks arise when companies confine themselves to the narrow goals reflected in these measures (*Etzioni/Lehman* (1967), pp. 2-3; *Weber* (1983), pp. 99-100). While indicators typically focus on single dimensions of organizational phenomena, multi-dimensional decisions may require combinations of several indicators to arrive at functional and effective conclusions.[13] Moreover, firms should scrutinize the validity and reliability of the measures to determine whether they are suitable for evaluating their goals (*Etzioni/Lehman* (1967), p. 11; *Schaltegger et al.* (2007), p. 121). Judgements based on indicators can be threatened if relationships between the indicators and issues of interests are unclear or if the indicators are manipulated or measured incorrectly (*Luft* (2009), pp. 311-316).

KPIs

KPIs[14] can be defined as "the financial or nonfinancial measures (metrics) used at different levels in organizations to evaluate success in achieving their objectives, KSFs, strategies and plans [...]" (*Ferreira/Otley* (2009), p. 271). Researchers argue that the success of a certain strategy depends on implementing or achieving the relevant KPIs (*Simons* (1995), p. 63; *Banker et al.* (2004), p. 2). This importance of KPIs differentiates them from indicators, as KPIs measure the key performance drivers with the greatest impact on the goal attainment (*Figge et al.* (2002), p. 271).

This importance of KPIs for the goal attainment forms the basis for **determining** a firm's KPIs. By reflecting on their business model, goals or stakeholder demands (*Epstein/Roy* (2001), pp. 589-592, *Searcy et al.* (2009), p. 35), firms can identify potentially important KPIs. As these factors are typically closely linked to a firm's industry, organizational structure and strategy (*Ittner/Larcker* (2001), pp. 377-381), relevant KPIs are likely to vary across firms and potentially even between business units. In addition to deducing appropriate and distinct KPIs on the basis of such reflections, firms can also base their selection on suggestions by reporting frameworks such as the GRI Standards (*Keeble et al.* (2003), p. 151). However, it is commonly argued that the extensiveness of such frameworks poses particular challenges for smaller firms, as they could be challenged with identifying KPIs material to management and stakeholders, measuring these indicators and providing sufficient resources to perform this process (*Clarke-Sather et al.* (2011), p. 254).

While the link between KPIs and goal attainment marks a central basis for the importance of the indicators, firms commonly struggle to find direct causalities regarding this link (*Chenhall* (2003); *Van der Stede et al.* (2006)). To implement and interpret KPIs, firms can establish implicit or explicit **causal models** between the expected performance drivers (e.g., employee training) and the objectives pursued (e.g., increased sales revenues) (*Kaplan/Norton* (1996), pp. 30-31).[15] Such leading KPIs that are linked to outcome measures of a strategy can hence provide a "dashboard" for managerial decision-making (*Perrini/Tencati*

---

[13] See *Munda* (2005) for examples of sustainability decisions based on multiple indicators.

[14] In the literature, other frequently used terms for KPIs are key performance measures (e.g., *Ferreira/Otley* (2009)) or critical performance variables (e.g., *Simons* (1995)).

[15] Researchers suggest using strategy maps and cause-effect-relationships to visualize and develop such causal models (*Kaplan/Norton* (1996), pp. 30-31).

(2006), p. 304; *Schewe et al.* (2009), pp. 6-7; *Eccles/Krzus* (2010), p. 89). Important KPIs are typically implemented in a firm's performance measurement system to support managerial decision-making and to provide an instrument for monitoring and aligning individual behavior (*Simons* (1995), pp. 63-85; *Luft* (2009), pp. 309-310; *Ferreira/Otley* (2009), pp. 271, 275). Hence, KPIs can provide guidance and structure for managerial decisions or could be linked to monetary incentives to promote beneficial actions towards the firm's goals (*Epstein/Roy* (2001), pp. 593-594). In connection with regular control and review of the indicators, KPIs can foster the accountability of organizational actors to make important contributions towards corporate goal achievement (*Keeble et al.* (2003), pp. 151-152).

When managing on the basis of KPIs, firms should also consider the weighting and number of these KPIs. Concerning the **weighting**, the relative importance of KPIs with regard to goal attainment should be reflected in the firm's KPI system (*Luft* (2009), p. 316; *Küpper et al.* (2013), pp. 480-481). By establishing realistic cause-and-effect relationships between input and output measures, KPI users can interpret the indicators and potential interdependencies more efficiently and accurately (*Schaltegger et al.* (2007), p. 119; *Luft* (2009), p. 310). With regard to the appropriate **number** of KPIs employed in a firm, researchers argue that limiting KPIs to a few central indicators improves the users' focus on the respective indicators (*Ferreira/Otley* (2009), pp. 271). While no absolute number is considered to be ideal, the recommended maximum of KPIs typically ranges between five and 25 (*Kaplan/Norton* (1996), p. 162; *Parmenter* (2010), p. 87). Nonetheless, researchers consider the optimum number of KPIs to be firm-specific (*Kaplan/Norton* (1996), p. 162).

Definition of nonfinancial KPIs

On the basis of the discussions above, the term nfKPIs can be defined. The first part of the definition combines the definition of indicators with the definition of its subgroup of KPIs. As KPIs comprise both financial and nonfinancial measures, nfKPIs are separated from financial KPIs in the second part of the definition. This differentiation is based on the definition of nonfinancial information. As highlighted in Figure 2-4, this study combines the three above mentioned elements for the following **definition of nfKPIs:**

> ***NfKPIs** condense and approximate the key performance drivers of the organizational goals in a quantitative or qualitative form, are provided outside the financial statements and are neither calculated on the basis of an accounting standard nor do they refer directly to financial statement information.*

As nfKPIs mark the **key performance drivers** of a firm's organizational goals, these indicators reflect a sub-section of nonfinancial information. In terms of the three dimensions of nonfinancial information, nfKPIs highly contribute to a firm's economic, environmental and social goals (Figure 2-5). In this context, the allocation of nfKPIs with regard to the individual dimensions is likely to vary across firms depending on the importance of the firm's economic, environmental and social goals. As firms' economic goals are commonly regarded as superior to the goals related to the other two dimensions, it can be expected that economic nfKPIs exceed environmental and social nfKPIs both in terms of their extent and importance.

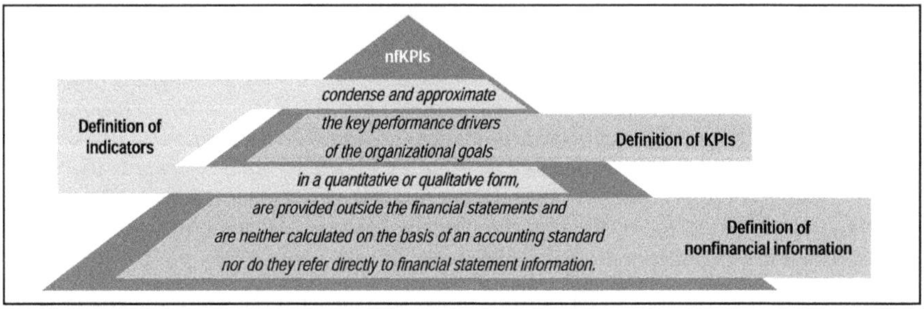

Figure 2-4: Elements of the definition of nfKPIs

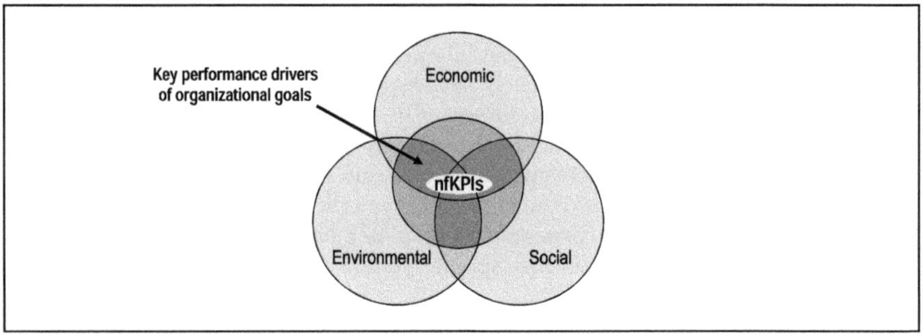

Figure 2-5: Dimensions of organizational goals in terms of nfKPIs

2.1.3 Management reporting

Management reporting comprises a variety of suitable media through which nfKPIs can be reported. Using a broad definition, management reporting describes the information transfer of facts, events, relationships and processes concerning a company and its environment (*Blohm* (1974), p. 15; *Freidank/Weber* (2008), p. 396). Depending on the audience of the particular information, such communication can be differentiated into internal and external management reporting (*Blohm* (1974), p. 15; *Koch* (1994), p. 49; *Freidank/Weber* (2008), p. 396). These two types of management reporting comprise several reporting media, which are discussed in the following (Figure 2-6).

Internal management reporting comprises all information transfer processes within or between the governing bodies (i.e., executive and supervisory board) and the departments of the firm (*Theisen* (2007), pp. 5-8; *Freidank/Hinze* (2014), p. 454). Internal management reporting with regard to nfKPIs is based on strategic or operational nonfinancial information which could for example be provided by sustainability accounting (*Fischer et al.* (2009), pp. 271-277). In contrast, **external management reporting** provides a company's external stakeholders with relevant backward- and forward-looking information in qualitative or quantitative form (*Böcking* (1998), p. 44; *Freidank/Hinze* (2014), p. 454).

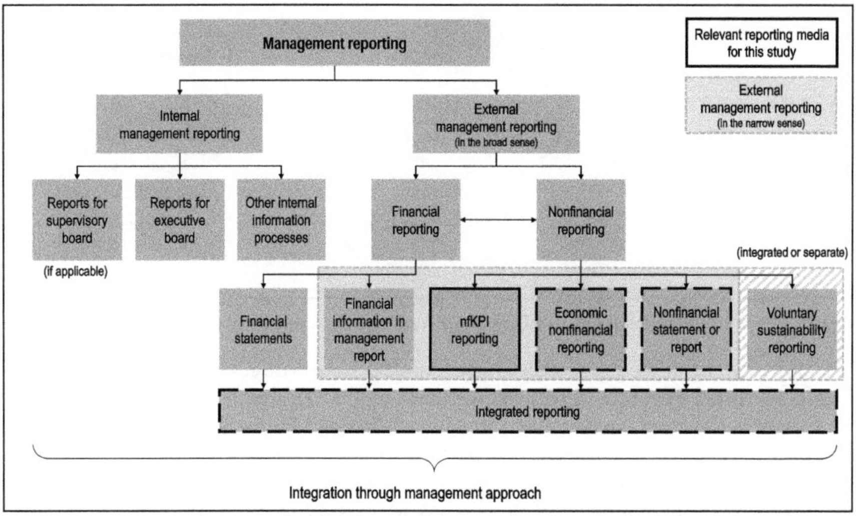

Figure 2-6: Types and media of management reporting (based on *Freidank/Weber* (2008), p. 399; *Freidank/Hinze* (2014), p. 454)

Although the objectives of internal and external management reporting diverge, the concept of the **management approach** integrates the information used for the internal management of the group into the reporting towards external stakeholders (*AKEU* (2002), p. 2339; *Merschdorf* (2012), pp. 33-40).[16] As a consequence of this approach, external stakeholders can gain insights into the information environment of the firm's executive board.

External management reporting (in the broad sense) is also referred to as **business reporting**, which comprises financial and nonfinancial reporting (*Noll/Weygandt* (1997), p. 59). **Financial reporting** represents financial accounting information communicated in the financial statements and specific sections of the management report (*Freidank/Weber* (2008), p. 396; *Fink et al.* (2013), pp. 3-5). In this context, the term management report (in the narrow sense) refers to a separate document which complements the financial statements (*Hartmann* (2006), p. 13; *Fink et al.* (2013), pp. 3-5). Such management reports fulfil a dual function as they allow for the reporting of both financial and nonfinancial information.

Nonfinancial reporting supplements the financial reporting information through nonfinancial information regarding the economic, environmental and social performance of the firm (*Brooks/Oikonomou* (2018), pp. 2-3). As a result, nonfinancial reporting supports the firm's stakeholders in gaining a complete understanding of a firm's performance. This type of management reporting comprises several mandatory and voluntary reporting media: nfKPI reporting, economic nonfinancial reporting, nonfinancial statements or reports and voluntary sustainability reporting. Figure 2-7 indicates the dimensions of nonfinancial information covered by these nonfinancial reporting media.

16 See section 2.2.1.2 for a discussion of the management approach for nfKPIs in management reports.

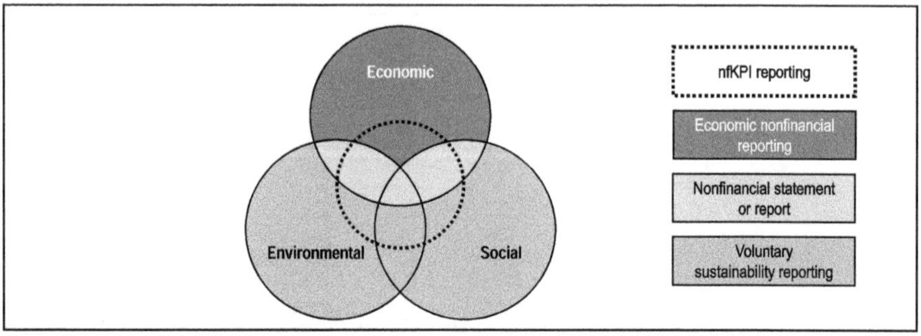

Figure 2-7: Dimensions of nonfinancial information covered by nonfinancial reporting media

The dotted circle in the figure above indicates **nfKPI reporting**, which refers to the mandatory disclosure of nfKPIs in the management report. This type of reporting marks the core reporting medium analyzed by this study. While nfKPI disclosures can be presented independently in the management report, it is also possible to integrate these disclosures in other nonfinancial reporting media. Thus, it is important to further differentiate these media according to the nonfinancial dimensions which they cover. With regard to the economic dimension of nonfinancial information, particular firms provide **economic nonfinancial reporting** information on specific topics such as corporate governance, research and development (R&D) or strategy reporting (*AKEU* (2002), p. 2338; *Freidank/Weber* (2008), pp. 397-399). While these topics and reports focus on economic issues, they may show interlinkages to nfKPIs. For example, a research intensive firm could provide an R&D report which contains several innovation-related KPIs. While the general preparation of these reporting media is not considered in the context of this study, it considers the preparation process of nfKPIs included in such reporting media.

As **nonfinancial statements or reports** shall disclose nonfinancial information relevant for both the economic position and the environmental and social effects of corporate actions, this reporting medium contains disclosures which cover the overlapping areas between the economic dimension and the other two nonfinancial dimensions. However, this form of reporting is only mandatory for a small number of large firms.[17] In this context, the statements shall also include nfKPI disclosures, which mark a subsection indicated by the overlaps with the economic dimension, the dotted circle and either of the other two dimensions in the figure above. Disclosures on these nfKPIs may also be mandatory for non-listed firms, while they are exempt from providing other disclosures of the nonfinancial statements. Thus, the preparation process of these particular mandatory disclosures is also examined in this study. **Voluntary sustainability reporting** provides a platform for voluntary disclosures on environmental or social issues, when they do not overlap with economic information. These disclosures can also be substantiated by nfKPIs, which can be integrated in the management report (*Müller/Stawinoga* (2013), p. 118) or published in a separate sustainability report (*Blaesing* (2013)). Due to the voluntary nature of this information, the preparation process of these nfKPIs is not analyzed in this study. While traditional external

[17] See section 2.2.1.2 for a discussion of the requirements regarding nonfinancial statements or reports.

management reports separate financial, nonfinancial, mandatory and voluntary reporting media, the concept of **integrated reporting** combines and interlinks these media within one report (*Hannen* (2017)). In the context of this study, nfKPI preparation processes for integrated reports are examined whenever these disclosures reflect mandatory nfKPI disclosures in management reports.

2.2 Management reporting on nonfinancial KPIs

This section discusses requirements and guidance related to nfKPI disclosures in management reports. As part of the regulatory requirements on nfKPIs, the historical development and status-quo of the provisions of the HGB and GAS are presented. Subsequently, several voluntary reporting frameworks for preparing nfKPIs are contrasted and discussed with regard to their suitability. Finally, the section indicates the assurance requirements for this type of disclosures.

2.2.1 Regulatory requirements

2.2.1.1 Historical development

Before nfKPI reporting was first required by German law in 2004, such indicators were reported in the management reports on a **voluntary basis**. In this context, firms commonly disclosed economic, ecologic or social nfKPIs connected to their course of business such as the number of employees or indicators about corporate health care and accident prevention (*Kropff* (1980), p. 526; *Adler et al.* (1995), pp. 186, 214-215).

In the year 2003, the **modernization directive (2003/51/EC)** introduced major changes with regard to nfKPI reporting (Directive 2003/51/EC art. 1 par. 14 in combination with Directive 78/660/EEC art. 46). The directive was transferred into German law through the **Bilanzrechtsreformgesetz (BilReG)** on 4 December, 2004 and became effective for reporting periods starting 1 January, 2005 (*Kajüter* (2004), pp. 197-198; BGBlt. 2004 part I no. 65, p. 3176; *Wolf* (2005), p. 438; *Fink/Keck* (2005), pp. 137-138). The directive follows a recommendation by the European Commission regarding the disclosure of ecological aspects (*European Commission* (2001); *Lange* (2004), p. 984). In line with these recommendations, changes were introduced to improve the information content and comparability of management reports and to strengthen the reporting on ecological and social aspects necessary for the understanding of a company's course of business and economic position (*BT-Drucksache* 15/3419, p. 30; Directive 2003/51/EC, rec. 9).

On 7 December, 2004, the Accounting Standards Committee of Germany (ASCG) adopted **GAS 15**. This standard was announced by the Federal Ministry of Justice (FMJ) on 26 February, 2005. After the publication by the FMJ and in accordance with § 342 (2) HGB, the GAS are assumed to be generally accepted accounting principles (*Ernst* (1998), pp. 1030-1031; *Scheffler* (1999), p. 412; *Spanheimer* (2000), pp. 1004-1005; *Ebke/Paal* (2013), pp. 2444-2446). GAS 15 included the reporting on nfKPIs within the principle of "focus on sustainable value creation" (GAS 15.30-35 (2005); *Fink/Keck* (2005), p. 140). The requirements exceeded the scope of § 315 (1) sent. 4 HGB by demanding disclosures on nfKPIs whenever these had a substantial effect on the economic position or course of business or whenever the company's management expected them to have a substantial influence on the probable development of the firm (*Greinert* (2004), pp. 56-57; GAS 15.31 (2005); *Fink/Keck* (2005), p. 140). In 2010, GAS 15 was amended by German Amendment Accounting Standard No. 5 (GAAS 5) to further clarify the requirements regarding nfKPIs for management report preparers (*Kajüter et al.* (2010), p. 462). The amendment added the requirement to include nfKPIs that "are regularly assessed by management and regularly form the basis of the management's decisions" (GAS 15.31 (2010)). GAAS 5 also clarified that not only qualitative but also quantitative nfKPIs shall be provided if necessary for the understanding of the course of business and economic position (GAS 15.32 (2010)). Moreover, a list of non-exhaustive examples was provided for nfKPIs (GAS 15.145-147 (2010)).

After conducting a critical review of the requirements and a survey of the practicality of the standards (*Kajüter et al.* (2010), pp. 457, 462), the resulting insights were used to **develop GAS 20** (GAS 20.B2). The standard was adopted by the ASCG on 2 November, 2012 and announced by the FMJ on 4 December, 2012. GAS 20 summarizes, extends and replaces GAS 5 and GAS 15 (GAS 20.238-241 (2012); *Lackmann/Stich* (2013), p. 236). Especially in the case of nfKPIs a revision of the GAS became necessary to strengthen the growing importance of nonfinancial information in practice (GAS 20.B26). For this reason, requirements regarding nfKPIs were reclassified from the standard's section on the principle of "focus on sustainable value creation" to the section on the "report on economic position" (GAS 20.B13, GAS 20.B26). Although GAS 20 is only mandatory for group management reports according to § 315 HGB (GAS 20.1), the application of the standard is recommended for management reports whenever it substantiates the requirements of § 289 HGB (*IDW* (2017), par. 1351-1353). For disclosures which exceed the requirements of the HGB, the application of GAS 20 is recommended for management reports (GAS 20.2).

The pace of changes to the management reporting regulation increased in the years following BilReG (*Fink et al.* (2013), p. 6). As a result of economic problems in Europe following the global financial crisis, the European Commission concluded – among other things – that corporate reporting on social and ecological manners should be raised to an equally high level in Europe across all industries and sectors (*European Commission* (2011), pp. 14-15; Directive 2014/95/EU rec. 1; *Kirsch et al.* (2018), p. 52). This goal led to the development of the so-called **CSR directive** (Directive 2014/95/EU)[18] which came in effect on 22 October, 2014. On 10 March, 2017, the German legislator transformed the directive one-to-one into German law through the **CSR-Richtlinie-Umsetzungsgesetz (CSR-RUG)**, which was effective for firm years beginning after 31 December, 2016 (*Kajüter* (2017), p. 617). The CSR directive and the CSR-RUG extensively changed the requirements for ecological and social management reporting of certain large companies (*Glaser* (2015), p. 55; *Kajüter/Wirth* (2018), p. 1606).[19]

Due to the implementation of the CSR-RUG, the ASCG **reviewed** GAS 20 to substantiate the regulatory requirements and to provide guidance for preparers of nonfinancial statements or reports (*Schmotz/Schmidt* (2017), p. 2877). In this context, the standard setter

---

[18] For the development process of the directive see *Monciardini* (2016).

[19] For an overview of the adoption of the directive in all EU member states see *GRI et al.* (2017).

expanded GAS 20 by the sections 232 to 305, which **clarify and substantiate** the requirements of the CSR-RUG. GAAS 8 amended GAS 20 in September 2017 and became effective for reporting periods beginning 1 January, 2017. A summary of the development of regulations and standards regarding the management reporting on nfKPI is illustrated in Figure 2-8.

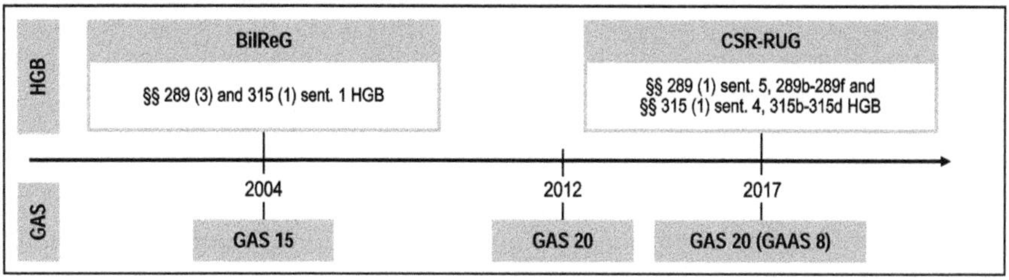

Figure 2-8: Historical development of nfKPI regulation

2.2.1.2 Current regulation

The regulation of nfKPIs in management reports is **twofold** in the HGB and GAS, respectively. On the one hand, some firms have to include the most important nfKPIs in their analysis of the course of business and economic position. On the other hand, particular firms of public interest also have to include nfKPIs on nonfinancial matters in their nonfinancial statements. These requirements of the HGB and GAS are discussed in this section.

Disclosure of the most important nfKPIs in the management report

§ 289 (3) HGB demands that large corporations (in the scope of § 267 (3) HGB) include the **most important nfKPIs** for their business activities in their management report, if the nfKPIs are material for an understanding of the course of business and position of the firm (GAS 20.105). By limiting the disclosure obligations to large corporations, the legislator follows the principle of proportionality of information depending on the type and size of a firm (*Kirsch et al.* (2018), p. 22). In addition, § 315 (1) sent. 4 HGB sets out congruent disclosure requirements for the group management report. However, group management reports always have to include nfKPIs that are relevant for the understanding of the economic position or the course of business (*Fülbier/Pellens* (2013), p. 1363).

GAS 20 further **limits** the requirements by mandating that only nfKPIs used for the internal management of the group have to be reported (GAS 20.106; *Fink et al.* (2013), p. 146-147). Whenever the management uses quantitative nfKPIs for the internal management which are material for knowledgeable users, the firm shall also disclose these nfKPIs in a quantitative form in the management report (GAS 20.108). However, in contrast to their level of detail used for the internal management, nfKPIs can be aggregated on a higher level in the group management report (GAS 20.109). Moreover, firms have to present and discuss material changes between nfKPIs from the previous and the current reporting period (GAS 20.113).

Neither the HGB nor its explanatory memorandums contain a **definition of nfKPIs** (*Schmidt* (2012), p. 51; *Fisch/Mujkanovic* (2015), p. 213; *Hinze* (2016), p. 1171; *Richter et al.* (2017), pp. 570-572). However, the law suggests information regarding environmental or staff-related nfKPIs as examples. The legislator clarifies that this should neither be seen as an exhaustive list nor as an emphasis on these matters (*BT Drucksache* 15/3419, p. 31). Substantiating the requirements of the HGB, GAS 20.11 defines a KPI as a "measure that is used to assess an aspect of an entity's performance", containing either qualitative or quantitative information. The term "nonfinancial" is not further defined by GAS 20. However, GAS 20.107 lists a catalogue of examples for nfKPIs in five categories:

- **Customer-related**: e.g., customer base or customer satisfaction indicators;
- **Environment**: e.g., energy consumption or emission indicators;
- **Employees**: e.g., staff composition or employee satisfaction indicators;
- **Research and development**: indicators which are not already reported in the R&D report according to GAS 20.46-51;
- **Social reputation of the group**: e.g., indicators on CSR or social involvement.

Companies can also disclose **sustainability related nfKPIs** (GAS 20.110). Whenever companies use such nfKPIs for their internal sustainability measurement, they are required to disclose this connection (GAS 20.111). In this context, GAS 20.112 suggests "presenting the connection to economic, ecological and social issues for individual indicators", which follows the GAS's definition of sustainability (GAS 20.11).[20] To support the preparation of sustainability related nfKPIs, GAS 20.110 suggests using generally accepted frameworks. If companies base their disclosures on frameworks such as the German Sustainability Code, the GRI Standards or the United Nations (UN) Global Compact (*Fink et al.* (2013), p. 153), they need to disclose the frameworks applied for their sustainability reporting (GAS 20.111.).[21]

According to the HGB and GAS, the **most important nfKPIs** have to be reported. This emphasis implicitly suggests that nfKPIs can be classified into most important and (less) important indicators (*Barth et al.* (2014), p. 53). Thus, the HGB and GAS 20 indicate the minimum requirements for nfKPI disclosures. It is also possible to disclose important or less important indicators voluntarily. In the latter cases, the management of the firm has to differentiate between the most important indicators and those of lower importance (*Kirsch et al.* (2018), p. 22).

Furthermore, only those nfKPIs shall be included in the analysis of the economic position that are material for its understanding (GAS 20.106 in accordance with GAS 20.32-33). This requirement is based on the **materiality principle** of the HGB. According to this principle, management reports have to include all information that is necessary for the decision-making of the firm's stakeholders and whose omission could potentially damage

[20] This definition of sustainability shows strong resemblance to the definition of sustainability of the GRI (*Lackmann/Stich* (2013), p. 237; GRI Standards 101, p. 28).

[21] Although the term "based on" is not explicitly clarified, it is assumed that this term comprises both the full usage of a reporting framework and cases in which firms only use such frameworks as an orientation for their reporting on sustainability nfKPIs (GAS 20.B28; *Lackmann/Stich* (2013), pp. 239-240).

these stakeholders (*Leffson* (1987), p. 183; *Baetge et al.* (1989), p. 22). While the management has to determine material nfKPIs, it often faces substantial scope for discretion (*Ossadnik* (1993), p. 1763; *Hartmann* (2006), p. 33). Particularly the industry structure or the business activities of the firm can point towards those nfKPIs that are relevant for an understanding of the course of business or economic position of the firm (*Grottel* (2018), par. 206).

The **scope of analyzing nfKPIs** corresponds to the requirements regarding the analysis the course of business and economic position. Hence, preparers have to present a "balanced and comprehensive" analysis of nfKPIs (§ 289 (3) HGB in accordance with § 289 (1) sent. 2 HGB). In this context, firms have to balance positive and negative disclosures on nfKPIs and include all material factors which affected the course of business, performance and economic position of the firm (*Kirsch et al.* (2018), p. 21).

In addition, the most important nfKPIs used for the internal management shall be **included in the management forecast** (GAS 20.126). Forecasts of nfKPIs need to be consistent with regard to their object of reference and to their determination method (*Fink et al.* (2013), p. 166). This consistency allows for a comparison of forecasts from the prior period with the actual development of the indicators (GAS 20.57). According to GAS 20.127, companies have to forecast their most important nfKPIs for a period of at least one year after the reporting date.[22] These forecasts have to describe and explain the direction and intensity of the expected change in comparison to the nfKPIs of the current period (GAS 20.128).[23] Such qualified comparative forecasts can be provided verbally or through quantitative point or interval forecasts (GAS 20.130; *Fink et al.* (2013), p. 270). Comparative or qualitative forecasts are not allowed. Table 2-1 provides a summary and examples for the different types of nfKPI forecasts. According to GAS 20.120, material assumptions underlying the forecasts have to be disclosed. Because of the strong connection between nfKPIs in the management forecast and those in other chapters, the reporting on these nfKPIs needs to be consistent throughout the report (*Barth et al.* (2014), pp. 52-53).

Type of forecast	Example	Permission
Point	"We expect CO_2–Emissions of 530 million tons in 2020."	✓
Interval	"We expect CO_2–Emissions of 500 to 560 million tons in 2020."	✓
Qualified comparative	"We expect slightly decreasing CO_2–Emissions in 2020."	✓
Comparative	"We expect decreasing CO_2–Emissions in 2020."	✗
Qualitative	"We expect a satisfactory level of CO_2–Emissions in 2020."	✗

Table 2-1: Types of forecasts for nfKPI according to GAS 20.128 (based on *Fink et al.* (2013), p. 171)

22 Should companies foresee factors which could affect their economic position after the management forecasting period, these have to be included and analyzed in the management report (GAS 20.127).

23 The direction describes a positive or negative trend (e.g., growing, decreasing) of the expected change, the intensity points out its strength (e.g., substantial, significant, slight) (GAS 20.129).

By requiring the management to both determine the most important nfKPIs and to disclose those used for the internal management of the group, the GAS applies the **management approach** (*Lackmann/Stich* (2013), p. 240).[24] This management approach reflects the GAS principle of conveying the perspective of the management (GAS 20.B13; *Fink et al.* (2013), pp. 69-71). The principle tries to ensure that information disclosed in the management report both conveys the information "through the eyes of management" (SEC release 33-6835 (1989)) and provides the reader with information used for the internal management of the firm. As this approach ensures flexibility for preparers and avoids a checklist mentality, the GAS does not require particular nfKPI disclosures (GAS 20.B13; *Böcking/Althoff* (2017), p. 248). **Overall,** the requirements of the HGB and GAS regarding the most important nfKPIs are largely congruent with the nfKPI reporting discussed in section 2.1.3. However, by mandating only the most important nfKPIs, the legislator uses a narrower understanding of nfKPI reporting.

Disclosure of nfKPIs in the nonfinancial statement

In addition to disclosing the most important nfKPIs in their management report, certain public interest entities also have to present a **nonfinancial statement** according to §§ 289b-289e HGB and §§ 315b-315c HGB. This nonfinancial statement has to include those nonfinancial disclosures that are necessary for an understanding of the course of business, performance and economic position of the firm *as well as* of the effects of its business activities on particular nonfinancial matters (§ 289c (3) HGB). Thus, as depicted in Figure 2-9, the CSR-RUG uses a different understanding of material nonfinancial disclosures as compared to that of nfKPIs according to § 289 (3) HGB (*Kajüter* (2017), pp. 620-621).

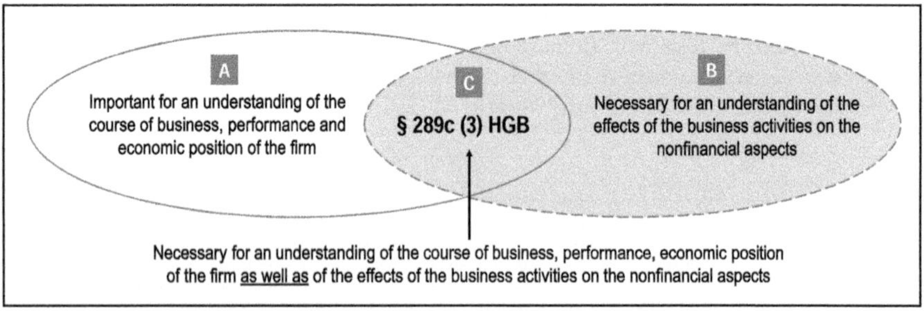

Figure 2-9: Material nfKPI according to § 289c (3) HGB (based on *Kajüter* (2017), p. 621)

Building on the discussions in section 2.1.3, **commonalities and differences in the understanding of materiality** between nfKPIs according to § 289 (3) HGB and nonfinancial disclosures according to the CSR-RUG can be determined (*Kajüter* (2017), pp. 622-623). On the one hand, the economic dimension of nonfinancial information resembles disclosures that are important for an understanding of the course of business, performance and

[24] For an overview over the management approach see *Merschdorf* (2012), pp. 40-94, and *Kajüter* (2019b), pp. 7-11.

economic position of the firm (subsection A). In this context, firms could for example report on sales personnel trainings or customer satisfaction. On the other hand, the information necessary for an understanding of the effects of the business activities on the nonfinancial matters summarizes the environmental and social dimension of nonfinancial information (subsection B). Disclosures in this subsection could for example resemble the degree of recycled waste from production or the number of reported discrimination incidents. The information on the intersection of these dimensions (subsection C) marks nonfinancial information from the economic dimension which can be linked to the environmental, social or both dimensions. Common examples are the employee satisfaction or resource consumption during the reporting period. While the CSR-RUG solely mandates information contained in subsection C, § 289 (3) HGB will typically mandate more nfKPIs as these could span into all three subsections (*Kajüter* (2019a), par. 249). However, as discussed in section 2.1.3 (Figure 2-7), nfKPIs focus on specific indicators in the economic, environmental and social dimensions as well as in their intersection. Hence, nonfinancial statements or reports are likely to contain more information included in the intersections between the three dimensions as compared to nfKPIs.

According to § 289b (1) HGB, large corporations, limited liability business partnerships (§ 264a HGB) or cooperatives (§ 336 HGB) have to cumulatively meet three criteria in to be counted as **public interest entities** which have to prepare a nonfinancial statement. First, firms need to exceed the thresholds of § 267 (3) sent. 1 HGB to be classified as large. Second, such firms have to employ more than 500 people on average during the financial year. Both the first and second threshold have to be met in two consecutive reporting periods (*Kajüter* (2019a), par. 221). Third, the firms must be capital market oriented companies according to § 264d HGB on the balance sheet date or financial institutions and insurance companies (§§ 340a (1a+b), 340i (5+6) HGB and §§ 341a (1a+b), 341j (4+5) HGB). Parent public interest entities in the form of corporations or limited liability business partnerships (§ 264a HGB) have to disclose a nonfinancial group statement if they meet similar criteria (§ 315b (1) HGB). GAS 20.232 further clarifies the scope of preparers by pointing out that the sum of employees of the groups shall include employees from both the parent firm and the subsidiaries included in the financial statements. Particular parent companies are exempt from disclosing a nonfinancial group statement if they are themselves subsidiaries (§ 315b HGB) (*Kajüter* (2017), p. 618; *Rimmelspacher et al.* (2017), pp. 229-230).

As depicted in Figure 2-10, firms can choose between three **different publication formats**[25] for their nonfinancial statements: nonfinancial disclosures integrated in different sections of their management report, a separated section in their management report or as a separate nonfinancial report (*Kajüter* (2017), pp. 618-619; GAS 20.241-256). These options enable companies to continue their current reporting practice (e.g., separate sustainability reports or integrated reports) and allow companies without one of these reporting formats to choose either of these (*Kajüter* (2016), p. 238). Moreover, the legislator offers this flexibility to account for the problem that nonfinancial data is often available at a later point in time as compared to financial data (*Kajüter* (2016), p. 234). However, separate **nonfinancial**

[25] In the literature, the number of potential publication formats varies depending on the level of differentiation of these formats (*Ruhnke/Schmidt* (2017), pp. 2561-2562).

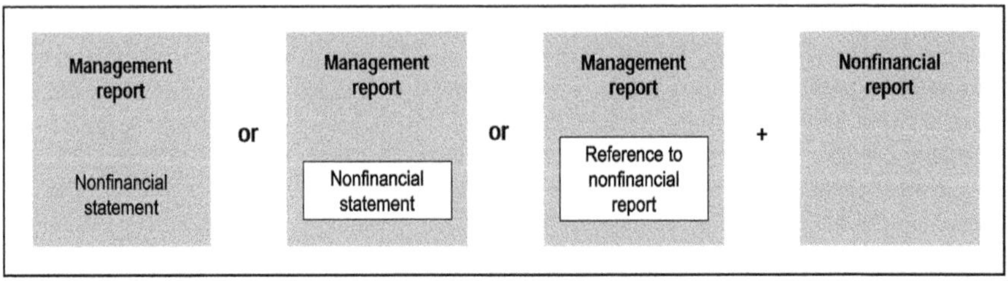

Figure 2-10: Alternative reporting formats for nonfinancial information (based on *Kajüter* (2017), p. 619)

reports need to fulfill the same minimum content requirements (§ 289c HGB) as nonfinancial statements in the management report. Nonfinancial reports can be prepared as individual reports or they can be included in a corporate report other than the management report, either integrated in different sections or as a separate section of the corporate report (*Schmotz/Schmidt* (2017), p. 2878). Furthermore, nonfinancial reports need to be published either simultaneously with the management report or – if the management report refers to the nonfinancial report – on the firm's website at the latest four months after the reporting date (§ 289b (3) HGB).[26] Similar rules apply to parent companies (§ 315b HGB), which have the possibility to combine their nonfinancial statement (or report) and the nonfinancial group statement (or report) according to § 315b (1) sent. 3 HGB.

The legislator does not require specific nfKPIs, justifying that such indicators would arise from the individual business models (*BMJV* (2016), p. 47). § 289d HGB allows companies to use national, European or international **reporting frameworks** for preparing their nonfinancial statements. GAS 20.298-300 further substantiate that firms may apply multiple reporting frameworks or parts of these. However, companies are required to disclose either the frameworks applied or provide reasons for not using a guideline ("apply-or-explain principle", *Kajüter* (2017), p. 623). Section 2.2.2 discusses the most important voluntary frameworks applicable for preparing nonfinancial statements. In addition to such frameworks, the European Commission provides preparers with a **non-binding guideline** on corporate disclosures of nonfinancial information (*European Commission* (2017)). While the application of the guideline is neither mandatory nor does the guideline reflect a reporting framework in the sense of § 289d HGB (*Mock* (2017), pp. 2146-2147),[27] it provides specific interpretations and guidance related to the CSR directive, including on the disclosure of nfKPIs (*European Commission* (2017), pp. 13-14).

[26] If published online, the management report needs to contain a reference regarding the place and form of the publication of the nonfinancial report. The nonfinancial report then needs to be made available for at least ten years. While a reference with regard to the expected time of publication seems reasonable, it is not required by law (*Kajüter* (2016), p. 234).

[27] Due to the legal nature of this guideline, firms may neither be held liable for applying or not applying the guideline nor do not need to disclose its (non-)application (*Kajüter* (2019a), par. 220).

Regarding the contents of nonfinancial statements or reports, § 289c (1) HGB requires firms to disclose a description of their **business model** to support an understanding of the material nonfinancial matters (*Kajüter* (2017), p. 621). As a core part of the regulation and a minimum requirement for nonfinancial information in the management report (*Schmotz/Schmidt* (2017), p. 2878), § 289c (2) HGB names five **nonfinancial matters** that shall be presented in the nonfinancial statement: ecological, employee and social matters, respect for human rights as well as anti-corruption and bribery matters. The order of the list neither reflects different priorities nor a fixed structure, therefore companies may choose their own order of topics (*BMJV* (2016), p. 42).[28] Moreover, § 289c (2) HGB lists **examples** for nonfinancial matters that could be reported if appropriate:

1) **Environmental matters:** greenhouse gas emissions, water consumption, air pollution, the usage of renewable and non-renewable energies or the protection of the biological diversity;
2) **Employee matters:** activities to ensure gender equality, rights of employees and unions, implementation of the fundamental principles of the International Labour Association, working conditions, social dialogue, health protection or workplace safety;
3) **Social matters:** dialogues on the municipal or regional level, or activities for the protection and development of local communities;
4) **Respect for human rights:** prevention of human rights violations;
5) **Anti-corruption and bribery matters:** instruments in force to fight corruption and bribery.

These examples specify the nonfinancial matters by using a principle-based approach and offer guidance on potentially relevant nonfinancial information (*BT-Drucksache* 18/9982, p. 47). However, the German legislator explicitly states that these examples shall not be interpreted as a conclusive checklist (*BMJV* (2016), p. 42). Other nonfinancial matters such as customer related-matters could also be considered material and would therefore have to be disclosed (*Kirsch et al.* (2018), p. 59).

Specifying the disclosure requirements regarding the nonfinancial matters, § 289c (3) HGB lists particular **disclosures on the reportable matters** that have to be provided whenever deemed material:[29]

1) Descriptions and results of the **policies** pursued by the company including the **due-diligence processes** used;
2) descriptions of particular material **risks** resulting from the business activities, business relations, products or services and descriptions of how they are managed;
3) the **most important nfKPIs** that are relevant for the business activities and
4) **references** to figures in the financial statements and explanations, whenever necessary for the understanding of the nonfinancial information.

---

[28] Regardless of the order, the nonfinancial statement needs to be structured, to follow the principle of clarity (*Kajüter* (2016), pp. 234-235).

[29] For a detailed analysis of the requirements see *Kajüter* (2017), pp. 621-623, and *Kirsch et al.* (2018), pp. 63-68.

While the requirement of § 289c (3) no. 5 HGB to disclose the **most important nfKPIs** appears to be similar to that of § 289 (3) HGB, it varies in scope as compared to the latter (*Glaser* (2015), p. 56). In the case of nfKPIs in the nonfinancial statement, the legislator demands a separate presentation of nfKPIs in addition to including these into the analysis of the economic activities (*Kajüter* (2016), p. 236; *BT-Drucksache* 18/9982, p. 51). This separate presentation can be achieved if nfKPIs are easy to identify and to detect, for example by presenting them in a table (GAS 20.285; GAS 20.B88). Irrespective of their separate presentation, nfKPI disclosures on reportable matters can still refer to nfKPIs included in the analysis of the course of business and economic position (GAS 20.244; GAS 20.256; *Schmotz/Schmidt* (2017), p. 2880). Nonetheless, firms have to pay attention to the interplay between nfKPI disclosures in the consolidated nonfinancial statement and in the rest of the group management report to avoid redundancies and overlaps (*Kajüter* (2016), p. 238).

While the CSR-RUG refrains from suggesting specific nfKPIs, GAS 20.286 provides several **examples** on nfKPIs regarding each of the five nonfinancial matters. In a similar vein, the non-binding guideline of the EU Commission substantiates the requirements of the directive by advising to disclose general and sector specific nfKPIs in accordance with those nfKPIs used for internal management and risk assessment (*Sopp/Baumüller* (2017), p. 381). Although each section of the guideline provides examples for nfKPIs, these indicators are rather superficial and limited to selected circumstances (*Sopp/Baumüller* (2017), p. 378; *Kajüter* (2019a), par. 220).

Whenever firms do not follow policies in the sense of § 289c (3) no. 1 HGB, they are nonetheless required by § 289c (4) HGB to justify clearly why no policy is followed (*comply-or-explain clause*). While the **comply-or-explain** clause is solely directed at missing policies rather than nfKPIs, it seems plausible that firms without policies for particular nonfinancial matters might not be monitoring relevant nfKPIs. However, whenever material nfKPIs exist, they have to be disclosed despite of the comply-or-explain clause (*Richter et al.* (2017), p. 569). GAS 20 further clarifies that certain disclosures on reportable matters can be omitted, although they are material according to § 289c (3) HGB (GAS 20.291). If disclosures on the particular nonfinancial matters are material, the missing policies, due diligence processes and results of the policies can be omitted (GAS 20.292). If disclosures are not material, reporting groups can also omit disclosures on risks, the most important nfKPIs and references to amounts reported in the consolidated financial statements (GAS 20.293). This clarifies that material nfKPIs always have to be reported, regardless of missing policies for a nonfinancial aspect.

According to the **exemption rule** of § 289e (1) HGB, firms can refrain from providing specific disclosures in their nonfinancial statements under very restrictive conditions (*Kajüter* (2019a), par. 279). For the exemption rule to apply, three conditions have to be met cumulatively. First, the disclosures have to refer to impending developments or matters in the course of negotiation (GAS 20.302). This first condition provides room for discretion as the unprecise wording of the term "in the course of negotiation" is neither clarified by the law nor the GAS (*Kajüter* (2019a), par. 281). Second, the executive board of the firm reasonably has to expect severe disadvantages by the disclosure. GAS 20.305 substantiates that such disclosures would incur considerable and sufficiently quantifiable damage to the firm, for example by significantly weakening its position in the market. Finally, the omission of the disclosure shall not obstruct the overall understanding of the course of business, performance, economic position and effects of the corporate activities (*Winkeljohann/Schäfer* (2018), par. 2; *Kirsch* (2018), p. 232). Whenever the reasons for omitting the disclosures are no longer applicable, the disclosures have to be included in the nonfinancial statement of the following period (§ 289e (2) HGB). Overall, it is expected that the exemption rule is rarely used in practice (*Kirsch et al.* (2018), p. 69).

2.2.2 Voluntary reporting frameworks

As identified in the previous section, firms can voluntarily apply **national or international reporting frameworks** when preparing nfKPIs for management reports or nonfinancial reports, respectively. In this context, various institutions have published frameworks on the preparation of nonfinancial information (*UNEP et al.* (2010), pp. 18-74; *FEE* (2016), pp. 7-10). Moreover, the CSR directive suggests several national, European or international frameworks that could be used to prepare nonfinancial statements and reports (Directive 2014/95/EU par. 9). However, only few frameworks provide specific guidance on nfKPI disclosures. On the one hand, these frameworks could support preparers with identifying material nfKPIs in the context of their preparation process On the other hand, the scope and extent of the frameworks could also impede the preparation depending on, for example, the size or industry of the firm. Hence, the most important frameworks are presented and discussed in the following.

National frameworks

The **German Sustainability Code** – also referred to as *Deutscher Nachhaltigkeitskodex* (DNK) – of the German Council for Sustainable Development (*Rat für Nachhaltige Entwicklung*, RNE) mandates a minimum set of 20 nfKPIs for all industries (*FEE* (2016), p. 20; *RNE* (2017), p. 8). These nfKPIs are based on two international frameworks published by the GRI and by the Society of Investment Professionals in Germany (DVFA) and the European Federation of Financial Analysts Societies (EFFAS) (*Velte/Stawinoga* (2016), p. 843; *RNE* (2017), p. 18). Moreover, the DNK was updated to be compliant with requirements of the CSR-RUG (*RNE* (2017), p. 7). To declare conformity with the DNK, firms are obliged to report on 20 nfKPIs in their corporate reports (*RNE* (2017), p. 18). However, non-applicable nfKPIs can be omitted through a comply-or-explain approach (*Velte/Stawinoga* (2016), p. 843). Moreover, firms are compliant with the DNK if these nfKPIs are reported in accordance with other frameworks (e.g., GRI, Integrated Reporting Framework, UN Global Compact) (*RNE* (2017), p. 19). The DNK is used by both listed and non-listed firms, including public-sector firms and medium-sized companies (*Velte/Stawinoga* (2016), p. 844; *RNE* (2017), p. 9). The advantage of applying the DNK when preparing nfKPIs thus lies in the limited amount of indicators mandated by the framework, which could particularly simplify the preparation processes of small firms. However, as the nfKPIs are general rather than industry-specific, firms may be required to measure nfKPIs which are not material according to their business model or industry, which could increase the efforts connected to the preparation.

The **Sustainability Accounting Standards Board (SASB) Standards** mark a national framework published in the US (*SASB* (2017)). While this framework primarily focuses on voluntary sustainability disclosures in Securities and Exchange Commission (SEC) filings of US-listed firms (*Ewelt-Knauer et al.* (2018), pp. 1677-1678, *SASB* (2017), p. 10), these standards are also suitable for preparing nfKPIs in management reports (*FEE* (2016), p. 8). The SASB Standards comprise 79 industry-specific sets of environmental, social and governance nfKPIs that should be integrated in the firms' financial reporting (*Ewelt-Knauer et al.* (2018), p. 1678, *SASB* (2017), p. 10). On average, the industry-specific indicator sets mandate around 13 to 14 nfKPIs (*Ewelt-Knauer et al.* (2018), p. 1681). For each indicator, the standards mandate specific disclosures which are often currency-denominated to link them to effects on the economic position of the firm (*Ewelt-Knauer et al.* (2018), p. 1685). While the SASB Standards are widely used by US-listed firms (*Rodriguez et al.* (2017)), their application is less common in Germany (*EY* (2014), p. 12; *Kajüter/Wirth* (2018), pp. 1611-1612). Hence, the framework could be suitable for German firms listed on a US stock exchange (*Ewelt-Knauer et al.* (2018), p. 1685). Similar to the DNK, the relatively low number of nfKPIs required by the SASB could simplify the preparation for listed or non-listed as well as large or small firms. Moreover, the industry-specific nfKPI sets support the preparation processes, as the mandated nfKPIs are likely to be material and may already be applied for managing the firm. However, as the standards focus on environmental and social indicators, firms may lack guidance on preparing economic nfKPIs.

European frameworks

As discussed in the previous section, the non-binding guideline of the EU Commission is not considered to be a voluntary framework in the sense of § 289d HGB (*Mock* (2017), pp. 2146-2147). However, the European federations **DVFA and EFFAS** provide a framework which mandates the disclosure of general and sector specific nfKPIs in corporate reports (*DVFA/EFFAS* (2010)). According to this framework, nfKPIs can be categorized into the dimensions environment, social, governance and long-term viability (*DVFA/EFFAS* (2010), p. 7). Furthermore, all firms should provide the same general selection of nine nfKPIs in their reporting. In addition, the framework distinguishes nfKPI sets for each industry sector, which have been identified through surveys of investment professionals (*Bassen/Kovacs* (2008), pp. 187-190). Firms can choose to adopt less nfKPIs in their reporting, if they consider that the measurement of particular nfKPIs is uneconomical (*Bassen/Senkl* (2010), p. 259). Hence, these nfKPI sets both offer guidance for sector specific nfKPIs that likely are material for the preparers and provide firms with the flexibility to forego disclosures. This support could be particularly helpful for smaller preparers of nfKPIs for management reports. Nonetheless, the standard is hardly used in practice (*Pedell et al.* (2014), p. 547; *Stawinoga/Velte* (2015), pp. 42-43). Moreover, as the framework was last updated in 2010, it may not reflect recent developments in nonfinancial reporting.

International frameworks

In addition to national and European frameworks, preparers can also choose to apply international frameworks. The **International Integrated Reporting Framework** of the IIRC suggests using quantitative and qualitative nfKPIs in an integrated report to explain the value creation of a firm (*IIRC* (2013), p. 8; *Hannen* (2017), pp. 29-33). However, the framework explicitly states that it does not prescribe the disclosure of particular nfKPIs but leaves the preparation and presentation of material nfKPIs to preparers (*IIRC* (2013), p. 7). Nonetheless, material nfKPIs shall be consistent across reporting periods, alterations of the indicators shall be explained (*IIRC* (2013), p. 23). Therefore, the framework is particularly important for including nfKPIs in integrated reports or as guidance for preparers who include their most important nfKPIs according to § 289 (3) HGB in their management report. Other preparers of nfKPIs may lack specific guidance for selecting nfKPIs and could, thus, prefer applying another reporting framework.

The reporting framework developed by the GRI have evolved as the "de-facto standard" for sustainability reporting worldwide (*Blaesing* (2013), pp. 57-70; *Fink et al.* (2013), pp. 45-47). **GRI Standards** – as the most recent version of the GRI reporting frameworks – provide guidance on integrating nfKPIs in corporate reports such as sustainability reports (*Stojanović-Blab/Blab* (2017)). Preparers can choose between a core and a comprehensive version of the report (GRI Standards 101, pp. 21-26). The core option contains the most important elements and background information of the firm's sustainability strategy and performance, including at least one nfKPI for each material aspect identified. The comprehensive option demands more detailed information and descriptions, including all indicators related to those aspects identified as material. Within their report, firms shall disclose financial and nonfinancial indicators on their economical, ecological and social impacts.[30] These indicators shall be embedded in narrative descriptions of how the firm manages the economic, ecologic and social impacts on material aspects (GRI Standards 103-1, 103-2). While the core and comprehensive options require firms to include a maximum of 69 or 136 nfKPIs respectively (*Stojanović-Blab/Blab* (2017), p. 314), nfKPIs shall be selected based on their materiality (GRI Standards 101, pp. 10-11). Overall, the extent of nfKPIs and the coverage of all three dimensions of nonfinancial information provides comprehensive support for preparers of nfKPIs. However, particularly preparing the comprehensive option of the GRI Standards is likely to be resource-intensive and is mostly directed at preparers of separate sustainability reports or integrated reports. Hence, the standards may be applied by large rather than small preparers of nfKPIs.

Discussion

As all of the above-mentioned frameworks can be applied voluntarily for preparing nfKPIs, preparers can choose one or more **suitable frameworks** according to their individual needs. To determine the suitability of a framework, preparers can consider several potential effects of these framework on the preparation of nfKPIs. First, the **number of required indicators** is likely to affect the elaborateness of the preparation process of nfKPIs. In this regard, smaller preparers with fewer resources for the preparation of nfKPIs could prefer frameworks such as the DNK or that of the DVFA and EFFAS. Nonetheless, as large firms or preparers of integrated or separate sustainability reports may be less affected by the costs

---

30 In addition to these dimensions, the guideline demands disclosures on strategy, organizational profile or the identification of material information (*Stojanović-Blab/Blab* (2017), pp. 309-310).

related to the preparation, these firms may prefer the extensive nfKPI sets of the GRI. Second, **industry-specific nfKPIs** required by a framework could simplify the preparation process. While the general nfKPIs of the DNK could require firms to provide additional, non-material nfKPIs, frameworks such that of as the SASB may provide better support regarding the identification of material indicators. Third, however, the suitability of a particular framework also depends on the **dimensions of nonfinancial information** covered by the framework. In this regard, the SASB Standards could be less suited for firms aiming to cover economic, environmental and social nfKPIs. In this context, the extensive GRI standards provide a better overview over nfKPIs from all nonfinancial dimensions. Nonetheless, the SASB Standards and the International Integrated Reporting Framework provide suitable guidance for firms which aim to integrate their nfKPIs in their financial reporting.

In summary, the suitability of a particular voluntary reporting framework remains an individual decision of the preparers of nfKPIs. Moreover, firms can also choose to partially apply such frameworks. As the choice of a framework is likely to influence not only the disclosures but also the preparation process of nfKPIs, the potential effect of such frameworks on the design of the preparation process of nfKPIs is examined in the empirical analysis.

2.2.3 Assurance

In addition to the requirements of HGB and GAS and the guidance of voluntary frameworks, nfKPI disclosures in management reports are subject to **mandatory assurance**. As assurors are likely to be involved during the finalization of nfKPI disclosures, this section presents the regulatory requirements regarding the assurance of nfKPIs.

Medium-sized and large German corporations (§ 267 (2) and (3) HGB) and commercial partnerships on equal terms (§ 264a (1) HGB) must have their report audited according to § 316 (1) HGB and § 316 (2) HGB for group management reports, respectively.[31] The **object and scope of the audit** is determined in § 317 (2) HGB, which demands that the (group) management report – including mandatory disclosures such as the most important nfKPIs according to § 289 (3) HGB – shall be audited as to whether it:

- is consistent with the associated financial statements and with insights gained in the course of the audit,
- conveys a true view of the firm's economic position,
- appropriately describes opportunities and risks of the firm's future development and
- has been prepared in accordance with the relevant regulatory requirements.

Similar to the audit of financial statements, auditors have to provide **reasonable assurance** for the management report.[32] Hence, auditors have to apply the same diligence and intensity in the audit of management reports as compared to auditing financial statements (*Wiechers*

[31] Voluntary management reports allow but do not require a statutory audit. For a general overview of audit requirements regarding management reports see *Selchert et al.* (2000), *Fink et al.* (2013), pp. 287-294, and *Kajüter et al.* (2017), pp. 802-803.

[32] For a comparison of different audit scopes see *Fink et al.* (2013), p. 288, and *IAASB* (2016), pp. 14-15.

(2000), p. 135). When auditing the management report, auditors have to adhere to professional rules codified in the *IDW PS 350 neue Fassung* (IDW PS 350 n.F.) issued by the Institute of Public Auditors in Germany (*Institut der Wirtschaftsprüfer in Deutschland e. V.*, IDW) (IDW PS 350 n.F., p. 2). In addition to various other audit requirements mandated by the standard (*Zwirner et al.* (2016)), auditors have to familiarize themselves with the preparation process of the reporting firm (IDW PS 350 n.F., par. 39-40). This knowledge serves as a basis for evaluating potential risks for material errors in the management report (*Kolb/Plömpel* (2017), p. 743). Furthermore, the auditors have to evaluate the truthfulness of the internal management system and the appropriate disclosure of associated nfKPIs (IDW PS 350 n.F., par. 54). The most important nfKPIs included in the internal management system have to be in accordance with the report on economic position and with the management forecast (IDW PS 350 n.F., par. 54, 60). Moreover, auditors have to verify the completeness, relevance and documentation of the respective nfKPIs (IDW PS 350 n.F., par. 60). Therefore, it is likely that auditors are involved in the final stages of the preparation process or even earlier.

Both the corporate governance declaration[33] and the nonfinancial statement or report are subject to a **limited audit scope**. According to § 317 (2) sent. 4, 6 HGB, auditors solely need to validate the disclosure of mandatory minimum information required in §§ 289b-f and 315b-d HGB.[34] When firms publish a separate nonfinancial report subsequently to their management report, the auditor of the management report has to determine whether the required disclosures have been made (§ 317 (2) sent. 5 HGB) (*Ruhnke/Schmidt* (2017), p. 2562; *Seidler* (2018), p. 1068).[35] If the corresponding information of the nonfinancial statement is integrated into different sections of the management report and is audited in accordance with § 317 (2) sent. 4 HGB, the management report could contain information with different levels of audit (*Kajüter* (2017), pp. 623-624). Therefore, management reports should clearly indicate the respective level of audit to their readers (*Kajüter* (2017), p. 624).

When firms prepare their management report as an **integrated report**,[36] auditors could be faced with a combination of mandatory and voluntary nfKPIs (*Naumann/Schmidt* (2015), p. 405; *Durchschein/Haller* (2018), p. 1811). Such voluntary nfKPIs could for example include non-mandatory nfKPIs required by GRI or references to additional nfKPIs on the firm's website (IDW PS 350 n.F., par. 17, A8). In this context, IDW PS 350 n.F. differentiates between disclosures that are typical for management reports ("*lageberichtstypisch*") and those that are untypical ("*lageberichtsfremd*") (IDW PS 350 n.F., par. 14-16). The latter

33 According to § 289f HGB and § 315d HGB, respectively.

34 The German regulator chose not to mandate an external audit of the nonfinancial statement as allowed by the CSR directive 2014/95/EU. This decision was justified by the expected additional burdens on the preparing firms (*Kajüter* (2016), p. 237; *BMJV* (2016), p. 33).

35 In case the auditor identifies that a nonfinancial report has not been published, he or she has to amend the audit opinion according to § 316 (3) sent. 2 HGB.

36 While integrated reports can also be prepared in the form of an integrated report separate of the management report or as a "one report" (*Durchschein/Haller* (2018), p. 1809), neither of these options are relevant for this study. On the one hand, separate integrated reports are not subject to mandatory reporting requirements. On the other hand, no German firm provides a "one report" (*Durchschein/Haller* (2018), pp. 1809-1810).

refers to disclosures which are neither required by HGB nor GAS 20 (IDW PS 350 n.F., par. 20 k; *Freidank et al.* (2018), pp. 684-685). In principle, such disclosures are part of the audit scope (*Zwirner et al.* (2016), p. 9). However, if disclosures are untypical and clearly separated from those that are typical for management reports, auditors are not required to audit the former (IDW PS 350 n.F., par. 15). If these types of disclosures are not clearly separated from one another, auditors can choose not to audit untypical disclosures (IDW PS 350 n.F., par. 15). In both cases, auditors have to refer to the non-audited information in the audit opinion (IDW PS 350 n.F., par. 16; *Durchschein/Haller* (2018), pp. 1811-1812). Moreover, non-audited information can be assured voluntarily on the basis of national or international audit standards (*Naumann/Schmidt* (2015), pp. 410-414; *Durchschein/Haller* (2018), p. 1811).[37] For such assurance services, firms can choose between certified public auditors or other assurance service providers (*Höschen/Vu* (2008), p. 378). Moreover, firms can also determine the scope and depth of the assurance (*Rauschenberg* (2014), pp. 323-326; *Haller/Durchschein* (2016), pp. 190-192).

In addition to external assurance, the management report is audited by the **supervisory board** of the firm according to § 171 (1) AktG (*Hennrichs/Pöschke* (2017), p. 123). The supervisory board has to audit the legality and appropriateness of the management report (*Kirsch/Huter* (2017), pp. 1020-1022). As the audit scope includes the nonfinancial statement or report, supervisory board members are required to conduct a deeper audit level as required for statutory auditors (*Kajüter* (2017), p. 624). However, according to § 111 (2) sent. 3 AktG the supervisory board may issue an external audit of the nonfinancial statement or report. Nonetheless, supervisory boards could mark important gatekeepers in the preparation process.

2.3 Preparation process

After having established the relevant terminology and requirements regarding the preparation and assurance of nfKPIs, this section develops a **conceptual framework of the preparation process of nfKPIs**. To provide an overview over the general phases and steps of preparation processes, section 2.3.1 presents and discusses several practitioner guidelines for preparation processes of management reports. Concerning more specific guidance on preparing nfKPIs, section 2.3.2 sheds light on the concept of materiality and guidelines for materiality analysis processes for material nfKPIs. Finally, section 2.3.3 draws from these discussions to derive a conceptual framework for the preparation process of nfKPIs.

2.3.1 Preparation processes of management reports

In the context of management reporting, **preparation processes** comprise the participants, actions, disclosure alternatives, timelines and relationships between these elements (*Gibbins et al.* (1990), p. 126). As preparation processes are firm-specific, it is likely that preparation processes differ from firm to firm. Hence, it is likely that firms could seek guidance for organizing their preparation process of nfKPIs in management reports. However, other than

[37] Such standards are for example the International Standard on Assurance Engagements (ISAE) 3000 (revised), the AccountAbility 1000 Assurance Standard (AA1000AS) or the IDW PS 821.

the general guidance contained in GAS 20, the German regulator does not provide practical guidance on how management reports in general and nfKPIs in particular can be prepared. Nonetheless, several **practitioner guidelines** are available for preparers of management reports.

Kolb et al. provide a **general project guideline** for the preparation of a management report in accordance with German legislation (*Kolb et al.* (2016), pp. 317-327). As depicted in Figure 2-11, the authors suggest that the preparation process consists of four phases:

1. Determining **relevant contents,**
2. planning the **responsibilities and timetable,**
3. preparing a **draft** of the management report and
4. **finalizing** the management report.

In the first phase, firms identify **mandatory and voluntary contents** for their management report (*Kolb et al.* (2016), pp. 319-320). With regard to nfKPIs, firms determine whether or not they are required to disclose this type of information. In addition to this, preparers can decide to extend their nfKPI reporting through additional or more detailed nfKPIs. After deciding on the relevant contents of the report, firms should determine the structure of the report. This structure can be used to collect initial ideas or keywords. Overall, this first phase typically takes place before composing the first draft, to relieve the workload for the preparers (*Kolb et al.* (2016), p. 320).

Based on the report's structure, firms should plan the composition of the report with regard to the **responsible persons and timetable** of the process (*Kolb et al.* (2016), pp. 321-322). In this second phase, preparers identify both the persons responsible for coordinating the preparation process and other participants of the process.[38] Depending on the individual

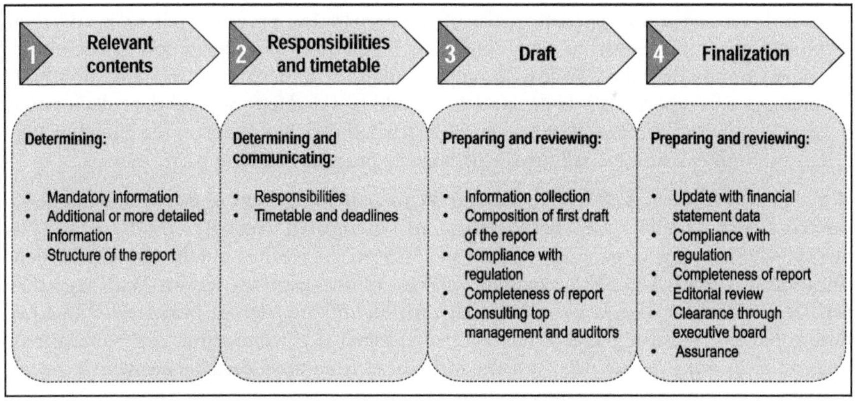

Figure 2-11: Phases of the preparation process of the management report for nfKPIs (based on *Kolb et al.* (2016), pp. 319-327)

[38] While the firm's management is responsible for the preparation of the report, the coordination of the preparation process is often delegated to the head of external reporting or investor relations (*Kajüter* (2013), p. 127; *Kolb et al.* (2016), p. 321; *Kolb/Plömpel* (2017), pp. 741, 743).

firm, relevant nfKPIs could for example be provided by the sales department (e.g., customer satisfaction scores) or human resources (HR) (e.g., employee turnover ratio or total head-count) (*Kolb et al.* (2016), p. 321). The timetable of the preparation process is aligned with important deadlines such as the audit of the report and the submission of the report to the firm's owners. Moreover, sections such as nfKPIs should be prepared before the end of the reporting period to facilitate subsequent composition and finalization activities. Subsequent to the planning activities, responsibilities and individual deadlines should be communicated to other participants of the preparation process.

In the third phase, preparers collect the relevant information for the management report and assemble a **first draft** (*Kolb et al.* (2016), pp. 323-325). Relevant nfKPIs can for example be drawn from internal reports to the firm's management and can be aggregated for the draft. Management reports from previous reporting periods can be used as templates and as a basis for comparing the development of nfKPIs. When preparing the first draft of the management report, preparers should take the relevant regulation and the materiality of the information into account. If possible, the firm's top-management and auditors should be consulted during the composition of the first draft.

In the **finalization** phase, data from the financial statements and notes is incorporated into the management report (*Kolb et al.* (2016), pp. 326-327). Once again, preparers should review the compliance with regulation and the completeness of the entire report. Moreover, an editorial review should be carried out to improve its wording and layout of the report. After a final review and clearance through the firm's top-management, statutory auditors provide their audit opinion based on their audit of the report, its underlying processes and documentation.

As these four phases describe **general tasks of the preparation process**, the guideline provides little guidance on the participants of the preparation process, their roles and their communication. Moreover, as the guideline is focused on the preparation of the overall management report, it sheds little light on particularities of preparation processes of nfKPIs for management reports. While the guideline could be suitable to address the collaboration in large firms with fixed processes and multiple participants, the phases of the guideline may be hard to implement for small firms with flexible processes and few participants.

While the guideline of *Kolb et al.* focuses on the preparation process of management reports, *Behncke/Streck* discuss the **preparation of integrated reports** (*Hillmer* (2014), pp. 397-398). Using a case study of Munich Airport, the authors briefly address the identification of nfKPIs and the preparation process of an integrated report. With regard to nfKPIs, the authors suggest a short checklist for identifying relevant indicators.[39] In addition to presenting participants of the reporting process (e.g., teams from communications, finance, accounting, group development and experts from functional departments), the authors separate the preparation process into four steps:

---

[39] According to the checklist, preparers should ask themselves a) whether clear definitions for nfKPIs exist, b) reliable measurement methods are available for these nfKPIs, c) whether these methods offer accurate or approximate results, d) whether management can influence these nfKPIs and e) which consequences are linked to missing nfKPI goals (*Hillmer* (2014), p. 398).

1) Structuring and prioritizing contents,
2) preparing texts and collecting information,
3) reviewing content and auditing,
4) language editing and layouting.

The authors also suggest separating the process into a financial part and an editorial part for nonfinancial information (*Hillmer* (2014), p. 398). Separating the preparation of financial and nonfinancial information into parallel processes could decrease the complexity of coordinating the preparation of an integrated report (*Thiele et al.* (2015), p. 67). With the exception of this separation of tasks, this preparation process shows strong similarities with the guideline suggested by *Kolb et al.* Hence, this guideline could also be more suitable for large preparers of integrated reports rather than small firms with less complex collaboration.

To support preparers of business reports, the International Federation of Accountants (IFAC) has issued a best-practice guideline including 11 **principles for effective business reporting processes** (*IFAC* (2013), pp. 6-7).[40] These principles constitute parts of a general preparation process of business reports depicted in Figure 2-12. Several principles directly address phases of the materiality analysis and management report preparation process discussed above (i.e., planning of roles and responsibilities, stakeholder engagement, defining reporting contents, analysis and interpretation, assurance and evaluation). The remaining principles support the preparation process in different stages (i.e., top-management commitment, frameworks and standards, reporting processes and systems and the use of technology). While the IFAC guideline provides general guidance on how these principles should be implemented or improved (*IFAC* (2013), pp. 8-20), it does not provide specific guidance on how to prepare nfKPIs for the management report.

In addition to the best-practice guideline of the IFAC, a number of publications look at the **optimization of reporting processes** (*Panitz*/Waschkowitz (2010), pp. 65-75; *Burghardt/Weigel* (2015); *Panitz/Touré* (2015); *Thiele et al.* (2015)). However, these studies

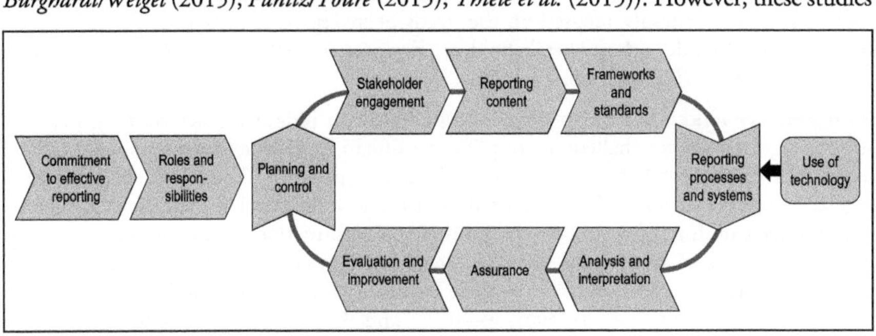

Figure 2-12: IFAC principles for effective business reporting (based on *IFAC* (2013), p. 7)

40 The IFAC broadly defines business reports as "financial and regulatory reporting; environmental, social, and governance (ESG) reporting (or sustainability reporting); and, increasingly, integrated reporting." (*IFAC* (2018)).

do not analyze the preparation process in detail. Nonetheless, *Panitz/Touré* and *Thiele et al.* hint at several organizational effects of implementing integrated reporting, such as the co-operation of departments, improved data systems and compliance (*Panitz/Touré* (2015), pp. 134-141; *Thiele et al.* (2015), pp. 212-218).

Overall, the guidelines provide a basis for structuring the preparation process of management reports in general. However, the guidelines appear to be more suitable for large firms with high a high number of process participants and fixed processes. Nonetheless, the general phases identified by the guidelines appear suitable for describing the processes of both large and small preparers. Thus, the guidelines provide a suitable basis for a conceptual model of the preparation process. Before deriving this conceptual model in section 2.3.3, the following section sheds light on the guidance for determining material nfKPIs in preparation processes.

2.3.2 Materiality analysis

As shown in the previous section, preparation processes rely heavily on determining relevant reporting contents. In this context, the concept of **materiality** plays an important role in the identification, selection and disclosure of nfKPIs. Due to their multidimensional nature, nfKPIs are subject to a different materiality concept as compared to financial information. In financial accounting, materiality allows preparers to focus their reporting on the most relevant disclosures which could affect decisions of report users (*Messier et al.* (2005), p. 155; *Amel-Zadeh* (2018), p. 3). As interpretations of material information regularly diverge between disclosing firms, auditors and users of disclosures (*Holstrum/Messier* (1982), p. 48; *Edgley et al.* (2015), p. 4; *FEE* (2016), p. 10), the concept of materiality entails an allowable level of discretion in reporting judgments (*Brennan/Gray* (2005), p. 3). However, the scope of materiality differs strongly between financial and nonfinancial information due to different underlying users regarding the information. While the materiality of financial information is commonly focused on the needs of investors, nonfinancial information is intended for a broader group of stakeholders (*Edgley et al.* (2015), p. 5; *Haller/Durchschein* (2016), p. 188; *FEE* (2016), pp. 10-12).

As materiality reflects a firm-specific concept based on judgment, determining material nfKPIs regularly proves challenging to preparers due to considerable discretion and lack of experience (*Edgley* (2014), p. 257; *Lai et al.* (2017), p. 534). To assist preparers in this regard, a number of regulations, standards and frameworks provide definitions and guidance for determining the materiality of nonfinancial information. Similar to the materiality principle in financial accounting, the CSR directive **defines** materiality from a user perspective by demanding that information shall be "necessary for an understanding of the undertaking's development, performance, position and impact of its activity" (Directive 2014/95/EU art. 1 (1) no. 1). In contrast, the IIRC and GRI take on a broader perspective of materiality. Extending the user perspective, the IIRC defines material information as being decision-relevant for investors or managers and influential to the short-, middle- and long-term value creation of a company (*IIRC* (2013), p. 18; *IIRC/IFAC* (2015), p. 25). The GRI further extends the principle by mandating that material information substantially influences the decision-making of the stakeholders *or* reflects significant economic, ecologic and social impacts of the firm (GRI Standards 101, p. 10-11). Particularly the conjunctions "or" in the GRI Standards and the "and" in the CSR directive indicate a narrower understanding of material nonfinancial information of the directive (*Kajüter* (2017), pp. 620-621). Hence, preparers of nfKPIs could be challenged by the higher number of material nfKPIs according to frameworks of the GRI as compared to limited disclosure requirements of the HGB and GAS regarding the most important nfKPIs or nonfinancial statements (*Barth et al.* (2014), p. 54; *Kajüter/Wirth* (2018), p. 1612).

Despite such definitions of material information, firms are typically challenged by applying these materiality principles when determining nfKPIs for external reporting (*EY* (2013), p. 5; *Calabrese et al.* (2017), p. 440). Although the non-binding guideline of the **European Commission** offers guidance with regard to the materiality principle of the CSR directive, these particular suggestions are criticized for being arbitrary and rather obvious (*Sopp/Baumüller* (2017), p. 379). To support preparers, voluntary frameworks such as the International Integrated Reporting Framework or the GRI Standards present **applicable guidance for identifying material nfKPIs** (*FEE* (2016), pp. 10-12). As these two frameworks reflect the most widely used reporting frameworks for nonfinancial information, their suggestions are analyzed in detail in the following.

The **IIRC** suggests a six step process to determine material information for integrated reports (Figure 2-13) (*IIRC/IFAC* (2015), pp. 12-24).[41] First, firms should determine those subsidiaries, activities and relationships of the entity that shall be included in the materiality analysis process. Steps two to four suggest "filtering" the material topics by identifying, evaluating and prioritizing material aspects (*IIRC/IFAC* (2015), pp. 15-21). To identify the relevant aspects for internal and external stakeholders,[42] firms can analyze their six forms of capital (*Eifert/Briem* (2015), pp. 134-135).[43] The importance of these aspects can be determined by judging the probability and effect of their occurrence. Financial or nonfinancial aspects can be classified using the nature (e.g., financial or reputational), area (internal or external) and time frame (short-, medium- or long-term) of their effects. Subsequently, aspects should be prioritized depending on current or expected effects on corporate value creation. The most important aspects are then considered material. In steps five and six, firms set boundaries for reporting on material aspects and determine disclosures related to the materiality analysis process, its results and the role of those persons responsible for this process (*IIRC/IFAC* (2015), pp. 23-25).

---

[41] This six step process substantiates the four step materiality analysis process suggested in the International Integrated Reporting Framework (*IIRC* (2013), pp. 18-20). According to the IIRC, integrated reports should both apply and disclose this process (*IIRC* (2013), pp. 18, 29).

[42] Stakeholders are defined as "any group or individual who can affect, or is affected by, the achievement of a corporation's purpose" (*Freeman* (2010), p. VI). Examples for typical stakeholders include shareholders, investors, employees, suppliers, customers, the general public, nongovernmental organizations (NGOs) or the media (*Azzone et al.* (1997), pp. 700-701; *Freeman* (2010), p. 55).

[43] The six forms of capital suggested by the International Integrated Reporting Framework are financial, manufactured, intellectual, human, social and relationship and natural capital (*IIRC* (2013), p. 11). For an overview of the capitals and their relation to the firm's value creation process see *Hannen* (2017), pp. 21-23.

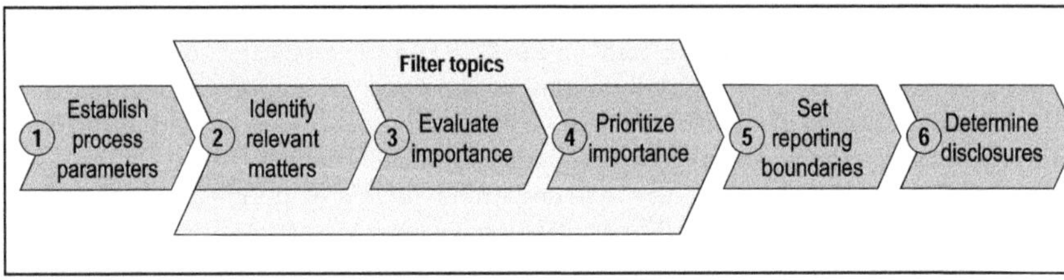

Figure 2-13: Materiality analysis process in the context of integrated reporting (based on *IIRC/IFAC* (2015))

The **GRI** also provides non-binding guidance on how to structure the process of defining material aspects and reporting boundaries.[44] The four steps of the process comprise the identification, prioritization, validation and review of material aspects while including four major reporting principles of sustainability context, materiality, completeness and stakeholder inclusiveness (*GRI* (2015a), pp. 32-40). This process is presented in Figure 2-14.

According to the GRI, the **identification** of relevant topics is connected to defining boundaries for events within or outside the firm. This approach serves the sustainability context principle of the GRI by presenting a firm's performance in a broader economic, ecologic and social context (*GRI* (2015a), pp. 33-35). In the **prioritization** stage, the firms should engage with internal and external stakeholders to categorize relevant topics.[45] Topics can be categorized according to the two materiality dimensions: influence on stakeholders' decision-making and significance of the firm's economic, ecologic and social impacts. Through determining thresholds for these dimensions, companies can differentiate material and non-material topics. Depending on the topics' priority, firms determine the prominence and level of detail of resulting disclosures. In the context of material topics, the GRI suggests including associated indicators when data is available and of sufficient quality (*GRI* (2015a), p. 38). Firms should then **validate** the disclosures to ensure the completeness of the disclosures. Subsequently, clearance for publication should be provided. While the prioritization step of the GRI materiality process is similar to that of the IIRC, the latter does not explicitly suggest validating the information identified. After the publication, firms should **review** the information to provide feedback for upcoming reporting phases.

While materiality analysis processes suggested by the IIRC and the GRI are similar to a certain degree, this study uses the suggestions of the GRI as a framework for analyzing the materiality analysis processes of the case firms. The GRI approach appears to be a **suitable analysis framework** for several reasons. First, as the GRI Standards aim for nonfinancial

44 Although is not mandatory to follow this guidance to be in accordance with GRI Standards, firms are required to comply with the overarching reporting principle of materiality (*GRI* (2015a), p. 32; GRI Standards 101, p. 7; GRI Standards 102-46). While the GRI have transitioned disclosure requirements on the materiality process from GRI G4-18 to GRI Standards 102-46, the associated guidance on the materiality analysis process remains part of the implementation manual of the G4 and is subject to revision in the future (*GRI* (2017), p. 1).

45 According to the GRI, the principle of stakeholder inclusiveness should be applied throughout the materiality analysis process, albeit with varying intensity (*GRI* (2015a), p. 32).

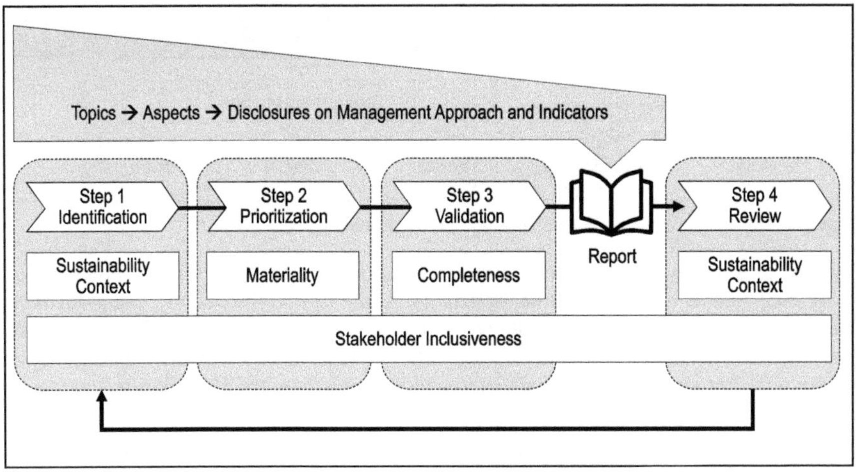

Figure 2-14: Materiality process according to GRI (based on *GRI* (2015), p. 32)

and sustainability reporting rather than an integration of financial and nonfinancial information, this type of materiality analysis should provide a more focused approach for determining nfKPIs. Second, the guidance on the GRI materiality analysis process provides more detailed explanations and requirements as compared to that of the IIRC. Third, the underlying nonfinancial reporting principles are integrated more clearly in the GRI materiality analysis process. Finally, the GRI guidelines and standards are more widely used for determining nfKPIs as compared to the International Integrated Reporting Framework (*KPMG* (2017), p. 28; *Kajüter/Wirth* (2018), pp. 1611-1612). Moreover, the materiality analysis process of the GRI can also be informative for firms preparing nfKPIs in accordance with HGB and GAS. While it is likely that such preparers use a narrower understanding of materiality as well as less extensive analysis processes, the GRI process nonetheless provides a comprehensive framework for identifying and categorizing the phases of the firm's materiality analysis processes.

2.3.3 Conceptual framework for the preparation process

As the above mentioned guidelines and frameworks lack a comprehensive conceptual model for the **preparation process of nfKPIs for management reports**, this section aims to derive a conceptual model for this process. Drawing from the discussions above, the preparation process comprises two interrelated sub-processes: the materiality analysis and the composition process (Figure 2-15). These sub-processes entail particular phases, which are presented in the following.

The aim of the **materiality analysis process** is to identify the mandatory and voluntary disclosures of the nfKPI reporting. This process entails the identification and prioritization of nfKPIs. In the **identification phase** firms apply internal or external methods (e.g., observations, surveys or peer comparisons) to compile an initial list with potentially relevant

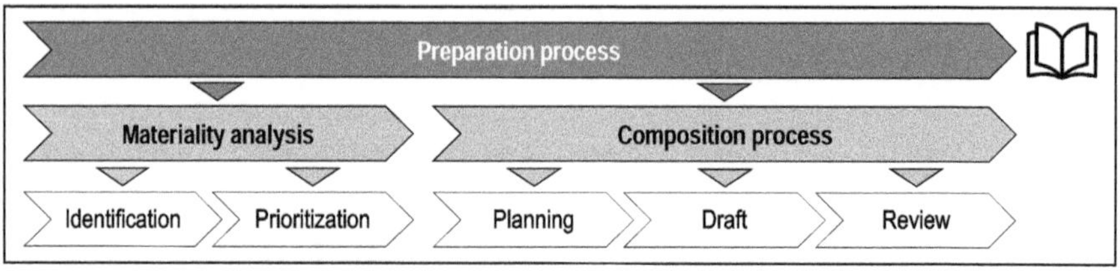

Figure 2-15: Sub-processes of the preparation process of nfKPIs

nfKPIs. In addition, preparers determine reporting boundaries by deciding whether disclosures shall comprise nfKPIs internal or external to the firm. Subsequently, the **prioritization phase** uses the list of potentially relevant nfKPIs to select those nfKPIs that are considered material. To do so, the firms judge whether nfKPIs match their understanding of materiality. For their subsequent decision-making regarding nfKPI disclosures, preparers can use different approaches (e.g., workshops or reporting thresholds).

Building on material nfKPIs identified in the materiality analysis, the **composition process** comprises the steps necessary for preparing these nfKPI disclosures for the management report. This process entails the planning, drafting and review of the nfKPI reporting. On the basis of the material nfKPIs, preparers use the **planning phase** to determine the concept of the nfKPI reporting as well as the responsibilities and timeline of the composition process. Moreover, the resulting concept of the composition process is then communicated to participants of the process. Subsequently in the **drafting phase**, the firms collect the material nfKPIs by using various sources of information for nfKPIs. This information is then validated and subsequently assembled in a first draft of the nfKPI reporting for the management report. This draft is then finalized in the **review phase**. In this phase, the draft is reviewed by different types of reviewers and the resulting feedback is communicated to the responsible writers who then incorporate the feedback. The composition process is completed once the statutory audit has been carried out and clearance has been provided by the top-management and the supervisory board.

This conceptual framework emphasizes the **role of the materiality analysis process** by differentiating it from the phases of the composition process. This differentiation is justified by the specific challenges of identifying multidimensional nfKPIs on the basis of demands by various report users. As these materiality judgments are subject to discretion, the resulting selection of nfKPIs could have considerable effects on the following composition process of. While it could be possible for firms to conduct their materiality analysis during or after the planning phase, the specific phases of materiality analysis can nonetheless be differentiated from the planning phase.

In the context of various heterogeneous preparation processes in practice, the design of preparation processes and their particular phases is likely to differ between companies. Depending on influencing factors such as firm size or listing, a firm's process phases could comprise fewer or less formalized methods for preparing nfKPIs as compared to those of other firms. Furthermore, preparation processes of individual firms could change over time due to internal or external changes as well as reporting routine. For example, it could be expected that firms do not carry out an extensive materiality analysis if stakeholder demands or existing nfKPIs have not changed significantly as compared to previous reporting periods. Nonetheless, this **conceptual framework** provides both a general structure for analyzing the phases of the preparation process of nfKPIs for management reports as well as the flexibility to account for variations between and within firms. Therefore, this framework serves as a foundation for empirically analyzing the design of the preparation process of nfKPIs (section 6.2.1).

3 State of research

This chapter critically discusses **previous contributions to the literature**. Building on the foundations of this study, this chapter summarizes the literature on the preparation of nfKPIs and on the preparation process of corporate reports (Figure 3-1). The first strand of the literature looks at the particularities of preparing nfKPIs for internal and external reporting purposes (section 3.1). A second strand focuses on the phases, participants and influencing factors of preparation processes of corporate reports, such as management reports, sustainability reports or integrated reports (section 3.2). On the basis of results and shortcomings of extant literature, section 3.3 identifies the intersection of both strands of the literature as a **research gap** this study aims to address: the preparation process of nfKPIs for management reports.

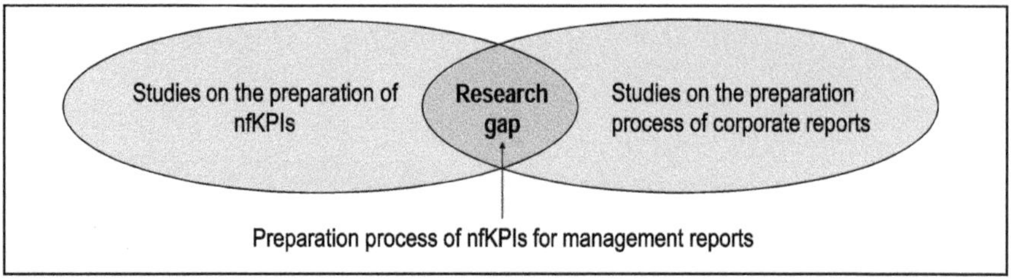

Figure 3-1: Identification of research gap

A large portion of the literature presented in this chapter deals with the preparation of **voluntary corporate reports** (e.g., sustainability reports). Although such voluntary reports differ from mandatory management reports in terms of both regulatory requirements and the firms' motivations to publish the report, these studies remain informative about the underlying relations and challenges connected to the preparation process of nfKPIs.

3.1 Studies on the preparation of nonfinancial KPIs

Studies on the preparation of nfKPIs analyze the development, measurement and selection of nfKPIs for internal and external reporting. Building on the literature of the internal and external usage of nfKPIs (section 2.1.2), these studies provide insights into the particular tasks and challenges connected to the reporting of such indicators. The majority of the literature looks at the preparation of nfKPIs in the context of sustainability reports and internal reports. While two studies look at the preparation of nfKPIs for the management report, these studies do not provide in-depth analyses of the preparation process.

Development of indicators

A strand of the literature looks at how nfKPIs are **developed**. This strand examines how relevant nfKPIs are identified and included into nfKPI frameworks. Building on early research which analyzes how countries and communities develop and report sustainability indicators (e.g., *Hardi/Zdan* (1997); *Bossel* (1999); *Giovannini/Linster* (2005)), the studies at hand transfer such processes to the nfKPI reporting of corporations.

Keeble et al. provide one of the first studies that looks at the process of identifying and implementing sustainability performance KPIs on different corporate levels (*Keeble et al.* (2003)). The researchers develop a **model process of compiling nonfinancial indicators** and selecting the most important KPIs for a KPI framework that can be used at either group or project levels (*Keeble et al.* (2003), p. 152). Two case studies, which indicate how the model approach can be used in practice, demonstrate this model process. While the authors present guidance and practical examples for selecting nfKPIs relevant for the firm and its stakeholders, they do not address the specific steps and challenges of selecting the most important nfKPIs.

To examine the indicator development process of a Canadian utility company, *Searcy et al.* interview 20 experts involved in the process (*Searcy et al.* (2005, 2008, 2009)). Drawing from the observations of the case study, the authors suggest an **indicator design process** and show which experts from within or outside the company could be involved in such a process (*Searcy et al.* (2005), pp. 36-39). A multitude of departments (such as corporate planning, communications or environment) has participated in the development process in the case company. Moreover, the authors discover that relevant indicators were identified "through a process of structured brainstorming, individual meetings, and professionally facilitated critical reviews" (*Searcy et al.* (2009), pp. 35-36), highlighting methods for identifying indicators. The study suggests that it "is the process of developing issues and indicators that is transferable, not the issues or indicators" (*Searcy et al.* (2008), p. 148), supporting the notion of commonalities between identification processes of different firms. However, the generalizability of the results can be questioned, as they are based on a single case study. Furthermore, the authors only briefly addressed the issue of identifying the most important KPIs for the company (*Delai/Takahashi* (2011), p. 464).

Adams/Frost examine **how sustainability performance KPIs are developed and used** within companies as a result of sustainability reporting (*Adams/Frost* (2008)). The authors interview 15 experts involved in sustainability accounting and reporting of four British and three Australian corporations identified as best-practice reporters. Drawing from the varying KPI development processes, the authors find that firms are mostly challenged by finding suitable social and economic indicators, developing targets linked to values or objectives and adapting comparable KPIs across regions. Similar to *Searcy et al.*, the authors identify a multitude of participants across all hierarchical levels of the organizations. However, the number of people involved[46] and the formality of the process vary significantly (*Adams/Frost* (2008), p. 292), which can partly be explained by the case companies being in different organizational stages of initiating sustainability reporting processes. The authors highlight that sustainability reporting processes which are being initiated are "influenced and constrained by existing processes" of corporate financial reporting (*Adams/Frost* (2008), p. 300). This points to the importance of the available organizational processes for the introduction of sustainability reporting. While providing an overview of potential best-practice processes, the study provides only few insights into the specific **organizational challenges** of nfKPI reporters. As the authors suggest themselves, in-depth studies of the reporting processes could uncover the "location and reach of the sustainability reporting function within the

46 The number of participants ranges from two indirectly involved persons to 60 who are actively involved.

organization and the degree of formality versus informality" in collecting and reporting the data (*Adams/Frost* (2008), p. 300).

Materiality analysis

Building on research regarding the development of nfKPIs, another strand of the literature examines the process of determining nfKPIs relevant for reporting. While several practical guidelines are available for the materiality analysis process (section 2.3.2), research is largely silent on how these **materiality decisions** are carried out in practice. *Arena/Azzone* build on the GRI materiality process and develop a four step identification process of sustainability KPIs, which the authors then test in a case study of a small and medium-sized enterprise (SME) from the Italian steel industry (*Arena/Azzone* (2012)). *Calabrese et al.* review specific quantitative instruments that can be used for the materiality analysis of sustainability reports and test these in a case study of an Italian SME (*Calabrese et al.* (2016)).[47] While providing insights into the advantages and disadvantages of certain indicators and instruments, the studies do not tap into the processes of decision-making and report preparation. *Edgley et al.* look at the role of assurors in the materiality process and find that the intensity of engagement and negotiations between assurors, companies and important stakeholders influences materiality decisions (*Edgley et al.* (2015)). While showing that the interaction may lead to varying interpretations of materiality between companies and contexts, the authors only shed light on the process from the assurors' points of view.

Solomon/Edgley interview 24 CSR managers from UK FTSE100 companies to determine **materiality analysis processes for sustainability information** in the operating financial review (OFR) (*Solomon/Edgley* (2008)).[48] As a part of their study, the researchers look into processes of gathering sustainability information and of determining its materiality. The interviews reveal a broad continuum of materiality processes ranging from highly integrated and formalized processes to informal processes based on ad-hoc information. These processes are contrasted across the cases on a high-level basis. However, specific phases, actors and challenges within the process are not analyzed in depth. A caveat of the research is the sole focus on CSR managers, which were often less involved in reporting processes than financial managers or accountants (*Solomon/Edgley* (2008), pp. 332, 334). Although the study is set around sustainability reporting in the OFR, these disclosures were voluntary.

Internal measurement of nfKPIs

In addition to examining how material nfKPIs are determined, researchers look into the measurement processes of such indicators (*Frost et al.* (2012); *Spence/Rinaldi* (2014)). These studies explore processes related to both the internal and external reporting of nfKPIs. Focusing on the measurement of nfKPIs for internal reporting, *Spence/Rinaldi* shed light on how corporations use sustainability accounting to govern suppliers (*Spence/Rinaldi* (2014)). Using a case study of a UK supermarket and focusing on an individual supply chain, the

---

[47] *Hsu et al.* (2013) present and discuss a similar quantitative model.

[48] The OFR is a narrative reporting format similar to the German management report. At the time of the study, a mandatory preparation of the OFR had been proposed but has later been repealed.

researchers interview eight senior managers involved in this particular supply chain. The authors discover that measuring sustainability issues within the supply chain was problematic because of the complexity of those issues and "the difficulty of either measuring them in any meaningful way or finding an expert whose advice was reliable" (*Spence/Rinaldi* (2014), p. 445). In combination with the requirement to report these issues, managers find themselves in a "conundrum between needing to present 'progress' on sustainability issues while knowing that the measures are inadequate" (*Spence/Rinaldi* (2014), p. 445). These results show challenges of monitoring and reporting nonfinancial issues in general and within supply chains. Moreover, the results point towards the potential **importance of functional** experts in the management and reporting of nonfinancial issues. However, the findings are limited to a single case study and one isolated supply chain.

In a case study of an Australian local government authority, *Frost et al.* interview 20 managers of the organization regarding the **internal collection and external reporting of information on sustainability matters** *(Frost et al. (2012))*. The authors find a discrepancy between the external perception and the actual internal processes of the organization's sustainability accounting. Although the organization was considered to be leading in sustainable actions, its measuring processes and the integration of sustainability information in decision-making were insufficient (*Frost et al.* (2012), p. 224). The biggest challenges of sustainability accounting identified by the authors are organizational restructuring, measurement difficulties, integration into data systems, understanding of sustainability issues by staff and support from top-management for these issues (*Frost et al.* (2012), pp. 218-223). While the authors interview a broad range of managers and consultants involved in the sustainability accounting and reporting of the organization, the focus of the study lies on the firm's environmental management system (*Frost et al.* (2012), pp. 202-203) rather than on the preparation of information for the sustainability report. Despite offering initial insights into the measurement process of sustainability information, the findings are limited to a single organization in the public sector.[49]

Preparation of nfKPIs in the context of management reporting

Two studies look at some parts of the preparation process of nfKPIs in the context of German management reports. While these studies provide an **initial link** towards the preparation process of nfKPIs for German management reports, they present solely superficial and partial insights into this preparation process.

Through interviewing experts responsible for the management reporting of 23 non-capital market oriented companies in Germany, *Haller et al.* look at the relevance of nfKPI in the internal and external reporting environment of the respective companies and whether necessary reporting processes are in place (*Haller et al.* (2014)). While the authors show that most private companies in their sample primarily disclose management reports to comply with the regulation (87%) and provide only restrictive information within the report (52%),

[49] For a similar study on an SME manufacturing organization see *Durden* (2008).

almost half of the companies also use it to provide the necessary information for stakeholders (48%) (*Haller et al.* (2014), pp. 2542-2543).[50] The authors also look at the **responsibilities for the measurement and reporting processes** within the firm. In one half of the firms, the parent company is responsible for the measurement of nfKPI, while in the other half this is carried out by the subsidiaries. The persons responsible for selecting nfKPI are either the Chief Executive Officer (CEO) (50%), functional departments (19%), the accounting department (13%) or the Chief Financial Officer (CFO) (13%) (*Haller et al.* (2014), pp. 2544-2545).[51] The authors also show that different functional departments participate in the measurement process of nfKPI. While the study provides insights into the nfKPI reporting environment of private companies, the focus lies on the measurement process of nfKPIs and related reporting goals. The study sheds only limited light on the materiality assessment of nfKPIs and on the composition process and its participants. Furthermore, through interviewing one expert per firm, the study provides an overview rather than an in-depth analysis of the firms' processes.

As a part of a study on the CSR risk management practice of German HDAX companies, *Schramm* looks at the **identification and collection of nfKPIs** for management reports before GAS 20 came into effect (*Schramm* (2012)). A short email survey was sent out to the investor relations (IR) departments of all HDAX companies in 2010, resulting in a final sample of 59 companies (*Schramm* (2012), pp. 98-101, 108). The survey yields that the identification of material nfKPIs is rarely formalized. In most cases (95%), the departments that are responsible for external communication (IR, public relations or financial reporting) are also fully or at least partly responsible for identifying nfKPIs. The HR department is involved in the identification processes in almost half (45%) of the companies. In contrast to this, the CSR (27%) and environmental department (18%) are less involved. However, as the survey is directed at the identification and collection of nfKPIs, it neither inquires into other phases of the preparation process of such indicators nor into the organization and coordination of such processes. Furthermore, the author focuses his analysis solely on the perceptions of the IR department without justifying the suitability of this department for answering surveys regarding the identification process of nfKPIs. Although the survey consists of five open-ended questions, the resulting answers are rather short – in most cases only one sentence – and insufficient for examining the identification and collection of nfKPIs in depth.[52] Nonetheless, the study indicates potential participants of the preparation process of nfKPIs.

In **summary**, studies on the preparation of nfKPIs tap into the tasks and challenges related to the preparation. While some studies provide overall guidance regarding the identification and selection of nfKPIs, the results remain rather vague regarding the particular steps and

---

[50] About 87% of the reporting firms state that their most important stakeholders for the management report are capital providers, referring primarily to banks (70%). Other important stakeholders of the reports are customers (26%) and suppliers (17%).

[51] In the remaining cases, nfKPIs are selected on the basis of demands from for example customers or auditors (*Haller et al.* (2014), p. 2545).

[52] The answers to the survey are disclosed by the author (*Schramm* (2012), pp. 270-278).

participants of these processes. Furthermore, the studies refrain from comprehensively analyzing and contrasting factors which influence the preparation of nfKPIs. Moreover, as most studies focus on internal or sustainability reporting, their results may not be directly transferable to a mandatory nfKPI reporting environment.

3.2 Studies on the preparation process of corporate reports

Studies on the **preparation process of corporate reports** analyze the participants and phases of existing or recently established reporting processes. Some of these studies connect potential internal and external influencing factors with the design of reporting processes. The literature looks at the preparation of financial statements, management reports, integrated or sustainability reports. These studies look into potential explanations for heterogeneous preparation processes and resulting disclosures.

Participants of the preparation process

One strand of the literature examines interactions between **participants** involved in the preparation of corporate reports. These studies identify various departments and stakeholders involved in such preparation processes. Moreover, several studies identify differences in the preparation processes and examine these in the light of organizational structures and individual motives.

In a foundational study, *Gibbins et al.* look at the **participants of the financial disclosure process** and the influence of consultants, auditors and regulation on both the process and respective outcomes (*Gibbins et al.* (1990)). The researchers use a grounded theory approach to develop a model for financial disclosure processes by interviewing 11 Canadian companies and nine external participants such as lawyers or auditors. Instead of a theoretical sampling approach, the authors use a selective sampling plan which reflects whether the firm is listed on a capital market, whether it is subject to product regulations and whether participants are internal or external stakeholders of the firm (*Gibbins et al.* (1990), pp. 123-124). The authors identify the degree of accounting regulation acceptance and firm-specific interpretations of such regulation as two important factors influencing the preparation of financial disclosures (*Gibbins et al.* (1990), pp. 130-131). In addition to external factors such as market pressures or consultants, financial disclosure decisions also depend on internal factors such as intra-firm politics and organizational structures (*Gibbins et al.* (1990), pp. 133-133). While the authors identify these internal factors as important enablers of financial disclosures, their research does not look at the individual behavior and roles of the participants. Although the sampling approach does not match the theoretical sampling approach suggested by grounded theory, it provides valuable dimensions for the sampling of case studies for this study.

In her study on the preparation process of sustainability reports, *Adams* identifies **internal context factors** which could influence the extent and nature of sustainability disclosures (*Adams* (2002)). The author uses her findings from interviews with four German and three British large chemical and pharmaceutical companies to construct a framework of possible internal and external influencing factors of sustainability reporting. In addition to traditional external determinants such as company size and company origin, *Adams* identifies that company boards, committees, governance procedures and the involvement of stakeholders and accountants can influence the reporting process and disclosures resulting from this process (*Adams* (2002), p. 244). The author suggests that the level of involvement and the specific attitudes of the participants are reflected in disclosure decisions. *Adams* calls for more engagement with reporting companies to determine how attitudes, communication and organizational processes influence the extent and quality of nonfinancial reporting (*Adams* (2002), pp. 245-246). The author also indicates that more academic work needs to be conducted on the interplay between external and internal influencing factors. While the study provides exploratory insights into internal influencing factors of sustainability reporting, it only slightly touches on the process steps of preparing nonfinancial information for external reporting. Although the majority of the case firms are German, the findings are limited to two relatively similar industries.

Building on insights of both authors, *Osann* looks at the voluntary disclosure of intangible resources in management reports (*Osann* (2010)). The author uses a grounded theory approach to examine the **interactions and motives in the disclosure processes** related to intangible resources. *Osann* interviews 17 managers from 13 German publicly listed companies, who are responsible for the preparation of the management report. As a part of his study, the author finds exploratory evidence for promotor structures and their communication in the preparation process of the management report (*Osann* (2010), pp. 105-107). The promotor roles and their potential motives for influencing disclosures are grounded in a framework of the overall instrumentalization of the management report. The study finds that disclosure decisions are influenced by the diverging goals and actions of the participants. In connection to this, the author argues that organizational structures and workflows have a decisive impact on the disclosure of immaterial resources (*Osann* (2010), p. 259). While this study offers exploratory insights into the preparation process of management reports, it focuses more on the roles and motives of the promotors in the instrumentalization of the management report than on their contributions to the phases of the preparation process. In the course of his study, the author often does not differentiate between the preparation process of the immaterial resources and that of the overall management report. Hence, it is difficult for the study to clarify particularities of preparing nonfinancial and qualitative information such as immaterial resources. These particularities may differ from those of mandatory disclosures such as nfKPIs, as disclosures on immaterial resources were voluntary at the time of the study. Moreover, the study draws its conclusions from rather short interviews – on average 45 minutes – with the responsible coordinators (*Osann* (2010), p. 93). While these experts can provide an overview over the preparation process, in-depth interviews with departments responsible for the measurement of nonfinancial information or with gatekeepers involved in the finalization of the preparation process could provide critical insights into their particular challenges in disclosure processes.

Similar to *Osann*, several studies have looked into the **motivations of managers** who participate in the preparation process of sustainability disclosures. *O'Dwyer* interviewed 29 Irish executive managers regarding their views on sustainability and identifies a tendency to use sustainability as a business case for shareholder value maximization while neglecting its broader societal scope (*O'Dwyer* (2003)). *Spence* picks up on these insights and looks at how such motivations are reflected in sustainability reports of large UK firms and which conflicts arise from diverging motives during the preparation process (*Spence* (2007)). Through interviews with five executives and 20 sustainability managers the author identifies various motivations for sustainability reporting attributable to the business case, such as risk management, peer pressure, efficiency and internal champions. It is highlighted by the researcher that conflicts often arise due to the incompatibility of such business goals with sustainability (*Spence* (2007), pp. 869-870). *Baettie/Smith* use a survey of 93 CFOs from UK listed firms to look at the goals and perceived benefits and costs of the voluntary disclosure of intellectual capital (*Beattie/Smith* (2012)).[53] The authors find that companies mostly disclose such nonfinancial information to establish trustworthiness with their important stakeholders while refraining from disclosing sensitive information. Although these three studies reflect on motives and challenges of participants of the reporting process, they fall short on discussing how and when these can occur during the preparation process.

Searcy/Buslovich interview 35 individual experts from Canadian firms regarding the preparation of sustainability reports (*Searcy/Buslovich* (2014)). The authors find that the majority of the firms consult external stakeholders for the preparation of reports and that most firms recognize the importance of materiality analysis (*Searcy/Buslovich* (2014), p. 156). Relevant reporting data is collected exclusively by internal staff, while responsibilities for the collection may rest on a single person, small teams or entire departments. The coordination of the data collection varies significantly across companies and the authors agree with *Adams/Frost* that there is "little consistency in reporting lines, reporting functions, and the degree of formality between sustainability reporting teams in different organizations" (*Searcy/Buslovich* (2014), p. 161). The authors note that such **differences between reporting processes** are "likely to lead to disparities in the final reports" and that "different paths will not lead to the same destination" (*Searcy/Buslovich* (2014), p. 167). While acknowledging that their findings are restricted to the Canadian business environment and that single interviews provide only limited insight into the corporations, the authors call for further research in other countries and for in-depth case studies of reporting processes. Although the study is based on a setting of voluntary sustainability reports, the authors briefly discuss the benefits of mandatory reporting requirements and call for further research on the "strengths and limitations of this in a sustainability reporting context" (*Searcy/Buslovich* (2014), p. 168).

In their study on the determinants of Management's Discussion and Analysis of Financial Condition and Results of Operations (MD&A) documents prepared by SEC registrants, *Tarca et al.* interview managers responsible for the MD&A preparation of 26 companies from the US, Canada, UK and Australia about their views on the role and content of the MD&A in their financial reporting (*Tarca et al.* (2011)). One part of the study looks at the **preparation process of the MD&A**. The authors describe the preparation process as a "highly structured" and formalized process which involves multiple departments (*Tarca et al.* (2011), p. 47). They note that some participants, such as information providers and reviewers, are typically less involved in the preparation process as compared to external re-

---

[53] The authors look at the voluntary disclosure of intellectual capital within and outside of annual reports (*Beattie/Smith* (2012), p. 477).

porting teams. These findings point towards differences in the distribution of responsibilities and roles. While the researchers shortly discuss the role of the board of directors in determining relevant information and the storyline of the MD&A (*Tarca et al.* (2011), p. 48), the authors do not address roles of the process participants and the communication between these persons in detail. Nonetheless, the study sheds light on important players of the preparation process in an international setting.

In contrast to other studies on the preparation process of corporate reports, two recent studies on the preparation process of MD&As use **large sample surveys** to shed light on such processes (*Amel-Zadeh et al.* (2018); *Brown et al.* (2019)). For their study on the association between internal preparation processes of MD&As and reporting disclosures, *Amel-Zadeh et al.* surveyed 193 investor relations managers (IRMs) on the preparation process of US listed firms (*Amel-Zadeh et al.* (2018)). Through their survey, the authors find that such processes are significantly heterogeneous (*Amel-Zadeh et al.* (2018), p. 4). The study finds that processes vary with regard to the involvement of particular departments such as accounting, marketing or IR in the process. Connecting organizational structures with reporting disclosures, the study shows that the involvement of non-accounting departments such as marketing can be associated to an increase in optimistic disclosures (*Amel-Zadeh et al.* (2018), p. 25). While this study provides first large scale insights into the heterogeneity of reporting processes and its participants, the survey touches only lightly on the phases of the preparation process of the MD&A. Moreover, the authors base their findings on the perception of IRMs on the preparation process while concluding that IRMs take on a limited role in terms of both disclosure decisions and the composition process of MD&As in comparison to other process participants (*Amel-Zadeh et al.* (2018), p. 3).

Brown et al. further examine the US setting by surveying and interviewing IRMs of US listed firms regarding their role in interacting with analysts and investors (*Brown et al.* (2019)).[54] The results show that CFOs and IRMs have considerable influence on disclosures in the MD&A as perceived by the IRMs (*Brown et al.* (2019), p. 66). These IRMs also state that preparing company disclosures such as MD&A sections is one of the most important tasks on which their performance is evaluated by superiors (*Brown et al.* (2019), p. 68). These results hint at the **importance of CFOs and IRMs in the management reporting process**. However, as the study is based on the perception of the IRMs, inferences regarding their actual role should be drawn with caution. Moreover, the study looks at a US setting of listed companies in which the MD&A plays a different role than for example the German management report.

Since 1994, the German Institute for Ecological Economy Research and the future e.V. regularly analyze sustainability reports from German public and private companies and publish these in a ranking (*Gebauer/Hoffmann* (2009)).[55] The studies regularly include 157 large firms – public and private – and 40 SMEs. As a part of the studies, the researchers also survey the sample companies regarding the preparation of their sustainability report.[56] The

---

[54] The authors surveyed 610 IRMs and interviewed 14 of these for in-depth insights into the survey results.

[55] For the collected publications connected to the rankings see http://www.ranking-nachhaltigkeitsberichte.de/publikationen/publikationen-aller-rankings.html (accessed 13.03.2019).

[56] The survey regularly yields around 60 responses of large firms and around 60 from SMEs.

researchers find that the **responsibility for the preparation** often lies with departments associated with CSR, sustainability or environment, while in other companies it is coordinated by corporate communications, cross-functional teams or other departments (*Gebauer/Rotter* (2009), p. 15; *Westermann et al.* (2009) p. 6; *Gebauer/Glahe* (2011), p. 14; *Fünning et al.* (2016), p. 10). Responsible departments vary not only across the groups of public and private firms but also within the respective groups. This points towards heterogeneity in the coordination of preparing sustainability reports and in turn to potential differences in the preparation processes. A limitation of the studies is the focus on the responsible department for the preparation of the sustainability report while the role of other potential participants is not included in the survey. Moreover, the survey neither inquires into the reasons for the heterogeneous organization of the preparation process nor into the challenges connected to this process.

Another study of the preparation process of German management reports is provided by *Knauer/Wömpener* (2011). The researchers focus on the **regulation of management forecasts and their preparation process** in German management reports. The authors interview the coordinators of management forecasting processes for financial information in six publicly listed and three private companies as well as six auditors (*Knauer/Wömpener* (2011), pp. 191-192). The study documents goals and challenges of management forecasts and shows that the management accounting department is strongly involved in the preparation of financial forecasts. According to the interviewees, planning tools and processes are rarely audited, which points to a low involvement of auditors in this regard (*Knauer/Wömpener* (2011), p. 196). Nonetheless, the experts stress that the forecasts and underlying assumptions are often discussed with auditors, which commonly causes frictions (*Knauer/Wömpener* (2011), p. 199). While the study looks into how forecasting information is obtained, the subsequent process of preparing the management report is not examined. Moreover, the management forecasts of the firms were of financial nature. Hence, the study does not provide insights into the specific challenges of preparing nonfinancial forecasts. The authors themselves suggest an in-depth case study approach to analyze the preparation process of management forecasts in detail (*Knauer/Wömpener* (2011), p. 204).

In addition to this study, *Rauhut* provides an overview over the preparation process of the management report in a large German chemical company (*Rauhut* (2012)). The author points out major steps of the preparation process and specifically looks at the preparation of management forecasts (*Rauhut* (2012), pp. 43-44). While he presents reasons for the selection of the relevant KPIs, he provides limited information on the preparation process itself. Nonetheless, the case study is helpful in showing a **sample schedule** for preparing a management report.

Introduction of nonfinancial reporting

In the context of the preparation process of corporate reports, several studies look at the particular challenges related to the introduction of sustainability reports and integrated reports, respectively. These studies particularly explore challenges and drivers of the introduction of nonfinancial reporting.

A foundational work of the introduction process of sustainability reporting and accounting is the study of *Gray et al.* (1995). The authors conduct interviews with 27 experts involved in the change processes of 21 firms from the UK and New Zealand to look at the role and influence of accountants in organizational change towards sustainability reporting. From the findings, *Gray et al.* develop a **continuum of accounting participation** in organizational change which ranges from accountants willingly promoting change to being reluctant to changes in status quo.[57] The study looks into reasons for such reactions and discusses the relationship between changes in the organization and accounts. The authors also identify particular gateways – the so-called organizational membrane – over which "jolts for change" could enter the organization (*Gray et al.* (1995), p. 230).[58] A limitation of this study is its sole focus on the role of accounting in organizational change towards sustainability reporting, disregarding other potential participants such as top managers or sustainability departments. Furthermore, no formal sampling approach was conducted in the study (*Gray et al.* (1995), p. 222), which limits the transferability of the results.

In a subsequent study, *Adams/McNicholas* focus on the process of introducing sustainability reports and the hurdles connected to this introduction (*Adams/McNicholas* (2007)). The researchers participated in the introduction process of a sustainability report in an Australian state-owned organization.[59] The study documents the organizational learning process of introducing sustainability reporting and determines key **challenges and drivers of the preparation process of sustainability reports.** One major limitation of the introduction process is the responsible managers' lack of experience (e.g., in identifying sustainability KPIs or engaging stakeholders in the reporting process) (*Adams/McNicholas* (2007), pp. 396-397). In addition, preparers are also challenged by limited time and resources to prepare the report and to simultaneously interact with stakeholders and auditors (*Adams/McNicholas* (2007), p. 392). In this particular case, the authors identify the CEO and managers participating in the introduction process as important process supporters (*Adams/McNicholas* (2007), p. 397). While this study offers first insights into the challenges of introducing sustainability reporting within organizations, the results are limited to one case study of a state-owned and highly regulated utility company. Nonetheless, the results explain why organizations could be reluctant to introduce sustainability reporting.

Other researchers also look at the introduction of sustainability reporting processes. In a case study of an Irish overseas aid agency, *O'Dwyer* finds that the **power of the executive board over the introduction process** can be a cause of conflict (*O'Dwyer* (2005)). In the context of the case, substantial changes have been prevented because of diverging motives between the executive board, report preparers and external stakeholders (*O'Dwyer* (2005),

---

57 The continuum developed by *Gray et al.* (1995) is further developed by *Larrinaga-González et al.* (2001) in a Spanish setting and extended by *Tilt* (2006) towards the relationship between organizational change and changes in reporting.

58 These jolts of change can stem from personal values of the participants in the reporting process or from external values they are exposed to.

59 In particular, they participated in project meetings of the responsible introduction team, provided feedback and reviewed the report after publication.

p. 292).[60] As identified by the author, board members most strongly interfered in the finalization process of the report (*O'Dwyer* (2005), p. 287). The timing of the interference indicates the role of executives in the finalization of corporate reporting. In another study, *Buhr* identifies internal change agents and external experts as major **drivers for the initiation of sustainability reports** of two Canadian organizations (*Buhr* (2002)). The author also finds that existing reporting processes are used as a basis for newly introduced nonfinancial reporting. Moreover, the lack of top-management support with regard to initiating the processes or to providing information appears to be a potential obstacle. While both studies provide valuable insights into key drivers and participants of the preparation process, the findings are limited to firms without previous experience and routine of preparing nonfinancial information for corporate reports. Moreover, both studies are based on one and two cases respectively, limiting the transferability of the findings.

In a study of the introduction process of integrated reporting in five German companies which were part of the IIRC pilot project, *Thiele et al.* identify different **organizational structures underlying the introduction.** While some companies set up cross-functional teams, others have integrated the process into existing organizational structures (*Thiele et al.* (2015), pp. 67-68). The study also points out differences between the responsibilities of coordinating and approving the report. It is noted that all companies lack standardized data systems and analysis tools, which complicates the integration of nonfinancial data into existing IT systems (*Thiele et al.* (2015), p. 96). While the authors provide insights into the implementation process of integrated reports, their results are discussed on a rather general level and shed light on only a few selected parts of the implementation process.

In a case study of an Italian multinational company, *Contrafatto* looks at the **processes through which sustainability reporting is institutionalized** (*Contrafatto* (2014)). Through interviews with 11 managers involved in the sustainability reporting process, the author finds evidence for three stages of institutionalization processes (*Contrafatto* (2014), p. 427). The first phase of initializing sustainability reporting revolves around the construction of a common meaning system which is promoted by several key players within the firm (*Contrafatto* (2014), p. 421). In the second stage, the case firm establishes rules and routines in connection to sustainability reporting. The author identifies several facilitating factors for the development of rules, such as stakeholder pressures, peer comparisons, normative pressures from sustainability guidelines and internal governance mechanisms (*Contrafatto* (2014), pp. 423-424). Moreover, the study provides a brief overview of the routines and participants of the preparation process. Regarding the third stage, the author identifies several organizational changes which could support and reinforce the institutionalization of sustainability reporting (*Contrafatto* (2014), pp. 425-427). While the study focuses mostly on factors influencing rules and routines established in the case firm, the author falls short on providing in-depth insights into how these rules and routines are designed and applied by participants of the preparation process.

---

60 *Bebbington et al.* (2009) identify similar drivers such as the role of the board or governance processes.

Influencing factors of preparation processes

Another strand of the literature examines factors influencing the preparation of corporate reporting. In addition to analyzing the influence of external factors, these studies discuss internal factors such as resources, reporting processes and the resistance towards sustainability values which could influence the preparation processes of corporate reports.

In an attempt to answer the call for more research on internal influencing factors of sustainability reporting, *Husillos et al.* interview 30 managers of 20 Spanish listed and non-listed corporations on the **interplay between internal and external factors** influencing the preparation process of sustainability reports (*Husillos et al.* (2011)). The authors identify case companies based on a purposeful sampling approach, using size, listing and ownership as selection criteria (*Husillos et al.* (2011), pp. 199-200). In addition to external influencing factors such as stakeholder interests and pressures, the study identifies corporate values, resources, capabilities and change processes as important internal drivers of the preparation process of sustainability reports (*Husillos et al.* (2011), pp. 202-211). Moreover, the researchers find that individual participants could use their strategic positions to shape sustainability disclosures through their values and views, influencing the final report (*Husillos et al.* (2011), pp. 211-213). While the authors provide insights into external and internal influencing factors, the largest part of the analysis focuses on external factors. In contrast to their research goal, the authors provide little evidence on interlinkages between internal and external influencing factors which influence the preparation processes.

Bouten/Everaert look at the preparation process of the annual report and reasons for the (non-)inclusion of CSR information (*Bouten/Everaert* (2015)). The study is based on interviews with 16 managers responsible for the annual report preparation in 14 Belgian listed firms. The sample includes both companies which voluntarily report on sustainability issues and ones that do not disclose such information. The authors find that the **degree of resistance towards sustainability values** could drive the non-disclosure of sustainability information in annual reports (*Bouten/Everaert* (2015), p. 40). Moreover, they argue that "a limited amount of human and economic resources available for the reporting process and the absence of reporting skills might be considered material hurdles" to the decision to provide sustainability-related information (*Bouten/Everaert* (2015), p. 27). Furthermore, the authors point out that traditional reporting routines and low pressures from stakeholders or peers could cause companies to not change their reporting processes. Overall, the researchers only provide top-level categorizations of reporting processes (e.g., amount of people involved or availability of reporting structures) and use these as indicators for material hurdles to categorize firms within a theoretical continuum (*Bouten/Everaert* (2015), p. 34). Similar to other studies, *Bouten/Everaert* do not look into the interplay between participants of the reporting process, for which reasons they suggest further research to examine decision processes such as the finalization of the report (*Bouten/Everaert* (2015), p. 40).

Role of auditors in the preparation process

As an intercept between the literature on participants and on influencing factors of the preparation process, several studies look at the specific **influence of auditors in the preparation process of disclosures**. As for financial accounting decision-making, *Gibbins et al.*

develop a model of client-auditor negotiations and test this model through a survey of 93 Canadian audit partners (*Gibbins et al.* (2001)). The researchers find that auditors could shape financial disclosures and act as gatekeepers in the decision process, depending on factors such as the complexity of the issue, the client-auditor history or the auditor's expertise (*Gibbins et al.* (2001), pp. 537-539). Furthermore, a related research stream dealing with the voluntary assurance of sustainability reports can be informative for the preparation and assurance of nfKPIs in management reports. In an international interview study of 50 auditors and 21 preparers of sustainability reports, *Clausen/Loew* find that the audit of such reports is perceived to highly increase the data quality and information system processes, which could be related to improvements in reporting processes (*Clausen/Loew* (2005), pp. 75-76). While the researchers argue that this could be a sign for auditors acting as sparring partners for the company through challenging their accountability, the authors remain silent on further explanations regarding the effect of auditors on data quality.

Drawing from 36 interviews with sustainability assurance providers from Western European Big 4 audit firms, *O'Dwyer* shows how assurance providers use different tactics on their clients to raise demand for the assurance of their sustainability reports (*O'Dwyer* (2011)). The author shows that assurors regularly offer their clients assistance in improving sustainability data systems and in setting up reporting processes for sustainability reports (*O'Dwyer* (2011), pp. 1247-1248). Auditors could hence act as change agents within the organization. Although this study provides only limited insights into the actual role of assurors within the preparation process of nfKPIs, it indicates how and where assurors could exert influence in reporting processes. Other studies provide contradicting evidence. *Kaspersen/Johansen* look at the reasons for and activities connected to changing social and environmental information systems to increase the auditability of the resulting CSR report (*Kaspersen/Johansen* (2016)). In their study of a multinational company, data systems were transformed without significant support from the company's audit firm. Moreover, *Owen et al.* show that the process of social audits could be captured by managers which force auditors to follow the business case of social reporting (*Owen et al.* (2000), p. 86).[61] Overall, the three studies appear to be **inconclusive** with regard to the influence of auditors on the disclosure process, as the results suggest a range between low to considerable influence.

In **summary**, studies on the preparation processes of corporate reports provide potential explanations for the heterogeneity of such processes and resulting disclosures. While the studies establish potential external and internal influencing factors, the effects of these factors on the processes are mostly analyzed for isolated phases of the preparation process. In contrast to this, this study provides insights into the entire preparation process and analyzes how and where influencing factors could affect the design of such processes.

3.3 Summary and research gap

Overall, studies on the **preparation of nfKPIs** offer first insights into particular phases, participants and challenges of preparation processes. While these studies shed light on the role of functional experts in developing, measuring and selecting nfKPIs and on particular

---

61 *Ball et al.* (2000) provide a similar argument for audits of the environmental report.

measurement problems, preparation processes are not examined in detail. Although the studies of *Schramm* and *Haller et al.* discuss the preparation of nfKPIs in a German management reporting context, they provide similarly superficial insights into preparation processes (*Schramm* (2012); *Haller et al.* (2014)). This study aims to address these gaps by providing detailed insights into the processes related to identifying and composing nfKPIs.

As a closely related research stream, studies on the **preparation processes of corporate reports** indicate the heterogeneity of such processes and present potential internal and external influencing factors. However, none of the studies provide overall insights on the design of preparation processes and associated effects of influencing factors. Furthermore, as almost all studies deal with the preparation of mandatory financial reporting or voluntary nonfinancial reporting, particularities of preparing mandatory nonfinancial reporting have not been looked at in-depth so far. While it is likely that the preparation of mandatory nfKPI reporting shares common traits with the other two types of processes, specific challenges could arise due to factors such as diverging motivations for mandatory nonfinancial reporting or the combination of traditional mandatory reporting media or processes with multidimensional nfKPIs. Taking both studies on nfKPI reporting and preparation processes of corporate reports into account, several factors point towards a current gap in the literature.

First, from a methodological stand point, most studies are based on either single case studies or comparative case studies with about one or two experts from each firm. While single case studies provide a basis for theory building or contrasting, the generalizability of their results is severely limited. In contrast to this, comparative case studies or surveys with individual case experts provide a broad basis for comparing processes while being limited to the perspective of the respective experts. These methodological shortcomings are circumvented in this study by examining and contrasting **multiple case studies from several internal perspectives** such as coordinators, information providers or executives.

Second, from a theoretical perspective, authors have looked at preparation processes in terms of organizational change, individual or group decision-making (e.g., mental models or the business case of nfKPI disclosures) or the interplay between internal and external influencing factors. Other organizational theories such as behavioral decision theory or the promotor model have so far been considered only rudimentarily. Solely the work of *Osann* provides first insights into the existence of promotor structures in the preparation processes (*Osann* (2010)). However, the author neither discusses the promotor roles in the light of extant theory nor determines their contributions to the phases of the preparation process. Hence, the study at hand looks further into the **role of participants in the preparation process** and draws from organizational theories to explain particular roles of participants and the communication between these persons.

Third, the German management reporting regulation and practice provides a particularly interesting setting for analyzing mandatory nfKPI reporting. As described in section 2.2, nfKPI reporting has been mandatory in Germany since 2004, in contrast to other European or non-European countries. Moreover, German regulation on filing financial and management reporting provides rare insights into the nfKPI disclosure behavior of private firms.

While significant differences in disclosures between public and private preparers of management reports point towards "two different worlds of reporting" (*Kajüter* (2013), p. 127), few researchers have looked at *how* private firms prepare these disclosures. In addition, comparisons of the internal preparation processes of private firms' management reports with respective processes of public firms are scarce. Furthermore, only few studies have looked into this particular German setting thus far. Hence, this study **exploits the particularities of the German mandatory reporting setting for nfKPIs** for both public and private firms.

Therefore, this study **addresses the calls for research** on the preparation processes of mandatory nfKPI reporting (*Searcy/Buslovich* (2014), p. 168). To do so, it examines the phases and participants of the preparation process of nfKPIs in management reports. This study further contributes to extant literature by linking the results with organizational theories and analyzing them on the basis of potential influencing factors.

4 Theories and theoretical framework

Drawing from the findings of the literature review, few researchers have found conclusive links between external or internal pressures and nonfinancial disclosure processes in organizations (*Husillos et al.* (2011), p. 196). To address these missing links, the following chapter presents three relevant organizational theories which focus on different organizational perspectives surrounding disclosure decision processes (*Brühl/Orth* (2008), p. 36; *Scherer/Marti* (2019), pp. 15-16): institutional theory, behavioral decision theory and the promotor model. These theories are then combined to form a suitable theoretical framework for analyzing the design and influencing factors of the preparation process of nfKPIs for the management report.

4.1 Institutional theory

Institutional theory aims at explaining why organizations[62] in similar settings develop resembling organizational structures (*Larrinaga-González* (2007), pp. 150-155). It is assumed that organizations succumb to external pressures by altering their structures to further legitimize themselves towards their stakeholders (*Meyer/Rowan* (1977), pp. 352-353). For accounting researchers, institutional theory provides a valuable link between external expectations, organizational structures and disclosure decision processes (*Rahaman et al.* (2004), pp. 40-41; *Deegan/Unerman* (2011), pp. 361-362).

In the context of institutional theory, the process of adapting and assimilating an organizational structure to that of other organizations with similar characteristics is referred to as **isomorphism** (*DiMaggio/Powell* (1983), p. 149). *Dimaggio/Powell* identify three mechanisms which induce organizational change (*DiMaggio/Powell* (1983), pp. 150-152). First, *coercive isomorphism* marks a reaction to formal and informal external pressures from regulators and other important stakeholders. In corporate reporting, such pressures are commonly imposed upon organizations through regulatory requirements (*Contrafatto* (2014), p. 418), for example in the form of the directives 2003/51/EC and 2014/95/EU mandating nfKPI reporting. Second, *normative isomorphism* is induced by common norms and rules which are typically developed by professional associations (*DiMaggio/Powell* (1983), p. 152). In the case of nfKPI reporting, relevant norms and rules could stem from associations such as GRI, IIRC or RNE. Finally, when facing uncertainties regarding their goals or environment, firms could imitate other organizations (*mimetic isomorphism*) (*DiMaggio/Powell* (1983), p. 151). For example, firms reporting nfKPIs could benchmark their preparation processes against those of other firms to determine how they could better identify material nfKPIs or to optimize their processes.

While these types of isomorphism describe dynamic processes of organizational change, over time "specific organizational procedures, practices and structures, including (social) accounting, become institutionalized" (*Contrafatto* (2014), p. 418). Thus, previously adapted reporting activities become routines which form a relatively stable organizational

[62] In the context of this study, the term organizations refers to private sector companies while many organizational researchers also understand organizations to be structures such as schools, churches or governments. For a discussion of the term organizations see *Berger et al.* (2019), pp. 124-125.

structure (*Burns/Scapens* (2000), p. 5). In this context, institutional theory can help identify and analyze external pressures with regard to their influence in the change and **institutionalization** of organizational structures (*Fogarty* (1996), p. 245; *Adams/Larrinaga-González* (2007), pp. 344-345; *Laine* (2009), p. 1045).

The **context of nfKPI reporting** appears to be particularly suitable for institutional theory, as preparers face recent changes in regulatory requirements and growing stakeholder pressures. As institutional theory also examines organizational reactions towards both internal and external pressures, it provides a valuable link to theories of internal organizational processes. In this context, behavioral decision theory could provide explanations for the activities related to preparation processes of nfKPIs. This theory is introduced in the following section.

4.2 Behavioral decision theory

An influential research stream of organizational theory – based on the works of *Barnard*, *Simon*, *March/Simon* and *Cyert/March* – argues that organizations adapt themselves to their environment through shaping and adjusting internal decision-making processes (*Barnard* (1938), p. 6; *March/Simon* (1958); *Cyert/March* (1963); *Simon* (1976), pp. IX, 1). As a result of its focus on the characteristics and determinants of human actions comprising decision processes, this theory is commonly referred to as **behavioral decision theory** (*Berger et al.* (2019), p. 122).

Proponents of this theory argue that humans have limited capacities to process information (*bounded rationality*) and need to be motivated to participate in organizational decisions (*Barnard* (1938), p. 14; *March/Simon* (1958), p. 6; *Simon* (1976), pp. XI-XII). According to *Simon*, the popular assumption of objective and rational human behavior reflects an idealized image of decision-makers (*Simon* (1976), pp. 80-84)). Rational behavior implies complete knowledge of any possible decision alternative – including its consequences – and the ability to choose the best alternative with regard to an overall goal. However, in reality, **bounded rationality** is assumed to impede rational decisions through three restrictions (*Simon* (1976), pp. 81-84):

1) Humans cannot grasp the **entirety of decision alternatives** available, therefore they focus on the alternatives they perceive to be most relevant.
2) Humans have **fragmented knowledge** regarding the fundamentals and context of a decision. It is neither possible nor reasonable to gather all relevant information.
3) The human brain is unable to **grasp and anticipate every consequence of a decision** at once.

The **main research goal** of behavioral decision theory is to understand how rational decision-making can be achieved under the restrictions of bounded rationality (*Barnard* (1938), pp. 186-189; *Simon* (1976), pp. 110-115). The theory looks at decision-making processes within the organization and at mechanisms used to coordinate and control the alignment of individual decisions with organizational goals. In this context, an important task of organizations is to reduce the complexity and uncertainty of a decision environment (*Simon* (1979), p. 501). *Simon* suggests **five measures** for organizations to shape decision-making criteria of individuals to a certain extent: division of labor, standard practices, hierarchy, communication and indoctrination (*Simon* (1976), pp. 102-103).[63]

Organizations break down their overall-goals into sub-goals which **divide the labor** between their members and focus their attention (*March/Simon* (1958), pp. 156-157; *Simon* (1976), pp. 102-103). This does however not resolve the complexity of the overall goals and could lead to goal incongruences between departments with diverging and independent goals (*March/Simon* (1958), pp. 121-129). In the context of the preparation process of a management report, several individuals could fulfill subtasks to achieve the overall goal of preparing nfKPI disclosures. By declaring certain decision-making procedures as **standard practices**, an organization supports its members by requiring specific actions and simplifying the search for alternatives (*March/Simon* (1958), pp. 139-142). For nfKPI preparation processes, such standard practices could entail training for measuring nfKPIs or timelines for coordinating the process.

Decisions can be transferred within an organization through formal authority in **hierarchical structures** or through informal relationships within or outside of the organization. In these contexts, the **communication** within an organization simplifies the complexity of an overall goal by breaking it down into information packages. These packages are shared with different individuals over formal and informal communication channels (*Simon* (1976), pp. 107-108). Particularly in situations where superiors lack detailed knowledge about the decision context of a subordinate – for example if the subordinate has expert knowledge regarding particular nfKPIs – an organization needs to rely on the subordinate's individual decision-making (*Simon* (1976), p. 238; *Berger et al.* (2019), p. 129). To promote rational and non-opportunistic behavior, organizations can influence the decision-making criteria of its members by using **indoctrination**. Through training the members' knowledge and skills or increasing their identification with organizational goals (e.g., the firm's primary goals with regard to nfKPI reporting), individuals can be moved to make independent decisions favorable to the organization (*Simon* (1976), pp. 198-219).

Behavioral decision theory provides a useful theoretical basis **for this study** for several reasons. First, this theory can provide explanations for organizational structures which support the decision-making in preparation processes of nfKPIs for management reports. Second, this theory links organizational structures with the decision-making behavior of individual participants. This link supports a better understanding of the relationship between the preparation process, its participants and resulting nfKPI disclosures. Finally, the behavioral decision theory serves as a basis for the promotor model, which is introduced in the following.

4.3 Promotor model

Building on the findings of behavioral decision theory, researchers have developed a theory of complex decisions within organizations which is commonly referred to as the **promotor model** (*Witte* (1972), p. 156). Proponents of this theory show how certain organizational

[63] Some individual decision-making criteria such as personal values and experience are difficult if not impossible to change (*Simon* (1976), pp. XXVII, 123, 270).

structures and constellations of actors can lead to effective decision-making in the context of innovation processes (*Witte* (1988a), p. 148).

Comparable to innovation processes, preparation processes of nfKPIs for management reports comprise complex procedures that are typically carried out by multiple participants, in several steps and over different time frames (*Witte* (1988b), p. 223). **Both innovations and nfKPI reporting** involve decision processes in which various steps such as generating ideas, developing concepts, collecting information and evaluating alternatives lead to a final decision. As nfKPI reporting resembles a fairly new form of corporate reporting that has only recently been adopted by reporting firms, it can be assumed that identifying and preparing nfKPIs for disclosure represents an innovation in many firms' reporting processes. In the context of the broad scope of nfKPIs, it is also highly likely that firms' preparation processes require the collaboration of participants from different departments with diverse sets of skills. In the light of these parallels, the promotor model is deemed appropriate for this study.

This theory is grounded on the **basic assumptions** that both the willingness and ability to contribute towards the innovation process are rather weak (*Witte* (1973), p. 6). These circumstances are referred to as barriers of will (*not wanting*) and barriers of capability (*not knowing*). To innovate successfully, an organization has to overcome these barriers (*Witte* (1977), pp. 49-52). Individual tendencies to preserve the status quo can create **barriers of will.** In contrast to the status quo, the risks and opportunities of innovations are unknown to process participants. Thus, it is difficult for the individual to determine possible benefits or drawbacks of an innovation. This uncertainty regarding the outcome of the innovation can affect an individual's willingness to participate in an innovation process (*Barnard* (1938), pp. 92-93; *Witte* (1973), p. 7; *Simon* (1976), pp. 110-122). When an organization adds nfKPIs to its management report, participants of the preparation process could be reluctant to participate in the process because of expected efforts for determining and reporting additional KPIs. Moreover, participants may not be able to assess whether nfKPIs included in the management report are of benefit to themselves or their department.

Barriers of capability exist because participants are unaware of the innovation object and its effects on organizational processes (*Witte* (1977), pp. 51-52). To adopt innovations in organizations, goals and decision criteria typically need to be revised and transformed into actionable tasks. Hence, adopting innovation requires problem-solving capabilities, particularly in the case of complex innovations that link multiple disciplines, departments and individuals. As for nfKPIs, organizations might struggle to define, identify or measure such indicators. Expert knowledge from other departments could be necessary to identify, collect and finalize nfKPIs for the management report.

According to *Witte*, "the amount of kinetic energy available within the organization to overcome barriers" determines the success of innovation processes (*Witte* (1977), p. 47). Promotor model is based on the assumption that these specific energies are provided by different persons who perform separate tasks within the innovation process (*Hauschildt/Kirchmann* (1999), p. 92). These persons who provide the energy to start and continue this process up to the final decision are referred to as **promotors** (*Witte* (1973), pp. 15-16). However, to surmount these barriers organizations typically need different energies to mobilize the participants' willingness (barriers of will) and to provide expert knowledge (barriers of capabilities) (*Witte* (1973), pp. 7-8). As a solution, researchers suggest three types of promotors: power promotor, know-how promotor and process promotor.

The **power promotor** uses his or her hierarchical power to actively and intensively encourage an innovation process (*Witte* (1977), p. 54). This is done by sanctioning opponents and protecting the ones in favor of the innovation (*Shepard* (1967), p. 473). Power promotors ideally hold a high ranking management position to provide the necessary power to advance the innovation and to surmount barriers of will (*Witte* (1973), p. 17). The **know-how promotor** actively provides his or her specific expert knowledge to support the innovation (*Witte* (1977), p. 54). To help an organization overcome barriers of capabilities, know-how promotors build up their own knowledge and share it with other members of the organization. The hierarchical position of know-how promotors is typically irrelevant, as he or she uses expert knowledge to argue in favor of the innovation. Know-how promotors persuade and encourage others to participate in the innovation process (*Witte* (1977), p. 55).

The **process promotor** is able to overcome organizational and administrative barriers which obstruct an innovation (*Hauschildt/Chakrabarti* (1988), p. 384).[64] A process promotor knows the organization and understands which persons are affected by an innovation. He or she connects the know-how promotor with the power promotor by mediating between technical, economical and hierarchical mindsets. The process promotor uses diplomatic skills and knowledge about process participants to act as a "salesman" for the innovation (*Chakrabarti/Hauschildt* (1989), p. 161). The process promotor is responsible for coordinating the innovation process (*Hauschildt/Chakrabarti* (1988), p. 385). After convincing the power promotor that the innovation is in line with organizational goals, the process promotor separates the main decision problem into sub-decisions and delegates these to know-how promotors. Following this, the process promotor summarizes the results and communicates these to the power promotor who makes the final decisions.

Acting as the coordinator of the innovation process, the process promotor plays an integral part in the **communication network** (*Chakrabarti/Hauschildt* (1989), pp. 166–168). The most important information relationships are shown in Figure 4-1. Know-how promotors connect themselves with like-minded persons of a company's suppliers or product users, who stimulate and challenge their ideas. The power promotor is introduced to these ideas and deals with opponents and functional managers to promote the innovation. Occasionally, the power promotor calls on consultants for external expertise. In the center of this network, the process promotor mediates between the other promotors and gathers information from the parties surrounding the promotors. This process promotor collects specialized technical knowledge and communicates this knowledge to top managers. Therefore, the process promotor communicates within and across hierarchical levels (*Chakrabarti/Hauschildt* (1989), p. 168).

64 Other researchers label this key person as "process helper" (*Havelock* (1973), pp. 8-9) or "product champion" (*Rothwell et al.* (1974), p. 264). For a meta-analytic review regarding the participants in innovation processes see *Chakrabarti/Hauschildt* (1989), pp. 161-165.

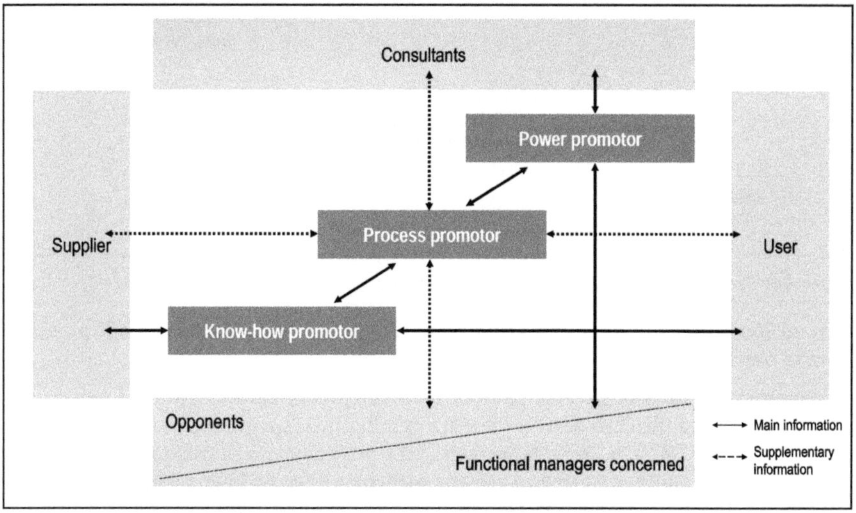

Figure 4-1: Flow of information in promotor model
(based on *Chakrabarti/Hauschildt* (1989), p. 167)

Research shows that when persons within an organization collaborate as a **troika of promotors**, the success of an innovation becomes more likely (*Hauschildt/Kirchmann* (2001), p. 49). A division of labor between know-how, process and power promotors seems to outperform the two promotor model of power and know-how promotors. In contrast to this, Anglo-American research focuses more strongly on the role of single individuals acting as promotors, so-called **champions** (*Roberts/Fusfeld* (1988); *Achilladelis et al.* (1971); *Howell et al.* (2005), p. 642).[65] While researchers argue in favor of a collaborative promotor constellations (*Hauschildt/Schewe* (2000)), it is recognized that champions could play a more decisive role in radical innovations as compared to incremental innovations (*Rost et al.* (2007), p. 358).

In the context of the **preparation process of nfKPIs for the management report**, the promotor model seems adequate. As shown in Figure 4-2, the CFO of a firm could act as a power promotor as he or she is typically the executive who is in charge of preparing the management report, including the preparation of nfKPIs. While it is likely that the CFO of a small firm also prepares the report him- or herself, it is common for CFOs of a large firms to delegate the task of coordinating and preparing nfKPIs. They could, for example, delegate this to the accounting or sustainability department, which take on the role of process promotor. Acting as know-how promotors, functional departments – which commonly use nfKPIs for their operational tasks – provide the process promotor with necessary data and analyses for nfKPIs. This top-down approach inherent in the preparation process differs from the innovation process, which assumes that know-how promotors initiate and carry

[65] The champion role is analogous to the personal union of promotors suggested by *Witte* (1973), p. 20.

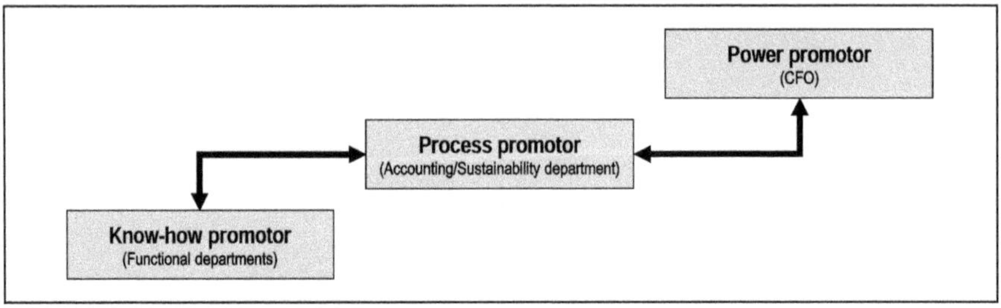

Figure 4-2: Promotors in the context of nfKPI reporting

forward innovations (bottom-up) (*Hauschildt* (2004), p. 200). However, both processes seem to overlap in central aspects.

As **promotor roles** typically emerge from informal circumstances instead of explicit job descriptions, it is difficult to observe these actors in business environments (*Folkerts* (2001), p. 34; *Rost et al.* (2007), p. 345). Nonetheless, the promotor model tries to identify particular roles which can be allocated to specific participants of the innovation process (*Witte* (1973), pp. 15-20; *Pulczynski* (1991), pp. 194-199; *Walter* (1998), pp. 99-115). Researchers have tried to categorize such roles, which results in a vast amount of role descriptions for promotors (*Chakrabarti/Hauschildt* (1989), p. 162). Drawing from these various role descriptions, the roles of promotors can be characterized by two criteria (*Day* (1994), p. 150; *Hauschildt* (2004), p. 197):

- Promotors actively **contribute** to specific phases of the innovation process.
- Promotors use **sources of power** such as resources or capabilities to promote innovations.

Contributions of promotors can be defined as activities necessary for overcoming barriers between or within the phases of the process (*Walter* (1998), p. 66). These activities require certain personal or structural powers (**sources of power**) to enable the individual to surpass potential obstacles related to the innovation (*Chakrabarti/Hauschildt* (1989), p. 165; *Folkerts/Hauschildt* (2002), p. 8; *Hauschildt* (2004), p. 197). Promotor roles can comprise multiple contributions or sources of power (*Chakrabarti/Hauschildt* (1989), p. 165). For example, a know-how promotor could discover a possibility for innovation and continue to work on finding a solution. Furthermore, a power promotor might not only hold hierarchical power but could also provide access to material resources.

Power sources related to the **preparation process of nfKPIs for management reports** could overlap with those of innovation processes. Table 4-1 contrasts examples of phase-specific contributions and sources of power in innovation processes to those of preparation processes of nfKPIs. While expertise regarding nfKPIs may be concentrated in functional departments (know-how promotors), CFOs (power promotors) could provide hierarchical power and resources such as budgets and additional personnel. Process promotors such as the accounting department could use their organizational knowledge and relationships to functional departments to communicate reporting goals and to manage the preparation process. As contributions of promotors are closely tied to particular phases of the preparation process, they are likely to differ as compared to the phases of the innovation process. The preparation process could, for example, be initiated by top-management delegating the responsibility for preparing nfKPIs to the process promotor.

Contributions of promotors			
Innovation processes		Preparation processes of nfKPIs (Examples)	
1	Stimulation of the process	1	Initializing preparation process (e.g., delegation of preparation tasks)
2	Solution development	2	Measurement of nfKPIs (e.g., collection of data)
3	Process management	3	Process management (e.g., coordinating tasks)
4	Decision	4	Decision (e.g., clearance of management report)
5	Realization		
Sources of power			
Innovation processes		Preparation processes of nfKPIs (Examples)	
1	Expertise	1	Expertise (e.g., knowledge regarding energy consumption)
2	Hierarchical power	2	Hierarchical power (e.g., top-management position)
3	Access to material resources	3	Access to material resources (e.g., budgets or data)
4	Organizational knowledge and communication intensity	4	Organizational knowledge and communication intensity (e.g., mediate between process participants

Table 4-1: Contributions and sources of power in innovation and preparation processes (based on *Chakrabarti/Hauschildt* (1989), p. 166)

While promotor roles can be differentiated on the basis of their contributions and power sources in innovation processes (*Folkerts* (2001), p. 38), such roles may not always be clearly assigned to individual participants of the process. As depicted in Figure 4-3, three types of **role distribution** can exist (*Folkerts/Hauschildt* (2002), pp. 8-9):

- **Role exclusivity**: one person occupies only one role.
- **Role combination**: one person occupies more than one role (personal union).
- **Role plurality**: multiple people occupy the same role.

In the case of role exclusivity, promotor roles can easily be assigned, as the role is solely taken on by one individual. In the other two cases, roles could be jointly taken on by one individual (role combination) or one role could be divided up to two or more individuals (role plurality). This role distribution view of the promotor model adds to the notion that promotor constellations could differ from the traditional troika of promotors.

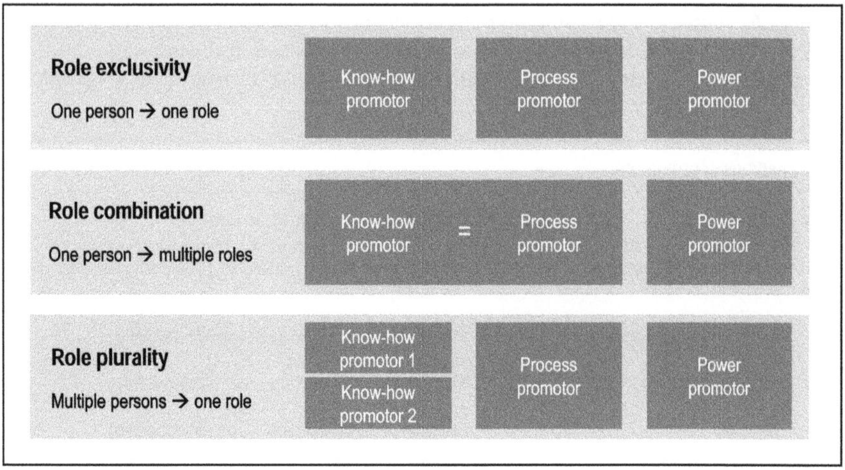

Figure 4-3: Role distributions in the promotor model (based on *Folkerts/Hauschildt* (2002), p. 9)

4.4 Theoretical framework

The previous sections of this chapter have introduced three theories which can be applied to preparation processes of nfKPIs for management reports. In the following, these theories are integrated into a theoretical framework (Figure 4-4) to provide an overall understanding of the design and influencing factors related to preparation processes of nfKPIs for management reports.

As an overarching theoretical concept, **institutional theory** serves as a basis for linking pressures external and internal to the firm with internal disclosure decision processes. The three types of isomorphism provide explanations for changes to organizational processes as reactions to external and internal pressures. Moreover, this model is also adequate for analyzing how institutionalized preparation processes have been adapted to environmental pressures. Building on this perspective, the **behavioral decision theory** takes a closer look at the organizational structures related to disclosure decisions. In the context of preparation processes for nfKPI disclosures, the theory offers explanations for particular organizational structures which shape decision-making regarding nfKPI disclosures. Taken together, the institutional theory and the behavioral decision theory explain how preparation processes of nfKPIs for management reports could be adapted to external and internal pressures to ensure appropriate disclosure decisions.

In addition to the other two theories, the **promotor model** provides explanations for the division of labor and communication within preparation processes. Therefore, this theory supports an understanding of the roles, collaboration and dynamics of the participants involved in preparation processes of nfKPIs. While this theory focuses on explaining particular organizational structures in the disclosure process, combining it with the other two theories can offer important links between organizational structures and environmental pressures.

In summary, **all three theories interlink** and can, therefore, be seen as consistent and suitable for this theoretical framework. On the basis of this framework, both the design of the preparation process and potential influencing factors can be explored.

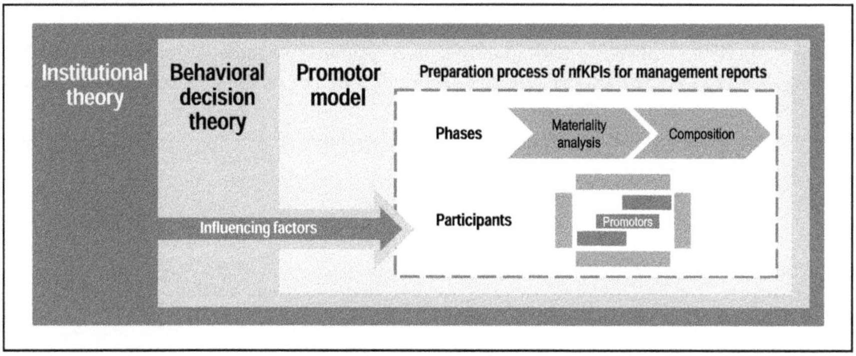

Figure 4-4: Integrated theoretical framework

5 Research approach

This chapter develops a suitable research approach for grasping the design and influencing factors of the preparation process of nfKPIs for management reports. As illustrated by Figure 5-1, the research approach of this study comprises the research strategy, design and process. The qualitative research strategy selected for this study (section 5.1) reflects the underlying scientific positioning and state of research (*Llewellyn* (1994), p. 18; *Bryman/Bell* (2015), pp. 37-38). In accordance with the research strategy, section 5.2 identifies case studies as a suitable research design. This research design comprises frameworks of appropriate methods for collecting and analyzing data (*Ahrens/Chapman* (2006), pp. 822-823; *Bryman/Bell* (2015), pp. 48-49). Finally, section 5.3 describes the particular methods applied in the research process of the present study.

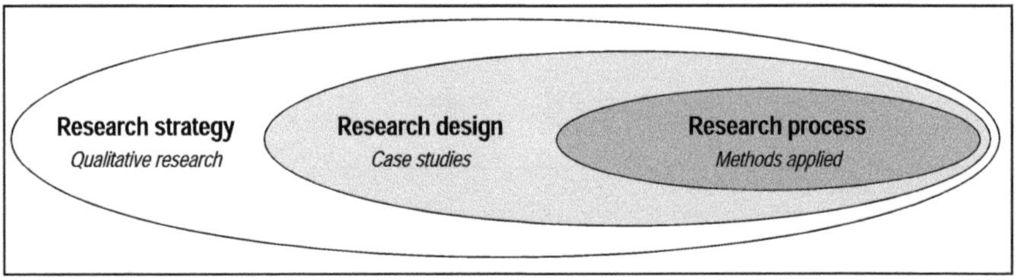

Figure 5-1: Research approach of the present study

5.1 Research strategy

5.1.1 Overview

As established in the scientific positioning (section 1.2), this study follows an empirical research strategy. Overall, empirical research comprises quantitative and qualitative research strategies or combinations of these methods (*Döring/Bortz* (2016), pp. 32, 180; *Brühl* (2017), p. 85). To find indications for the most suitable strategy for this study, these strategies are contrasted in the following.[66] Table 5-1 highlights important differences between qualitative and quantitative research strategies.

Overall, the present study calls for a qualitative research strategy. The **constructivist** position underlying this study can be seen as a strong indicator for this type of research strategy. A qualitative research strategy enables the researcher to approach underlying social realities in an open and communicative manner while taking the context into account (*Wrona* (2005), pp. 192-193). Moreover, the exploratory nature of qualitative research is deemed suitable for the study at hand (*Lamnek/Krell* (2016), p. 95). This study transfers extant **theories** and previously separate research streams into the field of preparation processes of nfKPIs for management reports to develop and explore theoretical relationships within this

[66] Both qualitative and quantitative research methods reflect collective terms which subsume various research designs and perspectives (*Wrona* (2006), p. 191).

field (*Edmondson/Mcmanus* (2007), p. 1160). The underlying research questions aim to examine processes and their contexts as **targets of inquiry** (*Eisenhardt* (1989), p. 536; *Gläser/Laudel* (2010), p. 28), thus providing another argument for qualitative research. In contrast to quantitative research, the **sample selection, data collection and data analysis** of qualitative research better reflects the comparative and interpretational nature of this study and supports the discovery of underlying relationships within and across the sample (*Flick* (2014), pp. 141-142). While qualitative research commonly does not aim for **generalizations** with regard to the population, deliberately constructed samples serve to explore extant or emerging theories (*Lamnek/Krell* (2016), p. 178).

Criteria	Quantitative research	Qualitative research
Theoretical position	Positivism	Constructivism
Theory	Basis for testing, explanatory	Result to be developed, exploratory
Target of inquiry	Causal relationships between variables	Qualities, processes, meanings, context
Sample selection	Representative, random	Theoretical, deliberate
Data collection	Standardized	Open
Data analysis	Statistical	Interpretational
Generalization	With regard to population	With regard to theory

Table 5-1: Differences between quantitative and qualitative research strategies (based on *Wrona* (2005), pp. 191-192, *Denzin/Lincoln* (2011), p. 8, and *Flick* (2016), p. 26)

5.1.2 Principles of qualitative research

As a consequence of its constructivist positioning, qualitative research follows particular research principles. Although qualitative research encompasses various research designs, the following principles can act as "common denominators" across them (*Döring/Bortz* (2016), pp. 63-64; *Lamnek/Krell* (2016), p. 33):

- Openness,
- research as a means of communication,
- reflexivity of object and analysis,
- circularity of research,
- flexibility and
- explication.

The principle of **openness** states that researchers should remain open to new dimensions and developments occurring during the research process (*Reichertz* (2009), Par. 27; *Breuer* (2010), p. 40). While researchers should still familiarize themselves with regard to the research topic and the methods applied, they should be able to lay aside their theoretical mindset to critically question and doubt the theoretical status quo (*Hitzler* (1991), p. 297).

The second principle recognizes **communication** between the researcher and the research subject as a fundamental component of the research process (*Küchler* (1983)). By engaging in an open "dialogue" with their research subjects, researchers can match their knowledge with the perspective of the research subject (*Lamnek/Krell* (2016), p. 242). Furthermore, the research process and research subject are assumed to be **reflexive** (*Lamnek/Krell* (2016), p. 36; *Haynes* (2017), pp. 284-285). Both the research subject and the researcher subjectively reflect on the behavioral patterns within the context of the research situation (*Denzin/Lincoln* (2011), p. 11; *Flick* (2017), p. 29). While research subjects reflect on behaviors from their own perspective, researchers examine and document their own subjective observations. Qualitative researchers deliberately use this subjectivity to draw conclusions from their findings and to develop or improve theories (*Döring/Bortz* (2016), p. 70).[67]

Unlike quantitative research, qualitative research follows a **circular** research process (*Döring/Bortz* (2016), p. 67). Qualitative research typically comprises successive, individual cycles of data collection and analysis, through which the research design can be refined and improved throughout the research process. This procedure is strongly connected to the principle of **flexibility**, which aims to ensure that the research process can react to characteristics of a research subject by adding important discoveries to an inquiry or by adjusting the research direction (*Lamnek/Krell* (2016), p. 37; *Döring/Bortz* (2016), p. 67). The combination of a circular and flexible research process implies starting with a broad scope which is narrowed down more and more. Finally, the principle of **explication** demands from researchers to disclose all steps of their research process, especially their underlying rules for gathering and interpreting qualitative data (*Lamnek/Krell* (2016), p. 36). Such disclosures support the audience of the study in verifying procedures and interpretations conducted by the researcher (*Kaiser* (2014), pp. 126-128; *Döring/Bortz* (2016), p. 70; *Mayring* (2016), p. 38).

5.2 Research design

5.2.1 Overview

Having identified the suitability of a qualitative research strategy for this study, the appropriate research design is selected. Among the most common research designs in social sciences,[68] the **case study method** is argued to be suitable when exploring processes and activities (*Creswell* (2014), pp. 13-14). The following section defines this research design and argues for its appropriateness.

Definition

Eisenhardt defines a case study as a research design "which focuses on understanding the dynamics present within single settings" (*Eisenhardt* (1989), p. 534). By categorizing it as a

[67] For an overview regarding the use of subjectivity in qualitative research see *Breuer et al.* (2019), pp. 108-128, and *Breuer et al.* (2011).

[68] The five most common research designs are identified as case studies, grounded theory, ethnography, narrative research and phenomenological research (*Creswell* (2014), pp. 13-14).

research design, a case study is recognized as being more than an isolated and specific research technique of social sciences (*Lamnek/Krell* (2016), p. 285). On the contrary, it can be understood as a **framework of methods and techniques** comprising the entire research process from its preparation to data analysis and presentation (*Stoecker* (1991), pp. 96-100; *Yin* (2018), pp. 15-16; *Flyvbjerg* (2011), p. 301; *Bryman/Bell* (2015), pp. 48-49).

Moreover, the definition indicates the **scope** and **operationalization** of the case study method. According to *Yin*, case studies investigate "a contemporary phenomenon in depth and within its real life context, especially when the boundaries between phenomenon and context are not clearly evident" (*Yin* (2018), pp. 15). In contrast to quantitative research designs, case studies deliberately include the context of a phenomenon into their inquiry (*Yin/Davis* (2007), pp. 77-79). Moreover, as case study researchers obtain their observations from various types of sources, they need to merge and triangulate their data for further analyses (*Yin* (2018), p. 15). These analyses may be directed by theoretical preconceptions to facilitate the collection and analysis of data (*Yin* (2018), p. 15). However, certain groups of qualitative researchers (e.g., grounded theory researchers) critically discuss the extent of theory integration in case study research (*Corbin/Strauss* (2015), pp. 28-29, 52-55).

Selection rationale

As the case study method has been used in several studies relevant for this study (e.g., *Adams* (2002); *Adams/Frost* (2008); *Osann* (2010); *Husillos et al.* (2011); *Searcy/Buslovich* (2014)), it resembles a thoroughly tested and recognized research design. Additionally, several reasons speak for selecting this research design for the study at hand: appropriate research questions, exploratory context, multiple perspectives, context-relatedness of the research and complex phenomena.

According to *Yin*, case studies are suitable for addressing "what", "how" and "why" questions (*Yin* (2018), pp. 9-10). Such questions show that case studies can enable researchers to investigate relationships between certain variables and phenomena. Moreover, case studies fit **research questions** which focus on contemporary events and which do not require researchers to interfere with interaction processes (*Yin* (2018), pp. 12-13).[69] As the research questions of this study resemble "how" and "why" questions, the case study method appears to be suitable to address the present research questions.

In the **exploratory context** of the preparation of nfKPIs for management reports, case studies can be used to advance the understanding of this novel and vague research problem (*Merchant/Van der Stede* (2006), p. 118; *Lamnek/Krell* (2016), p. 290). This study uses cases to explore relevant dimensions of organizational processes and relationships connected to the preparation process. The open and flexible research approach enables the researcher to shed light on new and previously neglected characteristics (*unfreeze thinking*) (*Eisenhardt* (1989), p. 546). Hence, the case study method can also contribute to existing streams of

[69] For research questions requiring control over certain behavioral aspects, experiments may be better suited than case studies. When analyzing non-current events without direct access to events, historical methods may be preferable to case studies (*Yin* (2018), pp. 9-11).

literature on nfKPI reporting or the preparation of corporate reports by "revitalizing", expanding or specifying them (*Locke* (2001), p. 97). Through analyzing and documenting the cases in detail, results from this study may be used to guide future research in the respective field (*Kromrey et al.* (2016), pp. 104-105). Thus, this study tries to link "rich qualitative evidence to mainstream deductive research" (*Eisenhardt/Graebner* (2007), p. 25).

Another important aspect of case studies is the opportunity to include **multiple perspectives** in the research. First, conducting interviews with various actors of the preparation process of nfKPI can shed light on individual perspectives, which help with challenging extant theory from different angles. Second, case studies help to reveal how participants of the preparation process of nfKPIs use their values and powers to shape the outcome of the preparation process (*Cooper/Morgan* (2008), p. 163). Third, case studies challenge perspectives of the existing literature by explicitly contrasting outliers or extreme cases – which are often dropped from samples of quantitative research – to typical cases (*Eisenhardt* (1989), p. 546; *Cooper/Morgan* (2008), p. 162). By explaining how and why these cases differ from one another, this study aims to provide a foundation for advancing existing theories (*Bailey* (1992); *Walton* (1992), p. 129; *Ragin* (1992), p. 218).

According to *Yin*, case studies are preferable to other research designs when phenomena cannot be separated from their **contexts** (*Yin* (2012), p. 4). This is the case if phenomena and contexts mutually influence each other as in preparation processes of nfKPIs (*Cooper/Morgan* (2008), p. 160). These processes are grounded in the structures, values and environment of the reporting firms. Through studying these processes in conjunction with their contexts, the cases provide the researcher with an in-depth and fundamental understanding necessary to analyze individual characteristics and interactions comprising preparation processes (*Cooper/Morgan* (2008), p. 164). By getting in close contact with the key persons involved in the process, the researcher receives exclusive data on their experience and gains access to other important persons and supporting documents (*Gibbins et al.* (1990), p. 122; *Bloomfield et al.* (2016), p. 371).

Another advantage of case studies is an ability to address **complex phenomena** (*King et al.* (1994), pp. 9-12; *Yin* (2012), p. 4; *Cooper/Morgan* (2008), p. 160). These phenomena typically comprise numerous – often non-quantifiable – variables which form multi-level cause and effect relationships (*Locke* (2001), p. 95; *Wrona* (2005), p. 18). Therefore, these phenomena often cannot be causally explained by isolated variables. Management reports are prepared by numerous participants and in the case of nfKPIs these participants likely represent diverse departments. Within the context and boundaries of their role in the organization, participants act according to their individual values and powers. Case study research can grasp such complex and contradictory phenomena by a rich narrative which describes the diversity and ambiguity of the situation at hand (*Ahrens/Dent* (1998); *Flyvbjerg* (2006), pp. 237-241).

Despite its advantages, case study research has several **caveats** which need to be considered when using this particular research design: the role of theory, generalization, subjectivity and limited resources. The **role of theory** in case study research is subject to heavy discussions. While some researchers support the notion of remaining open by working without "preconceptions" of theory (*Holton* (2007); *Glaser* (2012)), others fear that abandoning prior knowledge for the sake of openness – if possible at all – could lead to findings which fail to address significant gaps or flaws in the literature (*Hanson* (1965), p. 19; *Siggelkow* (2007), p. 21). This study assumes that theory, instead of obstructing openness in qualitative research, can extend the *repertoire to interpret* (*Wrona/Gunnesch* (2016), p. 729). As a result, theory provides more options for interpreting data or for reflecting on the findings. So long as researchers are doubtful about their previous knowledge, they can use their repertoire for inspiration when analyzing and explaining their findings (*Davis* (1972), p. 22; *Maxwell* (2013), pp. 49-53; *Wrona/Gunnesch* (2016), p. 270; *Reichertz* (2017), pp. 284-286). However, it is important that researchers reflect on and disclose their theoretical preconceptions (*Bourdieu/Wacquant* (1992), pp. 36-46).

Researchers commonly criticize that findings from case study research can only be **generalized to a limited degree** (*Steinke* (1999), p. 170; *Yin* (2018), pp. 20-21). Particularly financial reporting researchers tend to demand from research designs to yield *statistically generalizable* results (*Lukka/Kasanen* (1995), pp. 78-81; *Cooper/Morgan* (2008), p. 173). However, to expand existing theories, this study deliberately choses case studies and contrasts these to extant theories (*analytical generalization*) (*Yin* (2018), pp. 27-42, 55). Case studies can identify specific contexts and prerequisites in which certain phenomena can occur, which enables researchers to make inferences across populations (*Cook/Campbell* (1979), pp. 71-73; *Lukka/Kasanen* (1995), pp. 75-78). Hence, the generalizability of these analyses depends on the variation of conditions between the selected case studies (*Kleining* (1982)). Through applying techniques such as selective sampling or systematic comparisons this study compares and contrasts the case studies, which in turn improves the generalizability of the findings (*Flick* (2014), pp. 522-524; *Lamnek/Krell* (2016), pp. 178-180).

Data and findings from case studies are typically **subjective** with regard to researchers and interview partners. On the one hand, due to their individual preconception and skills, different researchers are likely to ask different questions and to arrive at divergent interpretations (*Breuer et al.* (2011), p. 428). While the use of theory may reduce the subjectivity of the researcher (*Wrona/Gunnesch* (2016), p. 727), this study is based on continuous reflections on the researcher's subjectivity and provides extensive disclosures of the research process and resulting theory building (*Steinke* (1999), p. 231). On the other hand, the subjectivity of interview partners can be linked to their limited personal perspective and distorted response behavior (*Döring/Bortz* (2016), p. 325). This subjectivity is mitigated and triangulated in this study through including multiple process participants per case firm (*Bebbington et al.* (2007), p. 369).

Finally, a major drawback of case study research is that both the capabilities of researchers and the access to relevant information are **limited resources** (*Bloomfield et al.* (2016), p. 370). In semi-structured expert interviews, researchers need to both moderate and document the interview, which is strenuous and prone for error (*Döring/Bortz* (2016), pp. 363-364). The number of case studies in research projects is typically small as these projects depend on the consent and collaboration of expert participants (*Bloomfield et al.* (2016), pp. 370-374). Moreover, the preparation, implementation and processing of case studies is time consuming for researchers which limits the amount of data that can be collected.

Thus, researchers have to carefully consider potential benefits and challenges of case studies for their respective research question. The specific drawbacks may not be averted completely, but a careful preparation and purposeful quality criteria can reduce their negative effects. In the context of this study, the case study method appears to be an adequate research design.

5.2.2 Case study design

According to *Yin*, case study designs **can differ across three dimensions**, as depicted in Figure 5-2 (*Yin* (2012), pp. 7-9; *Yin* (2018), p. 48). First, case study designs can be differentiated into single and multiple-case study designs. Second, within these case studies, researchers may focus either on single (*holistic*) or multiple (*embedded*) units of analysis. Third, the objective of case study research can be of exploratory, descriptive or explanatory nature. As illustrated by the dotted lines in Figure 5-2, the boundaries between the cases, their respective subunits and the contexts in which they are embedded are typically blurred and rather vague. This study defines each company[70] as a separate case study.

A **single case study** design enables researchers to analyze specific phenomena in depth (*Cooper/Morgan* (2008), pp. 165-166; *Yin* (2018), pp. 49-54). This can be especially relevant for testing theories in optimum conditions (*critical cases*), analyzing *extreme* or *unique cases*, examining common situations in *typical* or *representative cases*, accessing previously

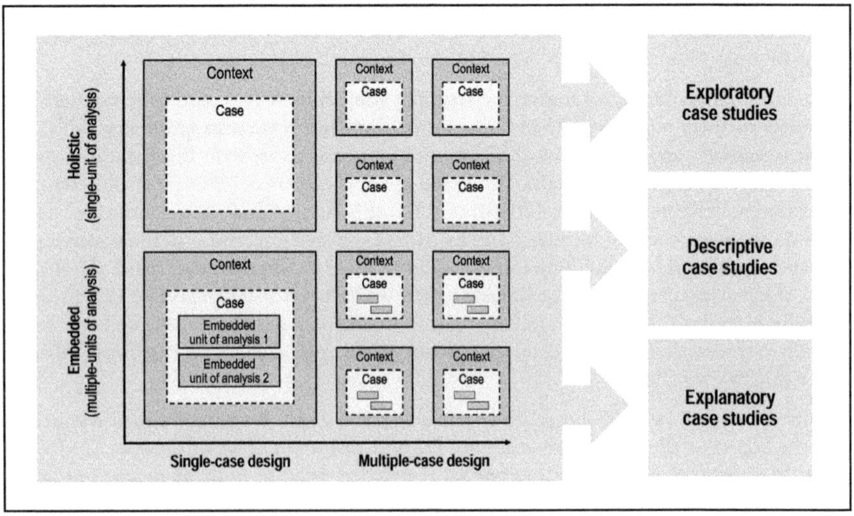

Figure 5-2: Case study designs
(based on *Yin* (2012), p. 8)

[70] As all sample firms in this study are incorporated in the form of a group, this study understands the group as a single entity and, hence, as an individual case study.

inaccessible phenomena (*revelatory cases*) or studying the changes within one case over a period of time (*longitudinal cases*).

The **multiple-case study** design – also known as comparative designs – contains two or more case studies which are examined with more or less equal research methods (*Eckstein* (1975), pp. 85; *Bryman/Bell* (2015), pp. 71-72). These cases are then compared with each other to provide a basis for theory-building or testing (*Eisenhardt* (1989), pp. 540-541; *Yin* (2018), pp. 54-60). Multiple-case studies follow a replication logic comparable to experiments, in which cases are chosen because researchers anticipate equal (*literal replication*) or contrasting findings (*theoretical replication*) (*Yin* (2018), p. 54). Similar to experimental research, contradictory findings would propose a revision and retesting of initial theories. Due to the possibility to distinguish between case characteristics, inquiries based on multiple cases are deemed to be more robust than single case studies (*Herriott/Firestone* (1983), p. 14). However, single cases can be better suited in certain settings and typically require less resources than multiple-case studies (*Yin* (2018), p. 55). This study is based on a multiple-case study design to allow for analyses of firms with similar or diverging characteristics. Thus, this approach can enable the researcher to extend underlying theories through including both typical and extreme cases into the analysis.

Holistic case study designs focus on the global character of a particular case study rather than on its subunits (*Yin* (2018), pp. 51-53, 60-61). These designs are typically chosen if a phenomenon cannot be separated into logical subunits or if an underlying theory is in itself global and holistic. In contrast to holistic designs, **embedded case study** designs examine various separate subunits within a case study. These case studies examine information flow, decision processes and resulting networks between multiple individuals to reveal general phenomena within groups, organizations or societies (*Schnell et al.* (2018), pp. 223-225). Through focusing on internal processes and roles of participants, embedded case studies can shed light on critical details of case studies which could otherwise be dismissed in favor of an abstract, generalist theory. For these reasons, this study uses an embedded case study design with individual participants and sub-processes as embedded units of analysis. A caveat of embedded case studies could be seen in the tendency of putting too much emphasis on the subunits. This caveat is mitigated by summarizing the analyses of the subunits to provide an analysis of the overall case.

The purpose of **exploratory** case studies is to gain a better understanding of new or under-researched topics and to develop relevant dimensions and hypotheses for future research (*Yin* (2012), pp. 29-32; *Lamnek/Krell* (2016), pp. 290-292). **Descriptive** case studies comprehensively describe a phenomenon and the context it is situated in. This serves as a basis for developing concepts and theories or for operationalizing future research (*Kromrey et al.* (2016), pp. 104-105). **Explanatory** case studies look into causal relationships to explain how events have happened (*Yin* (2012), p. 5; *Mayring* (2010), p. 235). This study leverages on all of these objectives of case studies to address the research questions at hand. Rich descriptions of the individual case studies provide a basis for exploring and explaining the preparation processes of nfKPIs for management reports both within and across cases.

In summary, this study uses a **multiple embedded case study design** to explore, describe and explain the preparation process of nfKPIs for management reports. The following section explains the implementation of this case study design throughout the research process.

5.3 Research process

This section discloses and explains the **research process** conducted for the study at hand. While qualitative research typically follows a cyclic research process (*Baetge/Prigge* (2006); *Flick* (2014), pp. 136-139), the phases of this research can be divided into the preparation, analysis and presentation (*Wrona/Gunnesch* (2016), p. 731).

Figure 5-3 shows the steps included in these three stages of the **research process**. As initial parts of the preparation phase, the research motivation (chapter 1), conceptual foundations (chapter 2), relevant literature (chapter 3) and underlying theories (chapter 4) have been presented in the previous chapters. In addition, this chapter lays out further steps taken in preparing the study at hand. The previous sections have explained and justified the selection of a qualitative research strategy (section 5.1) and the case study method (section 5.2). In the following, the selection of the cases (section 5.3.1) and the data collection process (section 5.3.2) are explained. Section 5.3.3 points out the coding procedures comprising the analysis phase. To provide meaningful results, this study follows several quality criteria which ensure a thorough and correct application of the aforementioned research strategy and research method (section 5.3.4). Chapters 6 and 7 present and discuss these results.

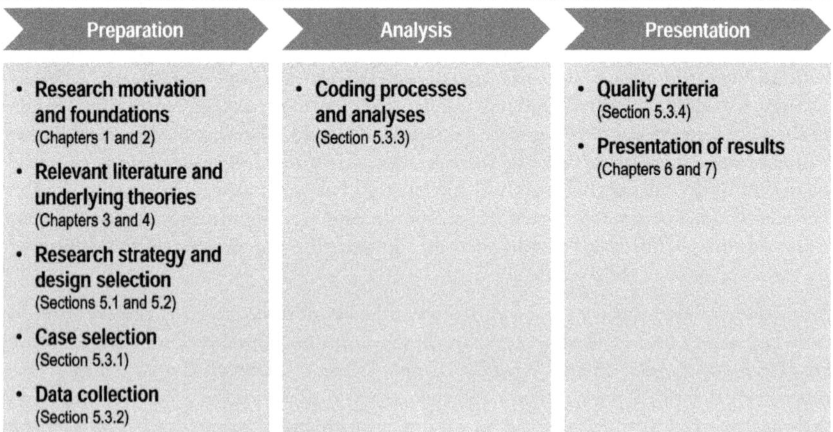

Figure 5-3: Research process of this study (based on *Wrona/Gunnesch* (2016), p. 731)

5.3.1 Sample selection

In contrast to quantitative findings that show statistically representative characteristics of a population, case study research typically aims to provide rich and insightful information on the causes or consequences of specific phenomena (*King et al.* (1994), pp. 46-49; *Flyvbjerg*

(2011), p. 306). However, the smaller sample size of case study research makes its findings more vulnerable to sampling errors as compared to findings of large sample quantitative methods (*King et al.* (1994), pp. 152-155; *Kelle/Kluge* (2010), p. 42). Hence, to avoid distorted findings in case study research, it is crucial to select cases that are **relevant** for the research question and for the respective area or group investigated. In this context, several different sampling strategies have evolved:

1) **Counterexamples**: The sample is made up of *crucial cases*, which are highly likely to offer counterevidence to initial hypotheses or extant theories. These hypotheses or theories are then refined and further challenged until additional cases do not provide any more counterevidence (*Cressey* (1953), pp. 13-17; *Lindesmith* (1968), pp. 3-22).
2) **Theoretical sampling**: This sampling process has been developed for the grounded theory method and applies to situations when research fields are novel or initial hypotheses are vague (*Glaser/Strauss* (1967)). Researchers follow a circulating sampling process which alternates between analyzing one case and then searching a follow-up case based on categories developed in the previous case. Such follow-up cases may be chosen because they are very different or very similar to prior cases. The sampling process is completed when the last case does not provide additional relevant differences or similarities (*theoretical saturation*).
3) **Selective sampling**: [71] Whenever researchers possess prior knowledge regarding variables or determinants, they can use this knowledge to develop and define selection criteria for their sample (*Schatzmann/Strauss* (1973), pp. 38-43; *Kelle/Kluge* (2010), p. 50; *Lamnek/Krell* (2016), pp. 184-185). In contrast to theoretical sampling, both sample size and selection criteria are determined in advance and data is analyzed after all case data has been collected.

For this study, the **selective sampling method** appears most appropriate for several reasons. First, selective sampling can be used for theory-driven research questions (*Merkens* (1997), p. 104; *Wrona/Gunnesch* (2016), pp. 734-735). This study follows such research questions, as it tries to establish a link between the design of the preparation process of nfKPIs for management reports and extant organizational theories such as institutional theory and promotor model. Second, this study can build on characteristics and determinants developed in previous research on the preparation of nfKPIs and the preparation process of corporate reports. As both topics have not been researched in combination before, this study could be seen as exploratory to some degree. While exploratory studies typically call for theoretical sampling, this study tackles the research problem by conducting the selective sampling process after an initial exploration of the research phenomenon (*Coyne* (1997); *Lamnek/Krell* (2016), p. 185).[72] Third, selective sampling provides a sampling plan containing all relevant characteristics and manifestations, which exposes researchers to the full heterogeneity of the field (*Lamnek/Krell* (2016), p. 185). This sampling plan does not result in a statistically

[71] This method is also referred to as purposeful sampling (*Coyne* (1997), p. 624).

[72] As an initial exploration of the field, an interview was conducted with an auditor who was involved in multiple preparation processes of nfKPIs for management reports. Resulting insights were combined with characteristics from extant literature to develop dimensions for the sample selection. Moreover, the dimensions and sample were revised after the first expert interviews.

representative sample but rather in a range from typical to rare or extreme cases (*Merkens* (1997), p. 100; *Kelle/Kluge* (2010), p. 55). Consequently, such sampling plans provide an opportunity to contrast unusual with typical cases to uncover organizational structures and to challenge extant theories (*Kelle/Kluge* (2010), p. 52). This selective sampling method is often chosen for interview studies in financial accounting (e.g., *Gibbins et al.* (1990), p. 123; *Graham et al.* (2005), p. 10; *Dichev et al.* (2013), p. 9; *Brown et al.* (2015), p. 7).

This study bases its selective sampling approach on selection criteria previously identified in the literature (*Gibbins et al.* (1990), p. 123; *Husillos et al.* (2011), p. 200; *Knauer/Wömpener* (2011), p. 191). The following selection criteria aim to identify typical and **critical cases**. While it is difficult to determine such cases from outside of the case firms (*Flyvbjerg* (2006), pp. 230-231), critical cases are assumed to be present when a case firm's disclosure of nfKPIs varies strongly in comparison to its peer companies. This could point to a high likelihood of differences in the internal preparation of the reporting in contrast to typical peer firms. Such indicators could for example be seen in firms providing best-practice nfKPI reporting.

Initially, cases are differentiated on the basis of three **key selection criteria.** As a first criterion, firms were selected according to being either **publicly listed or privately owned** (Figure 5-4).[73] While both types of firms face external demands from equity and debt capital providers (*Gibbins et al.* (1990), p. 123), management reporting practices of these groups reflect two different "worlds of management reporting" (*Kajüter* (2013), p. 127). Therefore, diverging outcomes and settings of public and private firms could be a possible indicator for differences in preparation processes of nfKPIs. The second criterion is reflected in the **size of the firms.** Both large and small firms are selected to account for potential effects of

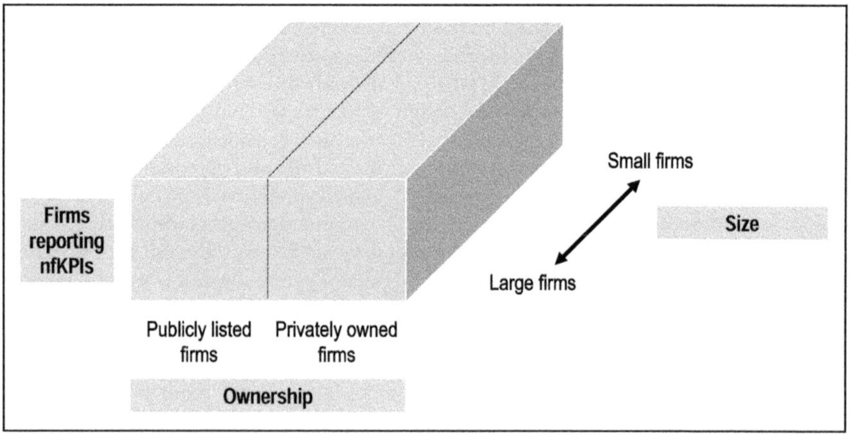

Figure 5-4: Key sample selection criteria

[73] In the following, the terms *public* and *private* are used to identify and differentiate the firms belonging to the particular groups.

the organizational size on the preparation process. Finally, only firms **which report nfKPIs** in their management report are selected. This limitation is deemed necessary to provide insights into the design of preparation processes.

As the actual design of the preparation process is difficult to determine from outside a company, these key selection criteria can only provide an initial indication. Therefore, the sampling for this study is also guided by additional criteria, which could indicate the design of the preparation process. First, the **scope** of nfKPI reporting is considered when selecting the sample firms. This scope can for example range between quantitative or qualitative nfKPIs or between nfKPIs relevant for the understanding of the course of business and nfKPIs relevant for the management of the group. Therefore, firms can be differentiated according to how extensive or restrictive they report on nfKPIs. Second, the **media and formats** of nfKPI reporting are considered. Firms with integrated reports, additional separate sustainability reports and those with chapters on nfKPIs in their management reports are included in the sample for this study. Thus, organizational effects of different reporting venues and formats can be further examined and compared. Third, the **industry** of the firms is considered in the final sampling. To provide a basis for comparing and contrasting, firms from different and similar industries are selected. Finally, the case firms are sampled with regard to their **location** and – to a certain degree – the **availability of interview partners** due to personal contacts. As the majority of interviews for this study is conducted on-site, firms from the wider region around the researcher's location were preferred over similar firms from other regions. Whenever possible and in line with the sampling plan, firms and interview partners were accessed through personal contacts (*convenience sampling*, *Bryman/Bell* (2015), pp. 200-201). However, several firms were also contacted through cold-calling the potential case firms.

The **selection of firms** is based on publicly available information such as the firms' annual reports from 2016 and earlier. A content analysis was conducted of the nfKPI disclosures in the management reports of firms listed in the HDAX. In combination with the other identification criteria, two large firms from the German HDAX were selected. In addition to this, a smaller firm listed on a German stock index for small companies was selected.[74] An initial sample of 100 private firms from three different size groups based on employee headcount was randomly selected from the AMADEUS database, excluding financial institutions. This sample was extended by private firms which had received awards for their management reporting, firms which were based in the wider region of the researcher and firms to which the researcher had personal contacts. In accordance with the above mentioned selection criteria, four suitable private firms were selected for the final sample of the present research project. The following Table 5-2 depicts all seven case firms with regard to their number of employees and their sales revenues in 2016. The overall sample size and composition reflects the goal of this study to enable in-depth analyses of the individual preparation processes while ensuring a broad basis of different firms for meaningful cross-case comparisons. For confidentiality reasons, all firm names are disguised as pseudonyms and data on company fundamentals has been approximated.[75]

74 This firm was identified through a list of all firms subject to CSR-RUG (*Kluge/Sick* (2016), pp. 12-24).

75 A detailed company profile for each of the case firms is presented in section 6.1.

	Firm name	Industry	Number of employees	Sales revenues
Public firms	HealthCo	Health care/agriculture	> 50,000	> € 5 billion
	ChemCo	Chemistry	> 25,000	> € 5 billion
	PrintCo	Manufacturing	> 1,000	> € 0.1 billion
Private firms	LogCo	Logistics	> 10,000	> € 1 billion
	FashCo	Retail	> 10,000	> € 1 billion
	TechCo	Manufacturing	> 5,000	> € 1 billion
	AgCo	Retail	> 5,000	> € 5 billion

Table 5-2: Fundamental data of sample firms (approximated)

5.3.2 Data collection

This section explains the data collection process of this study. Section 5.3.2.1 discusses the suitability of expert interviews for this study. Next, section 5.3.2.2 describes the phases of the interviewing process. Finally, section 5.3.2.3 presents an overview of the resulting interview data and discusses this data on the basis of the goals of this study.

5.3.2.1 Method selection

For case study designs in qualitative research, several different data collection methods can be selected: content analysis, observations and interviews (*Lamnek/Krell* (2016), pp. 279-283). When examining the preparation process of nfKPIs for management reports, several reasons speak for **interviews** as the most appropriate method for gathering the necessary data.[76] First, it is difficult or even impossible to observe the preparation process in practice. It is deeply rooted in the daily routine in practice and is carried out by multiple persons at various points in time. Second, interviews enable the researcher to gather background information and to establish relationships with the interviewees which facilitate access to other participants of the firm's preparation process. Third, the possibility to ask open-ended questions and to hold dynamic dialogues typically yields rich information which allows the researcher to examine the complex relationships embedded in preparation processes.

In social science literature, various types of interviews have been developed and discussed (*Helfferich* (2011), pp. 35-37). To identify the interview type suitable for this study, the **purpose of the interviews** is derived from the overall research goals (*Gläser/Laudel* (2010), p. 40). As this study aims to determine the design and influencing factors of the preparation process of nfKPIs for management reports, exclusive and detailed knowledge of process

[76] For a general discussion of the interview method see *Trinczek* (2009), pp. 226-229, and *Döring/Bortz* (2016), p. 356.

participants is necessary to reconstruct and analyze these processes (*Pfadenhauer* (2009), p. 99). Drawing from previous research (chapter 3), the preparation process of management reports is typically carried out by managers, accountants and specialists from functional departments of the respective firms. These participants serve as **experts**, who have specific knowledge in the field of preparation processes and who are able to communicate this knowledge to others (*Hitzler* (1994), pp. 21-24; *Bogner et al.* (2014), pp. 13-14).

Such expert interviews offer several **advantages** (*Lamnek/Krell* (2016), p. 690).[77] A certain degree of openness in the interviews allows the experts to explain, structure or evaluate the research object. This provides the researcher with helpful information for developing theories and possibly novel theoretical dimensions. As experts are accustomed to communicate in a concise and time-efficient manner, expert interviews can cater to their particular communication style (*Meuser/Nagel* (2009), pp. 31-32; *Trinczek* (2009), pp. 229-230). Moreover, the guideline-based design of the expert interview balances openness with a focus on the specific knowledge of the expert regarding the preparation process of nfKPIs (*Lamnek/Krell* (2016), p. 690).

An **interview guideline** is a central instrument of expert interviews, as this type of interviews is normally used in either semi-structured or structured interview situations (*Meuser/Nagel* (2009), p. 31; *Atteslander* (2010), p. 134; *Helfferich* (2011), p. 164). Depending on the interview situation, different interview guidelines may be appropriate. Semi-structured interviews are based on a semi-standardized interview guideline which contains open questions for the particular experts (*Döring/Bortz* (2016), p. 358).[78] While the guideline suggests a sequence of questions, both the order and composition of questions can be changed during the interview, if necessary. Structured interviews require a standardized interview guideline containing a non-modifiable sequence of closed questions (*Döring/Bortz* (2016), pp. 358-359). For this study, a **semi-structured interview guideline** seems appropriate. This method provides openness to further explore the research field while ensuring certain degree of standardization to categorize and compare the case studies. Moreover, this approach is prevalent in the literature on disclosure processes (e.g., *O'Dwyer* (2002), p. 411; *Osann* (2010), p. 83; *Husillos et al.* (2011), p. 196).

Interviews with experts can be classified into explorative, systematizing and theory-generating (*Meuser/Nagel* (1991), pp. 445-448; *Vogel* (1995), pp. 74-75; *Bogner/Menz* (2009a), pp. 46-48; *Flick* (2014), pp. 228-229). Interviews carried out for this study carry elements of all three types, reflecting the research objectives of this study. The **explorative** part of the interviews sheds light on the design and influencing factors of the preparation process. Other parts of the interviews aim to **systematize** the experts' detailed knowledge to *describe* such preparation processes (*Gläser/Laudel* (2010), p. 12). Finally, the interviews also serve as a **theory-generating** method. Experts are asked to *explain* their role in the preparation

[77] Some researchers critically discuss, whether or not expert interviews can be seen as an independent type of interviews. For an overview on the methodological discussion see *Bogner/Menz* (2009b), pp. 13-19.

[78] In the literature, this type of guideline is often referred to as semi-structured (*Husillos et al.* (2011), p. 199; *Bouten/Everaert* (2015), p. 28). This terminology is also applied in the present study.

process, which is used for constructing a theoretical model of the preparation process and its influencing factors (*Helfferich* (2011), p. 162).

As with any research method, expert interviews have specific **drawbacks**. Controlling the interview situation might be difficult, as experts can be prone to self-promotion and jargon (*Pfadenhauer* (2009), p. 85). Moreover, experts could be holding back relevant information (*ice-berg effect*) or could try to reverse the interview situation by engaging in a discussion with the interviewer regarding questions of interest to the expert (*Vogel* (1995), pp. 79-81). These drawbacks can be reduced in the course of the interview when the interviewer is accepted by the interviewee as a well-informed quasi-expert (*Trinczek* (1995), p. 65). Thus, a considerable amount of time was spent in preparing and pre-testing the expert interviews (*Kaiser* (2014), pp. 136-144).

5.3.2.2 Interviewing process

The interview process of this study consists of four parts depicted in Figure 5-5. First, a relevant expert of the case firm was identified and has assured his or her commitment to participate in the interview. Second, the individual interview was prepared taking into account prior knowledge regarding the firm and its preparation process of nfKPIs for the management report. Third, the interview was conducted either on-site or via telephone. Fourth, data gathered in the interviews was processed and potentially used for identifying and interviewing additional experts in the firm. These particular steps are further explained in the following.

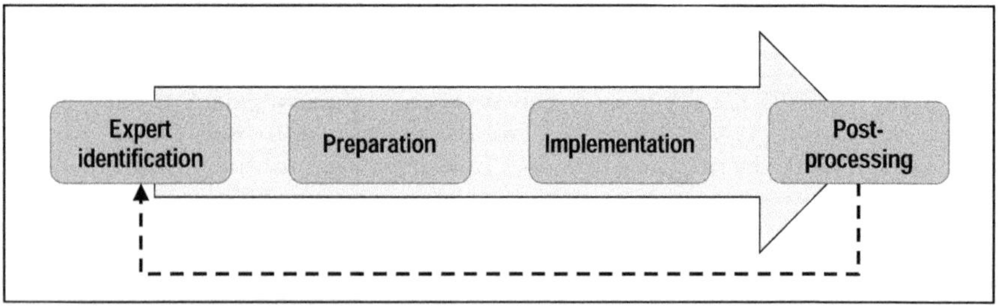

Figure 5-5: Interviewing process

Expert identification

The process of identifying the experts relevant for this study is depicted in Figure 5-6. In most cases, the participation of an **initial contact person** in the preparation process of the management report was not observable from the outside. Instead, initial contacts were chosen if their involvement in the process was perceived to be likely based on their department and position.[79] This was typically the case for the head of external reporting. In some cases, persons from IR or corporate communications departments were used as initial contacts

[79] The likeliness of an involvement of particular persons in the preparation process was derived from an analysis of the literature depicted in chapter 3.

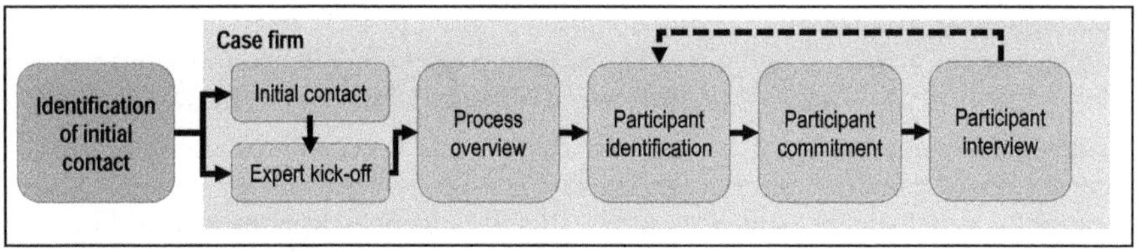

Figure 5-6: Expert identification process

when they were mentioned in the management report. However, it was assumed that financial accountants would possess a stronger gatekeeper role, for which reason it was preferred to contact these experts to ensure the commitment of the case firm.

The **initial contact persons** were called by telephone to explain the motivation and objectives of this study and to briefly describe the research design. They were then asked to describe their role in the preparation process of nfKPIs for the management report and – if possible – to provide an **overview** of this process. Whenever these initial contacts were not responsible for the coordination of the management report preparation, they were asked to **identify** the coordinators of the process. When contacting the coordinators of the process, they were informed about the study in a kick-off telephone call which – in almost all cases – proceeded with a **commitment** to participate in the study.[80] All interview partners also received a short summary of the research project. For each case company, the first interviews were **conducted** with the coordinators of the preparation process of the management report. Interviews were carried out in person, thus establishing a personal contact with the coordinators which enhanced the commitment to support this study.[81]

The results of these first interviews were then used to **identify further participants** of the preparation process of nfKPIs. With the support of the coordinators, participants were contacted and asked for their commitment to participate in the study. As indicated by the dashed line in Figure 5-6, experts often provided additional information which was used to identify and contact further participants of the processes. This type of interviewee selection is referred to as **snowball sampling**, as the researcher gains and accumulates access to other interviewees through the network of a previous interviewee (*Noy* (2008), p. 300; *Bryman/Bell* (2015), pp. 434-436). This type of sampling is suited for research questions that look at non-public and sensitive topics – such as the preparation process of nfKPIs for management reports – for which the knowledge and support of participants is crucial (*Biernacki/Waldorf* (1981), p. 141). The researcher deliberately controlled the development of the expert sampling within the firm to identify the most important actors within the process. Such selectiveness does not contradict the snowball sampling approach but prevents it

80 Only one large non capital-market oriented company declined to participate in this study in advance. The coordinator of the process justified the firm's decision by pointing out that nfKPIs were less important for their management report than for those of capital-market oriented companies.

81 After participating in an initial interview, the coordinator of the preparation process of the management report of a large private company declined to establish interviews with other process participants. This decision was justified by the fact that other interviews were currently not possible. Thus, this case was excluded from the final sample to ensure in-depth data and expert triangulation.

from becoming autonomous (*Biernacki/Waldorf* (1981), p. 143) and – metaphorically – turning into an "avalanche" sampling. This sampling approach is in line with prior research (*Kornberger et al.* (2011), p. 518; *Lander et al.* (2013), p. 134; *Kenno et al.* (2017), p. 90).

To determine the suitability of the interview experts in the context of the research goals, the interviewees were differentiated according to five types of departments: executive board, accounting, sustainability, communications, IR and functional departments. As the members of the **executive board** are responsible for the preparation of the management report, these experts were selected to provide insights into decision-making processes of preparing nfKPIs for communication to firm owners and other stakeholders. All executive interviews were conducted with CFOs of the respective companies, as these individuals typically supervise the preparation of the management report on behalf of the executive board. Members from the **accounting department** were selected based on the assumption that the CFO would typically delegate the task of preparing the management report. Moreover, participants from the sustainability department were interviewed. As this department is regularly involved in the preparation of sustainability reports and stakeholder communication, it was likely that this department would be involved in coordinating the preparation of the nfKPI sections or to at least provide information for its preparation. Furthermore, the **communications and IR departments** mark particular experts involved in the external communication of some firms. Hence, these departments were assumed to support the preparation through coordinating the preparation, writing nfKPI sections or reviewing the report with regard to its alignment with the firm's external communication. Finally, as nfKPIs can reflect a broad spectrum of operational information, **functional departments** were selected as interview experts. This selection was based on the assumption these experts could provide the coordinators of the report with specialist knowledge regarding nfKPIs.

Preparation

To prepare and conduct the interviews, a comprehensive **semi-structured interview guideline** was developed. This guideline serves two purposes, as it provides a structure for the research field at hand and serves as an auxiliary tool for data collection (*Bogner et al.* (2014), p. 27). Initially, to provide a **structure** for the present field of research, the guideline is derived from the research questions, foundations and theories underlying this study. Subsequently, the field of research was refined by selecting a qualitative research strategy, case study design and the appropriate type of interviews and guideline. Thus, structuring the field of research marks the first step undertaken to prepare the guideline (Figure 5-7).

Following this, research questions were transformed into actionable questions in the guideline to support the **data collection**. As an initial step, relevant interview questions were **collected** on the basis of the research questions (*Helfferich* (2011), p. 182). Subordinate questions were derived from the foundation on nfKPI reporting, a literature review[82] and the theoretical framework to form an initial pool of interview questions.

---

[82] Relevant questions were derived from interview guidelines of previous studies (*Osann* (2010); *Husillos et al.* (2011); *Knauer/Wömpener* (2011); *Tarca et al.* (2011); *Bouten/Everaert* (2015)).

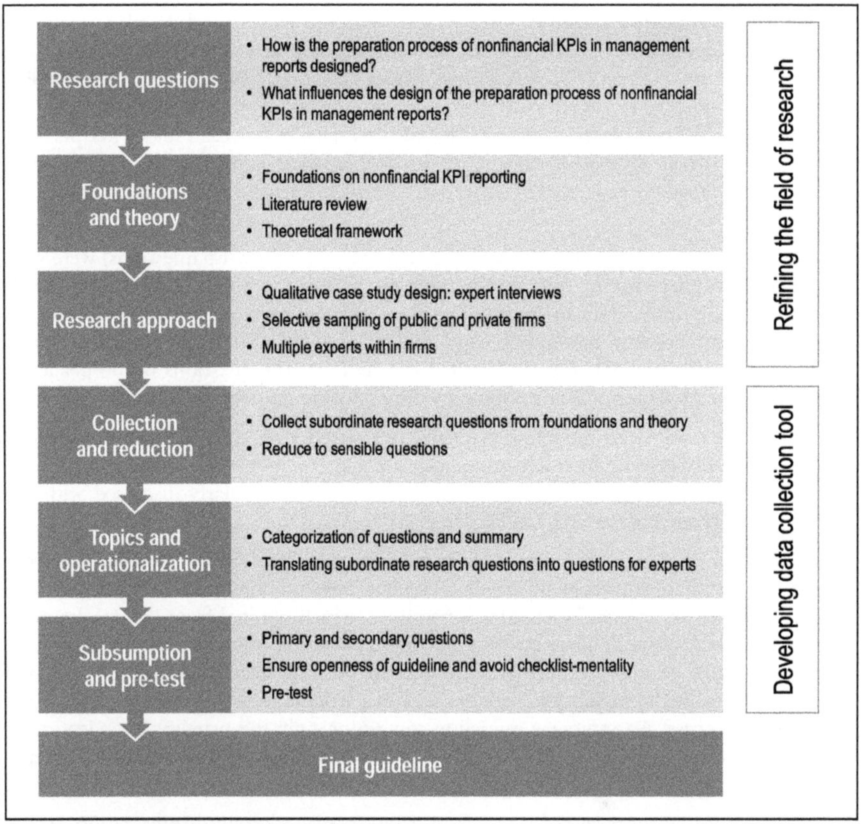

Figure 5-7: Development of the interview guideline

Subsequently, this pool of questions was **reviewed and reduced**. In accordance with *Helfferich*, questions were revised to eliminate or alter any of these which:

- evoke short factual statements,
- could likely not be answered by the interviewees,
- inquire previous knowledge of the researcher without being open for other results or which
- reflect the general, overarching research question, which may not be answered from the subjective viewpoint of the interviewee (*Helfferich* (2011), pp. 182-185).

Resulting questions were then **categorized** into different topics which reflect dimensions of analysis within the research field (*Bogner et al.* (2014), p. 33; *Kaiser* (2014), pp. 56-58). Whenever necessary, these questions were **operationalized** by transforming them into questions prompting experts to elaborate on individual topics of interest (*Gläser/Laudel* (2010), p. 113; *Helfferich* (2011), p. 185). In accordance with *Hopf*, questions were rephrased to

a) offer a large enough spectrum for answers, b) promote specific and detailed responses, c) inquire the involvement of participants in the preparation process or d) offer insights into personal views and contexts of the respective expert (*Hopf* (1978), pp. 99-101). However, to enable an objective reconstruction of the preparation process, most questions were directed towards the organizational knowledge of the expert rather than his or her personal views or skills (*Meuser/Nagel* (2009), pp. 33-34). Nonetheless, some questions were specifically directed at values and views of the expert to explore their role in the preparation process.

For the final interview guideline, secondary questions (e.g., follow-up questions) were **subsumed** under higher-ranking primary interview questions (*Kaufmann* (2015), p. 51). This hierarchy of questions serves to shorten and focus the interview guideline on the highest level to avoid a "checklist-mentality" (*Hopf* (1978), p. 102) and to reflect the natural train of thought (*Helfferich* (2011), p. 180). At the same time, the questions on deeper levels reflect the principle of openness through providing valuable support and points of reference.

The preliminary interview guideline was then **pre-tested** with an experienced auditor of nfKPIs in management reports. Resulting feedback and experiences were used to adjust the guideline. Moreover, the development of the guideline was regularly discussed with the doctorial supervisor and research colleagues.

Moreover, each interviewee received a **tailored interview guideline** matching his or her role in the preparation process of nfKPIs. The questions were extracted from the overall pool of interview questions depicted in Appendix A, which resulted from the development process described above. The interview guidelines comprised four categories of questions: 1) goals and role of nfKPI reporting, 2) phases of the preparation process, 3) roles and communication in the preparation process and 4) particularities and development of the preparation process. An interview guideline containing only the primary interview questions was provided to every interviewee before the interview to allow for a thorough preparation (*Bogner et al.* (2014), pp. 30-31).

Prior to each initial interview of a case firm, substantial background information on the firm was collected and analyzed (*Buhr* (2002), p. 20). This collection typically comprised annual reports, separate sustainability reports, presentations for investors and stakeholders, corporate websites, press-releases and corporate magazines. In combination with insights from kick-off meetings, this information was used to slightly **adapt the interview guideline** to the case firm. After each interview, the order and composition of the interview guideline was critically reviewed and slightly altered if necessary (*Kaufmann* (2015), p. 51).

Implementation

After agreeing on an interview date and providing an interview guideline to the experts, the **interviews** were preferably carried out face-to-face at the respective location of the company. In exceptional cases, follow-up interviews were conducted via telephone. Face-to-face interviews were preferred for several reasons. First, direct and personal contact enabled the researcher to pick up and react to non-verbal communication from the interviewee (*Busse* (2003), p. 30). In contrast to telephone interviews, the interviewer was able to interpret the reasons for silence and was less inclined to fill the void while potentially cutting off valuable answers (*Christmann* (2009), p. 176; *Gläser/Laudel* (2010), p. 168).[83] Second, the direct contact facilitated trust (*Gläser/Laudel* (2010), p. 154), which was critical for gaining access to internal information and a commitment to finding further interview partners. Interview partners often used the interview situation to present internal documents of the preparation process to the researcher, providing insights which may not have been presented in other forms of interview. Finally, the interview situation could be controlled to a certain degree by the researcher as distractions or attempts to multi-task during the interview could be noticed and reacted to (*Gläser/Laudel* (2010), p. 153).

A major **drawback** of vis-à-vis interviews is that on-site interviews are both time consuming and costly in terms of travel expenses. For this reason, the distance of possible case companies was considered in the sample selection process. Some researchers also argue that problematic interviewer effects[84] are higher in face-to-face interviews than for example in telephone interviews (*Groves/Magilavy* (1986), p. 255). While such effects could not be avoided completely, potential effects were factored in during the preparation to identify and potentially mitigate these effects whenever they occur (*Vogel* (1995), pp. 78-82; *Abels/Behrens* (2009), pp. 142-150). While researchers argue that the quality of telephone interviews is mostly equal to face-to-face interviews (*Irvine et al.* (2010)), the latter were always preferred for reasons mentioned above.

All interviews were **conducted** by the author of this study. Interviews were started with an introduction of the researcher and a brief summary of the research project (*Huber/Power* (1985), p. 176; *Spradley* (2011), pp. 78-80). The interviewees were then assured anonymity of both the case company and their identity. Following this, almost all interviewees agreed to a tape recording of the conversation.[85]

Post-processing

Subsequent to the interviews, interview postscripts and transcripts were prepared as a basis for data analysis. **Interview postscripts** contain relevant information that was gathered prior to, during or after the interviews and which is not covered by the recording (*Flick* (2014), pp. 387-388; *Kaiser* (2014), pp. 86-88). The information includes for example insights from emails or telephone calls, protocols of the interview situation or preliminary interpretations. Such postscripts provided context and background knowledge, which allowed for a better interpretation of the interviews.

Interview recordings were converted into **interview transcripts**, providing a written record of the conversations. The rigorous preparation of transcripts as "verbatim accounts" for the

---

[83] For an overview over benefits and drawbacks of telephone interviews see *Christmann* (2009), p. 176.

[84] The term interview effects refers to the influence of the verbal or non-verbal interaction between interviewer and interviewee, which could alter the responses of interviewees (*West et al.* (2013), p. 279). Common examples of such effects are for example the above-mentioned iceberg effects or feedback effects (i.e., the interviewee tries to reverse the interview situation by asking questions him- or herself) (*Vogel* (1995), pp. 78-82).

[85] Solely the investor relations representatives of ChemCo declined the request for recording for reasons of confidentiality. In this case, the interviewer took notes throughout the interview.

research is important to strengthen the trustworthiness of the research (*Poland* (1995), pp. 306-307). Transcripts were prepared through a four step **transcription process**. First, transcription rules were developed to provide guidance for a consistent and verbatim transcription of the interviews:[86]

- Conversations were transcribed verbatim (as said) without summarizing statements,
- separate paragraphs were used for each statement and were assigned with corresponding abbreviations to identify the respective speaker,
- acknowledging sounds of the interviewer ("Mhm", "aha", etc.) and filler words ("uhm", "yeah", etc.) were omitted unless they were important for the understanding of the statements,
- short pauses in statements were indicated (e.g., "(...)"),
- language and punctuation were marginally smoothed and
- non-verbal remarks were added in parentheses (e.g., "[Laughter]").

As a second step, student assistants transcribed the audiotapes following these rules. Interviews were transcribed in the language in which they were conducted, hence all transcripts were in German.[87] Third, the transcripts were reviewed and anonymized by the researcher to provide correct data that could not be traced back to specific companies or persons (*Gläser/Laudel* (2010), p. 190; *Bogner et al.* (2014), pp. 89-90; *Kuckartz* (2018), p. 171-172).[88] This step further improved the quality of the documents and enabled the development of initial ideas regarding the analysis.

5.3.2.3 Interview data

As described in the previous sections of this chapter, the findings of the seven case studies are primarily based on interview data from various participants of the firms' preparation process of nfKPIs for the management report. In addition, the interview data is triangulated by other internal and external data sources. The interviews for this study took place during a six month period between **May and October 2017**. In total, **29 different experts** were interviewed yielding around **31 hours of interview data**. These interviews ranged from a minimum of 54 minutes to a maximum of 135 minutes, with an average interview length of 64 minutes. Appendix B provides a complete list of all interviewees.

Experts were **selected** in such a way as to ensure meaningful and balanced within-case and cross-case analyses. On the one hand, each case study had to comprise a diverse set of key participants of the preparation process to allow for an in-depth within-case analysis. On the other hand, the amount of experts in each case firm was constantly compared across the sample. This comparison allowed the researcher to balance the interview data both within and between the public and private firms (*Oswald* (2010), pp. 188-191).

86 The transcription process and rules were developed in accordance with *Kuckartz* (2018), pp. 164-171.

87 Quotations used for the analysis were translated into English. In accordance with the literature, the quotations were – in rare occasions – marginally altered (e.g., the order of words) to improve the translation (*Adams* (2002), p. 230).

88 Further measures were taken to ensure ethical research (e.g., deleting the audiotapes and ensuring secrecy regarding the interview companies and partners) as suggested by *Helfferich* (2011), pp. 190-192.

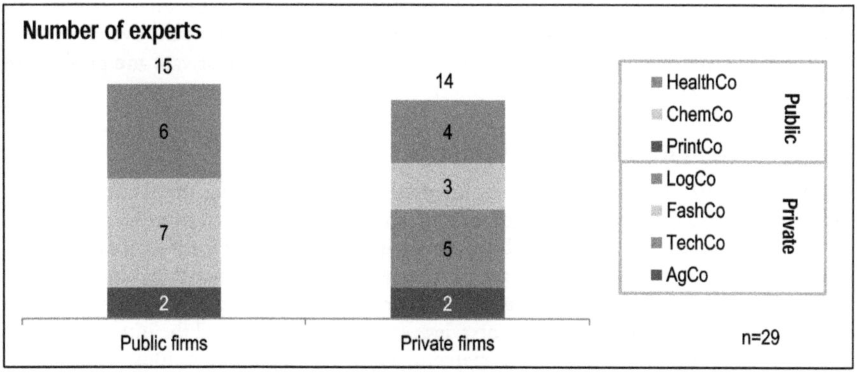

Figure 5-8: Number of experts

Overall, as depicted in Figure 5-8, 15 experts from public firms and 14 experts from private firms were interviewed. These interviews account for 16 and 15.2 hours of interview data respectively (Figure 5-9). This distribution shows that interview data on the level of public and private firms is relatively **balanced**, which reflects the goal of this study to analyze the preparation processes of both public and private firms. While the two case studies of HealthCo and ChemCo comprise the highest number of interviewees, each represent around one fifth of the total number of interviews or interview hours, respectively. Moreover, the combined length of interviews of these two firms (12.6 hours) is largely matched (10.4 hours) by the two private firms with the most interviews (TechCo, LogCo). Thus, it can be assumed that HealthCo and ChemCo do not create an imbalance in the sample.

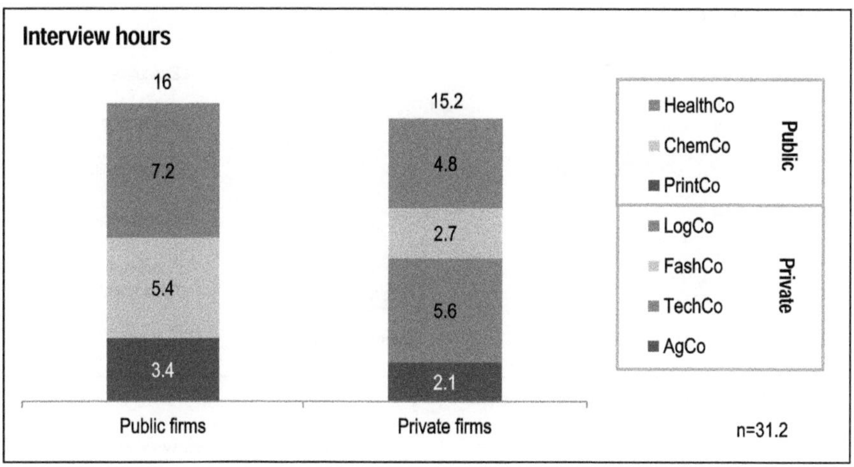

Figure 5-9: Interview hours

Although the number of expert interviews and the interview hours also diverge within the public and private sample groups, this divergence approximately reflects the overall size and complexity of the preparation processes. Thus, the interviews in the private and public firm groups, respectively, also seem to be balanced.

Interview data by departments of the experts

The departments of the experts play an important role in evaluating the suitability of the individual experts and the diversity of selected participants of the preparation process. All interviewees were able to answer to the interview questions relevant for their particular role in the preparation process. Thus, it can be assumed that they are knowledgeable about the preparation process of nfKPIs. Moreover, no expert rejected to participate in the study upon receiving the interview guideline. All interviewees claimed to have read the interview guideline prior to the interview and were prepared to answer all relevant questions.

The interview statistics of the **public firms** in Figure 5-10 show that one third (five experts, 5.6 hours) of the interviews were carried out with the accounting departments of the firms as potential coordinators of the management reports. Moreover, two experts (2.6 hours) from the sustainability departments were interviewed to address the involvement of these departments in the coordination of the preparation process. In addition, about one quarter (four experts, 4.1 hours) of the interviews involved the functional departments as information providers. These interviews included three experts from quality, environment, health and safety (QEHS) departments and one expert from the procurement department. Accounting for about one third of the subsample, three IRMs (1.9 hours) and one CFO (1.4 hours) provided insights into the review and decision-making related to the preparation processes in public firms.

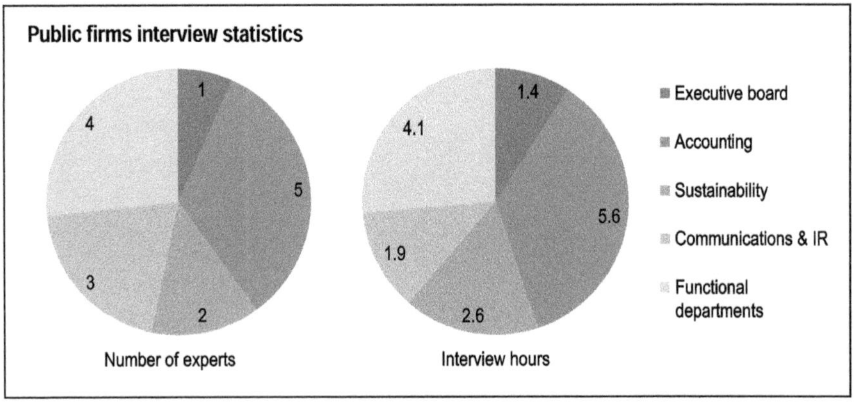

Figure 5-10: Public firms interview statistics

With regard to the **private firms** (Figure 5-11), about half of the interviews were conducted with participants from the accounting departments (six experts, 7.6 hours). One interview

(1.1 hours) was carried out with an expert from the communications department, who coordinated the preparation of the nfKPI section of the management report. Sustainability departments were not involved in the preparation processes. Similar to the public firms, about one quarter of the interviews (four experts, 3.4 hours) involved the functional departments of private firms. Out of these interviews, two were conducted with QEHS specialists and two with experts from the HR department. Finally, one fifth of the interviews (three experts, 2.9 hours) were conducted with CFOs of the sample firms.

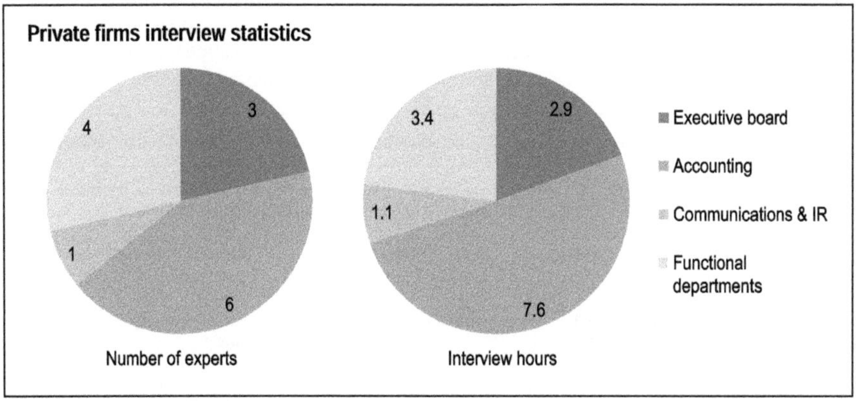

Figure 5-11: Private firms interview statistics

The interview statistics illustrate that this study circumvents the shortcomings of previous literature identified in chapter 3 by integrating perspectives of process participants from various departments. About half of the interviews capture the perspectives of the process coordinators, who provide integral knowledge about the preparation process and establish contacts to other participants. A similar number of interviews has been conducted with experts from functional, communications, IR departments or executive boards. Overall, the distribution of firms and experts **enriches the analysis** of this study through multiple case studies and perspectives.

5.3.3 Data analysis

The raw textual data of the interview transcripts represents the starting point of the qualitative data analysis. To analyze the data, texts are condensed through **coding** to "arrive at statements that can be generalized in one way or the other" (*Flick* (2014), p. 370). In a first step, rough analyses provide overviews and summaries of the preparation processes (*Flick* (2014), pp. 370-371). In a second step, detailed analyses result in categories and interpretations of the data. Data segments are labeled with codes to categorize, summarize and document relevant text passages at the same time (*Charmaz* (2006), p. 43). For the study at hand, such content analyses were not conducted on a "freestyle" basis as the coding procedures were deliberately chosen to match the underlying theoretical positions of the research (*Lamnek/Krell* (2016), p. 199). This approach promotes interpretations that are adequate for the research problem at hand and safeguards inter-subjectively traceable results (*Lincoln/Guba* (1985), pp. 316-317; *Steinke* (2017), pp. 326-327).

Coding procedures can range from very open and flexible (e.g., *theoretical coding*) to strictly rules-based, almost quantitative methods (e.g., *qualitative content analysis*) with various methods in between this spectrum (e.g., *structuring-thematic coding*) (*Lamnek/Krell* (2016), pp. 482-483). The procedures can also be differentiated by how they structure the data and by the goals, problems and limitations connected to their application. While differing in their approach to categorizing and analyzing data, all three methods provide frameworks for structuring and understanding the data (*Forman/Damschroder* (2008), p. 39; *Miles et al.* (2014), pp. 70-80). A comparison of the three methods is presented in Table 5-3.

Criteria	Theoretical coding	Structuring-thematic coding	Qualitative content analysis
Openness to data	Open coding	Identification of issues in cases and comparison to other cases	Rules-based and pre-defined content analysis
Structuring of data	Axial and selective coding, constant comparison	Development of a thematic structure for analysis of cases	Separate content analyses for summarizing and structuring data
Application	Theory generation (grounded theory)	Comparison of cases	Reduction of large amounts of data
Problems of application	Vague stopping-criteria for coding	Preceding case analyses increase time required for analysis process	Strict rules and procedures are often difficult to apply
Limitations	Flexibility of method is linked to practical experience of researcher	Rather suitable for studies with pre-defined comparative groups	Contradiction between qualitative principles and rigorous orientation of the method towards quantitative methods

Table 5-3: Comparison of coding procedures for qualitative data (based on *Flick* (2014), pp. 377-378)

Theoretical coding is part of the grounded theory research design. Grounded theory aims to develop theory from data in an iterative research process (*Corbin/Strauss* (1990); *Bryman/Bell* (2015), pp. 584-585). In grounded theory, coding is integrated into the process of data collection and continuous sampling (*Flick* (2014), pp. 403-410). While this research design is very flexible, the underlying rules and methods are rather abstract and do not provide sufficient stopping criteria for regarding the theoretical saturation of case comparisons or categories (*Flick* (2014), p. 417; *Bryman/Bell* (2015), pp. 592-593). Critics and founders of theoretical coding and grounded theory research agree that this research design requires sufficient experience and skills – often comparing it to a type of art or craftsmanship (*Strübing* (2002), p. 332). Overall, this type of coding is not seen as suitable for this study.

On the opposite end of the spectrum, the **qualitative content analysis** of *Mayring* is seen as a research design that is independent from the data collection, as it is typically carried out after the data collection without influencing the sampling or collection process (*Kuckartz* (2010), pp. 92-93; *Mayring* (2015)). This research design specifies a seven step framework to reduce the data to a predefined level of abstraction (*Mayring* (2015), pp. 61-

64). While this rules-based framework enables researchers to tackle larger amounts of data than other research designs, its focus seems to be oriented more towards describing the data rather than building or examining theories (*Kuckartz* (2010), pp. 95-96). The strict rules on how to categorize and summarize the data make it less suitable for rather open and explorative research questions as those examined in this study (*Mayring* (2017), p. 474).

The drawbacks of theoretical coding and qualitative content analysis at either end of the continuum call for a coding method which balances their specific advantages and disadvantages. The **structuring-thematic coding** approach marks a coding method within this continuum which is specifically suitable for reconstructing processes embedded in individual case studies and contrasting these in a multiple case study design (*Flick* (2014), pp. 376-377). This method also allows the researcher to integrate previous knowledge for examining and refining existing theories (*Kuckartz* (2010), p. 85). As this method seems to be the most promising for the research question at hand, it is briefly described in the following.

Structuring-thematic coding

While structuring-thematic coding can take on different forms,[89] a well-grounded method was developed by *Hopf* and colleagues (*Hopf et al.* (1985), pp. 42-43; *Hopf et al.* (1995), pp. 29-30; *Hopf/Hartwig* (2001)). Their method supports a **theory-driven analysis** of the data by integrating the coding into the development process of the interview guideline (*Kuckartz* (2010), p. 86). Nonetheless, open and flexible interview situations are ensured and researchers remain attentive towards irregularities or contradicting evidence.

As a first step of the **structuring-thematic coding process** depicted in Figure 5-12 (*Kuckartz* (2018), pp. 100-111), both the interview guideline and initial thematic categories were derived from the research questions and theoretical foundation. After collecting the data, initial thematic categories were used for a preliminary analysis of the first 7.5 hours of interviews. These transcripts were read from top to bottom and thematic categories were assigned to relevant text passages. After completing the first thematic coding, text passages were sorted by thematic categories to refine the dimensions and characteristics of these broad categories into more precise sub-categories.[90] With this refined system of categories, the entire data was coded – including the data that was already coded with thematic categories. Sub-categories were determined and differentiated in accordance with the underlying research questions. Resulting categories and codings were then used as a basis for the within-case and cross-case analyses (*Kuckartz* (2010), pp. 88-91).

Structuring-thematic coding is particularly **suitable** for data that was generated with theory-based interview guidelines (*Kuckartz* (2010), p. 91). This method also provides a structured framework of quality criteria which increase the inter-subjectivity of the coding process. Moreover, it is suited for analyzing and comparing pre-defined groups of single case studies (*Flick* (2014), p. 428). However, the coding process itself also points to a **drawback** of the

[89] For an overview see *Flick* (2014), pp. 420-428.

[90] Sub-categories were created to provide precise summaries while ensuring a manageable depth of codings. This was done by creating sub-categories that were as straightforward as possible and as differentiated as necessary (*Kuckartz* (2018), p. 106).

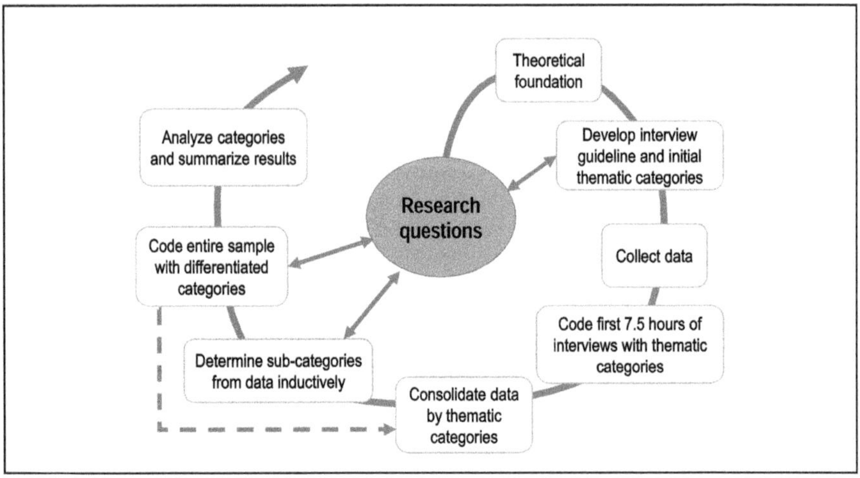

Figure 5-12: Thematic coding process
(own illustration based on *Kuckartz* (2018), p. 100)

method. Due to several stages of coding, refining and case analyses, the structuring-thematic coding method can be more time-consuming than theoretical coding or qualitative content analysis (*Flick* (2014), p. 428; *Kuckartz* (2018), p. 110).

Nonetheless, the time required was reduced through using **qualitative data analysis (QDA) software**. This software supported the research process by increasing the efficiency of the data coding and data analysis processes while ensuring the integrity and quality of the analysis (*Miles et al.* (2014), pp. 46-52; *Kelle* (2017), p. 500). The coding process was carried out with the software MAXQDA, which supports the structuring-thematic coding approach. The guidelines of *Kuckartz* were used for constructing the codes and for integrating these in the MAXQDA software (*Kuckartz* (2010), pp. 64-71; *Kuckartz* (2018), pp. 180-185).

5.3.4 Review of the research process

To present their empirical research as trustworthy and valid, researchers need to convince other researchers of the reliability and credibility of their findings (*Wrona* (2005), pp. 202-208; *Flick* (2016), p. 261; *Messner et al.* (2017), pp. 433-436). **Quality criteria** support researchers in this task, as they help to evaluate and legitimize the data collection and analysis (*Steinke* (1999), p. 11). Hence, such quality criteria serve as objectives and touchstones for assessing whether researchers have adhered to methodological requirements (*Lamnek/Krell* (2016), p. 141). However, as quality criteria are closely connected to the respective scientific positioning (*Wrona* (2005), pp. 202-203; *Lamnek/Krell* (2016), p. 142), four different positions regarding the use and the type of evaluation criteria for qualitative research have been developed and discussed in the literature:[91]

1) **Rejection of quality criteria:** based on a postmodernist world-view, researchers argue that no frame of reference for quality criteria could exist (*Smith* (1984), p. 383; *Richardson/St. Pierre* (2018), p. 820). This is justified by the assumption that no measurement method is universally correct because all qualitative research is seen as subjective and, thus, constructed (*Steinke* (1999), p. 50).
2) **Adoption of quantitative quality criteria:** according to this position, qualitative research shall be judged on the basis of the positivist quality criteria of objectivity, reliability and validity (*Krippendorf* (1980), pp. 129-168; *Steinke* (1999), p. 43; *Mayring* (2015), pp. 123-129).
3) **Development of new quality criteria**: supporters of this position suggest that quality criteria shall be on the basis of scientific and methodological positions of qualitative research.[92] It is argued that such criteria could better reflect the characteristics of the qualitative research process than quantitative quality criteria (*Flick* (2014), p. 489; *Steinke* (2017), pp. 320-321).
4) **Adaption of criteria towards common core objectives:** a fourth research stream identifies common core objectives of quality criteria from quantitative and qualitative research approaches. On this basis, researchers derive suiting quality criteria for qualitative studies (*Kelle et al.* (1993), pp. 40-41). Therefore, quality criteria address key methodological problems present in both research approaches (*Cook/Campbell* (1979), pp. 52-55, 73-74; *Wrona* (2006), p. 204).

The first three positions are seen as **inappropriate for this study** for several reasons. The first position is criticized for fostering arbitrariness and a potential lack of transparency of qualitative studies (*Steinke* (1999), p. 51). With regard to the second position, researchers criticize that qualitative research should not be evaluated with quality criteria primarily established for hypothesis testing and experimental research (*Steinke* (1999), pp. 160-165; *Wrona* (2006), pp. 202-203). In contrast to quantitative research, causalities are typically developed rather than tested and qualitative research situations are normally not replicable. Therefore, this position also appears to be unsuitable for this study. Although proponents of the third position have developed various catalogues of quality criteria suited for qualitative research (*Lincoln/Guba* (1985), pp. 289-331; *Kirk/Miller* (1986), pp. 13-21; *Noyes et al.* (2008), p. 580), no common and consensual set of core criteria exists. Hence, when using an individual pool of quality criteria, readers of the study are challenged with determining whether or not the selected criteria are appropriate (*Döring/Bortz* (2016), p. 107). As this third approach could impede the inter-subjective traceability of the findings, developing new quality criteria is not seen as suitable for this study.

This study follows the fourth approach of using quality criteria for qualitative research which share **common core objectives** with quality criteria for quantitative research (i.e.,

[91] For discussions regarding the different positions on quality criteria see *Steinke* (1999), *Wrona* (2006), pp. 202-208, and *Flick* (2014), pp. 487-510.

[92] For the discussion regarding the development of specific quality criteria for qualitative research see *Lincoln/Guba* (1985), pp. 289-331, *Flick* (1987), pp. 250-259, and *Mishler* (1990), pp. 416-423.

validity, reliability and objectivity). In the following, central problems and threats of these criteria are identified to derive suitable quality criteria (*Wrona* (2006), p. 205). Table 5-4 provides an overview over the discussion and presents the quality criteria applied in this study. These criteria are applied throughout the research process, some focusing on the development of the research design while others support the data collection and analysis processes.

Criteria	Core objectives of criteria	Quality criteria in quantitative research	Quality criteria in this study
Internal validity	Validity of variables in the model	• Operationalization	Closeness to data (one researcher, personal interviews, in-vivo codes, quotes, QDA software, verbatim transcripts); comprehensibility (communicative validation, triangulation)
		• causalities of variables	Structuring-thematic coding, permanent comparison, analytical induction
External validity	Generalization	Representative sample	Selective sampling, communicative validation
Reliability	Consistency of research process and data	Extent of measurement errors	Procedural reliability (documentation of research process, QDA software, quotes)
Objectivity	Independence from researcher	Standardized methods	Documentation and disclosure of subjectivity and reflexivity in the research process

Table 5-4: Quality criteria for qualitative research deducted from quantitative criteria (based on *Wrona* (2006), p. 208)

Validity

In quantitative research, the **validity** of measurement describes the "accuracy with which a description of particular events (or a set of such descriptions) represents the theoretical category that it is intended to represent and captures the relevant features of these events" (*Hammersley* (1992), p. 67).[93] This validity is separated into internal and external validity.

The **internal validity** shall ensure that changes in the dependent variable are caused by changes in the independent variable and not by other interfering variables (*Friedrichs* (1990), p. 100; *Johnson* (1997), p. 288; *Schnell et al.* (2018), p. 193). Therefore, the internal validity safeguards the operationalization and causality of variables (*Wrona* (2006), p. 202).

With regard to the **operationalization** in qualitative research, conclusions of a researcher shall be closely based on the data and shall be comprehendible for others (*Wrona* (2005), pp. 40-41; *Steinke* (2017), p. 321). This study ensures the **closeness to the data** through several means. First, all interviews were conducted by the researcher himself. Hence, first

93 For other researchers, validity reflects the "truthfulness of findings" (*Altheide/Johnson* (1994), p. 487) or whether a study has measured what should have been measured (*Friedrichs* (1990), p. 100).

hand insights were gained in the interview situations and interpretations were based on the interview context. Second, personal interviews improved the accuracy of interview results by ensuring that informants were experts in their respective field and by identifying and reacting to sensitive issues (*Huber/Power* (1985), pp. 174-178). Third, empirical results are presented in combination with "in-vivo codes" and data citations to limit the scope of interpretation (*Wrona* (2006), p. 205; *Flick* (2014a), pp. 406).[94] Fourth, using QDA software enabled a close and efficient analysis of the data (*Wrona* (2006), p. 205; *Kuckartz* (2010), pp. 19-20). Finally, transcripts of the interviews were prepared as verbatim accounts, thus reflecting the actual wording of the interview and establishing the trustworthiness of the data (*Poland* (1995), pp. 306-307). Tape-recordings were transcribed in German to base interpretations closely on the underlying meaning. The coding was conducted in English and "in-vivo" codes or citations were translated into English as closely to the original wording and meaning as possible (*Adams* (2002), p. 230; *Bouten/Everaert* (2015), p. 30).

Concerning the **comprehensibility** of conclusions, the internal validity was increased by debriefing interviewees to verify transcripts and by discussing preliminary interpretations (*communicative validation*) (*Lincoln/Guba* (1985), pp. 308-309; *Mayring* (2015), p. 127). In addition to communicative validation, several forms of **triangulation** were used to increase the internal validity (*Johnson* (1997); *Flick* (2018), pp. 454-455). *Data triangulation* was carried out by examining the preparation process of nfKPIs for the management report through the perspectives of various participants. Also, participants provided internal documents, spreadsheets or timelines of the processes. These different data sets helped to find multiple sources of evidence for interpretations of the processes. These interpretations were supported by an extensive *theory triangulation*, based on the theoretical considerations in chapter 4. Multiple theoretical lenses were used as an extensive framework for analysis of the design and influencing factors of the preparation processes (*Bennett* (1997), p. 97). Moreover, *researcher triangulation* was used on several occasions to audit the research process and to discuss central results of the study. In this context, the research progress was regularly discussed with the supervisor and other research assistants.

In addition to the operationalization, uncertain **causalities** stemming from alternative explanations pose another threat to the internal validity (*Wrona* (2006), p. 206). In quantitative research, different interpretations of empirical phenomena could lead to opposing hypotheses, which are then critically analyzed and contrasted (*falsifiability*). Transferred to qualitative research, researchers analyze and contrast their data to arrive at potential causal relationships (*Johnson* (1997), p. 287). To ward off the threat of arriving at wrong conclusions, methods were applied which question interpretations by searching for counterevidence (*Wrona* (2006), p. 206). In addition to the structuring-thematic coding approach of this study (section 5.3.3), methods such as the permanent comparison or the analytical induction were used to challenge the codings and interpretations.[95] Drawing from the permanent comparison, interpretations were scrutinized with counterexamples from other

94 "In-vivo" codes resemble code labels directly derived from expressions of interviewees (*Kruse* (2015), p. 379).

95 For the permanent comparison see *Strauss/Corbin* (1996), pp. 63-74, and *Goulding* (2002), pp. 68-69. For the analytical induction see *Bühler-Niederberger* (1985), pp. 478-480.

cases or extant theory. On the basis of the analytical induction, preliminary categories and interpretations were contrasted to additional cases to further improve the conclusions drawn from the findings.

The **external validity** safeguards that the empirical results can be generalized with regard to other points in time and circumstances as compared to those of the sample (*Cook/Campbell* (1979), p. 71). This quality criterion cannot directly be transferred to qualitative research because of the non-representative and non-replicable sampling of this type of research (*Strauss/Corbin* (1996), p. 215; *Wrona* (2006), p. 206; *Lamnek/Krell* (2016), p. 178). Addressing the underlying core objective of generalizability, a selective sampling approach was chosen to contrast between typical and extreme cases. Cases were selected on the basis of several external criteria (e.g., size, listing, format of nfKPI reporting) to ensure that the sample reflects typical and extreme cases. Moreover, verifying interpretations through communicative validation also enhanced the external validity of the results (*Lincoln/Guba* (1985), pp. 295-298).

Reliability

The quality criterion of **reliability** is defined as the "stability of findings" (*Altheide/Johnson* (1994), p. 487) for cases where phenomena are examined by other researchers or at different points in time (*Hammersley* (1992), p. 67). The corresponding consistency is typically approximated through the extent of measurement errors (*Wrona* (2006), p. 202). However, qualitative research situations are typically not repeatable as the results depend on the time, place and subject of the study. Hence, it is impracticable and often impossible to use quantitative methods to determine measurement errors of the methods applied (*Steinke* (1999), pp. 144-158). To present qualitative studies as dependable, researchers shall be able to explain that the research process both accurately captures phenomena and consistently draws conclusions from the findings (*procedural reliability*) (*Kirk/Miller* (1986), pp. 49-51; *Wrona* (2006), p. 207; *Flick* (2017), pp. 490-492). Consequently, this study secures the procedural reliability and inter-subjective verifiability by rigorously documenting and disclosing the research process (*Kirk/Miller* (1986), pp. 72-73; *Lillis* (2006), p. 470). This chapter derives indications for the research method and explains in detail how data was selected, collected and analyzed. Theoretical preconceptions are discussed in chapter 4 and integrated into the analysis (*Wrona/Gunnesch* (2016), p. 740). Moreover, using QDA software supports the structured and comprehensive analysis of the data. Within the analysis chapter, exemplary interview quotes are presented and contrasted when they reflect typical or extreme answers to the questions (*Deegan/Blomquist* (2006), p. 355). This way, quotes can illustrate practitioners' views and establish trustworthiness with regard to the interpretation of the researcher.

Objectivity

In quantitative research, findings are understood as **objective** if they are intersubjectively traceable (*Popper* (2005), p. 21). This is typically achieved by standardized methods of data collection and analysis (*Lienert/Raatz* (1998), pp. 7-9). However, the deliberate use of subjectivity in qualitative research is incompatible with the quantitative approach to objectivity

(*Steinke* (1999), pp. 142-144; *Döring/Bortz* (2016), p. 70). Therefore, a careful documentation and communication of the research process enables intersubjective comprehensibility (*Steinke* (1999), p. 207; *Wrona* (2006), p. 207). To ensure the intersubjective comprehensibility of this study, the use of subjectivity and reflexivity in the research process is disclosed.

Overview of implementation

Figure 5-13 provides an outline of how the embedded multiple case study design of this study was implemented. Data from each case firm was **collected** through publicly available documents, interviews with several participants of the preparation process of nfKPIs and – if available – internal documents provided to the researcher. This data was then **analyzed** for each individual case firm. These **within-case analyses** shall provide an overview of the company profile and the preparation process of nfKPIs.

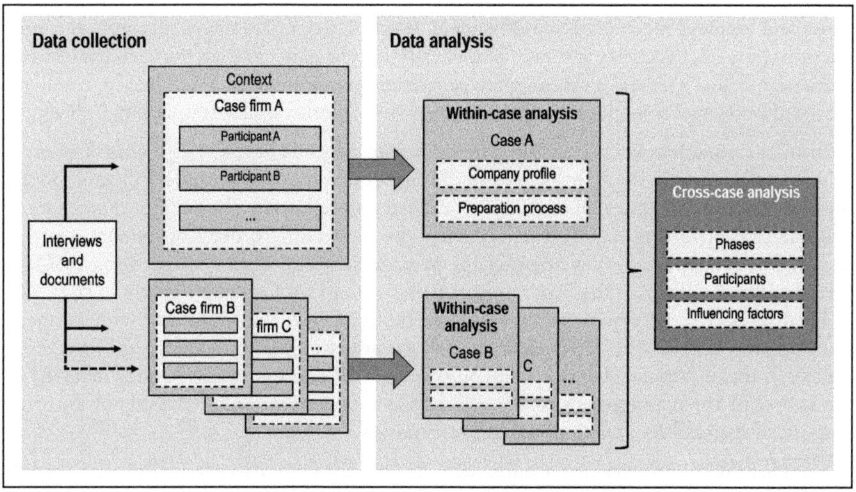

Figure 5-13: Embedded multiple case study design of the study

Subsequently, **cross-case analyses** were conducted on several units of analysis. Through analyzing the **phases** of the preparation process, similarities and differences of the process steps were identified. On the basis of this, **participants** of the preparation process were analyzed. Using the promotor model discussed in chapter 4, the influence of particular organizational structures on the design of the preparation process was analyzed and critically discussed. From these analyses, first explanations for the design of the preparation process for nfKPIs in management reports were derived. Finally, internal and external **influencing factors** were identified and analyzed with regard to their influence on the design of the preparation process. The results of the cross-case analyses shall both **extend present theory** and provide **implications for preparers** of nfKPIs for management reports. The results of both the within- can cross-case analyses are presented in the following chapter.

6 Empirical results

This chapter presents the empirical results of this study. Section 6.1 illustrates the company profiles and preparation processes of the seven case study firms. Subsequently, section 6.2 provides cross-case analyses of the cases with regard to the design and influencing factors of the preparation processes.

6.1 Within-case analyses

6.1.1 HealthCo case

6.1.1.1 Company profile and nfKPI reporting

HealthCo is a world-leading producer of health care and agricultural products for both supplier and consumer markets. The company generates more than € 5 billion in sales revenues and employs more than 50,000 people. HealthCo operates internationally with production sites, R&D centers and sales branches across the globe and on every continent. Far more than half of the firm's revenues are generated outside of Germany. HealthCo's shares are listed on German stock exchanges on major stock market and sustainability indices.

HealthCo's **organization** is structured in accordance with its business segments. The executive board supervises these segments and the corporate support functions. In the corporate support function for financial accounting and external reporting, the head of management and quarterly reporting (HMQR) coordinates the preparation process of the management report. She is supported by a manager for management and quarterly reporting (MQR). Her supervisor reports to the head of accounting who in turn reports directly to the CFO of HealthCo. The IR department, supervised by the CEO, communicates with financial stakeholders. Within this department, one of the investor relations managers (IRM) specializes in the nonfinancial and sustainability related IR communication and is involved in the review of the management report. HealthCo's supervisory board consists of an equal amount of shareholder and employee representatives.

While HealthCo's primary target is financial success, the firm strives to include sustainability into its practices as a necessary condition. The group aims for several **nonfinancial targets** with regard to R&D (e.g., number of drugs in development phase), sustainable procurement (e.g., ratio of evaluated suppliers), production (e.g., number of plant incidents and CO_2 emissions in tons) and HR (e.g., number of work-place accidents and the degree of management diversity). These nfKPIs reflect intersections between the economic dimension of nonfinancial information and the two other dimensions, except for the purely economic R&D nfKPIs. The nonfinancial targets are neither part of HealthCo's internal management system nor are they included in the compensation of the executive board. However, they are used for the operational management of the respective support functions and business lines. In addition to these nonfinancial targets and in accordance with the GRI G4 guidelines, HealthCo uses other economic, environmental and social nfKPIs for the operational management of the firm. However, the preparation process of these voluntary nfKPIs is not considered in this study.

HealthCo's **sustainability activities** are supervised by the QEHS support function, which is supervised by the Chief People Officer (CPO). Amongst other tasks, the department conducts materiality analyses and prepares the reporting on nfKPIs. A manager of the sustainability department (MSD) – a sub-department of the QEHS department – coordinates the preparation process, together with colleagues from the sustainability department. QEHS related nfKPIs are collected in a QEHS database which is coordinated by a small team headed by the database manager (DBM). In addition, other nfKPIs are provided by business lines or supporting functions such as procurement. In the procurement team, a manager for sustainable procurement (MSP) coordinates the sustainability activities of the support function and collects relevant nfKPIs for internal and external reporting. Table 6-1 presents the interview partners of HealthCo participating in the nfKPI preparation process.

Title	Abbreviation	Department
Head of management and quarterly reporting	HMQR	Financial accounting
Management and quarterly reporting	MQR	Financial accounting
Manager sustainability department	MSD	Sustainability
Manager sustainable procurement	MSP	Procurement
QEHS database manager	DBM	QEHS
Investor relations manager	IRM	Investor relations

Table 6-1: Interview partners at HealthCo

With the financial year ranging from January to December, HealthCo prepares its financial statements according to IFRS. The financial statements are complemented by a group management report. HealthCo uses an **integrated reporting format** for its management report. In a separate chapter of this report, linkages between financial and nfKPIs are explained. The chapter discusses the overall goals and strategies, the internal management system of the group and the sustainability related activities of the business lines and corporate support functions. While nonfinancial targets are provided, they are neither included in the report section on the internal management system nor in the management forecast. The remainder of the chapter provides analyses of the most important nfKPIs and refers to more detailed overviews of these and other nfKPIs on the company website. Both qualitative and quantitative nfKPIs are provided. In accordance with the CSR-RUG, a separate table provides references to relevant sections in the report which cover nonfinancial matters. As a part of the management report, nfKPIs are audited with reasonable assurance while those on the website are audited with limited assurance. Both the nfKPIs for the management report and the website are prepared according to GRI G4 guidelines and UN Global Compact.

HealthCo's most important **goal for nfKPI reporting** is transparency towards its stakeholders. Through disclosing its nonfinancial goals and performance, stakeholders shall be enabled to assess HealthCo's goal attainment. Moreover, HealthCo wants to demonstrate its commitment to take responsibility for its actions. Another important goal of integrating nfKPIs in its management report is to present interlinkages between financial KPIs and nfKPIs in HealthCo's business. In this context, the firm aims to underline the growing importance of nfKPIs and to provide stakeholders with a complete picture of its course of business. As HealthCo's stakeholders increasingly demand credible and valid nfKPIs, the firm strives to meet this demand by providing audited information in its management report and on its website. Complying with regulation and guidelines is a minimum goal for HealthCo, as the firm actively engages in various regulatory and industrial initiatives and strive for best-practice reporting. Overall, HealthCo uses a broad understanding of materiality regarding nfKPIs, which includes the most important nfKPIs according to § 289 (3) HGB, material nfKPIs according to CSR-RUG as well as voluntary nfKPIs in accordance with the GRI G4 guidelines.

The integrated report of HealthCo addresses a broad range of **report users**. Capital market participants such as investors, analysts and rating agencies are an important target group of HealthCo's nfKPIs.[96] While rating agencies already receive nfKPI-related information through questionnaires, HealthCo also adapts its disclosures in the management report of the following period to match the answers provided in the questionnaires. In addition, HealthCo uses the report to actively address concerns raised by NGOs or the general public. The firm wants to show regulators and politicians that it is acting sustainably. HealthCo also addresses nfKPIs in the management report to inform its employees.

6.1.1.2 Preparation process of nfKPIs

HealthCo's preparation process of nfKPIs reflects the integrated reporting approach of the firm. The overall preparation process of the management report is **coordinated** by the accounting team supervised by the HMQR and MQR. They are responsible for planning and implementing the overall timetable, coordinating the editorial software and providing the IT system for collecting the proof documents for the audit. Most tasks related to the nfKPIs are carried out by MSD and her team members from the sustainability reporting team. In addition to these two teams, a large number of other participants are involved in the preparation process of nfKPIs. The following section provides an outline of the phases and participants of this process. Figure 6-1 summarizes the participants and the flow of information involved in the preparation process.

6.1.1.2.1 Materiality analysis

HealthCo's materiality analysis is coordinated by the sustainability department which organizes and carries out the process in accordance with GRI G4 (*GRI* (2015a), pp. 32-40; *GRI* (2015b), p. 17). Figure 6-2 illustrates the materiality analysis process. HealthCo separates this process into an identification and prioritization phase. To **identify relevant nfKPIs** for its stakeholders, the department uses a two-pillar model: a large-scale stakeholder survey and ongoing stakeholder contact. As the first pillar of its materiality analysis, the sustainability department conducts a **global stakeholder survey** every two to three years. The department selects representatives of particular internal or external stakeholder groups and provides them with a questionnaire. In this questionnaire, the stakeholders state

[96] While nfKPIs have previously been largely a topic for sustainability-oriented investors, HealthCo experiences an increasing interest regarding nfKPIs from rather financially-oriented investors and analysts.

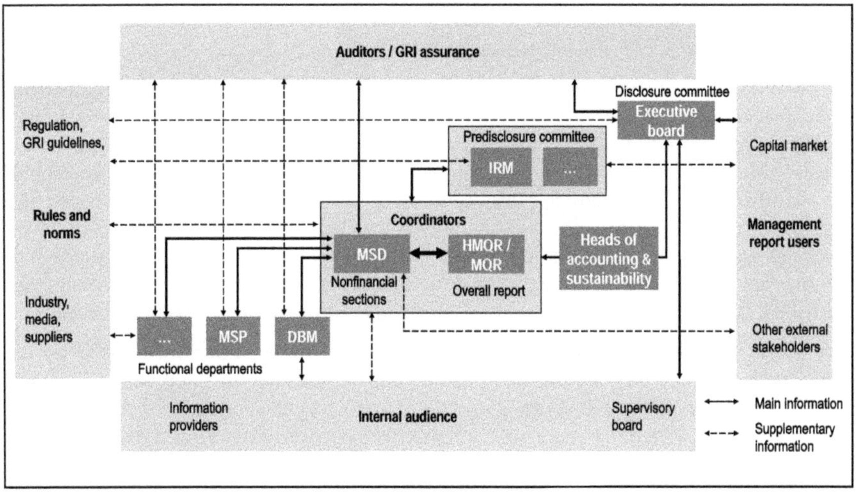

Figure 6-1: Participants and information flow in HealthCo's preparation process of nfKPIs

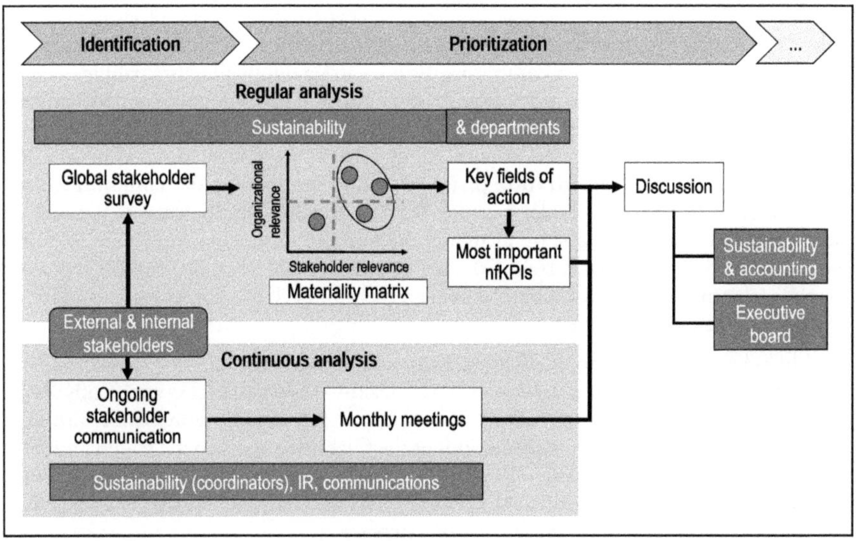

Figure 6-2: Materiality analysis process at HealthCo

their perceived importance of sustainability issues and their opinion on the importance of these issues for HealthCo and its suppliers.[97] Through this approach, HealthCo is able to

[97] In addition, the questionnaire also asks respondents to judge HealthCo's performance and quality of communication in these areas.

identify relevant topics within and outside the organization while simultaneously involving stakeholders in the identification process.

In the following **prioritization phase**, HealthCo builds on these relevant topics identified in the survey. The sustainability department ranks the topics according to their importance for the stakeholders and for HealthCo. These two dimensions form a **materiality matrix** which helps to prioritize those nonfinancial topics with the highest relevance for stakeholders, HealthCo or both of them. Specific economic and reputational thresholds provide guidance for the prioritization. The sustainability team then organizes a workshop in which highly relevant topics are condensed into key fields of action.[98] In this workshop, fields of action from the previous reporting period are integrated into those that have newly been identified. These fields are then discussed with and confirmed by the executive board.

The fields of action identified enable HealthCo to derive the **most important nfKPIs**. Together with the persons responsible for sustainability issues within the business lines and support functions, the sustainability department discusses goals for the fields of action and resulting nfKPIs. Whenever such goals and nfKPIs have previously been reported, possible adjustments are evaluated. Resulting goals are discussed with the CPO, IR and corporate communications. The finalized goals are then communicated to the accounting department.

As the second pillar for involving stakeholders in its materiality analysis, HealthCo uses its ongoing communication with various stakeholders to determine current and upcoming demands for nfKPIs. **Stakeholder communication** is carried out by the sustainability department from a local level up to participation in global initiatives. In terms of **identifying relevant topics for nfKPI reporting** in the management report, relevant events, demands or performance data are gathered whenever they arise in the stakeholder communication during the year. In the **prioritization phase related to the stakeholder communication**, these topics are discussed in regular meetings between the IR, communications, accounting and sustainability departments. By including the findings of the ongoing communication into the materiality analysis, HealthCo aims at ensuring an up-to-date nfKPI reporting which is relevant for its stakeholders. Moreover, this approach is not as complex and costly as the global stakeholder survey.

HealthCo bases the selection of nfKPIs on three important **criteria**. First, by actively engaging stakeholders in its materiality analysis, HealthCo bases the selection of nfKPIs on the demand of its stakeholders. Second, an important factor is the compliance with GRI G4. In addition to following the suggestions of the GRI with regard to the materiality analysis process, HealthCo takes the GRI's required and recommended nfKPIs into account. As part of the compliance with GRI G4, the materiality analysis process is disclosed in HealthCo's report. The third criterion is consistency:

> *"In general and throughout the management report we put emphasis on consistency. It also applies to the sustainability department – which filters out the nonfinancial information – to keep the report somewhat consistent in comparison to previous years. It is*

98 This workshop includes several internal stakeholders, for example IR, who provide feedback on the selection of the fields of action.

basically a requirement, which not only refers to financial but also to nonfinancial indicators." (HealthCo MQR)

In contrast to the integrated reporting approach of HealthCo, it is notable that both the accounting and IR department are involved only in late stages of the selection of nfKPIs and the setting of nfKPI goals:

"From my point of view, this process does not fit in with the integrated approach. Because basically we should have a stronger role as investor relations with regard to selecting nonfinancial KPIs, because if you follow the logic of integrated reporting, they should be equally important. Hence it is not optimal, I would say, that it is an internal solution that one department provides some of the goals and the other department provides the other goals. [...] This is an artificial separation which has evolved historically which we want to tackle with the upcoming materiality analysis." (HealthCo IRM)

Overall, it can be seen that HealthCo's materiality analysis process is comprehensive. Due to its application of GRI G4, the materiality analysis reflects a broad **understanding of materiality**. Thus, the process yields both the most important nfKPIs as well as important nfKPIs for voluntary sustainability reporting. In accordance with the research questions, this study focuses on HealthCo's preparation process of the most important nfKPIs.

6.1.1.2.2 Composition process

HealthCo's composition process entails the planning, draft and review phase for nfKPI disclosures in the management report. These phases are presented in the following.

Planning

The composition process of HealthCo's management report is based on a **formal and detailed schedule** to meet the tight publication deadline of the integrated report by the end of February. This schedule is managed by the accounting department on the basis of a scheduling tool. The schedule includes the preparation steps, responsible persons and deadlines necessary for the particular sections of the management report. HealthCo's accounting and sustainability departments have divided up the management report sections among themselves depending on the financial or nonfinancial nature of the information. In addition, the process is subdivided into quantitative and qualitative parts:

"We distribute our tasks, we call them numbers-critical and numbers-uncritical. And numbers-uncritical are all written texts, such as those with regard to sustainability. And at the beginning, we create a very, very detailed timetable, which contains all chapters and everything that we need for them: 'Who has to deliver, to whom, until when.' Hence, everyone knows what to do. And we deal with this numbers-uncritical part in the old year, anything we can already do and write. This results in a complete collection of the numbers-uncritical parts." (HealthCo MQR)

The sustainability department is responsible for coordinating the nonfinancial section. The **concept** of the report builds on the nfKPI reporting content identified in the materiality analysis process. On the basis of this content, the sustainability department creates a report template which serves as a structure for the draft of the nonfinancial report section. The

schedule planning process of this nonfinancial section takes place during the summer and is closely aligned with the schedule of the overall management report. The planning phase is summarized in Figure 6-3.

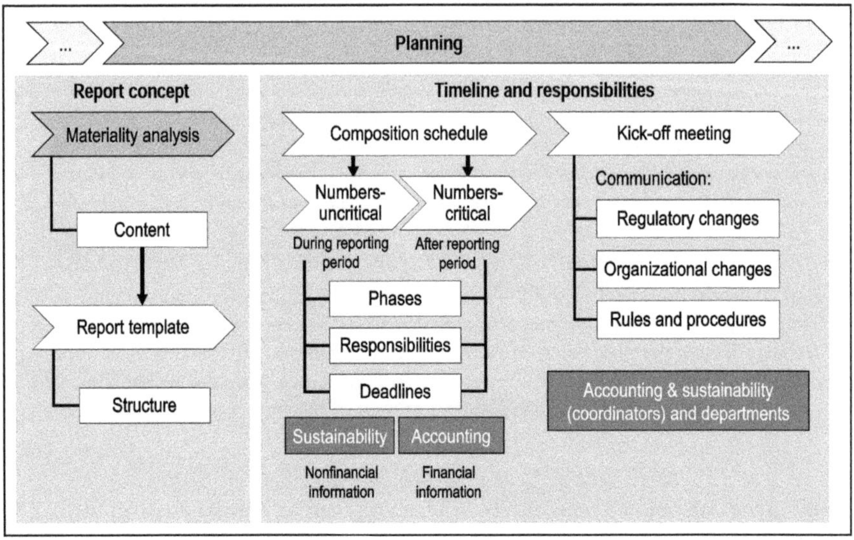

Figure 6-3: Planning phase at HealthCo

Between the end of August and the beginning of September, the accounting and sustainability reporting teams jointly organize a **kick-off meeting** for all participants of the preparation process of the management report. These participants include contact persons for financial KPIs or nfKPIs within the business lines and the HR, legal and risk management department.[99] In total, about 60 persons participate in the kick-off meeting. During the meeting, general issues are addressed which typically affect all participants. Such issues could for example resemble changes in regulations or guidelines and changes to the organizational structure, which could affect the preparation process, structure or content of the report. Moreover, the coordinators explain general procedures and requirements of the preparation process such as complying with materiality and consistency principles, using matter-of-fact language and providing proper documentation for statements and KPIs.

Draft

In addition to communicating relevant requirements, the kick-off meeting also marks the start of the **collection** of nfKPIs for the management report. This collection phase is depicted in Figure 6-4. As HealthCo strives for finishing the numbers-uncritical part before

[99] In some cases – such as for the MSP of the procurement department – one contact person is responsible for both the financial and nfKPIs within a department. In other cases, business lines provide one contact person for financial and nonfinancial information each.

the end of the reporting period, nfKPIs for the first draft are collected between September and the end of November. The firm uses an editorial software to coordinate the writing and editing of the management report. With the help of this software, all participants can mutually access and edit the management report draft, which contains the draft structure, texts from the previous year and notes regarding responsibilities. In addition, participants can access a separate database for proof documents regarding disclosures.

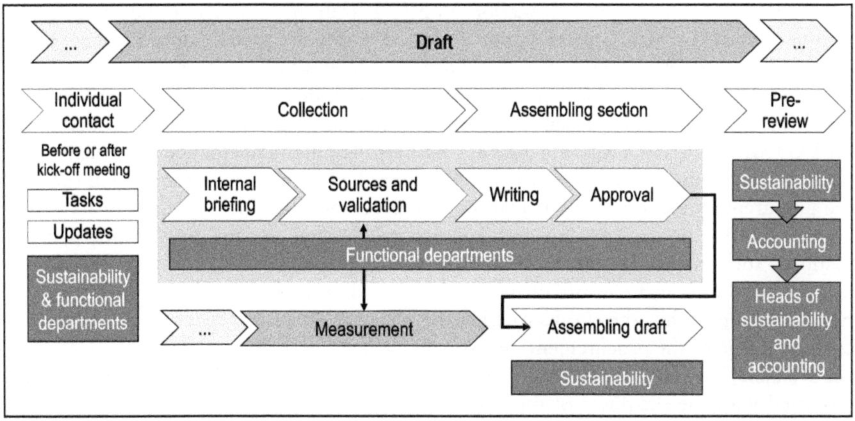

Figure 6-4: Drafting phase at HealthCo

To collect nfKPIs from the departments, the sustainability team **individually approaches** the contact persons. They discuss department specific tasks in the composition process and potential updates regarding nfKPIs. This communication typically takes place after the kick-off meeting, but some departments may have already been contacted beforehand, for example in the case of larger organizational changes.

To organize the **collection and assembling of the nfKPI sections within the departments**, many contact persons use their own detailed schedules. Such internal collection and assembling tasks typically start ahead of the kick-off meeting. This is for example the case for the procurement department and the QEHS database team. The collection and assembling of the departments' management report sections on nfKPIs are described in the following.

In August, the MSP briefs around 30 persons within the **procurement department** who provide her with the necessary nfKPIs. While the following collection is structured around the overall reporting deadlines, the MSP is autonomous in how and when she collects the necessary data. The MSP and her sustainable procurement team use various internal and external **sources** to collect information on nfKPIs. An internal reporting team accesses and structures quantitative procurement data. This quantitative nonfinancial data on sustainability audits and supplier ratings is continuously measured for a specialized sourcing database. In contrast, qualitative nonfinancial data such as supplier training is manually measured once a year. To collect this information, the MSP sends out reminders to the responsible experts to update the data and to provide sufficient proof documents. Financial information such as procurement costs or the number of contracts are drawn from SAP databases. In addition to the information from the internal reporting team, an internal procurement communications team provides descriptions on the organization of the procurement department. External information is accessed in the form of industry averages of supplier ratings and through analyzing sustainability reports of competitors.

When the MSP receives the information on nfKPIs from her colleagues, she compiles the information in the management report draft and writes the procurement section. In the course of the **writing process**, she writes texts on the basis of raw data or rephrases texts from her colleagues to make them clearer and more understandable for external readers. The MSP considers the information demands of sustainability rating agencies as well as the GRI G4 and the UN Global compact as minimum requirements for the procurement reporting section and makes sure that these are complied with. Due to the limited space in the procurement section of the management report, the MSP includes those nfKPIs that are material to the organization and external stakeholders. Additionally required information – such as recommended GRI indicators – is included in the online report. Moreover, the MSP only includes nfKPIs which are backed up by internal management mechanisms. On top of this, she checks whether the messages are in accordance with the aspired external image of the procurement department. Whenever quantitative information is not yet available, the MSP leaves blank spaces to be updated in January. All edited texts are discussed with the providers of the nfKPIs. Before the draft is sent out to the MSD in November, the MSD incorporates feedback from the head of the procurement department.

In the QEHS department, the DBM is responsible for **collecting and writing sections on health, safety and environment (HSE) data.** This type of data comprises mostly quantitative information such as CO_2 emissions, work-place accidents or waste volumes of production sites as well as qualitative information such as International Organization for Standardization (ISO) certifications of HealthCo sites. Throughout the year, the DBM handles information requests from internal and external stakeholders and is thus continuously involved in collecting HSE data. To identify potential alterations to HealthCo's measurement of nfKPIs, the IR and sustainability department regularly meet with the DBM to discuss upcoming trends in regulatory requirements, reporting guidelines or information demands of stakeholders:

> *"I am involved, because if investors ask new questions or demand more detailed information, then we typically ask ourselves: 'Do we have that information, can we get it and if yes: how fast and in which quality?' Thus, I am involved on a regular basis. We have meetings twice a year with the colleagues who coordinate the requests from investors as well as rating or ranking agencies. We then give each other updates: 'What's new, what do you think is increasingly being demanded, in which directions do we need to change our reporting?' And this is a continuous improvement process." (HealthCo DBM)*

However, the DBM occasionally participates in stakeholder meetings to answer questions regarding data availability and to implement the demands in the data measurement processes. Whenever changes to the reporting process are necessary, the DBM coordinates the adjustments to the database, questionnaires, guidance documents and definitions of nfKPIs. In September, her team briefs all suppliers of information on changes in the preparation process and presents both the timeline and responsibilities.

HealthCo's HSE-related nfKPIs are collected in a **QEHS database**. This database was developed in-house and has been improved over the years to meet the rising demand regarding nfKPIs. At every HealthCo site, nonfinancial data is gathered for HSE topics, summarized according to pre-defined processes, validated and then analyzed for internal or external reporting purposes. Certified users on the site-level receive a long questionnaire to gather and enter the relevant nonfinancial data. To ensure the consistency of the data, every user is personally trained by DBM and her team and receives guidelines on how to identify and enter the correct information. This data is then approved by a supervisor, who double-checks the data based on a four-eye-principle.

When nfKPIs have been uploaded in late November, the DBM and her team of internal audit specialists **validate the nfKPIs**. Every auditor approaches five to ten sites and checks their entire questionnaire. The auditors test the plausibility of calculations, look into outliers and check for subsequent mistakes. Any mistakes or uncertainties are marked in the system and are automatically forwarded to the on-site user. Following these notifications, the auditors and users discuss potential changes to the data and implement these if necessary. The data entry system is regularly audited by internal auditors on-site. To ensure the quality of data validation and on-site audits, the internal auditors are regularly trained and change their audit sites each year. In advance to the audit of the management report draft, the statutory auditors carry out site audits.[100] They examine the QEHS data and its preparation processes. The DBM and her colleagues accompany the statutory auditors, help them understand the processes and provide access to proof documents.

Her continuous contact with production sites and HSE projects supports the DBM in **writing** the management report section on HSE. As an overall structure of the section, the DBM uses the draft template in the editorial software, which includes texts from the previous year and notes for sections or information to be added or altered. When writing the section, the DBM and her team select the relevant HSE-related nfKPIs from the QEHS database to describe and explain their development. Other than occasionally approaching internal departments such as logistics or transport security, the DBM and her team do not use additional internal or external sources of information. Completed texts are sent to the responsible experts either for approval or as requests for explanations or documentation. Once approved, the DBM sends the texts to internal experts for a review of issues such as energy or resources. After this, she notifies the MSD that the draft is complete.

To ensure that participants meet the schedule, the sustainability team sends out reminders to inform the writers of upcoming or missed deadlines. Once drafted texts are handed over to the sustainability team, they conduct a critical **pre-review**. Particular care is given to the compliance with regulation and guidelines, continuity, balance of reporting topics and to

---

100 While the management report is audited by financial auditors, the sustainability related information and processes are audited by specialized sustainability auditors from the same audit firm.

whether stakeholder demands are met accordingly. Questions and feedback are directly discussed with the writers, who either justify why these disclosures are necessary or agree on rephrasing their section. When texts are agreed upon, the sustainability team shares the draft version with the accounting team. The HMQR and MQR review the texts with particular attention to the materiality of the information. Moreover, they check whether the nfKPIs are well aligned with the rest of the report, aiming for a good balance of the level of detail and extent of both nfKPIs and financial KPIs. Any feedback is discussed with the sustainability team and potentially looped back to the writers. Subsequently, the heads of the accounting and sustainability departments also provide feedback on the draft.

Review

After the initial review, the management report chapter on the interlinkage between financial and nfKPIs is handed out to a **review panel** consisting of colleagues from IR and communications (Figure 6-5).[101] The panel has split up this chapter into three sections of related contents.[102] The review panel then successively discusses these sections in three separate meetings between October and the end of November. Before these meetings, the IR team collects their feedback on the sections. This team typically pays attention to the report's compliance with regulations and the understandability of the texts. Moreover, they make

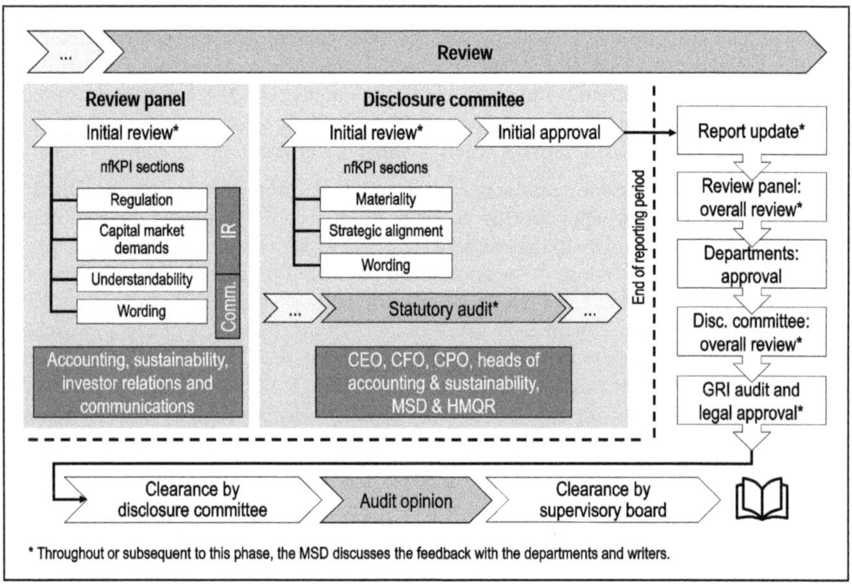

Figure 6-5: Review phase at HealthCo

101 In some sessions, the executive assistants participate as well.

102 For example, one review section would be a combination of corporate governance and strategy-related nfKPIs.

sure that the report satisfies the capital market's demand for relevant information while being in line with the information communicated to investors throughout the year. The IRM consolidates the feedback from her colleagues and represents the IR team in the review panel. While the IR feedback focuses mostly on the content, the communications team helps with improving the wording and understandability of the report. Parallel to this, the legal department reviews the report for regulatory conformity and potential litigation risks. The MSD forwards the feedback to the initial writers to discuss potential changes or questions regarding specific disclosures. In the procurement department, for example, the MSP reviews the feedback and contacts specific experts to find a compromise, if necessary.

In the beginning of December, the report draft is sent to the **disclosure committee**, which has one week to review the texts before their meeting. The committee consists of the CEO, CFO, CPO, the heads of IR, communications, sustainability and accounting, the MSD and HMQR. The committee critically discusses the entire nfKPI chapter with regard to issues such as materiality, strategic alignment or wording. In this context, HealthCo's executives typically discuss the level of detail with regard to nfKPI disclosures to prevent information overload and to ensure that all nfKPIs have a comparable level of detail:

> *"It is always addressed in every committee meeting: 'That is too long, too detailed. Is this necessary?'" (HealthCo HMQR)*

Parallel to this review, the draft is sent to HealthCo's auditors. After resulting feedback is implemented, the majority of the nfKPI section receives preliminary clearance before Christmas. Once the final data is available in January, the remaining financial and nonfinancial information is included into the report and existing sections are **updated** where necessary. In the middle of January, the review panel meets again to provide feedback on the entire management report, including the nfKPI section. The functional departments also receive the report to approve their sections. In the end of January, the disclosure committee meets again to review the final draft of the entire annual report, including the management report.

As HealthCo's **auditors** have already been auditing nfKPI databases and processes throughout the year, they focus their audit of the respective management report sections on the texts and figures. In connection to this, they typically discuss the relevance of nfKPIs for the management of HealthCo's operations or the group in general, the materiality and verifiability of nfKPIs and the wording of the report. They continuously provide the MSD with their feedback in large Excel-sheets which remark necessary documentation or changes for specific sections. Proof documents can be downloaded from a specialized database or requested from the responsible experts. Feedback and changes are discussed between the writers, the sustainability team and the auditors. The auditors typically issue their audit opinion in the beginning of February. After the audit, the auditors provide recommendations for improvements of the preparation process or the report itself. Parallel to the statutory audit, a certified GRI auditor checks whether HealthCo's nfKPIs are complete and in accordance with the GRI guidelines.

Once the annual report is completed, the legal department checks the disclosures and provides **clearance** for the publication. Before the executive board approves the entire report in February, the top managers within the business lines and departments have to certify and approve their respective report sections. After this, the supervisory board receives the annual report to conduct their audit and to provide clearance for the annual report. For the final publication of HealthCo's print and online formats, both an external agency and internal graphic and web designers illustrate the texts, tables and images to finalize the report.

In summary, the preparation process of HealthCo has several key characteristics. First, the preparation process comprises a large number of participants and processes. It is coordinated by the sustainability and accounting departments. Second, the integrated reporting format seems to affect not only the nfKPI disclosures but also the collaboration between process participants. In this context, external demands from stakeholder surveys, rating agencies and the GRI G4 guidelines also seem to drive the elaborateness of the materiality analysis, measurement and validation of the nfKPIs. In addition, as HealthCo follows goals for its most important nfKPIs, the importance of these nfKPIs also appears to be reflected in these particular phases of the preparation process. Third, as the firm applies a broad understanding of materiality based on that of GRI G4, a high number of nfKPIs are considered material by the preparers. This high number further drives the elaborateness of the process. Fourth, the publication date of the management report in the end of February seems to drive the pressure regarding a timely preparation of nfKPIs. Fifth, HealthCo's internal and external auditors are strongly involved in the audit of the nfKPIs, which adds to the elaborateness the preparation process. Finally, the hierarchical organization of the firm is particularly reflected in the high number of feedback stages with regard to the review process.

6.1.2 ChemCo case

6.1.2.1 Company profile and nfKPI reporting

ChemCo is a world-leading supplier of chemicals for manufacturing companies in various industries. The company employs more than 25,000 people and generates more than € 5 billion in sales revenues. ChemCo's business model is international as production facilities are located on all continents and far more than half of the firm's revenues are generated outside of Germany. ChemCo's shares are listed on German stock exchanges and are part of major stock market and sustainability indices.

The **organization** of ChemCo reflects its international business and the target market orientation of its business segments. ChemCo's executive board supervises the business segments and corporate support functions. Within the financial accounting department, a manager for the management and quarterly reporting (MQR) coordinates the preparation of the management report. Her supervisor, the head of external reporting (HER), supervises the preparation process of the financial report. He is supervised by the head of accounting who reports directly to the CFO. The CFO also supervises the IR department, in which several investor relations managers (IRM) communicate with financial stakeholders through various channels. The supervisory board of ChemCo is comprised of shareholder and employee representatives to equal parts.

According to its **sustainability strategy**, ChemCo aspires to have zero incidents on its sites and zero accidents of its employees. Furthermore, the firm strives for zero CO_2 Emissions by 2050. Each goal is reflected in nfKPIs, namely the number of work place and plant incidents as well as CO_2 emissions in tons. These nfKPIs reflect intersections between the economic dimension of nonfinancial information and the environmental and social dimensions. All of these nfKPIs are used for the management of both the business lines and the group. Moreover, the nfKPIs are used as incentives in the production lines. While the focus group management is on financial KPIs, nfKPIs targets affect the variable compensation of ChemCo's executives. In addition to these nfKPIs relevant for the management of the group, ChemCo reports on several other economic (e.g., number of patents), environmental (e.g., water consumption) and social (e.g., employee satisfaction) nfKPIs which are material but not used for the management of the group. Overall, ChemCo reports evenly about each of the nonfinancial dimensions.

ChemCo bundles **sustainability related tasks** in the QEHS support function, which is supervised by the CPO. Management accountants of the QEHS department are responsible for collecting, validating and analyzing nfKPIs related to production, environment and safety. The safety related nfKPIs – including the important nfKPIs on incidents – are controlled by the head of safety controlling (HSC) who supervises a team of safety controllers (SC). As part of the QEHS department, the sustainability department is responsible for preparing the sustainability report. This process is coordinated by a manager of the sustainability department (MSD) and her colleagues. The interview partners participating in ChemCo's preparation process of nfKPIs are presented in Table 6-2.

Title	Abbreviation	Department
Head of external reporting	HER	Financial accounting
Management and quarterly reporting	MQR	Financial accounting
Manager sustainability department	MSD	Sustainability
Head of safety controlling	HSC	QEHS
Safety controller	SC	QEHS
Investor relations manager 1	IRM1	Investor relations
Investor relations manager 2	IRM2	Investor relations

Table 6-2: Interview partners at ChemCo

ChemCo follows a **two report strategy**. On the one hand, the firm publishes a separate sustainability report. This report discusses and analyzes the most important and other material nfKPIs in detail.[103] In accordance with CSR-RUG, the separate nonfinancial report draws from ChemCo's sustainability report to disclose material nfKPIs related to the nonfinancial matters. This report is published about two month after the balance sheet date. On the other hand, ChemCo uses its group management report to disclose the most important nfKPIs on an aggregated level. This group management report complements the financial statements which are prepared in accordance with IFRS for the financial year from

[103] The sustainability report of ChemCo follows the GRI guidelines and is published a few months after the annual report.

January to December. In the management report, the most important nfKPIs are included in a separate chapter which presents ChemCo's sustainability strategy and information on QEHS and employees. The chapter includes qualitative and quantitative information on nfKPIs. In this chapter, nfKPIs on incidents and CO_2-emissions are highlighted as the most important nfKPIs for ChemCo. In addition, these nfKPIs are included in the chapter on the control system and the remuneration report of the executive board. The development of these quantitative nfKPIs is analyzed and compared to previous years. Moreover, they are included in the management forecast for the firm. While ChemCo's management report states its compliance with the UN Global Compact, the report is not prepared on the basis of other reporting guidelines. Overall, ChemCo's understanding of material nfKPIs in the management report includes the most important nfKPIs according to § 289 (3) HGB as well as some material nfKPIs according to CSR-RUG, while most of the latter are disclosed in the nonfinancial report.

An important **goal of the nfKPI reporting** of ChemCo is to present the sustainability of its business to the capital market:

> *"Of course we also want to be seen as a sustainable company by the capital market. That [ChemCo] is attractive to capital-market oriented investors. So, this is of course a reputation we would like to have, we would like to achieve and hence we pursue this with our activities." (ChemCo MSD)*

Moreover, by reporting their efforts with regard to incidents and accidents, ChemCo also wants to assure the general public that it is able to handle the dangers inherent in the chemical business. At the same time, the firm tries to balance financial and nonfinancial topics so that each topic's relevance is reflected in the level of detail covered in the report.

ChemCo targets a smaller **core audience** with its management report than with its sustainability report. An important audience for ChemCo's nfKPIs in the management report are capital market participants such as investors or analysts. The majority investors expresses a stronger interest in ChemCo's financials, while still expecting that ChemCo "is not bare on this issue [nfKPIs] as a company in the chemical industry" (*ChemCo IRM1*). However, a growing number of investors – especially those focused on sustainable investments – demand specific nonfinancial information to gain an understanding of ChemCo's value drivers and its competitive advantages. The management report also targets analysts, who are mostly interested financials while also showing some interest in HR-nfKPIs. In addition to the capital market, the management report is directed at potential and current employees of ChemCo. The firm uses nfKPIs to provide them with credible information on headcounts or social benefits and to highlight the relevance of these topics. While ChemCo addresses safety and emissions nfKPIs to all stakeholders including NGOs, neighbors of ChemCo's plants and politicians, the demand for more detailed QEHS nfKPIs is more extensively met in the sustainability report.

6.1.2.2 Preparation process of nfKPIs

The MQR finds herself in the center of ChemCo's preparation process of nfKPIs for the management report. Apart from the MQR, the preparation process of nfKPIs comprises the HER and other selected members of the finance department, a number of people from the business lines, participants from the R&D, strategy, controlling, IR, legal and QEHS departments as well as the executive board. While the sustainability department uses similar databases and contact persons for the preparation of the sustainability report, the coordination of this process is independent from the preparation process of the management report. Figure 6-6 summarizes the participants of the preparation process.

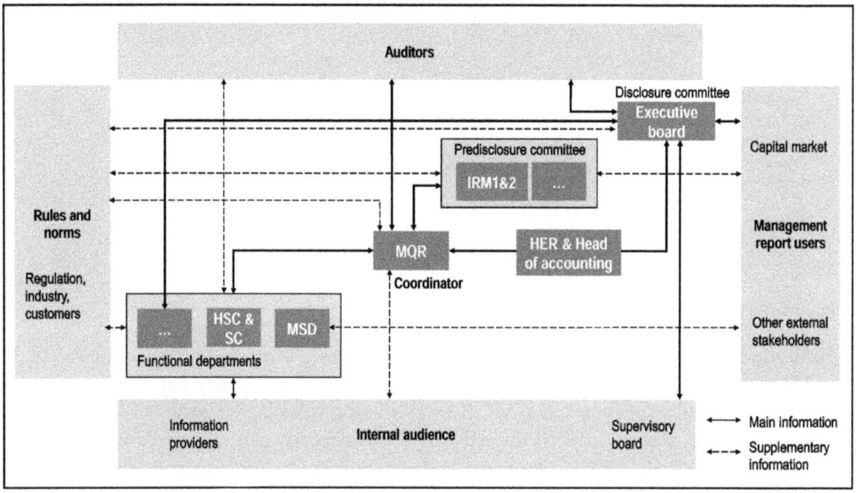

Figure 6-6: Participants and information flow in ChemCo's preparation process of nfKPIs

6.1.2.2.1 Materiality analysis

To determine material nfKPIs for the management report, ChemCo takes on a different **perspective** as compared to the materiality analysis of the sustainability report:

> *"In the case of the management report, we do of course look at materiality from the perspective of the organization, while for the sustainability report we base the materiality analysis on the perspective of the stakeholders. That is a totally different approach which coincidentally leads to the same result, or maybe on purpose, or maybe inherent in the system." (ChemCo MQR)*

Although the different perspectives yield the same most important nfKPIs, the materiality analysis processes for the two reports differ significantly. While the materiality analysis for nfKPIs in the sustainability report is mostly based on a large-scale stakeholder survey which carried out every two to three years, the materiality analysis process of the management report is less formalized and involves less participants. The materiality analysis process of nfKPIs for the management report is depicted in Figure 6-7.

Early in September or October, the MQR initiates the **identification phase** of the material analysis process by individually approaching the persons of reference for respective nfKPIs

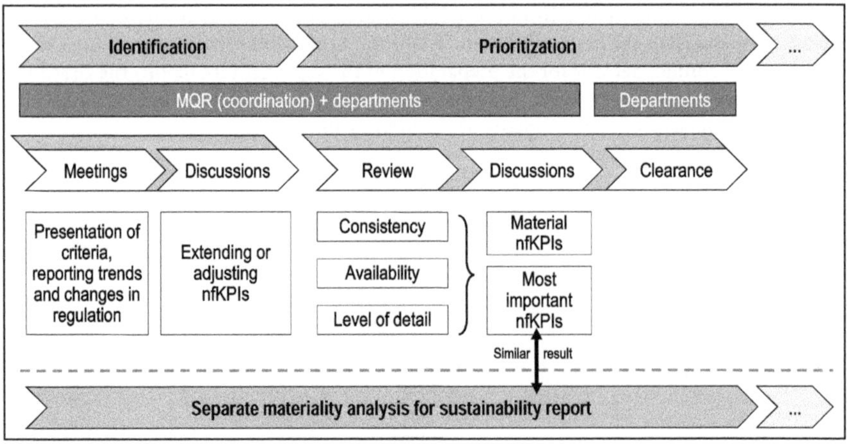

Figure 6-7: Materiality analysis process at ChemCo

within the business lines and corporate support functions. When GAS 20 came into effect, the MQR presented a list of criteria to the business lines to identify the most important nfKPIs. In the following years, the MQR used existing nfKPIs as a basis of discussion. To identify potential adjustments in the nfKPIs of the departments, she explains changes in regulation and describes nfKPIs reported by peer companies. Subsequently, the MQR and the departments discuss potential adjustments and try to find consensus on whether ChemCo is able and willing to extend or adjust the nfKPIs of the respective department. External stakeholders are not explicitly included in the identification of relevant nfKPIs. Moreover, reporting boundaries are limited to the ChemCo group and do not include external suppliers.

For ChemCo's materiality analysis of nfKPIs for the management report, several principles and criteria play a central role. First of all, the principle of continuity is a major pillar of selecting nfKPIs. If nfKPIs are selected, they should also be reported in future periods. Second, only those nfKPIs that are material for the major stakeholders of the management report are reported. Finally, nfKPIs should also be auditable. This means that nfKPIs have to be measurable, available in time and need to be based on sufficient documentation in case of site audits. To identify the **most important nfKPIs**, ChemCo has developed a set of criteria that provide guidance for discussions about the significance of nfKPIs:

1) Regular reporting to the executive board,
2) regular internal analyses of the nfKPIs,
3) nfKPIs as a basis for remuneration,
4) external expectations regarding the nfKPIs and
5) actions are derived from the nfKPIs.

Moreover, the nfKPIs shall also be relevant for the company on the group-level. While these criteria do not need to be fulfilled all at once, nfKPIs which are used for the remuneration of executives are deemed to be the most important ones.

After the MQR and the departments have agreed on certain nfKPIs which match the criteria, the **prioritization stage** takes place. In this phase, the MQR and the departments check whether the nfKPIs identified are consistent with regard to the selection criteria as well as prior material nfKPIs. It is also checked, whether nfKPIs are available and reportable in time for the management reporting process. Furthermore, the MQR and the departments reconcile the nfKPIs with legal requirements to determine the level of detail required. Resulting material nfKPIs as well as the most important nfKPIs are then discussed within the departments and released by the head of department before the report is composed.

6.1.2.2.2 Composition process

The composition process marks the second part of ChemCo's preparation process of nfKPIs for the management report. This process entails the phases of planning, drafting and reviewing.

Planning

After the content of the nfKPI section has been determined in the materiality analysis, ChemCo initiates the **planning phase** of the composition process (Figure 6-8). The content of the nfKPI section forms the basis for the report template, which comprises an initial structure of the respective section among other management report sections. This report template is developed by the MQR, the functional departments and the accounting department.

The composition process is based on a detailed plan coordinated by the MQR. This plan is recorded in the **scheduling tool** used for ChemCo's financial reporting. For most of the process steps regarding nfKPIs, the MQR approaches the responsible persons with specific

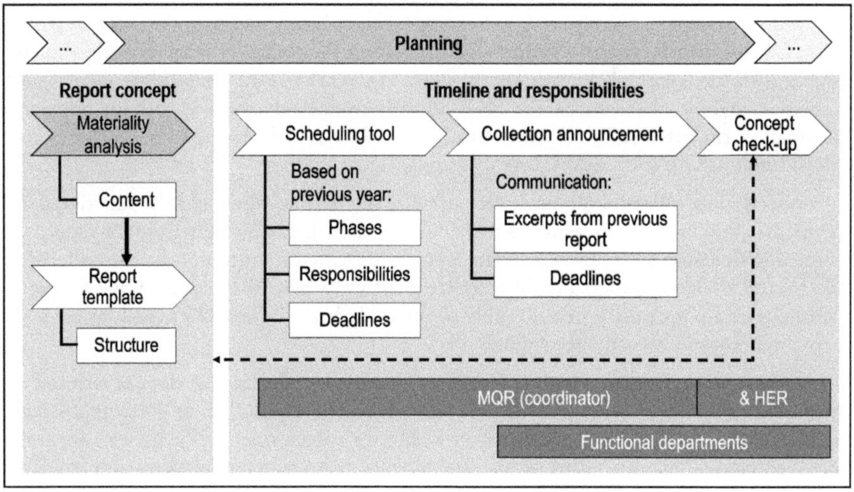

Figure 6-8: Planning phase at ChemCo

guidance. This approach is preferred as compared to email reminders, as most participants are involved in the preparation process only once a year. To prepare the scheduling tool for the upcoming composition process, the schedule from the previous reporting period is carried forward and adjusted depending on feedback received or expected changes in the process. The MQR is autonomous in adjusting and coordinating the schedule of the preparation process, building on her experience in preparing ChemCo's management report. Hence, no particular planning meetings are carried out.

To **communicate** the timeline and responsibilities, the MQR engages in direct discussions with the functional departments. This collection announcement is mostly carried out via email or telephone. The MQR reminds the departments in advance that she needs information on particular nfKPIs for the management report. She also provides them with the respective texts of the previous management report.

Subsequent to the collection announcement, the MQR personally meets with or calls the responsible persons to talk about potential **changes or news regarding the nfKPIs**. Once the MQR has collected first concepts for the nfKPIs, the MQR and HER discuss whether or not changes are necessary within the nfKPIs section. Moreover, they check whether these changes suit into the planned length of the management report. If departments can assure continuity and convince the MQR and HER of the importance of additional nfKPIs, such nfKPIs may get selected. In contrast, if departments are hesitant to provide nfKPIs for material issues in their respective management report section, the MQR and HER investigate whether nfKPIs should in fact be presented. Following the discussions, the MQR informs the departments on the agreed upon nfKPIs concept in the report.

Draft

The collection announcements of the MQR mark the start of the **collection** of nfKPIs. This process is depicted in Figure 6-9. In some business lines or departments such as R&D, the MQR contacts a central coordinator who gathers the necessary information from colleagues with the respective knowledge or access to the nfKPIs. In other departments, such as the sustainability department, the MQR directly contacts the persons with the respective information on nfKPIs. In all cases, the MQR asks the departments for the previously agreed upon nfKPIs for the first draft of the respective section.

In connection to collecting the necessary nfKPIs, the business lines and the functional departments carry out the **measurement** of nfKPIs for ChemCo's management report. In contrast to financial KPIs, for which data is typically gathered continuously, the underlying data for the nfKPIs is gathered in different frequencies. While nfKPIs relevant for the group management are measured on a monthly or quarterly basis, other nfKPIs such as environmental KPIs are measured once a year.

To promote the correctness and traceability of nonfinancial data, the **data is entered** on the basis of a four-eyes-principle. Specific individuals are responsible for entering the data, which is then approved by another person within their department. The manner in which data is entered differs depending on the data type. Data on material incidents and accidents is manually transferred from an incident management system into the sustainability database. This database also contains sustainability related data, which is entered manually on

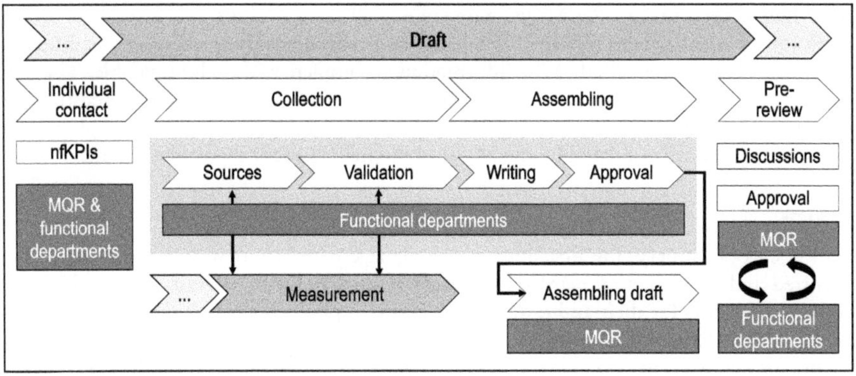

Figure 6-9: Drafting phase at ChemCo

the basis of extensive questionnaires used for preparing the sustainability report. However, the majority of environmental nfKPIs is not available during the preparation process of the management report. This is mostly caused by measurement bottlenecks regarding the large volume of environmental data, complex technical calculations and a lengthy GRI audit. Data on HR is available in a separate SAP system which can be accessed by the HR department. All persons involved in entering and approving the data receive mandatory manuals and training. In case of questions, they can contact the sustainability or safety controlling department. Data is automatically consolidated in the database and can be used for further analyses and for internal or external reports. In addition to the four-eyes-principle, the data **validation** is based on regular plausibility checks through the QEHS department.

During or shortly after gathering relevant nfKPIs, the departments start **writing** their respective sections:

> *"First we go ahead and write the safety management approach, how [ChemCo] is organized, our internal management systems, which goals do we follow, which measures we have taken throughout the year and an outlook on what we are planning for future years. Then we slowly receive the first metrics from our systems. When they are available, we send them out to our colleagues who supervise these topics and to the sustainability department. And then we write the texts for each section." (ChemCo HSC)*

In the safety controlling department, one of the SC drafts the texts and discusses these with the HSC. In addition, the SC consults colleagues of the safety and the sustainability department to agree on the contents of the texts and to align the wording with the sustainability report. To write a particular section, the department starts with a description of the nfKPIs, compares them to the previous year and provides explanations for deviations. Any explanations and examples are validated with the person responsible for the particular nfKPI.

The draft is then sent to the MQR, who collects all section drafts and **assembles a first draft** for the management report.[104] While doing so, she aligns the wording of the different sections and checks on whether the information is complete and understandable. The sections are then looped back to the departments a few times to discuss potential questions or changes. This entire communication process is carried out via email and telephone, all changes are manually updated by the MQR in the management report document.

Review

By the end of January, the first draft of the management report including the nfKPIs is finalized and sent out to ChemCo's **auditors** (Figure 6-10). The auditors have between three to four days for their audit, during which they approach the functional departments to check the origin and correctness of the nfKPIs, the preparation process of the management report and the sustainability database.[105] Many of these processes and the data systems have already been audited throughout the year. Site audits are conducted in autumn at selected ChemCo sites across the globe to audit data entry processes and reporting systems for the most important nfKPIs. The auditors discuss their feedback with both the responsible department and the MQR. If all parties agree on changing the respective section, the MQR adjusts the draft document.

Parallel to the audit, the first draft is sent out to a **pre-disclosure committee**. This committee is comprised of participants from various departments such as strategy, management accounting, finance, R&D, HR, QEHS, legal and IR. The participants read both the management report and financial statements and provide the MQR with feedback and proposals for modifications. While nfKPIs are rarely discussed in the committee, typical comments raised would question the understandability or level of detail of specific nfKPIs. This feedback is forwarded to the departments, who implement it or provide comments. Alterations are included in the draft document by the MQR. Subsequently, the report is approved by the HER and head of accounting and is then handed over to the CFO.

After implementing potential feedback from the CFO, the MQR hands over a near final draft to the **disclosure committee** in the course of February. This committee is comprised of the executive board of ChemCo. Regarding nfKPIs, the board typically discusses the wording and tone of the nfKPIs. While the management forecast is an important and difficult topic for the committee, the forecast for ChemCo's most important nfKPIs is already determined in December and is typically only slightly adjusted. The MQR forwards any feedback from the disclosure committee to the departments and ChemCo's auditors. After implementing their feedback and receiving clearance from the disclosure committee, the MQR prepares the final document of the management report. She provides this document to the auditors, who provide their audit opinion. Subsequently, the audit committee of the supervisory board receives the management report a few days before the supervisory board

[104] A few departments discuss their nfKPIs section directly with their responsible member of the executive board. After the text is cleared, it is sent to the MQR to be included in the first draft.

[105] Sustainability related nfKPIs are audited by the sustainability auditor team of ChemCo's audit firm. These sustainability auditors are also responsible for auditing ChemCo's sustainability report.

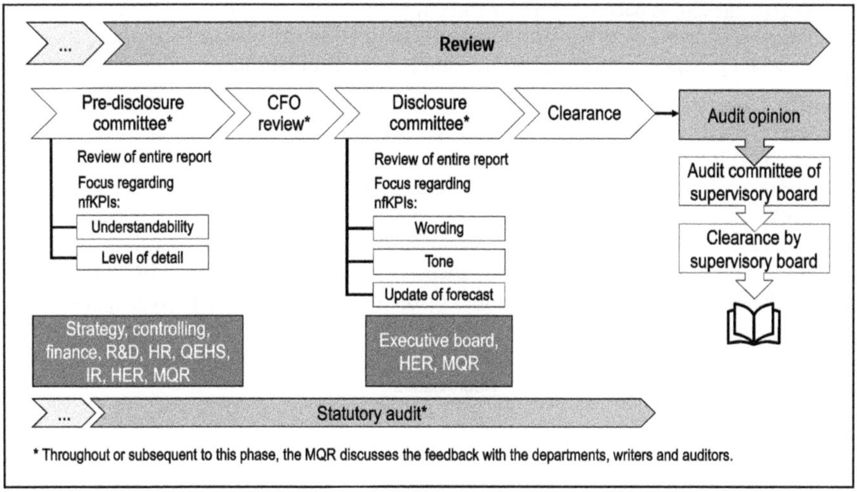

Figure 6-10: Review phase at ChemCo

meeting. The supervisory board rarely comments on ChemCo's nfKPIs. After the clearance of the supervisory board, the management report is prepared for publication.

In summary, the preparation process of ChemCo's nfKPIs for the management report has several specific characteristics. First, the preparation process is coordinated by one person rather than a team of preparers. Furthermore, the MQR as the coordinator draws from several decades of experience to prepare the nfKPI section of the management report. Second, although ChemCo publishes a separate sustainability report, its preparation process is separated from that of the nfKPI section of the management report. Although both reports are based on a different understanding of material nfKPIs, they yield the same most important nfKPIs. Third, these most important nfKPIs are connected to elaborate materiality criteria, measurement approaches and review procedures. While some of these nfKPIs are measured on a yearly basis, others are measured at higher frequencies such as quarterly or monthly. Fourth, the functional departments of ChemCo appear to be strongly involved in the preparation process, as they have considerable influence in the materiality analysis and the composition process. Fifth, the hierarchical structure of the firm is reflected in the two disclosure committees in place during the review phase. Thus, the review of ChemCo's nfKPI section is subject to multiple feedback loops.

6.1.3 PrintCo case

6.1.3.1 Company profile and nfKPI reporting

PrintCo is a manufacturing company which supplies technologies and services to the print industry and other manufacturing industries. The company employs more than 1,000 people and generates more than € 0.1 billion in sales revenues. PrintCo is listed on a German stock exchange and is part of a stock market index for small companies. PrintCo's business is international as the firm has sites for production, sales and services in Europe, America and Asia and generates about half of its revenues outside of Germany.

PrintCo's **organization** comprises only few administrative departments. The members of the executive board of the company handle several administrative tasks themselves. Among others, the CFO of PrintCo handles mergers and acquisition or IR tasks himself. The head of external and internal reporting (HEIR) supervises the external and internal accounting of PrintCo and reports directly to the CFO. PrintCo's supervisory board consists of two thirds of shareholder representatives and one third of employee representatives. The heads of the departments dealing with nonfinancial issues (e.g., production, HR, compliance) report directly to the supervising member of the executive board. The participants interviewed for this study can be found in Table 6-3.

Title	Abbreviation	Department
Chief Financial Officer	CFO	Executive board
Head of external and internal reporting	HEIR	Financial and management accounting

Table 6-3: Interview partners at PrintCo

PrintCo's **interest in nonfinancial issues** stems primarily from a focus on resource efficiency. This focus is mostly driven by considerations regarding PrintCo's production costs and demands from their customers to provide resource efficient products. While financial KPIs are relevant for the group management of PrintCo, nfKPIs are not linked to specific goals and are used subordinately in decision-making. PrintCo's most important nfKPIs span from the economic (e.g., participation in trade fairs), environmental (e.g., energy-savings related to new products) and social dimension (e.g., donations to charity or number of staff trainings) of nonfinancial information. Although most nfKPIs do not appear in the main reports to the executive board,[106] line managers and heads of production or quality departments receive reports on specific nfKPIs and can address these to their supervising board member if necessary. PrintCo does not have a designated sustainability department.

With a financial year from January to December, PrintCo prepares its financial statements according to IFRS, which are complemented by a group management report. The firm publishes a **separate section on nfKPIs in its management report**. Before the CSR-RUG came into effect, this section comprised mostly qualitative information on compliance matters and communication activities with customers, the general public and investors. A section on HR included a mixture of quantitative and qualitative data such as headcounts or employee qualifications. This section on nfKPIs was included in the management report to be compliant with GAS 20. After the CSR-RUG became effective, PrintCo presents its nfKPIs in a separate chapter of the report which covers the relevant nonfinancial matters. The particular matters mostly include qualitative nfKPIs and are not prepared in accordance with sustainability guidelines, although the report notes that the UN Global Compact and

[106] Solely HR-related nfKPIs are reported to the board on a regular basis. These are, however, not part of the internal management system of the firm.

the DNK have been considered in the preparation. Overall, nfKPIs are neither included in the chapter on the control system nor in the management forecast. In addition to the management report, PrintCo does not publish a separate sustainability report. While PrintCo's nfKPIs cover all three dimensions of nonfinancial information, the nfKPIs reflect the intersection between the three dimensions as well as some purely economic nfKPIs. Thus, the firm's understanding of material nfKPIs is in accordance with § 289 (3) HGB as well as the CSR-RUG while leaving out environmental or social nfKPIs that do not intersect with the economic dimension.

PrintCo follows several **goals with regard to nfKPI reporting**. A major goal has been to fulfil the regulatory requirements while trying not to "over-fulfil" them (*PrintCo HEIR*). Moreover, PrintCo uses nfKPIs to enable its investors to gain a more holistic understanding of the firm:

> *"Then there are some specific topics, which are interesting for investors to see: the company is well-positioned in that field and is taking care that there will be enough people to do this in the future, well qualified people. That we are facing up with current topics that are important for the future. To show we are headed in this direction. That is the picture, which I mean [PrintCo] has to provide to the capital-market and for this, we pick out the respective instruments we need for the reporting." (PrintCo CFO)*

To a limited degree, PrintCo also understands nfKPIs in the management report as a marketing instrument to promote a favorable image of the company to its stakeholders.

So far, only large listed customers have shown interest in the nfKPI reporting of PrintCo, mostly because they are required to report on nfKPIs from their supply chain. No current or potential investor has approached the CFO regarding nfKPIs. Neither has PrintCo received feedback from banks or employees. Similarly, the attention from the public, NGOs or the media towards PrintCo's nfKPIs is rather low. Despite the lack of feedback, PrintCo still understands these stakeholders to be the most important **audience of the nfKPIs** in their management report.

6.1.3.2 Preparation process of nfKPIs

Before the nonfinancial statement has been introduced, the CFO was responsible for writing the management report and the HEIR for writing the notes. From financial year 2017 onwards, the HEIR is responsible for preparing the nonfinancial statement of PrintCo. The preparation timeline of the nonfinancial statement is structured around major supervisory board meetings at which the board discusses the suggestions of the CFO and the HEIR with regard to the format, content and audit of the nonfinancial statement. Figure 6-11 summarizes the participants of the process.

6.1.3.2.1 Materiality analysis

As a consequence of the CSR-RUG, the **materiality analysis process** and its participants have changed to a certain degree. An overview of PrintCo's materiality analysis process before and after the CSR-RUG has come into effect is provided in Figure 6-12.

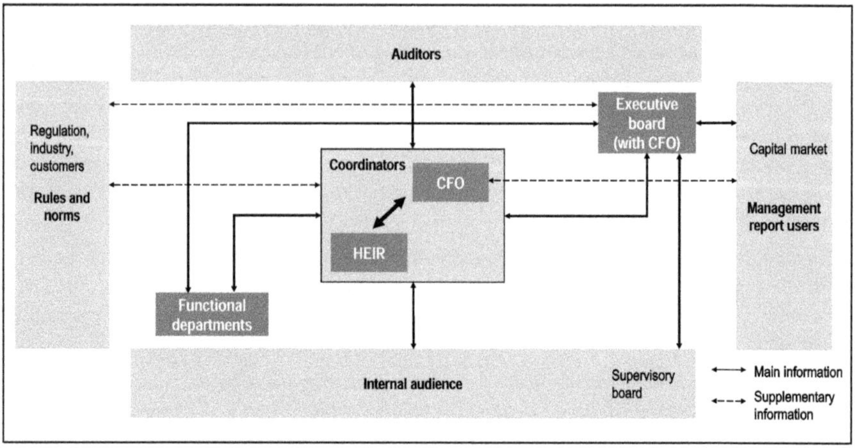

Figure 6-11: Participants and information flow in PrintCo's preparation process of nfKPIs

Before the CSR-RUG came into effect, the CFO started with the **identification phase of the materiality analysis** by reflecting on important issues which came up throughout the year. This procedure typically took place a few weeks before the end of the financial year. He prepared an overview of nonfinancial topics – typically related to employees, customer communication or governance – that had come up in day-to-day tasks or executive board meetings. This approach focuses almost exclusively on an internal perspective of the firm, excluding internal and external stakeholders from the identification process.

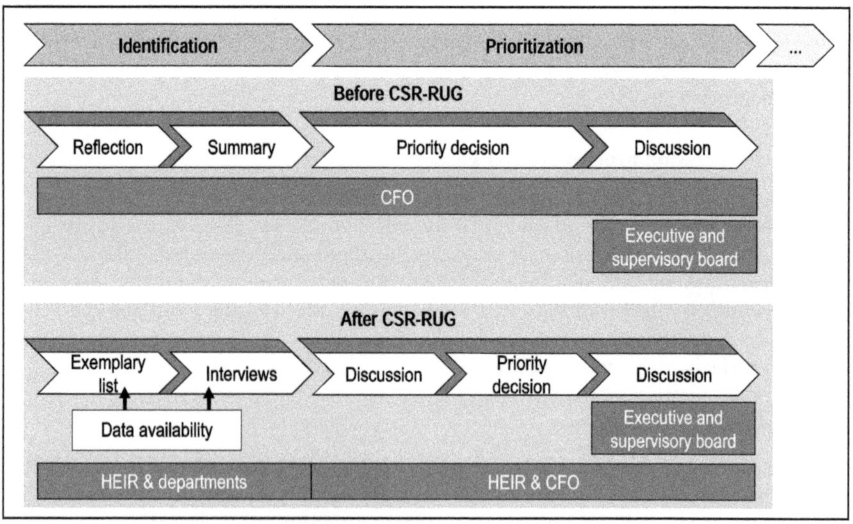

Figure 6-12: Materiality analysis process at PrintCo

After the CSR-RUG became effective and as a first step of the **identification phase for the nonfinancial statement**, the HEIR draws from various sources to assemble a list of potential and existing nfKPIs. On the basis of the five nonfinancial matters, the HEIR collects ideas for nonfinancial topics and nfKPIs from the literature, workshops and from sustainability or annual reports of peer companies. This research is necessary, because PrintCo had only reported on two of these five matters prior to the nonfinancial statement. Throughout her research, the HEIR considers the relevance of the information for PrintCo's organization. Moreover, the HEIR evaluates nfKPIs with regard to the **availability of data**. To do so, the HEIR conducts interviews with operational departments such as production or procurement. In their meetings, she shortly explains the requirements of the CSR-RUG that are perceived to be relevant for the respective department and provides examples of nfKPIs from other companies' reports. Building on this, the HEIR asks for potential nfKPIs:

> *"I have talked to the head of production and found out that we are already prepared for energy audits, if these should take place. For this, we have already collected a lot of data so I thought: 'Okay, we are already measuring data there!' [...] Such things, I have realized only once I talked to the departments. [...] I was astonished that for every matter we somehow have at least something." (PrintCo HEIR)*

Through these insights, the HEIR can also determine whether nfKPIs are available throughout the PrintCo group or only for a few subsidiaries. The availability of nonfinancial data is quite heterogeneous within PrintCo. In most cases, data from large German production sites is precise and accessible, while smaller sales and service subsidiaries typically have less precise or no data. Hence, PrintCo limits the reporting of certain nfKPIs to those provided by material subsidiaries, thus excluding other subsidiaries by "drawing a circle" (*PrintCo CFO*) within the group. Hence, reporting boundaries are limited to relevant nfKPIs within the organization, those related to suppliers are not included in the materiality analysis.

After collecting an overview of potential topics, material information is identified in the **prioritization phase**. While there are no formal **decision criteria** for material nfKPIs at PrintCo, an important factor is whether they perceive that a nfKPI contributes towards a favorable presentation of PrintCo. Selected topics should show how well PrintCo is doing and potentially provide explanations for PrintCo's success. Moreover, the CFO and HEIR use their experience and knowledge of PrintCo's business to determine the importance of a nfKPI for the firm's business. Therefore, PrintCo applies rather soft criteria to determine material nfKPIs. In prior years, the CFO has selected the material nfKPIs himself. Since the CSR-RUG came into effect, the HEIR discusses material KPIs with the CFO, while the CFO is still responsible for making the final decision.

6.1.3.2.2 Composition process

Subsequently to its materiality analysis process, PrintCo carries out its composition process of nfKPIs for the management report. The phases of the composition process (planning, draft, review) are presented in the following.

Planning

The **planning phase** of the composition process starts at the same time as the preliminary audit in October or November. Figure 6-13 illustrates the most important steps of this phase.

To plan the concept of the nfKPI section of the report, the CFO and HEIR schedule a meeting and use the previous management report and its specific sections as a rough **structure** for the new management report. They then allocate the respective **responsibilities** based on section headlines.

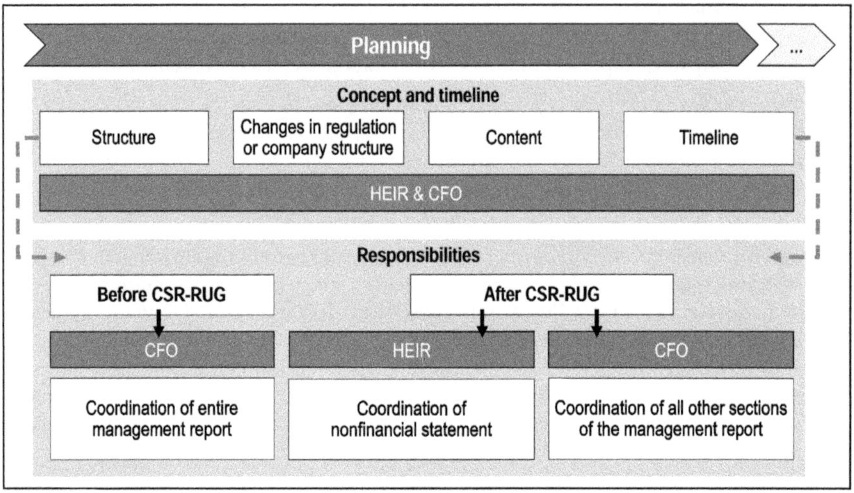

Figure 6-13: Planning phase at PrintCo

Subsequently, the CFO and HEIR note important **changes in regulation or in their company structure** and integrate these into the structure of the report. Material nfKPIs determined in the materiality analysis, which resemble the content of the section, are categorized into the relevant sections of the report structure. These nfKPIs, potential changes in regulation or the company structure as well as the structure of the nfKPI section form the concept of the nfKPI section. As nfKPIs had not changed significantly before the CSR-RUG came in effect, the CFO used to carry forward nfKPIs and their structure from the previous management report to simplify the planning. After conducting his materiality analysis in December, the CFO updated the nfKPI section where necessary. With the CSR-RUG in effect, the materiality analysis of PrintCo is carried out prior to the planning process to consider resulting nfKPIs in the planning. In the context of implementing the CSR-RUG, the HEIR has also developed a structure and concept for the nonfinancial statement, which was discussed with the CFO, the executive board, the supervisory board and PrintCo's auditors. In addition to the contents identified for the nfKPI section, the CFO and HEIR reflect on feedback they have received for the previous reports from their auditors.

Finally, the CFO and HEIR determine the **timeline** and responsibilities of other participants in the composition process. While overall deadlines are adjusted to meet the final publication date, no particular deadlines are fixed regarding the preparation of nfKPIs. Both the CFO and the HEIR attempt to finish the nfKPI sections by January, in time before the preparation of the financial statements. In previous years, other participants have neither been involved in the planning phase nor briefed regarding the composition timeline. In the course of planning the nonfinancial statement, other participants have shortly been briefed regarding deadlines of the composition process of the nonfinancial statement. No process management software is used.

Draft

Following the planning phase, the draft for the narrative sections of the management report including the nfKPIs is prepared between November and January. To **collect** the necessary nonfinancial information, the CFO or HEIR approach the heads of the departments (i.e., HR, production, procurement and legal) and the compliance manager (Figure 6-14). In previous years, the CFO has used the following approach to contact the departments:

> *"In the past, I basically approached specific people or departments in the company with regard to the management report and asked them: 'I recall some topics that came up last year. Can we contribute something reportable about them?' And then I basically asked them to provide me with the necessary information. Then I transferred that into the nfKPI section in the report." (PrintCo CFO)*

Through this, the CFO gathered information on specific material nfKPIs which he had selected in the materiality analysis. The heads of the departments prepared the necessary documentation on nfKPIs such as trade fairs or press relations. To prepare the nonfinancial statement, the HEIR asks her contact persons in the departments for an explanation on what PrintCo is doing in relation to the nonfinancial matters relevant to the department. Arising topics are then discussed so that the HEIR can gain an understanding of the nfKPIs.

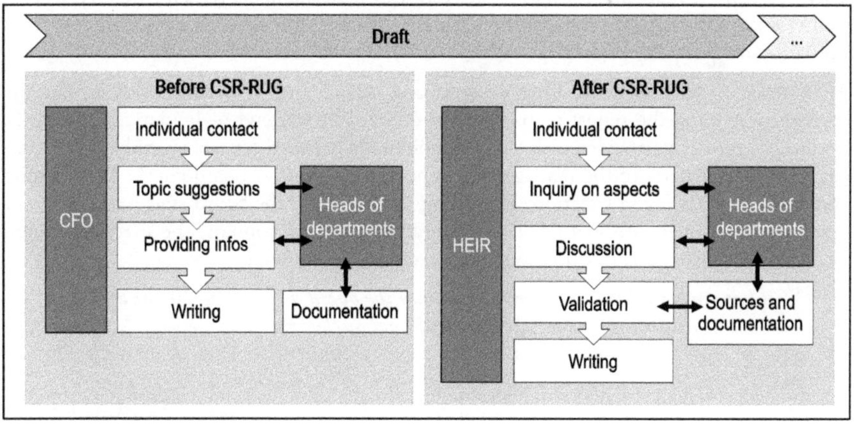

Figure 6-14: Drafting phase at PrintCo

Depending on the respective department, different **data sources** provide the HEIR with information on nfKPIs. Production sites of PrintCo have separate data systems for measuring specific nfKPIs, which have mostly been introduced to fulfill necessary requirements such as energy audits. However, these systems are isolated and are not used to monitor specific nfKPI goals. Thus, the HEIR talks to several heads of production to gather the necessary data. By collecting and validating the data herself, she tries to ensure a similar depth in measurement and to check for inconsistencies in the measurement methods to avoid "comparing apples with oranges" (*PrintCo HEIR*). The HR department provides the HEIR with access to an HR Cockpit with data regarding HR-KPIs (e.g., employee headcounts or the aggregated staff deployment in production facilities) measured on a global and frequent basis. The HEIR uses this database and related internal reports to collect the information relevant for the management report. The information collected is sufficient for the HEIR to prepare the nfKPIs on HR, hence she contacts the head of HR solely in case of additional questions. Other data such as the adherence to the compliance directive is supervised by a compliance manager. The manager provides the HEIR with the necessary information and documentation.

Subsequently, the HEIR takes the information gathered and **writes** the texts for the nonfinancial statement. No additional external data is needed for the nfKPIs with an exception of management reports from peer companies to identify acceptable practice and sector averages for nfKPIs. Most of the nfKPIs can be collected and written out as texts before the financial data is finalized in January. Before the CSR-RUG came in effect, the CFO prepared all texts for the nfKPI section of the management report. No persons other than the CFO and HEIR respectively write the nfKPI section of the management report.

Review

To conduct a **preliminary review** of the nfKPIs, the supervisory board receives a draft of the nonfinancial statement in December (Figure 6-15). This review serves as a basis for the discussion on the reporting format. Moreover, the board members validate the nfKPI selection to ensure the completeness of the nfKPIs. However, members of the board base their validation on company knowledge rather than on formal audit procedures.

After updating the first draft after the reporting period, the CFO and HEIR initiate the **review** by sending the report to the executive board by the end of January. The board's feedback is typically provided directly in person or via handwritten notes on the draft. Similar to the other parts of the management report, the executive board checks the wording and content of the nfKPI section. Regarding the wording, the board suggests changes or demands additional information, if necessary. In terms of content, the executive board mostly questions critical information on markets and technology:

> *"You have to consider that my colleagues from the board will ask me: 'What the hell is this about?' […] In their opinion, we should not disclose this much, especially because some of this information reflects our company's competencies. They don't really like that. Particularly if we mention specific customers or product details. […] That is why my colleagues are right – and please don't take this the wrong way – by asking me, what the hell this is about. They are specifically triggered to say that this is our know-*

how, our standards for customers and technology, so that they prefer not be so transparent in this regard." (PrintCo CFO)

Such criticism is typically raised after a larger restructuring of the nfKPI section, recently in connection with the initial implementation of GAS 20 or the CSR-RUG. In addition, the board reviews the correctness and consistency of the nfKPIs. The draft is then looped back to the CFO and the HEIR to include potential adjustments.

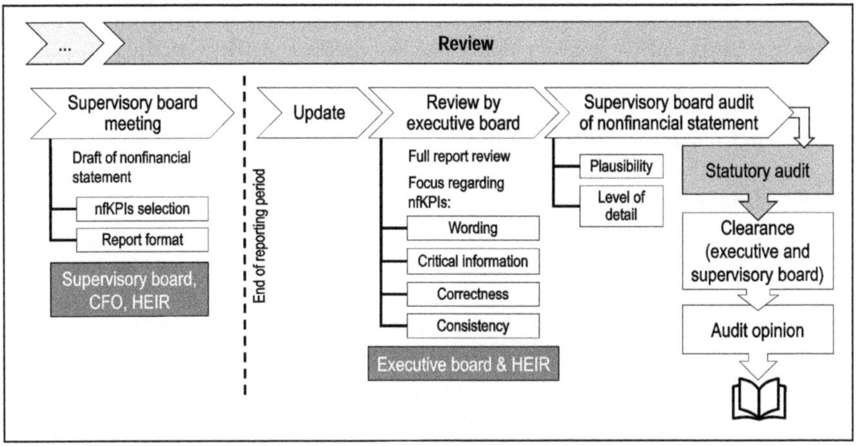

Figure 6-15: Review phase at PrintCo

The **audit committee of the supervisory board** audits the nonfinancial statement without the support of a statutory auditor. To do so, they receive the respective section after the review of the executive board. The audit committee then scrutinizes the data measurement process of the nonfinancial matters and the criteria for identifying material nfKPIs. Parallel to this audit, the management report draft is released for the **statutory audit.** In prior years, auditors have critically reviewed the plausibility of the nfKPI section, resulting in little feedback regarding this information. More feedback occurred if the nfKPI section had been restructured. In such cases, auditors typically asked PrintCo for additional, more specific or quantitative information. Subsequently, relevant feedback from the supervisory board or the auditors is incorporated into the report.

Two weeks before the publication, the final draft of the management report is sent to the supervisory board. One week later, the members of the board have a meeting in which they discuss the report. This meeting is also attended by the CFO, HEIR and statutory auditor. In this meeting, the board members scrutinize the materiality of the nfKPIs and check that nfKPI disclosures do not exceed the requirements. After the supervisory board meeting, the final feedback is incorporated, approved by the auditor and then **cleared for publication** in the beginning of March.

In summary, PrintCo's preparation process has several important characteristics. First, the preparation process is largely carried out solely by the CFO and HEIR. Thus, the majority of the tasks are combined in these two participants. The functional departments appear to be involved solely as providers of information. Second, the firm has experienced significant changes to its preparation process due to the CSR-RUG. The regulation appears to affect the materiality analysis, measurement and review of the preparation process. Third, the supervisory board of PrintCo is often consulted with regard to nfKPI disclosures and carries out the audit of the nonfinancial statement by themselves instead of delegating this audit to the statutory auditor. Hence, this board acts as an important gatekeeper in the process. Fourth, the participants involved in the preparation base their materiality decisions on the compliance with regulatory requirements and consider a report users such as investors, large customers, banks and the general public as the key audience of nfKPIs in the management report.

6.1.4 LogCo case

6.1.4.1 Company profile and nfKPI reporting

LogCo is one of the leading providers of logistics services in Europe. The company employs more than 10,000 people and generates over € 1 billion in sales revenues. The firm's business is international, as LogCo maintains warehouses and service offices across Europe and Asia. Around one third of the firm's sales revenues is generated outside of Germany. LogCo is a privately owned company which is fully controlled by a family foundation.

The business lines and service solutions of LogCo provide a structure for the **organization** of the company. Along with the corporate support functions, the business lines and service solutions are supervised by the executive board. The head of accounting (HA) is responsible for the preparation of the management report, which he provides directly to the CFO. The coordination of the preparation process is handled by the assistant to the CFO (CFOA). LogCo does not have a supervisory board as a result of its legal form. The interview partners involved in the preparation process of nfKPIs for LogCo's management report are listed in Table 6-4.

Title	Abbreviation	Department
Chief Financial Officer	CFO	Executive board
CFO assistant	CFOA	Executive assistance
Head of accounting	HA	Financial accounting
Manager human resources strategy	HRS	HR

Table 6-4: Interview partners at LogCo

LogCo's **interest in nonfinancial nfKPIs** is driven mostly by business motives. Employee related matters such as the results from a new feedback system, employee surveys or qualification programs are closely monitored by the HR department and are regularly reported to the executive board. Within the department, the HR strategy manager (HRS) is responsible for preparing the employee related nfKPI section of the management report. Environmental nfKPIs such as resource efficiency and CO_2 emissions of its fleet and buildings are regarded as important as long as they provide a competitive advantage for LogCo over other logistics providers. However, LogCo does not have a dedicated sustainability department to measure and report such nfKPIs. Therefore, only some environmental KPIs are measured for tender processes of large customers. Overall, the main focus of the executive board lies on the financial performance of the group while nfKPIs support executive and operational decision-making.

LogCo prepares its financial statements according to the HGB, which are complemented by a group management report. The firm's financial year reflects the calendar year. LogCo uses a **separate chapter within its management report** for its reporting on nfKPIs. This chapter contains individual sections on innovation-related activities, employees and environmental aspects. Thus, the firm provides nfKPIs from all three nonfinancial dimensions. Apart from the employee headcount, the chapter includes solely qualitative nfKPIs such as employee or sustainability related projects. The chapter was initially introduced in the management report when BilReG came into effect. Up to now, the format and overall content of the chapter have not changed significantly. The section on the internal management system of the group states that financial KPIs are material for the management of the group. In addition to this, it refers to the existence of nfKPIs and highlights the importance of employee-related nfKPIs. LogCo does not prepare a separate sustainability report and does not rely on voluntary frameworks such as the DNK or GRI Standards to prepare its nfKPIs for the management report. The firm's financial report is neither provided in print nor on the website. However, as required by law, LogCo publishes its financial report in the German Electronic Federal Gazette. Overall, LogCo's nfKPIs reflect the understanding of materiality of § 289 (3) HGB. Although these nfKPIs show overlaps with those required by the CSR-RUG, PrintCo only touches on few of the nonfinancial matters mandated by this regulation as the firm is not subject to the regulation.

LogCo's main **goal for reporting nfKPIs in the management report** is to meet the legal obligations while providing as few details as possible:

> *"Ultimately, I believe that the emphasis of our management report lies on fulfilling the legal requirements. And – in principle – to share and convey as little information as allowed by these requirements. We want to fulfil them, for sure. But we see neither an obligation nor a benefit in providing more information than absolutely required." (LogCo HA)*

As LogCo participates in a very competitive industry, the firm is reluctant to disclose information which could affect its competitive advantages. Although several nfKPIs are accessible for the management of the group in a high level of detail, the firm sees it as a "tightrope walk" (*LogCo CFO*) to ensure that the nfKPIs are disclosed to the public only on a general level of detail. A secondary goal is to provide a reasonably favorable presentation of LogCo's nonfinancial development. LogCo wants to present the performance of its activities with respect to its employees and the environment as indicators for its successful growth strategy. To a limited extent, these disclosures are also used for marketing purposes. The HR department understands the management report as a platform for presenting LogCo as an attractive service provider and employer. Bad news are reported whenever material, but disclosures perceived as damaging are avoided when possible to prevent leaving a bad impression of the firm.

LogCo sees its owners, debt capital providers, customers and employees as the **key audience of its nfKPI reporting**. While the owners of LogCo show high interest in environmental and employee related matters, they receive more frequent and more detailed information through private communication channels as compared to the information in the management report. Debt capital providers such as banks, leasing companies and other creditors are interested in nfKPIs only to a limited extent. Nonetheless, they use this information to inform themselves about the overall course of LogCo's business. Although specifically large listed customers are increasingly interested in LogCo's nfKPIs, the majority of the communication is based on financial information because of the strong industry focus on cost reduction. For its potential and current employees, LogCo wants to present itself as an attractive employer who is supporting sustainable business practices.

6.1.4.2 Preparation process of nfKPIs

The preparation process of nfKPIs in LogCo's management report is structured around the HA and the CFOA. While the preparation of the overall annual report is assigned to the HA, the CFOA is responsible for coordinating the preparation process of the management report including the nfKPIs. In addition to these two, contact persons from the HR, logistics and facility management departments, the HER and the executive board are involved in the preparation process of nfKPIs for the management report. The participants of the preparation process and their communication channels are summarized in Figure 6-16.

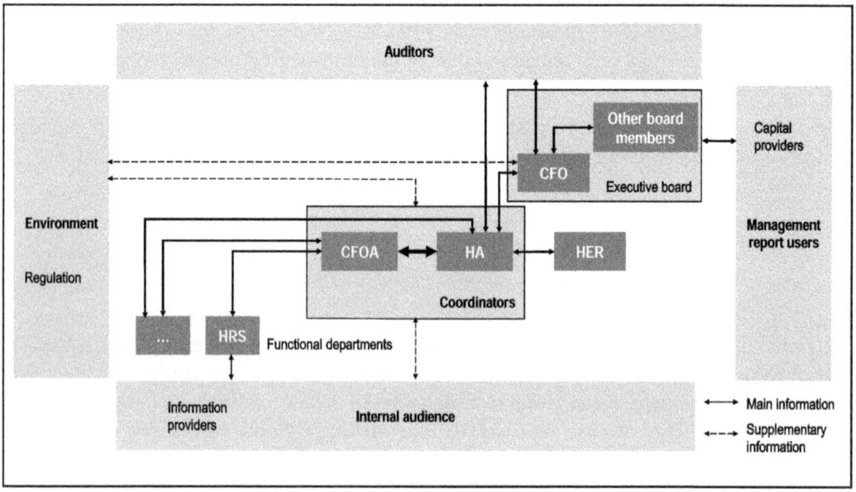

Figure 6-16: Participants and information flow in LogCo's preparation process of nfKPIs

6.1.4.2.1 Materiality analysis

At LogCo, the materiality analysis process for the management report is **embedded** in multiple phases of the composition process and is separated into **two stages**, as depicted in

Figure 6-17. In the first stage – which takes place during the planning phase – the participants determine material nfKPI sections of the report. Subsequently during the collection phase, the second stage aims at determining resulting material nfKPIs for these sections.

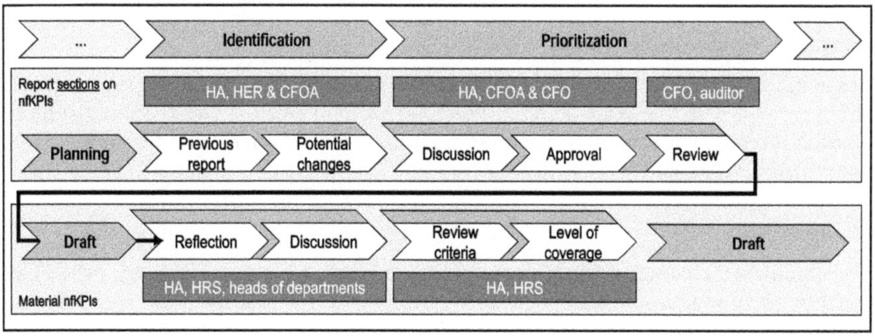

Figure 6-17: Materiality analysis process at LogCo

In the **first stage**, the HA, CFOA and HER **identify potentially material nfKPI sections** for LogCo's management report. This stage takes place during the planning meeting for the preparation process timeline and contents. The participants' selection is based on nfKPIs from the previous report and changes in LogCo's organization or relevant regulation. Reporting regarding nfKPIs is limited to the internal view of the LogCo group, excluding suppliers from the scope of reporting. In the **prioritization phase of the first stage**, the nfKPI sections are then discussed with the CFO, who provides feedback and an approval for the initial selection. Following this, the statutory auditor of LogCo also reviews and approves the selected sections. The coordinators then include the sections in the management report draft and assign a responsible contact person in the respective department.

During the collection stage of the composition process, the **second stage** of the **identification of nfKPIs** takes place within the departments. When the HRS receives the request to provide texts on employee related nfKPIs for the management report, she organizes a short meeting with her colleagues. In this meeting, the team identifies important projects of the HR department which have occurred throughout the reporting period. As LogCo does not have a department or person responsible for environmental nfKPIs, the HA determines material environmental nfKPIs for the management report. To identify and select the nfKPIs, the HA reviews articles and documents on LogCo's environmental activities and approaches the heads of logistics and facility management to ask for their opinion on environmental nfKPIs.

To **prioritize material nfKPIs in the second stage**, LogCo applies several criteria. The most important criterion for material nfKPIs for LogCo is the compliance with legal requirements. When nfKPIs were first included in LogCo's management report to comply with § 289 (3) HGB, nfKPIs related to employees and the environment were selected as relevant for the group. Moreover, LogCo wants to ensure continuity when selecting nfKPIs. In this context, the management report of the previous reporting period provides a basis and guideline for the materiality analysis of current nfKPIs. Besides implicitly considering the interests of report readers when identifying material nfKPIs, LogCo's external stakeholders are not included in the materiality analysis process. Moreover, no stakeholders have demanded the inclusion of specific nfKPIs.

6.1.4.2.2 Composition process

As identified above, the composition process of LogCo's nfKPIs for the management report is intertwined with the materiality analysis process. Nonetheless, the specific planning, drafting and review phases of the composition process can be differentiated from the materiality analysis process.

Planning

To coordinate the **composition process** of nfKPIs for the management report, the CFOA and HA use a rough schedule based on the sections of the management report (Figure 6-18).[107] In September, the HA and HER discuss the overall timeline of the preparation process of the annual report. This timeline also schedules a meeting for around mid-December during which the management report is planned. A few weeks before this meeting, the HA and HER meet with LogCo's statutory auditor who provides checklists for the preparation of the annual report – including the management report and nfKPIs. The auditors also indicate changes in the legal requirements. In a planning meeting in December, the HA, HER and CFOA discuss the legal requirements, contents, contact persons and deadlines of the overall management report, including nfKPIs. The previous management report is used as a basic framework to plan the contents, participants and schedule. The contents and timeline are then discussed with and approved by the CFO.

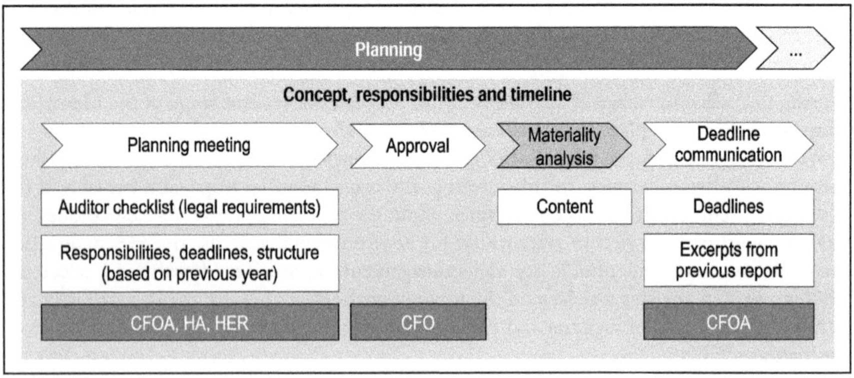

Figure 6-18: Planning phase at LogCo

The composition process for nfKPIs and other narrative information is **coordinated** by the CFOA. This narrative information is assembled in a draft before the financial information is available for the management report. Before the Christmas holidays, the CFOA asks the

[107] The preparation process of LogCo's management report is not supported by a project management tool.

HRS to provide texts on nfKPIs related to employees by the end of January. The same deadline applies to the HA, who provides texts on environmental aspects of LogCo's activities. No specific **guidelines on the contents** of the sections are provided other than the relevant texts of the previous management report.

Draft

LogCo's drafting phase begins when the CFOA contacts the HRS and HA (Figure 6-19). The **composition process for the specific sections** of the management report is organized differently for the nfKPIs related to employees and environmental activities. Within the **HR department**, the HRS coordinates the collection process. When the contents of the section are agreed upon in the initial HR materiality meeting, the HRS assigns the writing tasks to those colleagues who are responsible for the selected HR projects. Moreover, she forwards the previous report to the colleagues without providing writing criteria or requiring specific information.

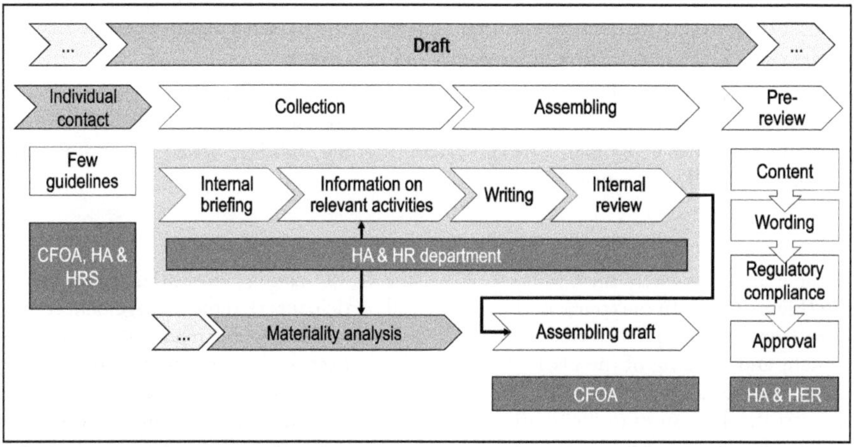

Figure 6-19: Drafting phase at LogCo

Once her colleagues have written the respective sections, the HRS collects the texts and includes these in a draft document. Subsequently, the HRS thoroughly **reviews the section on HR-related nfKPIs** to check its materiality, truthfulness and correctness. The HRS rephrases the texts wherever necessary to increase their readability and to optimize their appeal and authenticity. Any changes are discussed with the writers. The information on the employee headcount is provided to the HRS by the personnel administration, who draw the information from an SAP-based database. External sources are not used and the HRS does not analyze the HR reporting of peer companies. Once the HRS decides that the texts are finished, she forwards the texts and documentation on the HR projects and the employee headcount to the CFOA.

For the section on **environmental nfKPIs**, the HA collects the relevant information and prepares the respective texts. To collect the information, the HA speaks to different contact persons such as the head of logistics or the head of facility management. These contacts shortly explain and discuss the relevant activities which have occurred throughout the reporting period in relation to environmental nfKPIs. In addition, the HA draws from information on LogCo's environmental activities which he has picked up in management meetings, news articles or internal presentations throughout the year. Based on this information, the HA selects material projects and shortly describes these. For each of these projects, the HA collects documentation for the auditors. The HA does not use management reports of peer companies as benchmarks. Once the section on environmental nfKPIs is completed, the HA forwards the draft and documentation to the CFOA.

As part of organizing the composition phase, the CFOA sends out reminders to the contact persons whenever necessary. Once the CFOA receives the texts from the HRS and the HA, he includes them in the **draft of the management report**. He then reviews the texts with respect to their plausibility and their spelling. However, major changes are left open for the following review meeting. Similar to the writers, the CFOA does not benchmark LogCo's management report with those of peer companies. External sources such as market studies or industry forecasts are only used by him for writing the financial report sections.

Prior to a **review meeting with the CFO**, the HA and HER receive the complete draft of the management report. They check whether the sections related to HR and environmental activities are complete, comprehensible and in accordance with regulation. In case of questions, the respective departments are contacted. After the draft is reviewed and approved by the HA and HER, it is forwarded to the CFO.

Review

In the middle of March, the CFO, HA, HER and CFOA conduct an **initial review meeting** (Figure 6-20). In the course of the meeting, all participants read the management report from front to end. Their review of the nfKPIs in the management report focuses on the content and wording of the nfKPI chapter. With respect to the **content**, the participants check whether all material nfKPIs are included. To determine missing information, they contrast the disclosures to the nonfinancial developments they have encountered throughout the year in management meetings or corporate events. In addition, they examine and discuss the credibility of the information. Information deemed as implausible is reconfirmed with the departments or left out of the report. Moreover, information which could shed a negative light on LogCo is only included in the report when it is absolutely necessary for the understanding of the course of business. Furthermore, the participants critically examine the level of detail of nfKPIs. Descriptions and explanations of projects related to nfKPIs should remain on a general level to avoid overemphasizing specific nfKPIs and to provide a balanced report. In terms of the **wording** of the report, the style of language is aligned across the various texts to achieve a consistent and comparable tone. In addition, texts are reviewed with respect to their conciseness, clarity and understandability. Changes in wording are directly implemented in the draft, questions related to the content of the sections are discussed with the departments after the meeting.

Once the feedback is included in the management report around the middle of March, the document is forwarded to LogCo's statutory auditors. When **auditing the nfKPI chapter**,

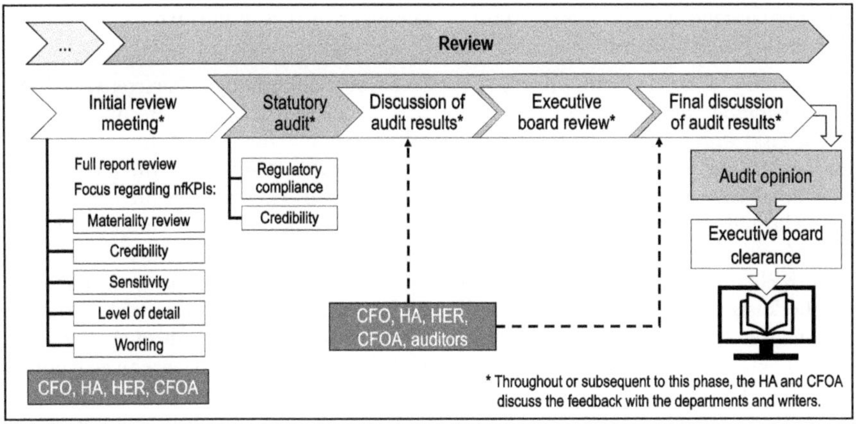

Figure 6-20: Review phase at LogCo

the auditors' focus lies on the compliance with regulations and on the wording. The communication with the auditors is mostly handled by the HA, who is supported by the HER and CFOA. The HA provides auditors with documentation on the nfKPI sections and answers to questions. If the auditors request more documentation or explanation regarding nfKPIs, the HA approaches the departments to discuss the auditors' questions. However, the auditors typically provide minor feedback regarding nfKPIs. After the audit, a final meeting is scheduled with the CFO, HA, HER, CFOA and the statutory auditors to discuss remaining critical issues.

During the audit of the management report, a second review meeting with the CFO, HA, HER and CFOA is scheduled for the end of March. In this meeting, the updated report is reviewed once more. The focus of this meeting lies on passages that have been altered or which were identified as critical. Passages which have previously been agreed on and which have received clearance by the CFO are left aside. The departments are contacted to discuss remaining questions or requests for changes. After including this feedback, the report is sent to the other members of the **executive board**. The board members have about one week to provide their feedback to the CFO. Feedback regarding nfKPIs typically concerns only the wording of the texts:

> *"After the management report has been audited, it is sent to my colleagues from the board, who also read it. From our Chief Operating Officer, comments are quite rare. Our CEO and Chief Marketing Officer sometimes have minor comments. It could be one or two sentences of the texts, which might be discussed." (LogCo CFO)*

After the feedback from the board has been included in the report in the beginning of April, the CFO and the auditors schedule a final meeting to discuss remaining questions and changes. Shortly after this, the auditors issue their audit opinion and the executive board provides clearance for the annual report.[108] The report is then **published** in the German Electronic Federal Gazette.

In summary, the preparation process of LogCo has several important characteristics. First, the preparation process of the management report is coordinated by two persons, who share several tasks with regard to the preparation of nfKPIs. Second, the CFO of the firm is closely involved in discussions regarding the materiality of nfKPIs as well as in the review. This close involvement indicates low hierarchies between the participants of the preparation process. Third, the materiality analysis process of LogCo is embedded in the composition process. Moreover, the materiality analysis is separated into two stages which determine material nfKPI sections and, subsequently, material nfKPIs. Fourth, the preparers strongly rely on checklists provided by the firm's auditors. Hence, the firm's auditors take on an important role with regard to the monitoring of regulatory changes. Fifth, due to its legal form, LogCo does not have a supervisory board. Hence, the final management report is only cleared by the executive board and the statutory auditor. Sixth, the firm is very restrictive with regard to its nfKPI reporting as it operates in a very competitive industry. Its management report is solely published in the German Electronic Federal Gazette and not in print. Moreover, the firm provides solely qualitative nfKPIs.

6.1.5 FashCo case

6.1.5.1 Company profile and nfKPI reporting

FashCo is one of the largest textile retailers in Germany. The firm employs more than 10,000 people and has a turnover of more than € 1 billion. The firm's business is national as it is focused almost exclusively on Germany. FashCo is a privately held company which is controlled by the descendants of FashCo's founder.

The **organization** of the company is structured around FashCo's retail process and location management. FashCo's executive board supervises the product assortment, procurement, logistics and sales connected to the retail process, the real estate management and corporate support functions. As the head of external and internal reporting (HEIR), the HEIR is responsible for FashCo's internal and external financial communication and reports directly to the CFO. The HEIR has been in office for more than five years. She supervises a manager for external and internal reporting (MEIR), who is responsible for coordinating the preparation process of the management report. As a result of FashCo's legal form, the firm does not have a supervisory board. The interview partners of the preparation process of nfKPIs for FashCo's management report can be seen in Table 6-5.

FashCo's **interest in nonfinancial issues** is strongly tied to the firm's corporate values and culture. The firm has incorporated sustainability goals and standards within its departments. These goals and standards are developed and monitored by a cross-functional sustainability team. This team consists of the heads of several departments such as communications, quality, procurement and HR as well as the CEO of FashCo. While the primary

[108] The clearance dates typically vary depending on the finalization of the annual report. However, the latest possible deadline is the end of April, when the report has to be handed over to financial institutions.

goals within the functional departments are financial, nfKPIs are used as frameworks and minimum requirements for FashCo's decisions. As an important factor, the HR department monitors the development of the employee headcount and the qualification of FashCo's employees. The real estate department monitors the energy efficiency of FashCo's retail locations and the procurement department reviews the compliance of suppliers with social accountability standards. Overall, FashCo's understanding of nfKPIs focuses on the social and environmental dimension of nonfinancial information. Thus, the firm understands material nfKPIs as those nfKPIs on the intersections of the three nonfinancial dimensions as well as voluntary nfKPIs from the environmental and social dimension.

Title	Abbreviation	Department
Chief Financial Officer	CFO	Executive board
Manager external and internal reporting	MEIR	Financial and management accounting
Head of external and internal reporting	HEIR	Financial and management accounting

Table 6-5: Interview partners at FashCo

With a financial year from July to June, FashCo prepares its financial statements according to the HGB. These financial statements are accompanied by a group management report. As FashCo is not subject to the CSR-RUG, it does not provide a nonfinancial statement. The nfKPIs of FashCo are presented in a **separate chapter within its management report**. This chapter contains individual paragraphs on the nonfinancial topics of social commitment, sustainable procurement and energy efficiency. All paragraphs are narrative and do not contain quantitative information. The employee headcount is provided in a different chapter of the management report and contains a table and a verbal explanation of the headcount's development. FashCo first included the chapter on nfKPIs after GAS 20 came into effect. Since then, the content and format of the chapter has not changed significantly. In addition to an updated HR section, solely the section on resource efficiency is changed on a yearly basis to account for the development of current projects. Although the management report does not contain a section on the internal management system of the group, the report states that nfKPIs are relevant for the management of the group. The chapter on nfKPIs is not prepared in accordance with voluntary frameworks such as the DNK or GRI Standards. However, the firm publishes a separate sustainability report, which explains sustainability related projects in more detail and with more quantitative information as compared to the nfKPI chapter of the management report.[109] FashCo's financial report is neither provided in print nor on the firm's website. As required by law, the firm publishes its financial report in the German Electronic Federal Gazette.

The main **goal of FashCo's reporting on nfKPIs** is to fulfil regulatory requirements:

> *"We prepare our management report on the basis of GAS 20. I mean, the wording is not particularly compulsory, but it can be interpreted that if they explain the course of*

[109] The sustainability report is published on an infrequent basis and is not prepared in accordance with sustainability reporting guidelines. The report is prepared by the sustainability team, the accounting department is not involved in the preparation.

business, nfKPIs are requested. This means we have a sort of obligation and want to fulfil this requirement. And yes, we pursue this as our primary goal." (FashCo MEIR)

"Preparing our management report – including nfKPIs – is a sort of compulsory exercise for us. If possible, we would definitely reduce our disclosures." (FashCo CFO)

As FashCo's owners, banks and customers receive detailed information through private communication channels, the management report serves primarily to comply with requirements. To avoid revealing competitive advantages, FashCo aims to provide as few disclosures as possible with regard to nfKPIs. Nonetheless, the firm seizes the opportunity to disclose their corporate values and to substantiate this with nfKPIs. In this context, the firm wants to present goals and performance related to sustainability activities.

As FashCo does not address nfKPIs towards specific stakeholders, the firm sees the general public as an **audience for its nfKPI disclosures**. Although the management report documents FashCo's nfKPIs for owners and banks, these groups receive more detailed reports and information through more frequent, private communication channels. While the owners show interest and support for the sustainability activities of FashCo, banks are mainly interested in financial information. The latter use nfKPIs to gain a broader understanding of the firm's development. Moreover, nfKPIs are also provided for customers, employees and suppliers as a documentation of FashCo's values and nonfinancial performance.

6.1.5.2 Preparation process of nfKPIs

The MEIR acts as the center of FashCo's preparation process of nfKPIs for the management report (Figure 6-21). In addition, contact persons from the real estate, procurement, communications and HR department, the HEIR and the executive board are involved in the preparation process of nfKPIs for FashCo's management report.

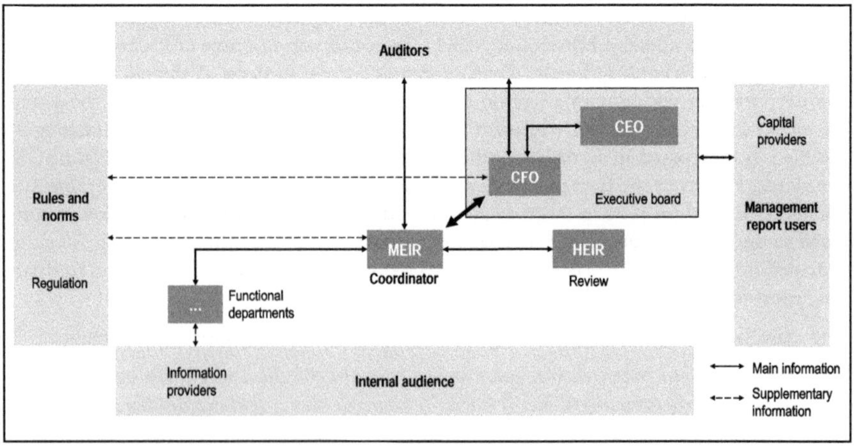

Figure 6-21: Participants and information flow in FashCo's preparation process of nfKPIs

6.1.5.2.1 Materiality analysis

The **materiality analysis process for FashCo's nfKPIs** is embedded in the planning phase of the composition process (Figure 6-22). During the planning meeting for the management report, the CFO and MEIR **determine nfKPIs** which they deem necessary for an understanding of FashCo's course of business. To **identify** relevant nfKPIs, the CFO and MEIR draw from nonfinancial developments which they have observed and documented throughout the reporting period. Neither the CFO nor the MEIR receive demands or suggestions regarding nfKPIs for the management report. Moreover, internal or external stakeholders are not included in the identification of relevant nfKPIs. Following the initial discussion, the CFO scrutinizes the relevance of previous nfKPIs and evaluates whether new nfKPIs need to be added. FashCo's nfKPIs comprise both nfKPIs relevant for the organization and nfKPIs on supply chain related information such as product and supplier certifications.

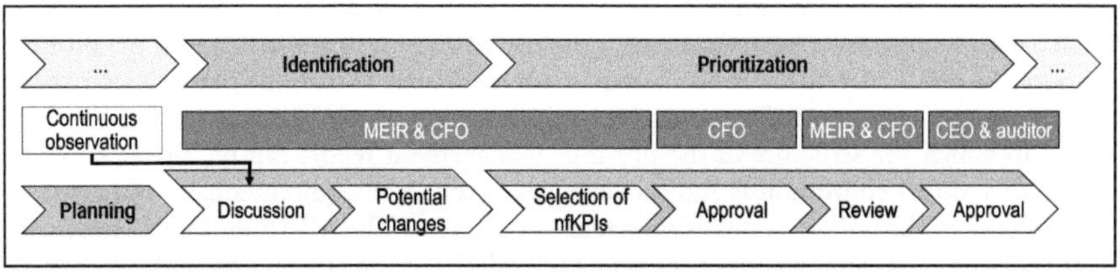

Figure 6-22: Materiality analysis process at FashCo

Subsequently, the CFO and MEIR **prioritize** nfKPIs by establishing an initial selection of important nfKPIs on the basis of relevant nfKPIs identified in the discussion. To identify material nonfinancial nfKPIs for the management report, the CFO and MEIR apply several implicit **criteria**: corporate values, accessibility, regulatory requirements, demand by stakeholders and sensitivity of information. Initially, the CFO and MEIR check whether the nfKPIs reflect and substantiate the corporate values and culture of FashCo. Material nfKPIs shall be used to explain and document how FashCo's nonfinancial activities and performance are linked with the corporate values and culture. In addition, sufficient information regarding the nfKPIs needs to be accessible to support explanations and analyses. Furthermore, the nfKPIs shall be necessary for an understanding of the course of business. It is also scrutinized, whether the nfKPIs could be of value to the various stakeholders of the management report. Moreover, no internal information shall be provided, which could reveal competitive advantages. Subsequent to selecting material nfKPIs, the CFO approves the preliminary selection.

The CFO and MEIR check the communication about nfKPIs in FashCo's other reporting media such as the sustainability report or the website. By conducting this **review**, they validate their selection of material nfKPIs and safeguard that the nfKPI disclosures are consistent with those in other communication channels. The selection is discussed with and approved by both the statutory auditors and the CEO.

6.1.5.2.2 Composition process

FashCo's composition process entails the planning, drafting and review phase. This section describes the individual phases in the context of the preparation of nfKPIs for the management report.

Planning

> *"All in all, it is a very short time frame. The process is: taking the previous report, handing this to the respective departments and discussing it with them. The departments give us their feedback, update the information, this is incorporated. First quality control is done by myself, the second through [CEO], and out with the report. [Laughter]" (FashCo CFO)*

As summarized in the quote above, FashCo's **composition process** for the management report is rather straightforward. This process – including the nfKPIs – takes place after the financial statements have been finalized in the end of August. Around the time of this finalization, the CFO schedules a short meeting with the MEIR to plan the preparation process of the management report (Figure 6-23). In this meeting, the MEIR and CFO discuss the extent to which the structure of the previous management report can be carried forward. FashCo's auditors continuously indicate changes in the legal requirements for the management report to the MEIR and CFO throughout the year. The MEIR and CFO then conduct the materiality analysis and discuss how the nfKPIs can be integrated in the report. By the end of the meeting, a loose deadline is set for the finalization and audit of the management report. The CFO then approves the concept and deadlines of the management report.

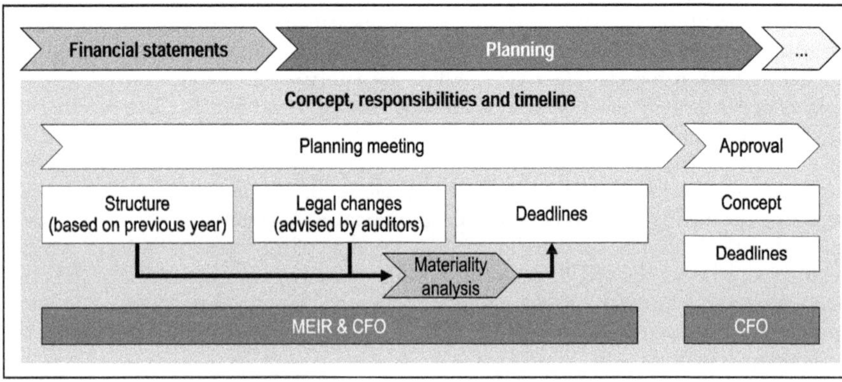

Figure 6-23: Planning phase at FashCo

The MEIR uses a **guideline** on the basis of the previous management report to coordinate the composition process of FashCo's current management report. While the guideline contains notes on how to obtain and transform specific financial figures for the management report, it does not contain instructions on how to prepare the nfKPI section of the management report. Other participants of the preparation process are not briefed regarding timelines or reporting contents in advance to the collection of the nfKPIs.

Draft

Subsequently, the MEIR begins **collecting** the information for the management report (Figure 6-24). To obtain the nfKPIs, the MEIR approaches the heads of the real estate, procurement, communications and HR departments and discusses previous and potentially new material nfKPIs. Before these discussions, the MEIR has been collecting relevant information and ideas for the nfKPI section throughout the reporting period. Whenever the MEIR considers this information as relevant for the management report, she addresses it during the discussions with the departments. Other than asking for a swift implementation, the MEIR sets no explicit deadlines for the preparation of the information. Apart from handing out the previous nfKPI section to the departments for orientation, the MEIR provides no specific guidelines for the preparation of particular nfKPI texts. The MEIR allows the departments to provide nfKPIs in their preferred format. Thus, some departments contact the MEIR to provide verbal feedback on nfKPIs, others send short text drafts on their particular section of the report.

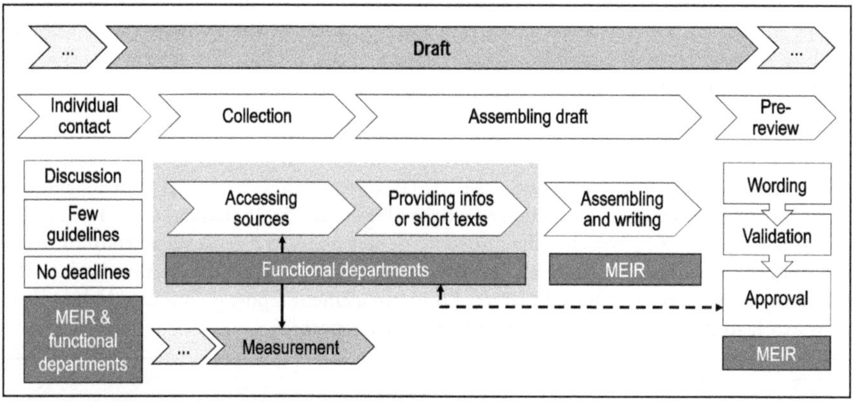

Figure 6-24: Drafting phase at FashCo

When **collecting** nfKPIs for the MEIR, the heads of the departments rely on different **sources of data.** To obtain information on the energy efficiency of FashCo's retail locations, the real estate department draws data from a centralized energy management database. This database is used for monitoring and controlling the energy usage and efficiency of FashCo's retail locations. The head of the real estate department provides the MEIR with a description of the energy management database and qualitative explanations of current improvements and goal attainments. The procurement department provides the MEIR with an update on sustainable sourcing goals and standards. While the department has access to detailed information on the certification of suppliers and the production locations of particular products, the head of procurement provides only general and qualitative sustainable sourcing goals for the nfKPI section of the management report. For FashCo's social commitment, the MEIR approaches the communications department to ask for one or two highlights from the reporting period. The HR administration draws the current employee headcount from an SAP database and provides this information to the MEIR, who updates the table and descriptions in the HR section of the report. For every nfKPI included in the management report, the MEIR also receives written or numerical documentation from the departments.

The MEIR includes texts provided by the departments in a **draft of the management report**. For nfKPIs which have been provided to her on a verbal basis, the MEIR writes the respective texts. To do so, the MEIR builds on the wording of previous reports:

> *"There is no point in pretending: some paragraphs, which recur from year to year, of course have a certain share of 'copy-paste' in them. If you reword some of it, you check whether it is still correct. But you don't need to reinvent the wheel each year. To frame it more positively: we try to ensure a certain continuity. [Laughter]" (FashCo HEIR)*

When **reviewing** the nfKPI section, the MEIR pays particular attention to the wording of the texts to make sure that they are understandable and written in a similar tone and style. However, most nfKPI paragraphs of the report are not updated significantly. Whenever the MEIR has changed or created a paragraph, she forwards it to the responsible head of the department to ask for their feedback and approval. The MEIR also validates the plausibility of the documentation to determine the correctness of the nfKPIs. Throughout the drafting phase, the MEIR updates the CFO on the progress of the composition.

Review

Whenever larger sections are finished, the MEIR forwards these to the CFO or schedules a short meeting to **review** the particular sections (Figure 6-25). If changes exceed minor rewordings, the MEIR approaches the respective departments to discuss the alterations. After the feedback has been incorporated, the MEIR forwards the respective section back to the CFO for another review. Once the draft of the management report is completed, the MEIR forwards it to the CFO who then reviews the entire report.[110]

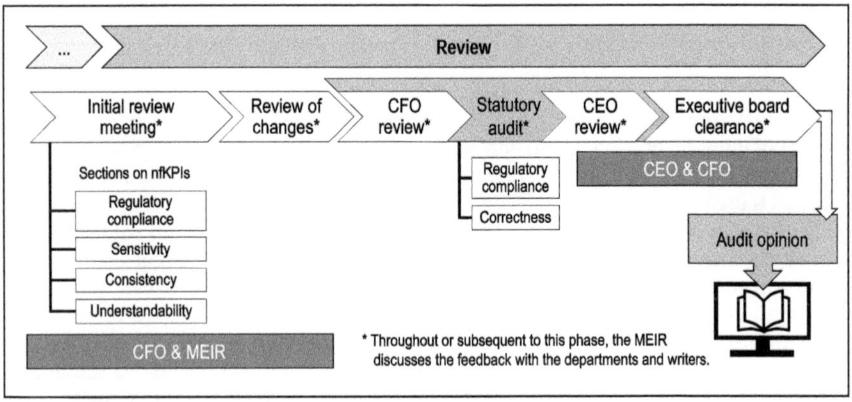

Figure 6-25: Review phase at FashCo

110 The draft is also shortly reviewed by the HEIR and the assistant to the CEO.

Both the MEIR and the CFO do not have specific **criteria or checklists** for the review of the nfKPI chapter. Particularly in the case of changes to the legal requirements, the CFO and MEIR examine whether the nfKPI chapter is compliant with the regulation. Moreover, the CFO and MEIR try to ensure that the nfKPI chapter does not reveal sensitive information. Furthermore, the MEIR and CFO compare the contents of the nfKPI chapter to those of the previous year to check the consistency of the disclosures. They also review the texts with regard to understandability and potential inconsistencies. Feedback or changes are communicated to the writers in the departments and incorporated in the report when agreed upon.

Parallel to this, the draft and documentation is sent to FashCo's **auditors**. Their focus lies on the correctness of the nonfinancial information and the compliance with legal requirements. The auditors contact the MEIR in case of questions or when they need documentation. However, the auditors rarely discuss or provide feedback for the nfKPI chapter of FashCo's management report.

After the feedback from FashCo's auditors is incorporated, the CFO forwards the final draft of the management report to the **CEO**. This feedback loop takes about two days, after which the feedback by the CEO is incorporated. After this, both the CEO and CFO provide their clearance for the management report.[111] FashCo's statutory auditor then reviews the changes to the report and provides an audit opinion. Typically by the end of October, the annual report is finished and forwarded to the German Electronic Federal Gazette for publication.

In summary, the preparation process of FashCo's nfKPIs for the management report has several important characteristics. First, the preparation process of nfKPIs takes place after the financial statements of the firm have been completed. Second, due to FashCo's legal form and low reliance on external financing, the firm is not subject to tight publication deadlines. Thus, the timeline of the preparation process is rather flexible. Third, the firm publishes qualitative nfKPIs which mostly reflect the environmental and social dimension of nonfinancial information. Hence, the firm's understanding of material nfKPIs is more related to that of the CSR-RUG and the GRI Standards and includes less economic nfKPIs as suggested by § 289 (3) HGB. Fourth, despite having a sustainability team and publishing a separate sustainability report, FashCo's preparation process shares only few resources with its sustainability reporting. Fifth, the preparation process is primarily carried out by two persons (CFO and MEIR). The close collaboration of these actors indicates flat hierarchies.

6.1.6 TechCo case

6.1.6.1 Company profile and nfKPI reporting

TechCo is a world-leading manufacturer and service provider for technologies in the water processing and building systems industries. The firm has more than 5,000 employees and

[111] Due to FashCo's legal structure, only the CEO and CFO are accountable for the publication of the management report.

generates more than € 1 billion in sales revenues. With both production and sales and services sites located in America, Europe and Asia, the firm's business is international. More than half of TechCo's sales revenues are generated outside of Germany. TechCo is a privately held corporation which is not listed on a stock-exchange. Almost all shares are held by a family foundation.

TechCo's is **organized** according to its segments. The executive board supervises these segments along with the corporate support functions. As an assistant to the CFO, the investor relations manager (IRM) coordinates the preparation process of the management report.[112] TechCo's supervisory board consists of two thirds of shareholder representatives and one third of employee representatives.

TechCo's **interest in nfKPIs** is derived from its strategy of market and technology leadership. TechCo considers product quality (e.g., complaint rates), employees (e.g., diversity trainings), procurement (e.g., number of suppliers) and resource efficiency (e.g., recycling rate of products) as important drivers for obtaining and sustaining these leadership positions. Overall, these nfKPIs focus mostly on the economic and social dimension of nonfinancial information, while the environmental dimension is covered partly by resource efficiency. As the nfKPIs can be found mostly within the economic dimension or within the intersection of the dimensions, the nfKPIs reflect primarily those mandated by § 289 (3) HGB and are partly congruent with the CSR-RUG.

The business lines and functional departments closely **monitor** these nfKPIs in their operational activities. Board members responsible for operational departments or HR receive frequent reports on the development of relevant nfKPIs. However, the main focus of the overall management of the group lies on financial KPIs. The QEHS department prepares QEHS-nfKPIs, which are reported directly to the Chief Operating Officer (COO) by the head of database management (HDBM) and her colleagues. One of these colleagues, the database manager (DBM), is responsible for preparing the management report section on quality related nfKPIs. In a similar vein, the HR department prepares HR-related nfKPIs which are reported within the department and to the CEO. In the department, an HR manager (HRM) is responsible for the narrative internal and external HR communication, including the preparation of the management report section on HR-nfKPIs. TechCo does not have a dedicated sustainability department. The interview partners who participate in the preparation process of nfKPIs for TechCo's management report are listed in Table 6-6.

TechCo prepares its financial statements according to IFRS, which are complemented by a group management report. The firm's financial year reflects the calendar year. The firm is not subject to the CSR-RUG. TechCo reports its nfKPIs in a **separate chapter within its management report**. This chapter contains individual sections on quality, HR, resource efficiency and production. Except for a few quantitative measures such as employee headcounts or the improvement rate of warranty costs, the chapter contains solely qualitative information on nfKPIs. This chapter on nfKPIs was first included shortly after GAS 20 came into effect. Although the report states that the internal management system of the

[112] As TechCo is a privately held company, the term investor relations refers to the communication with the family foundation, banks and minority shareholders.

group is based on financial KPIs, it refers to nfKPIs as important drivers for the group's development. It is noted however, that financial KPIs are more relevant for the group's management. The chapter on nfKPIs is not prepared in accordance with voluntary reporting frameworks such as the GRI Standards or the DNK.

Title	Abbreviation	Department
Chief Financial Officer	CFO	Executive board
Investor relations manager	IRM	Executive assistance
Head of database management	HDBM	QEHS
Database manager	DBM	QEHS
Human resources manager	HRM	HR

Table 6-6: Interview partners at TechCo

TechCo follows several **goals with its reporting on nfKPIs**. While it is a basic goal of TechCo to comply with the regulatory requirements, the firm aims to use the requirements to its advantage. To do so, TechCo follows a best-practice approach with regard to its reporting and benchmarks itself with large listed and non-listed firms:

> *"We are part of the forefront and we have won several awards for our annual report. We are up front with the other large non-listed companies, which are significantly larger than we are [...] and we benchmark ourselves with them a bit: what do they do, what do we do. Because we think that a good annual report is a kind of 'business card' for our company. It is a communication medium, a marketing medium which fully depicts our business through showing not only the economic, financial performance in an adequate format, but also through presenting other aspects which could be of interest to various stakeholder groups." (TechCo CFO)*

This best-practice approach reflects several motivations for TechCo's nfKPI reporting. First, TechCo wants to highlight the performance of both its financial and nfKPIs and to explain how particular projects have contributed to TechCo's achievements. The firm uses the disclosures as a marketing tool to establish a positive image of TechCo in the eyes of its business partners as well as current and future employees. Moreover, nfKPIs are included to provide a holistic picture of the company for the management report readers and to meet their diverging interests. By selecting key departments (e.g., quality or HR) as providers of nfKPIs for the management report, TechCo wants to appreciate the importance of the departments for the company's business. Despite being transparent in many aspects, TechCo also limits its disclosure of nfKPIs. The firm does not disclose nfKPIs which reflect sensitive information or shed a negative light on the company.

TechCo regards all of its stakeholders as the **audience of its nfKPI reporting**. However, the varying needs of these stakeholders may be addressed through different sections of the management report. The group's shareholders, banks and other debt providers have shown little interest in nfKPIs so far. Nonetheless, these stakeholders use the nfKPI chapter to inform and reassure themselves about the development of the group aside from the financial results. The specific sections on nfKPIs shall also address the interests of employees, customers and suppliers. TechCo's nfKPI chapter informs its staff about the firm's nonfinancial performance and credits the efforts of the QEHS, HR or procurement departments through disclosing their contribution to the company's success. In addition, nfKPIs are targeted towards potential future employees to present TechCo as a successful and sustainable employer. Furthermore, nfKPIs shall provide customers and suppliers with evidence regarding the quality and sustainability of TechCo's products.

6.1.6.2 Preparation process of nfKPIs

The IRM is located in the center of the preparation process of nfKPIs in TechCo's management report (Figure 6-26). Apart from the IRM, contact persons from the QEHS, HR, procurement and compliance departments as well as the executive board are involved in the preparation process of nfKPIs for the management report.

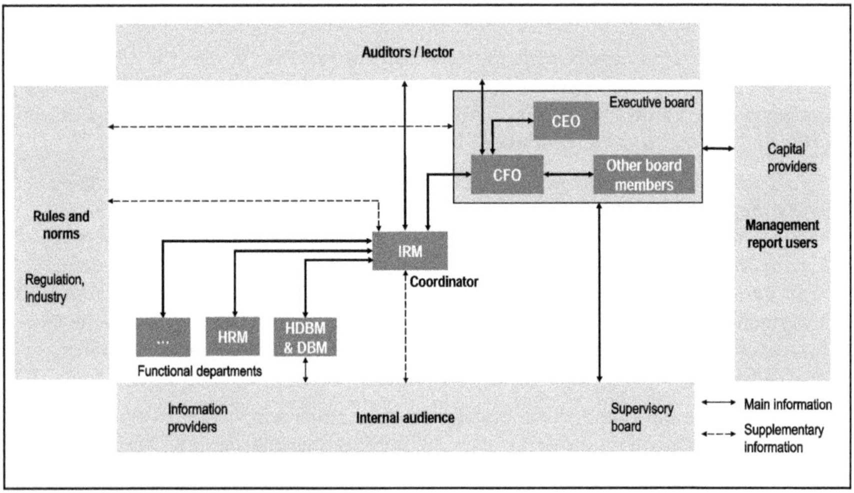

Figure 6-26: Participants and information flow in TechCo's preparation process of nfKPIs

6.1.6.2.1 Materiality analysis

TechCo determines material nfKPIs in **two separate stages**, which are illustrated in Figure 6-27. Both stages take place each year when the participants review the materiality of previous and new nfKPIs. In the **first stage of the identification phase**, the IRM identifies a list of nfKPI sections for the management report. The IRM selects a section if she perceives it to be material for an understanding of TechCo's business model and its performance. Resulting sections are then discussed with the CFO.

In the identification phase, TechCo applies several **criteria**. As a basis for their selection, the IRM and CFO consult the requirements according to § 289 (3) HGB and the associated requirements of GAS 20. On this basis, they identify nfKPI sections which they deem relevant for TechCo's industry and business model:

> *"A decision criterion is the importance we believe a KPI has for an external person. First of all, information on employees is always important. If we did not have that, we would have failed that objective. Of course, as a premium supplier, we always talk about quality. That is important. Then the criterion of external perception. What is expected from [TechCo], what we should report?" (TechCo CFO)*

Based on TechCo's quality leadership strategy, sections such as HR, quality and resource efficiency have been identified and confirmed as important each year. Furthermore, the IRM and the CFO reassess whether nfKPIs related to these sections may be demanded by external stakeholders and if the nfKPIs would add to the reader's understanding of TechCo's course of business.

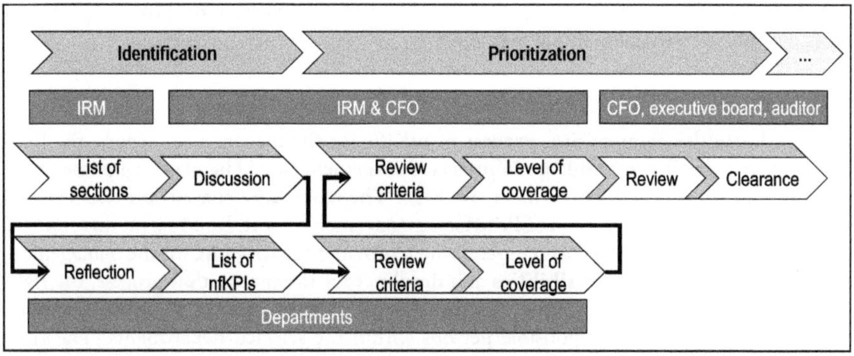

Figure 6-27: Materiality analysis process at TechCo

In the **second stage of the identification phase**, the IRM approaches the departments responsible for the respective sections. The selected departments reflect on and identify material nfKPIs for their section of the management report. Furthermore, they determine potential contact persons for the information. In the **first stage of the prioritization phase**, the departments determine material nfKPIs. In this context, they pay particular attention to the availability and continuity of the nfKPIs. Available nfKPIs may be those which have emerged during the year or those which are reported within the department. To provide continuity with previous reports, the departments follow up on prior nfKPIs by addressing developments or results of these nfKPIs in the reporting period. After selecting material nfKPIs, the departments determine the appropriate level of coverage.

The **second stage of the prioritization phase** builds on the nfKPIs suggested by the departments. The IRM and CEO analyze the state of the art and best practice of nfKPI reporting of large listed and non-listed peer companies. This analysis is done to confirm the selected nfKPIs, to determine the level of detail of the disclosures and to examine which nfKPIs may not be disclosed. Overall, these reporting criteria support TechCo's stronger focus on economic and firm-internal nfKPIs. Reporting boundaries are set within the group, external suppliers are not considered. By involving functional departments in the materiality analysis, TechCo considers the demands of internal stakeholders. External stakeholders are, however, not engaged in the process other than through considering their potential demands.

After the material nfKPIs have been identified by the IRM and CFO, the CFO **reviews the nfKPIs** for the management report. To do so, he re-applies his decision criteria and compares the nfKPIs selected to the relevant issues from prior board meetings or market developments. This selection is then discussed with the other members of the executive board and subsequently approved by them. The board discusses the selection with the statutory auditor who then confirms the selected nfKPIs.

6.1.6.2.2 Composition process

Subsequently to its materiality analysis process, TechCo carries out its composition process of nfKPIs for the management report. The phases of the composition process (planning, draft, review) are presented in the following.

Planning

To coordinate the **composition process** of nfKPIs for the management report, the IRM neither uses a detailed schedule nor a project management tool. The planning phase of the composition process is depicted in Figure 6-28. The materiality analysis process provides the **content** of the nfKPI section of PrintCo's management report. Building on this content, the IRM creates an initial report template which provides the structure for the management report. To determine **responsibilities** and deadlines for the preparation process, the IRM carries forward and adjusts those of the previous preparation process. By mid-September, the IRM approaches the responsible persons within the selected departments. The IRM individually asks them to provide a first draft for their respective management report section by the end of November. This particular communication of the planning deadlines marks an overlap with the drafting phase of the composition process.

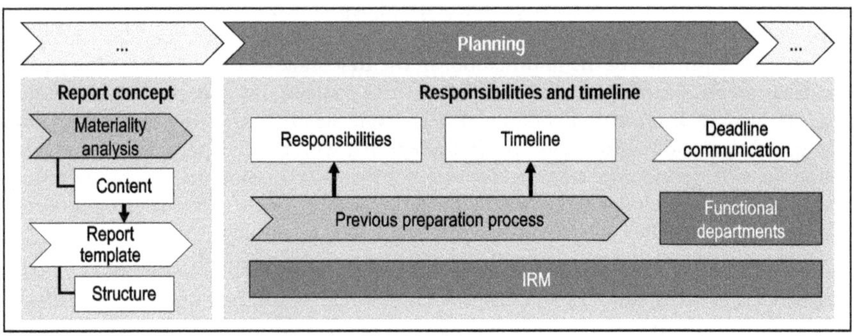

Figure 6-28: Planning phase at TechCo

Draft

Simultaneously to communicating the deadlines of the composition process, the IRM initiates the drafting phase of the nfKPIs. This phase is summarized in Figure 6-29. When contacting the functional departments, the IRM provides few **guidelines on the contents** of the nfKPI sections except for providing excerpts from the previous report:

> *"I do offer them certain guidelines: "What has changed? Were there any restructurings in the organization?' I try to give them some hints, what might be interesting for the reader, hence some kind of guidance. But I leave them enough space, because I have made the experience that if I narrow it down too much, I don't receive back much in return. I'd rather get a jumbled mess which I need to structure and shorten down. My colleagues are very forthcoming and I don't want to block that." (TechCo IRM)*

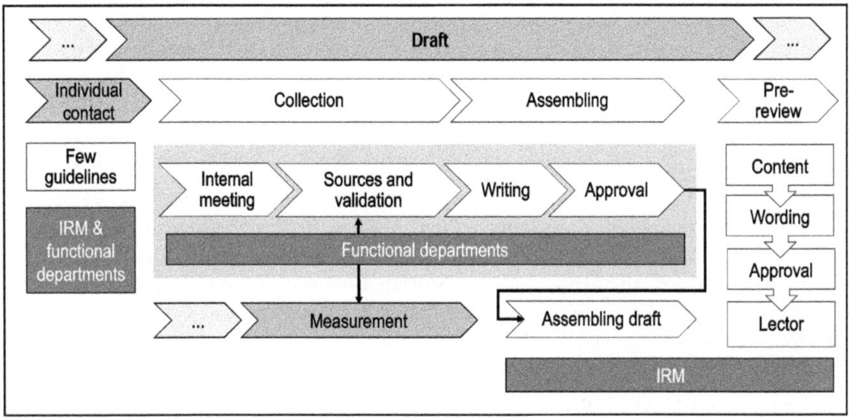

Figure 6-29: Drafting phase at TechCo

Furthermore, the IRM occasionally hints towards certain events she deems relevant to the report. When nfKPIs were first included in the management report, the IRM met with the selected departments to explain TechCo's goals for the nfKPI reporting and reasons for selecting the particular department. She briefly explained the regulatory requirements and her expectations regarding the section. To provide an understanding for the reader, the nfKPI sections had to include a description of the department, its most important projects and links from the nfKPIs to the performance of the company. This open approach initially posed difficulties for the departments, as they were insecure about which information was required and expected. However, building on feedback and experience throughout the following years, the departments became more experienced in the preparation of their sections. Over the course of the years, the IRM has kept her requirements for the nfKPI section open:

> *"For me personally, regarding the softer, verbal information, I prefer this open or less structured process. My contact persons are very diverse and I don't want to press them into a structure. From my experience, if I let them do it and just follow up at certain points, it is much easier and more constructive for everyone." (TechCo IRM)*

The **collection within the selected departments** is organized by the responsible contact persons in these departments. For the **QEHS department**, the DBM coordinates the collection of the quality-related nfKPIs and writes the texts for the draft. The DBM has not documented this process and does not use planning tools. Once the DBM receives the request for a draft from the IRM, the DBM organizes a meeting with colleagues who are responsible for major quality-related projects. In this meeting, the participants recall the course of the past year and brainstorm on potential highlights, projects and improvements which are reportable and are perceived to be interesting for readers. The DBM asks the managers to explain their project and the development of related KPIs. While taking notes, the DBM tries to reflect on the explanations to determine whether they are understandable for outsiders.

Some of these projects and nfKPIs have been summarized and analyzed in an internal annual quality report, which is used as a basis for discussion in the meeting. This report and other accessible internal reports are prepared on the basis of a **QEHS database**. This SAP-based database contains nfKPI data which is continuously being **measured** by TechCo's production sites on the basis of internal questionnaires and detailed guidelines. The plausibility of the data is regularly checked by the QEHS team. Production sites are infrequently audited by external QEHS auditors. The statutory auditors of TechCo are not involved in any site audits.

When **writing the section on quality-related nfKPIs**, the DBM draws from the discussions of the manager meeting and the analyses from internal reports. Once a particular paragraph is finished, the DBM asks the associated manager for feedback. By the end of November, the DBM has completed two or three feedback loops with the managers, the HDBM and the head of QEHS. Missing figures are left blank in the draft to be updated by the middle of January. The DBM then forwards the draft to the IRM.

Similar to the DBM, the HRM does not follow a formal process for preparing **HR-related nfKPIs** for the management report section. Once the HRM receives the request from the IRM, she meets with her supervisor to agree on the topics for the report section. Most HR-related information for the management report is already known to the HRM from her day-to-day HR communication tasks. For explanations on specific projects such as top-management training or diversity management, the HRM approaches the colleagues responsible for the respective projects. These colleagues provide the HRM with presentations, reports or short explanations on the topics. As the only quantitative figure, the employee headcount is provided to the HRM by an HR reporting team with access to an SAP-based HR-database. Due to the confidentiality and sensitivity of the information, only the employee headcount is disclosed as a quantitative nfKPI in the management report. When analyzing the management reports of competitors as part of her research on potential HR projects, she uses this opportunity to benchmark their reporting practice to that of TechCo's HR department.

When the HRM has gathered the respective information, she starts **writing the particular paragraphs of the HR section**. Throughout this process, she continuously meets with her supervisor to discuss the current content and wording of the draft and to receive feedback on potential improvements. Once the draft is finished and approved by her supervisor, the HRM forwards it to the IRM.

When the IRM receives the texts from the departments and assembles these into a draft document, she **reviews** these texts with regard to content and wording. With respect to the **content**, the IRM ensures that the texts do not reveal sensitive information, that the volumes of the sections are well-balanced and that the texts are not too detailed for readers. However, if the IRM is unsure about the appropriateness of the level of detail, she leaves this decision to the CFO and CEO. Through her experience with coordinating TechCo's management report, the IRM has developed an intuition for the requirements of the CFO and CEO. Concerning the **wording**, the IRM asks the departments for clarification whenever she thinks that texts contain too much technical jargon or when she does not understand them. When appropriate, she rephrases texts to align the tonality and writing style of the report.

Whenever paragraphs or sections have been changed, the IRM contacts the department to discuss suggested changes and to request approval for the texts. When the IRM contacts the QEHS department, the DBM coordinates the **feedback** with the responsible managers and the head of the department. In the HR department, the HRM directly discusses the feedback from the IRM with her supervisor. After the feedback is incorporated, the IRM sends the draft to an **external lector**, who is experienced in proofreading management reports of listed and non-listed firms. The lector provides feedback on the wording and clarity of the texts and provides suggestions for improvement. This feedback is forwarded to and discussed with the departments.

Review

Once the feedback from the lector has been included in the draft by mid-December, the IRM hands the preliminary draft of the management report to the CFO (Figure 6-30).[113] The CFO applies several **criteria when reviewing the nfKPI chapter**:

> *"If the texts go into too much detail – you realize this while reading – I cut the flow of information at a particular point. I just look at it from the perspective of an external reader: 'Do I understand what is written there? Is this interesting to me? Or am I rather interested in a summary?' And in case of many disclosures, I might not be interested at all. Moreover, some things may not be intended for disclosure to outsiders. For example if it refers to our customers or if it could raise our competitors' attention. It is a blend of different criteria." (TechCo CFO)*

In addition to aiming for understandable, concise and precise texts, the report shall convey the messages of the executive board. To do so, the CFO checks the balance between topics and how they are interlinked. Moreover, the CFO tries to identify texts which are contradictive or which could create false impressions. His goal is to provide the "right messages in

---

[113] This draft includes other narrative chapters of the management report, e.g., risks and opportunities, in addition to the nfKPI section.

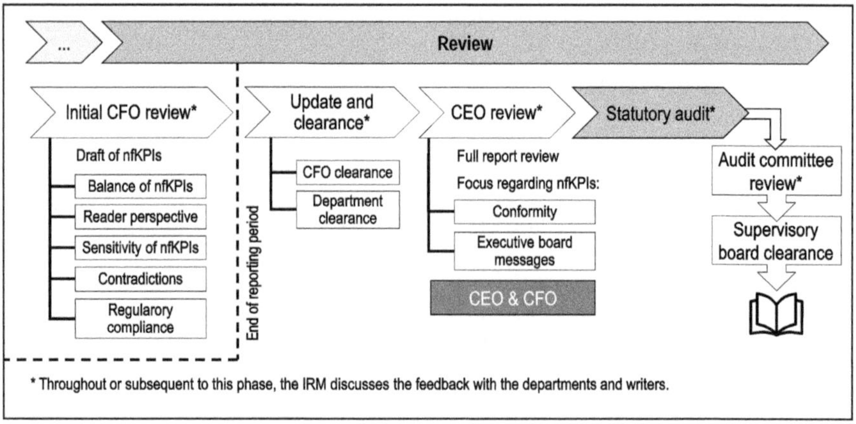

Figure 6-30: Review phase at TechCo

the right manner with the right intention" (*TechCo CFO*). Finally, he verifies the compliance with regulatory requirements.

Any comments and requests for changes are discussed with the IRM, who communicates the **feedback** to the departments. By the end of December or the beginning of January, the departments have included the feedback and approved the narrative parts of the management report. Subsequently, the CFO provides his preliminary clearance for the nfKPI chapter.

As soon as the missing information is available around the middle of January, the nfKPI chapters of the management report are **updated**, along with chapters containing financial statement information. Once the information is included, the CFO reads the entire management report and provides feedback to the IRM. By the end of January, the feedback has been incorporated into the report and cleared by the heads of the departments.

The draft is then sent to both the CEO and the statutory auditors. Both have a timeframe of about one week to read the report and to provide their feedback. Concerning nfKPIs, the **CEO** particularly reviews the conformity of the disclosures with his messages on TechCo's performance. Once the CEO has read the report, he meets with the CFO to discuss the management report. Through reconciling their viewpoints, the CEO and CFO align the messages of the report. Any feedback is communicated to the departments by the IRM. Once the heads of the department approve the changes, the feedback is incorporated into the report.

The **statutory auditors** of TechCo carefully read the nfKPI chapter and request documentation for any quantitative information. The IRM provides them with the necessary documentation. Thus, none of the departments are in contact with the auditors. Feedback is mostly provided on the wording of the nfKPIs and on the coherence of the texts. Occasionally, the auditors recommend to include more quantitative nonfinancial information in the report. However, the nfKPI chapter is not a key focus within the audit of the financial report. Once the feedback of the CEO and CFO is included in the report, the auditors review the changes and provide their audit opinion.

Following the audit opinion, the annual report is handed to the audit committee of TechCo's **supervisory board**. Parallel to the audit of the audit committee, the annual report website and the layout of the print report are prepared by a communications agency. After the audit of the financial report through the audit committee, the report is discussed in the supervisory board meeting and cleared for publication in March.

In summary, the preparation process of TechCo's nfKPIs for the management report has several characteristics. First, TechCo applies a best-practice approach with regards to its management report and the respective nfKPI disclosures. In accordance with this best-practice approach, the preparation process of nfKPIs for the management report is elaborate with regard to the materiality analysis, measurement and composition of the report. Second, while the IRM and CFO coordinate and review the nfKPI section, the functional departments of TechCo are closely involved in determining material nfKPIs and preparing the disclosures of the information. Third, the IRM provides little guidance to the departments on how to compose the nfKPI disclosures. Fourth, the firm publishes qualitative nfKPIs with a focus on economic nfKPIs and the main focus of the group management lies on financial KPIs. In contrast to the qualitative disclosures, the firm uses several nfKPI databases which entail quantitative nfKPIs. Fifth, the timeline and responsibilities of the process are not documented in detail by the IRM. This low documentation indicates that the preparation process is organized in a rather informal manner.

6.1.7 AgCo case

6.1.7.1 Company profile and nfKPI reporting

AgCo is one of the leading retailers and service providers for agricultural products in Germany. The firm employs more than 5,000 people and generates more than € 5 billion in sales revenues. The firm's business is focused mostly on the German market with less than one quarter of sales being generated abroad. AgCo is a non-listed stock corporation whose shares are held by cooperatives, employees and other shareholders related to the agricultural industry.

AgCo is **organized** according to its business segments. Along with the corporate support functions, these segments are supervised by the executive board. The head of finance supervises the head of external reporting (HER), who is responsible for the preparation process of the management report. In addition to the HER, a public relations manager (PRM) from the communications department is responsible for the narrative parts of the management report, including the preparation of the nfKPI chapter. AgCo's supervisory board is comprised of shareholder and employee representatives to equal parts. The interview partners who participate in the preparation process of nfKPIs for AgCo's management report are presented in Table 6-7.

Title	Abbreviation	Department
Head of external reporting	HER	Financial accounting
Public relations manager	PRM	Communications

Table 6-7: Interview partners at AgCo

AgCo's **interest in nfKPIs** is driven by the perceived importance of the firm's employees and a growing sense of responsibility for sustainability issues. A cross-functional sustainability project-team, which consists of representatives from every business line and corporate support function, is responsible for developing AgCo's sustainability strategy and integrating it in AgCo's operations. While the sustainability team is responsible for developing sustainability indicator systems, several quantitative nfKPIs are already measured and used for AgCo's operational activities. In addition to the employee headcount, the HR department measures and analyzes training rates, employee turnover and the degree to which target achievements are met. Within the business lines, several nfKPIs related to production such as utilization of production capacity are monitored and reported. AgCo's marketing department also monitors the firm's number of social media followers. Therefore, AgCo's nfKPIs reflect all three dimensions of nonfinancial information.

With a financial year from January to December, AgCo prepares its financial statements according to the HGB, which are complemented by a group management report. As AgCo is not subject to the CSR-RUG, it does not prepare a nonfinancial statement. The company reports its nfKPIs in a **separate chapter within its management report**. This chapter contains individual sections on employees, social media presence and sustainability. The nfKPIs within this chapter are mostly qualitative. However, quantitative information is provided on measures such as employee headcount, training rates, degrees of production quantity target achievement, social media followers, resource efficiency or the utilization of production capacity of selected business lines. The chapter on nfKPIs was included in the management report when GAS 20 came into effect. Although it is disclosed that the internal management system of the group is based on financial KPIs, it refers to nfKPIs as evaluation criteria for the management of the group. The chapter on nfKPIs is not prepared in accordance with voluntary reporting frameworks. In addition to the management report, a sustainability report is published on AgCo's website. The separate report provides detailed explanation of AgCo's sustainability strategy and analyzes qualitative and quantitative nfKPIs for AgCo's fields of action.[114] AgCo's management report, however, only refers to the sustainability report without disclosing important environmental nfKPIs. Overall, nfKPIs in AgCo's management report reflect purely economic nfKPIs and economic nfKPIs which overlap with the environmental or social dimension. Hence, its focus lies on the most important nfKPIs in accordance with § 289 (3) HGB as well as a few indicators related to the CSR-RUG understanding of material nfKPIs.

[114] The sustainability report is published on a two-year basis and is prepared in accordance with the GRI G4 guidelines. The report is prepared by the sustainability team without involving the accounting department.

The most important **goals of AgCo's reporting on nfKPIs** are to emphasize the importance of AgCo's employees and to convey the firm's values. Through reporting the employees' contribution to the firm's success, the executive board appreciates the achievements of AgCo's employees. In this context, the management report is also used to convey the firm's qualities as an employer to its shareholders and potential employees. Moreover, nfKPIs are disclosed to show how the management of the group incorporates the firm's values into its actions and business relations.

While AgCo regards all stakeholders as the **audience for nfKPIs in the management report**, its shareholders are seen as the core target group of the disclosures. As its shareholders are closely tied to the agricultural industry, AgCo understands them as multipliers for its messages towards customers or potential employees. Moreover, AgCo provides nfKPIs as a source of information for AgCo's current and potential employees. Moreover, the disclosures are also directed at politicians and the general public. Although nfKPIs are also provided for AgCo's partner banks, they have so far shown little interest in this type of information.

6.1.7.2 Preparation process of nfKPIs

The PRM forms the center of AgCo's preparation process for nfKPIs in the management report. While the HER is responsible for the preparation of the annual report, all narrative sections of the management report including the nfKPIs are prepared by the PRM. Besides these two, contact persons from the business lines, the HR, social media and sustainability department, the heads of the finance and management accounting departments as well as the executive board are involved in the preparation process of nfKPIs for AgCo's management report. Figure 6-31 summarizes the information flows between the participants of the preparation process of AgCo.

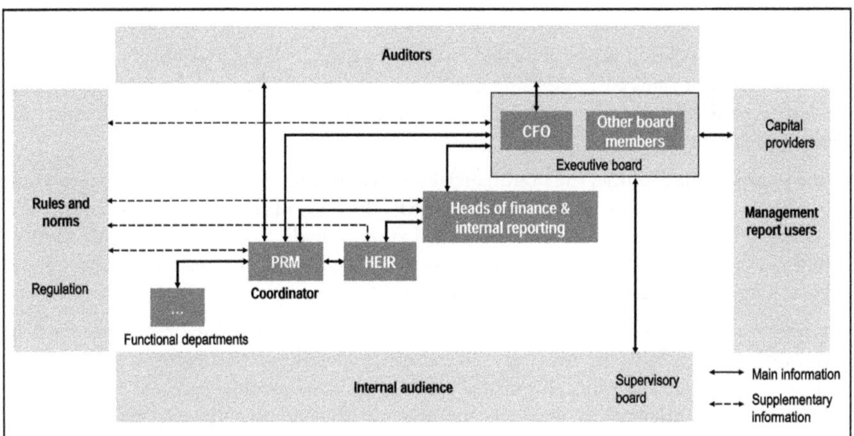

Figure 6-31: Participants and information flow in AgCo's preparation process of nfKPIs

6.1.7.2.1 Materiality analysis

At AgCo, the PRM **determines material nfKPIs** prior to the composition process of the management report. The materiality analysis process is depicted in Figure 6-32. Throughout the reporting period, the PRM continuously monitors the development of AgCo's nfKPIs and receives notifications from the functional departments:

> *"This is experience. We basically observe the business lines throughout the year and we are in close contact with them. And of course, they notify us on what could become interesting for our target groups and update us on what we already disclose. But I cannot remember any scene in which it was debatable. It basically leaps at you, which topics you include in the management report and which could be covered in more detail than in the previous year. But if you monitor the course of business and the development of [AgCo] throughout the year, it falls right into place. In October or November, the topics just come tumbling down at you." (AgCo PRM)*

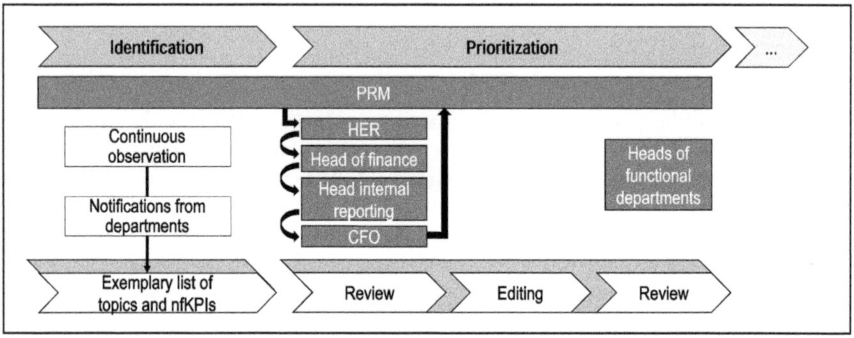

Figure 6-32: Materiality analysis process at AgCo

During the **identification phase** carried out in October, the PRM assembles a broad list of nonfinancial topics and corresponding nfKPIs. Except for notifications from internal stakeholders to the PRM, no other internal or external stakeholders are included in the identification of relevant nfKPIs.

In the **prioritization phase**, the nonfinancial topics and nfKPIs, the PRM uses a circulation procedure to provide his suggestions to the HER, the head of finance, the head of internal reporting and the CFO. Each of these participants provide feedback for the selection of nfKPIs. After incorporating this feedback, the PRM approaches the heads of the functional departments to discuss the selection of nfKPIs.

To determine material nfKPIs, AgCo applies several **criteria**. The legal requirements help determine which nfKPIs are necessary. Moreover, to determine the relevance of the information, the preparers consider the perspective of specific stakeholders and the AgCo group. However, this examination is based on experience rather than consultations with stakeholders. AgCo also tries to ensure the consistency of nfKPI disclosures through carrying forward nfKPIs from the previous reporting period. These KPIs are then contrasted to nfKPIs identified in the current materiality analysis process:

"You have to see – an annual report is published once a year. This means, we collect these topics and we have a look at whether these nfKPIs are followed up on to ensure consistency. But also: 'What is our basis? What happened during the year?' And when we feel that certain topics are still of interest and that we still pursue them, we disclose this information again in the current report." (AgCo HER)

6.1.7.2.2 Composition process

AgCo's composition process entails the planning, draft and review phase for nfKPI disclosures in the management report. These phases are presented in the following.

Planning

After determining material nfKPIs in October, AgCo's **composition process** for the nfKPIs follows in November (Figure 6-33). The timeline of the composition process is determined in an initial **planning meeting** between the heads of the finance and management accounting departments, the HER and the PRM. In this meeting, the participants carry forward the timetable of the previous composition process and align it with the date of the shareholder's meeting in May, which marks the final deadline of the management report. After this meeting, the progress of the management report composition is monitored and discussed in weekly meetings between these participants.

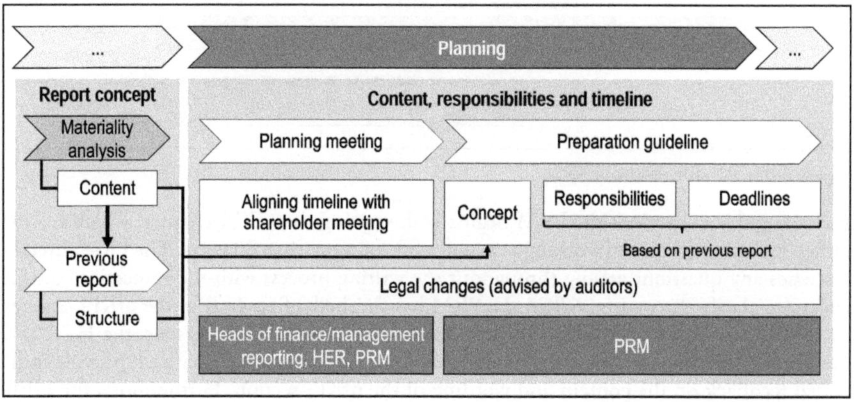

Figure 6-33: Planning phase at AgCo

To coordinate the composition process, the PRM uses a detailed **guideline** on the basis of the previous management report and the results from the materiality analysis. This guideline includes notes on process steps, deadlines, contact persons and previous data sources. Changes to legal requirements for the management report are known to the HER and the PRM as they are continuously informed about these changes by AgCo's statutory auditors throughout the year.

Draft

Following the planning phase, the PRM **collects** the nfKPIs for the management report, as depicted in Figure 6-34. As the PRM has been monitoring AgCo's internal and external media throughout the reporting period, he has already pooled information on the various nfKPIs. On this basis, the PRM assembles an outline of the nfKPIs for the respective topics. Next, he individually approaches the heads of HR and of one selected business line, the responsible persons for AgCo's social media marketing and contact persons in the sustainability reporting team. On a bilateral basis, they discuss the suggested structure and alterations to the nfKPIs. Apart from these internal sources, neither the PRM nor the HER analyze the nfKPI reporting practice of AgCo's competitors to gain insights for AgCo's preparation process or disclosures.

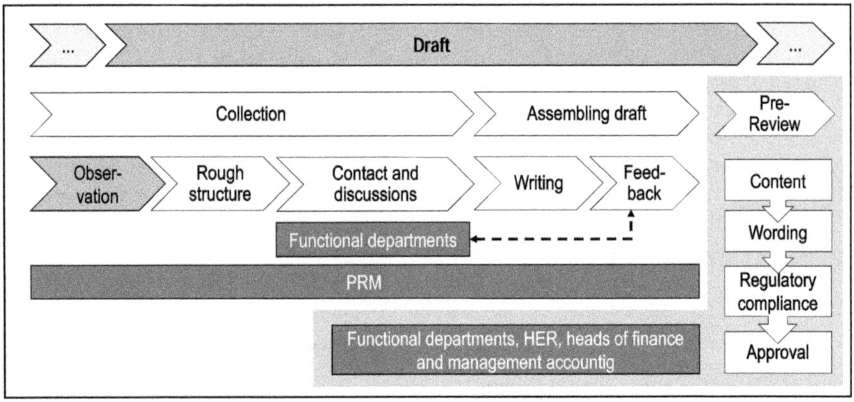

Figure 6-34: Drafting phase at AgCo

Following this collection, the PRM begins with **writing** the nfKPI chapter, which is simplified by his experience of working as a journalist for more than 20 years. The PRM directly discusses any questions arising throughout the writing process with the respective contact person to clarify the matter. When the PRM has finished a first draft of the nfKPI chapter by mid-December, he forwards this draft to the respective contact persons, the HER and the heads of the finance and management accounting department. They each provide individual feedback on the content and wording of the nfKPI section. Furthermore, the HER and the heads of the finance and management accounting department validate the regulatory compliance of the nfKPI sections. Subsequently, all participants approve the respective section.

Review

In the beginning of January, the PRM asks the HR department for the final quantitative HR-related nfKPIs. Moreover, he asks the head of the selected business line for a final production utilization ratio and requests an **update** from the social media manager on the number of followers on social media channels. Along with these numbers, the PRM includes the feedback he has received for the nfKPI chapter by Mid-January (Figure 6-35). Such feedback is typically minor and commonly refers to wording or understandability. By the end of January, the nfKPI section and other largely narrative parts of the management report are preliminarily finished. Using these texts as a basis, a graphic designer prepares the layout of the report.

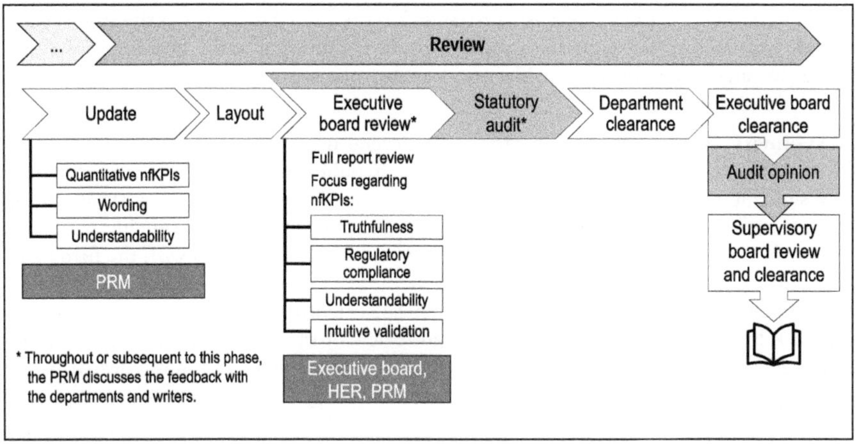

Figure 6-35: Review phase at AgCo

After the financial statement data is incorporated into the management report, the report draft is forwarded to every member of the executive board by the end of February. The members of the board have about one week to **review** the report and to provide their feedback to the CFO. The CFO pools the feedback and contacts the HER and PRM to coordinate the adjustments. In previous years, AgCo's executive board had been included earlier in the review stage. However, due to complications regarding the coordination of the feedback, the feedback loop of the executive board was changed:

> *"I mean one thing we have changed about the process is that the executive board is included in the process at a relatively late stage with a well advanced draft of the management report. This facilitates the coordination of feedback, especially when we get closer and closer to the printing deadline." (AgCo PRM)*

The board members apply several **criteria** when reviewing the nfKPIs. They examine the truthfulness of the disclosures and check whether these reflect the course of business. The board also investigates the relationships underlying the statements using their knowledge about the development of the nfKPIs. Moreover, it is checked whether the texts are understandable and clear.

Parallel to the review of the executive board, the management report is sent to AgCo's **statutory auditors**. Similar to the executive board, the auditors do not receive earlier drafts of the management report. The PRM provides the auditors with documentation on the nfKPIs. The auditors then review the statements and examine the documentation. In case of questions, they approach the PRM. However, the auditors typically provide little feedback regarding nfKPIs.

The feedback from auditors and the executive board is incorporated into the report by the PRM and discussed with the responsible contact persons from the departments. After receiving clearance from the departments, the executive board and statutory auditors review the final changes. Both the board and the auditors provide clearance for the report by the end of March. The annual report is then handed to the audit committee of the **supervisory board**, who audits the report for a supervisory board meeting at the beginning of April. Once the supervisory board provides its clearance, the report is printed in time for the shareholders' meeting in May.

In summary, AgCo's preparation process has several important characteristics. First, the PRM as the process coordinator has a background in public relations rather than accounting or sustainability. These skills support him in observing relevant nfKPI information during the year and in writing the respective nfKPI texts. Second, while the firm provides a separate sustainability report, the management report shares only few resources with the firm's sustainability reporting. Moreover, the nfKPIs disclosed in the management report reflect mostly qualitative nfKPIs. Third, the hierarchical structure of the firm is reflected in the feedback loops of the materiality analysis and review of the report. Fourth, AgCo's functional departments are involved in the preparation process only to a limited degree, as the PRM carries out most tasks related to the materiality analysis and draft preparation.

6.2 Cross-case analyses

Based on the single case analyses, this section derives the design and influencing factors of the preparation process of nfKPIs for management reports. To shed light on the design of the preparation process, the cases are compared and contrasted with regard to phases (section 6.2.1) and participants (section 6.2.2) of the process. Section 6.2.3 integrates the results of the within-case and cross-case analyses to derive influencing factors of the process. All three sections discuss the findings in the light of extant literature and theories.

6.2.1 Phases of the preparation process

This section differentiates the phases of the preparation process of nfKPIs for the management report. In this context, this section identifies procedures and methods used for the preparation. In accordance with the foundations of this study, the overall preparation process is separated into the materiality analysis and composition process. The materiality analysis (section 6.2.1.1) consists of the identification and prioritization of material nfKPIs. The composition process (section 6.2.1.2) comprises the planning, draft and review phases.

6.2.1.1 Materiality analysis

6.2.1.1.1 General characteristics

Building on the conceptual model of the preparation process developed in the foundations of this study, one of the first steps of the preparation of nfKPIs is to determine relevant contents through materiality analyses. Prior research observes that materiality analysis processes of companies appear to be evolved to different degrees (*Solomon/Edgley* (2008), p. 338; *Manetti* (2011), pp. 118-119; *Jones et al.* (2016), pp. 226-227). Researchers discuss the evolution of materiality analyses on the basis of the extent of formalization and the range of report users considered. Similarly, the **general characteristics** of the case firms' materiality analysis processes can also be differentiated according to the extent of formalization and range of report users considered. In addition, materiality analysis processes can vary with regard to their timing in the preparation process as well as their elaborateness between subsequent reporting periods. As these four general characteristics apply for the entire materiality analysis process rather than individual phases of this process, this section discusses these characteristics individually before analyzing the identification and prioritization phases.

Formalization

The formalization of materiality analyses reflects "the control of job activities by administrative rules and procedures" (*Organ/Greene* (1981), p. 238). In accordance with this definition, the formalization of materiality analyses can be differentiated based on whether firms adhere to external or internal norms (rules) (*Montagna* (1968), pp. 142-143) and whether they have established particular sequences and techniques (procedures) to facilitate the materiality analysis of nfKPIs (*Gibbins et al.* (1990), p. 133).

As the first differentiating characteristic, **sustainability reporting guidelines** can provide external rules which structure the materiality analysis process. HealthCo is the only firm in the sample using the GRI G4 guidelines for its integrated management report. Its materiality analysis process for nfKPIs is explicitly structured according to the recommendations of GRI G4-18. The recommendations of the guidelines hence serve as a set of rules for HealthCo's materiality analysis process. The other two public firms refer to their compliance with the UN Global Compact (ChemCo, PrintCo) and the DNK (PrintCo), which do not particularly serve as guidelines for structuring the materiality analysis process but rather for supporting the identification of nfKPIs. Thus, these guidelines serve as decision criteria without particular influence on the overall structure of the process. None of the private firms uses sustainability reporting guidelines to determine nfKPIs for its management report. These firms may not use sustainability reporting guidelines because of cost-benefit considerations to ensure lean and fast materiality analysis processes. Furthermore, firms with separate sustainability reports based on GRI (ChemCo, AgCo) show that the materiality analysis processes are not formalized according to reporting guidelines although respective processes exist within the firms. Therefore, the firms' materiality analysis processes could be decoupled between sustainability and accounting departments.

In contrast to sustainability reporting guidelines, firms' internal **reporting criteria** play a more important role for the case firms in providing rules and structures for materiality analysis processes. While most criteria are applied in either the identification or prioritization phase, some criteria shape the overall structure of the firms' materiality analysis processes. These criteria are consistency and regulatory compliance.

All sample firms stress the particular importance of **consistency** as a rule underlying the materiality analysis process, which is in line with extant research (*Searcy/Buslovich* (2014), p. 158). Hence, both public and private firms compare newly identified material nfKPIs to those identified in previous reporting periods. However, firms differ in their application of the consistency principle. Firms such as LogCo and FashCo strongly base their understanding of materiality on the consistency principle by carrying forward previous selections and subsequently evaluating potential changes to the nfKPIs. Although HealthCo and ChemCo also pay attention to the consistency of the nfKPIs, the principle is incorporated in a later stage of the materiality analysis, namely after relevant nfKPIs have been identified. The point of time at which the consistency principle is incorporated into the materiality analysis could point towards a greater openness for identifying additional nfKPIs. This openness seems to be applied by the larger public firms (HealthCo, ChemCo) and voluntary best-practice reporters such as TechCo. While this open and rather flexible approach could indicate a lower degree of formalization in the materiality analysis of these particular firms, the extent of formalization of the preparation process is also influenced by several other decision criteria.

Similar to the consistency principle, the **compliance with regulation** is regarded as an important criterion for all firms. However, PrintCo and all private firms except TechCo try to meet rather than exceed the requirements:

> *"I believe our supervisory board interprets the reporting requirement on nonfinancial information in a similar manner as we do. It has to be fulfilled, but not over-fulfilled." (PrintCo HEIR)*

> *"Honestly, I abide by what GAS 20 requires. That's what we will include. There won't be more which will be included [in the management report]." (FashCo CFO)*

> *"As long as we don't have to, we won't ask anyone to translate [nfKPIs] into numbers. These things could actually be operationalized and put into numbers." (LogCo CFO)*

This approach of meeting rather than exceeding regulation points towards a narrow interpretation of the term materiality (*Solomon/Edgley* (2008), pp. 341-343), particularly in the case of private firms (*Haller et al.* (2014), p. 2542). Thus, the interpretation and implementation of regulatory requirements can affect the internal rules underlying the materiality analysis. The effect of increased regulatory requirements on the materiality analysis process can be seen in the case of PrintCo. The firm significantly altered its materiality analysis process, adopted an additional sustainability reporting guideline and discloses additional nfKPIs in its nonfinancial statement because of the requirements of the CSR-RUG. In a similar vein, ChemCo expresses that its materiality analysis is an "evolving process" (*ChemCo MQR*) which is adapted to regulatory requirements and reporting trends.

In addition to the application of internal and external rules, the formalization of materiality analysis processes is also expressed in the **usage of particular methods and procedures**. However, as these methods and procedures (e.g., materiality matrix or stakeholder engagement) are specific to the phases of the materiality analysis process, they are examined in the context of the identification and prioritization phases in the following sections.

Range of report users considered for management report

In addition to the extent of formalization of the materiality analysis, the materiality analysis process is also shaped by the firms' understanding of its report users. In this context, the **range of report users considered for the management report** differs strongly across the case firms. HealthCo uses the broadest range of management report users in the sample by considering the demands of employees, shareholders and many other external stakeholders. The other two **public firms** (ChemCo, PrintCo) explicitly target a smaller core audience with their management reports. Both consider capital market participants as their main audience for nfKPIs. In addition, ChemCo also targets current or future employees and other external stakeholders who are interested particularly in plant safety and emissions. However, the firm's separate sustainability report addresses a larger audience with more detailed nfKPIs. PrintCo recognizes that thus far few report users including the capital market have shown interest in its nfKPI reporting. Similar to findings from extant literature, the differences between the public firms show that both an integrated reporting format (HealthCo) and a mixture of company size, industry and visibility (HealthCo, ChemCo) could have an effect on a firm's range of report users (*Hahn/Kühnen* (2013), p. 13).

Most **private firms** in the sample consider only business-related report users such as owners, employees, customers and suppliers when determining material nfKPIs, which is in line with extant research (*Haller et al.* (2014), pp. 2542-2543). Solely FashCo and AgCo explicitly state that their nfKPI reporting is also addressed at a broader, general public. Nonetheless, as the latter address a larger audience through their separate sustainability reports, the firms' focus of the management report lies on nfKPIs material for the business of the firms. Moreover, with FashCo and AgCo being active in socially (fashion) and environmentally (agriculture) critical industries, a broader range of report users might be driven by their membership in critical industries comparable to the cases of HealthCo and ChemCo.

Overall, the range of report users seems to be **reflected** in the materiality analysis. While firms with broad ranges of report users show rather elaborate materiality analyses and engage more of these users in the process, firms with narrow ranges conduct rather intuitive and less inclusive processes.

Timing of the materiality analysis process

The preparation processes of the case firms also differ with regard to the **timing of the materiality analysis process** during the preparation process. This timing appears to reflect the role of the materiality analysis for the particular firm. Most firms (all public firms, TechCo, AgCo) conduct a **separate materiality analysis** before the composition process of the management report. By doing so, preparers allow for more time and diligence regarding the materiality analysis and aim to relief the work-load of the composition process. As a result, materiality analyses include various methods and procedures for identifying material nfKPIs which are either structured according to detailed timelines (HealthCo, ChemCo, TechCo, AgCo) or are flexible and less structured (PrintCo). In contrast, LogCo and FashCo have **embedded the materiality analysis** into their composition process. While the phases and procedures of their materiality analysis can still be distinguished from the composition process, these have strong overlaps. The materiality analyses of these firms also have particularly low degrees of formalization as compared to the other firms and appear to play a subordinate role in the preparation process. Figure 6-36 illustrates the difference between separate and embedded materiality analyses.

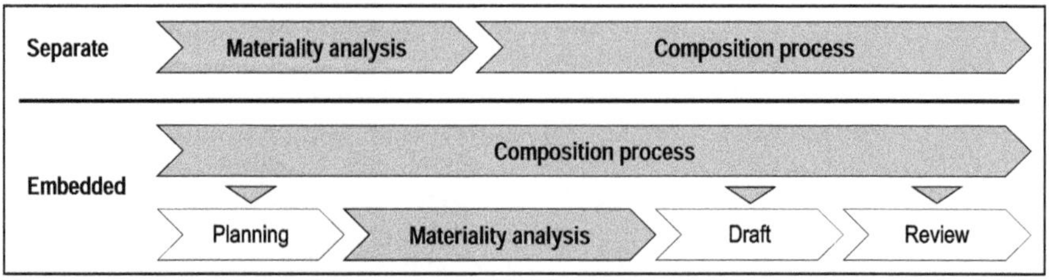

Figure 6-36: Separate and embedded materiality analyses

Elaborateness of materiality analyses

The materiality analysis processes of the case firms also vary in their **elaborateness in subsequent reporting periods**. In some reporting periods, the materiality analysis processes may be conducted through formal means, extensive discussions and research to determine nfKPIs relevant according to changes in regulatory requirements or reporting guidelines. In other reporting periods, these processes may be rather lean by mostly carrying forward previous nfKPIs. In spite of less elaborate processes, the case studies show that firms always carry out the general steps of the materiality analysis. While firms might use less formal methods of identifying and prioritizing nfKPIs, participants of the process nonetheless check that no other nfKPIs have evolved to be material and that previously reported nfKPIs are still material.

6.2.1.1.2 Identification

As identified in the foundations of this study, the materiality analysis process begins with the **identification phase**. In this phase, preparers compile a list of relevant nfKPIs and determine boundaries for the reporting of such nfKPIs (Figure 6-37) (*GRI* (2015a), pp. 33-35). This section discusses this phase in the light of the case studies.

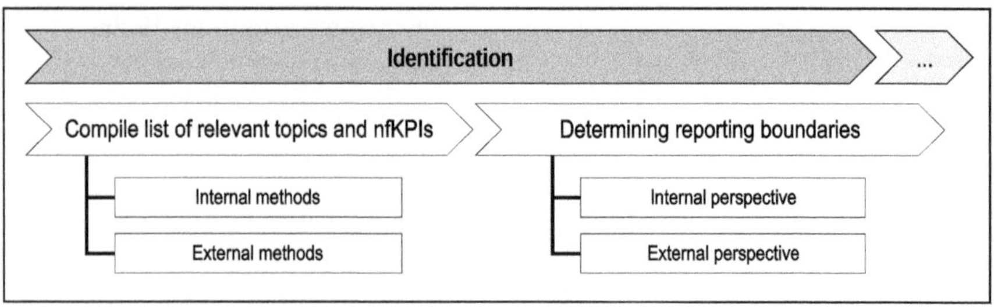

Figure 6-37: Stages of the identification phase

Compile list of relevant topics and nfKPIs

The case companies use a broad range of **methods to compile a list of relevant nonfinancial topics and nfKPIs**. These methods reflect internal or external perspectives on the relevance of particular issues or nfKPIs (*Günther/Muschallik* (2017), p. 424). Figure 6-38 presents the methods analyzed in the following.

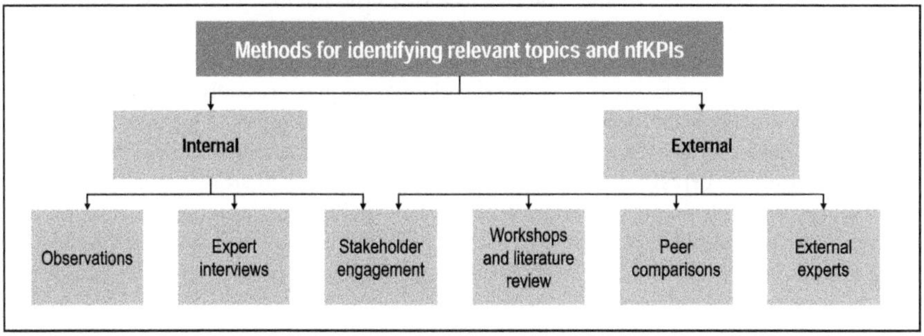

Figure 6-38: Internal and external methods for identifying relevant topics and nfKPIs

Common methods focusing on an **internal perspective** are observations and expert interviews. Comparable to extant research findings (*Searcy et al.* (2009), pp. 35-36), **observations** are heavily used by the private firms in the sample. While the majority of observations reflects recurring nfKPIs, which have been reported in previous periods, some observations reflect current nfKPI developments of interest (*Tarca et al.* (2011), pp. 47-48). At FashCo and AgCo, the identification of nfKPIs is carried out through observing the internal reporting related to the nonfinancial development of the firm. This approach is rather informal and based on experience. LogCo and TechCo scrutinize their observations through an explicit set of criteria to identify relevant nfKPI sections for the management report. In the public firms, internal observations appear to play a less important role than for private firms. Solely the CFO of PrintCo also based his initial selection of nfKPIs on internal observations, before the firm was required to prepare a nonfinancial statement.

One **explanation** for the use of such informal, criteria-based observations could be that some coordinators of the preparation process are well enough informed about the nonfinancial development of the firm to have a high-level overview of the nfKPIs:

> *"You have to have a good understanding of the entire firm, the entire group, to determine, whether it is really an important factor. We are a manufacturing company, there it is easy to see that production and quality are very important. Employees. All of this is relatively easy." (TechCo IRM)*

Another explanation for the use of informal observations could be drawn from contrasting these to formal and quantitative identification methods suggested in the literature (e.g., *Hsu et al.* (2013); *Calabrese et al.* (2016)). While such methods can provide a comprehendible and objective selection of nfKPIs, informal and unsystematic methods of analysis may be better suited – particularly for private firms – from a cost-benefit perspective.

Some case companies use **internal expert interviews** to identify relevant nfKPIs (*Günther/Muschallik* (2017), pp. 424-425).[115] All public sample firms integrate experts from the functional departments in the identification phase. These firms argue that engaging internal experts in discussions regarding relevant nfKPIs helps them determine the availability of data and the significance of the nfKPIs for the departments. In the case of the private sample firms, LogCo and TechCo include internal experts in the identification phase of their materiality analysis. In contrast to the public firms, LogCo and TechCo do not schedule meetings with the functional departments but rather request a selection of nfKPIs. Moreover, the functional departments are engaged in the identification process after the general nfKPI sections have already been identified by coordinators and executives. This points to differences in the degree of involvement of functional experts in the selection of nfKPIs. These differences could be explained by a better overview of the coordinators in private firms regarding the availability and relevance of particular nfKPIs. Furthermore, all four private firms provide functional experts with particular guidance in the form of criteria for identifying nfKPIs. However, in TechCo's case the coordinator purposefully provides little guidance to ensure that the departments have few restrictions in selecting nfKPIs. This implies that the engagement of experts could also be differentiated by the level of restrictions placed on them in the form of guidelines and identification criteria.

Consistent with prior research (*Searcy/Buslovich* (2014), p. 156), public firms appear to put stronger emphasis on the **external perspective** in their identification phases. The only private firm which explicitly includes the external perspective is TechCo. As the most common method, HealthCo, ChemCo, PrintCo and TechCo analyze the nfKPI reporting of **peer companies.** All firms conduct this analysis to conform to peer companies' nfKPI reporting. Both PrintCo and TechCo place particular emphasis on this analysis to determine an acceptable industry-standard selection of nfKPIs. While peer analysis appears to be a common approach for public firms, most private firms in the sample make limited use of this method:

> *"From time to time, we have a look at our competitors' reports [...] to get some input." (FashCo HEIR)*

> *"Currently, we do this to a very limited extent. [...] we have a position in the market which is difficult to compare to other logistics companies." (LogCo HA)*

In contrast to this, TechCo conducts a peer analysis of listed companies and best-practice reporters to provide high-quality reporting:

> *"We are non-capital market oriented. We are not subject to securities trading regulation or any other stock exchange rules. At one point, we have taken up the claim to act as if we were listed on a stock exchange and we have set a high quality standard for our external reporting." (TechCo CFO)*

In addition to the peer analysis, HealthCo and PrintCo explicitly mention an external analysis based on **workshops and literature reviews** used to identify relevant nfKPIs. This particular method seems to be useful for preparers who have to extend their nfKPI reporting because of regulatory changes, such as PrintCo. In HealthCo's case these methods are used

[115] Section 6.2.2 discusses the role of experts as know-how promotors in the preparation process.

to train participants to ensure regulatory compliance. In contrast to the suggestions of extant research (*Arena/Azzone* (2012)), the sample firms do not explicitly include **external experts** such as consultants or auditors in the identification phase of nfKPIs. However, this method could be particularly helpful for first time reporters or firms that were subject to major organizational or regulatory changes.

One method of combining internal and external perspectives is **stakeholder engagement.** This combined method is solely used in HealthCo's identification phase for nfKPIs. The firm identifies a range of relevant nonfinancial topics through a regular global survey of external and internal stakeholders and through ongoing stakeholder communication. Overall, this combined method provides the highest form of stakeholder inclusion as compared to other methods identified in the sample. Moreover, HealthCo marks the only firm which applies structured methods of stakeholder identification and prioritization (e.g., *Bryson* (2004); *Boesso/Kumar* (2009)). Therefore, HealthCo is able to base the material nfKPIs on the demands of its internal and external stakeholders.

Overall, the analysis indicates a strong **emphasis on internal methods** in the context of identifying material nfKPIs, which is consistent with findings in the literature (*Searcy/Buslovich* (2014), p. 158). This emphasis could be strongly connected to the degree of stakeholder engagement in the identification phase. While HealthCo's engagement process shows a strong reliance on internal and external stakeholder input, other firms show low engagement to none at all. However, most firms (PrintCo, FashCo, TechCo, AgCo) consider the perceived or expected interests of stakeholders in the identification process. This indirect engagement of external stakeholders can be justified by the lower costs for the firms (*Günther/Muschallik* (2017), p. 424). Nonetheless, these methods lack the opportunity to verify that resulting nfKPIs in the reports reflect stakeholder demands.

Determining reporting boundaries

Reporting firms also determine **boundaries for the reporting** of nfKPIs during the identification phase (*Jones et al.* (2016), p. 226). However, most firms determine these reporting boundaries implicitly and from an organizational perspective. As an exception from these cases, HealthCo takes on both an internal organizational perspective and an external perspective by including nfKPIs that are related to suppliers. The other two **public firms** limit their disclosures to the internal organization for diverging reasons. While ChemCo takes on an external perspective in its separate sustainability report, nfKPIs in the management report solely reflect the organizational view of the firm. This difference in perspective points towards the potential role of the reporting format on the preparation process. In the case of PrintCo, nfKPIs are further limited to material subsidiaries and production sites because of data availability issues.

Similarly, the **private companies** identify nfKPIs from within the organization. FashCo and AgCo explicitly state that only nonfinancial information relevant for the overall group is considered, excluding information relevant only for particular segments. However, FashCo provides selected nfKPIs regarding supply chain related certifications. While this extension of reporting boundaries could be explained by the firm being part of a critical industry, AgCo as a firm with a similarly critical industry (agricultural industry) does not extend reporting boundaries. Hence, given that most public and private firms in the sample focus on internal boundaries, the firms' nonfinancial impacts caused by supply chain activities are rarely included in the materiality analysis. Nonetheless, the results indicate the potential role of several influencing factors such as industry or reporting format.

In summary, the identification phase yields an initial selection of nfKPIs or nonfinancial topics. In contrast to findings in the literature (*Adams/Frost* (2008), pp. 293-294), the case firms do not seem to be particularly challenged by identifying material nfKPIs. However, this divergence from the literature can be explained by the emphasis on internal methods and the strong focus on internal boundaries. Moreover, firms simplify their identification phase by carrying forward material nfKPIs from previous years. Firms appear to use more elaborate methods when identifying material nfKPIs for the first time or after major organizational or regulatory changes took place. Nonetheless, nfKPIs are identified each year, albeit on the basis of previously selected nfKPIs which are reviewed to a limited degree with less elaborate methods than in previous periods.

6.2.1.1.3 Prioritization

In the **prioritization phase** of the materiality analysis, material nfKPIs are determined on the basis of the relevant nfKPIs identified. The prioritization phases of the case firms comprise two stages: determining a firm's understanding of materiality and the decision-making regarding material nfKPIs. These stages illustrated in Figure 6-39 are analyzed in the following.

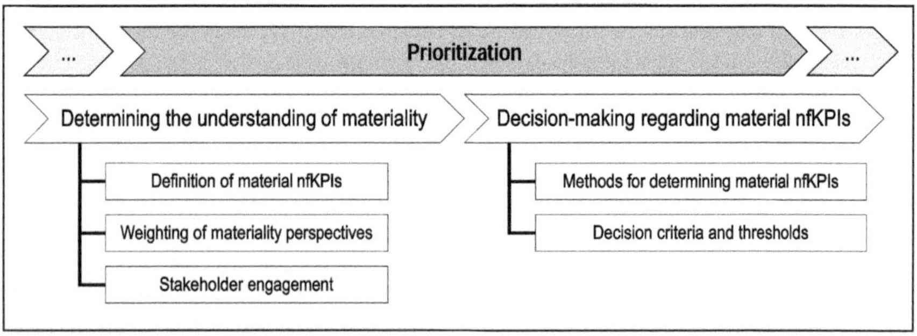

Figure 6-39: Stages of the prioritization phase

Determining the understanding of materiality

As a basis for their materiality assessments, firms **determine their understanding of materiality**. This stage comprises the firm's definition of material nfKPIs, the weighting of materiality perspectives and the engagement of stakeholders. Regarding the **definition of material nfKPIs**, the case firms choose between the different definitions by § 289 (3) HGB, the CSR-RUG, GAS 20 or voluntary reporting frameworks such as the GRI Standards or the International Integrated Reporting Framework. While all case firms comply with the requirements of § 289 (3) HGB, the public firms also apply the materiality definition of the CSR-RUG in their nonfinancial statements or reports. In addition, HealthCo broadens its understanding of material nfKPIs by applying the GRI G4 guidelines. As a consequence of applying these materiality definitions, all public firms consider economic, environmental and social nfKPIs equally. In contrast, some private firms focus their reporting on selected dimensions such as the environmental and social dimension (FashCo) or emphasize the economic dimension (TechCo, AgCo). Therefore, the private firms seem to apply a narrower definition of materiality as compared to the public sample firms.

In addition to the definition of material nfKPIs, firms can also determine material nfKPIs with regard to the nfKPIs' influence on stakeholder assessments and decisions (*stakeholder perspective*) and with regard to their significance on the organization's economic, ecologic and social impacts (*organizational perspective*) (*GRI* (2015a), p. 36). These **materiality perspectives** can be included in the prioritization process in various degrees (*weighting*). HealthCo's prioritization phase serves as an example for an equal **weighting** of the two perspectives. On the basis of a materiality matrix, HealthCo incorporates both perspectives in equal parts into its materiality assessment. In contrast to this approach, the other two public firms put stronger emphasis on the organizational perspective. ChemCo justifies this emphasis by stating that the stakeholder perspective is covered in the firm's sustainability report. PrintCo primarily addresses the organizational perspective by defining material nfKPIs as information which provides an added value to an understanding of the firm's business. Nonetheless, both firms indirectly consider their stakeholders' demands when selecting material nfKPIs.

Similar to the latter two public firms, most private case firms put **higher emphasis on the organizational perspective** when determining material nfKPIs. FashCo and LogCo appear to focus mostly on the organizational perspective. Both derive material nfKPIs with the goal to provide information necessary for an understanding of the course of business, as required by § 289 (3) HGB and the respective requirements in GAS 20. In contrast, the other two private firms include the stakeholder perspective to a higher degree. TechCo includes the stakeholder perspective by assuming that stakeholders consider business related nfKPIs as material. Thus, the organizational perspective also prevails in the case of TechCo. While AgCo recognizes the shareholder perspective as equally important to the organizational perspective, its focus on shareholders points towards a higher importance of the organizational perspective.

While all firms consider stakeholders in the materiality analysis, the skewed weighting of perspectives appears to be connected to the **range of report users** considered in the analysis.[116] Firms with a range limited to those users in direct connection with their business (e.g., owners, banks, employees, customers, suppliers) seem to place higher emphasis on the organizational perspective of material nfKPIs. This emphasis becomes evident in the case of firms which publish separate sustainability reports (ChemCo, FashCo, AgCo). These firms stress that they particularly emphasize the organizational perspective in their management report and target it mostly towards their business-related report users, while their sustainability reports are targeted towards a larger audience. The other private firms and PrintCo also address business-related report users and emphasize the organizational perspective. It can be assumed that all of these firms understand management reports as target media for

---

116 For a discussion of the firms' ranges of report users refer to section 6.2.1.1.1.

a business-related audience, justifying a focus on the organizational perspective. In contrast to this understanding, HealthCo's integrated reporting approach appears to support a broader range of report users and perspectives. In connection with considering all report users, HealthCo follows both the stakeholder and organizational perspective when prioritizing material nfKPIs.

In connection to the range of report users considered, the materiality analyses also vary with regard to the **engagement** of stakeholders in the prioritization phase (*Searcy/Buslovich* (2014), p. 158). None of the case firms directly engages **external stakeholders** in the prioritization phase. However, in HealthCo's case, the stakeholder input from the identification phase is considered in the prioritization phase. All other sample firms consider external stakeholders' interests only indirectly by reflecting on which nfKPIs could be of interest to these groups. For the latter firms, this difference in external stakeholder engagement is in line with their higher focus on the organizational perspective in the prioritization phase.

In contrast to the external stakeholder engagement, all case firms except for FashCo engage only those functional departments or support functions as **internal stakeholders** in their prioritization phases which provide the material nfKPIs for the management report. Other internal stakeholder groups (e.g., employees from departments not involved in the preparation) are only indirectly considered in the prioritization by, for example, reflecting on their potential demands. Therefore, most materiality analyses engage only a small range of stakeholders. While this engagement of internal and external stakeholders could be connected to the firm's understanding of materiality (*Edgley et al.* (2015), p. 14), the effects of the engagement appear to depend on the methods of engagement and on the decision-making regarding material nfKPIs. Hence, the decision-making stage regarding material nfKPIs is analyzed in the following.

Decision-making regarding material nfKPIs

After identifying relevant nfKPIs and determining the understanding of materiality, firms can conduct their **decision-making regarding material nfKPIs**. This decision-making stage entails the methods applied for determining material nfKPIs as well as the decision criteria and thresholds. Overall, the case firms apply a multitude of **methods to determine material nfKPIs.** The methods applied by the case firms differ strongly in their degree of formalization (*Adams/Frost* (2008), p. 293). On the one end, HealthCo uses workshops to prepare a materiality matrix and to condense resulting nonfinancial topics into key fields of action. This approach is highly structured and includes a multitude of participants. On the other end, FashCo bases the prioritization on a discussion between the CFO and the coordinator, which is implicitly guided by several criteria. Settling within the range of this spectrum, the remaining case firms support their decision-making through including functional departments in the selection of material nfKPIs or with an individual set of explicit or implicit criteria.

While most firms include **functional departments in decision-making processes** regarding material nfKPIs during the prioritization phase, the level of inclusion of these department differs across the sample. In the **public firms**, functional departments are included in the prioritization phase. However, while the decision-making regarding material nfKPIs is mostly carried out between coordinators and the departments at HealthCo and ChemCo, the functional departments of PrintCo only provide information for the decision-making of the coordinator and the CFO. In the case of ChemCo, departments appear to be particularly powerful through being responsible for the approval for the selected nfKPIs. ChemCo justifies this approach with trying to not impose nfKPIs on the departments.

Similar to HealthCo and ChemCo, the functional departments of the **private firms** LogCo, TechCo and AgCo are engaged in the prioritization phase. In TechCo's case the departments prioritize nfKPIs which then serve as a basis for the prioritization through the CFO and IRM. The prioritization decisions of LogCo's functional departments are embedded in the collection phase. In a comparable manner, AgCo's functional departments are engaged in the prioritization phase after the finance department and the CFO have reviewed the initial suggestions of the coordinator. Contrary to the other case firms, FashCo's functional departments are not included in the prioritization of material nfKPIs. This is justified by the overview of the CFO and coordinator over the nfKPI development of the firm. Overall, the results reflect the findings in the literature (*Haller et al.* (2014), p. 2545), which show that top-management is involved in most firms' prioritization phases. Through including functional departments in the prioritization phase, the materiality analysis of nfKPIs comprises a multi-level decision-making process. Thus, materiality decisions could be influenced by the number, background and positions of the participants involved. Moreover, important materiality decisions could also be made prior to the involvement of executives.

The decision-making stages of the case firms also differ with regard to their **decision criteria and thresholds** for material nfKPIs. These differences are highlighted by the spectrum of criteria and thresholds in the **public firms**. On the one hand, HealthCo uses fixed thresholds such as revenues or the probability and severity of reputational risks to determine material information. On the other hand, PrintCo bases its priority decisions on the compliance with the regulatory requirements of § 289 (3) HGB and the CSR-RUG as a decision criterion:

> *"There is no process behind this, in which we delineate the materiality. It is rather that whenever we find that the information reflects a truthful image of [PrintCo], then these are material topics. And they will be included. And all others, that are not material, are not included." (PrintCo HEIR)*

ChemCo settles within this spectrum with a fixed catalogue of decision criteria based on both GAS 20 and the consistency principle. Overall, solely HealthCo uses quantitative thresholds to determine material information.

While none of the **private firms** uses fixed or explicit thresholds for their prioritization decisions, all firms stress the compliance with regulatory requirements as an important decision criterion. TechCo additionally draws from peer comparisons and the perceived importance of particular nfKPIs for an understanding of the group. In this case, the external criteria can be explained by TechCo's best-practice reporting approach. In contrast to TechCo, the decision criteria of the other private firms reflect a narrow perspective of materiality, as they are oriented towards providing minimum disclosures rather than best-practice.

In summary, the materiality analyses of the case firms yield a selection of material nfKPIs. Such indicators are typically based on internal perspectives, decision criteria such as regulatory compliance and are commonly selected without engaging external stakeholders. Nonetheless, functional departments are often involved in the selection of material nfKPIs, albeit to varying degrees. Similar to the identification phase, the prioritization phases of the individual case firms also differ in their elaborateness across reporting periods. Changes in organizational structures or regulatory requirements provide similar drivers for using more elaborate prioritization processes. Nonetheless, in all case firms the prioritization of nfKPIs is carried out each year. These nfKPIs provide the content for the management report, whose composition process is analyzed in the following section.

6.2.1.2 Composition process

6.2.1.2.1 General characteristics

In accordance with the conceptual model of the preparation process, the **composition process** comprises the steps necessary for preparing disclosures on material nfKPI for the management report. While the conceptual model distinguishes the planning, drafting and review phases, the analyses indicate that composition processes in general can be differentiated according to several overarching characteristics. First, the phases of the composition processes of the case firms can be differentiated according to the extent of process formalization. Second, case firms use different IT systems to support the composition. Third, preparers have different levels of experience regarding the composition. Fourth, firms differ with regard to the resources available for the composition process. This section sheds light on these differentiating characteristics which occur across all phases of the composition process.

Extent of process formalization

Similar to the materiality process, **composition processes** of the case firms vary with regard to their formalization (Figure 6-40). On the one side, composition processes of large firms such as HealthCo and ChemCo are rather **formal**. These processes involve various departments and a large number of participants, resulting in high coordination efforts. In combination with the need to provide documentation for internal governance mechanisms and statutory auditors, the procedures and responsibilities of the process are documented in detail. Moreover, several hierarchical levels are involved in approving the content of the report. Finally, such processes involve fixed deadlines which are rigorously enforced to ensure a timely preparation of the report.

On the other side, **informal** composition processes of nfKPIs tend to comprise a small number of participants. Smaller firms such as PrintCo, FashCo and AgCo involve only a handful of departments while the preparation of the report is coordinated by only one or two persons. Such processes are normally rather straightforward and do not require the coordinators to document the phases and participants of the preparation process. A rather flat hierarchy in the organization enables the preparers to directly gather feedback from departments or executives. Furthermore, deadlines tend to be rather soft. These case firms stress that such informal processes are beneficial and suitable:

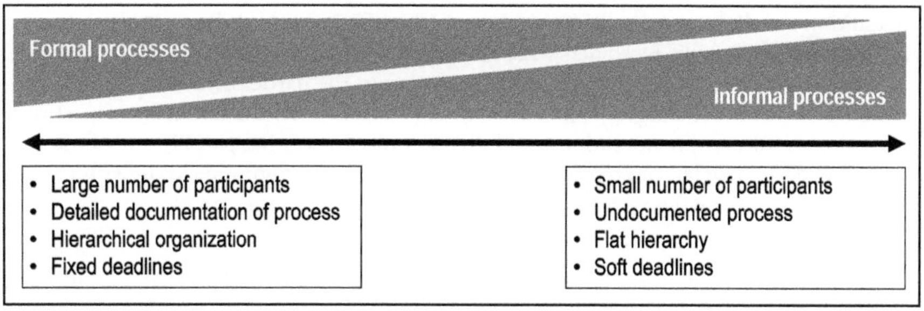

Figure 6-40: Continuum of formal and informal composition processes

> *"In our firm, the process is as lean as this, because it basically falls back on us two [CFO and HEIR] first of all. We don't have five more levels of hierarchy, where information has to be channeled upwards to us in several loops. This does not take place here. And it will not be the case. Because from our position, we will search the path of least resistance for us." (PrintCo CFO)*

> *"We have other parts of the management report which we are dealing with and this means that we try to keep processes as lean as possible so that we can start and finish particular sections quickly." (AgCo HER)*

While the case firms mentioned above have either formal or informal processes, some processes can be categorized somewhere between these two extremes of the **continuum**. TechCo, for example, involves a large number of participants while the process is undocumented, hierarchies are flat and deadlines are rather soft. Overall, the results are in accordance with extant literature (*Adams/Frost* (2008), p. 300; *Searcy/Buslovich* (2014), p. 161)

IT systems

Some case firms recognize that **IT systems** support the speed and efficiency of the preparation process. While a variety of these tools are used in individual phases of the composition process, particularly IT systems for editing, scheduling and documenting are used across the phases of the composition processes of nfKPIs.

The two large public firms HealthCo and ChemCo use mutually accessible **editing software** for writing the management report. At HealthCo, this software is accessible for all participants. In the case of ChemCo, the assembling of the draft is channeled through the coordinator. It is only in the review phases of ChemCo's preparation process that this software is accessible to the reviewers of the report. In these two cases, the editing software simplifies the access of other participants to the draft document. However, ChemCo only choses to leverage potential benefits of the editing software during the review phase. This can be explained by the exclusive role of the coordinator, who uses the collection of texts to remain in close contact with the writers. In all other firms, the texts and figures of the management report draft are collected by the coordinator and assembled in a central document. In these firms, an editing software is not considered due to its expected high implementation costs.

In addition to editing software, HealthCo and ChemCo use **scheduling tools** to organize the procedures, send out reminders to the participants and provide documentation for the preparation process. Such reminders can be sent out to the participants directly and automatically by the scheduling tool (HealthCo). Apart from this, the reminders can also be forwarded to the coordinators who would then approach the other participants of the process (ChemCo). The last approach particularly improves the communication with participants who are only involved in the preparation process once a year:

> *"In the finance department, we know about the deadlines, but it is nice to have documentation for it. And if there are delays, we can determine that this or that task was too late. We do of course have the colleagues in the scheduling tool, who provide the nonfinancial sections. But to be honest, as they only do this once a year, I would often get calls: 'Oh, I have received an email, what do I have to do now?'" (ChemCo MQR)*

While these scheduling tools particularly support large, complex processes, these tools require regular maintenance and administration. The latter provide potential justifications for the fact that other, smaller case firms refrain from using such tools. In a similar vein, solely HealthCo and ChemCo use an IT database for collecting the **documentation** for the audit of the nfKPI sections. In all other firms, either the coordinators collect the documentation themselves or the documentation remains in the departments.

Experience

Next to IT systems, many firms explicitly mention that **experience** supports their composition process. This characteristic refers to the knowledge of key participants of the process regarding tasks and responsibilities connected to the preparation process:

> *"That the process is based on as much routine as possible with regard to the timing. So that you know that this and that has to be done in September. You know beforehand what you have to do." (TechCo HDBM)*

> *"The process at [AgCo] works seamlessly. All participants know about what they have to do when. The process is well-established and provides a stable platform to react flexibly to possible changes in requirements." (AgCo PRM)*

Almost all case firms mention or show particular experience in composing the nfKPIs for the management report. This experience simplifies several parts of the composition process such as the identification of responsibilities, the training of functional departments or the review of nfKPI sections. Nonetheless, such experience could be missing in cases of organizational changes or changes to the reporting. For example, when preparing the first nonfinancial statement, PrintCo's coordinator was challenged with identifying material nfKPIs or finding relevant contact persons in the functional departments for collecting nfKPIs.

Available resources

An important factor which supports the composition process are the **resources available** for the preparation process (*Searcy/Buslovich* (2014), p. 162). The most important of such resources are staff and time:

"Time is also always an important factor. Setting your time horizon too short makes it difficult to write a good report, from my point of view, because it might get lost in the day-to-day tasks." (LogCo CFO)

"We don't have personnel or resources for this. [...] Maybe large firms can afford to do that, where they have a team of people that don't do anything else than that. But here this is not the case. This has to be done in addition to the typical tasks." (FashCo CFO)

"We don't want to build a huge Moloch for the preparation process of the management report. Instead, we want it to pass through as efficiently as possible. That takes up a lot of time, but it does not have to take up an unnecessary amount of time from a high number of employees. We take care that we channel the tasks and that we involve as few people as possible." (AgCo PRM)

Particularly smaller and private firms point out that these factors limit the composition process for nfKPIs, as most participants including the coordinators prepare the nfKPI sections in addition to their day-to-day tasks. In contrast, particularly HealthCo and ChemCo have designated coordinators and departments for the preparation of the report.

However, the **time** available for the composition also marks an important limitation for HealthCo and ChemCo, as short publication deadlines shorten the leeway in the process:

"You have hardly any capacities at the sites for providing the data. The validation is very, very complex, very time intensive, very extensive. And if you want to have some answers from the sites and it's Chinese-New-Year in that week, then we have a problem. Then we don't have any room to say: 'Doesn't matter, just send it next week.' No, that doesn't work. The time horizon is really, really short and there is no room for unexpected issues. And that is what drives this pressure and what proves a big challenge." (HealthCo DBM)

"No, we don't have much influence in this regard. When the deadline for the management report is set and it has to be finished by that day, the financial community is in the lead. We can't just say: 'Finish it four weeks later, that would be enough.' We can't adjust anything in this regard. In the case of our sustainability report, we have a little more leeway because it can be published later and the publication date is also not as strict." (ChemCo HSC)

In summary, the case firms show considerable differences with regard to the overall extent of formalization, IT systems, experience and available resources. In the following, the composition processes of the case firms are contrasted with regard to the planning, drafting and review phases.

6.2.1.2.2 Planning

As identified in the conceptual model of the preparation process, the planning phase of the composition process of nfKPIs entails the planning of the responsibilities and timeline of the composition process. Moreover, the planning phase draws from the relevant contents determined in the materiality analyses. The results show that materiality analyses and planning phases are sometimes embedded in the composition process phases. Nonetheless, the stages of the planning phase can be identified (Figure 6-41). First, firms initiate the necessary planning procedures. Second, preparers determine the tasks related to the composition process, which reflect the report concept, process timeline and responsibilities of the process participants. Finally, these tasks are communicated to the other process participants. These stages are examined in the following

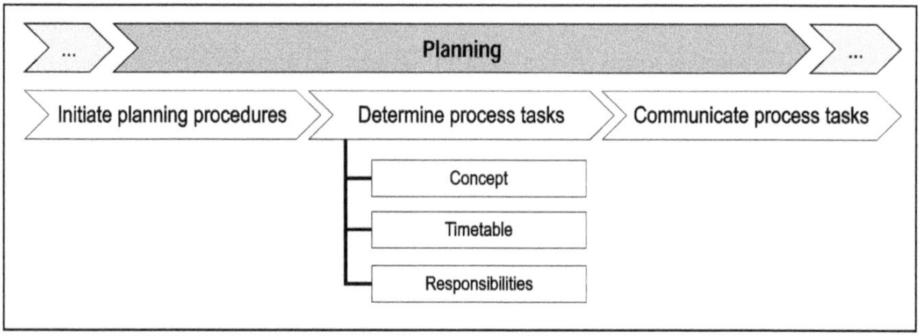

Figure 6-41: Stages of the planning phase

Initiate planning procedures

As a first step of the planning phase, the preparers **initiate the planning procedures**. The procedures used for planning the composition of management reports differ across the case studies. At the HealthCo, the planning is carried out over a planning period of multiple weeks and includes several members of the accounting and sustainability departments. Most other sample firms (PrintCo, LogCo, FashCo, AgCo) set an individual meeting for planning the composition process. In contrast to the other firms, ChemCo and TechCo schedule no meetings, as the planning is carried out by the person responsible for coordinating the composition.

Initially, such **differences in planning procedures** could be justified by differences in the scope of the composition process, using HealthCo as an extreme example for a process with many participants and procedures. However, the latter two cases of ChemCo and TechCo involve a larger scope of participants and procedures in their composition processes than the group of firms with individual meetings. Hence, other factors might provide better explanations for the differences in procedures. At ChemCo and TechCo, the planning processes are carried out by the responsible coordinators. In other firms such as PrintCo, LogCo and FashCo, the planning process also involve top-managers. In these firms, the CFO is either directly involved in the planning or approves the planning shortly after it has been conducted. Therefore, planning procedures reflect the scope of the preparation process, the role of the coordinators and top-management involvement.

Determine process tasks

In the course of the planning procedures, the case firms **determine tasks related to the composition process**. In the following, the specific steps carried out to determine tasks related to the report concept, process timetable and responsibilities of the process participants are analyzed.

Concept

To develop a **concept** for the nfKPI section of the management report, the case firms discuss the contents and structure of the nfKPI disclosures. The **contents** of the disclosures are determined in the materiality analysis process. Due to the different timing of the materiality analyses in the case firms, preparers consider the contents of nfKPI sections at different points in time of the planning phase. In some firms (ChemCo, PrintCo, TechCo, AgCo), material nfKPIs have already been determined by the time of planning. In other firms (PrintCo in previous years, LogCo), material nfKPIs are determined after the planning phase. In contrast to these firms, FashCo determines material nfKPIs during the planning meeting. Similarly, HealthCo's materiality analysis and planning phase take place simultaneously. However, in this case both processes are conducted independent of each other. As a result, the report concept is adjusted once the results of the materiality analysis are available.

Despite of the varying availability of the contents at the time of the planning, all firms determine or review the **structure** of the report during this phase. Whenever material nfKPIs have not yet been determined, firms base their planning on previous report contents. Nonetheless, all case firms assemble newly or previously determined nfKPIs into an initial structure of the report. Particularly in the private firms of the sample, the structure serves as a basis for planning the report. Similarly, PrintCo uses the structure of the nonfinancial statement to plan its drafting phase. By noting the timetables and responsibilities in a document containing the report structure, the firms assign and coordinate the composition process on this basis. In contrast to the smaller case firms, HealthCo and ChemCo base their planning on detailed scheduling tools. For these two firms, the structure of the report serves as an initial template of the report.

Timetable

Almost all firms plan the **timetable** of their composition process before the end of the reporting period. Solely FashCo conducts the planning meeting regarding the management report after the reporting period, once the financial statements have been prepared.

The firms use varying approaches to plan the timetable of the composition process. Firms typically start their planning by setting a **final preparation deadline**. Stock corporations typically choose the shareholders' meeting as an important external deadline (all public firms, TechCo, AgCo). Private firms with other legal forms such as LogCo comply with the publication deadline of the banks (LogCo). However, FashCo does not set a final deadline. This lack of a deadline can be explained by low external pressures due to low reliance on external financing.

Final deadlines help the case firms to construct a timetable with sufficient buffer for each phase of the composition process. To identify **timeframes and interim-deadlines** for the phases, all firms adjust previous timetables to the current final deadline or to previous publication dates (FashCo). Such timetables are documented in schedule planning tools (HealthCo, ChemCo) or in electronic documents (PrintCo, LogCo, FashCo, TechCo,

AgCo). These tools and documents vary strongly with regard to their level of detail. While schedule planning tools contain detailed information regarding the preparation steps, the documents range from very detailed to-do lists (LogCo) to a rough overview of important deadlines without process descriptions (PrintCo, TechCo). In all firms, the preparation of nfKPIs is included in the overall timeline of the management report composition.

In the **following phases** of the composition process, timelines are coordinated and implemented in a comparable manner. At HealthCo and ChemCo, the coordinators monitor the schedule on the basis of the schedule planning tool and send reminders to the responsible persons. Similar to this, the coordinators in most other firms (PrintCo, LogCo, TechCo, AgCo) monitor deadlines and communicate reminders. Solely at FashCo, no deadlines are communicated to the preparing experts. However, the experts are advised to provide their information as soon as possible.

Responsibilities

In most sample firms, with the exception of HealthCo and ChemCo, the planning of responsibilities for particular nfKPI sections is rather intuitive and straightforward. Coordinators identify responsibilities from the previous report's list of responsibilities and compare it with their knowledge about organizational changes. Responsibilities are either documented in electronic lists (LogCo, FashCo, AgCo) or not at all (PrintCo, TechCo):

> *"There are not that many participants and I used to have an Excel list to see who I would have to contact. It's all in my head now. It would of course be bad, if let's say I dropped dead. I should document the responsible persons somewhere so that a third person could have access to this. [...] As I said, it is a very simple process." (TechCo IRM)*

Solely at HealthCo and ChemCo, the two largest sample firms, the coordinators continuously monitor organizational changes and adjust their planning tools accordingly. This monitoring also enables the firms to provide briefings ahead of the preparation process to persons who have become responsible for a particular task for the first time.

Communicate of process tasks

At the end of the planning phase and as a transition to the drafting phase, several sample firms (HealthCo, ChemCo, LogCo, TechCo) use briefings to **communicate** deadlines, contents and responsibilities to the participants of the composition process. A particularly large briefing is carried out by HealthCo, which uses a **kick-off meeting** to provide all participants with relevant information regarding the composition process. However, this meeting is limited to general procedural information and does not address tasks related to specific reporting contents. This approach is deemed necessary by HealthCo to prepare participants:

> *"And that's why we use this pre-reporting process, which helps the reporting process run more smoothly. We believe that you always have to engage the participants. [...] Because in the last years the participants always had other issues to deal with and then blindly trotted into the preparation process. Our colleagues behave this way, because they do more things than just reporting." (HealthCo MSD)*

Other firms (ChemCo, LogCo, TechCo) combine the communication of deadlines with an **individual briefing** of the drafting phase through addressing responsibilities and deadlines alongside with reporting contents and excerpts from previous reporting periods. The sample firms apply this approach to minimize time expenses and bureaucracy. In contrast, PrintCo, FashCo and AgCo do not brief other participants of the preparation process. In these firms, the coordinators approach the other participants in the drafting phase to begin the collection of nfKPIs. **In summary**, the case firms use various formal and informal procedures to plan their composition processes and to communicate the associated tasks and responsibilities.

6.2.1.2.3 Draft

Subsequently to the planning phase, the case firms prepare a draft for the nfKPI section of the management report. Such drafting phases can be differentiated into several stages, namely the collection and validation of nfKPIs as well as the assembling of the respective draft (Figure 6-42). This section sheds light on the similarities and differences between the case firms with regard to these stages of the drafting phase.

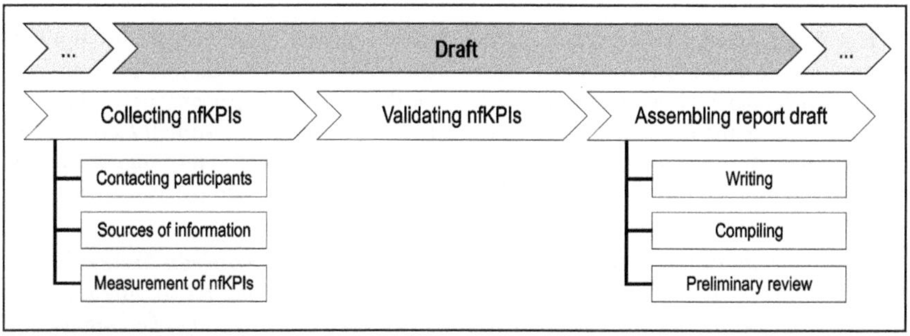

Figure 6-42: Stages of the drafting phase

Collecting nfKPIs

The **collection of nfKPIs** marks the first step of the drafting phase. This collection entails the contacting of participants, the sources of information and the measurement of nfKPIs. These stages are analyzed in the following.

Contacting participants

To initiate the collection, the coordinators of the management report typically **contact** the information providers. Such contact methods differ with regard to their timing, content and form. As for the **timing**, most coordinators in the sample firms contact the functional departments at the end of or shortly after their planning phase. As mentioned above for the communication at the end of the planning phase, most private firms (LogCo, FashCo, TechCo) jointly communicate deadlines, responsibilities and tasks to the responsible departments to reduce the disruption of the departments' non-reporting workflows. One exception is marked by AgCo, where the coordinator assembles a rough structure of the nfKPI section himself, before approaching the departments. In this case, the strain on the departments is relieved even further. In contrast to this, HealthCo and ChemCo engage their information providers earlier and more intensively to ensure that data is available in time. This approach can be justified by the scope of the collection paired with the need to meet time critical publication deadlines. A similar case can be made for PrintCo, in which the novel regulation of the CSR-RUG made it necessary to engage information providers earlier and more intensively.

Regarding the **content** of the contact, coordinators commonly provide excerpts from previous management reports and assign particular collection tasks. While HealthCo and ChemCo approach departments with specific tasks and pre-determined nfKPIs, PrintCo and the private case firms provide few guidelines to their departments. While these differences in openness indicate a lower degree of formalization of collection processes in smaller and private firms, the flexibility and freedom does not indicate a higher decision power of departments in preparation processes as compared to HealthCo and ChemCo. Although HealthCo and ChemCo approach their departments with pre-determined nfKPIs, these nfKPIs have been developed in collaboration with departments during the materiality analyses.

As regards the **form of contact**, all coordinators in the sample firms individually approach the responsible persons of the selected departments. Almost all firms do this in the form of personal meetings or briefings. Solely at LogCo, the responsible persons are notified via email to provide the necessary nfKPIs. Similar to findings in the literature (*Osann* (2010), p. 221), firms mostly refrain from formal contact media such as group meetings or surveys. Preparers deem such forms as too inflexible and time-consuming and perceive such media to provide low synergies:

> *"Actually, we do this on a bilateral basis with the respective department. There is no large meeting, but we talk to the specific departments, to minimize the time spent on this issue. Because they all have their specific tasks to do, and why should for example the R&D department sit in a meeting while we are discussing HR issues? Well, for selected issues we do this, but apart from that we prefer the focused approach and preferably only with those persons, who can truly contribute to the issue." (ChemCo MQR)*

Following the initial contact, many functional departments organize **internal meetings** to initiate the collection of nfKPIs. These meetings range from large briefings (HealthCo), over a department internal brainstorming on topics and tasks (LogCo, TechCo) to the distribution of individual composition tasks (ChemCo). Moreover, such meetings can be used to structure the department internal collection or to generate ideas regarding the nfKPI reporting. In the remaining firms, coordinators and responsible contact persons in the departments discuss the necessary tasks on a bilateral basis. These diverging types of contact between and within the departments mark the gateway to the sources and measurement of nfKPIs.

Sources of information

The collection of nfKPIs evolves around the particular **sources of information**, which connect the coordinators of the processes with the nfKPIs that are being measured in the firm

(Figure 6-43). As identified in the contacting stage, the coordinators of the preparation process request and collect information on nfKPIs from sources internal or external to the firm. To meet the information demands of the coordinators, the sources draw nfKPIs from various locations at different levels of measurement. The particular linkages between coordinators, sources and the measurement are discussed in the following.

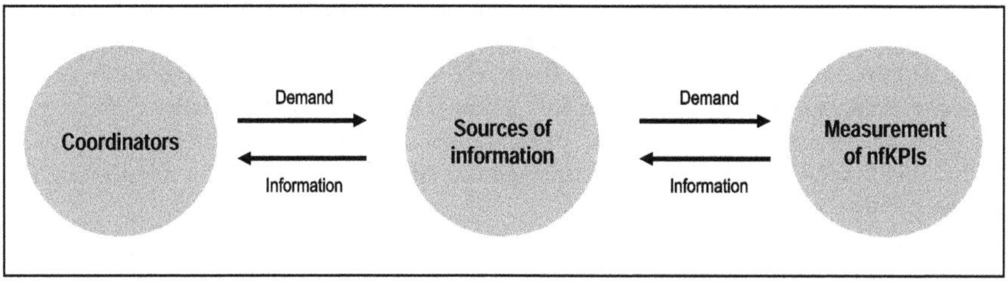

Figure 6-43: Role of sources of information in the collection of nfKPIs

To collect relevant nfKPIs for the management report, the coordinators and functional departments predominantly use internal sources. Lesser used **external sources** provide the reporting firms with supportive information for their analyses of the course of business and economic position. HealthCo – which draws the largest reporting boundaries – enhances its reporting through external information from industry initiatives, supplier ratings and public media. In addition and similar to most other case firms, HealthCo consults peer companies' management reports to benchmark their own reporting. Merely LogCo and AgCo refrain from analyzing other reports, as their reporting and business model are hardly comparable to those of other firms.

Concerning **internal sources**, the coordinators and functional departments use a variety of sources to collect nfKPIs. Building on the findings from the case studies, internal sources for nfKPIs can be differentiated according to the **types of sources**: data systems, documents and experts. **Data systems** constitute specific nonfinancial databases which provide structured and interactive access to nfKPIs. While all sample firms draw quantitative, HR-related nfKPIs from an SAP-based database for managing HR information, only few other departments use databases. In the sample firms, examples for databases can be seen in the sustainability (HealthCo, ChemCo), safety (ChemCo), procurement (HealthCo), production (PrintCo, AgCo), quality (TechCo) or facility management (FashCo) departments. In addition to providing information for the management report, these databases can be used for managing the firm on an operational or group level. Some databases provide the most important nfKPIs for the management of the group, as apparent in the cases of the safety and sustainability databases at ChemCo or the procurement database at HealthCo. These nfKPIs are connected to top-management incentives and are closely monitored by the responsible department. Hence, measurement and reporting processes of these nfKPIs are rather elaborate. In contrast to this, the other nonfinancial databases of the case firms are primarily used for the operational management of the particular department. Hence, such databases are available and accessible solely in the functional departments. In such cases, coordinators typically depend more strongly on functional departments to provide the information.

In addition to databases, **internal documents** such as presentations or newsletters provide another source of nfKPIs. In contrast to databases, internal documents lack interactivity and are prepared by humans, who process the underlying data. Similar to databases, internal documents can be used for the strategic or operational management of the firm. In addition, documents such as internal newsletters or presentations provide media for communicating nonfinancial developments within a department or across the firm. While coordinators of large firms such as HealthCo and ChemCo also use internal documents to stay informed about nonfinancial developments, these firms rely more heavily on information intermediaries and databases. In contrast, smaller and private firms tend to collect their nfKPIs mostly on the basis of internal documents. Particularly the coordinators at PrintCo, LogCo, FashCo and AgCo collect documents throughout the year and use these for drafting the management report.

Finally, the analyses indicate that information can also be collected from **experts**. These experts are persons in the firms with particular know-how regarding nfKPIs. In every case firm, either such persons provide the coordinators of the management report with necessary information regarding nfKPIs or the coordinators are experts themselves. To provide the information, experts collect nfKPIs through their day-to-day tasks in the department, from databases or documents or from other experts within the department. Experts can reflect either individuals, teams or entire departments (*Searcy/Buslovich* (2014), p. 161). As expert knowledge reflects an important part of the role of know-how promotors, this source of information is analyzed in detail in section 6.2.2.3.

Overall, these types of sources provide access to the nfKPIs measured within the firm. The diverse types of nfKPI measurement comprised in the sources are analyzed in the following.

Measurement of nfKPIs

The **measurement of nfKPIs** can be differentiated according to the methods of measurement, the measurement frequency and the object of measurement. With regards to the **methods of measurement**, the nfKPIs provided by internal sources are subject to either automatic or manual methods of measurement. **Automatic** measurements are primarily used in the context of databases, providing access to a constant stream of nonfinancial data through electronic measurement systems. In the sample firms, such automatic measurements are applied for example in the product quality database of TechCo and the real estate management database of FashCo. While this automatic measurement enables the case firms to continuously monitor the state of production and energy efficiency, it also simplifies the measurement procedures for the particular departments. In PrintCo's case, despite using automated production measurement systems, nfKPIs have to be manually collected from the decentralized production sites, as their databases are not interconnected.

In contrast to these automatically measured nfKPIs, most other nfKPIs are measured **manually**. HealthCo, ChemCo and TechCo use extensive questionnaires to measure nfKPIs in their subsidiaries. This standardized method provides access to local nfKPIs in a timely, comparable and reliable manner. The relevant data is typically entered on the basis of the four-eyes-principle, with independent individuals being responsible for entering and approving the data. Such questionnaires are regularly updated to match the needs of internal and external stakeholders (HealthCo, ChemCo). Moreover, the participants involved receive extensive training and guidance to ensure consistency. While TechCo also provides its participants with guidance, global training has thus far not been conducted due to a lack of resources. Resulting data is included in a database (HealthCo, ChemCo) or in internal reports (TechCo). In contrast to using formal questionnaires, other firms rely on regular analyses for internal reports (FashCo) or on ad-hoc requests for nfKPIs (LogCo, AgCo). Finally, manual measurements can also be based on the experience of participants throughout the reporting period. Especially coordinators and information intermediaries in smaller and private firms (PrintCo, LogCo, FashCo, AgCo) use their know-how or observations on the nfKPI development to gather relevant data.

In connection with these measurement methods, the measurement of nfKPIs is subject to different **frequencies of measurement**. While automatically measured KPIs are uploaded continuously, other nfKPIs may be measured on a regular or irregular basis. Regular measurement periods of the case firms range from monthly over quarterly to yearly measurement. Irregular measurements occur directly after particular events, such as the documentation of training in HealthCo's procurement department, or are requested on-demand, such as the number of AgCo's social media followers. Particularly in the case of measuring nfKPIs manually on a yearly basis, persons responsible for measuring are challenged due to missing routines or a high concentration of tasks at year-end:

> *"Surely, a challenge is to have all data in the system at that point in time. We want to change from a yearly reporting to quarterly or monthly reporting so that users and measurement experts get used to this rhythm. Because if you knock on their door once a year and ask for the data [...] then a considerable number of users come back to you and say: 'Uhm, please send me the link to the tool again, I have forgotten my password, where do I have to enter what?' They don't do this often enough. Or they say: 'I am new to the department and my previous colleague hasn't told me anything about environmental things, which should enter in a database.'" (ChemCo HSC)*

In addition to the frequency of measurement, firms also deal with the **object of measurement** in the measurement stage. The firms' nfKPIs as the object of measurement can be differentiated according to the type of nfKPI, the inclusion of subsidiaries as well as the aggregation of these nfKPIs.

While the **types of nfKPIs** measured differ for each firm, general characteristics regarding the topic area and the quantitative or qualitative nature of the nfKPIs can be identified in measurement stages of the case firms. The **topic area of the nfKPIs** resembles the department from which the nfKPI originates (e.g., HR-related nfKPIs) or the specific nonfinancial dimension into which the nfKPIs can be categorized (e.g., environmental dimension). As each firm provides HR nfKPIs, this type of data is commonly available in the case firms. However, while this type of data is being measured in the firms, the accessibility of the data as well as the possibility to disclose these nfKPI are limited due to the sensitivity of the information:

> *"It's not that we don't want to communicate numbers. But specifically in the area of HR we have a lot of sensitive issues that are not communicated externally." (TechCo HRM)*

In the case of environmental nfKPIs, the measurement can be challenging for the firms, as these nfKPIs often depict effects or events external to the firm. While ChemCo has attempted to include these effects or events in its automatic measurement, the firm recognizes the complexity of these issues:

> *"For environmental data, for example CO_2 emissions, we do not need to calculate this by hand but we can draw the data from the databases of the sites. This could mean energy usage on the basis of gas, coal or other sources of energy. The site has included its specific mix in the database, even from utility companies, so that the system can calculate CO_2 emissions automatically. [...] For other issues, we do not have databases at the sites. Hence, it is actually calculated somewhere at the site and provided in Excel reports." (ChemCo HSC)*

Moreover, the case firms also highlight differences and difficulties in the measurement of **quantitative as compared to qualitative nfKPIs**. Most case firms, such as LogCo, argue that measuring qualitative nfKPIs is easier for them than measuring quantitative indicators:

> *"We report solely qualitative and no quantitative nfKPIs, as they are relatively easy to obtain. Describing projects is quite easy, whereas if you want to collect quantitative KPIs and describe these, it is always connected to far more effort. Because you have to maintain them, check whether they are correct and they have to be auditable. And this is significantly more complex than if you just have a look at which measures you have taken which ensure or support a positive development of the firm." (LogCo HA)*

In contrast, both the coordinators of FashCo's report and the responsible person for HealthCo's procurement nfKPIs propose that quantitative KPIs could be easier to measure:

> *"Quantitative KPIs are easier. Qualitative KPIs – if you look at the GRI and the measurement of impact. There is on the one hand the impact of the supply chain on society and the environment. That's really challenging, if you look at the market and try to measure the impact on society. There are always some examples at hand, but I doubt that one should stick one's neck out to claim that we have had this and that impact. That is really, really difficult." (HealthCo MSP)*

> *"Qualitative KPIs are always a bit harder to collect and to put in a nutshell." (FashCo MEIR)*

In HealthCo's case, the difficulty seems to be grounded in the topic of measurement (*societal impacts*), as societal impacts reflect effects of corporate actions outside of the firm which appear to be difficult to quantify. A similar case can be seen at FashCo, where the coordinator indicates the difficulties of collecting and analyzing qualitative nfKPIs as opposed to quantitative KPIs. However, it could be argued that such difficulties of measurement could stem from the preparers' tendency to prefer quantitative over qualitative information. Both the MSP and MEIR share professional backgrounds which require quantitative skills as procurement manager and management accountant, respectively.

ChemCo, PrintCo and TechCo recognize the difficulties of **including small or foreign subsidiaries** into nfKPI measurement processes. Particularly the smaller firms PrintCo and TechCo highlight that the costs of implementing such measurement systems neither reflect current needs nor do they outweigh potential benefits.

While all firms measure and analyze nfKPIs for internal purposes, the nfKPIs are **aggregated or transformed** for the management report. Quantitative nfKPIs such as those from HealthCo and ChemCo are aggregated in accordance with GRI and GAS 20, respectively. The disclosures of both firms are oriented towards the highest possible levels of aggregation to avoid disclosing competitive advantages. However, both firms recognize that the regulation does not offer large leeway for aggregating nfKPIs at higher levels of detail due to requirements of regulations or guidelines. Private firms such as FashCo and TechCo deliberately choose to verbalize internal information. While the firms admit that providing quantitative measures could be more informative, they stress that they try to reduce the level of detail of critical information disclosed:

> *"I am not a big fan of this [topic of nfKPIs], because I come from a world of metrics. If you do something like this, I would like to have more quantitative measures in there, through which you can actually benchmark yourself. But of course I understand that particularly in family firms, these things are dealt with carefully." (TechCo CFO)*

Overall, the analyses show that the case firms differ strongly with regard to how they contact participants, which sources of information are applied as well as how the nfKPIs are measured. In conjunction with these nfKPIs collected, the validation of the information marks a following step of the drafting phase.

Validating nfKPIs

Parallel to or after measuring the nfKPIs in the case firms, the **nfKPIs are validated.** Material nfKPIs are validated with regard to their consistency, correctness and completeness respectively. To safeguard a **consistent** understanding of the nfKPIs throughout the measurement, firms take on different approaches. HealthCo and ChemCo provide the persons responsible for measuring the data with extensive **manuals and training:**

> *"We have definitions, which are rooted in the systems, that whenever someone new is providing us with data or fulfilling the role as HSE manager at the particular site, then this person is trained. People who provide us with environmental data receive a video training, where they can ask one-on-one questions and receive consultation. In addition, we provide a large array of support documents, guidance documents, which are also linked in the system. We also provide training on-site, which means that 60, 70, 80% of all [HealthCo] sites, who provide data relevant for production, have seen me at one point or the other. And I have consulted the sites, which has also been documented." (HealthCo DBM)*

Such formal validation procedures are applied by these firms to ensure the reliability and auditability of the nfKPI data. However, these procedures require a lot of effort and resources.

In contrast to providing such formal guidelines for measurement, smaller firms such as PrintCo and TechCo use **direct communication** as a method to verify the consistency of data:

> *"And I do of course make sure that we are not comparing apples with oranges, checking that we have what we need. That everyone is measuring the data consistently. That's*

of course something I would check. Because if you are asking for such data, everyone might have a different understanding of what they would have to provide." (PrintCo HEIR)

"It requires a lot of individual communication. Because from my experience, documentation is rarely read. Of course you need documentation as a reference, but individual communication is more important." (TechCo HDBM)

Informal validation procedures appear to be suitable for these firms, as they face lower internal and external requirements regarding nfKPI data quality. Internally, it is possible that these nfKPIs do not require high levels of validation as they are not used for managing the group. With regard to the external management report disclosures, nfKPIs are often solely provided in a qualitative manner, for which reason the preparation and statutory audit could be less extensive as compared to nfKPIs of HealthCo and ChemCo.

In addition to the consistency of nfKPIs, the case firms use different methods to validate the **correctness and completeness** of the nfKPIs. By checking the nfKPIs through a four-eyes-principle when they are entered in the database, HealthCo and ChemCo apply a first level of validation. This validation procedure provides an initial approval of the data and strengthens the validity of the measurement by assigning responsibilities. As a second level, the firms conduct thorough site audits to verify that the measurement processes are carried out correctly. Such audits are carried out throughout the reporting period by the departments responsible for collecting and validating nfKPIs. Finally, the departments responsible for collecting the nfKPIs regularly review these indicators with regard to their plausibility. While none of the other case firms use such extensive validation procedures, TechCo relies on irregular site audits by external experts.

All other case firms rely mostly on plausibility checks. Such **plausibility checks** are carried out by comparing current nfKPIs with previous reporting periods or by reviewing the documentation for the nfKPIs. The strong reliance on plausibility checks can be explained by a lack of staff and time to validate nfKPIs more thoroughly. In this context, applying plausibility checks might enable the firms to simplify the validation of their nfKPIs.

In summary, the validation of nfKPI measurement processes appears to be most formal for firms with elaborate data systems (HealthCo, ChemCo). As most other firms rely on informal validation methods – with the exception of TechCo – these methods appear to simplify the firms' validation.

Assembling of draft

After collecting and validating the nfKPIs, firms use this information to **assemble the draft** of the nfKPI related management report sections. This assembling phase of the preparation process of nfKPIs for the management report comprises the writing and compiling of nfKPI sections into a draft of the management report as well as the preliminary review of this draft. In most case firms (HealthCo, ChemCo, LogCo, TechCo), the **writing** of the nfKPI sections is carried out by the functional departments. These sections are then approved by experts and supervisors within the department and handed over to the coordinator of the report who compiles them into the draft document. In two other case firms (PrintCo,

FashCo), the functional departments provide information or short texts to the coordinators. Thus, the majority of texts is written by coordinators who compile these into the draft. This approach is comparable to the case of AgCo, where the coordinator initially prepares a rough draft of the report and then discusses it with the functional departments.

In firms where **functional departments carry out the writing**, department internal coordinators collect information and texts on nfKPIs from the internal experts and typically write sections for the report themselves. Some coordinators rely mostly on information which is already available to them (e.g., the DBM at HealthCo) and contact internal experts for particular project descriptions or approval. This approach enables the coordinators to decrease the efforts of coordinating several experts in the departments. In a few cases (e.g., sustainability nfKPIs at ChemCo and LogCo), the coordinators of the management report directly contact department experts to gather information on nfKPIs. This approach is chosen to avoid using a department internal coordinator (ChemCo) or because of missing internal coordinators (LogCo).

When writing, some of the department coordinators use **decision criteria** for creating relevant texts or tables. In an integrated reporting environment such as for HealthCo, the responsible writers in the case firms check whether nfKPI sections cover all necessary GRI indicators. Moreover, some writers (HealthCo, LogCo, TechCo) also try to convey a positive image of their department through the nfKPI section. Conversely, all writers try to avoid disclosures which contain confidential information or which could shed a negative light on their department or the firm. Furthermore, HealthCo provides all departments with a communication guideline for management report information. This guideline contains principles for HealthCo's management reporting and suggests particular words and phrases. The purpose of this guideline is to promote consistent communication across the various departments involved, which in turn simplifies the review of the texts.

In spite of these decision criteria, writers are often **challenged** with addressing the perspective of the reader. Department internal writers in the case firms aim to address this perspective by writing understandably for external and non-expert readers of reports (HealthCo) or by ensuring that the report is not overloaded with information (LogCo). The responsible writer in TechCo's QEHS department tries to address this perspective by putting herself in the role of a management report reader:

> *"As I'm not involved in every topic, I need to have them [functional managers] explain that to me. And I try to do that by verbalizing and reflecting on the topic to see if I have understood it correctly. Thus, I am a kind of reference user. If I understand it, then someone who is not as involved in these topics might also understand it. It should not be written in hieroglyphics and it should be easy to understand what has happened." (TechCo DBM)*

Subsequently, the contact persons in the departments forward information or texts to the **management report coordinators** either in person, in writing or through mutually shared editorial software. The coordinators then **compile** the information in a first draft of the management report. If these coordinators write texts for the report, they apply similar decision criteria and face similar challenges as compared to writers in the departments. While coordinators may be more challenged with describing department specific nfKPI information, they are typically well informed about report user demands and reporting requirements. Information which is currently unavailable is left blank until measured and accessible. Contrary to occasional findings in the literature (*Searcy/Buslovich* (2014), p. 156), none of the case firms use external writers for the preparation of nfKPI sections.

When compiling the draft or shortly after this procedure, the coordinators conduct a **preliminary review** of the management report draft. Upon reviewing texts or information received, coordinators often contact the functional departments in case of questions or ambiguities:

> *"Sometimes you need to remind and consult the departments again, otherwise you'll get texts which you cannot read. I ask some particular candidates to provide me with the information in time, then I revise the texts and send them back to the departments. Some need a bit more guidance, others need less." (ChemCo MQR)*

In this context, the coordinators particularly highlight their task of ensuring the **readability** of the nfKPIs and aligning the language of these sections with that of the remaining management report:

> *"Then I take the information which I receive and have a look at whether I can directly use it for the management report. Perhaps I have to adjust the wording so that the report appears to be cast in one piece. [...] We do have at least some stylistic aspirations." (FashCo MEIR)*

> *"The departments send me their texts, I read them. I check whether I understand this, make adjustments, possibly consult the departments again. [...] And then at the end, they receive the texts again and I say: 'I have adjusted the text to the language of the report. Have I misstated your information?' And then they have a look at it and tell me whether or not it is correct. Thus, the last authorities are the functional departments." (TechCo IRM)*

The last quote indicates that the coordinators may seek **approval** for particular changes conducted in the draft document. While most firms recognize that linguistic changes are often agreed to by the functional department, changes to the content can sometimes result in discussions between the departments and coordinators:

> *"From the functional departments, some might say: 'We have the sole control over our texts, they are our intellectual property. You assemble and coordinate the report, but this means that we have the final say with regard to the wording.' And this is a real fight, at some points it is incredibly tough, lengthy and unpleasant." (ChemCo MSD)*

In most firms, the preliminary review is limited to an **interaction** between the coordinators of the report and the departments (ChemCo, PrintCo, LogCo, FashCo, TechCo). At HealthCo, the review successes from the coordinators in the sustainability department over the financial reporting team to the heads of these two departments. In this case, the financial reporting team conducts an additional review to align the wording of the nonfinancial parts with the financial sections of HealthCo's integrated report. In a similar manner, the coordinator of AgCo's management report discusses his draft with the accounting and finance departments. This difference between HealthCo and AgCo compared to the other case firms can be explained by the fact that the coordinators of the management reports are not part of the accounting department, which supervises the preparation of the management report in all case firms. In addition to a preliminary review by the coordinator and the departments, HealthCo and TechCo also use feedback from external lectors. Such lectors check the readability and clarity of the report ahead of the review phase.

With regard to the **timing**, almost all case firms conduct this preliminary review of the nfKPI sections before the end of the reporting period. By doing so, the firms aim to complete the drafting phase before the financial statement closing process begins. The sole exception is FashCo, where nfKPIs are prepared after the financial statements.

While the tasks of the assembling stages appear to be similar across the case firms, these stages particularly appear to differ depending on the involvement of functional departments in the writing of the nfKPI sections. **In summary**, the drafting phases of the case firms generally resemble the overall steps of the drafting phase of nfKPIs for the management report. Nonetheless, the findings indicate strong differences across the case firms within the collection, validation and assembling phases.

6.2.1.2.4 Review

After the drafting phase, the case firms **review** the nfKPI section of the management report. Review phases can be separated into the critical reading of the draft, feedback, audit and clearance of the nfKPI section of the management report (Figure 6-44).

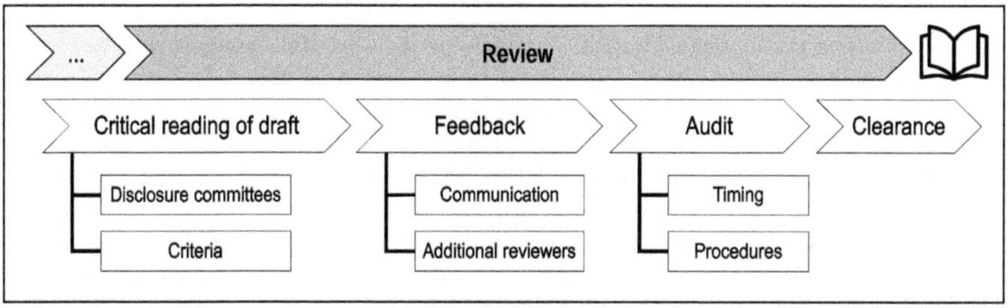

Figure 6-44: Stages of the review phase

Although almost all case firms complete their nfKPI section drafts before the end of the reporting period, only some firms initiate their review phase within this period (HealthCo, PrintCo, TechCo). All three firms apply this **timing** to relieve the drafting and review phase of the financial sections of the management report after the reporting period:

> *"And we deal with this numbers-uncritical part in the old year. Everything we can prepare and write ends up in a comprehensive numbers-uncritical part. This part is reviewed by our different committees and it is discussed in an executive board meeting. There it is discussed and it is ideally like this: the executive board nods it through and we have finished this part. Because in January and February – you can imagine – we are very, very, very busy with the numbers. [Laughter] And we also need to update those numbers-uncritical sections which contain figures." (HealthCo HQMR)*

"I can already deal with the majority or 99% in advance. Then this issue does not arise during the normal closing processes. Hence, it is a bit more relaxed, if my colleagues do not exceed the deadlines." (TechCo IRM)

In these firms, the preliminarily approved nfKPI sections are **updated** once the latest information on the nfKPIs is available. In the remaining firms, the review phase is conducted after the reporting period. While some firms purposefully forward the entire management report for an initial review to simplify the coordination of the review (AgCo), other firms point out that some of the necessary information for the nfKPI sections is only available after the reporting period (ChemCo, LogCo, FashCo).

Critical reading of the draft

In the majority of the case firms (HealthCo, ChemCo, LogCo, AgCo), the **critical reading of the draft** is organized in a formal and hierarchical way. This formalization is indicated by **multiple review levels** during the review phase:

"Basically this draft is transferred hierarchically. That means everything is first agreed on a working level. And then, once it climbs the hierarchical ladder from the heads of the departments up to the executive board, all feedback is collected through a cascading procedure. This way, we can make sure that all comments and remarks have been taken into account once the document is reviewed by the executive board." (HealthCo MQR)

Such review levels entail different review committees: pre-disclosure committees, CFO reviews and disclosure committees.

In the two largest public firms HealthCo and ChemCo, a **pre-disclosure committee** reads the nfKPI sections before these are reviewed by the executive board. In addition to the coordinators of the preparation process, these committees comprise participants from the communications (HealthCo), IR (HealthCo, ChemCo) or various other departments such as management accounting or strategy (ChemCo). Members from the IR departments of both firms review the nfKPIs from the perspective of the capital market and align the information with the communication provided to investors throughout the reporting period. While the communications team at HealthCo focuses on the alignment of the management report with the overall communication strategy, the pre-disclosure committee members of ChemCo focus on reviewing the financial and strategic messages of the report:

"In the pre-review committee, we do not often discuss nfKPIs. If we do, the focus lies on understandability and the level of detail." (ChemCo IRM1)

Using a pre-disclosure committee might be necessary for HealthCo and ChemCo due to the size of the organizations and the scope and extent of the reports.[117] These committees support the coordinators in aligning the report with extant communication and by preparing the draft for a review through the executive board. Hence, this preliminary review can raise the quality of the draft to relieve the executive board from some of its tasks related to the review of the report.

[117] In HealthCo's context, the pre-disclosure committee subdivides the review of the nfKPI chapter into three individual sections to provide more in-depth feedback as compared to a single review session.

Before handing the drafts to the executive board, most **CFOs** individually review the nfKPI drafts. The coordinators at PrintCo, FashCo and TechCo integrate their CFO in the review whenever individual sections are finished, marking a "rolling process" (*PrintCo HEIR*). In these cases, the CFO still reviews the entire draft again once completed. Similar to the last step of this review, the CFOs of ChemCo and LogCo receive the final draft of the management report and provide their feedback. In these cases, the CFO typically shares any feedback through mutual meetings with the coordinators (LogCo) or in writing (ChemCo). Such preliminary reviews enable CFOs to provide early feedback and to potentially align the draft to their messages.

In each firm, a **disclosure committee** – consisting of the executive board of the case firm – reviews the management report, including nfKPI sections. The coordinators of the management report attend these review meetings or receive written feedback. Such disclosure committee reviews can take place subsequently to the pre-disclosure committee review (HealthCo) or the CFO review (ChemCo, FashCo, TechCo), after the update of the management report (PrintCo, AgCo) or after receiving feedback from the statutory audit (LogCo). By conducting this review, the executive board follows the requirement to confirm the truthfulness of the management report and its compliance with regulation. In addition, the committee also reviews the messages, tone and alignment of the report with the strategic communication of the firm.

Depending on the case firm, the disclosure committee reviews differ significantly with regard to the **degree of formalization**. In one firm, the committee schedules a meeting in which the management report is extensively discussed (HealthCo). In other firms, the executive board members individually review the report and provide feedback to the coordinators (ChemCo, PrintCo, LogCo, AgCo). The latter approach is justified by the difficulty to find common time-slots for the firms' executives. At TechCo and FashCo, the CEO informally discusses his feedback with the CFO:

> *"It takes less than two days. [...] He receives the report document, either electronically or in print. Provide feedback, quickly incorporate it into the report, and then the whole thing is done. [Laughter] [...] We have really short lines of communication here." (FashCo CFO)*

The latter two cases also point towards a role of specific executives. In both firms, the CEO and CFO are more involved in the review as compared to the other board members. Thus, these actors could exert more influence on the nfKPI disclosures.

Throughout the critical reading of the nfKPI disclosure draft, a variety of **assessment criteria** is applied in the case firms: language, message, level of detail and the correctness and completeness of the nfKPIs. With regard to the **language**, potential differences in writing styles are aligned to create the impression of a common voice in the report:

> *"The type of language is something where we regularly see that other persons who are not from the financial community use a different wording and language. And they get to the heart of things differently – I try not to be judgmental here – as compared to in other parts of the report." (HealthCo MQR)*

This language review appears to be particularly important in the case of nfKPIs, due to the variety of departments and persons involved. Moreover, writers vary significantly with regards to their familiarity with the external communication strategy of the firm. To align potential differences in writing, reviewers simplify department or firm specific wording to improve the readability and understandability of the report. Such language reviews are typically conducted by internal journalists (HealthCo, AgCo), pre-disclosure committees (HealthCo, ChemCo) or by the coordinators of the report (PrintCo, LogCo, FashCo, TechCo) before the final draft is handed to the executive board. This type of review indicates that reviewers attempt to relieve executives from this particular task to enable them to focus more strongly on other review criteria.

One of these criteria important for the review by executives is the **message** inherent in the nfKPI disclosures. Reviewers particularly scrutinize whether nfKPI disclosures are in line with the messages and performance presented in the management report. In the case of HealthCo's integrated report, the reviewers examine whether the explanations of nfKPIs share a "common theme" (*HealthCo HMQR*) with the explanations of the financial sections. At TechCo, the CEO specifically checks whether the nfKPIs are in accordance with his messages in the editorial letter. In addition to the internal consistency, the two large public firms explicitly make sure that nfKPIs are aligned with external communication. Executives and representatives of the IR department make sure that the messages of the nfKPIs meet the demands of the capital market and that they are in accordance with the previously communicated "equity story" (*HealthCo IRM*). Furthermore, representatives of the sustainability departments make sure that the communication meets demands of various external stakeholders such as NGOs or the general public. Similarly, private firms with sustainability reports (FashCo, AgCo) align their nfKPI reporting with this type of external reporting.

The case firms similarly consider external demands and expectations when reviewing the **level of detail** of the nfKPI sections. Many firms explicitly take on a reader perspective to determine whether investors, owners or other stakeholders might need more or less detailed information (e.g., HealthCo, FashCo, TechCo). Reviewers in the pre-disclosure and disclosure committees also consider such perspectives in their final review of the materiality of the nfKPIs. However, all firms note that nfKPIs determined in the previous phases are typically accepted as material and that additional nfKPIs have not yet been suggested. However, particularly financially oriented reviewers (e.g., accounting, IR, CFO) question the relevance of selected details regarding nfKPIs:

> *"My financial colleagues, they often address the relevance. We know the report quite well and can reply that the particular information is required by GRI or maybe something else. (HealthCo MSD)*
>
> *"If he [LogCo's CFO] reads something he cannot retrace, then he says: 'How can this be? I don't believe this, I can't imagine this.' Something like that. Then we discuss, whether it could be true or not. And in case of doubt, we leave it out. In this case, we rather do less than more." (LogCo CFOA)*

In this context, the level of detail is often discussed with regard to **sensitive information.** Case firms agree that they try to avoid disclosing information which could reveal competitive advantages or which could put the firm in an unfavorable position. Especially private firms state that they are cautious regarding sensitive or very detailed information. In these firms, reviewers make sure that nfKPI sections mostly provide readers with a general understanding rather than in-depth insights:

> *"There should definitely not be internal information in the report, which is not intended for externals. And we shouldn't create a competitive disadvantage through disclosing this, if our competitors discover our advantages. It's not always the negative information that's critical, because positive aspects could be copied." (FashCo MEIR)*

> *"It is a tendency, that customers can see what is happening, what are they doing, how are they structured. Thus, they can see that there are structures and processes in the background. A good, overall feeling for the firm. However, with regard to quality-related reporting, the most interesting facts – those that really count – can only be found in our internal reports." (TechCo HDBM)*

Finally, reviewers also scrutinize the **correctness and completeness** of the nfKPIs. All review committees check – to the best of their knowledge – whether the nfKPIs are correct, truthful and in accordance with regulation:

> *"[The disclosure committee] for example checks particular statements, whether they are accurate. They also check the backgrounds of these statements, if there are problems of understanding or need for clarification. Overall, it is both an understanding of the numbers and the statements." (AgCo HER)*

This task of auditing the correctness and completeness of the nfKPIs is closely linked to the executive board's task of approving the final management report. While pre-disclosure committees and other participants (e.g., coordinators and auditors) also pay attention to the correctness and completeness of the disclosure, the final responsibility of ensuring the correctness and completeness lies in the hands of the executive board.

Feedback

Throughout the review phase, the coordinators of the preparation process receive **feedback** and changes regarding the nfKPI sections from the reviewers. The coordinators then forward this feedback to the respective writers from the departments. This commonly takes place after major committee meetings, updates to the report or in the course of the statutory audit. In some firms (HealthCo, ChemCo, TechCo), the department internal coordinators distribute the feedback to their colleagues in the department. After the feedback has been discussed, the coordinators forward the draft back to the reviewers. In most case firms, feedback can loop several times before subsequent phases of the review begin:

> *"Exactly, [IRM] looks at the report and judges whether she understands our section from her point of view. And then a lector reviews it. This bounces back to [IRM]. Then it is passed on to [CFO] and then back to us whenever there have been corrections. And this way, the whole thing works like ping-pong." (TechCo DBM)*

Sometimes coordinators and reviewers in the case firms **refrain** from communicating feedback to the departments, if they have only slightly changed the wording of the nfKPI section. This approach shortens the feedback process, as some firms have realized that such changes are approved by the departments in most cases anyway:

"Typically, they [the functional departments] gladly accept editorial changes if you say: 'This is how we can express this a little bit more elegantly, more neatly, more colloquially and not so technical.' They sometimes tend to use rather technical language." (ChemCo MQR)

Particular **challenges** can occur if departments are unwilling to accept changes in wording or when nfKPI sections have already been approved by executives responsible for the particular department. Moreover, coordinators can be challenged with being intermediaries between the departments and the reviewers:[118]

"There are sometimes conflicts. One investor relations manager from the review panel says that it has to be this way and another person from the business segment counters that he doesn't want it this way. We have conflicts, depending on which worlds clash, and it's our task to mediate. That is true for both the financial and the nonfinancial parts." (HealthCo HMQR)

The review phase of nfKPIs in the management report is sometimes supported by other **internal and external reviewers**. In the two large public firms, the legal department reviews the report and provides clearance for its publication. At TechCo, an external lector reviews the writing style of the management report. Furthermore, to ensure the compliance of its management report with GRI, HealthCo carries out an external GRI audit by an independent GRI audit agency. This auditor serves as a "watchdog" (*HealthCo MSD*) by validating that all required GRI disclosures have been included in the report.

Audit

An external review conducted by all case firms is the **statutory audit** of the management report.[119] These statutory audits differ with regards to their timing, audit procedures and feedback through the auditors. With regard to the **timing**, the statutory audit of most management reports is carried out shortly before, simultaneous to or shortly after the disclosure committee review. The statutory auditors of HealthCo and ChemCo conduct site-audits throughout the reporting period to audit the preparation process of nfKPIs. By the time of the audit of the management report, these auditors have already validated preparation procedures, documentation and early drafts. This timing is necessary for auditing the nfKPIs of such large public firms, as the auditors have around one week to audit the management report drafts. While auditors of most other case firms have a similarly short time span, the extent of both the reports and preparation processes is significantly smaller as compared to HealthCo and ChemCo. Solely at LogCo, the audit is stretched for a longer period of time and includes multiple discussion sessions between the CFO, the auditor and the coordinators.

[118] These challenges are discussed in more detail in connection with the role of process promotors in section 6.2.2.1.

[119] In accordance with the audit requirements discussed in section 2.2.3, all case firms are required to have their management reports audited with reasonable assurance. In addition, auditors of all three public firms' nonfinancial statements have to validate that these statements contain the mandatory minimum information required by the CSR-RUG.

The timing of the audit is strongly connected with **audit procedures** carried out to examine nfKPI disclosures and preparation processes. Auditors commonly contact the coordinators of the management report to gain access to documentation and processes of the preparation process. Both HealthCo and ChemCo provide the auditors with access to document databases containing proof documents related to the management report. In the other case firms, documentation is either centrally collected by the coordinators (PrintCo, FashCo, TechCo, AgCo) or provided to the auditors by the writers in the departments (LogCo). Typical documentation of nfKPIs includes for example intranet articles, training material, surveys or production data. For most firms, the statutory audit of the measurement process is carried out almost exclusively on the basis of such documentation, in contrast to the audit of preparation process procedures at HealthCo and ChemCo. This sole reliance on documentation indicates a rather low comprehensiveness of the audit which can be explained by the lack of nfKPIs used for the management of the group as well as the qualitative nfKPI reporting of the respective firms. As these nfKPIs are not part of the internal management system, it is likely that auditors perceive nfKPIs as less important as compared to financial KPIs. Moreover, as these nfKPIs are often disclosed in a qualitative manner, it is likely that these indicators are not based on elaborate measurement processes and databases. Hence, auditors may be inclined to use less comprehensive audit procedures.

These differences in audit comprehensiveness also reflect differences in the **focus** of the statutory audit regarding nfKPIs. In most firms, a particular focus of the auditors lies on the materiality, relevance, validity and plausibility of nfKPIs. With regard to the materiality and relevance of nfKPIs, auditors determine whether the information provided in the management report is material and whether other material information is missing. In this context, auditors often propose more quantitative nfKPI disclosures or discuss the relevance of the nfKPIs for the management of the firm:

> *"One topic which we really like to discuss again and again is the relevance of the non-financial goals for the management of the firm. We have a table with goals in the report. And if they were relevant for the management, we would have to include them in the management forecast. This is always a popular topic. We say: 'No, that's not relevant for the management.'" (HealthCo HMQR)*

> *"In the beginning, it was noted that we had not written enough or that we should include more indicators, key figures or – if unavailable – at least descriptions. They [the auditors] then sometimes said: 'Can't you have a look at whether you have something on this here or there?'" (PrintCo HEIR)*

> *"The extent [of the nfKPI disclosures] is often discussed, whether or not we report too much. And also that we should provide more quantitative KPIs here and there, if possible. But that's not a big deal for them [the auditors]. They tick it off their list and then it's done. That's the feeling I get: 'There are some disclosures, it is not nonsense, then that's it.' [Laughter]" (TechCo CFO)*

While auditors of HealthCo suggest an extension of nfKPI disclosures with regard to forward-looking disclosures, other firms' auditors indicate adding quantitative disclosures to existing qualitative disclosures. These suggestions indicate that auditors attempt to extend their audit mandate towards auditing the preparation of such quantitative disclosures.

Another common focus of the audit procedures is the **validity and plausibility** of statements or figures related to nfKPIs:

> *"Most of the time, they [the auditors] contact the departments directly, because most of the time their questions concern the contents: 'Where does the number come from and is it correct?'" (ChemCo MQR)*

In this context, auditors try to assess the correctness of the information. Auditors of firms with more quantitative information tend to check the correctness by auditing processes and documentation. For most other firms, the statutory audit of the measurement process is carried out almost exclusively on the basis of documentation.

The **feedback** of the auditors is typically provided to the coordinators or the CFO through large Excel files or meetings. In case of critical feedback, the case firms engage in discussions with their auditors:

> *"There are some things where we say: 'We don't want that.' And then he [the auditor] says: 'Yes, but it has to be included, otherwise we can't accept this.' From time to time we have tough discussions and at the end we always find a joint solution." (LogCo CFO)*

While such discussions are in line with findings of extant literature on the audit of annual reports (*Gibbins et al.* (2001), p. 558; *Knauer/Wömpener* (2011), p. 199), the case firms acknowledge that such discussions are rather rare in the case of nfKPIs.

Clearance

After the draft has been reviewed and feedback has been implemented, high-ranking participants provide **clearance** for the final management report. Most case firms (HealthCo, ChemCo, FashCo, TechCo, AgCo) consider the approval by the **responsible departments** to be important:

> *"Internally, the departments have to provide mirror certificates. [...] That means, the executive board discharges itself from the responsibility by having the top-managers approve these things through their signature. The managers certify that all stated data and facts are correct to the best of their knowledge." (HealthCo MSD)*

> *"The final authority is always the functional department. I don't publish anything, if the departments haven't reviewed it and told me: 'Yes, that's correct, I would sign that off like this.'" (TechCo IRM)*

Subsequently, the **executive board** provides clearance for the management report and the financial statements and signs the documents as required by § 245 HGB. For listed companies, this clearance is explicitly published in the mandatory responsibility statement according to § 297 (2) sent. 4 HGB.[120] Furthermore, the auditors issue their **audit opinion** (§ 322 HGB) and provide their audit report to the supervisory board or the executive board, respectively (§ 321 HGB).

---

[120] As a part of this responsibility statement, the executive board approves that to the best of its knowledge, the management report includes a fair review of the course of business and the financial position of the firm (*Fink et al.* (2013), pp. 263-267).

Moreover, in all case companies in the legal form of a stock corporation (HealthCo, ChemCo, PrintCo, TechCo, AgCo), the **supervisory board** audits the annual report. An initial audit is conducted by the audit committee of the board, which is often guided by the audit report of the statutory auditor. The committee then presents its results to the remaining supervisory board. In all of these case companies, the supervisory board questions the statements and figures of nfKPI sections. After discussing with the executive board or the coordinators, the supervisory boards agree to the disclosures of the nfKPIs. In the case of the nonfinancial statements, the supervisory boards of HealthCo and ChemCo delegate the audit of the statement to the statutory auditor. As PrintCo's supervisory board carries out the audit of the statement without the help of a statutory auditor, the supervisory board members question the coordinators of the preparation process:

> *"Our supervisory board is really close to our business. The supervisory board is able to judge as good as we [CFO and HEIR] can what's material and what's not. So they don't need special processes to inquire into how we delineated this and that. [...] And it will be some kind of question and answer session, I can imagine, where they would say: 'Why this topic and why is it reported this way?' Maybe, I don't know. Or: 'How did you come up with this number?' But I suppose it won't be more than that." (PrintCo HEIR)*

After the approvals, the documents are **finalized** for publication. Layouts for report websites and printed reports are prepared for the final texts and metrics. Particularly in the case of HealthCo this finalization phase is time-critical, as the firm uses multiple report formats (i.e., print, online extensions and website). Most layouts are already prepared during the composition process. All case firms with print reports use external agencies for the layouts of their annual report. Firms which do not publish their report in print or online (LogCo, FashCo) upload the report document on the website of the German Electronic Federal Gazette.

In summary, the review phases of the case firms differ significantly with regard to the number of review committees, feedback loops and audit comprehensiveness of the statutory auditors. As statutory auditors and supervisory boards often do not particularly question nfKPI disclosures, the disclosures are often approved at this last stage of the preparation process.

6.2.1.3 Discussion

Overall, the preparation processes of the case firms are **in line with the conceptual model** presented in the foundation of this study (section 2.3.3). In accordance with this model, preparation processes consist of materiality analyses and composition processes. While the case firms are similar with regard to the overall phases and stages comprised in these processes (Figure 6-45), the design of these individual phases as well as the timing of the materiality analysis in the preparation process differ significantly across the sample.

Considered as a whole, preparation processes of the case firms differ with regard to their **degree of formalization**. In the course of their materiality analyses and composition processes, firms apply diverse sets of formal or informal rules and procedures, forming a continuum of preparation processes. While preparation processes of large or more hierarchical

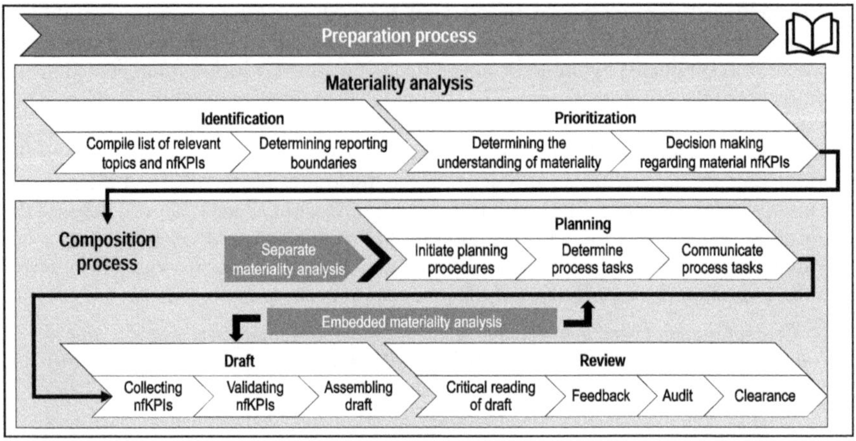

Figure 6-45: Phases and stages of the preparation process

firms seem to be rather formalized, less formalized processes seem to be present in small firms with less process participants and less early publication deadlines. These results extend findings in prior literature, which present initial evidence for varying levels of formalization across preparation processes (*Adams/Frost* (2008), p. 300; *Searcy/Buslovich* (2014), p. 161).

In their **materiality analyses**, firms determine the content of their nfKPI sections by identifying relevant nfKPIs and prioritizing nfKPIs deemed material. Firms tend to use more elaborate processes when determining nfKPIs for the first time, as a reaction to changing regulatory requirements or when updating their materiality analysis through stakeholder surveys. In other circumstances, firms tend to use less elaborate processes when carrying forward and reviewing their previous materiality analyses. In terms of elaborate processes, HealthCo conducts the most elaborate materiality analysis. As the only case firm conducting the materiality analysis process suggested by GRI, HealthCo provides an example for integrating internal and external stakeholder perspectives and methods into their materiality analysis. While other case firms also include internal and external perspectives into their analyses, they do so indirectly and with a strong focus on organizational perspectives. Moreover, most case firms focus on a smaller, more business-related range of report users. Overall, the case analyses show that a broad understanding of materiality is reflected in rather elaborate materiality analysis processes while firms with a narrow understanding appear to use less elaborate rules and procedures to determine material nfKPIs. These findings regarding the decision-making processes of material nfKPIs are in line with prior literature (*Solomon/Edgley* (2008), p. 338).

Although the rules and procedures applied in the materiality analysis processes of the case firms vary across the firms and between reporting periods, all processes comprise the identification and prioritization phases suggested by the conceptual framework. With regard to the **timing of materiality analysis processes**, such processes can be carried out as a separate process before composing the management report or as an embedded analysis during the planning or drafting phases of the composition process. Despite the differing timing of materiality analysis processes, all case firms strongly rely on the resulting selection of material nfKPIs for their composition process. Hence, this dependence on the analysis supports the separation between the materiality analysis process and the composition process in the conceptual model. Nonetheless, the materiality analysis process described in the conceptual framework should not be understood as a process preceding the composition. Materiality analyses processes rather reflect an individual set of tasks providing the basis for the composition of nfKPI disclosures.

As for **composition processes**, firms plan their preparation process for nfKPIs, compose a draft and review this document for publication. Similar to materiality analyses, such processes can also vary in their elaborateness. Firms which compose nfKPI sections for the first time or adjust it to changing requirements tend to use more elaborate processes as compared to firms which carry forward and update previous texts.

While the general phases of the composition processes of the case firms largely reflect the phases and stages suggested by the conceptual framework, the analyses reveal several differences regarding the rules and procedures applied in these processes. In the **planning phase**, nfKPI preparation processes are typically scheduled before the end of the reporting period to relieve the workload of the preparers during the preparation process of financial disclosures. Moreover, preparers differ with regard to their planning of responsibilities for the nfKPI sections. To account for the number of persons involved from non-accounting departments and for the need to document preparation processes for the audit, larger public firms tend to use more extensive planning tools as compared to smaller and private firms.

In the **drafting phase**, case firms draw from a multitude of sources for collecting and assembling nfKPIs for the management report. Interfaces to databases and experts in various departments represent an important difference to other parts of the management report:

> *"I believe this is the main difference as compared to financial reporting. That there are more interfaces within the group. The coordinative effort is much higher." (ChemCo HER)*

Furthermore, particularly firms with quantitative nfKPI reporting are challenged by the measurement frequencies and validation of nfKPIs for the management report. Another difficulty of nfKPI reporting lies in the writing. On the one hand, experts from the departments are well-informed about the development of nfKPIs. However, these experts are typically challenged with writing texts on nfKPIs. On the other hand, coordinators of the report are experienced in writing for management report users while lacking specific expert knowledge on the nfKPIs. These challenges related to writing are commonly mitigated through several feedback loops between coordinators and experts.

Subsequently, the case firms **review** the nfKPI sections of the management report draft. While some firms conduct their reviews of nfKPIs before the end of the reporting period, most firms conduct their nfKPI reviews together with those of other parts of the management report. Nonetheless, significant differences exist with regard to the number of review committees, feedback loops and audit comprehensiveness of the statutory auditors. However, the cases also indicate that reviewers such as executives, supervisory boards and auditors often provide little feedback with regard to nfKPIs. This lack of feedback is likely connected to the role of nfKPIs for the internal management system of the firm. As nfKPIs that are used for the management of the group are commonly reported on more extensively and are often connected to management incentives, reviewers need to review more information and this information is likely to be considered more important. Therefore, reviewers are likely to engage in more discussions and to provide more feedback on the particular disclosures. In contrast, reviewers in firms with solely qualitative information tend to face fewer disclosures which are commonly perceived to be less important as compared to financial KPIs. Hence, the elaborateness of the review between such firms can differ. Nonetheless, the general stages of the review phases suggested by the conceptual model are present despite of these differences in the extensiveness of reviews.

Overall, the analyses confirm the conceptual model developed in the foundations of this study. In this context, the conceptual model supports the notion that while firms may differ with regard to their rules and procedures applied in the preparation process, these firms share common phases of preparing nfKPIs for management reports (*Searcy et al.* (2008), p. 148). Therefore, these phases provide a basis for comparing and contrasting firms' preparation processes of nfKPIs for management reports. In addition, the findings indicate that participants of the preparation processes seem to take on different roles in connection with the preparation process.

6.2.2 Participants of the preparation process

This section determines the roles and communication of participants in the preparation process of nfKPIs for management reports. In accordance with the promotor model, three types of promotors can be identified: process promotors, power promotors and know-how promotors. For each of these promotors, contributions and powers related to the preparation process are discussed. Moreover, participants within the case firms fulfilling these roles are identified. Subsequently, the communication and collaboration between these actors is analyzed. Resulting findings regarding these roles are discussed in the light of the promotor model to derive an adjusted promotor model for the preparation process of nfKPIs in management reports.

6.2.2.1 Process promotor

To identify **process promotors** roles in the case firms, this section examines the contributions and powers of these actors in the preparation process of nfKPIs for the management report. In comparison to the literature on process promotors in innovation processes (*Chakrabarti/Hauschildt* (1989), p. 161; *Walter* (1998), p. 99), certain actors of the preparation process of nfKPIs for management reports provide similar **contributions and powers** in the process. While process promotors contribute to the preparation of nfKPIs by managing the preparation process, they use their powers of organizational knowledge and communication competency to support this contribution (Table 6-8). These contributions and powers are analyzed in the following.

Contributions	Powers
Process management • Determine tasks and participants • Coordinate tasks of participants • Exchange information • Mediate between participants	Organizational knowledge Communication competency

Table 6-8: Contributions and powers of the process promotor

Determine tasks and participants

An initial contribution of the process promotor is to **determine tasks and process participants**. Process promotors do so by coordinating the majority of the steps in the planning phase of the preparation process. While the content and structure are developed in accordance with the executives of the firm, process promotors are responsible for preparing and managing the **timelines and tasks** of the preparation process. This contribution is particularly supported by the promotor's organizational know-how:

> *"The planning process begins in the middle of December. […] Then [HER], [HA] and I go through the steps that have to be done: who does what and until when does it have to be done." (LogCo CFOA)*

Most of the time, process promotors of the case firms carry forward and adjust timelines of previous preparation processes. However, process promotors may also need to develop a new timeline as in the case of PrintCo's nonfinancial statement. In the latter case, this was closely aligned with and approved by the firm's executives and the supervisory board. This approval indicates a potential necessity to seek approval for the timelines and tasks from superiors of the process promotor.

As it becomes evident in the example of LogCo above, process promotors also determine the **participants** of the preparation process during the planning phase. For most process promotors, the participants are already known from previous years or from continuous monitoring of organizational changes:

> *"One should not overestimate this. This company is so small, you are so close to all topics that you know both where to find the data and in how far it is available. Thus, you can collect it relatively quickly." (PrintCo HEIR)*

> *"[PRM] knows all participants and directly contacts them: 'Please provide me with this or that information.'" (AgCo HER)*

At HealthCo and ChemCo, responsibilities are planned and documented in scheduling tools. In this context, ChemCo's MQR is in close contact with the administrator of the scheduling tool regarding changes in responsibilities:

> *"There is a [ChemCo scheduling tool] administrator who manages the tool and contacts the persons and says: 'Have a look at it, I have copied it from last year. I know we had this and that change, I might need new responsible persons. Or is something missing*

there?' And then before the closing starts, we update the schedule. It is activated ahead of the closing process." (ChemCo HER)

"In the past, each year we have asked the departments: 'Who is the person of contact, who organizes the coordination for the department?' We have seized to do so, because it is always the same persons. And I mean, if something changes, we can discuss this on a bilateral basis." (ChemCo MQR)

Coordinate tasks of participants

Another contribution of the process promotor is to **coordinate the tasks of the process participants**. This coordination can be differentiated according to the person responsible for coordinating and to the communication of these tasks. With regard to the responsibility for coordination, the process promotor can coordinate the tasks by acting as a "single point of contact" (*ChemCo HER*). In such cases, all communication between process participants is **channeled** through one person. This approach is used by the majority of the case firms (ChemCo, LogCo, FashCo, TechCo, AgCo) as it appears to provide clear responsibilities and communication channels:

"I mean the role which [MQR] is taking on is so prominent that they [functional departments] cannot keep their information from her. They have to be open with her. And they do that." (ChemCo HER)

Alternatively, process promotors can also act as a team of coordinators (HealthCo) or a **constellation** of process promotors and other promotors (PrintCo). In HealthCo's case, the coordination tasks are divided up within the sustainability department to tackle the extent of the preparation process. As for PrintCo, both the HEIR and the CFO coordinate the preparation of the report. This is justified by the CFO's experience as previous coordinator of the nfKPI section of the report and his contacts to other participants of the process.

As a part of coordinating process-related tasks, process promotors **communicate** with the respective participants to ensure that the process is carried out correctly and in time:

"I would say that we have control over the process, and by 'we' I mean our core team of accounting, communications and us, but in the end this does not work without the gear train. We are those who keep the whole thing together and who have to kick each other and especially our editorial members, to ensure that all deadlines are met, that information is provided, that this information is sound, that text are re-worded and that the translation is reviewed." (HealthCo MSD)

Process promotors can choose to communicate these tasks to other participants either by providing very specific or rather general and open tasks. These communication approaches could be related to the extent of formalization of the preparation process:

"I believe we already do this here. This clear communication of the timetable and individual tasks. Responsibilities are clearly assigned: 'You have to do this and this up until then.' A good communication." (HealthCo HMQR)

"For me personally, regarding the softer, verbal information, I prefer this open or less structured process. My contact persons are very diverse and I don't want to press them

into a structure. From my experience, if I let them do it and just follow up at certain points, it is much easier and more constructive for everyone." (TechCo IRM)

As identified in the planning phases of the case firms (section 6.2.1.2.2), process promotors use several **communication media** (e.g., briefings, meetings or emails) to communicate the tasks to the participants. These media can range between informal personal meetings to formal and impersonal means such as large briefings. As apparent in the cases, most process promotors appear to prefer informal and personal communication, whereas meetings seem to be used as kick-off procedures in large case firms.

Moreover, process promotors also **monitor** the progress of the preparation process and contact participants with reminders if necessary. Through carrying out this task, process promotors aim to ensure that the responsible persons carry out their particular tasks in time. While at HealthCo and ChemCo this monitoring is mostly carried out by the scheduling tools, coordinators in smaller firms carry out these tasks themselves:

"[CFOA] is the one who has to collect everything for the management report. If deadlines are not met, he first calls the particular person and tries to remind them. And then we either get the information, we receive it a little later or at some point it has to escalate and I get involved. But sooner or later we have all information." (LogCo HA)

Exchange information

In addition to coordinating the tasks of participants, process promotors also **exchange information between the process participants.** The task of exchanging information with participants is connected to the tasks of collecting nfKPIs, including these into a draft of the management report and forwarding information from one participant to the other.

As process promotors are responsible for organizing the collection of nfKPIs, their tasks largely reflect those included in the drafting phase described in section 6.2.1.2.3. In particular, process promotors **contact** information providers to communicate demands from the executive board or external stakeholders:

"Yes, there are also impulses from the outside. Be it that you see what others are doing, what is trending. New regulation. You have to observe what comes from the outside. And then we have to deliver this to the departments, because they of course don't necessarily know what is 'en vogue' in terms of management reporting." (ChemCo MSD)

"With regard to the information providers, it is important to me that I can rely on a team which does not do this for the first time, who know the requirements. Then it is a quite lean process, because they know what they need to deliver so that I can write." (PrintCo CFO)

"I communicate only through [IRM]. She forwards the information to me. I receive it and if there are issues up for discussion, then I hand it back to her." (TechCo CFO)

Through forwarding demands and requirements to the information providers, the process promotor can **access the various sources of information** such as databases, internal documentation or expert knowledge.

Subsequently, process promotors distribute the collected information by assembling the report draft. In all case firms, process promotors are responsible for assembling the draft of the nonfinancial KPI sections for the management report. For some process promotors, the task of collecting nfKPIs is connected to **writing nfKPI sections**. In such cases, this separation of tasks is justified by the promotor's knowledge regarding the requirements from regulators or report users (PrintCo), a lack of coordinators in the departments (LogCo) or the efficiency and experience of the coordinator in writing (AgCo). Moreover, FashCo's process promotor writes some nfKPI sections because some departments provide her with verbal information rather than texts. Thus, it becomes evident that particularly process promotors from small and private firms engage in the writing of these sections. These contributions are closely linked to the promotor's organizational know-how:

> *"If we told our head of production that he should write something on energy consumption, he would provide me with a four page report which I could not use anyway. I believe, he does not have a good feeling for what belongs into a management report. He is not familiar with GAS 20. I think it makes sense that you collect the information and that you filter what you need. And this is then verbalized for the report." (PrintCo HEIR)*

> *"Then we communicate with the departments for the environmental KPIs. I would call the head of transport, our facility management department or the building maintenance. At some point I have some information and then we try to process this accordingly." (LogCo HA)*

> *"The reporting on nfKPIs is an easy task for me. Thus it is done relatively quickly and we can finish it relatively timely." (AgCo PRM)*

> *"Most of the time, I leave this to the departments. It's totally different. Some provide me with verbal information, because we just talk on the phone. Sometimes some people also like to provide me with something in writing. Yes, there are no requirements." (FashCo MEIR)*

In the course of **assembling** the sections, the process promotors also conduct preliminary reviews. During these reviews, the process promotors are often in contact with the functional department to ask for clarification and to seek approval for changes to texts.

In addition to exchanging information with functional departments, the process promotors also exchange information with other participants of the preparation process. After the draft is prepared, process promotors **forward** it to the reviewers. Depending on the review committee existing in the firm, the draft is provided to a pre-disclosure committee, the CFO or a disclosure committee. Depending on the timing of the review and the completion status of the report, reviewers may receive single nfKPI paragraphs, the nfKPI section of the report or the entire management report. Similarly, process promotors also provide **auditors** with documentation and report drafts. With regard to documentation, process promotors provide auditors with access to databases containing proof documents on disclosures (e.g., HealthCo) or sending relevant documentation to the auditors on demand, the latter being used by every case firms. While most auditors receive the nfKPI disclosures in the form of a final draft during the review phase, some firms such as HealthCo provide their auditor with the disclosures earlier to allow for a thorough audit of the preliminary disclosures. However, this forwarding of information is commonly not limited to the mere exchange of information. As these actors often provide the process promotors with feedback and messages for the functional departments, these exchanges of information also point towards the promotor's contributions of mediating between process participants.

Mediating between participants

Process promotors act as mediators between the other participants involved. The process promotor **mediates** between departments and reviewers by resolving uncertainties and conflicts between participants. As process promotors are responsible for mediating feedback during the preparation process, they forward this feedback and explain it to the relevant participants:

> *"We are involved the whole time. We pass everything back to the initial writer. If the executive board says 'This is stupid, we want this changed.', then we forward this feedback. And then the writer might say: 'It is not that stupid, I had a reason for this.' And then, we have to coordinate this feedback back to the executive board: 'No, it is correct this way.' And hence, we are involved in the entire process." (HealthCo HMQR)*

> *"And there can always be some feedback [from the disclosure committees]. And if there are comments on particular topics, then I approach the departments again and say: 'If it is valid, can we adjust something in this text or is it reasonable? The colleagues don't quite understand it.' Then we can talk about it before it is handed to [CFO]. Similarly, when [CFO] has comments, we also go back again quickly, in the sense of: 'Can we do this again?' Insofar, I ask the colleagues that I always have a contact person during this short time-frame." (ChemCo MQR)*

These quotes indicate that in some occasions, the process promotor also has to communicate negative feedback when nfKPIs were scrutinized or removed:

> *"And I also believe that we are always the messengers. If the disclosure committees decide: 'This should be totally different. We don't like this.' Then we go back to the person, who has written the document and say: 'Please re-write this.' That is not always easy. Or even worse – which happens often – when we remove some parts. Someone has put in a lot of effort and we cut it out. As a consequence, the people who have written the text are a bit frustrated of course." (HealthCo HMQR)*

Therefore, process promotors need to carefully communicate the feedback between the participating parties. This communication is supported by the promotor's power of communicative competency.

In addition, promotors pass on the demands and requirements from particular participants and try to achieve an agreement between opposing parties:

> *"In such cases, conflicts can arise. The investor relations representative says that it should be reported as so and so and the person from the segment says: 'I don't want that!' Basically, depending on which worlds clash, we do have conflicts and we have to try to*

mediate. And that is apparent for the financial and for the nonfinancial parts." (HealthCo HMQR)

"Generally for the nonfinancial KPIs, the individual departments are a driving force. There are some that say that they would like to report a lot. They make suggestions and then we discuss with them, if the continuity is secured or not. And there are others, who are more restrained and who would like to say as little as possible, and we have to motivate them to say a bit more. In the end, it is the individual department which agrees that they want something and are able to do it. And we are the integrative bracket." (ChemCo HER)

In this regard, process promotors can also act as a "sparring partner" when discussing particular views and opinions with process participants. Similarly, promotors also draw from their particular power of communication competency:

"You are, I would say, a kind of sparring partner, because you receive comments which are partly justified, partly not or sometimes just up for discussion. To clarify why some things are written down the way they are, you sometimes have to engage in a discussion on whether you want to do it this way or another." (HealthCo MQR)

Powers of the process promotor

The above mentioned contributions of the promotors are closely linked to their **powers**: organizational know-how and communication competency. As part of their powers, process promotors draw from their **organizational know-how** to fulfil their coordinating tasks (*Walter* (1998), pp. 117-118). This know-how can be separated into an overview over the business operations of the firm and into knowledge regarding the organizational structures and persons of contact in the firm.

Process promotors use their knowledge regarding the **business operations** to for example determine material information or to collect information. This knowledge can span from a general overview of the firm (PrintCo) over an involvement in relevant projects (TechCo) to an observation of the departments reporting nfKPIs (AgCo):

"We know our business processes very well. Looking at my example from earlier, that it does not make much sense to report on the fleet emissions of our cars, nobody cares about that. Nor is it interesting to anyone within the company. And therefore we do not report it. It is basically not material. Those matters that are material for this firm, we know about them and those are reported." (PrintCo HEIR)

"Through my tasks I see relatively much of what happens in the group. I am aware of the sentiments or projects in which I am involved. There you might say: 'Oh, this might be important, this should be included.'" (TechCo IRM)

"That's experience. We observe the departments over the entire year and we are always in dialogue with them." (AgCo PRM)

In this context, the example of FashCo shows that the process promotor's knowledge of business activities can be closely related to their knowledge regarding the **organizational structures and relationships** (*Walter* (1998), pp. 117-118):

"There is a lot of information available. Especially regarding the market development and our course of business of the last year. We from management accounting are very well informed. We are very well connected to other departments. You can hardly argue that information is available at one point in time. But it's rather that you have your eyes and ears open over the entire year because of the normal course of business." (FashCo MEIR)

The process promotor uses this power of organizational know-how to fulfil tasks such as determining participants or identifying material nfKPIs. Overall, the cases show that experience and thorough documentation regarding the coordination of the preparation process **support** the organizational know-how of the process promotors. Moreover, these factors can also simplify the task of writing and reviewing nfKPI sections.

Process promotors also draw from their **communication competency** to fulfil their tasks of coordinating the preparation process (*Walter* (1998), p. 117). As discussed above, the majority of the tasks of the process promotor require communication. Therefore, process promotors use their communication skills to connect themselves with other participants and to exchange information between them (*Walter* (1998), pp. 122-123). This power is closely related to the promotors' contribution of mediating between other participants. In some cases, process promotors need to be diplomatic and sensitive about addressing particular issues:

"You have to phrase it relatively carefully. And most of all, you should not give the person who has written the initial document and who has put in a lot of effort the feeling, that he has not done a good job. Instead, you have to say that there are different opinions and there is this Mr. 'So and So' from investor relations and he has more information. I believe it is important to not frustrate the initial writer, because next time he would say: 'This is all going to be cut out anyway.' We have heard that before. And that applies to all parts of the report. You have to make sure that you keep everyone motivated and say: 'Come on, you are making an important contribution, even if we have re-written this part.'" (HealthCo HMQR)

Process promotors in the case firms

Building on the discussions above, participants with promotor roles within the case firms are identified in the following. Furthermore, potential role distributions are compared, contrasted and discussed according to the literature (*Folkerts/Hauschildt* (2002), p. 9). Table 6-9 summarizes the results.[121]

The coordinators of **HealthCo's** preparation process take on promotor roles. The HMQR and MQR serve as process promotors for the financial sections of the report and for the overall coordination of the management report preparation. While these participants are well experienced in coordination and communication tasks, they cooperate with the sustainability team around MSD, who act as process promotors for nonfinancial reporting. In this context, the MSD and her team carry out the coordination and communication tasks related to the nfKPI sections. The cooperation between both coordinators points towards a

121 See Appendix B for the list of interview partners, abbreviations and departments.

role plurality of the promotor role. Moreover, the persons of contact in the functional departments (such as the DBM and MSP) take on several process promotor tasks within the department to coordinate the collection of relevant nfKPIs. As the majority of tasks of these participants are related to their expertise and know-how regarding nfKPIs, these participants combine multiple promotor roles.[122]

Firms	Role exclusivity	Role combination	Role plurality
HealthCo	-	DBM, MSP (know-how)	HMQR, MQR, MSD
ChemCo	MQR	-	-
PrintCo	(previously: CFO)	CFO (power)	CFO, HEIR
LogCo	-	HRS (know-how)	CFOA, HA
FashCo	MEIR	-	-
TechCo	IRM	HDBM, DBM, HRM (know-how)	-
AgCo	PRM	-	-

Table 6-9: Process promotor role distribution in the case firms

At **ChemCo**, the process promotor role is exclusively assigned to the MQR (role exclusivity). As a single point of contact, the MQR coordinates process tasks and channels the communication between the different participants. Within the functional departments, participants such as MSD, HSC and SC do not take on process promotor tasks as they are solely involved with measuring the data and writing their respective nfKPI sections.

In **PrintCo's** case, the process promotor role is shared by the CFO and HEIR (role plurality). While the CFO has coordinated the preparation of the entire management report himself in previous years (role exclusivity), the HEIR is now responsible for the preparation of PrintCo's nonfinancial statement. Moreover, as the CFO also takes on his tasks as executive of the firm, he shows a role combination with the power promotor role.[123]

At **LogCo**, the tasks of coordinating and communicating nfKPI sections are shared by the CFOA and HA (role plurality). While the CFOA takes on the majority of tasks, the HA supports him and is responsible for the preparation process. In addition, the HRS coordinates the preparation of the HR-related nfKPIs within her department. As she takes on multiple roles in the preparation process (know-how promotor), a role combination exists in her case.

At **FashCo**, the preparation process for nfKPIs is coordinated by the MEIR, who takes on the process promotor role by herself (role exclusivity). No other participant of FashCo's preparation process shares similar contributions or powers.

The IRM coordinates the preparation of **TechCo's** management report – including the nfKPIs – and communicates with all participants of the preparation process. As the IRM takes on these tasks by herself, she assumes process promotor role exclusively. Within the

[122] For a discussion of the know-how promotor role see section 6.2.2.3.

[123] For a discussion of the power promotor role see section 6.2.2.2.

functional departments, contact persons such as HDBM, DBM and HRM take on parts of the promotor role such as determining tasks and responsibilities or exchanging information to coordinate the collection of nfKPIs within their departments. As these participants fulfil this role in conjunction with other tasks requiring functional expertise, a role combination between process promotor and know-how promotor roles can be identified.

The PRM of **AgCo** takes on all coordination and communication tasks of the preparation process for nfKPIs. As the HER is mostly involved in coordinating the financial parts of the management report, the process promotor role is exclusively taken on by the PRM. Other participants do not show traits of process promotors.

Overall, the **distribution of process promotor roles** is mixed across the case firms. The coordinators of the preparation process show either role exclusivity or role plurality. Role exclusivity appears to be more common in smaller and private firms. However, the case of ChemCo acts as a counterexample. In this case, the long-term experience and organizational knowledge of the MQR seems to be beneficial from streamlining the coordination of the process. Role plurality occurs within the same department (LogCo), across departments that are responsible for reporting (HealthCo) or across hierarchical levels (PrintCo). While the role plurality in LogCo's case is justified by the lower experience and responsibility of the CFOA, the cooperation of different departments in HealthCo's case is particularly driven by the integrated reporting approach of the firm. In the case of PrintCo, the CFO combines the roles of power and process promotor. This combination is justified by the firm's small size and the lean preparation process. In all three cases, the collaboration of different persons appears to be beneficial due to their specific circumstances.

In addition to process coordinators, several contact persons in the functional departments show **role combinations** with process promotor roles. This combination between process promotor and know-how promotor roles tends to occur within functional departments where nfKPIs are not centrally available. In contrast to this, ChemCo's HSC and SC do not act as process promotors because of the standardized measurement of the QEHS nfKPIs.

6.2.2.2 Power promotor

Subsequently to discussing the role of the process promotor, this section aims at identifying **power promotors** in the case firms. Similar to the previous section, this section identifies contributions and powers of these participants in the preparation process of nfKPIs for the management report.

Comparable to prior literature on power promotors in the innovation process (*Witte* (1973), p. 12; *Witte* (1977), p. 54; *Walter* (1998), p. 99), specific participants of the preparation process of nfKPIs for management reports provide similar **contributions and powers** in the process (Table 6-10). While the majority of tasks are congruent, power promotors in preparation processes of nfKPIs are responsible for initializing the process. In innovation processes, such contributions are typically carried out by know-how promotors. In this context, promotors initiate the process by developing initial ideas for innovations (*Chakrabarti/Hauschildt* (1989), p. 166). In addition to initializing the preparation process, power promotors also contribute to the process by making decisions and dealing with opponents and proponents of nfKPI disclosures. To do so, power promotors use both their hierarchical position and access to material resources. These contributions and powers are described and analyzed in the following.

Contributions	Powers
Initialize the preparation process	High ranking hierarchical position
Decision-making	Access to material resources
• Determining material nfKPIs and nfKPI goals • Review of the management report • Providing feedback • Clearance of the management report	
Dealing with opponents and proponents	

Table 6-10: Contributions and powers of the power promotor

Initialize the preparation process

In the beginning of the preparation process, the power promotor – being responsible for the preparation of the management report – **initiates** the preparation process of the management report, including nfKPIs. In almost all case studies, the coordinators of the report initiate the preparation process. At first glance, one could assume that coordinators take on this contribution of power promotors. However, as executive boards remain responsible for the preparation, the task of initializing the preparation appears to be **delegated** to the coordinators (*Tarca et al.* (2011), p. 48). In all cases, this division of labor is part of the routine of the preparation process. Therefore, executives typically do not explicitly approach the responsible coordinators to initialize the process:

> *"It's interesting to see it from their [CEO and CFO] point of view. How they view the process. As functions which step in later in the process, who delegate or who evaluate the topics from a specialist point of view." (HealthCo MQR)*

> *"All of our executives are responsible, but [HA] is responsible for the core coordinating tasks. Most of the coordination is done by [HER] and myself." (LogCo CFOA)*

Solely in two cases, the CFO explicitly initiates the preparation process. When he was preparing the report by himself in previous years, the CFO of PrintCo would approach the departments to start the process. Moreover, the CFO of FashCo **actively initiates** the preparation process by approaching the MEIR:

> *"[The planning phase begins] when we are almost done with the financial statements. The responsibilities are sorted out relatively clearly. The CFO knows that he can approach me again. It's on my radar, in terms of my yearly planning, that I will start after the financial statements are finalized." (FashCo MEIR)*

Another part of the initialization of the preparation process is to introduce the reporting on nfKPIs to ensure truthful management reporting compliant with regulatory requirements.

As shown in previous research (*Adams* (2002), p. 244; *Frost et al.* (2012), pp. 218-223), the executive board could have an important influence in introducing this type of reporting. While all case firms have already introduced nfKPI reporting, the firms stress that top-management support for these issues could be crucial to initialize the reporting on nfKPIs. This contribution is supported by the executive board's hierarchical position and their access to material resources. Nonetheless, the boards typically delegate the operative contributions of the introduction to coordinators of the preparation process:

> *"I would find it very important if we had a real commitment of the top-management with regard to nonfinancial KPIs. The executive board has to back this up. It has to carry it into the entire organization. Only then we have a chance to structure the processes accordingly. That's exactly the point. Then it will work well and efficiently." (ChemCo MSD)*

Hence, the cases show that the contribution of initializing the process lies in the set of tasks of power promotors, who typically delegate this contribution to the process promotors. Solely executives who are more actively involved in the preparation process seem to actively initiate the preparation process.

Decision-making

A central contribution of power promotors is the **decision-making** with regard to nfKPI disclosures. This decision-making can be separated into several different steps: determining material nfKPIs and nfKPI goals, reviewing the report, providing feedback for the disclosures and providing clearance for publication. These steps are discussed in detail in the following.

Determining material nfKPIs and nfKPI goals

Power promotors are also responsible for identifying material nfKPIs, determining goals for nfKPIs and prioritizing relevant indicators. As part of the materiality analysis, the power promotor is responsible for **identifying material nfKPIs**. Similar to the initialization of the preparation process, power promotors in most firms **delegate** the task of identifying nfKPIs to the coordinators of the process (*Tarca et al.* (2011), pp. 47-48). The latter subsequently suggest these nfKPIs to the power promotor:

> *"We argue about what is actually used for the management, determine the expectations of the stakeholders and then we think about what is possible in which timeframe. And from this, we develop a suggestion. We compare this to the requirements and say that we have to do more here, or that we might have to limit this a little somewhere else. And from this, something evolves which is then discussed." (ChemCo HER)*

> *"That was our suggestion. We stated our vision of the section and that this reflects the regulation. Yes, we have developed this in the finance department and have discussed it with the responsible member of the executive board." (TechCo IRM)*

> *"We – particularly the communications and finance department in close cooperation – are involved in the materiality decisions. Then, of course, the executive board provides feedback." (AgCo PRM)*

In the cases of PrintCo and FashCo, the CFO is **directly involved** in the identification of nfKPIs. Moreover, before PrintCo had to prepare a nonfinancial statement, the CFO identified nfKPIs himself:

> *"Regarding the selection of the topics, I mean, we [CFO and HEIR] think about it together, about what should be reported and what is material." (PrintCo HEIR)*

> *"I get back to our CFO, we communicate very closely, and I briefly discuss the nonfinancial KPIs with him: 'Roughly the same basis as last year? Is there already something that should be included or left out? Or do we start with this?' Yes, and this is how we start the process." (FashCo MEIR)*

In contrast to other case firms, HealthCo and ChemCo set goals related to their nfKPIs. It could be assumed that **setting goals for nfKPIs** could be contribution of power promotors carried out by a firm's top-management. However, participants involved in determining such goals differ strongly across these firms. At HealthCo – where nonfinancial goals are not used for the management of the group – these goals are determined by the functional departments, reviewed by the sustainability department and discussed with the responsible executive:

> *"Our [CSR] department prepares the nonfinancial goals and agrees on them with the executive board. Of course we want to have their blessing for all of these. And in the context of the introduction of our integrated report, we have talked to our colleagues in accounting and showed them the nonfinancial goals. At that point, they had to swallow hard, because we have significantly more nonfinancial goals than financial goals. However, the financial goals outweigh the nonfinancial ones." (HealthCo MSD)*

> *"When evaluating our strategically relevant suppliers, we – that is my supervisor and me – are closely working together with [the CSR department] to sketch out new goals, to define them." (HealthCo MSP)*

In the case of ChemCo, the executive board is more strongly involved in determining the nonfinancial goals. This stronger involvement can be explained by the usage of nfKPIs for the management of the group. As a consequence, ChemCo also includes these indicators in their **management forecast**:

> *"When you have determined the most important nonfinancial KPIs, then you also have to say: 'I am forecasting this and that development. And I am also evaluated based on how well I have estimated this in the past.' This is something the CFO clearly has a look at and possibly not only [CFO], but the entire executive board." (ChemCo HER)*

In addition to being able to delegate tasks, power promotors are **supported** by their experience and overview over the company's business when determining material nfKPIs and goals related to nfKPIs is facilitated for:

> *"This results from the day-to-day business and executive board meetings. In my role I see a lot." (LogCo CFO)*

> *"This is basically connected to how long you have been working in the company and I have been working here for more than ten years. You are continuously involved in this in the course of the reporting period, we – as the executive board – deal with these issues*

as well. Thus, I would notice if something is missing, if I find something relevant although the functional department has not considered this material or if they said: 'Come on, I want this off my table quickly.' In this context, these issues rise up again. But it's basically connected to the fact that we also deal with these issues on the executive level." (FashCo CFO)

Subsequently to identifying relevant nfKPIs, the power promotor typically **selects** material nfKPIs that are then collected for the draft of the report. As seen in the case of FashCo, power promotors are supported in their selection of nfKPIs through an early communication of their demands regarding nfKPIs. While the entire executive board is responsible for the selection of nfKPIs, this task is often carried out by the CFO, as in the case of PrintCo:

"I can make my life easy, because I write the report. [Laughter] It's absolutely my decision, which is for sure agreed upon with the executive board. But so far it was the case that I have gained an overview over the nonfinancial KPIs and then I have decided on what we would report on." (PrintCo CFO)

"In the end, the selection of nonfinancial KPIs and the decision on that we really want to say there, lies in the hand of the executive board. They would ultimately say yes or no. [...] An early communication is definitely important. You should not collect some wild measures and put in additional effort. On the contrary, you should communicate with the executive board very early: 'Is this a topic you want to have included? Should we have a look at what we have available in this regard, or rather not?'" (FashCo MEIR)

Overall, the responsibility of executive boards for selecting material nfKPIs is grounded in their hierarchical position. While delegating tasks does not evoke this power, coordinators of the preparation process can gain considerable power in selecting and suggesting nfKPIs.

Reviewing the report

After receiving the draft of the report, the power promotors contribute to the preparation process by **reviewing the nfKPIs** in the management report. An important task of the power promotor is to check the **compliance of the report with the regulation**. Most cases show that the executive boards delegate this task to the coordinators, preliminary reviewers and the statutory auditors of the nfKPIs. Nonetheless, particularly CFOs of the case companies consider the regulatory compliance when reviewing the report:

"As the executive board, we stand back-to-back because we all know that particular regulations need to be complied with. We do that of course. For this, we have assigned responsibilities. It is one of my responsibilities to carry such topics into the executive board and to say: 'Listen up, people. Here and there we have to do something, because a new regulation has come up. We have to comply with this and we have to adapt ourselves to it.'" (PrintCo CFO)

"Exactly, the true and fair view of the IFRS has to be carried over to the management report. Okay, we also have our statutory auditor who has a look at it. But he is of course a bit further away from the topic." (TechCo CFO)

In addition to regulatory compliance, power promotors also review the **consistency** of individual nfKPIs and their consistency with regard to the other sections of the management report. This contribution is in line with the requirement to ensure consistent reporting (*Barth et al.* (2014), pp. 51-52):

> *"The indicators are the main focus of what I look at, because they are interlinked with various areas. […] I have to make sure from an investor relations perspective, that what is disclosed follows a common thread from the cover to the end of the report." (HealthCo IRM)*

> *"Of course, I read the sections multiple times and I read the management report from front to back. […] My task is to check that the individual aspects – and not only the nonfinancial KPIs but all aspects – fit together homogeneously. That there are no contradictions, because there are of course very different preparers involved in the process. So the different parts of the management report should be interlinked." (TechCo CFO)*

Furthermore, process promotors also review **messages** included in the nfKPIs. As seen in the case of LogCo and TechCo, the promotors commonly check that these messages are not too detailed, that they are balanced as compared to other disclosures and that they are clear enough to not be misunderstood:

> *"If someone from HR would write about an individual project in an individual country, then we would take this out and write something like: 'We have different programs in different countries.' And then that's fine. Otherwise we would create the impression that there are no other programs anywhere else, if that one is described in detail. The entire report has to be consistent. It should yield a balanced picture of the firm." (LogCo HA)*

> *"I always try to have a common thread in the management report and to either send messages or to prevent particular messages. […] So that we don't give away too much information. And to not highlight things which could create a wrong impression for readers of the report. We should not make a mountain out of a molehill and vice versa. We really have to be careful about this. That we send the right messages in the right manner with the right intention." (TechCo CFO)*

Finally, power promotors also check that the management report is written in "**one voice**". The initial task of aligning the wording is often delegated to coordinators of the report, while the power promotors review the coherency of the wording:

> *"This is one of our tasks, to write the report in such a way that the reader gets the impression as if one person had written the report and not different people. One person writes this way, another one writes another way. Basically we are kind of an island here in the accounting department, which should be proficient in German. [Laughter]" (HealthCo HMQR)*

> *"Then I take the information I receive and have a look at whether I can directly use it for the management report. Or maybe I have to adjust the wording so that the report appears to be cast in one piece. […] We do have at least some stylistic aspirations." (FashCo MEIR)*

Similar to other contributions of power promotors, these particular review tasks appear to be taken on by executives as well as coordinators of the report. It becomes evident, that both actors try to ensure that management reports do not contain mistakes and provide the intended messages.

Providing feedback

Power promotors also contribute to the decision-making regarding nfKPIs by providing feedback to other participants of the process. In all case firms, several **preliminary feedback loops** are in place before the executive board provides its feedback. As part of this feedback, reviewers inform initial writers about other potential perspectives on the disclosures. HealthCo for example includes the investor relations department in this preliminary review to receive feedback on the potential reception of the nfKPI disclosures by the capital market:

> *"I would also say that details are dealt with in working groups beforehand. However, this does not mean that the executive level does not address changes or demands later on. That's part of the process. In the end, as part of its large extent, you have to somehow spread out and separate the process. And I think it is also important that the different departments, who address various stakeholders or contacts, are somehow involved in the process and provide feedback from their perspective." (HealthCo MQR)*

> *"We provide feedback – we always call this review – and I review the nonfinancial KPIs from my point of view and I mirror the feedback of the capital market. What would fit better or where could we be more ambitious than what we set as a goal. However, the authority for decision-making lies in the hand of the sustainability department. And we also have an executive responsible for sustainability. Thus, I have a pure review-feedback-function." (HealthCo IRM)*

These preliminary feedback loops show that the executive board typically delegates some of its feedback tasks to other participants of the process. Feedback is then usually coordinated and distributed by the process promotors, as described in the previous section. In many case firms, the CFO provides feedback for the management report draft before it is handed to the executive board. Such preliminary feedback loops appear to improve the management report draft to such an extent, that in most case firms the **executive board review** yields little or no feedback regarding nfKPIs. Nonetheless, executives commonly comment on the wording, content or message of the disclosures:

> *"And after we have coordinated the feedback from the CFO, the near final draft is passed onto the entire executive board. And there, you hope, that no material changes are demanded. But we had the case when we had some changes in the management report that some executives had comments about this. And we hope, that when we have such changes again, that this is not the case. In the normal process this does not happen. At the most, they would say: 'I don't like that phrase, or can't we remove that sub-clause?' Or something like that. Much more does not happen, typically. Because everything is already finely tuned." (ChemCo HER)*

> *"Usually they address product development, because that is their topic, product development and markets. That's the CEO and the technology officer. Typically, they would say something about that, if some technical content is written incorrectly. [...] And*

regarding the rest, they sometimes say: 'Well, if you think that this should go into the report, then it has to go in, right?'" (PrintCo HEIR)

"And then this is handed to my colleagues from the executive board, who also read that thing. Then we rarely get comments from [COO], who is more involved in the operative details. From [CEO and CMO] there might be some minor comments. Typically we would discuss one particular sentence. And that's the process." (LogCo CFO)

Clearance of the report

As one of the final decision-making tasks in the preparation process, the power promotor acts as a gatekeeper by providing **clearance** for the final management report. In this context, the executive board fulfils a corrective function:

"The management report is approved by the overall executive board. This means that I have a kind of regulative function. In the end, my colleagues say that they do not like the wording, would like some changes or additions which came into their heads. That does happen, but this is a team and on this level we deal with this topic." (PrintCo CFO)

"Basically, I am the first stage of quality control. Then the report has to be at 99%. I mean, when [MEIR] and I really don't have anything more to add, when I would say that I would publish it like this. [Laughter] And then [CEO] has a look at it. And he is basically the second stage of quality control. He has a few remarks, improvements or some additions and that's it. And after this, we sign it, the complete management report." (FashCo CFO)

After the approval, the report is handed to the supervisory board, if applicable. While the supervisory board itself does not act as a promotor in the preparation process, it takes on a gatekeeper role in the context of its corporate governance function. Hence, power promotors have to deal with this board by potentially defending disclosures provided in the management report. Such tasks mark another contribution of power promotors, which is addressed in the following.

Dealing with opponents and proponents

In the course of determining and collecting material nfKPIs, power promotors deal with persons who **support or impede the disclosure of nfKPIs**. This contribution differs slightly from the power promotor tasks suggested in the innovation process literature (*Walter* (1998), pp. 102-103). While power promotors in innovation processes sanction opponents and support proponents (*Witte* (1977), p. 54), power promotors in preparation processes aim to balance contributions of opponents and proponents. This balance could be achieved by limiting contributions from participants who willingly provide more nfKPIs than necessary or by demanding more contributions from participants who refuse or oppose such disclosures. In most case firms, power promotors do not need to actively deal with opponents or proponents as such behaviors either do not occur or they fall within the – typically implicit – boundaries of acceptable disclosures:

"I would say that those people involved in determining our reporting principles provide the scope of what is possible and what isn't. This question sounds a bit political, but I believe that it's not the case that someone is holding back information." (HealthCo MQR)

"There are some that say that they would like to report a lot. They make suggestions and then we discuss with them, if the continuity is secured or not. And there are others, who are more restrained and who would like to say as little as possible, and we have to motivate them to say a bit more." (ChemCo HER)

While the CFO of LogCo recognizes some tendencies of proponents using nfKPI disclosures as marketing for their department, he tolerates these tendencies. The CFO justifies his stance by the rather low importance of nfKPIs in the management report:

"And there is of course the goal of the departments to present their department in a positive light. But also of course, which is particularly welcomed by my colleagues from the executive board, to see this as an advertising block. This is kind of the image I see, where not much is quantified. [...] I would not see the importance of this as so immense. I don't believe that after we have published the report that these KPIs are important for any analyses or evaluations of our company. At least not now. On the contrary, I believe most of the people who access the report in the German Electronic Federal Gazette will quickly scroll over this part – if they read it at all – to read the financial topics." (LogCo CFO)

Moreover, in some cases power promotors **themselves** promote disclosures on nfKPIs. In HealthCo's case, this was connected to enhancing disclosures on R&D nfKPIs. Similar to the cases above, such suggestions are discussed within the board. Nonetheless, suggestions by other executives may carry more weight as compared to those of individual functional departments:

"It was more about how the topic was marketed. We have an executive responsible for R&D. And he wanted this topic to be more 'sexy', to show how much we do and how innovative we are, you know?" (HealthCo HMQR)

In this context of dealing with opponents and proponents of nfKPIs, the power promotor also communicates with statutory auditors and the supervisory board:

"And in the end, the supervisory board has a look at the management report with an auditing eye. Although the board members are sometimes so far away from the business operations, that they accept this and find it interesting, but they don't get involved in the sense of: 'This should be phrased as such and such.'" (PrintCo CFO)

"Once the draft is finished, it is sent to our statutory auditors. They give us their input on the report and sometimes on changes in the legal requirements. But if they take on an extreme position, then we often do not agree. This can lead to controversial discussions and arguments." (LogCo CFO)

As both actors serve as internal and external **governance mechanisms**, power promotors defend the nfKPI disclosures provided in the management report, if necessary. However, both the quotes and case studies indicate that the intensity of these engagements may differ.

Overall, power promotors in preparation processes of the case firms appear to be mindful about potential proponents and opponents. Nonetheless, it seems that both proponents and opponents act in a tolerable manner. For this reason, it appears that power promotors may not need to get deeply involved. These circumstances could be caused by a low interest in nfKPIs of the proponents and opponents or by a credible hierarchical potential of the power promotors to support the nfKPI disclosures. The latter indicates a power of the power promotor, which is discussed in the following.

Powers of the power promotor

Similar to the literature on power promotors in innovation processes, power promotors in preparation processes of nfKPIs draw their **powers** from their hierarchical position and access to material resources to support the preparation of management reports (*Walter* (1998), pp. 101-102).

With regard to their **hierarchical position**, power promotors typically hold top-management positions (*Witte* (1977), p. 54). Such positions equip power promotors with a credible hierarchical potential, despite not being constantly involved in the preparation process (*Witte* (1973), p. 17). Most firms concentrate the majority of these powers in the CFO, as he or she typically holds the responsibility for preparing the management report. However, particularly in larger firms with integrated reports or separate sustainability reports these powers are distributed across various executives:

> *"[After the pre-disclosure committee review] this is passed up to the executive board. We have an executive who is responsible for sustainability. He is not exclusively responsible for sustainability, but our [CPO] has a look at the report and discusses this." (HealthCo HMQR)*

> *"We have to contact the departments again and say: 'The auditors won't let this pass. Or we think they won't. Or this doesn't fit with our other disclosures.' We can just beg with a little bit of pressure, because in the end we have to meet our deadlines, to send the report to the entire executive board. But we can't say: 'Do it this way, we have decided that.' In the financial sections we can do that, as long as we know that our CFO supports this too." (ChemCo HER)*

> *"I am strongly involved in the group management report, because it is also a medium which we use to articulate the messages of the executive board. This is of course agreed upon with the CEO." (TechCo CFO)*

Next to the hierarchical position, power promotors also have **access to material resources** which support the process or could be used to sanction opponents (*Hauschildt/Chakrabarti* (1988), p. 384). In the case of the preparation process of nfKPIs, material resources can occur in the form of **access to important stakeholders**:

> *"Take for example investor meetings with sustainability investors. I never do these alone, but there are always people from [sustainability department] in the lead, accompanied by investor relations. And we have discussions right after we have met with an investor interested in sustainability." (HealthCo IRM)*

"Corporate communications is carried out by the executive board. Investor relations is also carried out by the executive board. Thus everything is a kind of personal union anyway." (PrintCo HEIR)

"Banks read our reports of course, although they have different sources of information. They do not rely on the management report alone. They have that, the direct contact, the meetings, they have a reporting system throughout the year." (LogCo CFO)

These circumstances show that in addition to executive boards, other participants such as coordinators or IR departments could hold these particular powers. This distribution indicates that the power promotor role could be shared by various participants.

Moreover, power promotors also decide on the **use of budgets and resources** for the preparation. Although the case firms did not explicitly mention particular pressures from the power promotors, a common theme emerged with regard to keeping the processes as lean as possible. This implicit optimization of budgets and staff resources could be an indicator for the credible hierarchical potential of the case firms' power promotors. These powers appear to be located mainly in the executive board:

"A challenge of the preparation process is that it requires a lot of money and resources to finish the report in this short time span." (HealthCo MSD)

"I mean it is basically good that our process is so lean and that we don't use up X man-hours or man-weeks. And that we don't tie up resources for an obligation which we have." (FashCo MEIR)

Power promotors in the case firms

In the following, the findings of the discussions above provide a basis for identifying participants with power promotor roles in the case firms (Table 6-11).[124] In addition, role combinations are highlighted. In all firms, the executive board is responsible for preparing the management report and therefore takes on the role of the power promotor. At first glance, this could be interpreted as a role exclusivity. However, all case firms show that the contributions and powers of power promotors are shared with other participants of the preparation process.

In addition to the executive board of **HealthCo**, several other participants contribute to the process. While the final decision on material nfKPIs rests with the executive board, other participants such as the MSP, MSD or IRM are involved earlier in the selection process and therefore show role combinations and role pluralities with regard to power promotor contributions. Moreover, as both the CPO and CFO are involved in the selection process to a similar degree, powers and contributions are not concentrated in one person within the executive board. Furthermore, various different participants are involved in the review of the management report, such as the pre-disclosure committee, the report coordinators and the executive board. Thus, a role plurality exists with regard to this particular contribution of the power promotor. Participants from IR or the sustainability department base some of their review criteria on their access to investors and stakeholders. Similarly, the coordinators

[124] See Appendix B for the list of interview partners, abbreviations and departments.

of the preparation process show a role combination with their process promotor role as they aim to balance contributions from supportive and restrictive information providers in the functional departments.

Firms	Role exclusivity	Role combination	Role plurality
HealthCo	-	MSP, IRM (know-how); MSD (process)	Executive board, MSP, IRM, SD, HMQR, MQR
ChemCo	-	MQR (process); HSC, SC, MSD (know-how)	Executive board, MQR, HSC, SC, MSD, HER, IRM1, IRM2
PrintCo	-	CFO, HEIR (process)	Executive board, CFO, HEIR
LogCo	-	HA (process, know-how)	CFO, remaining executive board, HA, HER
FashCo	-	MEIR (process)	CEO, CFO, MEIR, HEIR
TechCo		IRM (process)	CEO, CFO, remaining executive board, IRM
AgCo	-	PRM (process)	Executive board, PRM, HER, heads of finance and management accounting

Table 6-11: Power promotor role distribution in the case firms

In terms of selecting material nfKPIs for **ChemCo's** management report, the MQR collaborates with participants from functional departments (such as HSC, SC and MSD) to identify the most important nfKPIs. In addition to these tasks, all participants fulfil other process or know-how promotor roles in the process. While the selection of nfKPIs is approved by the executive board, the other participants contribute considerably to preparing this decision. In addition, the MQR and HER also aim to balance contributions of functional departments to safeguard a balanced report. Subsequently, participants such as the MQR, HER, IRM1 and IRM2 and the executive board take part in the review of the nfKPIs in the management report. In addition to the multiple roles taken on by the MQR, the HER, IRM1 and IRM2 use their particular powers to conduct the review. While the HER draws from his hierarchical powers, the IRM1 and IRM2 use their access to investors to review nfKPIs from a capital market perspective.

While the executive board at **PrintCo** mutually makes the final decisions regarding the publication of the management report, many of the contributions and powers in the preparation process are concentrated in the CFO. The CFO both holds hierarchical potential and carries out the majority of capital market communication. Nonetheless, a role plurality exists for the role of the power promotor. In previous years, the CFO contributed to other parts of the process, acting both as a know-how and process promotors (role combination). Now, the HEIR fulfils these tasks with regard to nfKPIs. As the HEIR is also involved in the selection of material nfKPIs and in the communication with supervisory board and auditors, she also shows signs of role combination and role plurality for parts of the power promotor role.

In **LogCo's** preparation process for nfKPIs, the CFO marks the executive with the majority of contributions and powers of the preparation process. However, he shares several of his power promotor contributions and powers with the HA. As the HA is particularly involved in the identification and review of nfKPIs, a role plurality and role combination becomes apparent. In addition, the HER of LogCo supports the HA in reviewing the report. As the HER solely takes on a review function and does not fulfil other roles, a role plurality exists with regard to the reviewers of the report.

In the case of **FashCo**, the executive board consists of the CEO and CFO who mutually provide clearance for the management report (role plurality). In addition to this contribution, the CFO takes on most of the power promotor tasks himself and applies his powers to manage the preparation process. The MEIR supports the CFO in the materiality analysis of the nfKPIs and in the review of the nfKPIs (role combination and plurality). Moreover, the HEIR participates in the review of the management report. As she is not involved in other parts of the preparation process, her support shows a role plurality with regard to the power promotor contribution of reviewing the report.

At **TechCo**, the final decision-making regarding the nfKPIs in the management report is concentrated in the CEO and CFO (role plurality). Besides providing clearance for the report, other members of the executive board are less involved in the report's finalization. While the CFO takes on many of the contributions and powers, the IRM supports the CFO in the materiality analysis and review of the report. In this regard, the IRM fulfils a role combination with her promotor role and shares some of the contributions related to the identification of material nfKPIs (role plurality).

In contrast to other CFOs in the case firms, the CFO of **AgCo** solely acts as a member of the executive board. Thus, the role of the power promotor is taken on by the executive board as a whole. Similar to the other case firms, some contributions of the power promotor are fulfilled by other participants of the process. The PRM is strongly involved in the materiality analysis of nfKPIs, which points to a role combination of power and process promotor contributions. Furthermore, the PRM is involved in the review of the nfKPIs, together with the HER and the heads of finance and management accounting. As the latter have considerable hierarchical positions and review both the material nfKPIs and the final draft of the report, a role plurality exists with regard to these contributions and powers of the power promotor.

Overall, the findings indicate that neither executive boards nor CFOs in particular appear to fulfil the power promotor role exclusively. Within executive boards, contributions and powers related to power promotors are regularly concentrated in the CFO, which reflects the responsibility of this actor to prepare the management report. Nonetheless, powers could also be shared as in the cases of HealthCo and AgCo.

While executive boards typically hold hierarchical powers exclusively, other typical contributions and powers of power promotors seem to be **shared** by multiple participants (role pluralities) in all case firms. With regard to role combinations, particularly process promotors appear to take on specific power promotor contributions (e.g., materiality analysis or reviewing reports). Moreover, some participants such as IRMs or supervisors of coordinators often take on particular review tasks without being involved in other steps of the process. Furthermore, know-how promotors are involved in the materiality analysis and the setting of goals for nfKPIs in the two large public firms.

In summary, the results show that firms seem to have divided powers among several participants and hierarchical levels, which indicates limited decision-making powers of executives in preparation processes of nfKPIs. Nonetheless, executives mark an important final gatekeeper for nfKPI disclosures (*O'Dwyer* (2005), p. 287; *Adams/McNicholas* (2007), p. 397).

6.2.2.3 Know-how promotor

This section determines the **know-how promotors** and their contributions and powers in the case firms' preparation processes of nfKPIs. Similar to the innovation literature (*Witte* (1973), pp. 18-19; *Chakrabarti/Hauschildt* (1989), p. 166; *Walter* (1998), pp. 103-105), several participants in the case firms use their contributions and powers to provide the necessary information on nfKPIs for the management report. To do so, these promotors measure nfKPIs and write the respective nfKPI sections by using their powers of specific expert knowledge and access to data. Table 6-12 provides an overview of these contributions and powers of such promotors, which are discussed in the following.

Contributions	Powers
Measurement of nfKPIs • Collection of nfKPIs • Validation of nfKPIs Writing of nfKPI sections	Expert knowledge Access to data

Table 6-12: Contributions and powers of the know-how promotor

Measurement of nfKPIs

In the context of their task to provide the necessary nfKPI data for the preparation of the management report, the know-how promotor coordinates the **measurement of the nfKPIs.** This contribution consists of the collection and validation of these indicators.

As an initial step of the measurement, the know-how promotor is **contacted** by the process coordinator who initiates the collection. When the coordinators approach contact persons in the departments, they either use single points of contact or approach multiple contact persons in the departments. While examples from HealthCo and ChemCo help contrast these types of contact, the fact that each firm uses both types of contact indicates that these types may not only vary across but also within firms:

> *"We have split tasks in such a way, that for each segment we have one contact person for the financial parts and one for the nonfinancial parts. Because we can't tour through every segment. We can't phone everyone across the segment. Here at [HealthCo], you*

would be busy with that for a long time. That's why we have a central person of contact who communicates into the segment and then reports to us." (HealthCo HMQR)

"In the past, we asked the departments each year: 'Who is the person of contact, who takes on the coordination for the department?' We have seized to do this, because it's always the same people anyway. And if something changes, we clarify this on a bilateral basis. Previously, we asked officially, because you like to have at best one person who organizes this for the entire department. However, especially in the sustainability department, there are more points of contact by now, which makes it easier for me to directly talk to the respective experts as compared to a coordinator. Then you have the direct contact and if the people do this each year anyway, it is easier if you directly exchange information." (ChemCo MQR)

As such coordinators or experts within the departments are responsible for measuring the data, they **coordinate the external and internal sources** consisting of databases, internal reports and expert knowledge regarding particular nfKPIs. Only few large case firms use databases for nfKPIs aside from HR information. In these case firms, know-how promotors manage such databases applied for nfKPI measurement. It becomes apparent, that the know-how promotors can support the measurement of nfKPIs through this access to relevant sources of data:

"My role in the [HealthCo] group is to manage the [global QEHS database of HealthCo]. This means that we develop reporting processes, which finally end up as KPIs, as information in the management report." (HealthCo DBM)

"We have different methods to get the data into the systems. One system is based on SAP, which draws its information from other SAP systems or from other tools. Through this, no one has to hand-collect information by running to subsidiaries and no one has to manually type information into Excel. We try to draw this from the system. [...] In other cases, where we do not have underlying data systems, we actually have to measure at business-level or site-level. The preparers usually do this on an Excel basis and there are dedicated persons in the business who have to enter this data into the systems." (ChemCo HSC)

"[Warranty-related costs] from selected and relevant subsidiaries are entered from Excel into SAP. This way, they are included in the business warehouse and are then analyzed. That's how the warranty-related costs come about. The scrap and rework costs are measured by group controlling. The subsidiaries report these to us and we analyze them. Supplier parts per million are accessible over SAP, the entire supplier management is managed through SAP. That's our quality-related nfKPIs. In the HSE, we demand a quarterly reporting by Excel and PowerPoint. This way, we just receive the numbers we need. They are not accessible in any system. That's why the people have to enter these into Excel and send them to us." (TechCo HDBM)

In the context of managing the databases, know-how promotors also **coordinate and train** persons responsible for measuring the data. Thus, know-how promotors are often not only responsible for accessing nfKPI data but also for maintaining the databases and measurement:

"The time horizon is really, really short and there is no room for unexpected issues. And that is what drives this pressure and what proves a big challenge. [...] I tackle this challenge by cautioning the persons responsible for measuring sufficiently early: 'You know, the yearly reporting always takes place, always at the same time. You have your thanksgiving in the USA. Be prepared that you prepare the data in time. And make sure to have one person ready who can provide answers to our questions.' Basically, this is proactive management." (HealthCo DBM)

"We have software solutions which also show you the differences compared to the previous year. And there are colleagues who still send us the data, although they see that the system shows a 1,000 per cent difference. There is a lack of self-reflection sometimes. But we have started doing live-training this year, thus we invest time to further improve and to develop these issues." (ChemCo SC)

"It does require a lot of personal communication, because documentation is rarely read, from my experience. You do of course need documentation as a reference, but personal communication is more important." (TechCo HDBM)

In these contexts, the particular expert knowledge is often distributed across departments. Hence, department internal coordinators act as process promotors to access this particular knowledge.

In some cases (HealthCo, LogCo, FashCo, AgCo), know-how promotors either have an overview over the respective nfKPI development or measure nfKPIs themselves. This type of measurement is particularly common among the smaller, private firms. In this context, know-how promotors act as **experts.**[125] Therefore, these promotors dispose over the respective information through internal reports or their individual knowledge. In comparison to nfKPI databases, this type of sources draws more intensively from the particular knowledge of coordinators:

"First we list all of our projects. And when we decide that one of them should be included in the management report, we go back to this list and have a look at what we can already write about this project." (LogCo HRS)

"We also collect some data for our internal reporting, which we can sometimes use directly for writing our management report." (FashCo MEIR)

"We ask our departments for the numbers. We already have a lot of the necessary information on our radar anyway. This is a normal, day-to-day process. We call or write an email. If for example I need the number of followers on Facebook or Instagram or somewhere else, I contact our social-media manager. I just use our portfolio, whatever is necessary for this occasion." (AgCo PRM)

In addition to the measurement of the data, know-how promotors are also responsible for **validating** the data. However, this validation of the data varies from extensive validation processes to plausibility checks. While HealthCo's know-how promotors extensively validate nfKPIs, know-how promotors from firms like TechCo fulfil fewer validation tasks:

[125] For a discussion of experts as a source of information for collecting nfKPIs see section 6.2.1.2.3.

"Validating the numbers is one of our main focuses in the [global QEHS database] management department. We spend the majority of our time validating whether or not the numbers we receive are plausible and what is driving these numbers. Which story you can write for the management report. If for example we see that a KPI has increased at a particular site, we specifically inquire what has happened and which things have changed. Through this, you basically get the explanations delivered directly to you." (HealthCo DBM)

"If water usages decline dramatically – this is also a KPI of ours – we are of course surprised and we approach the departments. We do of course do some plausibility checks. Sometimes you just realize that a decimal point has gotten out of place. That can happen. But sometimes you have no chance, then you can't check it at all. [...] Our statutory auditor would also not be able to check whether the water usage in India has been measured correctly." (TechCo HDBM)

These validation tasks are in accordance with the know-how promotors' contribution of managing the data measured for the management report. The different types of validation show that the accessibility of the data could differ for the persons responsible for the data management. As evident from TechCo's case, the importance of the data validation task could also vary with regard to the importance of auditable and correct nfKPIs.

Writing of nfKPI sections

In addition to the measurement of nfKPIs, know-how promotors are also responsible writing nfKPI sections. A large part of the experts in the case firms **write the respective nfKPI section** for their departments. In these cases, these participants provide numbers, texts or both for the nfKPIs collected:

"Everything related to the areas of environment, accidents and other HSE topics – all topics that are clearly HSE – I write them entirely, together with my team. My team are a couple of colleagues who support me with that. And I also provide the necessary documents and discuss my texts with the sites. For example, the energy consumption of the [HealthCo headquarters] has increased from X to Y, because more consumption from external customers has been included. Then I write to my colleagues from our firm: 'I would like to write the sentence like this. Would this be okay for you or do you want to change it?' This way I also receive a proof document for the statutory auditor." (HealthCo DBM)

"Then we consolidate all the numbers, which yields a KPI. We then write a short text and explanations. [...] This suggestion is then sent to [MQR], who collects the texts and includes them in the draft. And then we typically have two feedback loops looking like this: 'I have included this in the annual report, is it okay this way?' Or there could also be a question: 'I don't understand this, or there might be something missing.'" (ChemCo HSC)

"I think that some [department experts] were relieved that I do the writing. They only need to collect the information internally. [...] Some don't have a feeling for texts or for writing. It starts with finding an introductory sentence. It's already a hurdle to

> *write this sentence. And many don't write at all. And then we also have to translate this into English. I also do this." (TechCo DBM)*

To write the particular sections, the promotors typically draw from the data received from other participants. The quotes also indicate that the dependency of the writers on other sources can vary with regard to the knowledge of the particular data. Conversely, these writers can fulfil tasks that other know-how promotors may not be willing or able to do, as indicated in the case of TechCo.

As evident in the quotes above, know-how promotors often receive **feedback** from the other promotors. In some cases, this feedback is related to questions which are then discussed. In other cases, the know-how promotors are asked for approval in case of changes to the writing. These approaches point towards the collaboration between multiple know-how promotors in the respective department. Moreover, the approaches indicate that the expert knowledge of know-how promotors can help influence the content of the nfKPI sections:

> *"Any feedback is passed back to me. I have a look at whether I can accept these changes. If the changes are larger, I approach the individual content providers and try to find a compromise." (HealthCo MSP)*

> *"When the functional departments write something and you shorten or rephrase it, you typically send the part back to them and say: 'Have I included these points correctly? Did I understand it right or have I changed the content?'" (FashCo HEIR)*

> *"And then at the end, they receive the texts again and I say: 'I have adjusted the text to the language of the report. Have I misstated your information?' And then they have a look at it and say whether or not it is correct." (TechCo IRM)*

Overall, the cases show differences in the involvement of know-how promotors in writing the nfKPI sections. Know-how promotors seem to be more involved when the coordinators of the report are less knowledgeable about the particular nfKPIs. In such cases, the approval of know-how promotors in approving the contents becomes particularly important and highlights potential decision-making powers of know-how promotors.

Powers of the know-how promotor

Similar to know-how promotors in the innovation process, know-how promotors participating in the preparation process of nfKPIs use their expertise as a **power** to support the process (*Walter* (1998), pp. 103-104). In addition to their expertise, know-how promotors have access to the nfKPI data necessary for the preparation of the management report. These powers based on the access to nfKPI information point out a knowledge advantage of know-how promotors as compared to the other promotors (*Witte* (1973), p. 19).

The **expertise** of know-how promotors is particularly grounded in their involvement in specific nonfinancial areas. This knowledge sets them apart from other participants of the preparation process such as the coordinators of LogCo and FashCo. These coordinators recognize that their knowledge about particular nonfinancial topics is limited as they are not involved in these issues as part of their regular tasks:

"My biggest challenge lies in the numbers. I know why the numbers have gone up or down, I know the trend and then I prepare a pre-draft version for these topics in the nonfinancial section of the management report. Including everything that involves numbers: environmental impact, accidents and certificates. That's the larger scope, everything with CO_2 Emissions, waste, water, everything related to this." (HealthCo DBM)

"It's important to me that the individual experts write about their particular area. I could not say anything about HR. Of course, I have some half-knowledge and I can read the previous reports, but I do not have these deep insights into this area." (LogCo CFOA)

"I am dependent on the information from the other departments in the case of the nonfinancial KPIs. Be it that I get in contact with the functional departments, because they are experts in the field and can provide me with better information. And qualitative KPIs are always a bit harder to collect and to put in a nutshell." (FashCo MEIR)

These quotes also indicate the experts' power of **access to nfKPIs.** This power is connected to the know-how promotors' involvement with nfKPI databases, reports or other department internal experts. This particular power separates the know-how promotors from other promotors, as the access to nfKPIs can be restricted to a limited number of persons within the firm because of confidentiality reasons. For example, in the case of TechCo's HR data, the HRM is responsible for providing only non-sensitive HR data for the nfKPI disclosures. Moreover, access to data could also be limited due to its predominant usage for the operational management. For this reason, the coordinator of the report lacks access to this type of information and, hence, needs to contact the respective functional departments:

"I have to go directly to the functional departments, otherwise we don't get this information. In the course of preparing the report, I ask the colleagues to send me some documents. But that's very sensitive data which they treat confidentially because they are related to the analysis of weak-points. [...] I sometimes receive them before the end of the reporting period. But we don't have access to them." (ChemCo MQR)

"People would love to know everything. And this is my biggest challenge to slow down their curiosity. But this is normal for the HR department, that we can't provide clearance for all numbers, disclose all of them externally or internally, because this is confidential information. And yes, from this point on it is clear to us in the HR department, which information we can communicate and which we cannot." (TechCo HRM)

Know-how promotors in the case firms

On the basis of the discussions above, participants with know-how promotor roles in the case firms can be identified. Moreover, potential role distributions can be clarified (*Folkerts/Hauschildt* (2002), p. 9). Table 6-13 summarizes the results of this section.[126]

[126] See Appendix B for the list of interview partners, abbreviations and departments.

In the case of **HealthCo**, the functional departments act as know-how promotors for individual nfKPIs. On the one hand, the DBM, MSP and various contact persons in the departments contribute to the process with their expertise and access to specific databases (role plurality). On the other hand, these participants also fulfil process promotor roles by coordinating the collection of nfKPIs within their departments (role combination). In addition to their process promotor role, the MSD and her colleagues take on several know-how promotor contributions and powers by preparing texts for the management report (role combination and plurality).

At **ChemCo**, functional departments act as know-how promotors. The MSD, HSC, SC and other informants from the departments show contributions and powers of know-how promotors (role plurality). The HSC and SC, for example, manage the QEHS database of ChemCo and write the respective nfKPI sections. In addition, the MSD, HSC and SC are involved in the material analysis, indicating a role combination with power promotor tasks.

Firms	Role exclusivity	Role combination	Role plurality
HealthCo	-	DBM, MSP, MSD (process)	DBM, MSP, MSD, other functional departments
ChemCo	-	MSD, HSC, SC (power)	MSD, HSC, SC, other functional departments
PrintCo	-	CFO (power), HEIR (process, power)	CFO, HEIR, functional departments
LogCo	-	HRS, HA (process)	HRS, HA
FashCo	-	MEIR (process)	MEIR, functional departments
TechCo	-	HDBM, DBM, HRM (process)	HDBM, DBM, HRM, other functional departments
AgCo	-	PRM (process)	PRM, functional departments

Table 6-13: Know-how promotor role distribution in the case firms

The know-how promotor roles at **PrintCo** are shared by different participants of the preparation process. Before the CSR-RUG became effective, the CFO collected relevant nfKPIs and wrote the respective sections himself (role combination). The heads of the functional departments solely served as information providers (role plurality). In a similar vein, the HEIR collects and writes large parts of the nfKPIs for the nonfinancial statement (role combination). While functional departments still act as providers of information, they are consulted to a larger extent as compared to previous years (role plurality).

At **LogCo**, the role of the know-how promotor is taken on by multiple persons (role plurality). The HRS provides nfKPIs for the HR-related section of the management report. In addition, the HRS acts as a coordinator within her department to collect the relevant information (role combination). Similarly, the HA prepares the nfKPIs of the environmental section of the report. The HA takes on these know-how promotor tasks in addition to his process promotor role (role combination).

Similar to other case firms, multiple participants of **FashCo's** preparation process share the know-how promotor role. Most contributions with regard to nfKPI collection and writing are provided by the MEIR as the coordinator of the process (role combination). Functional departments provide the MEIR with information and texts for nfKPI sections (role plurality). However, in the case of departments which provide nfKPI information rather than texts, the participation of the departments in FashCo's preparation process is rather limited.

In **TechCo's** preparation process for nfKPIs, the functional departments take on the role of know-how promotors. While the HDBM, DBM, HRM and several other participants from functional departments carry out writing or measurement tasks (role plurality), some contact persons such as the DBM and HRM also act as process promotors by coordinating the collection within their departments (role combination).

Finally, the know-how promotor role at **AgCo** is mostly taken on by the PRM, who writes most of the nfKPI sections in addition to his process promotor role (role combination). Nonetheless, the PRM contacts individual departments to gather specific nfKPIs and to ask the departments for approval regarding the nfKPI sections. Hence, the departments also take on contributions and powers related to the know-how promotor role (role plurality).

In summary, the know-how promotor role is **shared** in all case firms. No case firm shows role exclusivity for the know-how promotor role. This type of role distribution seems to reflect the diverse nature of nfKPIs in the management report. As it can be observed in the case firms, various functional departments support the preparation process by collecting nfKPIs or writing corresponding nfKPI sections.

Moreover, **role combinations** with power or process promotor roles exist in all case firms. In smaller firms, the know-how promotor role appears to be mostly carried out by process coordinators and executives. In contrast to this, functional departments in larger firms (HealthCo, ChemCo) and private firms with extensive nfKPI reporting (TechCo) seem to take on process promotor roles in addition to their know-how promotor roles. This inverse relation could point towards a different importance of functional departments in the preparation process. However, in almost all case firms, the functional departments are asked for approval before the nfKPIs are cleared for publication. These results support previous findings in the literature, which indicate that functional departments appear to be important for the preparation of nfKPIs (*Spence/Rinaldi* (2014), p. 445).

6.2.2.4 Communication and collaboration among promotors

As the previous sections have identified the individual contributions and powers of promotors in the preparation process of nfKPIs, this section examines how these promotors communicate and collaborate in the preparation process.

Communication

The analyses reveal that the **communication** between participants of the preparation process can be differentiated with regard to the flow of information and types of communication. In addition to communicating with other promotors, the promotors of the preparation process are also in contact with other internal and external sources of information or contact persons (*Chakrabarti/Hauschildt* (1989), pp. 166-168). Figure 6-46 illustrates the **flow of information** occurring in the course of the preparation process, which differs according to the individual promotor roles.

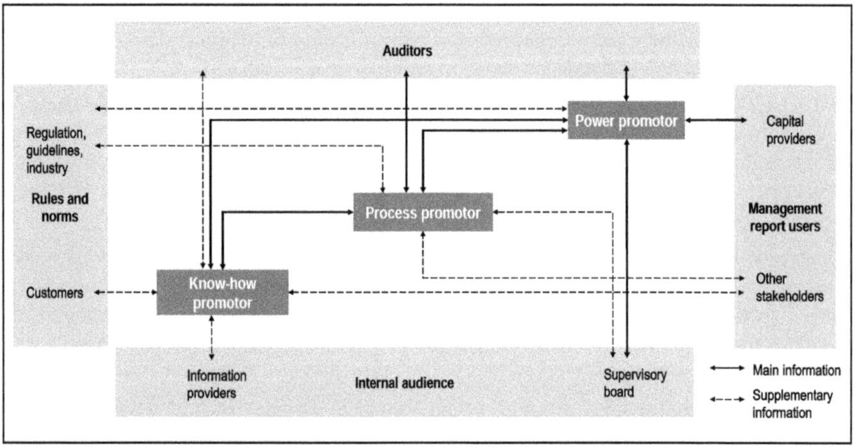

Figure 6-46: Flow of information among participants of the preparation process

In addition to measuring nfKPIs and writing report sections, **know-how promotors** draw additional information from customers, external stakeholders (e.g., NGOs or media) or information providers within functional departments. In some cases, know-how promotors are also involved in the audit process and provide the statutory auditors with documentation regarding the nfKPIs in the management report. The majority of communication regarding the collection and writing of the nfKPIs occurs between know-how and process promotors. However, in rare cases (ChemCo, PrintCo) know-how promotors are also directly in contact with power promotors. It becomes evident that particularly know-how promotors in the functional departments of the case firms are rarely involved in direct communication with external stakeholders. This circumstance indicates that the external communication is mostly carried out by other promotors.

In the center of the process, the **process promotor** mediates between the know-how and power promotors. In addition to managing this communication channel, process promotors observe the reporting of industry peers and ensure the compliance with regulations and guidelines. Depending on their contact to external stakeholders such as NGOs or the general public, some process promotors consider these demands in the preparation of the management report. An important point of contact is the statutory auditor of the report, whom the process promotor typically provides with report drafts and documentation. The process promotor then distributes resulting feedback to the other promotors. Finally, process promotors support power promotors in their communication with the supervisory board.

As the person responsible for the preparation of the report, **power promotors** are also responsible for the official communication connected to the management report. Similar to the process promotor, power promotors ensure that the management report is compliant with regulation and guidelines. Moreover, power promotors observe the reporting of industry peers and adjust their firm's reporting accordingly. In the course of the statutory audit, the power promotor is in contact with the auditors to defend the firm's reporting decisions. Subsequently, the power promotor also discusses these decisions with the supervisory board of the firm, if applicable. Finally, the power promotor officially publishes the management report for the general public and for capital providers in particular. Throughout the year, power promotors are in contact with capital providers and safeguard that their demands are reflected in the report.

In addition to the flow of information, the analyses reveal different **characteristics of communication** between participants. These types of communication can be differentiated according to the directness, degree of formalization and openness of the communication. Most case firms use **direct communication** between the promotors to support a lean and fast preparation process:

> *"We have a lot of direct contact. Basically, we have very flat hierarchies. It's not that I have to contact the secretary of the head of a department through some kind of official request for a meeting." (FashCo MEIR)*

> *"We have short communication channels. And I am happy, that there is no authority in between. […] Suppose that I would not report directly to the head of HR, but that there would be another manager in between who would pass it on to the head of HR. I believe, this would not make this process more efficient." (TechCo HRM)*

In contrast to direct communication between the key participants of the preparation process, particularly firms with a large number of participants use contact persons in the functional department as coordinators (section 6.2.2.1 or 6.2.2.3). Moreover, report drafts are passed through several **hierarchical levels** in some case firms (HealthCo, ChemCo, AgCo). This type of hierarchical communication seems to be necessary to handle the large size of participants and official hierarchical channels. In contrast to direct communication, messages are passed on through several hierarchical levels to the process promotors:

> *"Basically, this is transferred hierarchically. You can say it like this. That means, everything is first agreed on a working level. And then, when it goes upwards from the heads of the departments to the executive board, all feedback is collected through a cascading procedure. This way, we can make sure that all comments and remarks are taken into account when the document is reviewed by the executive board." (HealthCo MQR)*

A communication characteristic which is closely related to hierarchical communication is the **extent of formalization** of communication. While firms with various hierarchical levels such as HealthCo, ChemCo and AgCo appear to use more formal types of communication, in firms with rather flat hierarchies, participants communicate rather informally:

> *"We have an editing software, which means that the communication could also take place through this software. I would see whether or not a colleague has edited the document at a particular point in time, hence we could also communicate non-verbally. […] Nonetheless, it is important that you talk in some form, because it could lead to misunderstandings." (HealthCo MQR)*

"[The communication is] absolutely informal. [Laughter] Basically, we just exchange information. If you need something, then you call, send a mail or whatever, meet and talk about what should be included. Without any concept." (PrintCo HEIR)

"The review meeting is not cast in stone. But it happens in the course of October, via written correspondence. Because we are a decentralized company and a lot of our heads of department work in [AgCo site] and some of them here. And then we do this through a circulation procedure." (AgCo PRM)

On the one hand, formal means of communication comprise for example briefings, work groups, regular meetings or editing software. Such means typically require the participants to coordinate and plan the communication on a regular basis. In large firms, the communication is also commonly documented as evidence for audit procedures. On the other hand, informal communication takes place on a bilateral and on-demand basis. As this type of communication bypasses hierarchical exchanges, extensive preparation and documentation, it marks a fast, lean and cheap way to exchange information in preparation processes. While firms which heavily rely on formal communication also use informal communication in some cases, most small or private firms with informal communication do not use formal means of communication.

Furthermore, the communication between participants can differ with regard to their **level of openness**. While some promotors specify requirements from regulators, guidelines or stakeholders when communicating with other promotors, the cases show that most communication is done on an open basis:

"I would like to add that an open communication culture is important. That you can talk and brainstorm across departments without hierarchical thinking. Even if you discard everything afterwards, you at least have the chance to address each thought. This is important, because if you think in finished sentences and results, you will never make a step forward. You have to be able to look beyond your own nose and discuss freely. […] And as soon as someone is afraid that each statement might be scrutinized by their superior, then they might not be open." (ChemCo MQR)

"When I approach the departments, [the communication is] relatively open. I'm open for their input, because I think they are better informed about what is relevant. They do of course get informed that it is about the management report. That it is not an internal report but a public medium. And I tell them what we have communicated in the previous year, because some of them are only involved in the preparation process once a year. This way they have an orientation for what could be relevant and for the extent of the report." (FashCo MEIR)

"I initiate everything and then they deliver. And then it goes back and forth, for some a bit more and for others a bit less. Let's say it's an open communication." (TechCo IRM)

Overall, the case studies show several differences with regards to the flow of information and communication characteristics between participants. While the process promotors seem to coordinate most of the communication, other promotors also communicate with other stakeholders, depending on their contacts inside and outside of the company. Moreover, particularly the large and more hierarchical firms appear to use more formal and specific types of communication.

Collaboration

In addition to the communication between the participants, the results also indicate the collaboration between the promotors involved. In the following, procedures and challenges of the collaboration between promotors in preparation processes are analyzed.

From a **procedural perspective** (*Utterback* (1971), p. 125), process promotors act as important links between power promotors and know-how promotors (*Chakrabarti/Hauschildt* (1989), pp. 168-169; *Hauschildt/Chakrabarti* (1999), pp. 79-82). This linkage becomes evident in the contributions of process promotors during the preparation process. Figure 6-47 illustrates these contributions in the context of the typical contributions of the three promotors involved in the preparation process. Throughout the preparation process, the process promotor supports the collaboration by continuously mediating and exchanging information between promotors.

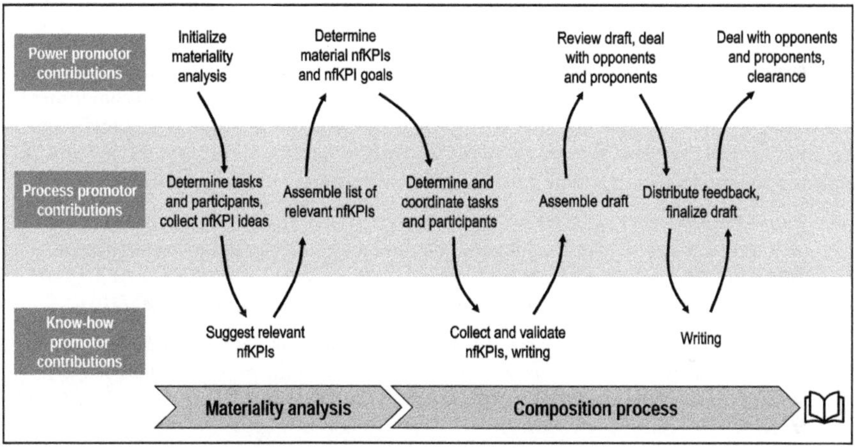

Figure 6-47: Typical collaboration between promotors in the preparation process (based on *Chakrabarti/Hauschildt* (1989), pp. 168-169)

Although the case studies show that individual roles can be combined, such **role combinations** appear to not affect the sequence of contributions in the process. On the contrary, role combinations would eliminate the collaboration between individual promotors. Therefore, role combinations could simplify the collaboration in the preparation process. For example, such role combinations simplify the collection of nfKPIs at PrintCo and LogCo:

> *"Due to the fact that there are only two persons involved in this process, it is relatively easy to coordinate the process." (PrintCo HEIR)*

> *"Most parts I can prepare together with [HER]. We already have most of the information, so that we can prepare these from here by accessing the sources of information*

available in the company. Because the more shoulders you split it on, the more complicated the coordination and collection of the information will become." (LogCo HA)

Nonetheless, prior literature on promotors stresses the importance of a close collaboration between the promotors in the process (*Hauschildt/Chakrabarti* (1999), pp. 81-82). However, the collaboration between promotors also poses **challenges**. In the integrated reporting context of HealthCo, the coordinators highlight the challenge of agreeing on the materiality and balance of nfKPIs. The coordinators recognize that the firm lacks a power promotor who could **mediate** between the sustainability and accounting departments before the report is passed upwards through the hierarchy:

"The problem with materiality is that we [sustainability and accounting] sometimes have different opinions without having an authority between us and the executive board. [...] There I see huge potential for improvement. We sometimes wear ourselves out on this. You discuss, discuss and discuss and there is no one on our level of hierarchy who can say: 'Come on, that is how we do it, I decide.' [...] They would have to be absolutely competent in both the financial and nonfinancial sections. So not just an accountant but also someone proficient in GRI. And who has a certain position in the hierarchy and who is also able to make decisions." (HealthCo HMQR)

Therefore, additional participants could support the process by mediating between process promotors from different backgrounds. Moreover, know-how promotors can sometimes be **unwilling** to change particular texts or to provide specific information. This unwillingness could potentially result in tensions between know-how and power promotors. For this reason, process promotors negotiate with know-how promotors to find a compromise:

"From the functional departments, some might say: 'We have the sole control over our texts, they are our intellectual property. You assemble and coordinate the report, but this means we have the final say with regard to the wording.' And this is a real fight, at some points it is incredibly tough, lengthy and unpleasant." (ChemCo MSD)

"And on the other hand, there could be the case that some do not want to be measured by KPIs. And then you have to say: 'People, you have a concept about which you are writing a lot. There has to be a KPI or two related to this.' [Laughter]" (ChemCo HER)

In this context, interviewees stress that it is of great importance that all participants are **committed** to contribute to the preparation process. Such commitment is argued to facilitate the collaboration between promotors:

"You need the commitment of all participants. It has to be clear for everybody that this is not an alibi exercise, which someone from company headquarters has come up with. But if you say: 'Hey, we need these KPIs!', then you have to make transparent what this is important for, for the business and for the management approach. And I believe that the people are then willing to do the extra work." (ChemCo HER)

"The preparation process is good, when it is lean, when it is efficient, when all participants work hand in hand. To do so, all participants should identify themselves with the process and should also be convinced of the nfKPI on a content-level." (AgCo PRM)

Both the communication and collaboration between the process participants indicate the **central role of process promotors**. While the cases show that the collaboration between promotors faces several challenges, this collaboration could be simplified through role combinations or the commitment of all participants to contribute to the process. The following section evaluates these findings in the light of the promotor model and discusses an adapted promotor model for explaining the roles and collaboration of participants of the preparation process.

6.2.2.5 Discussion

The results of the analyses above indicate the existence of **promotors in the preparation process of nfKPIs for management reports**. Moreover, the collaboration between these promotors appears to be effective with regard to the preparation of such disclosures. Nonetheless, the results also indicate specific differences between the promotor model of the innovation process and promotors in the preparation process of nfKPIs for the management report. Hence, this section examines the effectiveness of promotor structures in preparation processes and discusses an adapted promotor model based on the results of this study.

With regard to the effectiveness of promotor structures, the promotor model indicates the suitability of such structures for **dividing the labor** between various different participants contributing to the preparation of the report:

> *"We have to include all departments involved with the topics in the [HealthCo] group in time to achieve an optimum result with regard to the management report. Two departments won't handle this alone. You have to include the experts and most importantly, you have to include them in time." (HealthCo IRM)*

As expected by previous research (*Adams/Frost* (2008), p. 292; *Osann* (2010), pp. 259-260; *Tarca et al.* (2011), p. 47), the contributions of the process participants are distributed according to the particular powers of the persons involved. Although executive boards as power promotors are responsible for the preparation and hold the power to initialize and finish the process (*Witte* (1973), p. 56), they might lack the necessary time and knowledge to prepare the management report. These circumstances indicate the necessity of know-how promotors and support the notion that "data collection is carried out by those who are familiar with the data themselves" (*Adams* (2002), p. 244). Nonetheless, such know-how promotors would typically not be able to prepare the report by themselves and lack the authority to publish it (*Witte* (1973), p. 56). As moderators, process promotors connect the contributions of the know-how promotors and the power promotors to advance the preparation process (*Chakrabarti/Hauschildt* (1989), p. 168).

An efficient division of labor is deemed necessary as personnel resources are limited and relevant skills needed for the preparation are distributed across the organizations. With regard to **scarce resources**, the promotor model offers a helpful basis to determine key players and effective organizational constellations in order to refrain from using excessive or wrong resources for preparing management reports. In addition, the division of labor in the preparation process can be beneficial due to the diverse **distribution of skills** in the form of contributions and powers. Particularly as a consequence of the extent and complexity of preparation processes in large firms, the knowledge and skills necessary for the preparation of nfKPIs seem to be fragmented among process participants. Hence, these participants appear to be subject to bounded rationality. This bounded rationality is driven by a concentration of knowledge on nfKPIs in functional departments as compared to accounting departments or executive boards. Moreover, such know-how promotors lack the knowledge of reporting regulation or demands from stakeholders and face large hierarchical gaps towards other promotors. Thus, dividing the labor among these participants can serve as a solution for overcoming bounded rationality and for providing relevant nfKPI disclosures.

Despite of the effectiveness of using promotors in the preparation process, the results indicate that the general promotor model needs to be adapted to explain how promotors are involved in the preparation process. In this context, the role distribution, decision-making powers as well as the roles of champions and accountants reflect important characteristics of the involvement of promotors in the preparation process. While all case firms show the above mentioned promotor roles and division of labor, only a handful of firms indicate that individual promotor roles are taken on by one person exclusively. In this context, the promotor model also helps to understand how the roles of participants can be **distributed** in the preparation process. As summarized in Figure 6-48, participants from various departments typically take on multiple promotor roles (role combination). Moreover, individual promotor roles are commonly taken on by multiple participants (role plurality). Overall, such distributions indicate that the idealized promotor constellation based on three individuals should be rejected in favor of a shared contribution of participants. Nonetheless, all three promotor roles become apparent in the preparation processes and signalize that the collaboration of these roles supports the effectiveness of the process (*Hauschildt/Chakrabarti* (1988), pp. 382-383; *Hauschildt* (2004), p. 211).

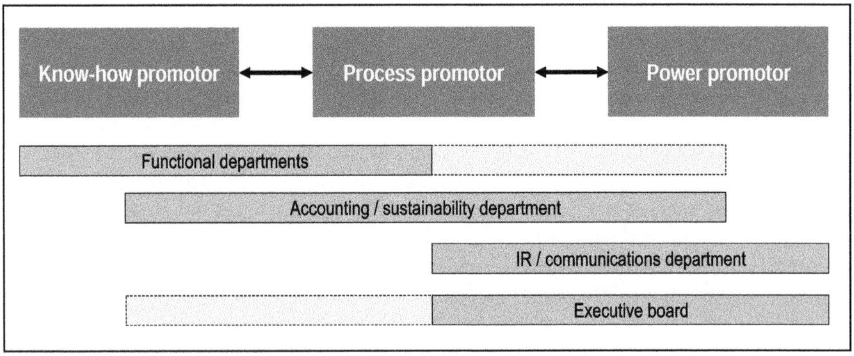

Figure 6-48: Distribution and concentration of promotor roles according to departments

The shared contributions of power promotors indicate that **decision-making powers** regarding nfKPI disclosures may not be concentrated in executive boards. In contrast, many cases show that process coordinators and functional departments have considerable powers in determining and selecting material nfKPIs. According to extant research (*Gibbins et al.* (1990), pp. 130-131; *Husillos et al.* (2011), pp. 211-213), such positions of power could be used to shape nfKPI reporting towards favorable disclosures from the perspective of functional departments or accountants. While the case studies show that participants rarely use these powers actively, these potential powers persist nonetheless. Such structures contradict previous findings of the power of CFOs and IR departments in determining management report disclosures (*Brown et al.* (2019), p. 66). Conversely, these findings of prior research are in line with cases of PrintCo or FashCo, where the CFO is closely involved in the coordination and writing of the report. Thus, it can be argued that the decision-making powers of executives depend strongly on their involvement in the preparation process and on their believable hierarchical potential to influence decisions of other promotors.

Despite signs for role combinations, the cases do not indicate so-called "**champions**" who combine all promotor roles in one person (*Chakrabarti/Hauschildt* (1989), p. 164). As noted by *Witte*, preparation processes solely carried out by individuals appear to be unrealistic in the light of large, complex organizations (*Witte* (1973), p. 5). Only a few case firms show that multiple roles are combined in relatively few participants (PrintCo, FashCo, AgCo). These examples indicate that role combinations could be more likely in small firms due to scarce resources and less elaborate preparation processes. Nonetheless, champion structures could increase risks related to the preparation process. The more tasks are bundled within one participant, the more the particular process becomes dependent on this particular participant. In combination with missing process documentation, this concentration could potentially lead to risks of lacking process independence with regard to such participants (*Kolb/Plömpel* (2017), p. 743).

In the context of the distribution of contributions, the cases also indicate the **role of accountants** in the preparation process of nfKPIs. Contrary to the assumption that accountants solely focus on numbers and financials according to their traditional roles (*Gray et al.* (1995), pp. 228-230; *Haller et al.* (2017), p. 415), almost all case firms show that accountants act as process promotors in the preparation process of nfKPIs. Only HealthCo and AgCo use process promotors from other departments as coordinators of the preparation process. Nonetheless, as most accountants stress their preference for quantitative rather than qualitative nfKPIs, some of these actors show tendencies of not being fully supportive of nfKPI reporting. Such tendencies are in line with findings of *Gray et al.* who show that the support of accountants for nonfinancial reporting could vary between being fully supportive to being defensive about the status quo (*Gray et al.* (1995), pp. 232-233). In combination with their central role in the preparation process, the level of involvement and attitudes of accountants could influence the nfKPI disclosure process (*Adams* (2002), p. 244).

Overall, the promotor model of preparation processes strongly resembles that of the innovation process. As shown above, contributions and powers of the promotor roles are similar to those of promotors in innovation processes. However, several **key differences** exist between both models. First, the contributions of know-how promotors vary strongly between the models. As the preparation process of nfKPIs follows a top-down approach, the process is initiated by power promotors rather than know-how promotors. Moreover, know-how promotors often solely act as providers of information. This difference strongly sets the role apart from know-how promotors in innovation processes, who take on an important role in initiating and developing an innovation. Nonetheless, some know-how promotors in preparation processes are responsible for selecting nfKPIs and writing the respective sections of the report. Second, the communication of the promotors with external and internal sources differs significantly. While the power and process promotors in preparation processes take on most communication inside or outside the company, know-how promotors in innovation processes communicate intensively with external actors such as suppliers or customers to develop an innovation (*Chakrabarti/Hauschildt* (1989), p. 166). Finally, the differences in promotor models reflect the nature of the overall tasks. The preparation process of nfKPIs for management report marks a periodically recurring process connected to clearly defined responsibilities and deadlines. Although innovation processes could also be standardized to a certain extent, these processes typically lack a recurring nature. This predictability of preparation processes supports the delegation of particular contributions and powers.

In summary, the findings across the case studies show the existence of promotors in the preparation processes of nfKPIs for management reports. Hence, an adapted promotor model provides a suitable framework for analyzing the participants of the process. The framework not only indicates potential roles and promotor constellations, but also highlights potential impacts of organizational structures and workflows on the disclosure of nfKPIs (*Osann* (2010), p. 259).

6.2.3 Factors influencing the preparation process design

After the previous sections have identified how preparation processes of nfKPIs for management reports are designed, potential **factors influencing the preparation process design** are identified and analyzed in the following. Drawing from the theoretical framework developed in in chapter 4 as well as findings in the previous literature, preparation processes appear to be influenced by several factors internal and external to the organization.

In line with **promotor theory**, supervisory boards mark internal parties opposing or supporting nfKPI disclosures. Moreover, the promotor model suggests communication channels between promotors and service providers in the form of consultants or auditors as well as between promotors and external management report users. Drawing from **institutional theory**, external pressures from regulators, standard setters and peer companies indicate external rules and norms which can potentially influence the preparation processes. While **extant research** commonly suggests these aforementioned influencing factors as well, researchers also argue that organizational characteristics such as firm size (e.g., *Hahn/Kühnen* (2013), p. 10) or report format (e.g., *Searcy/Buslovich* (2014), pp. 161-162) can influence preparation processes.

On the basis of the empirical findings of this study, this section discusses these **internal and external influencing factors** (Figure 6-49). These factors are used to explain differences and similarities in the design of preparation processes. Moreover, the empirical results are critically discussed in the light of previous findings in the literature and the theoretical framework of this study.

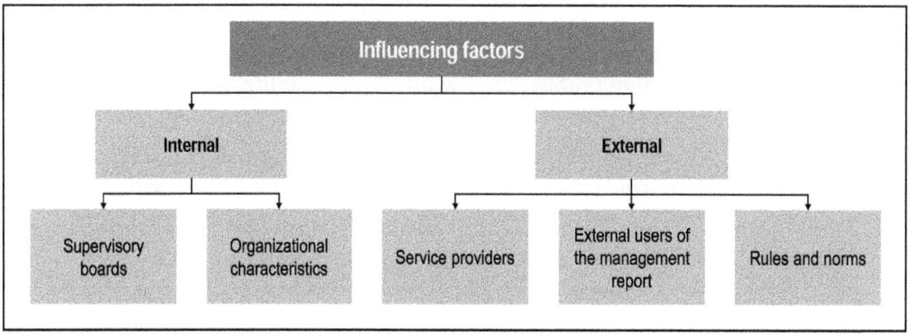

Figure 6-49: Overview of internal and external factors influencing the design of preparation processes

6.2.3.1 Internal factors

6.2.3.1.1 Supervisory boards

The promotor model identifies internal parties which communicate with promotors and which **oppose or support the preparation process of nfKPIs** (*Chakrabarti/Hauschildt* (1989), pp. 166-168). Supervisory boards, when reviewing the management report with regard to regulatory compliance, can act as potential opponents or supporters of nfKPI disclosures. Thus, the potential effects of these supervisory boards on the design of the process are considered in this analysis.

The **supervisory board** acts as an institutional representative of shareholders and exerts these shareholders' influence on the decision-making of the executive board (*Li et al.* (2008), p. 139). However, as part of the two-tier system, the supervisory board is separated from the executive board (*Dienes/Velte* (2016), pp. 2-4). Hence, supervisory board members have to overcome potential information asymmetries between themselves and the executive board to effectively monitor executive decision-making (*Bezemer et al.* (2014), p. 17). To do so, researchers expect supervisory boards to influence nfKPI reporting processes by for example questioning the disclosures or conducting audits (*Adams* (2002), p. 244; *Bezemer et al.* (2014), p. 26; *Dienes/Velte* (2016), pp. 4-6). Depending on the supervisory board's level of scrutiny or the consultations of the executive with regard to disclosures, the supervisory board could act as an opposing or supporting party, respectively.

Five of the seven case firms have a supervisory board. In almost all cases, supervisory boards are only involved in the review phase of the preparation process of nfKPIs. The boards act as "**gatekeepers**" by approving the management report for publication. In this context, particularly the executive board communicates with the supervisory board and answers to the supervisory board's questions regarding the nfKPIs in the report. However, the cases show that the supervisory boards rarely comment on nfKPIs. Moreover, supervisory boards delegate the audit of management reports to an audit committee. This audit committee, in turn, often bases its audit on the audit report of the case firm's statutory auditor:

> *"The supervisory board can delegate the audit, and they will most certainly delegate it to our statutory auditor." (HealthCo HMQR)*

These circumstances indicate a **low involvement** of the supervisory board in the preparation process of nfKPIs for the management report. Despite marking an important hurdle at the end of the preparation process, the few questions regarding nfKPIs seem to hardly influence the preparation process before and after the supervisory board review.

The case of PrintCo's nonfinancial statement marks an **exception**, as the audit committee of the supervisory board conducts the audit of the statement without the help of the statutory auditor:

> *"I mean there are supervisory board members that have been working together with this company for a considerable time. They know the company at least as well as the executive board. One or two of them actually know the firm longer than the present executive board. Therefore, we rely on the fact that they are actually close to the topic and that they know where the main areas of our business should be located." (PrintCo CFO)*

In PrintCo's case, the experience and expertise of the supervisory board could drive the willingness of the supervisory board to conduct the audit of the nonfinancial statement (*Dienes/Velte* (2016), pp. 5-6). Due to this willingness, PrintCo's supervisory board was consulted by the CFO and HEIR regarding the format and nfKPI disclosures of the nonfinancial statement. This consultation served to arrange an agreement regarding the nfKPI disclosures ahead of the final review, which simplified the nfKPI collection and the review of the nonfinancial statement. Thus, the board had a considerable influence on the design of the preparation process. While this influence might be driven by the experience of board members, the firm size and industry also play an important role for the supervisory board to become active in the preparation process. Due to the small firm size, the supervisory board has a good overview of the firm. Moreover, the statutory audit costs are high for a small firm like PrintCo. In the context of being supplier in an industry with a low visibility to external stakeholders, pressures for external audits of the nonfinancial statement are perceived to be low.

While the general results indicate that the role of the supervisory board in the preparation process provides low support for the **theoretical framework** of this study, findings from PrintCo's case demonstrate some support for this framework. From the perspective of **institutional theory**, the supervisory boards ideally drive coercive isomorphism by ensuring that the management reports comply with regulatory requirements. However, as the boards in most of the case firms appear to have little interest in nfKPIs and delegate the audit of nfKPIs, supervisory boards seem to be hardly involved in the nfKPI reporting processes. Thus, potential coercive pressures in these firms might be initiated by auditors rather than supervisory boards. Solely the supervisory board of PrintCo is involved early on in the selection of material nfKPIs and structuring the nonfinancial statement. While this involvement supports the notion of coercive pressures from supervisory boards, the higher board involvement is likely to be connected with other influencing factors such as firm size or industry visibility.

Regarding the perspective of **the promotor model**, the supervisory board ideally acts as a gatekeeper within the organization. According to this gatekeeper role, power promotors have to convince supervisory boards of the completeness and trustworthiness of the nfKPIs in the management report. However, in line with the findings regarding institutional theory, the support and opposition with regard to nfKPIs through supervisory boards appears to be rather low. Solely PrintCo provides an example in which the board supports the preparation of nfKPI disclosures by being involved in the preparation process at an early stage.

Nonetheless, these initial theoretical conclusions should be **differentiated**. On the one hand, it can be argued that supervisory boards tend to neither support nor oppose nfKPI disclosures because of a perceived low importance of the disclosures or the delegation of this gatekeeper role to auditors. On the other hand, it should be differentiated that the board's credible hierarchical potential might move preparers to consider potential demands by the supervisory board prior to the review and without direct interactions. Moreover, in accordance with the potential scope for discretion with regard to nfKPI disclosures, most supervisory boards might decide to waive their right to support or opposition to the disclosures if they consider the disclosures to be acceptable. Thus, supervisory boards tend to not make use of their high potential to influence the preparation process. Table 6-14 summarizes these theoretical findings.

	Institutional theory	Behavioral decision theory	Promotor model
Supervisory boards	Coercive isomorphism (low influence in general, higher for PrintCo) Higher influence possible due to hierarchical potential	-	Gatekeeper role (low), supportive role for nfKPI disclosures (PrintCo) Higher influence possible due to hierarchical potential

Table 6-14: Influence of supervisory boards on preparation processes

6.2.3.1.2 Organizational characteristics

In addition to supervisory boards, the preparation processes of nfKPIs also seem to be influenced by organizational characteristics. In line with extant literature and theory, the size and structure of the organization and the report format selected by the firm resemble important influencing factors.

Size and structure

In line with its role as a key sampling criterion and in accordance with previous findings, the **size of the organization** – measured by for example sales revenues or the number of employees – appears be an important driver for the design of the preparation process of nfKPIs. Extant research argues that the size of firms can be linked to higher visibility and stakeholder pressures (*Osann* (2010), pp. 257-258; *Hahn/Kühnen* (2013), p. 10), which could for example explain the involvement of more departments or stakeholders in their preparation processes (*Adams* (2002), p. 244; *Prado-Lorenzo et al.* (2009), p. 101). Moreover, researchers argue that larger firms can benefit from lower marginal costs of nonfinancial reporting (*Haddock* (2005), p. 801; *Baumann-Pauly et al.* (2013), pp. 700-702). In contrast to this, small firms might lack financial resources, time and personnel to establish structured and formalized reporting processes (*Borga et al.* (2009), pp. 164-165). Furthermore, researchers also argue that larger firms create higher amounts of nonfinancial data at higher frequencies (*Cohen et al.* (2012), pp. 78-81), potentially requiring firms to involve a large number of process participants in acquiring and reporting this data.

In line with these findings in the literature, the size of the **sample firms** appears to play an important role with regard to the design of the preparation process of nfKPIs for management reports. This factor is highlighted by several sample firms:

> *"This is probably caused by the size of our company, you know? For each topic, we have entire departments, whereas in a small firm one person would be responsible for everything." (HealthCo HMQR)*

> *"One should not overestimate this. This company is so small, you are so close to all topics that you know where the data is available and in how far it is available. Thus, you can collect it relatively quickly." (PrintCo HEIR)*

> *"Many things cannot be done, because this department is not that big. Therefore, I prepare the management report on my own. I don't know how it is done in large companies, how many people are involved there." (TechCo IRM)*

According to the findings, organizational size might affect the amount of data available, personnel involved and the use of formal structures. The **largest firms** HealthCo and ChemCo create significantly higher amounts of nfKPI data as compared to the smaller firms in the sample. Moreover, these firms also use formal and elaborate procedures to collect and report this data. In line with behavioral decision theory, this formalization indicates the use of standard practices and internal norms to deal with the amounts of data. These procedures and amounts of data also tend to require a higher number of participants necessary for handling the data when preparing a management report. In this context, large numbers of participants fulfil similar roles, which reflects role pluralities according to the promotor model. These results are in accordance extant research, which finds that the number of promotors is positively associated with firm size (*Folkerts* (2001), pp. 53-54) and that larger firms typically include more participants in their preparation processes (*Osann* (2010), pp. 219-220; *Searcy/Buslovich* (2014), pp. 161-162).

While **small firms** such as PrintCo or TechCo also create considerable amounts of nfKPI data, significantly less personnel collects and reports this data in comparison to large firms. These firms also use less standardized practices and recognize that although they apply norms such as internal guidelines, data is validated only to a limited extent. As small firms typically involve fewer participants in their preparation processes, individual participants in these firms often take on multiple roles (role combination). In these firms, participants such as coordinators and executives tend to contribute to the preparation process through multiple promotor roles, which can be explained by their overview over the nfKPI development in the firm and by the lack of personnel.

In addition to organizational size, the **overall structure of the organization** in the form of the number of hierarchies within a firm is also considered as influencing factor. The overall structure of the organization is argued to have an effect on both the design of the preparation process and resulting disclosures (*Fan/Ma* (2015)). While communication and decision-making processes in firms with rather flat **hierarchies** might be rather informal and lean, such processes can be more numerous and elaborate in firms with more hierarchical levels (*Tsai* (2002), p. 186):

> *"Internally, we of course have a number of feedback loops. Large company, many hierarchies." (HealthCo HMQR)*

> *"It reflects our company culture: hands on, very flat hierarchies. This results in low bureaucracy and no fixed deadlines. We don't have a specific department only tasked with writing the management report. It is basically woven into our day-to-day tasks." (FashCo HEIR)*

> *"You prepare the report, send it to your superior, then it is sent back to [IRM], who takes a look at it. [...] And management report texts have a much higher relevance as compared to website news. Of course you put effort in and for sure you ask two or three colleagues to read it over. But the coordination is not based on a large hierarchy." (TechCo HRM)*

From a **behavioral decision theory** perspective, the usage of hierarchies resembles a method for dealing with particular uncertainties regarding decision-making processes on nfKPI disclosures. In hierarchical firms such as HealthCo, ChemCo and AgCo, this way of dealing with uncertainties appears to be reflected in the hierarchical distances between particular promotors. Especially in the case of the power promotors, other promotors are situated several hierarchical levels beneath the executive board. Hence, the communication between these promotors traverses several levels of supervisors. While these hierarchies shall ensure that responsibilities regarding disclosure decisions are clearly assigned, these structures increase the time spent for communicating and preparing nfKPIs for management reports.

Overall, the organizational size and structure appear to be important influencing factors for the design of the preparation process. In combination with behavioral decision theory, it can be shown that these factors can influence standard practices and hierarchies connected to the preparation process. From a promotor model perspective, large or hierarchical firms tend to apply a higher extent of promotor structures while small or less hierarchical appear to combine promotor roles more often.

Report format

While research shows that **nfKPI reporting formats** such as standalone sustainability reports or nfKPI disclosures in annual reports can be associated with the extent of nfKPI disclosures (*Holder-Webb et al.* (2009), pp. 509-510; *Cohen et al.* (2012), pp. 75-78), much less is known about the effect of such reporting formats on the design of the preparation processes. The findings of this study indicate that reporting formats such as integrated reporting, separate sustainability reports or the type of nfKPIs reported can influence the preparation process.

Integrated reporting

In the case of **integrated reporting**, it is argued that coordinating and aligning both financial and nonfinancial information increases the complexity of the reporting process (*Thiele et al.* (2015), pp. 215-216). As the only firm in the sample with an integrated reporting format, HealthCo shows that integrating nonfinancial reporting into financial reporting processes strongly increase the coordination efforts of the process. The participants note that coordination efforts were particularly driven by the goal to harmonize financial and nonfinancial management reporting processes:

> *"The integration was also made easier for us because of our planning meetings a few years ago. It was really interesting, because we sat down in a small operative task force and created a dummy integrated report from our financial and nonfinancial reports. And it was great, because it combined the thinking schemes of the financial department and of our department, which led to a lot of discussions. But these discussions were all very interesting and never dismissive. They were discussions which showed the core idea of integrated thinking." (HealthCo MSD)*

> *"At that moment, when you merge two reporting formats, and this could also mean a combined report, I believe that it's essential that you try to harmonize the reporting by for example conducting a kick-off meeting. Otherwise you have just two documents in one, if you don't harmonize them. And the more integrated you are reporting, the more processual integrity you need to have." (HealthCo MQR)*

These statements and circumstances are supported by ChemCo, whose experts justify why their firm is not yet willing or able to harmonize processes to prepare an integrated report:

> *"And honestly, we don't see an added benefit. At the moment, we don't have the processes for a large integrated report. We have just talked about the fact that the availability of numbers and processes don't match, they are not harmonized. [...] We would have to put in a lot of effort and energy to be able to report in an integrated form." (ChemCo MSD)*

With regard to **behavioral decision theory**, the "harmonization" of financial and nonfinancial reporting processes mentioned in the statements affects the standard practices related to the preparation process. First, preparing both types of management report information likely increases the overall workload. Hence, preparers can be driven to restructure and streamline processes for both types of information to lower the overall workload. Second, including nfKPI reporting into the schedule of financial management reporting can increase the pressure on preparers to prepare nfKPIs in time and at sufficient quality and validity. Such challenges related to workload and pressure are in line with extant research (*Searcy/Buslovich* (2014), pp. 160-162).

In addition and in line with the **promotor model**, the integrated reporting approach seems to particularly affect the roles and collaboration of promotors. To cope with the increased workload, the sustainability department acts as a process promotor for the nfKPI chapter. Nonetheless, the team is fully involved in the entire preparation process and works closely together with the process promotors from the accounting department. Therefore, integrated reporting appears to affect the role plurality of the process promotor.

Separate sustainability reports

In addition to nfKPIs presented in their management report, several case firms prepare **separate sustainability reports** (ChemCo, FashCo, AgCo). While it is argued that such reports could be based on management reporting processes or could influence these processes (*Adams/Frost* (2008), p. 300; *Searcy/Buslovich* (2014), pp. 161-162), the case firms' management reporting processes appear to be largely **decoupled** from the preparation of the sustainability reports (*Tilt* (2006), pp. 9-10; *Laine* (2009), p. 1047). When preparing nfKPIs for their management reports, all three firms use only few common resources such as personnel or databases for both their preparation process for nfKPIs and the sustainability reporting processes. This decoupling appears to be driven by the diverging perspectives and goals of the reports. Moreover, the firms might not want their sustainability reporting to be assured with reasonable assurance. Overall, the cases point towards a limited motivation to harmonize sustainability reporting processes and management reporting processes.

In addition, this decoupling of the preparation processes can be driven by a lack of **top-management support** for combining preparation processes for nfKPIs and sustainability reporting processes (*Buhr* (2002), pp. 32-33; *Frost et al.* (2012), pp. 218-223; *Bouten/Everaert* (2015), pp. 39-40). Interview partners from ChemCo particularly highlight the potential role of top-management support for closer aligning reporting processes:

> *"And we won't go and say: 'We are going to prepare an integrated report, so that the executives think in an integrated way.' That is not going to happen. Someone from the executive board would have to appear and say: 'Alright, I want this to happen!'" (ChemCo HER)*

Overall, publishing a separate sustainability report appears to have a low influence on preparation processes of nfKPIs. With regard to the promotor model, firms with separate sustainability reports show a certain separation between promotor structures for the preparation of the management report and the sustainability report. However, the decoupling and lack of top-management support stand in contrast to the fact that all three case firms have established sustainability departments. Therefore, the **institutionalization of sustainability** in these firms appears to affect the preparation process of nfKPIs for management reports only to a low degree.

Type of nfKPIs

Another factor related to reporting formats is the **type of nfKPIs** reported. The preparation processes of quantitative nfKPIs, nonfinancial goals, forward-looking nfKPIs and most important nfKPIs appear to be more elaborate as compared to the preparation of qualitative nfKPIs.

The cases show that **quantitative nfKPIs** appear to increase the effort necessary for measuring, validating and documenting these types of indicators. Moreover, the firms note increased auditing procedures for this type of information:

> *"You have hardly any capacities at the sites for providing the data. The validation is very, very complex, very time intensive, very extensive. [...] The time horizon is really, really short and there is no room for unexpected issues. And that is what drives this pressure and what proves a big challenge." (HealthCo DBM)*

"I mean describing particular projects is relatively easy. In contrast, to measure particular quantitative figures and to describe these is connected to significantly higher efforts. You have to update them, you have to check that they are really correct, they have to be auditable. And all of this is much more complex." (LogCo HA)

"Regarding quantitative figures, I find it very, very important, that you have clear requirements about how figures have to be measured. A strict and stringent reporting process as the one used for financial KPIs. Auditing, well, that is complicated." (TechCo IRM)

Similarly, firms reporting **nonfinancial goals or forward-looking nfKPIs** experience high effects on reporting processes with regard to, for example, their materiality analysis or measurement of nfKPIs. In HealthCo's case, nonfinancial goals are derived and discussed on the basis of the materiality analysis and are approved by the executive board. Each nonfinancial goal has to be connected to a management system, which allows the firm to further ground nfKPIs in decision-making processes. Similar to this, ChemCo measures its **most important nfKPIs** on a monthly or quarterly basis, sets goals and discusses the goals and performance in the executive and supervisory boards. Moreover, the executives are incentivized with these goals and provide forecasts for these particular nfKPIs in the management report. Hence, these types of nfKPI reporting appear to require elaborate preparation processes.

In contrast to these types of extensive reporting, TechCo deliberately reports mostly **qualitative nfKPIs**. While quantitative information and nfKPI databases are used for internal reporting, the nfKPIs in TechCo's management report are "heavily slimmed down and kept on a rather generic level" (*TechCo HDBM*) to provide an overview rather than detailed analyses of nfKPIs. Restrictive disclosures are justified by internal criteria, namely that nfKPIs should not risk competitive advantages or shed a negative light on TechCo. Similarly, the report does not provide disclosures on nonfinancial goals. While TechCo sets and monitors nonfinancial goals internally, the CFO justifies a decision against their disclosure in the management report by pointing towards difficulties related to their reliability and sensitivity:

"Of course I have to say that we have difficulties with reporting quantitative statements. Qualitative is easier. [Laughter] Quantitative is more difficult, and particularly KPIs that are forward-looking are a challenge. And we are very careful in this regard. [...] It's a challenge to plan these things reliably, for example if you want to reach a particular quality level or other forecasts. [...] We are of course quite careful with these [nonfinancial goals], because we don't have to disclose them. Why should I commit myself to something that is difficult in our situation and which does not matter anyway. I mean which matters in the sense of whether or not our management report is signed off by our auditor. I don't have to make life extra hard for myself." (TechCo CFO)

Overall, potential effects of the type of nfKPIs on the design of preparation processes are in line with the theoretical framework of this study. From a **behavioral decision theory** perspective, the type of nfKPIs can influence the standard practices related to the preparation process. In HealthCo's case, for example, the reporting on nonfinancial goals increases the need for an elaborate measurement and validation of nfKPIs. To ensure timely and valid data, preparers can adapt standard practices such as formal materiality analysis criteria or frequent measurement of nfKPIs. Moreover, the type of nfKPIs also appears to affect **promotor structures**. In terms of promotor structures for quantitative and forward-looking nfKPI reporting, promotor structures appear to be more elaborate as compared to firms with qualitative nfKPI reporting. This can be explained by the need to involve more staff in the measurement and validation to ensure the availability and quality of the former type of information.

In summary, the largest effects of reporting formats on the design of preparation processes appear to be caused by integrated reports. The preparation processes of firms with separate sustainability reports indicate that the preparation of both reports seems to be mostly decoupled. Hence, the effect of such reports appears to be rather low. Finally, particularly the reporting on quantitative nfKPIs, nonfinancial goals, forward-looking nfKPIs and most important nfKPIs appears to have a strong effect on the preparation processes. The cases also show that small or private firms appear to avoid such disclosures, in part to avoid costly and elaborate preparation processes.

Summarizing the **influence of organizational characteristics** on the preparation process of nfKPIs for management reports, particularly organizational size and structure appear to be important influencing factors of the design of preparation processes. Moreover, integrated reporting formats and certain types of nfKPI reporting seem to affect the process design. Table 6-15 summarizes the theoretical discussions.

6.2.3.2 External factors

6.2.3.2.1 Service providers

Service providers involved in the preparation process are external advisors who "have an institutional reason for being nearby" (e.g., auditors) or who "are consulted on an ad hoc basis" (e.g., lectors or consultants) (*Gibbins et al.* (1990), p. 132). Although service providers show varying levels of involvement in the preparation process, they typically participate in the process directly. The following section analyzes the most important service providers involved in the preparation processes of the case firms: auditors, consultants and lectors.

Auditors

Prior research shows that **auditors** can take an important role in the preparation process of nfKPIs for management reports (*Gibbins et al.* (2001), pp. 537-539; *Edgley et al.* (2015), pp. 10-11). However, research is inconclusive regarding the level of involvement of auditors in the preparation process. While some studies indicate a high involvement in the preparation process (*O'Dwyer* (2011), pp. 1247-1248), others detect a rather low involvement of auditors (*Knauer/Wömpener* (2011), p. 196; *Kaspersen/Johansen* (2016), p. 733). On the basis of the present case studies and extant research, the roles of auditors as gatekeepers and change agents in the preparation process can be identified. Moreover, the influence of these roles on the design of the preparation process appears to be moderated by the comprehensiveness of the audit or auditor expertise. Figure 6-50 summarizes these characteristics of auditor roles, which are analyzed in the following.

	Institutional theory	Behavioral decision theory	Promotor model
Organizational size	-	Establishing standard practices and internal norms (large firms)	High number of process participants and role pluralities (large firms), role combinations (small firms)
Organizational structure	-	Hierarchical levels clarify responsibilities but increase preparation time (hierarchical firms)	Higher extent of promotor structures and communication between participants (hierarchical firms), role combinations (firms with flat hierarchies)
Reporting format			
Integrated reporting	-	Establishing standard practices to address workload and time pressure	Process promotor role of sustainability department
Separate sustainability reports	-	-	Decoupling of promotor structures between processes and potential lack of executive support
Type of nfKPIs	-	Establishing standard practices (materiality analysis, measurement, validation) for quantitative nfKPIs, nonfinancial goals, forward-looking nfKPIs and most important nfKPIs	More elaborate promotor structures for quantitative nfKPIs, nonfinancial goals, forward-looking nfKPIs and most important nfKPIs

Table 6-15: Influence of organizational characteristics on preparation processes

Gatekeepers

In their role as **gatekeepers**, auditors aim to ensure the "quality and integrity" of nonfinancial information for the stakeholders of the management report (*Wallman* (1995), p. 82). The results indicate that the gatekeeper role is reflected in the auditors' tasks of auditing nfKPI disclosures and informing their clients regarding regulatory changes.

With regard to their tasks of **auditing the nfKPIs**, auditors examine preparation procedures, documentation and the management report draft. However, the effect of auditor involvement on the preparation process is strongly influenced by the moderating factor of the audit comprehensiveness. In addition to this and consistent with findings in the literature regarding negotiations between auditors and clients (*Gibbins et al.* (2001), pp. 537-539; *Edgley et al.* (2015), p. 14), the auditors engage in client discussions to varying degrees. While some auditors engage in few discussions with their clients (LogCo, AgCo), others take a more active position (HealthCo):

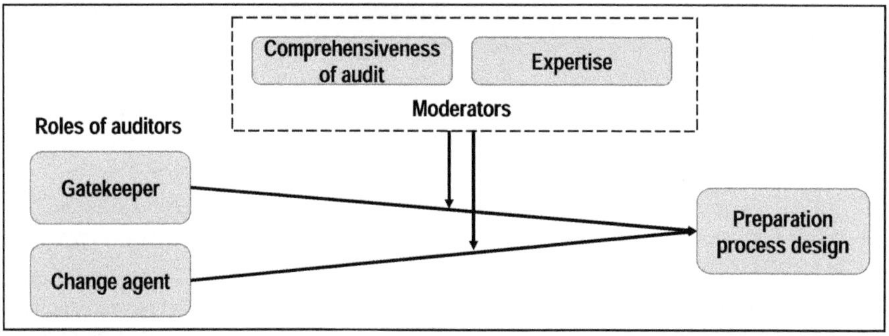

Figure 6-50: Characteristics of auditors in the preparation process

"The materiality and traceability are often discussed. A topic which we also often discuss is the relevance of the nonfinancial goals for the group management. We have a table with goals in our report. And if they are relevant for the group management, they also have to be forecasted. That is a very popular topic. We say: 'No it's not relevant for the management of the group.'" (HealthCo HMQR)

"There are some topics, for which the auditor suggests something. But in this case, it is limited to them providing us with a section title. They would suggest, that we should report something on the environment or IT. It would be less about them checking for particular types of information, as it is done in other areas." (LogCo CFO)

"Regarding nonfinancial KPIs, we rarely receive feedback from our auditors. Either it would be a wrong comma or that some statements should be a little bit more precise. But not the KPIs themselves. These are already 100% waterproof." (AgCo HER)

These differences in engagement indicate that while auditors aim for ensuring the compliance of disclosures with regulation, the interest of auditors with regard to nfKPIs can vary. This varying interest can reflect in the intensity of discussions between auditors and clients depending on the audit comprehensiveness, as auditors who are highly involved in the audit of preparation procedures or nfKPI databases are likely to find and discuss mistakes or opportunities for changes. Moreover, auditors might also engage in discussions out of commercial interests to deepen audit engagements.

Moreover, auditors act as a mouthpiece for **regulatory changes**. All auditors of the case firms inform the preparers regarding regulatory changes. While large firms such as HealthCo and ChemCo typically monitor regulatory developments, small and private firms appear to be more dependent on notifications and checklists provided by the auditors. These circumstances indicate a more important role of auditors with regard to regulatory compliance in private firms:

"I remember that [HealthCo's auditor] had checklists for the sustainability topics. And now we have met with them upfront to discuss the CSR-RUG. We had extensive meetings. They have also prepared a gap analysis regarding the matters we have not already

> *included. We always try to involve the auditors as early as possible." (HealthCo HMQR)*
>
> *"We are informed about major regulatory changes ahead of the preparation process. This way, we are informed about GAS 20 or other changes for which we have to provide the necessary information. We receive the notice in the fall so that we can incorporate this. Therefore, we don't forget important topics." (LogCo HA)*
>
> *"We of course have to check for regulatory changes. This is checked ahead of the process, but it is of course a cooperation with the auditors. They typically monitor these changes more closely than us." (FashCo MEIR)*

From an **institutional theory perspective**, the gatekeeper role of auditors can be seen as a driver for coercive isomorphism (*Baker et al.* (2014), p. 377). Through addressing and enforcing regulatory changes in the preparation processes of nfKPIs for management reports, the auditors safeguard their clients' compliance with regulation. Therefore, auditors particularly affect the preparation and review criteria of the preparation process. However, the strength of this coercive pressure varies strongly between the case firms. While coercive pressures might be smaller for firms which monitor regulatory changes themselves (HealthCo, ChemCo), these pressures induced by auditors might be stronger for smaller or private firms. Nonetheless, the effect of these pressures can also be moderated by other factors such as audit comprehensiveness.

Concerning the perspective of the **promotor model**, the gatekeeper role of auditors reflects an external opposing party. Thus, promotors within the firm try to convince auditors of the correctness of their nfKPI reporting. While all firms engage in this type of communication, the intensity of the opposition varies between the case firms. In HealthCo's case, auditors scrutinize the truthfulness of the importance of nfKPI goals for the management of the firm. In addition to their task to ensure the quality and integrity of nfKPIs, this scrutiny might also be driven by commercial interests of the auditors to extend the audit towards forward-looking reporting processes. In the case of smaller and private case firms, the audit comprehensiveness as a moderating factor might particularly influence the involvement and interest of the auditor with regard to the nfKPI audit.

Change agent

In addition to providing audit services, auditors can also offer consulting services to their clients (*Shockley* (1981), pp. 787-789). Auditors justify this through their insights into data systems and preparation processes. Using this access, auditors can act as **change agents** by consulting their clients on improving data systems or reporting processes (*Power* (2003), pp. 188-189; *Park/Brorson* (2005), pp. 1099-1100; *O'Dwyer* (2011), pp. 1247-1248; *Kaspersen/Johansen* (2016), p. 747).

In terms of data systems, auditors can support their clients in **improving the auditability of data systems** which might result in a better quality and accuracy of data (*Clausen/Loew* (2005), pp. 75-76; *O'Dwyer* (2011), pp. 1246-1248). In the case firms, auditors assert this influence only to a limited degree. As partially evident in the case of the two large public firms, the influence is likely to be particularly driven by audit comprehensiveness with regard to the nfKPI reporting systems. Due to their low involvement in auditing nfKPI data systems in other case firms, auditors seem to have few opportunities to justify additional consulting services:

> *"The auditors have benchmarked others which they see in this area. And they have always told us, that we are very well-positioned in this respect. [...] But find me an auditor who does not find anything. They always find something, which we can improve. [Laughter]" (HealthCo DBM)*

> *"After the site-audits, we receive a report which states what we could improve, but also with respect to our meetings or the content of the report. And after evaluating this, we look at the suggestions again and decide on which of these we can, want to or have to implement." (ChemCo HSC)*

Concerning the **improvement of reporting processes**, the cases show a similar involvement of auditors. While the statutory auditors of the case firms typically provide their clients with suggestions for improvements, their influence on the preparation processes appears to be limited:

> *"You get a note from the auditors, if they find something during the audit process, for example when a relevant process for the nonfinancial KPIs is incorrect. Then you have to take something out or reword it. We always ask for a big Excel-sheet with every line of text in it. This states whether proof documents were handed in, if they were sufficient or if the wording needs to be changed. [...] And then, at the end of the process, we receive notes [...] on where we have to improve." (HealthCo MSD)*

> *"Externally, we had some changes because the IDW and others have mandated more topics for the auditors. Then we added some report sections. But internally, I believe, we have had little changes." (LogCo CFO)*

Similar to the auditability of data systems, auditors of smaller or private case firms appear to be less involved in the audit of preparation processes. Hence, they seem to have less opportunities for convincing their clients to improve such preparation processes. Nonetheless, the influence of auditors might be moderated by the audit comprehensiveness.

From the point of view of **institutional theory**, the change agent role of auditors in the preparation processes indicates mimetic isomorphism. Through the audit firm's exposure to the reporting processes of other companies, their suggestions help align their client's data systems or reporting processes with those of other clients. However, in the context of this study, this effect appears to be rather low. While large public firms note that auditors benchmark their processes and provide recommendations, small and private firms appear to be largely unaffected by auditor recommendations regarding process improvements. Thus, other influencing factors such as size also appear to determine the influence of the auditors.

From a **behavioral decision theory** perspective, auditors might be involved in aligning data systems and reporting processes to establish standard practices. These practices in turn decrease uncertainties with regard to disclosure decision. Similar to mimetic isomorphism, this effect appears to be rather low in the case firms. Concerning the **promotor model**, the involvement of auditors as change agents might influence the tasks and communication of the promotors. Through changing data systems and reporting processes, know-how and process promotors have to fulfill other tasks to measure, collect and verbalize relevant nfKPIs. However, these effects seem to be apparent only in larger public firms. Overall, the change agent role of auditors appears to be rather limited. Furthermore, effects occurring in the case firms might be driven by moderating factors such as audit comprehensiveness.

Audit comprehensiveness as a moderator

While the management reports of all case firms are audited with reasonable assurance, the **audit comprehensiveness** within the preparation processes varies significantly. Particularly in the cases of HealthCo and ChemCo, the auditors conduct audits of data-systems, preparation process workflows and documentation. Substantiating previous findings in the literature (*Clausen/Loew* (2005), pp. 75-76), the two case firms note that this involvement of the auditors in the preparation process might – directly or indirectly – increase the quality of the nfKPIs:

> *"For the auditors, reasonable assurance means much, much higher documentation requirements at the sites, much more detailed processes at the sites which of course has an effect on the quality and on everything in the end." (HealthCo DBM)*

> *"Through raising this awareness we want to be able to include more of those KPIs in the management report, which we would like to have in there. We also want to achieve that they are available earlier and with a quality that is high enough for the audit at reasonable assurance, which is necessary for the management report." (ChemCo HER)*

Concerning the effect of audit comprehensiveness on the **quality of the nfKPIs**, the statutory auditors' high documentation requirements regarding nfKPI disclosures and measurement processes can motivate the HealthCo and ChemCo to increase the validity and availability of the data. However, these effects appear to be interlinked with the influencing factor of reporting formats. Due to their extensive nfKPI reporting, the preparers themselves already aim to ensure both a high reporting quality and sufficient documentation for these nfKPIs to use these nfKPIs for the internal management system.

In addition to higher documentation requirements related to a high audit comprehensiveness, auditors are typically engaged at an earlier stage of the processes through site-audits or by receiving early drafts. This engagement indicates a **higher involvement** of auditors in the process, which can result in more interactions between auditors and preparers. These interactions can increase the influence of auditors in their gatekeeper or change agent roles (*O'Dwyer* (2011), pp. 42-43). These effects of audit comprehensiveness can be contrasted to the audit of TechCo's measurement processes. As the firm uses quantitative nfKPIs on an operative level and does not engage auditors in site-audits, the firm is satisfied with a lower level of data validation. Hence, the effects of auditors as change agents are low in this case:

> *"He [the auditor] would also have no chance. He would also not be able to check whether the water usage in India has been measured correctly. There is no way he could audit that. So it's just about what do you derive from the data internally. All the way to internal pricing. You are not hurting anyone from outside the company. But you still want to use valid data." (TechCo HDBM)*

Similarly, in all case firms except HealthCo and ChemCo, auditors mostly concern themselves with auditing the documentation of nfKPIs. This can be explained by the firms **predominantly disclosing qualitative nfKPIs**. Moreover, some firms explain a lower audit comprehensiveness by the higher interest of auditors in quantitative or financial measures disclosed in the management report:

> *"If you write something on supplier relationships, then this is based on some kind of data source which is then attached to the draft. Through this, the auditor can have a look, if the input is in line with the text." (FashCo HEIR)*

> *"I think that because we don't have a lot of metrics in there, they [the auditors] probably don't take such a hard look at it. [...] Off and on, particularly when metrics appear in the report, we have to document them. But I think it lies in the nature of the audit that auditors have to check off the metrics, and we don't have many in there." (TechCo IRM)*

In this context, auditors occasionally **advise** their clients to include more quantitative measures in their reports. While this involvement indicates evidence for the role of auditors as change agents, the assertiveness of auditors in this regard is typically low. This non-compliance is particularly present in small or private firms. It provides an indicator for the importance of the firms' reporting goals and the rather low interest of auditors in the audit of nfKPIs in comparison to other parts of the management report:

> *"In the beginning, we didn't write enough. We were advised to include indicators or to at least explain why we didn't have an indicator. Then they said: 'Can't you have a look at whether you have indicators here or there?'" (PrintCo HEIR)*

> *"We always discuss the extent, that we write too much. That we should include some metrics here and there, if possible. These are always points of friction. But they are no big deal for them [the auditors]. They check it off their lists and then it's done. That's my feeling: 'They have written something, it's not nonsense, that's it.'" (TechCo CFO)*

Overall, a high audit comprehensiveness appears to increase the interaction between **promotors** and auditors. Such interactions might indicate a higher likeliness of promotors being influenced by auditors as change agents. Conversely, smaller and private firms with lower audit comprehensiveness show that this influence appears to be rather low. Furthermore, the audit comprehensiveness might also increase isomorphic behavior suggested by **institutional theory**. By improving the auditability and validity of nfKPI data, auditors support preparers in being more compliant with extant regulations. While such coercive isomorphism becomes apparent in larger case firms, auditors of smaller case firms with lower audit comprehensiveness seem to be less assertive with regard to providing more quantitative nfKPIs. While the cases indicate a potential link between audit comprehensiveness and these influences, the effects of audit comprehensiveness might also be driven by other factors such as the reporting format or size of the firm.

Auditor expertise as a moderator

Another moderator driving auditor effects is the **expertise** of the auditor. The expertise of auditors is linked to their knowledge of auditing and accounting, industry or client specialization, general business knowledge and their general problem-solving skills (*Bonner/Lewis*

(1990), pp. 5-6). In the context of auditing nfKPI disclosures, it becomes evident that auditors potentially need to rely more on audit skills related to nonfinancial reporting as compared to financial accounting. Similar to findings in the literature (*Gibbins et al.* (2001), p. 558), auditors with specific expertise in the audit of nfKPIs appear to be more involved in the preparation process. However, such auditors with high nfKPI auditing experience seem to be involved only in cases with high audit comprehensiveness. This becomes evident in the nfKPI preparation processes of HealthCo and ChemCo, whose processes are audited by specialized sustainability auditors. All other firms show an involvement of traditional financial auditors with less expertise in auditing nfKPIs:

> *"We have our own assurance team, which is from [HealthCo's audit firm], but the assurance for our nonfinancial parts has particular contact persons, who are in constant, continuous contact with the main auditor team. One team has the topical knowledge, the other the management report knowledge. However, at [HealthCo's audit firm] no one has typically worked in the sustainability sector. Thus, all of them have relatively good knowledge of the processes and the management report." (HealthCo MSD)*

> *"The auditors at [ChemCo's audit firm] are organized in such a way that the sustainability data is audited by a sustainability team in accordance with GRI and at limited assurance. These colleagues also audit the management report, with reasonable assurance." (ChemCo MQR)*

> *"For auditors, let's not fool ourselves, they have a very different focus: auditing profit and loss statements or financial statements. But we might have to dismiss the thought that they are good at auditing nonfinancial KPIs." (FashCo CFO)*

Due to a connection between auditor expertise and audit comprehensiveness as well as firm size, it is difficult to determine the **effects of auditor expertise** in the case studies. It can be argued that specialized, experienced auditors are more likely to provide better assurance for the quality and integrity of the information (gatekeeper role) or provide better feedback (change agent role). However, specialized sustainability auditors might lack the necessary knowledge of auditing nfKPIs with reasonable assurance as well as interlinkages of this information with other management report information. In combination with cost-benefit considerations, particularly small firms without separate sustainability reports might prefer regular statutory auditors over specialized sustainability auditors. Thus, effects of auditor expertise on the preparation processes of nfKPIs should be considered critically in combination with other influencing factors such as audit comprehensiveness or firm size.

While the literature notes the importance of **auditor tenure** as a part of the expertise of an auditor (*Shockley* (1981); *Gibbins et al.* (2001), pp. 540-541), this characteristic appears to have a low impact on the preparation processes of the case firms. This can be associated to the fact that most case firms have not changed their audit firm in recent years. These firms note that their auditors are well-integrated in their preparation processes. Solely HealthCo – which has recently changed its auditors – highlights potential frictions with regard to the coordination and focus of their new audit firm:

> *"And then you have to take a look at the assurance, particularly with the new [IDW] EPS 350 and so forth. Which does not become easier, if you have switched audit firms,*

like we have. [...] Because the later they audit the processes, the harder it will get if they say that they don't like something which [the previous audit-firm of HealthCo] would have agreed with." (HealthCo MSD)

"We have a close relationship with [LogCo's audit firm]. We have a situation in which we have been working with the same auditor for many, many years. We are not listed, thus we do not need to rotate auditors. In so far, this is a grown process, where we know a lot of topics from our history. And we also have fixed contact persons." (LogCo CFO)

As shown in HealthCo's case, a change in auditor likely drives the scrutiny of the auditors, which supports the gatekeeper role. From an **institutional theory** perspective, such changes can increase coercive isomorphism in the firms. In contrast to the case of LogCo, the short audit tenure of HealthCo's auditors also shows that the low experience of the audit firm with HealthCo can be problematic in the preparation process. Due to the low expertise of the auditors with regard to the firm and its processes, the **promotors** of the case firm potentially have more interactions with the auditors. These interactions might increase the resources applied for the preparation and lead to more discussions with auditors in their roles as gatekeepers and opposing parties. Moreover, as pointed out by LogCo's CFO, the audit tenure can be influenced by other factors such as the mandatory auditor rotation for listed firms.

Overall, audit comprehensiveness and auditor expertise can be seen as moderators for the effect of the auditors on the preparation process of nfKPIs for management reports. While audit comprehensiveness appears to be the factor with the highest influence on preparation processes, the auditor expertise appears to influence preparation processes to a lower degree. Nonetheless, this factor should be considered in combination with audit comprehensiveness and other influencing factors such as the reporting format and firm size.

Consultants

In addition to auditors, two case firms use **consultants** as service providers to improve their nfKPI reporting. While research suggests a variety of consulting services that can be used for preparation processes (*Gibbins et al.* (1990), pp. 132-133), HealthCo and ChemCo use specific GRI consultants. HealthCo uses such consultants to improve and validate their selection of GRI indicators. At ChemCo, these consultants check the alignment of the management report and the sustainability report in terms of sustainability information:

"We work with an agency, which supports us with the GRI validation. They send a GRI expert who checks that we have included everything. And where we are missing something. [...] Because we must need someone who is our watchdog." (HealthCo MSD)

"There is this preliminary meeting in which we are informed on the yearly changes, so that we can adjust the process to the requirements of GRI. We also have a consultant, who supports us in this. [...] And then we write the texts for the individual chapters: workplace safety, plant safety or environment. And we discuss these with the consultant and [ChemCo's auditor]." (ChemCo HSC)

From a **theoretical** point of view, these consultants might drive normative isomorphic behavior to comply with international sustainability reporting norms in the form of the GRI. However, the case firms show that the involvement of the consultants in the preparation process is rather technical and limited to the validation of the indicators and texts. Hence, their role cannot be seen as a driving force of isomorphism but rather as a supporting actor for other driving forces such as voluntary reporting frameworks. In this regard, GRI consultants might fulfil a gatekeeper role similar to statutory auditors. In addition to driving normative isomorphism as a part of this role, GRI consultants might be involved as an opposing party towards the promotors involved in the preparation. Nonetheless, the effects of this role on the preparation process appear to be weaker than for statutory auditors. This can be explained by the voluntary nature of GRI reporting in HealthCo's case and by the lower role of GRI compliance in the management report of ChemCo as compared to their sustainability report.

Lectors

Some case firms also use **lectors** as service providers to improve the understandability and readability of their management reports. HealthCo uses several lector services with regard to the structure and wording of their integrated report. Structural changes to their report are typically prepared by creating a new version of a previous report, which are discussed and improved internally before implementing major changes on the overall report. Although the firm has also used external lectors to align the wording of the report, the firm now uses an internal lector to safeguard that the tonality and wording of the report are in line with the communication strategy of the firm. In TechCo's case, the firm includes an experienced lector in their preparation process to align the wording and to receive hints on current reporting trends:

> *"Then, in the course of this summer, we had an agency create a dummy report of 2016. We talked to them about the structure, but they had to make suggestions from an external perspective. Moreover, they also have expert knowledge, because they are from the areas of management reporting and sustainability reporting. Their suggestions were then discussed up to the executive board." (HealthCo MSD)*

> *"And this year, we have something new, because a colleague from communications, who writes speeches, reviews the texts to ensure that the language style is not too different because of the number of people working on the report – including ourselves. To make it seem aligned. We have had an agency, which has done this for us. But you could notice that they are not involved in the company. Thus, we still needed to change the text in a couple of places." (HealthCo MSD)*

> *"We have an experienced lector who looks at the wording. He might notice something and say that something needs to be explained in more detail. [...] Naturally, the lector gives us hints on reporting trends and what this or that firm is reporting." (TechCo IRM)*

From a **theoretical perspective**, lectors might act as drivers for mimetic isomorphism by helping their clients align their nfKPI reporting with that of other firms. While the cases indicate that this can be the case for disclosures of nfKPIs, these forces do not significantly influence the design of the preparation process. Particularly HealthCo uses the services to improve the wording of the report. While the lector of TechCo provides hints on reporting topics, external reporting trends also observed by the IRM and CFO. Therefore, lectors seem to have low influence on the preparation process of nfKPIs for management reports.

In summary, auditors appear to be those service providers with the largest potential effect on the preparation process of nfKPIs for management reports. While their effects tend to be highest for their role as gatekeepers, some firms also show an influence of these actors as change agents for their preparation processes. As indicated by the results, the coercive and mimetic effects and the role as opposing party for promotors appears to be positively associated with the audit comprehensiveness and to a lower extent with other moderators such as auditor expertise. Similar to auditors, the largest two firms use GRI consultants as gatekeepers for their nfKPI disclosures, albeit with a lower effect on preparation processes as compared to auditors. Finally, lectors appear to affect nfKPI disclosures while exerting little influence on the preparation process of nfKPIs. Table 6-16 summarizes the influence of service providers on preparation processes discussed in this section.

	Institutional theory	Behavioral decision theory	Promotor model
Auditors	Coercive isomorphism (gatekeeper role rather low for most firms, higher for small or private firms and auditors with less tenure) Mimetic isomorphism (change agent role low for most firms, higher for firms with extensive nfKPI reporting)	Standard practices (low influence)	External opposing party (influence depending on audit comprehensiveness) Interactions of auditors and promotors can increase with higher audit comprehensiveness and lower auditor tenure
Consultants	Normative isomorphism (limited to validation and selection of nfKPIs, connected to application of voluntary reporting frameworks)	-	Opposing party to nfKPI disclosures (weaker influence as compared to auditors)
Lectors	Mimetic isomorphism (low influence)	-	-

Table 6-16: Influence of service providers on preparation processes

6.2.3.2.2 External users of the management report

In contrast to private companies, public companies are likely to face both higher reporting requirements from stock-exchanges and more external pressures from management report users due to higher visibility (*Haddock* (2005), p. 803; *Oliveira et al.* (2010), p. 581; *Husillos et al.* (2011), pp. 205-206; *Hope et al.* (2013), p. 1718). Researchers regularly find that pressures from **external users of the management report** affect disclosure decision processes (*Husillos et al.* (2011), pp. 203-205; *Contrafatto* (2014), pp. 423-424; *Bouten/Everaert*

(2015), p. 27). In addition to such pressures (*outside-in*), some firms actively address their stakeholders (*inside-out*) to legitimize or present their business in a favorable manner (*Maas et al.* (2016), pp. 239-240). Hence, participants of preparation processes might be challenged by adequately addressing both individual stakeholder demands and firm internal reporting goals in the preparation process of management reports:

> *"This is another exciting process: how we deal with this tension between the mass demands from outside and our reporting processes. In this case, mass does not mean mass stakeholders but rather relevant stakeholders, who become more and more detailed in their questions and in the indicators which they throw at you." (HealthCo MSD)*

The results show that a variety of **key external users of the management reports** exist (Figure 6-51), which vary with regard to their influence on the preparation process: equity capital providers, other capital market participants, debt capital providers and other key external stakeholders. This section sheds light on the relationship between pressures from these management report users and the preparation process of nfKPIs.

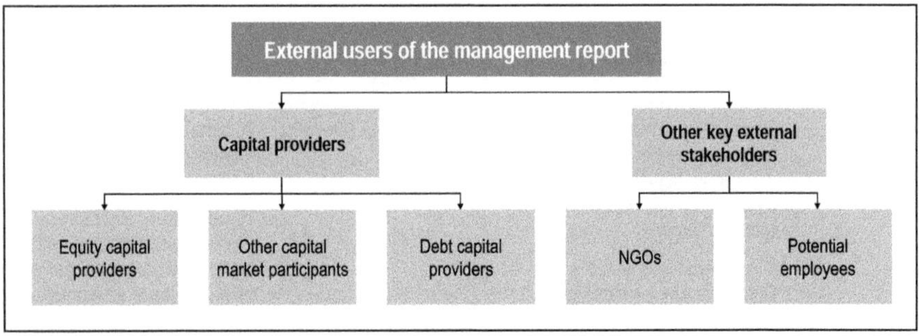

Figure 6-51: Overview of key external users of management reports

Equity capital providers

For all case firms, **equity capital providers** are important management report users. These stakeholders are either directly or indirectly involved in different stages of the preparation process. Hence, providers of equity capital of listed and non-listed firms can influence the design of the preparation process through direct or indirect involvement with regard to for example the materiality criteria, reporting deadlines or review criteria, as indicated by the case firms.

As the only firm with **direct involvement** of equity capital providers in the preparation process, HealthCo is subject to several specific influences from its shareholders. With shareholders being part of the stakeholder survey to determine material nfKPIs, HealthCo directly includes their demands when selecting relevant indicators. Moreover, in the course of the ongoing stakeholder communication, the availability of relevant information is continuously checked and improved to meet the demands of these users. By being able to voice demands for particular nfKPIs, shareholders have a considerable influence on the selection of HealthCo's material nfKPIs which drives the resulting measurement of these nfKPIs.

Furthermore, the IR department takes on an indirect capital-market perspective when reviewing the report:

> *"There are situations in which the sustainability colleagues say: 'It's important to us to have a particular level of detail for this KPI, because we are well-positioned in this regard in comparison to other companies.' And then it's very well possible that we answer from our investor relations perspective: 'Yes, we understand, this is a very good KPI and it is important from the point of the feedback you receive or the guidelines. But an investor would not be interested in this,' this is a little exaggerated, 'rather provide the business case for the KPI you have explained in five sentences.'" (HealthCo IRM)*

While the other case firms involve equity capital providers only **indirectly**, the results demonstrate that this indirect involvement also influences the preparation process to some extent. In contrast to a direct involvement, the firms incorporate stakeholder demands in their preparation processes to a lower degree. In most firms, these demands are considered in the materiality analysis or the review of the draft by indirectly taking on an investor or owner perspective. However, most firms highlight that equity capital providers show low interest in the nfKPI reporting in the management report. Nonetheless, equity capital providers see nfKPIs as additional information on the course of business of which they are already informed. Particularly in the case of LogCo and FashCo, which are not registered as stock corporations, the firms inform their owners through different communication channels:

> *"For our owners, this part here is useless decoration. [Laughter] They don't need it at all. And they are not that interested in it. But this doesn't mean that they are not interested in these topics. But they have very different information channels and a totally different distance as compared to shareholders in a listed company." (LogCo CFO)*

> *"This is really just the reporting to fulfil the requirements. Internally, we have of course different reporting media which we use to inform our owners or the advisory board. We don't prepare the management report for them." (FashCo HEIR)*

> *"The annual report and the management report, everything we write in there is already known to our closest partners. It is directed more towards the general public." (TechCo CFO)*

Another indirect influence of equity capital providers can be seen in the **deadlines** for reports. Listed firms such as HealthCo and ChemCo are subject to tight deadlines to meet capital market demands for timely information. As a consequence, preparation processes need to be streamlined and fast-tracked, to achieve these deadlines:

> *"We have specific deadlines, and they tend to become shorter and shorter." (HealthCo HMQR)*

> *"No, we don't have a lot of influence when the deadline is determined by the management report. The financial community is in the lead here, we can't just say that four weeks later would also be okay. [...] Honestly, the deadline is the shareholders' meeting. The deadlines are a challenge. And a challenge is definitely to have all data available in the systems by that point of time." (ChemCo HSC)*

Therefore, capital market pressures can drive the time pressure connected to the preparation process. While almost all other cases firms' preparation processes are oriented towards deadlines such as shareholders' meetings, these firms do not recognize particular forces driving the deadlines. In contrast to the other cases, FashCo does not use deadlines because of its legal form and low pressures from owners or banks for particular publication dates. Nonetheless, the firm aims to complete its report in a timely manner to limit the resources spent on the preparation.

Overall, the results indicate that the demands of equity capital providers can influence the **preparation** process of nfKPIs for management reports with regard to the selection of material nfKPIs, the review of the report as well as the timeline of the process. Particularly in the case of large listed firms, the demands drive the time pressure related to the preparation. Furthermore, by integrating these stakeholders in the preparation process, stakeholders are in direct contact with promotors and institutionalize the perspective of stakeholders in the preparation of nfKPIs. However, particularly preparation processes of small and private firms appear to be less influenced by these actors. In most cases, this can be explained by the importance of other information channels as compared to the management report.

Other capital market participants

In addition to pressures from shareholders, HealthCo and ChemCo are also subject to demands and pressures from **other capital market participants** such as analysts or rating agencies. While these actors use the management report as a basis for their analyses, they also use other communication channels by approaching the process promotors or IR departments of the firms in case of questions. In addition to this, rating agencies send questionnaires to HealthCo and ChemCo to survey particular nfKPIs relevant to ratings or for the participation in sustainability indices. These interactions tend to move the firms to extend their measurement and reporting processes to include the relevant nfKPIs in upcoming management reports:

> *"The times are over, when you provided a rating agency with information and told them: 'This is non-disclosure, only you will receive the information.' Now they say that if you don't publish the information you gave them, then you will be punished by deduction of points." (HealthCo MSD)*

> *"Ratings and external requirements change our point of view, of course, and subsequently the reporting. There is a kind of trend in this direction." (ChemCo MQR)*

Therefore, reporting firms subject themselves to **normative isomorphism** by complying with the external norms of the rating agencies. As both HealthCo and ChemCo stress that they comply with the demands from rating agencies, these agencies have a considerable effect on the preparation processes. The effects become particularly evident in the selection and review criteria for material nfKPIs and in the measurement processes of these nfKPIs. For example, HealthCo and ChemCo consider additional environmental or social nfKPIs as material for their management report because these nfKPIs were included in the rating agency questionnaire. This effect is strongly based on the rating agencies' demands to also disclose these nfKPIs to other management report users in the following periods. In these cases, particularly process and know-how promotors are involved in the contact with the other capital market participants. It can be assumed, that these interactions provide an important motivator for changes in the preparation processes. Similar to results in the literature, sustainability index participation can be seen as a driver for the adoption of nonfinancial reporting (*Nikolaeva/Bicho* (2011), p. 150). While analyst contact seems to also affect the preparation process, they affect preparation processes in a similar manner as compared to rating agencies, albeit to a lower extent. However, such effects are likely driven by the visibility of firms, as small listed firms such as PrintCo do not appear to be a subject of interest to analysts or rating agencies.

Debt capital providers

In accordance with extant literature (*Claessens/Tzioumis* (2006), p. 266; *Haller et al.* (2014), p. 2542), particularly private case firms see **debt capital providers** as important audience for their management reports. This reliance can be explained by the firms' tendency to rely more on banks as sources of financing as compared to public firms. However, all private firms agree that their partner banks show low interest in their nfKPI reporting. In this context, the firms recognize a higher interest of banks in financial KPIs. In addition, the firms point out that their banks receive either more timely quarterly reports or are informed on nfKPIs through non-public communication channels:

> *"Banks read this as well, of course. They do not depend on our management report alone. They have the direct contact, the meetings, they have a reporting during the year." (LogCo CFO)*

> *"Financial institutions are basically focused mainly on financials. It's true. There is not much interest in nonfinancial KPIs. It's more that if I talk to the respective responsible person in the executive board, then we sometimes also talk about nonfinancials so that the person can gain a better understanding of our firm." (FashCo CFO)*

> *"I think that banks are basically more interested in our financial KPIs. But to integrate this in the overall context, at least for the bank representative who visited us, I had the feeling that she needed something to reassure her gut feeling. I don't know how to best describe this. She wanted to know, what the company is doing, where it is headed apart from the numbers." (TechCo IRM)*

As banks generally express little interest in the case firms' nfKPI reporting, the **involvement** and effect of banks on the design of the preparation process appears to be relatively low. Solely in the example of LogCo, the overall deadline of the preparation process is set by the reporting deadline set by the partner bank. Nonetheless, due to the low interest of LogCo's partner bank in nfKPIs, this reporting deadline is driven by the overall necessity to provide timely and audited financial statements:

> *"There is a calendar, which states at which points in time we have to present our results. We have external obligations, from which we can count back from. From a legal perspective, we have to be done on 30 June, publish it on 31 December, and we have to present our audited financial report to the banks by the end of April." (LogCo CFO)*

Hence, the overall effect of these actors on the preparation process of nfKPIs is considered to be low. Nonetheless, the case firms state that they provide their banks with nfKPI disclosures in the management report as a form of documentation.

Other key external stakeholders

In addition to capital providers, all case firms recognize that nfKPIs in their management report are directed towards **other key external stakeholders** from the general public. In accordance with their understanding of external management report users, the firms often target nfKPI disclosures at important management report users such as NGOs or potential employees.

Solely HealthCo actively addresses its nfKPI reporting towards **NGOs**, as the firm experiences high interests of these stakeholders in its nfKPI disclosures. Other case firms indicate that they experience a low interest and scrutiny from NGOs:

> *"We had an example where I said: 'This is nonsense, leave it out.' And then our colleague from the sustainability department showed me that this was actually published on the website of [NGO relevant for HealthCo]. And that we particularly wanted to write something about this topic to show that we don't want to cover something up. We don't harm the environment. It is always the question what to report and what not to report. By tendency, we rather report too much than too little." (HealthCo HMQR)*

> *"While it could happen that some organizations or shareholders ask questions about this in the shareholders' meetings of other stock corporations, we have never experienced that." (PrintCo HEIR)*

This factor points towards the potential **influence of public pressures** on the reporting processes. As HealthCo integrates NGO demands in its preparation process, this particular strength of public pressures might drive normative isomorphism within the firm. While NGOs do not publicize norms comparable to reporting guidelines, HealthCo complies with NGO demands to avoid confrontation and loss of legitimacy. Hence, this behavior is an indicator for implicit norms. Moreover, NGOs can be seen as opposing parties communicating with the process and power promotors. In this context, promotors try to address the demands of these parties to avoid losing legitimacy. While these effects appear to be particularly strong for HealthCo, other case firms are not subjected to comparable scrutiny from NGOs and associated effects on the preparation process. In addition, the effect of stakeholder pressures on the preparation process of nfKPIs for the management report might also be influenced by the reporting format. Firms with separate sustainability reports appear to experience less stakeholder pressures. Hence, the reporting format can play a role in shifting stakeholder scrutiny from the management report to other report types. Furthermore, NGO scrutiny might also be linked to other factors such as industry and firm visibility.

Another stakeholder group addressed by nfKPI disclosures are **potential employees**. Some case firms point out that their departments provide positive nfKPI information to attract potential employees. While most firms agree that the management report and its nfKPI sections also presents an HR marketing medium, the interview experts raise concerns regarding the importance of this reporting medium for recruiting purposes:

> *"It's about credibility. And at that point in time, when I say that we are advertising, seeking new employees and claiming that our staff is important to us, but we only have one page on employees in our management report, that is not the right proportion. I have to of course treat the topic with the according relevance." (ChemCo MQR)*

> *"Whether or not a normal job applicant looks at these things – I have no idea. [...] I believe a job applicant for technical tasks would have no idea that he could find something like this in the report." (PrintCo HEIR)*

> *"Also considering today's job applicants, when you apply as a business administration graduate, and particularly in the field of management accounting, finance and financial accounting, then you can have a look at the firm. [...] I believe this is good information over which you can determine in which risk environment the firm is acting, how we are treating our employees." (LogCo HA)*

While potential employees as report users can affect the motivation of the preparers to present positive information, the overall interest of these stakeholders appears to be unknown to most experts in the firms. Therefore, the effect on the preparation process appears to be rather low. Nonetheless, the potential usage of nfKPIs for shedding a positive light on specific departments can be seen as an influence of potential employees on the underlying reporting criteria of the preparation process.

In summary, external users of management reports reflect a considerable influencing factor on the design of the preparation process. Drawing from **institutional theory**, management report preparers demonstrate normative isomorphic behavior by adhering to the demands of their stakeholders. However, these effects appear to be valid only for larger listed firms, as PrintCo and private firms experience lower pressures from management report users and hence indicate less isomorphic behavior. Moreover, these effects also vary with regard to the type of management report users. While capital market participants and NGOs appear to influence the selection criteria, measurement processes and review criteria of large firms such as HealthCo and ChemCo, other types of management report users such as banks or future employees seem to have few effects on the preparation process of nfKPIs.

With regard to the **promotor model**, management report users appear to be in contact with various promotors in the course of the process. Some actors such as NGOs and rating agencies appear to act as opposing parties, whom promotors need to address and convince. At HealthCo, which directly involves its management report users in the preparation process, process and know-how promotors are in contact with these stakeholders. In the other case firms, the communication with management report users is typically limited to power promotors or the IR department. Moreover, these firms typically consider the demands of the management report users indirectly. However, the strength of such effects appears to be influenced by factors such as legal form, firm size or industry visibility as well. Table 6-17 summarizes the theoretical discussion.

	Institutional theory	Behavioral decision theory	Promotor model
Equity capital providers	Normative isomorphism (selection criteria, measurement processes and review criteria in large public firms)	-	Direct contact between promotors and report users (HealthCo through stakeholder survey, CFO or IR in other firms)
Other capital market participants	Normative isomorphism (selection criteria, measurement processes and review criteria in large public firms with analysts following or listed on sustainability index)	-	Rating agencies as opposing parties (large listed firms) Direct contact between promotors and report users (HealthCo, stakeholder survey)
Debt capital providers	Low effects (e.g., deadline for LogCo's management report)	-	Direct contact between promotors and report users (HealthCo, stakeholder survey, CFO or IR in other firms)
Other key external stakeholders	Normative isomorphism (selection criteria, measurement processes and review criteria in large public firms and through NGOs, lower effects through potential employees)	-	NGOs as opposing parties (large listed firms) Direct contact between promotors and report users (HealthCo, stakeholder survey, CFO or IR in other firms)

Table 6-17: Influence of external management report users on preparation processes

6.2.3.2.3 Rules and norms

In addition to service providers and management report users, firms preparing nfKPIs for their management reports are also subject to influences from external rules and norms. The analyses indicate an influence of implicit norms from a firms' industry, regulatory requirements and explicit norms from voluntary reporting frameworks on the design of the preparation process of nfKPIs. These influencing factors are discussed in the following.

Industry norms

In the literature, **industry** is seen as an important influencing factor for nfKPI reporting (*Adams* (2002), p. 225; *Cohen et al.* (2012), pp. 81-83; *Hahn/Kühnen* (2013), p. 13). Researchers argue that particularly firms from environmentally or socially critical industries or from industries with strong mimetic tendencies may be inclined to increase their nfKPI reporting. Analyses of the cases show that implicit industry norms influencing preparation processes can comprise general industry effects, peer firm comparisons and the firms' distance to consumers in the supply chain.

General industry effects

With regard to **general industry effects**, the sector affiliation of a firm can influence the relevance of particular nfKPIs, the dependency on know-how promotors and the participation in critical industries with regard to social and environmental impacts. The **relevance of particular nfKPIs** is strongly based on the industry a firm operates in. As most case firms consider the sector affiliation when determining material nfKPIs, such industry effects seem to be particularly present in the materiality analysis of the reporting process:

> *"A steel company has of course totally different nonfinancial KPIs than we do. Sustainability in their case revolves around the environment. In contrast, in our case it is always about procurement countries and their resources." (FashCo CFO)*

> *"When it became pressing for us due to GAS 20, we thought about which ones were important for us. We are a technology company, this means research and development. This is not included in our success factors, but it is such an important topic that it is presented individually. Then we asked ourselves, what is also important: employees, production, production systems, quality, resource efficiency and sustainability." (TechCo IRM)*

In addition to effects on the selection of nfKPIs, the literature on innovation processes suggests that firms from manufacturing industries could be **more dependent on know-how promotors** (*Chakrabarti/Hauschildt* (1989), p. 169; *Folkerts* (2001), p. 54). While this relationship is justified by the importance of R&D for these particular industries in the context of innovation processes, the importance of know-how promotors in the preparation process of nfKPIs for management reports is less driven by their ability to innovate but rather by their operational knowledge and access to data.

However, the case firms show **no clear relationship** between the industry and the importance of know-how promotors in the preparation process. Some case firms from manufacturing industries (HealthCo, ChemCo, TechCo) rely heavily on the participation of know-how promotors in the preparation process. Firms with retailing and logistics background (LogCo, FashCo, AgCo) show rather low involvement of know-how promotors. Initially, this could be seen as evidence for a relationship between manufacturing industry and participants in the nfKPI reporting process. Nonetheless, as the manufacturing company PrintCo also shows low involvement of know-how promotors, the influence of the industry can be mitigated by other influencing factors such as size or reporting formats.

In addition, other industry effects might be present as some researchers hypothesize that firms in critical industries with regard to social and environmental impacts (such as fashion and agriculture) increase their nfKPI reporting to comply with high stakeholder demands for this information (*Patten* (2002), pp. 766-767; *Lee/Hutchison* (2005), pp. 96-99). On the one hand, FashCo and AgCo have rather lean reporting processes with few know-how promotors involved. On the other hand, HealthCo indicates a relation between the **participation in an environmental critical industry** and effects on the preparation process. Drawing from these findings, industry classifications can be seen as "macro-level proxies"

(*Roberts* (1992), p. 609) while other related factors such as size, stakeholder pressures or reporting formats mitigate these industry effects.

Peer company comparisons

Apart from general industry characteristics, the preparation processes of firms can be influenced by **peer company comparisons** (*Husillos et al.* (2011), p. 208; *Contrafatto* (2014), pp. 423-424). Several firms (HealthCo, ChemCo, TechCo) compare their nfKPI reporting to that of other companies from the industry or best-practice reporters. These firms follow the goal of providing nfKPIs at a similar or better quality as compared to other preparers. Similarly, PrintCo conducts analyses of the reports of their largest customers to identify minimum acceptable standard disclosures regarding nfKPI reporting:

> *"When we publish something, I would say that it is the minimum requirement or maybe a bit more. And if we notice that everyone else would report much, much more, then we would also top up. And then we would have a look at what we would disclose and how we would design the processes around it." (PrintCo HEIR)*

However, all other firms (LogCo, FashCo, AgCo) state that they put low emphasis on peer comparisons. These firms recognize that they are hardly comparable to other peer firms (LogCo) or that the nfKPI reporting of their peers is not informative for their own reporting (FashCo, AgCo):

> *"Currently, we do this to a very small extent. But it is certainly something we should do in the future, having a look at what others in our environment are writing. However, we cannot compare ourselves to [large competitors of LogCo] and there are honestly very few companies that are comparable to our size. [...] Therefore, we have a position in the market which is hardly comparable to other logistics companies." (LogCo HA)*

> *"The topics are created internally. [...] Other influences come from outside, but not from our competitors. Afterwards, you of course have a look at what your competitor has done and which focus points they had, but that does not influence our work. [...] This comparison mostly focuses on their business practices and overall it is simply a source of information." (AgCo HER)*

From the perspective of **institutional theory**, such peer comparisons point towards mimetic isomorphism (*Hahn/Kühnen* (2013), p. 13). This isomorphic behavior can, for example, arise in the firms' materiality analyses when these firms consider disclosures of peer companies. As seen in the example of PrintCo above, mimetic isomorphism can drive the creation or change of reporting processes to provide the intended nfKPI disclosures. While this isomorphism appears to be present in the public firms and TechCo, the private firms conduct few peer analyses. Hence, such low pressures from peer comparisons can result in fewer changes to the reporting processes (*Bouten/Everaert* (2015), p. 27).

As this **isomorphic behavior** is based on the adoption of peer firms' nfKPI disclosures rather than an observation of their reporting processes, the preparers do not directly imitate preparation processes of peer firms. However, HealthCo's case indicates that some firms use industry meetings to exchange information on reporting processes. While such exchanges provide a possibility for mimetic isomorphism with regard to reporting processes, these meetings appear to be rather rare and are not mentioned by other case companies:

"I also had discussions with others from the industry in which we were open about some things. That's not a problem, we talk about nonfinancials and not about numbers. We also talk about processes and some years ago I was asked how we deal with HR reporting, how we would do that and how does the process work. And everyone is jealous regarding our [QEHS database] process for the QEHS information." (HealthCo MSD)

Distance to consumers

Another influencing factor related to the industry of the reporting firms is the **distance to consumers**. While the industries and associated business models of most sample firms are built on business-to-business transactions (ChemCo, PrintCo, LogCo), other case firms either exclusively sell their products to consumers (FashCo) or supply both businesses and consumers (HealthCo, TechCo). It is argued that consumer interactions can lead to higher visibility of corporate actions and increased pressures from consumers or other stakeholders, which moves firms towards more extensive sustainability reporting (*Haddock* (2005), p. 803; *Groves et al.* (2011), p. 540). Such effects of corporate visibility become particularly evident in the cases of HealthCo, PrintCo and LogCo. While the first is subject to high scrutiny by various stakeholders and provides extensive nfKPI disclosures, the latter two firms are hardly visible to the public and include stakeholder interests only to a small degree in their preparation processes.

Furthermore, firms with higher brand visibility might understand their management report as a platform for **marketing or brand building** (*Haddock* (2005), p. 803). Firms such as TechCo indicate that one goal of preparing a management report is to use it as a marketing medium for supporting its quality-leader image. However, in accordance with extant research (*Nikolaeva/Bicho* (2011), p. 150), the reporting formats and preparation processes of such firms show mixed indications for this relationship. On the one hand, HealthCo and ChemCo both conduct extensive nfKPI preparation processes although having strong differences in brand visibility. On the other hand, the consumer-oriented firm FashCo uses a less formalized and extensive preparation process as compared to the business-to-business oriented firm LogCo. Hence, it can be concluded that other factors might have a higher influence on the preparation process as compared to brand visibility.

In addition, business-to-business firms can be subject to **supply chain reporting scrutiny** by their business-to-business customers. The results of the analyses indicate that firms are often required by their customers to provide nfKPIs through non-public communication channels, which can affect measurement processes and the selection of additional material nfKPIs in the materiality analyses:

"As we supply many companies, we not only have to report ourselves but also provide our customers with information on what we have been doing. This is like a cascade running further and further. And for some years now, our businesses have been required to provide lots of surveys for nonfinancials and the environment." (ChemCo MQR)

"For particular customer businesses, these nonfinancial KPIs are strongly used, because I would not be able to evaluate them or provide offers. But we don't use them in that form in the management report. It's more a kind of general information medium, which is used for a very limited circle of KPIs." (LogCo HA)

However, as these cases indicate, supply chain reporting requirements appear to have little influence on reporting processes. Although suppliers appear to adapt their measurement processes of nfKPIs to fulfil demands of their customers for particular nfKPIs, this information appears to be largely used for non-public communication only. While public firms such as ChemCo can be required by other large public customers to provide documentation on their sustainability actions in the nfKPI section of the management report, smaller and private firms such as LogCo do not seem to face this type of pressure and, hence, do not adjust their preparation processes.

Relating these discussions to **institutional theory**, the conflicting results do not indicate more isomorphic behavior for firms with higher visibility or more consumer contact. While other influencing factors such as external users of management reports indicate explanations for this relationship, some business-to-business firms reveal mimetic isomorphism. When facing supply chain reporting requirements, supplier firms might adapt their reporting processes to provide large public customers with documentation on their nfKPI-related performance or sustainability of their products. However, this effect appears to be stronger for listed as compared to private firms, as non-listed firms seem to currently face less requirements from their customers to provide public documentation on their nfKPIs.

In summary, the diverse industry factors appear to influence the design of the preparation process of nfKPIs. Although general industry effects appear to influence the materiality of nfKPIs, effects stemming from the participation in producing or environmentally critical industry seem to be superimposed by other influencing factors such as size, stakeholder pressures or reporting formats. Moreover, particularly public and best-practice reporters appear to be subject to mimetic isomorphism induced by peer company comparisons. Finally, the distance to consumers, brand visibility and supply chain reporting scrutiny seem to have a low influence on preparation processes.

Regulatory requirements

Prior research finds that regulatory requirements for nfKPI disclosures can have a major influence on the reporting content (*Tarca et al.* (2011), p. 48; *Hahn/Kühnen* (2013), p. 13)) and consequently on reporting processes (*Gibbins et al.* (1990), p. 132; *Osann* (2010), p. 257). The results show that regulatory requirements influence the preparation process design in several phases. During the materiality analysis, regulatory requirements are used as thresholds for material nfKPIs. Moreover, the firms include these requirements in their review of the report to check the compliance of the report with regulation. While these influences become evident in all case firms, the particular effects on the individual processes appear to be strongly moderated by regulatory changes, reporting goals and the scope for discretion (Figure 6-52). Hence, these moderating effects are discussed in the following.

Regulatory changes

All case firms note that they adjust their preparation processes when existing **regulation is changed:**

> *"This is ultimately a living process which is and has to be continuously developed. Particularly in the context of ever changing regulatory requirements." (HealthCo MQR)*

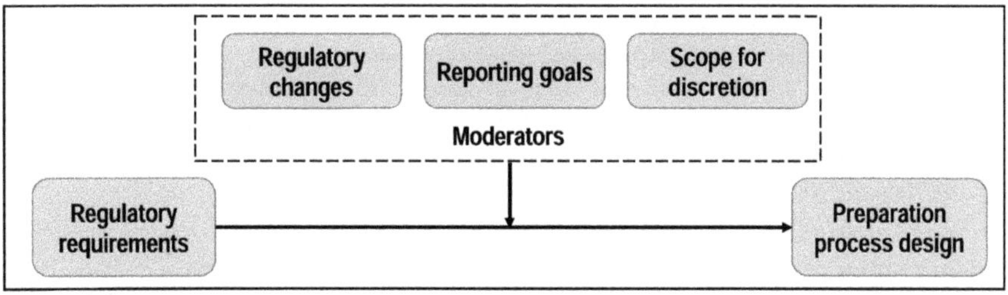

Figure 6-52: Effects of regulatory requirements on preparation process design

> *"Our processes are established. But each year something happens which we have to adjust to, such as changes in the regulatory environment and so forth. We are at this point again now. [...] It's not cast in stone, each year we add something new." (ChemCo MSD)*

> *"As long as we don't have to, we will not ask anyone to turn this into metrics." (LogCo CFO)*

Such changes are typically reflected in the materiality analysis process, as firms introduce criteria on the basis of regulatory requirements. Similarly, firms include new regulatory requirements into their review of the report. Particularly in the case of more detailed requirements, the **materiality analysis and the review of the report** can be influenced to a large degree:

> *"The most important decision criteria [in the review process] are the regulatory requirements. According to HGB, IFRS, GRI." (HealthCo IRM)*

> *"When GAS 20 was introduced, we first sat down internally and asked ourselves, which criteria we would be looking for. Not from the point of view that each of them would have to be fulfilled, but you need some kind of orientation and a basis for discussions to validate this." (ChemCo MQR)*

These changes to the process to comply with extant regulation provide evidence for coercive isomorphism in all case firms. In this context, the case firms highlight that regulatory changes can **increase the efforts and costs** of preparing nfKPIs for the management report:

> *"It is getting more and more, it's becoming more difficult. [...] And it is also connected to a certain audit effort, which has to be controlled and managed. For this you need to get other players on board. This is an additional task related to the regulation." (PrintCo CFO)*

> *"Well, if the legislators demand more information, then it basically means more efforts in the preparation process." (FashCo HEIR)*

> *"As I said, GAS 20 resulted in additional efforts. But ever since we introduced this process, particularly the collection in the departments, nothing much has been changed." (TechCo IRM)*

With regard to responsibilities, regulatory changes are typically **monitored and implemented** in the preparation process by the coordinators of the report. As indicated in the analysis of the promotor roles, executives are also aware of potential changes and monitor these. Moreover, auditors inform these participants of the preparation process in many firms in case of relevant regulatory changes. This communication indicates that the tasks of observing regulation are primarily carried out by process and power promotors of the firm, who are responsible for implementing such changes in the preparation processes. These findings are in line with findings in the literature (*Osann* (2010), p. 257).

From the perspective of **institutional theory**, the case firms' compliance with regulatory requirements regarding nfKPIs indicate coercive isomorphism (*Contrafatto* (2014), p. 418). All case firms institutionalize the compliance with regulatory requirements in their goals for management reporting and subsequently in their organizational structures. However, the degree and type of institutionalization appear to vary across the case firms. Listed firms, large firms and best-practice reporters seem to incorporate the monitoring of regulatory changes and the review of regulatory requirements to a high degree in their preparation processes. Smaller private firms indicate lower levels of institutionalization of regulatory requirements in their preparation processes. Hence, influencing factors such as size and reporting goals can help explain varying effects of coercive isomorphism.

Overall, regulatory changes mark an important influencing factor for the preparation process of nfKPIs for the management report. However, the effect of this factor is also connected to the reporting goals and scope for discretion.

Reporting goals

Similar to findings in the literature, all case firms follow the **goal** of meeting regulatory requirements with their nfKPI reporting (*Holland* (1998), pp. 260-261; *Tarca et al.* (2011), p. 48; *Haller et al.* (2014), pp. 2542-2543). However, several factors influence the firms' willingness to exceed the reporting requirements. As discussed above, such factors can be seen in the listing, size or industry. Some firms particularly show a **conservative attitude** towards nfKPI reporting (*Bouten/Everaert* (2015), p. 27), as long as specific nfKPI disclosures are not required by law:

> *"Now with this regulation, which has been introduced, our goal is definitely to fulfil the requirements. But on top of that, we currently don't see a benefit or usefulness in doing more than what we are required to do." (PrintCo CFO)*

> *"For me, these external requirements do not justify using something internally. On the contrary, one should report something which is used internally towards the outside. That's the effective direction, and not the other way around. […] And it's not beneficial to us to write something into the report." (LogCo CFO)*

> *"Honestly, I only keep to what is required by GAS 20. That's what we will include into the report. More will not be included. I won't include something just because we say that we like this or that a lot, that won't be the case." (FashCo CFO)*

Consistent with findings from previous analyses of this study, such conservative attitudes are reflected in the **resources** provided for the preparation of nfKPIs for the management report. The results indicate that particularly small and private firms which follow conservative goals have few participants in their preparation process and provide mostly qualitative nfKPIs in their management reports. Large public firms such as HealthCo and ChemCo see regulatory requirements as a minimum goal next to other goals. Thus, these latter firms use considerably more resources for the preparation of nfKPIs for the management report. Although being a private firm, a similar attitude is taken on by TechCo due to their best-practice reporting approach. While the firm provides more resources for the preparation process and follows more reporting goals as compared to other private firms, the private firm nature of TechCo is still reflected in several restrictions to its nfKPI reporting and in the extent of its preparation process.

Similar to the resources provided and also related to the attitudes towards regulatory requirements, the reporting goals also reflect the firms' **understanding of material nfKPIs**. On the one end, public and best-practice reporters apply a rather broad understanding of materiality which includes economic, environmental and social nfKPIs in accordance with § 289 (3) HGB, CSR-RUG and voluntary reporting frameworks. On the other end, small and private firms use narrow definitions of materiality by referring mostly to economic nfKPIs and some environmental or social nfKPIs in accordance with § 289 (3) HGB. Although all firms remain within the scope of regulatory requirements, the preparation processes of firms with a broader understanding of materiality appear to be more elaborate.

Therefore, the **firm's attitude towards regulatory requirements** seem to be driven by the reporting goals of the firm. However, as these goals are typically connected to the listing and size of the firm, potential effects of reporting goals on regulatory compliance should be analyzed in combination with such influencing factors.

Scope for discretion

In connection with attitudes and goals related to nfKPI disclosures, prior research argues that the **scope for discretion** in regulatory requirements can influence the preparation of nfKPI disclosures (*Gibbins et al.* (1990); *Bouten/Everaert* (2015), p. 27; *Haller et al.* (2017), p. 413). The cases show that the effect of the scope for discretion is strongly linked to the firms' underlying interpretations and reporting motivations. Whenever firms follow rather conservative and restrictive attitudes and goals, they can use a potential scope for discretion to provide solely the minimum required level of disclosures.

With regard to the interpretation of the regulation, preparers recognize that previous requirements of GAS 20 and HGB have been rather **vague** and without proper guidance. Hence, previous regulatory requirements have indicated a potential scope for discretion to the preparers. However, effects on the preparation processes vary significantly:

> *"You don't want a regulation, but for GRI 3.1 it was relatively easy, because you had guidance and you were able to build on this standard with the possibility to extend it with material information in a few areas. I find the GAS 20 not expressive enough in some parts. If you look back at what it said about nonfinancials, that was basically nothing." (HealthCo SD)*

> *"We prepare our management report on the basis of GAS 20. I mean, the wording is not particularly compulsory, but it can be interpreted that if nfKPIs explain the course of business, nfKPIs are requested. This means we have a sort of obligation and want to fulfil this requirement. And yes, we pursue this as our primary goal." (FashCo MEIR)*

On the one hand, HealthCo seems to interpret the scope of discretion of regulatory requirements as a **lack of guidance** for preparing nfKPIs. Nonetheless, the firm choses to provide extensive information on the basis of voluntary reporting guidelines such as those from GRI. Hence, the perceived lack of guidance can promote the usage of standard practices to deal with uncertainties during the preparation.

On the other hand, private firms such as FashCo use the scope of discretion to provide the **minimum possible disclosure level.** Similar to other private firms, the preparation process is kept rather lean to meet the requirement but not to over-exceed them in terms of the amount and level of detail of nfKPIs. Nonetheless, the cases also show that private firms could be willing to exceed the minimum requirements through higher disclosure levels whenever it is beneficial to them. This behavior can be seen in the case of LogCo. On the one side, LogCo uses the scope of discretion to select favorable yet truthful nfKPIs which can present the firm as an attractive, sustainable company with a positive future outlook. On the other side, the firm tries to apply the scope of discretion to refrain from disclosing sensitive information:

> *"We might decide against including nfKPIs because we do not want these things to leave the company. This could happen. However, there could always be a conflict of interest. But there certainly are grey areas. Not everything we know belongs into the report. However, my point of view differs from the one from our auditor. Moreover, my colleagues have a totally different view, because they are somewhat unburdened by laws, guidelines or checklists. They are rather thinking about how disclosures could affect the market, because they have different tasks of course in the company." (LogCo CFO)*

Thus, the firms' usage of the scope of discretion seems to be interlinked with their reporting goals. Therefore, the effects of the scope of discretion on the preparation process seems to be mixed.

The effects of **changes in the scope of discretion** can be seen in the case of PrintCo. The stricter requirements of the CSR-RUG appear to have decreased the scope of discretion. As it can be seen in the changes to the preparation process in this firm, the decreased scope of discretion has had an effect on the organizational structures and phases of the preparation process of nfKPIs:

> *"As we have been a little freer with regard to what we could report according to GAS 20, now we have to make sure that we exactly meet the regulatory requirements. [...] We were free with regard to what we wanted to write, but GAS 20 also required us to look at the materiality. But we didn't have to present results." (PrintCo HEIR)*

To meet the higher reporting requirements, the promotor roles were re-distributed within the firm. The CFO has assigned the MEIR with coordinating the nonfinancial statement due to expected efforts regarding the preparation. In addition, additional internal and external sources were tapped to provide sufficient information for the management report. Thus, a decreased scope of discretion can call for more elaborate preparation processes.

In contrast to PrintCo, changes in the scope of discretion caused by CSR-RUG appear to have had little effect on the preparation processes of **HealthCo and ChemCo.** As both firms have previously exceeded the minimum requirements with regard to nfKPI reporting, they were not required to adjust their preparation processes significantly. These circumstances provide further evidence for the link between the scope of discretion and other influencing factors. In combination, these influencing factors can **considerably affect** the design of the preparation process of nfKPIs.

Behavioral decision theory offers explanations for the institutionalization of regulatory requirements in internal disclosure decision processes. To conform to extant regulation or to address a potential lack of guidance in the requirements, firms establish specific standard practices. These practices can be implemented in the form of decision criteria in the firms' materiality analyses or review criteria during their review phase. However, particularly small and private firms seem to apply less strict decision and review criteria by showing conservative reporting attitudes and using the lower bounds of the scope of discretion. Moreover, such criteria serve not only as standard procedures in the preparation process but also as a form of indoctrination of the participants. Particularly those persons responsible for coordinating and reviewing the preparation seem to internalize the requirements to be able to sufficiently apply them in the preparation process. Overall, the theoretical framework indicates that regulatory requirements can affect the preparation process on several organizational levels.

Reporting frameworks

In addition to complying with regulatory requirements, firms can apply voluntary **reporting frameworks**. Several private firms do not apply frameworks when preparing their management reports (LogCo, FashCo, TechCo), which can be explained by cost-benefit considerations and diverging reporting goals. Nonetheless, the remaining case firms apply such frameworks in several forms: management reports are prepared in accordance with such frameworks (HealthCo), these frameworks are consulted or used in parts for the report preparation (ChemCo, PrintCo) or they are used for preparing a separate, individual sustainability report (ChemCo, AgCo).

While the private firms LogCo, FashCo and TechCo appear **reluctant** to implement voluntary reporting frameworks in their nfKPI reporting (*Spence/Lozano* (2000), pp. 50-51; *Husillos et al.* (2011), p. 207), several firms from the other group also show a particular reluctance to preparing their management reports in accordance with such frameworks (ChemCo, PrintCo, AgCo). This reluctance becomes particularly evident in the cases of ChemCo and AgCo, which also publish a separate sustainability report based on GRI. These firms prefer to include less extensive reporting frameworks such as UN Global Compact in their management report (ChemCo) or none at all (AgCo). The reluctance to use extensive frameworks such as GRI in their management report can be explained by the diverging goals and perspectives of the firms' management reports and sustainability reports. Moreover, as the publication dates of the reports differ strongly, the preparers might be unable to provide nfKPIs recommended by GRI in time during the preparation process of the management report.

In contrast to the other firms, HealthCo strongly bases its materiality analysis and the composition of its integrated report on the **GRI frameworks**. On the one hand, its materiality analysis is conducted according to the guidance of GRI G4-18 and includes several formal and informal means of including stakeholders in the process (*GRI* (2015a), pp. 32-40). On the other hand, the preparers use the nfKPIs recommended by GRI to measure their nfKPIs and review the conformity of the draft with the frameworks. Therefore, the framework significantly influences the preparation process of HealthCo. However, the process participants also criticize the efforts in connection to complying with several different reporting frameworks and to adjusting processes to changes in reporting frameworks:

> *"There are very many external demands regarding what you have to report and in which form. UN Global Compact, EU guidelines and many more have their own ideas. And they are all similar but not equal. [...] It shouldn't be necessary to invest too much into complying with these guidelines. On the contrary, you should be able to use your resources for implementing what you are reporting rather than report something just a tiny bit differently. This is one of the largest challenges for companies, because you adjust the systems, structure the processes and some people have to manage this." (HealthCo MSP)*

> *"A process is always easier when you have low influence from outside. That means if you have no regulatory changes, no changes from GRI, but that does not exist. Because in the next year, we will deal with [integrating a HealthCo acquisition], we will conduct a materiality analysis and then we change from GRI G4 to the GRI Standards. There are so many things which limit a good preparation for the process." (HealthCo MSD)*

From a **theoretical perspective**, reporting frameworks seem to influence the preparation process of nfKPIs through similar channels as compared to regulatory requirements. However, the low usage of such frameworks among the case firms results in rather low overall effects on the preparation processes of the case firms. Drawing from **institutional theory**, reporting frameworks mark normative isomorphic behavior which could drive firms to institutionalize nfKPI reporting in their disclosure processes (*Contrafatto* (2014), pp. 423-424). Such effects can particularly be seen in the case of HealthCo's materiality analysis process, nfKPI measurement and its compliance with nfKPI recommendations. Normative pressures could be increased by other influencing factors such as investors or rating agencies. In contrast to this case, frameworks have not particularly influenced preparation processes of nfKPIs of the other case firms. These circumstances can be explained by a reluctance to apply frameworks for a management report due to missing nfKPIs, diverging perspectives and goals between their management and sustainability report or due to cost-benefit considerations.

On the basis of **behavioral decision theory** and similar to regulatory requirements, reporting frameworks assist firms in establishing standard practices and supporting indoctrination of participants with regard to the preparation process. Similarly, **promotor structures** in the preparation process appear to be comparable to those related to regulatory requirements. However, HealthCo's case shows that know-how promotors can be more involved in checking the compliance with frameworks as compared to the compliance with regulation. This involvement appears to be connected to the more specific requirements inherent in the frameworks as compared to the rather vague regulatory requirements. Hence, these promotors have more specific guidance regarding the preparation. Overall, effects related to reporting frameworks seem to be present solely in the integrated reporting environment of HealthCo.

Summary

In summary, rules and norms appear to influence the preparation process of nfKPIs to varying degrees. Table 6-18 summarizes the findings with regard to the effects on the preparation process. While industry effects seem to influence the design of the processes, these implicit norms are commonly connected to or superimposed by other influencing factors. Regulatory requirements mark an important influencing factor, which varies in its influence depending on changes in requirements, reporting goals and the scope for discretion. Similar to industry effects, the influence of regulatory requirements on preparation processes is connected to other influencing factors such as firm size. Finally, reporting frameworks show significant effects on the preparation processes. However, such effects seem to solely be

	Institutional theory	Behavioral decision theory	Promotor model
Industry norms	Mimetic isomorphism (indirect effects due to peer analyses for materiality analysis, higher for public firms, higher for business-to-business firms with high visibility and consumer contact)	-	Higher dependence on know-how promotors in manufacturing firms (mixed results)
Regulatory requirements	Coercive isomorphism (high for all firms, high institutionalization of requirements in listed and best-practice firms)	Standard practices (criteria for selection and review of nfKPIs, stricter criteria in large and public firms) Indoctrination of participants through criteria	Responsibilities for monitoring requirements and communicating with auditors (process and power promotors) More elaborate processes in case of stricter requirements (e.g., nonfinancial statement of PrintCo)
Reporting frameworks	Normative isomorphism (basis for materiality analysis, measurement and review of HealthCo, low effect in firms with separate sustainability reports due to decoupling of preparation processes)	Standard practices (criteria for selection and review of nfKPIs, solely applied by HealthCo) Indoctrination of participants through criteria (HealthCo)	Higher involvement of sustainability department (coordination) and know-how promotors (measurement and review) as compared to regulatory requirements

Table 6-18: Influence of rules and norms on preparation processes

present in situations of integrated reporting, as other case firms use reporting frameworks either to a low degree or refrain from them completely when preparing their management report.

6.2.3.3 Discussion

Overall, several **internal and external factors influence** the design of the preparation process of nfKPIs for management reports (Figure 6-53). While supervisory boards and organizational characteristics mark important internal factors, preparation processes are also influenced externally by service providers, external users of management reports and the rules and norms of the firm. These factors influence the preparation process designs to varying degrees and are typically interlinked with other factors depending on the context of the particular firm. Moreover, the influence of these factors on the design of the preparation process can be explained by the theoretical framework of this study.

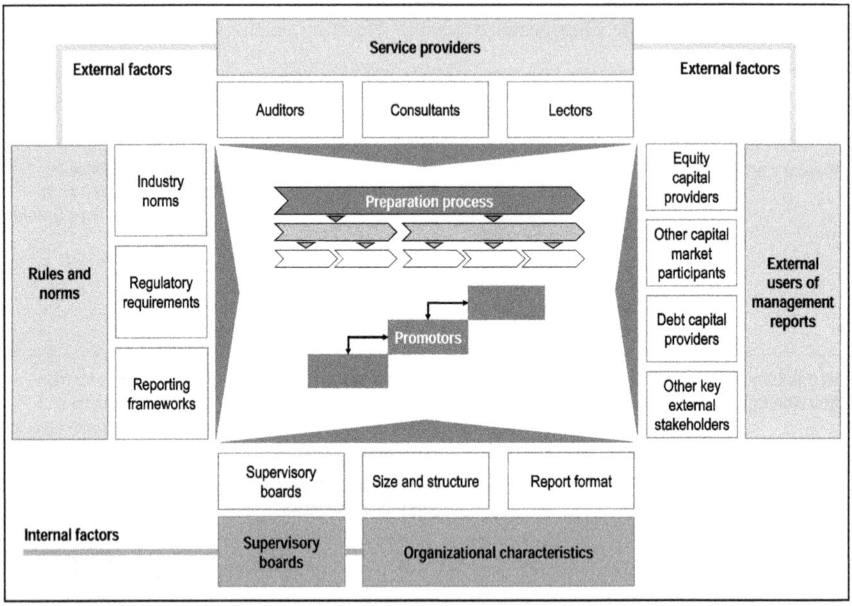

Figure 6-53: Overview of internal and external influencing factors

The existence of a **supervisory board** can influence the design of the preparation process. Acting as "gatekeepers" for nfKPI disclosures who ensure the compliance with regulatory requirements, supervisory boards mark a final hurdle in the preparation process and serve to safeguard compliance practices in the firms. However, the results demonstrate that the influence of supervisory boards appears to be rather low, as the board members seem to be mainly interested in financial KPIs and other disclosures as compared to nfKPIs. Solely in the case of PrintCo, the board is involved in the audit of nfKPIs, which increases its influence on the process. Despite the hierarchical potential of supervisory boards regarding the preparation process of nfKPI, they appear to show low interest in the preparation process and resulting disclosures.

Organizational characteristics comprise firm size, organizational structure and reporting formats, which strongly affect the design of preparation processes. The **size** of the organization influences the data and personnel available for the preparation of nfKPIs and seems to drive the formalization of reporting structures. While large firms typically apply extensive and formal preparation processes, small firms apply more informal and flexible processes due to a lower availability of time and resources. Moreover, the **structure** of the organization can explain the influence of hierarchies on the preparation processes. Hierarchical firms typically assign clear responsibilities and deploy several review levels between the report coordinators and the executive board. In contrast, less hierarchical firms show fewer review levels and more flexibility with regard to the preparation. Overall, these two factors can significantly influence the design of preparation processes.

In addition to the former organizational characteristics, the **reporting format** also affects the design of the preparation process. An integrated reporting format seems to have a significant influence on the preparation process with regards to its phases and participants. In contrast to this, the preparation processes of firms with separate sustainability reports appear to largely reflect those of firms without sustainability reporting. In this context of reporting formats, the types of nfKPIs reported influence the processes considerably. Particularly quantitative and forward-looking nfKPI disclosures can increase the extent of resources, formalization and audit procedures connected to the preparation process.

External **service providers** such as auditors, consultants and lectors are involved in preparation processes to different extents. Auditors show significant influence on the design of preparation processes. In their role as gatekeepers, auditors communicate regulatory changes throughout the preparation process and check whether reporting processes and disclosures are compliant with regulation. Hence, auditors seem to increase coercive isomorphic behavior of the reporting firms. For their second role as change agents, the case firms show low involvement of auditors in the improvement of data systems or in the benchmarking of reporting processes. Nonetheless, the cases indicate that these roles and their effects on the preparation processes can be moderated by audit comprehensiveness and the expertise of auditors. While consultants such as GRI consultants could take on similar roles and tasks as compared to auditors, the overall effect of these actors on preparation processes is lower as compared to auditors. This difference can be explained by the voluntary nature of applying GRI frameworks. Moreover, only the two large public firms engage such consultants. The effects of both auditors and GRI assurors are closely connected to effects from regulatory requirements and reporting frameworks. Finally, while lectors are typically involved in the review phase of the preparation process, the overall influence of these actors appears to focus mostly on disclosures rather than the design of the preparation process.

External users of management reports seem to have mixed influence on the design of preparation processes. Such users are typically directly or indirectly included in the materiality analysis or the review phase. Equity capital providers commonly have a large effect on the design of the processes, as these stakeholders reflect the most important target group for the firms' nfKPI reporting. However, preparers consider the demands of these stakeholders to varying degrees, depending on the stakeholders' interest in nfKPIs and the existence of non-public communication channels. Moreover, listed firms appear to include demands from other capital market participants such as analysts or rating agencies in their measurement processes of nfKPIs. Particularly for HealthCo and ChemCo, these capital market participants could drive normative isomorphism for complying with extant sustainability reporting frameworks or information demands from rating agencies. While the private firms also tend to depend more strongly on banks as important management report users, the interest of these banks in nfKPIs and a resulting influence on preparation processes seems to be rather low. Similarly, most firms consider other key external stakeholders such as NGOs or potential employees only to a limited extent. Solely HealthCo addresses pressures and demands from NGOs due to its high visibility and resulting public pressures. Overall, the influence of management report users seems to be connected to the direct or indirect consideration of demands as well as the interest of these users in nfKPIs.

Finally, preparation processes can also be subject to influencing factors from the **rules and norms**. Marking informal norms, a firm's industry can have important effects on preparation processes. General industry factors typically influence the relevance of particular nfKPIs. In addition, firms from manufacturing industries tend to rely more on the specialist knowledge of know-how promotors in the report preparation. Moreover, depending on the comparability of peer firms and best-practice aspirations, firms apply peer comparisons more or less intensively. Thus, peer comparisons appear to drive mimetic isomorphism. While a low distance to consumers can also indicate increasing pressures from external stakeholders, only few case firms show noticeable effects. In addition, the visibility of the firm (HealthCo) appears to have a higher effect on the reporting processes as compared to firms with branding interests (TechCo, FashCo, AgCo) or supply chain firms (ChemCo, PrintCo, LogCo). However, the overall effects related to visibility seem to be rather low and correlated with other influencing factors such as firm size. In contrast to this, regulatory requirements can significantly influence preparation processes through coercive isomorphism. Particularly regulatory changes seem to increase efforts related to the preparation of nfKPIs and require monitoring through promotors and auditors. However, these effects seem to be associated with the firms' reporting goals and the scope of discretion of the requirements. Furthermore, voluntary reporting frameworks can affect nfKPI preparation processes with regard to materiality analyses, measurement and reviews. These effects seem to be associated with integrated reporting formats, as solely HealthCo's preparation process shows influences from such guidelines. In summary, rules and norms appear to considerably influence preparation processes. Nonetheless, these factors are commonly interlinked with other influencing factors.

Throughout the analysis, it becomes apparent that the individual influencing factors often show interlinkages with the **listing status** of a firm. In terms of nfKPI reporting, public firms for example face higher regulatory requirements and are likely to be subject to more extensive pressures from their management report users (*Oliveira et al.* (2010), p. 581; *Hahn/Kühnen* (2013), p. 12) as compared to private firms. On the one hand, this interlinkage to other important factors indicates the potential importance of this influencing factor, which has also been used as a key selection criterion for the sample of the study. On the other hand, the listing status cannot easily be separated from these influencing factors. Hence, potential differences with regard to the preparation processes of public and private firms are contained in the results regarding the various influencing factors connected to the listing status.

Drawing from these findings, the initial sampling dimensions of organizational size and listing status can be seen as **key influencing factors** on the preparation process of nfKPIs. However, other factors also assert particular influence on preparation processes and indicate interlinkages with effects related to size and listing status. As one of these factors, reporting formats can considerably influence preparation processes, particularly regarding nfKPI measurement processes. Moreover, regulatory requirements in combination with auditors mark important influencing factors which drive materiality analyses and reviews of the reports.

In line with previous discussions in the literature, other influencing factors have shown **mixed or low effects** on the design of preparation processes. Effects from a firm's industry are evident, yet remain rather low. While the influence of external users of management report varies significantly depending on the type of user and the type of preparer, the overall effects also seem to be strongly interlinked with firm size and listing status. Overall, the analyses offer insights into interlinkages between internal and external influencing factors and their combined effects on preparation processes (*Husillos et al.* (2011), p. 199).

Moreover, the **theoretical framework** appears to be appropriate for explaining how particular factors influence the design of the preparation processes. **Institutional theory** can explain several external and internal drivers of change in preparation processes. Coercive isomorphism appears to be driven mostly by reporting requirements in association with listing status, as public firms face higher regulatory requirements regarding nfKPI reporting. Nonetheless, all firms institutionalize such requirements in several phases and roles in their processes. Moreover, auditors and supervisory boards support this isomorphic behavior, the latter albeit to a considerably lower degree. In this mandatory nfKPI reporting setting, normative isomorphism becomes apparent only in integrated reporting settings such as for HealthCo. The firm marks the only case in which nfKPIs in the management report are prepared on basis of GRI frameworks. In firms with separate sustainability reports, the preparation processes of management reports seem to be largely decoupled from the preparation of sustainability reports. Hence, forces driving normative isomorphism appear to be rather low in this mandatory nfKPI reporting setting. Finally, particularly industry factors such as peer comparisons drive mimetic isomorphism of the case firms. In this context, service providers such as auditors, lectors or consultants provide only limited support with regard to aligning the firms' preparation process with those of others. Hence, these forces can explain how specific influencing factors can drive the institutionalization of nfKPI preparation processes.

Behavioral decision theory provides explanations for the evolvement of specific organizational structures in the context of nfKPI reporting. In line with this theory, firms particularly develop standard practices (e.g., decision or review criteria) for their preparation processes. Such practices are mostly established to ensure compliance with regulatory requirements or – if applicable – voluntary reporting frameworks. For similar reasons, firms use indoctrination to safeguard that participants of the preparation process – particularly process and power promotors – consider requirements from regulators or frameworks. In addition, hierarchical levels may be used to assign specific responsibilities for disclosure decisions. Some firms seem to use several hierarchical levels to assign clear responsibilities with regard to the preparation and to ensure a thorough review of nfKPI disclosures. However, particularly smaller firms could be avoiding such structures due to a lack of flexibility. While these factors indicate the suitability of behavioral decision theory, several factors also affect the division of labor related to the preparation process.

In this context, the **promotor model** can explain the effects of influencing factors on the participants of the preparation processes. The extent of promotor structures seems to be driven significantly by organizational size, as large firms include more participants into their processes who provide individual promotor contributions and powers. Small firms tend to combine promotor tasks and roles to limit the amount of persons involved in the preparation. In addition to size, the reporting format strongly influences promotor structures. While the effect appears to be strongest for integrated reporters, firms with quantitative and forward-looking nfKPIs also use more elaborate promotor structures. Furthermore, changes in regulatory requirements can also affect promotor structures, particularly if the reporting requirements are extended as in the case of PrintCo's nonfinancial statement. In addition to the three key promotor roles, actors such as supervisory boards and auditors act as gatekeepers who safeguard compliance with regulatory requirements. In cases where management report users are engaged in preparation processes – for example in HealthCo's materiality analysis – these actors communicate particularly with process and power promotors. However, in most firms the demands from these users are only considered indirectly.

Overall, the theoretical framework offers three organizational perspectives suitable for understanding how the design of preparation processes can be influenced from within or outside of the firm. In combination with the findings on influencing factors, this section indicates particularly important factors influencing the design of the preparation process of nfKPIs for management reports.

7 Conclusions

7.1 Main results

The **research goals** of this study were to investigate the design and influencing factors of preparation processes of nfKPIs for management reports. These goals were followed by conducting case study analyses of publicly listed and privately held firms, which are required to report nfKPIs as part of their management report. Subsequently, the case studies were analyzed on a within- and cross-case basis. The first research question was addressed by describing the case firms' preparation processes (within-case analyses) and contrasting the **phases** and **participants** of these processes in the cross-case analyses. In the third part of the cross-case analyses, the second research question was addressed by determining **influencing factors** of the preparation process from the previous analyses.

This study applied a qualitative **case study design** to address the two research questions. Through conducting a selective sampling approach, three publicly listed and four privately held firms were analyzed. By choosing sample firms from different industries, sizes and with various reporting formats, the study aimed at analyzing a broad range of preparation processes. The study bases its empirical results on interviews with 29 experts from the case firms, reflecting participants from functional departments, corporate support functions (e.g., accounting, sustainability or IR) and the executive board. In addition to the interviews, external and internal company documents helped to triangulate and enrich the findings of the interviews. Through this approach, the analyses are grounded on multiple perspectives related to the preparation process of the management report. In the following, the main results of the respective analyses are summarized.

Within-case analyses

The within-case analyses provided rich and in-depth descriptions of the preparation processes of nfKPIs for the management report of the case firms. Initially, the cases individually described the company profiles, organizational structure and nfKPI reporting of the case firms. Subsequently, the analysis shed light on the process participants, materiality analysis and composition process of the firms. Thus, the within-case analyses serve as a basis for answering the research questions of this study. First, the cases highlight phases of the preparation process and methods applied for preparing nfKPIs for the report. Second, the varying contributions and powers of the process participants serve as evidence for promotor roles in the preparation process. Third, by pointing out the contexts of the individual cases, these analyses provide initial evidence for important influencing factors regarding the phases and promotors of the preparation process.

Cross-case analyses

Building on the within-case analyses, the **cross-case analyses** looked at the design of the process – consisting of the process phases and participants – and associated influencing factors. To derive the design and influencing factors, the analyses compared and contrasted the case descriptions and empirical results. While the study found evidence for general phases and roles connected to the preparation process, the analyses indicated that these two parts of the preparation process design can differ significantly across the sample. On the basis of a theoretical framework comprising institutional theory, behavioral decision theory and the promotor model, this study discussed internal and external reasons for particular organizational structures in the preparation processes. Moreover, results and interpretations were discussed in the light of previous findings in the literature.

Phases

In the first part of the cross-case analyses, the study discussed the **phases** of the preparation process of nfKPIs for the management report. This study presented that preparation processes differ with regard to their **extent of formalization**, depending on the rules and procedures applied for preparing nfKPI disclosures. Large and more hierarchical firms appear to use formal processes while small firms tend to use fewer deadlines, procedures and participants.

On the basis of the conceptual framework of the preparation process developed in the foundation of the study, it was shown that the preparation process comprises a materiality analysis of the nfKPIs and a composition process of the report. In the **materiality analysis**, the case firms identify relevant nfKPIs which are then prioritized to determine material nfKPIs. The results indicated that materiality analyses can differ with regard to the procedures and perspectives applied for identifying and prioritizing nfKPIs. Furthermore, firms engaged internal or external stakeholders to varying degrees. While HealthCo applied the most elaborate materiality analysis with multiple perspectives and stakeholders considered, particularly small firms focused on organizational perspectives and determined nfKPIs rather intuitively. Furthermore, while most firms determined their material nfKPIs before conducting the composition process, some firms integrated these processes. Finally, the elaborateness of materiality analyses can also vary depending on whether firms determine material nfKPIs for the first time or whether they update previous nfKPIs. Although it can be assumed that firms forego materiality analyses by carrying forward previously reported nfKPIs, findings demonstrated that all case firms conduct materiality analyses in each reporting period, albeit with varying levels of elaborateness.

Regarding the **composition process**, case firms planned the report concept, timeline and responsibilities of the preparation process, prepared a draft of the nfKPI sections and reviewed this draft for the publication of the final management report. Similar to materiality analysis processes, composition processes of the case firms differed with regard to their elaborateness. In contrast to the preparation of the rest of the management report, composition processes had certain particularities with regard to the preparation of nfKPIs. When planning the preparation, the composition of nfKPI sections was commonly scheduled before the end of the reporting period. Moreover, most composition processes included a large variety of participants from different departments. When collecting nfKPIs, firms relied on various types of databases, reports and experts. Firms also differed strongly with regard to their validation of nfKPI information, which ranged from extensive site-audits to plausibility checks. Coordinators of the process often assembled the nfKPI sections on the basis of information provided by the departments or through information they had gathered themselves. Subsequently, coordinators managed the review process between review committees and initial writers. Results also indicated that the review of nfKPIs appears to be rather unproblematic, as preparers tended to focus less on these indicators as compared to other contents of the report.

In **summary**, the results demonstrated that the overall phases of the preparation processes of nfKPIs were similar across firms. However, the procedures and rules applied in these process steps differed significantly across firms. Building on previous findings in the literature (e.g., *Adams* (2002); *Searcy et al.* (2008); *Osann* (2010)) and on the conceptual framework of the preparation process developed in the foundation of this study, it was discussed how and why general phases of preparation processes can differ across firms. As these differences also highlighted different organizational structures underlying the preparation processes, the second part of the cross-case analyses focused on process participants.

Participants

The second part of the cross-case analyses presented how **participants of the preparation process** contribute to the process and how they communicate and collaborate in this context. On the basis of the promotor model, the study identified three specific promotor roles in the preparation process of nfKPIs: process promotors, power promotors and know-how promotors. While these roles were identified depending on the contributions and powers of the participants, the results indicated that individuals can take on one or more different roles (role combination) or share roles with other participants (role plurality).

The role of the **process promotor** comprises the task of process management in the case firms. To manage the preparation process, these actors determined and coordinated tasks for the process participants, exchanged information between these participants and mediated between them whenever necessary. To carry out this contribution, process promotors drew from specific powers, namely organizational know-how and communication competency. This study found that process promotor roles were often taken on by individuals from accounting or sustainability departments, who coordinated the preparation process of nfKPIs. In few cases, process promotor roles were taken on by individuals from other departments (e.g., communications). Moreover, these roles can also be carried out by multiple persons from the same department or from different hierarchical levels (e.g., CFO and the HEIR). In addition, some members from functional departments can take on process promotor roles when collecting department-specific nfKPIs from colleagues in their departments.

Power promotors contributed to the preparation processes by initializing the preparation, making decisions regarding nfKPI disclosures and dealing with opponents and proponents of these disclosures. As power promotors were often responsible for the publication of the management report, they initiated the preparation process by commencing the process or by asking the process promotor to prepare the report. With regard to decision-making, power promotors determined material nfKPIs, reviewed the draft and provided feedback and clearance for the report. These contributions were supported by the power promotor's high-ranking hierarchical position and access to material resources. Results of this study revealed that the promotor role was commonly taken on by multiple persons the case firms. The executive boards of the case firms delegated particular contributions to other participants such as functional departments, coordinators or review committees. Hence, the results demonstrated that firms seemed to have divided powers among several participants and hierarchical levels, indicating limited decision-making powers of executives in preparation processes of nfKPIs. Nonetheless, the executive boards remained responsible for the final clearance of the report.

As providers of information on nfKPIs, **know-how promotors** provided several contributions and powers in connection with the preparation processes. These actors measured nfKPIs by collecting and validating the relevant information. Moreover, they were responsible for writing the respective sections of the report draft. These promotors were able to contribute to the process due to their powers of expert knowledge and access to the relevant data. The results demonstrated that know-how promotor roles were shared within the case firms due to the diverse nature of nfKPIs. Role pluralities were present because of multiple functional departments such as HR, production or facility management involved in the preparation process. Moreover, know-how promotor roles were often combined with other roles. This occurred when functional departments also carried out process or power promotor roles or when other process participants such as coordinators or executives took on know-how promotor roles. The latter case can exist when the persons responsible for preparing nfKPIs for the management report have access to nfKPI information without relying on the support from functional departments.

In addition, the case studies revealed the **communication and collaboration** between the various participants of the preparation process. In all case firms, process promotors found themselves in the center of the communication between all participants. They managed the flow of information and applied various forms of formal or informal communication to coordinate the preparation process. Furthermore, case firms used other communication channels of the process participants with internal or external sources such as supervisory boards, auditors or regulatory requirements. With regard to the collaboration of participants, process promotors took on an important role through mediating between know-how and process promotors. In this context, process promotors faced several challenges such as finding agreements on material nfKPIs or communicating changes of draft texts.

Overall, the analysis provided explanations for the division of labor between participants of the preparation process. On the basis of the discussion, an **adapted promotor model** can be seen as suitable for preparation processes. In contrast to previous literature, the analysis highlighted that accountants tend to play an important role in such processes. While results indicated that roles were not concentrated in one person exclusively – which would reflect the champion theory – particularly small firms showed tendencies of role distributions.

Influencing factors

Building on results from the previous analyses, the third part of the cross-case analyses addressed the second research question of the study. To do so, the analysis identified and discussed internal and external **influencing factors** on the design of the preparation process. As **internal influencing factors**, the study identified supervisory boards and organizational characteristics. While supervisory boards appeared to have rather low impacts on the design of the preparation process, several important organizational characteristics were analyzed. Particularly corporate size appeared to influence the design of preparation processes. As a consequence of their nfKPI reporting goals and available resources, large and public firms appeared to have more elaborate preparation processes as compared to small and private firms. In addition to this factor, the organizational structure appeared to influence hierarchies involved in the process. While other forms of reporting did not have strong effects on the process design, particularly integrated reporting, forward-looking nfKPIs and disclosures of nfKPI goals appeared to strongly affect the collaboration between participants and processes connected to measuring and auditing nfKPIs.

This study indicated that **external influencing factors** comprised service providers, external users of management reports and the rules and norms surrounding the firms. With regard to service providers, results demonstrated that neither consultants nor lectors influenced the design of preparation processes significantly. In contrast, auditors seemed to provide a strong force for coercive isomorphism by acting as gatekeepers with regard to regulatory requirements. While auditors influenced some firms' data systems and reporting processes to a limited degree, such effects were low in other firms, confirming mixed results in previous studies. Similar to service providers, the effects of external users of management reports on the design of preparation processes appeared to be mixed. The influence of report users was mostly limited as their demands were commonly considered only indirectly as part of the preparers' decision criteria. While equity capital providers reflected the most important user group for preparers, these users showed varying interest in nfKPIs and their influence appeared to be connected to other factors such as listing or industry norms. In addition to equity capital providers, debt capital providers and other external stakeholders often indicated low interest in nfKPIs and hence had low influence on most case firms' preparation processes. Nonetheless, firms recognized that these actors expected nfKPI disclosures. Finally, industry norms, regulatory requirements and reporting frameworks indicated important rules and norms influencing preparation processes. In terms of industry norms, peer company comparisons conducted by most firms indicated mimetic isomorphism while industry-membership and distance to consumers had only low effects on individual firms' preparation processes. Regulatory requirements were connected to strong coercive isomorphic behavior with regard to preparation processes as specific participants monitored regulatory changes and adjusted processes accordingly. Other than for integrated reporters, reporting frameworks had low influence on preparation processes.

In the **discussion** of the influencing factors, the key sample selection criteria of corporate size and listing status were confirmed as key influencing factors on the design of the preparation process. The effects of the listing status on the preparation process were derived from interrelated influencing factors such as management report users or regulatory requirements. In addition to organizational size and listing status, the discussion also highlighted other important influencing factors such as regulatory requirements in combination with auditors and demonstrated potential connections between influencing factors.

In this context, the underlying **theoretical framework** appeared to be suitable for explaining the linkage between influencing factors and the design of the preparation process of nfKPIs for the management report. In this context, institutional theory provided explanations for the influence of internal and external factors on different forms of isomorphic behavior. Coercive isomorphism was strongly institutionalized in the case firms, induced by regulatory requirements and supported by actors such as auditors and supervisory boards. Normative isomorphism seemed to be apparent solely in the case of integrated reports.

Moreover, mimetic isomorphism was driven more strongly by industry factors than by service providers. Behavioral decision theory can be used to explain the development of standard practices in reaction to regulatory requirements. Furthermore, indoctrination can be used to ensure the compliance with such requirements. In addition, hierarchical levels safeguarded decision-making processes in some firms. Finally, promotor structures can be linked to influencing factors. While organizational size reflected an important factor for the extent of promotor structures, other factors such as reporting format or regulatory requirements influenced the extent and constellations of promotor structures. Furthermore, internal and external sources can be linked to the communication channels of promotors.

7.2 Contributions and implications

This study provides several contributions and implications with regard to the preparation process of nfKPIs for management reports. In the following, theoretical and managerial contributions and implications of this study are discussed.

Theoretical contributions and implications

This study provides several **contributions to the literature**. By building on the previously separate research streams on preparation processes of nfKPIs and on the preparation of corporate reports, this study **bridges a gap** by addressing the preparation of nfKPIs in the mandatory reporting setting of management reports. Therefore, this study informs researchers on the particularities regarding the phases, participants and influencing factors of preparing mandatory nonfinancial information. In addition, this study addresses several calls for research on preparation processes of nonfinancial reporting (*Adams* (2002), pp. 245-246; *Osann* (2010), pp. 261-264; *Searcy/Buslovich* (2014), pp. 167-168). Hence, the findings of this study can be used as a basis for future research on preparation processes of nonfinancial reporting.

Furthermore, this study contributes to the literature **methodologically**. Previous studies in this field have focused on single case studies, on multiple case studies with single expert interviews or on surveys. As an extension to research, the present study is based on an embedded multiple case study design with experts from various hierarchical levels and departments. Hence, this research is based on a large number of interviews and perspectives. Results can thus shed light on the diverse challenges of participants of preparation processes. In addition, as this study looks at public and private preparers of nfKPIs for management reports, results can be transferred to both types of firms.

From a **theoretical** perspective, this study contributes to the literature by transferring the promotor model and behavioral decision theory to the preparation process of nfKPIs for management reports. Both theories provide suitable explanations for organizational structures surrounding such processes. Moreover, the theoretical framework of this study connects these two theories with institutional theory to further explain the design of the preparation process and associated influencing factors. Therefore, this model addresses and links several organizational levels and perspectives. As the results of this study demonstrate the suitability of this theoretical framework for analyzing the preparation process of nfKPIs for the management report, this framework could be further tested in this context. Moreover, the framework could be adjusted and further advanced to explore preparation processes of other mandatory or voluntary disclosures.

In addition, the study contributes to an understanding of **mandatory nfKPI reporting** in a reporting environment in which preparers have considerable experience regarding the reporting of nfKPIs. Therefore, effects of nfKPI reporting requirements identified in this study could be used to examine or compare effects of regulatory changes in other countries. Overall, this study contributes to the literature by advancing the understanding of preparation processes of nfKPIs for management reports.

Managerial contributions and implications

This study also provides several **managerial contributions and implications**. The study at hand informs **preparers** of management reports on the design and potential influencing factors of preparation processes. On the basis of the descriptions and analyses of preparation processes from multiple public and private firms, preparers can draw helpful conclusions for their own preparation processes. With regard to phases of the preparation process, preparers receive an overview over particular process steps and potential methods suitable for preparing nfKPIs for the management report. Moreover, typical participants and roles are discussed in the light of the promotor model, which could help preparers to reflect on their organizational structures surrounding their preparation process. Findings regarding the influencing factors can guide preparers in determining suitable organizational structures for their particular internal and external organizational environment. Additionally, the results of this study support and extend practitioner guidelines on preparation processes.

Statutory auditors receive insights on the role of assurance in the context of nfKPI reporting in management reports. This study indicates points of contacts between auditors and preparers throughout the preparation process. Moreover, it sheds light on the roles of auditors in the preparation process and on moderating factors influencing their involvement in the process. In this context and in combination with descriptions of collection and validation processes, auditors can identify their potential influence on the preparation process. Similar to preparers, auditors can also use this study to identify particular challenges related to the preparation of nfKPIs. This knowledge can support future audits of nfKPI disclosures.

Furthermore, this study supports **users of management reports** in understanding decision-making processes related to nfKPI reporting. Thus, users such as equity and debt capital providers, NGOs or the general public become aware of the organizational structures surrounding preparation processes. By pointing out external and internal influencing factors, this study can enable management report users to determine potential effects of a firm's context on the preparation process and resulting nfKPI disclosures. Hence, this understanding of the particularities and challenges of preparing nfKPI disclosures can support users in evaluating a firm's nfKPI disclosures.

Building on the results of this study, **regulators and standard setters** can gain a better understanding of the effects of regulatory requirements or reporting frameworks on the internal preparation processes of corporate disclosures. While results show strong effects of regulatory changes on organizational reporting processes, only few firms use nfKPIs for the internal management of the group. This implication could be particularly interesting to evaluate the European legislator's goal of increasing the usage of nfKPIs for internal decision-making (Directive 2014/95/EU, rec. 3; *Kajüter* (2016), p. 230). Standard setters such as the GRI could use the findings to gain an understanding of the materiality analysis processes of non-GRI users. These insights could be used to further improve the relevance and practicality of the frameworks for preparing nfKPI disclosures.

In addition to these individual contributions and implications, the foundations of this study provide all parties involved in nfKPI reporting with a better understanding of the associated **terminology**. These discussions provide a conceptual basis for converging the understanding of nfKPIs between regulators, standard setters and reporters (*Stolowy/Paugam* (2018), pp. 528-531). Overall, the results of this study are useful to all internal and external parties involved in the preparation process.

7.3 Limitations

Although a qualitative research design in the form of multiple embedded case studies was determined to be suitable for the present research questions, this research design is subject to several limitations. While the researcher major limitations were mitigated by a thorough review of the research process on the basis of quality criteria for qualitative research, some limitations of this study remain. The following theoretical and methodological limitations should be considered when evaluating the results of this study.

Theoretical limitations

An important theoretical limitation of behavioral decision theory and the promotor model is **generalizability**. Organizational researchers note that theoretical findings regarding firm internal decision processes may not easily be transferable to other organizations (*Berger et al.* (2019), pp. 161-162). Researchers and practitioners should be particularly cautious when transferring the findings to other disclosure decision processes of mandatory and voluntary information. Nonetheless, the generalizability of the results is supported by multiple case studies with various process participants. By contrasting extreme and typical cases, interpretations of this study are grounded on a variation of contexts which supports inferences across the population (*Cook/Campbell* (1979), pp. 71-73; *Lukka/Kasanen* (1995), pp. 75-78).

Moreover, the **reliability** of theoretical findings could be influenced by ex-post rationalizations and hidden motivations of research subjects (*Berger et al.* (2019), pp. 161-162). Similar to the generalizability, this study supports the reliability of the results through theoretical and methodological triangulation. Furthermore, by disclosing both the research process and evidence of the interviews in the form of quotations, the study safeguards the intersubjective verifiability of the interpretations and theoretical discussions (*Kirk/Miller* (1986), pp. 72-73; *Lillis* (2006), p. 470).

The **theoretical focus** of this study lies on the organizational structures surrounding the preparation process of nfKPIs for management reports. Therefore, neither decision-making characteristics of individual participants nor the effects on the extent and quality of nfKPI disclosures have been analyzed in-depth. While decision-making characteristics of individual participants have been considered in the light of decision criteria, this study does not shed light on personal characteristics and agendas of decision-makers involved in the preparation process. Although such characteristics are considered by *Osann* to a certain extent for the preparation of immaterial resources (*Osann* (2010), pp. 163-168), more research is necessary which links individual decision-making characteristics, organizational structures and influencing factors internal or external to the firm. Furthermore, this study has only considered effects of organizational structures on final nfKPI disclosures to a limited degree. Hence, further studies on the linkage between organizational structures and the extent and quality of disclosure outcomes are necessary. In addition, studies could look at the receptions of resulting disclosures on management report users (*Laine* (2009), p. 1048). Despite these limitations mentioned above, this study remains informative about the theoretical linkage between the design of the preparation process of nfKPIs and associated influencing factors.

Methodological limitations

Similar to the theoretical limitations, the results of this study cannot easily be **generalized** for methodological reasons. While comparisons between preparation processes of public and private firms show considerable similarities and differences, discussions regarding the effect of firm size should be interpreted with caution. As the two large public firms are significantly larger than the largest private firm, size effects in private firms' preparation processes could be driven by a lack of private firms of similar size as compared to HealthCo or ChemCo. However, as nfKPI disclosures from large private firms are typically rather reserved (*Haller et al.* (2014), pp. 2544-2545), it can be assumed that size effects may be less important for the preparation process design of private firms as compared to public firms. Nonetheless, this limitation calls for further investigations of size effects.

Furthermore, several potential **biases** may be present with regard to the expert interviews. First, around half of the interviews were carried out with coordinators of the preparation processes. While this could indicate an overreliance on the perspective of these actors, they reflect the actors most involved in the preparation process. Due to their overview over the process, these actors can also provide the most comprehensive account of the preparation processes as compared to other participants. Perspectives of the other participants support and triangulate the statements of the coordinators of the preparation process. Although it was not possible in some firms to access executives to include their perspective, this perspective can be approximated through interviews with the respective coordinators of the report and through executive interviews conducted with the majority of the other case firms. Second, as the coordinators serve as gatekeepers for acquiring additional expert interviews with other participants of the preparation process, the selection of experts might be biased towards participants favorable to the coordinators. While this risk could not be mitigated completely, the researcher ensured that the most important actors of the preparation process were included. Finally, the high involvement of the researcher with the interview experts in the context of personal interviews may result in potential interpretation biases. However, such biases were mitigated by applying quality criteria, disclosing subjectivity and by providing quotations as evidence for interpretations.

In addition, the comparisons and discussions in the cross-case analysis could be biased by the **subjectivity** of the researcher. However, the study accounts for underlying interpretations by referring to evidence in the individual case studies, by explaining his interpretative process and by connecting findings with a theoretical framework and extant literature. Therefore, the interpretations should be traceable intersubjectively.

7.4 Outlook

As indicated in the motivation of this study, preparers face a growing importance of both nfKPI disclosures and their preparation processes as well as increasing regulation for these types of disclosures. In line with the findings of this study, changes in regulatory requirements and are likely to affect preparation processes of nfKPIs in management reports. Therefore, this section closes with an outlook on forthcoming developments in nfKPI reporting regulation to determine potential changes and challenges for preparers in the future. Drawing from the findings and limitations of this study, this study closes with avenues for future research.

Regulatory outlook

In the light of recent changes to EU regulation on nonfinancial reporting and the goal of the European Commission to strengthen sustainability investments in European capital markets, current requirements are being scrutinized through several initiatives from regulators (*European Commission* (2018a), p. 2; *Schmotz/Schmidt* (2017), p. 1033). First, the European Commission has established a **high-level expert group on sustainable finance** (HLEG) which has developed recommendations for strengthening sustainability in EU regulation on reporting and financial policy (*HLEG* (2018), p. 6). While the expert group suggests several regulatory improvements affecting both reporting firms and capital market participants, some recommendations directly address nfKPIs. The HLEG suggests that investors should consider specific social indicators such as those from the International Bill of Human Rights or the International Labour Organization standards in their asset allocation decisions (*HLEG* (2018), pp. 86-87). As evident in the findings of this study, such capital market demands could drive the inclusion of these nfKPIs in the firms' management reports. Moreover, the HLEG also suggests requiring specific nfKPI disclosures of nfKPIs for particular industries such as the agricultural and food industries (*HLEG* (2018), pp. 89, 91), which could directly affect preparation processes of firms from these industries.

Second, the European Commission has established a **technical expert group** consisting of various stakeholder group representatives (i.e., business, finance, NGOs and researchers) which assist the commission in developing regulation related to sustainable finance (*Lanfermann* (2018), p. 1645). As a part of the tasks of the expert group, the non-binding guideline of the European Commission on nonfinancial disclosures (*European Commission* (2017)) shall be extended through disclosing metrics applied for determining climate-related risks and opportunities (*European Commission* (2018c), pp. 1, 5; *Schmotz/Schmidt* (2017), pp. 2882-2883). This update of the guideline indicates that the European Commission aims to increase climate-related disclosures (*Lanfermann* (2018), p. 1647), which could potentially affect the selection and preparation of relevant nfKPIs for the management report.

Third, the European Commission announced a consultation process ("**fitness check**") based on a broad range of stakeholders to scrutinize the effectiveness of EU reporting requirements (*European Commission* (2018b), p. 4). While this fitness check examines several forms of corporate reporting such as reporting requirements of financial institutions or the reporting of listed and non-listed firms, the consultation also touches on the perceived effectiveness of the CSR directive (*European Commission* (2018b), pp. 29-36). Although the consultation does not explicitly address nfKPIs, it surveys stakeholders regarding for example their perception of the effectiveness of the regulation, their view on the Commission's non-binding guideline or estimates of the implementation costs of preparing nonfinancial statements (*Schmotz/Schmidt* (2017), p. 1038). Depending on the outcome of the consultation, changes to the regulation on nonfinancial statements could affect the requirements regarding nfKPI disclosure. Overall, these three initiatives of the European Commission show strong overlaps (*Schmotz/Schmidt* (2017), p. 1038-1039).

On a global level, stakeholders and standard-setters are discussing whether the FASB and International Accounting Standards Board (IASB) should **mandate** nonfinancial reporting. Groups such as the HLEG (*HLEG* (2018), p. 58) and researchers (*Barker/Eccles* (2018), pp. 30-35) argue in favor of mandatory nonfinancial reporting imposed by these standard-setters. While the IASB has recently stated that it does not see the necessity to change its requirements in this regard, it has resumed to work on its management commentary project, which could provide a basis for nfKPI reporting in the future (*Lanfermann* (2018), p. 1647).

Future research

From a **theoretical** perspective, future research could shed light on decision-making characteristics of individual participants involved in preparation processes of nfKPIs. Building on theories from sociology or psychology, studies could link individual decision environments with organizational structures and resulting nfKPI disclosures. Moreover, studies could further extend the promotor model in the field of preparation processes. This extension could for example analyze the dynamics of promotor roles throughout preparation processes (*Hauschildt/Schewe* (1997), pp. 511-514; *Folkerts/Hauschildt* (2002), pp. 9-10). In addition, researchers could examine potential cross-country differences in promotor structures.

Future research can also approach this field with different **methodologies**. Similar to recent studies in the field of management reporting (*Amel-Zadeh et al.* (2018); *Brown et al.* (2019)), studies could use survey methods to collect large sample evidence on preparation processes. Such surveys could determine and contrast promotor structures in a large number of public and private companies reporting nfKPIs. These structures could then be discussed in the light of internal and external influencing factors to determine the importance of individual factors identified in this study. Moreover, such studies could develop recommendations regarding the effectiveness of particular organizational structures for preparing nfKPIs for management reports. When conducting surveys, researchers should be aware of potential biases in relation to single informants within the case firms. While process promotors may be well informed about the overall preparation processes, extending the surveys through other participants of the process could increase the reliability of the results and provide additional perspectives. As for qualitative research, authors could use case studies to examine challenges related to the first time adoption of nfKPIs or nonfinancial statements. In this context, researchers could identify barriers of will or capability inherent in introduction processes and discuss contributions of promotors to overcome such barriers.

In addition to preparation processes of nfKPIs, researchers could look at other **topics** related to the preparation of corporate reports. In a management reporting context, researchers could examine preparation processes of narrative sections on for example corporate governance or risk and opportunities. Furthermore, research could focus on the involvement of executive boards in the preparation process of management forecasts. It could also be of interest to compare preparation processes of different management report sections to identify variations in organizational structures or participant roles. Moreover, studies could focus on the preparation of other corporate reports such as sustainability reports. In this context, it could be particularly interesting to contrast materiality analysis processes of sustainability reports to those of management reports. Overall, various exciting research opportunities exist which could build on the results of the present study.

Appendix A

Pool of interview questions

I Goals and role of nfKPI reporting

- Which goals does your company pursue with regard to the reporting on nfKPIs in the management report?
- Which roles do other reporting media play with regard to your company's reporting on nfKPIs (e.g., sustainability report, website or direct stakeholder communication)?

II Phases of the preparation process of nfKPIs for the management report

- How does your company determine, which nfKPIs are relevant for understanding the course of business and the financial position of the firm?
- On the basis of these nfKPIs, how are material or the most important KPIs determined?
- In the beginning of the preparation of the management report, how is the reporting on nfKPIs planned?
- Which department or person manages and coordinates the preparation process of nfKPIs for the management report?
- How are the nfKPIs for the management report measured and collected?
- Which challenges exist with regard to the measurement and collection of nfKPIs?
- How are the respective sections on nfKPIs written for the first draft?
- How are nfKPIs finalized for the management report?

III Roles and communication in the preparation process for nfKPIs

- Which key persons are frequently involved in the process and provide support?
- How do you and the other participants communicate in the preparation process?
- In how far do you use information sources which are not directly involved in the preparation process (internal and external to your company)?
- Which groups or persons in your company follow particular goals with the reporting on nfKPIs?

IV Particularities and development of the preparation process of nfKPIs

- Which particularities exist with regard to the preparation process of nfKPIs in comparison to the preparation process of the remaining management report?
- In how far has the preparation process of nfKPIs changed over time through factors internal or external to the company?

Open questions regarding the potential for improvements

- From your point of view, what constitutes a good preparation process of nfKPIs for the management report?
- How satisfied are you with your current preparation process? Where do you see potential for improvement?
- Do you have further comments on this topic that are important for you?

Appendix B

Firm and job title	Abbreviation	Department
HealthCo		
Head of management and quarterly reporting	HMQR	Financial accounting
Management and quarterly reporting	MQR	Financial accounting
Manager sustainability department	MSD	Sustainability
Manager sustainable procurement	MSP	Procurement
QEHS database manager	DBM	Sustainability
Investor relations manager	IRM	Investor relations
ChemCo		
Head of external reporting	HER	Financial accounting
Management and quarterly reporting	MQR	Financial accounting
Manager sustainability department	MSD	Sustainability
Head of safety controlling	HSC	Safety
Safety controller	SC	Safety
Investor relations manager 1	IRM1	Investor relations
Investor relations manager 2	IRM2	Investor relations
PrintCo		
Chief Financial Officer	CFO	Executive board
Head of external and internal reporting	HEIR	Financial and management accounting
FashCo		
Chief Financial Officer	CFO	Executive board
Manager external and internal reporting	MEIR	Financial and management accounting
Head of external and internal reporting	HEIR	Financial and management accounting
LogCo		
Chief Financial Officer	CFO	Executive board
CFO assistant	CFOA	Executive assistance
Head of accounting	HA	Financial accounting
Manager human resources strategy	HRS	HR

(Appendix B continued)

Firm and job title	Abbr.	Department
TechCo		
Chief Financial Officer	CFO	Executive board
Investor relations manager	IRM	Executive assistance
Head of database management	HDBM	QEHS
Database manager	DBM	QEHS
Human resources manager	HRM	Human resources
AgCo		
Head of external reporting	HER	Financial accounting
Public relations manager	PRM	Communications

Table A-1: Interview experts in case companies

List of references

A

Abels, G./Behrens, M. (2009): Interviewing Experts in Political Science, in: Bogner, A./Littig, B./Menz, W. (eds.), Interviewing Experts, Houndmills et al. 2009, pp. 138-156.

Achilladelis, B./Jervis, P./Robertson, A. (1971): A Study of Success and Failure in Industrial Innovation – Report on project SAPPHO to SRC, Brighton 1971.

Adams, C. (2002): Internal Organisational Factors Influencing Corporate Social and Ethical Reporting, in: Accounting, Auditing & Accountability Journal, Vol. 15, No. 2, 2002, pp. 223-250.

Adams, C./Frost, G. (2008): Integrating Sustainability Reporting into Management Practices, in: Accounting Forum, Vol. 32, No. 4, 2008, pp. 288-302.

Adams, C./Larrinaga-González, C. (2007): Engaging with Organisations in Pursuit of Improved Sustainability Accounting and Performance, in: Accounting, Auditing & Accountability Journal, Vol. 20, No. 3, 2007, pp. 333-364.

Adams, C./McNicholas, P. (2007): Making a Difference – Sustainability Reporting, Accountability and Organisational Change, in: Accounting, Auditing & Accountability Journal, Vol. 20, No. 3, 2007, pp. 382-402.

Adler, H./Düring, W./Schmaltz, K. (1995): Rechnungslegung und Prüfung der Unternehmen, 6th edition, Stuttgart 1995.

Admiraal, M./Nivra, R./Turksema, R./Netherlands Court of Audit (2009): Reporting on Nonfinancial Information, in: International Journal of Government Auditing, Vol. 36, No. 3, 2009, pp. 15-20.

Ahrens, T./Chapman, C. (2006): Theorizing Practice in Management Accounting Research, in: Chapman, C. S./Hopwood, A. G./Shields, M. D. (eds.), Handbook of Management Accounting Research, Oxford 2006, pp. 99-112.

Ahrens, T./Dent, J. (1998): Accounting and Organizations – Realizing the Richness of Field Research, in: Journal of Management Accounting Research, Vol. 10, No. 1, 1998, pp. 1-39.

Altheide, D./Johnson, J. (1994): Criteria for Assessing Interpretive Validity in Qualitative Research, in: Denzin, N. K./Lincoln, Y. S. (eds.), Handbook of Qualitative Research, Thousand Oaks 1994, pp. 485-499.

Amel-Zadeh, A. (2018): Social Responsibility in Capital Markets – A Review and Framework of Theory and Empirical Evidence, URL: https://papers.ssrn.com/sol3/papers.cfm?abstract_id=2664547 (13.03.2019).

Amel-Zadeh, A./Scherf, A./Soltes, E. (2018): Creating Firm Disclosures, URL: https://ssrn.com/abstract=3234402 (13.03.2019).

Amir, E./Lev, B. (1996): Value-relevance of Nonfinancial Information – The Wireless Communications Industry, in: Journal of Accounting and Economics, Vol. 22, No. 1-3, 1996, pp. 3-30.

Arbeitskreis Externe Unternehmensrechnung der Schmalenbach-Gesellschaft für Betriebswirtschaft e.V. (AKEU) (2002): Grundsätze für das Value Reporting, in: Der Betrieb, Vol. 55, No. 45, 2002, pp. 2337-2340.

Arbeitskreis Externe Unternehmensrechnung der Schmalenbach-Gesellschaft für Betriebswirtschaft e.V. (AKEU) (2015): Nichtfinanzielle Leistungsindikatoren – Bedeutung für die Finanzberichterstattung, in: Schmalenbachs Zeitschrift für betriebswirtschaftliche Forschung, Vol. 68, No. 2, 2015, pp. 235-258.

Arena, M./Azzone, G. (2012): A Process-based Operational Framework for Sustainability Reporting in SMEs, in: Journal of Small Business and Enterprise Development, Vol. 19, No. 4, 2012, pp. 669-686.

Ashton, R. (2005): Intellectual Capital and Value Creation – A Review, in: Journal of Accounting Literature, Vol. 24, No. 1, 2005, pp. 53-134.

Atteslander, P. (2010): Methoden der empirischen Sozialforschung, 13th edition, Berlin 2010.

Azzone, G./Brophy, M./Noci, G./Welford, R./Young, W. (1997): A Stakeholders' View of Environmental Reporting, in: Long Range Planning, Vol. 30, No. 5, 1997, pp. 699-709.

B

Baetge, J./Fischer, T./Paskert, D. (1989): Der Lagebericht – Aufstellung, Prüfung und Offenlegung, Stuttgart 1989.

Baetge, J./Prigge, C. (2006): Anforderungen an verpflichtende, empfohlene und freiwillige Angaben des Konzernlageberichts, in: Der Betrieb, Vol. 59, No. 8, 2006, pp. 401-407.

Bailey, M. (1992): Do Physicists Use Case Studies? Thoughts on Public Administration Research, in: Public Administration Review, Vol. 52, No. 1, 1992, pp. 47-54.

Baker, C./Bédard, J./Prat dit Hauret, C. (2014): The Regulation of Statutory Auditing – An Institutional Theory Approach, in: Managerial Auditing Journal, Vol. 29, No. 5, 2014, pp. 371-394.

Ball, A./Owen, D./Gray, R. (2000): External Transparency or Internal Capture?, in: Business Strategy and the Environment, Vol. 9, No. 1, 2000, pp. 1-23.

Banker, R./Chang, H./Pizzini, M. (2004): The Balanced Scorecard – Judgmental Effects of Performance Measures Linked to Strategy, in: The Accounting Review, Vol. 79, No. 1, 2004, pp. 1-23.

Barker, R./Eccles, R. (2018): Should FASB and IASB Be Responsible for Setting Standards for Nonfinancial Information?, URL: https://www.sbs.ox.ac.uk/sites/default/files/2018-10/Green%20Paper_0.pdf (13.03.2019).

Barker, R./Imam, S. (2008): Analysts' Perceptions of 'Earnings Quality', in: Accounting and Business Research, Vol. 38, No. 4, 2008, pp. 313-329.

Barnard, C. (1938): The Functions of the Executive, Cambridge 1938.

Bartel, R. (1990): Charakteristik, Methodik und wissenschaftsmethodische Probleme der Wirtschaftswissenschaften, in: Wirtschaftswissenschaftliches Studium, Vol. 19, No. 2, 1990, pp. 54-59.

Barth, D./Rahe, I./Rabenhorst, D. (2014): Ausgewählte Anwendungsfragen zur Konzernlageberichterstattung nach DRS 20, in: Zeitschrift für internationale und kapitalmarktorientierte Rechnungslegung, Vol. 14, No. 1, 2014, pp. 47-56.

Bassen, A./Kovacs, A. (2008): Environmental, Social and Governance Key Performance Indicators from a Capital Market Perspective, in: Zeitschrift für Wirtschafts- und Unternehmensethik, Vol. 9, No. 2, 2008, pp. 182-192.

Bassen, A./Senkl, D. (2010): Ermittlung von Leistungsindikatoren nachhaltiger Unternehmensführung aus Kapitalmarktperspektive, in: Controlling – Zeitschrift für erfolgsorientierte Unternehmenssteuerung, Vol. 22, No. 4-5, 2010, pp. 256-261.

Baumann-Pauly, D./Wickert, C./Spence, L./Scherer, A. (2013): Organizing Corporate Social Responsibility in Small and Large Firms, in: Journal of Business Ethics, Vol. 115, No. 4, 2013, pp. 693-705.

Beattie, V./Smith, S. (2012): Evaluating Disclosure Theory Using the Views of UK Finance Directors in the Intellectual Capital Context, in: Accounting and Business Research, Vol. 42, No. 5, 2012, pp. 471-494.

Bebbington, J./Brown, J./Frame, B./Thomson, I. (2007): Theorizing Engagement – The Potential of a Critical Dialogic Approach, in: Accounting, Auditing & Accountability Journal, Vol. 20, No. 3, 2007, pp. 356-381.

Bebbington, J./Higgins, C./Frame, B. (2009): Initiating Sustainable Development Reporting, in: Accounting, Auditing & Accountability Journal, Vol. 22, No. 4, 2009, pp. 588-625.

Belkaoui, A./Karpik, P. (1989): Determinants of the Corporate Decision to Disclose Social Information, in: Accounting, Auditing & Accountability Journal, Vol. 2, No. 1, 1989, pp. 36-51.

Bennett, J. (1997): A Case for Theory Triangulation, in: Nursing Science Quarterly, Vol. 10, No. 2, 1997, pp. 97-102.

Benston, G. (1982): Accounting and Corporate Accountability, in: Accounting, Organizations and Society, Vol. 7, No. 2, 1982, pp. 87-105.

Berger, U./Bernhard-Mehlich, I./Oertel, S. (2019): Die Verhaltenswissenschaftliche Entscheidungstheorie, in: Kieser, A./Ebers, M. (eds.), Organisationstheorien, 8th edition, Stuttgart 2019, pp. 118-163.

Bezemer, P.-J./Peij, S./de Kruijs, L./Maassen, G. (2014): How two-tier boards can be more effective, in: Corporate Governance, Vol. 14, No. 1, 2014, pp. 15-31.

Biernacki, P./Waldorf, D. (1981): Snowball Sampling – Problems and Techniques of Chain Referral Sampling, in: Sociological Methods & Research, Vol. 10, No. 2, 1981, pp. 141-163.

Blaesing, D. (2013): Nachhaltigkeitsberichterstattung in Deutschland und den USA – Berichtspraxis, Determinanten und Eigenkapitalkostenwirkungen, Frankfurt am Main 2013.

Blohm, H. (1974): Die Gestaltung des betrieblichen Berichtswesens als Problem der Leitungsorganisation, 2nd edition, Herne et al. 1974.

Bloomfield, R./Nelson, M./Soltes, E. (2016): Gathering Data for Archival, Field, Survey, and Experimental Accounting Research, in: Journal of Accounting Research, Vol. 54, No. 2, 2016, pp. 341-395.

Böcking, H.-J. (1998): Zum Verhältnis von Rechnungslegung und Kapitalmarkt – Vom „financial accounting" zum „business reporting", in: Ballwieser, W. (ed.), Rechnungslegung und Steuern international, Düsseldorf 1998, pp. 17-53.

Böcking, H.-J./Althoff, C. (2017): Paradigmenwechsel in der (Konzern-) Lageberichterstattung über nicht-monetäre Erfolgsfaktoren, in: Der Konzern, Vol. 15, No. 5, 2017, pp. 246-255.

Boesso, G./Kumar, K. (2009): An investigation of stakeholder prioritization and engagement, in: Journal of Accounting & Organizational Change, Vol. 5, No. 1, 2009, pp. 62-80.

Bogner, A./Littig, B./Menz, W. (2014): Interviews mit Experten – Eine praxisorientierte Einführung, Wiesbaden 2014.

Bogner, A./Menz, W. (2009a): Das theoriegenerierende Experteninterview – Erkenntnisinteresse, Wissensform, Interaktion, in: Bogner, A./Littig, B./Menz, W. (eds.), Experteninterviews – Theorien, Methoden, Anwendungsfelder, 3rd edition, Wiesbaden 2009, pp. 61-98.

Bogner, A./Menz, W. (2009b): Experteninterviews in der qualitativen Sozialforschung – Zur Einführung in eine sich intensivierende Methodendebatte, in: Bogner, A./Littig, B./Menz, W. (eds.), Experteninterviews – Theorien, Methoden, Anwendungsfelder, 3rd edition, Wiesbaden 2009, pp. 7-31.

Boms, A. (2008): Unternehmensverantwortung und Nachhaltigkeit – Umsetzung durch das Sustainability Performance Measurement, Lohmar 2008.

Bonner, S./Lewis, B. (1990): Determinants of Auditor Expertise, in: Accounting and Auditing, Vol. 28, No. 1, 1990, pp. 1-20.

Borga, F./Citterio, A./Noci, G./Pizzurno, E. (2009): Sustainability Report in Small Enterprises, in: Business Strategy and the Environment, Vol. 18, No. 3, 2009, pp. 162-176.

Bossel, H. (1999): Indicators for Sustainable Development – Theory, Method, Applications – A Report to the Balaton Group, Winnipeg 1999.

Bourdieu, P./Wacquant, L. (1992): An Invitation to Reflexive Sociology, Cambridge 1992.

Bouten, L./Everaert, P. (2015): Social and Environmental Reporting in Belgium, in: Critical Perspectives on Accounting, Vol. 33, No. 1, 2015, pp. 24-43.

Brennan, N./Gray, S. (2005): The Impact of Materiality, in: Asian Academy of Management Journal of Accounting and Finance, Vol. 1, No. 1, 2005, pp. 1-31.

Breuer, F. (2010): Wissenschaftstheoretische Grundlagen qualitativer Methodik in der Psychologie, in: Mey, G./Mruck, K. (eds.), Handbuch Qualitative Forschung in der Psychologie, Wiesbaden 2010, pp. 35-49.

Breuer, F./Mey, G./Mruck, K. (2011): Subjektivität und Selbst-/Reflexivität in der Grounded-Theory-Methodology, in: Mey, G./Mruck, K. (eds.), Grounded Theory Reader, 2nd edition, Wiesbaden 2011, pp. 427-448.

Breuer, F./Muckel, P./Dieris, B. (2019): Reflexive Grounded Theory, 4th edition, Wiesbaden 2019.

Brooks, C./Oikonomou, I. (2018): The Effects of Environmental, Social and Governance Disclosures and Performance on Firm Value, in: The British Accounting Review, Vol. 50, No. 1, 2018, pp. 1-15.

Brown, L./Call, A./Clement, M./Sharp, N. (2015): Inside the "Black Box" of Sell-Side Financial Analysts, in: Journal of Accounting Research, Vol. 53, No. 1, 2015, pp. 1-47.

Brown, L./Call, A./Clement, M./Sharp, N. (2019): Managing the Narrative – Investor Relations Officers and Corporate Disclosure, in: Journal of Accounting and Economics, Vol. 67, No. 1, 2019, pp. 58-79.

Brühl, R. (2017): Wie Wissenschaft Wissen schafft – Theorie und Ethik, 2nd edition, Konstanz et al. 2017.

Brühl, R./Orth, M. (2008): Controlling und die Veröffentlichung von Informationen über immaterielle Ressourcen, in: Controlling & Management, Vol. 52, No. 1, 2008, pp. 28-39.

Bryman, A./Bell, E. (2015): Business Research Methods, 4th edition, Oxford 2015.

Bryson, J. (2004): What to Do When Stakeholders Matter, in: Public Management Review, Vol. 6, No. 1, 2004, pp. 21-53.

Bühler-Niederberger, D. (1985): Analytische Induktion als Verfahren qualitativer Methodologie, in: Zeitschrift für Soziologie, Vol. 14, No. 6, 1985, pp. 475-485.

Buhr, N. (2002): A Structuration View on the Initiation of Environmental Reports, in: Critical Perspectives on Accounting, Vol. 13, No. 1, 2002, pp. 17-38.

Bundesministerium der Justiz und für Verbraucherschutz (BMJV) (2016): Referentenentwurf des Bundesministeriums der Justiz und Verbraucherschutz – Entwurf eines Gesetzes zur Stärkung der nichtfinanziellen Berichterstattung der Unternehmen in ihren Lage- und Konzernlageberichten, URL: https://www.bmjv.de/SharedDocs/Gesetzgebungsverfahren/Dokumente/RefE_CSR-Richtlinie-Umsetzungsgesetz.pdf?__blob=publicationFile&v=1 (13.03.2019).

Burghardt, M./Weigel, C. (2015): Integrated Reporting bei deutschen Kreditinstituten, in: Freidank, C.-C./Müller, S./Velte, P. (eds.), Handbuch Integrated Reporting, Berlin 2015, pp. 655-676.

Burns, J./Scapens, R. (2000): Conceptualizing Management Accounting Change, in: Management Accounting Research, Vol. 11, No. 1, 2000, pp. 3-25.

Bushman, R./Indjejikian, R./Smith, A. (1996): CEO Compensation – The Role of Individual Performance Evaluation, in: Journal of Accounting and Economics, Vol. 21, No. 2, 1996, pp. 161-193.

Busse, G. (2003): Leitfadengestützte, qualitative Telefoninterviews, in: Kopp, R./Langenhoff, G./Schröder, A. (eds.), Methodenhandbuch – Angewandte empirische Methoden – Erfahrungen aus der Praxis, Dortmund 2003, pp. 27-36.

C

Calabrese, A./Costa, R./Ghiron, N./Menichini, T. (2017): Materiality Analysis in Sustainability Reporting, in: European Journal of Sustainable Development, Vol. 6, No. 3, 2017, pp. 439-447.

Calabrese, A./Costa, R./Levialdi, N./Menichini, T. (2016): A Fuzzy Analytic Hierarchy Process Method to Support Materiality Assessment in Sustainability Reporting, in: Journal of Cleaner Production, Vol. 121, No. 1, 2016, pp. 248-264.

Calabrese, A./Costa, R./Rosati, F. (2015): A Feedback-based Model for CSR Assessment and Materiality Analysis, in: Accounting Forum, Vol. 39, No. 4, 2015, pp. 312-327.

Chakrabarti, A./Hauschildt, J. (1989): The Division of Labour in Innovation Management, in: R&D Management, Vol. 19, No. 2, 1989, pp. 161-171.

Charmaz, K. (2006): Constructing Grounded Theory – A Practical Guide Through Qualitative Analysis, London 2006.

Chenhall, R. (2003): Management Control Systems Design Within its Organizational Context, in: Accounting, Organizations and Society, Vol. 28, No. 2-3, 2003, pp. 127-168.

Christmann, G. (2009): Expert Interviews on the Telephone, in: Bogner, A./Littig, B./Menz, W. (eds.), Interviewing Experts, Houndmills et al. 2009, pp. 157-183.

Cinquini, L./Passetti, E./Tenucci, A./Frey, M. (2012): Analyzing Intellectual Capital Information in Sustainability Reports – Some empirical evidence, in: Journal of Intellectual Capital, Vol. 13, No. 4, 2012, pp. 531-561.

Claessens, S./Tzioumis, K. (2006): Ownership and Financing Structures of Listed and Large Non-listed Corporations, in: Corporate Governance, Vol. 14, No. 4, 2006, pp. 266-276.

Clarke-Sather, A./Hutchins, M./Zhang, Q./Gershenson, J./Sutherland, J. (2011): Development of social environmental, and economic inficators for a small/medium enterprise, in: International Journal of Accounting and Information Management, Vol. 19, No. 3, 2011, pp. 247-266.

Clausen, J./Loew, T. (2005): Mehr Glaubwürdigkeit durch Testate? Internationale Analyse des Nutzens von Testaten in der Umwelt- und Nachhaltigkeitsberichterstattung, URL: https://www.borderstep.de/wp-content/uploads/2014/09/Clausen_Loew-Mehr_Glaubwuerdigkeit_durch_Testate_Langfassung-2005.pdf (13.03.2019).

Clausen, J./Loew, T./Klaffkle, K./Raupach, M./Schoenheit, I. (2001): Der Nachhaltigkeitsbericht – ein Leitfaden zur Praxis glaubwürdiger Kommunikation für zukunftsfähige Unternehmen, Berlin 2001.

Cohen, J./Holder-Webb, L./Nath, L./Wood, D. (2012): Corporate Reporting of Nonfinancial Leading Indicators of Economic Performance and Sustainability, in: Accounting Horizons, Vol. 26, No. 1, 2012, pp. 65-90.

Cohen, J./Holder-Webb, L./Zamora, V. (2015): Nonfinancial Information Preferences of Professional Investors, in: Behavioral Research in Accounting, Vol. 27, No. 2, 2015, pp. 127-153.

Contrafatto, M. (2014): The Institutionalization of Social and Environmental Reporting, in: Accounting, Organizations and Society, Vol. 39, No. 6, 2014, pp. 414-432.

Cook, T./Campbell, D. (1979): Quasi-Experimentation – Design and Analysis Issues for Field Settings, Chicago 1979.

Cooper, D./Morgan, W. (2008): Case Study Research in Accounting, in: Accounting Horizons, Vol. 22, No. 2, 2008, pp. 159-178.

Corbin, J./Strauss, A. (1990): Grounded Theory Research, in: Qualitative Sociology, Vol. 13, No. 1, 1990, pp. 3-21.

Corbin, J./Strauss, A. (2015): Basics of Qualitative Research – Techniques and Procedures for Developing Grounded Theory, 4th edition, Thousand Oaks et al. 2015.

Cormier, D./Magnan, M. (2003): Environmental Reporting Management, in: Journal of Accounting and Public Policy, Vol. 22, No. 1, 2003, pp. 43-62.

Coyne, I. (1997): Sampling in Qualitative Research – Purposeful and Theoretical Sampling – Merging or Clear Boundaries?, in: Journal of Advanced Nursing, Vol. 26, No. 3, 1997, pp. 623-630.

Crane, A./Matten, D. (2016): Business Ethics – Managing Corporate Citizenship and Sustainability in the Age of Globalization, 4th edition, Oxford 2016.

Cressey, D. (1953): Other People's Money – A Study in the Social Psychology of Embezzlement, New York 1953.

Creswell, J. (2014): Research Design – Qualitative, Quantitative, and Mixed Methods Approaches, 4th edition, Los Angeles et al. 2014.

Cyert, R./March, J. (1963): A Behavioral Theory of the Firm, Englewood Cliffs 1963.

D

Davis, W. (1972): Peirce's Epistemology, The Hague 1972.

Day, D. (1994): Raising Radicals – Different Processes for Championing Innovative Corporate Ventures, in: Organization Science, Vol. 5, No. 2, 1994, pp. 148-172.

Day, R./Woodward, T. (2004): Disclosure of Information About Employees in the Directors' Report of UK Published Financial Statements, in: Accounting Forum, Vol. 28, No. 1, 2004, pp. 43-59.

Deegan, C./Blomquist, C. (2006): Stakeholder Influence on Corporate Reporting, in: Accounting, Organizations and Society, Vol. 31, No. 4-5, 2006, pp. 343-372.

Deegan, C./Unerman, J. (2011): Financial Accounting Theory, 2nd edition, Maidenhead 2011.

Delai, I./Takahashi, S. (2011): Sustainability Measurement System, in: Social Responsibility Journal, Vol. 7, No. 3, 2011, pp. 438-471.

Denzin, N./Lincoln, Y. (2011): The Discipline and Practice of Qualitative Research, in: Denzin, N./Lincoln, Y. S. (eds.), The SAGE Handbook of Qualitative Research, 4th edition, Los Angeles et al. 2011, pp. 1-19.

Deutsche Vereinigung für Finanzanalyse und Asset-Management (DVFA)/European Federation of Financial Analysts Societies (EFFAS) (2010): KPIs for ESG – A Guideline for the Integration of ESG into Financial Analysis and Corporate Valuation, Version 3.0, URL: http://www.dvfa.de/fileadmin/downloads/Publikationen/Standards/KPIs_for_ESG_3_0_Final.pdf (13.03.2019).

Dichev, I./Graham, J./Harvey, C./Rajgopal, S. (2013): Earnings Quality – Evidence from the Field, in: Journal of Accounting and Economics, Vol. 56, No. 2-3, 2013, pp. 1-33.

Dienes, D./Velte, P. (2016): The Impact of Supervisory Board Composition on CSR Reporting – Evidence from the German Two-Tier System, in: Sustainability, Vol. 8, No. 1, 2016, pp. 1-20.

DiMaggio, P./Powell, W. (1983): The Iron Cage Revisited, in: American Sociological Review, Vol. 48, No. 2, 1983, pp. 147-160.

Dong, L. (2017): Understanding Investors' Reliance on Disclosures of Nonfinancial Information and Mitigating Mechanisms for Underreliance, in: Accounting and Business Research, Vol. 47, No. 4, 2017, pp. 431-454.

Döring, N./Bortz, J. (2016): Forschungsmethoden und Evaluation in den Sozial- und Humanwissenschaften, 5th edition, Berlin et al. 2016.

Durchschein, C./Haller, A. (2018): Integrierte Unternehmensberichterstattung – eine Herausforderung für die Berichterstattung des Wirtschaftsprüfers (Teil 1), in: Der Betrieb, Vol. 71, No. 31, 2018, pp. 1805-1814.

Durden, C. (2008): Towards a Socially Responsible Management Control System, in: Accounting, Auditing & Accountability Journal, Vol. 21, No. 5, 2008, pp. 671-694.

Dyllick, T./Hockerts, K. (2002): Beyond the Business Case for Corporate Sustainability, in: Business Strategy and the Environment, Vol. 11, No. 2, 2002, pp. 130-141.

E

Ebke, W./Paal, B. (2013): § 342, in: Schmidt, K. (ed.), Münchener Kommentar zum Handelsgesetzbuch, 3rd edition, München 2013, pp. 2436-2447.

Eccles, R./Ioannou, I./Serafeim, G. (2011): The Impact of a Corporate Culture of Sustainability on Corporate Behavior and Performance, in: Management Science, Vol. 60, No. 11, 2011, pp. 2835-2857.

Eccles, R./Krzus, M. (2010): One Report – Integrated Reporting for a Sustainable Strategy, Hoboken 2010.

Eckstein, H. (1975): Case Study and Theory in Political Science, in: Greenstein, F. I./Polsby, N. W. (eds.), Handbook of Political Science, Reading 1975, pp. 79-137.

Edgley, C. (2014): A Genealogy of Accounting Materiality, in: Critical Perspectives on Accounting, Vol. 25, No. 3, 2014, pp. 255-271.

Edgley, C./Jones, M./Atkins, J. (2015): The Adoption of the Materiality Concept in Social and Environmental Reporting Assurance, in: The British Accounting Review, Vol. 47, No. 1, 2015, pp. 1-18.

Edmondson, A./Mcmanus, S. (2007): Methodological Fit in Management Field Research, in: Academy of Management Review, Vol. 32, No. 4, 2007, pp. 1246-1264.

Eifert, E./Briem, C. (2015): Wesentlichkeitsanalyse – Identifikation, Bewertung, Priorisierung und Darstellung der relevanten Berichtsinhalte in der Praxis, in: Gleich, R./Grönke, K./Kirchmann, M./Leyk, J. (eds.), Integrated Reporting, Freiburg et al. 2015, pp. 129-147.

Eisenhardt, K. (1989): Building Theories from Case Study Research, in: Academy of Management Review, Vol. 14, No. 4, 1989, pp. 532-550.

Eisenhardt, K./Graebner, M. (2007): Theory Building from Cases – Opportunities and Challenges, in: Academy of Management Journal, Vol. 50, No. 1, 2007, pp. 25-32.

Elkington, J. (1997): Cannibals with Forks – The Triple Bottom Line of 21st Century Business, Oxford 1997.

Epstein, M./Roy, M.-J. (2001): Sustainability in Action, in: Long Range Planning, Vol. 34, No. 5, 2001, pp. 585-604.

Erkens, M./Paugam, L./Stolowy, H. (2015): Non-financial Information – State of the Art and Research Perspectives Based on a Bibliometric Study, in: Comptabilité-Contrôle-Audit, Vol. 21, No. 3, 2015, pp. 15-92.

Ernst, C. (1998): KonTraG und KapAEG sowie aktuelle Entwicklungen zur Rechnungslegung und Prüfung in der EU, in: Die Wirtschaftsprüfung, Vol. 51, No. 23-24, 1998, pp. 1025-1035.

Etzioni, A./Lehman, E. (1967): Some Dangers in "Valid" Social Measurement, in: The Annals of the American Academy of Political and Social Science, Vol. 373, No. 1, 1967, pp. 1-15.

European Commission (2001): Commission Recommendation of 30 May 2001 on the Recognition, Measurement and Disclosure of Environmental Issues in the Annual Accounts and Annual Reports of Companies, URL: https://eur-lex.europa.eu/legal-content/EN/TXT/PDF/?uri=CELEX:32001H0453&from=EN (13.03.2019).

European Commission (2011): Communication from the Commission to the Single Market Act – Twelve Levers to Boost Growth and Strengthen Confidence, URL: http://eur-lex.europa.eu/legal-content/EN/TXT/PDF/?uri=CELEX:52011DC0206&from=EN (13.03.2019).

European Commission (2017): Communication from the Commission – Guidelines on Non-financial Reporting (Methodology for Reporting Non-financial Information), in: Official Journal of the European Union, Vol. 60, C 215, 2017, pp. 1-68.

European Commission (2018a): Communication from the Commission to the European Parliament, the European Council, the Council, the European Central Bank, the European Economic and Social Committee and the Committee of the Regions – Action Plan – Financing Sustainable Growth, URL: https://eur-lex.europa.eu/legal-content/EN/TXT/PDF/?uri=CELEX:52018DC0097&from=EN (13.03.2019).

European Commission (2018b): Consultation Document – Fitness Check on the Framework for Public Reporting by Companies, URL: https://ec.europa.eu/info/sites/info/files/2018-companies-public-reporting-consultation-document_en.pdf (13.03.2019).

European Commission (2018c): Technical Expert Group on Sustainable Finance (TEG) – Overview of consultation plans, URL: https://ec.europa.eu/info/sites/info/files/business_economy_euro/banking_and_finance/documents/sustainable-finance-teg-consultations-plans_en.pdf (13.03.2019).

Ewelt-Knauer, C./Schneider, J./Blaß, J. (2018): Eine kritische und vergleichende Analyse der Nachhaltigkeitsberichterstattung nach den Standards der GRI und des SASB, in: Der Betrieb, Vol. 71, No. 29, 2018, pp. 1677-1685.

EY (2013): The concept of 'materiality' in Integrated Reporting, URL: https://www.ey.com/Publication/vwLUAssets/The_concept_of_materiality_in _Integrated_Reporting_-_July_2013/$FILE/EY-the-concept-of-materiality-in-integrated-reporting-july-2013.pdf (13.03.2019).

EY (2014): Pflicht oder Kür? Nachhaltigkeitsberichterstattung in Deutschland – Standortbestimmung, URL: https://www.ey.com/Publication/vwLUAssets/EY_Studie_-_Pfli cht_oder_Kuer/$FILE/EY-Studie-PflichtoderKuer-2014.pdf (13.03.2019).

EY (2015): Tomorrow's Investment Rules 2.0 – Emerging Risk and Stranded Assets have Investors Looking for More from Nonfinancial Reporting, URL: https://www.ey.com/Publication/vwLUAssets/investor_survey/%24FILE/CCaSS_In stitutional_InvestorSurvey2015.pdf (13.03.2019).

F

Fan, Y./Ma, M. (2015): The Effects of Organizational Structure on Management Earnings Forecast – Evidence from U.S. Multinational Firms, URL: https://ssrn.com/ab stract=2635563 (13.03.2019).

Federation of European Accountants (FEE) (2016): EU Directive on Disclosure of Non-financial and Diversity Information – Achieving good quality and consistent reporting, URL: https://www.accountancyeurope.eu/wp-content/uploads/FEE_position_ paper_EU_NFI_Directive_final.pdf (13.03.2019).

Ferreira, A./Otley, D. (2009): The Design and Use of Performance Management Systems, in: Management Accounting Research, Vol. 20, No. 4, 2009, pp. 263-282.

Fifka, M. (2012): The Development and State of Research on Social and Environmental Reporting in Global Comparison, in: Journal of Business Economics, Vol. 62, No. 1, 2012, pp. 45-84.

Figge, F./Hahn, T./Schaltegger, S./Wagner, M. (2002): The Sustainability Balanced Scorecard – Linking Sustainability Management to Business Strategy, in: Business Strategy and the Environment, Vol. 11, No. 5, 2002, pp. 269-284.

Financial Accounting Standards Board (FASB) (2001): Business and Financial Reporting – Challenges from the New Economy, Norwalk 2001.

Fink, C./Kajüter, P./Winkeljohann, N. (2013): Lageberichterstattung – HGB, DRS und IFRS Practice Statement Management Commentary, Stuttgart 2013.

Fink, C./Keck, B. (2005): Lageberichterstattung nach BilReG und DRS 15 – Eine kritische Würdigung, in: Zeitschrift für internationale und kapitalmarktorientierte Rechnungslegung, Vol. 5, No. 4, 2005, pp. 137-146.

Fisch, M./Mujkanovic, R. (2015): Leistungsindikatoren im Lagebericht, in: Praxis der internationalen Rechnungslegung, Vol. 10, No. 7-8, 2015, pp. 213-220.

Fischer, T./Sawczyn, A./Brauch, B. (2009): Nachhaltigkeit und Sustainability Accounting, in: Wall, F./Schröder, R. W. (eds.), Controlling zwischen Shareholder Value und Stakeholder Value, München 2009, pp. 262-307.

Flick, U. (1987): Methodenangemessene Gütekriterien in der qualitativ-interpretativen Forschung, in: Bergold, J. B./Flick, U. (eds.), Ein-Sichten – Zugänge zur Sicht des Subjekts mittels qualitativer Forschung, Tübingen 1987, pp. 247-262.

Flick, U. (2014): An Introduction to Qualitative Research, 5th edition, London et al. 2014.

Flick, U. (2016): Sozialforschung – Methoden und Anwendungen – ein Überblick für die BA-Studiengänge, 3rd edition, Reinbek 2016.

Flick, U. (2017): Qualitative Sozialforschung – Eine Einführung, 8th edition, Reinbek 2017.

Flick, U. (2018): Triangulation, in: Denzin, N. K./Lincoln, Y. S. (eds.), The SAGE Handbook of Qualitative Research, 5th edition, Thousand Oaks et al. 2018, pp. 444-461.

Flöstrand, P./Ström, N. (2006): The Valuation Relevance of Non-financial Information, in: Management Research News, Vol. 29, No. 9, 2006, pp. 580-597.

Flyvbjerg, B. (2006): Five Misunderstandings About Case-Study Research, in: Qualitative Inquiry, Vol. 12, No. 2, 2006, pp. 219-245.

Flyvbjerg, B. (2011): Case Study, in: Denzin, N./Lincoln, Y. S. (eds.), The SAGE Handbook of Qualitative Research, 4th edition, Los Angeles et al. 2011, pp. 301-316.

Fogarty, T. (1996): The Imagery and Reality of Peer Review in the U.S., in: Accounting, Organizations and Society, Vol. 21, No. 2-3, 1996, pp. 243-267.

Folkerts, L. (2001): Promotoren in Innovationsprozessen – Empirische Untersuchung zur personellen Dynamik, Wiesbaden 2001.

Folkerts, L./Hauschildt, J. (2002): Personelle Dynamik in Innovationsprozessen, in: Die Betriebswirtschaft, Vol. 62, No. 1, 2002, pp. 7-23.

Forman, J./Damschroder, L. (2008): Qualitative Content Analysis, in: Jacoby, L./Siminoff, L. A. (eds.), Empirical Methods for Bioethics, Amsterdam et al. 2008, pp. 39-62.

Franceschini, F./Galetto, M./Maisano, D. (2007): Management by Measurement – Designing Key Indicators and Performance Measurement Systems, Berlin et al. 2007.

Frank, U. (2007): Wissenschaftstheorie, in: Köhler, R./Küpper, H.-U./Pfingsten, A. (eds.), Handwörterbuch der Betriebswirtschaft, 6th edition, Stuttgart 2007, col. 2010-2017.

Freeman, R. (2010): Strategic Management – A Stakeholder Approach, Cambridge 2010.

Freidank, C.-C./Hinze, A.-K. (2014): Corporate Governance Reporting versus Integrated Reporting, in: Controlling – Zeitschrift für erfolgsorientierte Unternehmenssteuerung, Vol. 26, No. 8-9, 2014, pp. 453-462.

Freidank, C.-C./Scheffler, E./Simon-Heckroth, E. (2018): Trennung des Lageberichts von „übrigen Berichten", in: Die Wirtschaftsprüfung, Vol. 71, No. 11, 2018, pp. 683-692.

Freidank, C.-C./Weber, S. (2008): Corporate Governance als Objekt des Management Reportings, in: Gleich, R./Horváth, P./Michel, U. (eds.), Management Reporting, Freiburg et al. 2008, pp. 389-434.

Friedrichs, J. (1990): Methoden empirischer Sozialforschung, 14th edition, Opladen 1990.

Frost, G./Jones, S./Lee, P. (2012): The Measurement and Reporting of Sustainability Information within the Organization, in: Jones, S./Ratnatunga, J. (eds.), Contemporary Issues in Sustainability Accounting, Assurance and Reporting, Bingley 2012, pp. 197-226.

Fülbier, R. (2004): Wissenschaftstheorie und Betriebswirtschaftslehre, in: Wirtschaftswissenschaftliches Studium), Vol. 33, No. 5, 2004, pp. 266-271.

Fülbier, R./Pellens, B. (2013): § 315, in: Schmidt, K. (ed.), Münchener Kommentar zum Handelsgesetzbuch, 3rd edition, München 2013, pp. 1351-1379.

Fünning, H./Kreis, T./Scholl, G. (2016): Nachhaltigkeitsberichterstattung in der Praxis, URL: https://www.ranking-nachhaltigkeitsberichte.de/data/ranking/user_upload/2015/IOEW-future-Ranking_2015_Unternehmensbefragung.pdf (13.03.2019).

G

Gallopín, G. (1997): Indicators and Their Use – Information for Decision-making, in: Moldan, B./Bilharz, S. (eds.), Sustainability Indicators – A Report on the Project on Indicators of Sustainable Development, Chichester 1997, pp. 13-27.

Gebauer, J./Glahe, J. (2011): Praxis der Nachhaltigkeitsberichterstattung in deutschen Großunternehmen – Befragungsergebnisse im Rahmen des IÖW/future-Rankings 2011, Berlin 2011.

Gebauer, J./Hoffmann, E. (2009): Evaluating Extra-financial Reporting, in: Journal of Applied Accounting Research, Vol. 10, No. 3, 2009, pp. 224-234.

Gebauer, J./Rotter, M. (2009): Praxis der Nachhaltigkeitsberichterstattung in deutschen Großunternehmen – Befragungsergebnisse im Rahmen des IÖW/future-Rankings 2009, Berlin et al. 2009.

German Council for Sustainable Development (RNE) (2017): The Sustainability Code, URL: https://www.deutscher-nachhaltigkeitskodex.de/en-GB/Documents/PDFs/Sustainability-Code/The_SustainabilityCode_2017.aspx (13.03.2019).

Gibbins, M./Richardson, A./Waterhouse, J. (1990): The Management of Corporate Financial Disclosure – Opportunism, Ritualism, Policies, and Processes, in: Journal of Accounting Research, Vol. 28, No. 1, 1990, pp. 121-143.

Gibbins, M./Salterio, S./Webb, A. (2001): Evidence about Auditor-Client Management Negotiation Concerning Client's Financial Reporting, in: Journal of Accounting Research, Vol. 39, No. 3, 2001, pp. 535-563.

Giovannini, E./Linster, M. (2005): Measuring Sustainable Development – Achievements and Challenges, paper presented at Conference of European Statisticians, Statistical Commission and Economic Commission for Europe, United Nations, Geneva 2005.

Givoly, D./Li, Y./Lourie, B./Nekrasov, A. (2019): Key Performance Indicators as Supplements to Earnings – Incremental Informativeness, Demand Factors, Measurement Issues, and Properties of Their Forecasts, URL: https://ssrn.com/abstract=2990730 (13.03.2019).

Gladen, W. (2014): Performance Measurement – Controlling mit Kennzahlen, 6th edition, Wiesbaden 2014.

Gladwin, T./Kennelly, J./Krause, T.-S. (1995): Shifting Paradigms for Sustainable Development – Implications for Management Theory and Research, in: The Academy of Management Review, Vol. 20, No. 4, 1995, pp. 874-907.

Glaser, A. (2015): Corporate Social Responsibility (CSR) – Erweiterung der (Lage-)Berichterstattung um nicht-finanzielle Informationen zur Erhöhung der Unternehmenstransparenz in Umwelt- und Sozialbelangen, in: Zeitschrift für Internationale Rechnungslegung, Vol. 10, No. 2, 2015, pp. 55-57.

Glaser, B. (2012): No Preconceptions – The Dictum, in: Grounded Theory Review, Vol. 11, No. 2, 2012, pp. 1-6.

Glaser, B./Strauss, A. (1967): The Discovery of Grounded Theory – Strategies for Qualitative Research, New Brunswick et al. 1967.

Gläser, J./Laudel, G. (2010): Experteninterviews und qualitative Inhaltsanalyse, 4th edition, Wiesbaden 2010.

Global Reporting Initiative (GRI) (2015a): G4 Sustainability Reporting Guidelines – Implementation Manual, URL: https://www.globalreporting.org/resourcelibrary/GRIG4-Part2-Implementation-Manual.pdf (13.03.2019).

Global Reporting Initiative (GRI) (2015b): G4 Sustainability Reporting Guidelines – Reporting Principles and Standard Disclosures, URL: https://www.globalreporting.org/resourcelibrary/grig4-part1-reporting-principles-and-standard-disclosures.pdf (13.03.2019).

Global Reporting Initiative (GRI) (2017): Mapping G4 to the GRI Standards, URL: https://www.globalreporting.org/standards/media/1098/mapping-g4-to-the-gri-standards-disclosures-full-overview.pdf (13.03.2019).

Global Reporting Initiative (GRI)/CSR Europe/Accountancy Europe (2017): Member State Implementation of Directive 2014/95/EU, URL: https://www.globalreporting.org/resourcelibrary/NFRpublication%20online_version.pdf (13.03.2019).

Goulding, C. (2002): Grounded Theory – A Practical Guide for Management, Business and Market Researchers, London et al. 2002.

Graham, J./Harvey, C./Rajgopal, S. (2005): The Economic Implications of Corporate Financial Reporting, in: Journal of Accounting and Economics, Vol. 40, No. 1-3, 2005, pp. 3-73.

Gray, R. (2002): The Social Accounting Project and Accounting Organizations and Society, in: Accounting, Organizations and Society, Vol. 27, No. 7, 2002, pp. 687-708.

Gray, R. (2005): Taking a Long View on What We Now Know about Social and Environmental Accountability and Reporting, in: Electronic Journal of Radical Organisation Theory, Vol. 9, No. 1, 2005, pp. 6-36.

Gray, R./Milne, M. (2004): Towards Reporting on the Triple Bottom Line – Mirages, Methods and Myths, in: Henriques, A./Richardson, J. (eds.), The Triple Bottom Line – Does it all Add Up?, London 2004, pp. 70-80.

Gray, R./Walters, D./Bebbington, J./Thompson, I. (1995): The Greening of Enterprise, in: Critical Perspectives on Accounting, Vol. 6, No. 3, 1995, pp. 211-239.

Greinert, M. (2004): Weitergehende Anforderungen an den Konzernlagebericht durch E-DRS 20 sowie das Bilanzrechtsreformgesetz, in: Zeitschrift für internationale und kapitalmarktorientierte Rechnungslegung, Vol. 4, No. 2, 2004, pp. 51-60.

Grewal, J./Reidl, E./Serafeim, G. (2015): Market Reaction to Mandatory Nonfinancial Disclosure, URL: https://ssrn.com/abstract=2657712 (13.03.2019).

Grochla, E. (1978): Einführung in die Organisationstheorie, Stuttgart 1978.

Grottel, B. (2018): § 315, in: Grottel, B./Schmidt, S./Schubert, W. J./Winkeljohann, N. (eds.), Beck'scher Bilanz-Kommentar – Handels- und Steuerbilanz §§ 238 bis 339, 342 bis 342e HGB, 11th edition, München 2018, pp. 2041-2075.

Groves, C./Frater, L./Lee, R./Stokes, E. (2011): Is There Room at the Bottom for CSR?, in: Journal of Business Ethics, Vol. 101, No. 4, 2011, pp. 525-552.

Groves, R./Magilavy, L. (1986): Measuring and Explaining Interviewer Effects in Centralized Telephone Surveys, in: Public Opinion Quarterly, Vol. 50, No. 2, 1986, pp. 251-266.

Guidry, R./Patten, D. (2012): Voluntary Disclosure Theory and Financial Control Variables – An Assessment of Recent Environmental Disclosure Research, in: Accounting Forum, Vol. 36, No. 2, 2012, pp. 81-90.

Günther, J./Muschallik, M. (2017): Identifikation wesentlicher Themen im Rahmen der Nachhaltigkeitsberichterstattung, in: Zeitschrift für internationale und kapitalmarktorientierte Rechnungslegung, Vol. 17, No. 10, 2017, pp. 421-425.

H

Haddock, J. (2005): Consumer Influence on Internet-based Corporate Communication of Environmental Activities, in: British Food Journal, Vol. 107, No. 10, 2005, pp. 792-805.

Hahn, R./Kühnen, M. (2013): Determinants of Sustainability Reporting – a Review of Results, Trends, Theory, and Opportunities in an Expanding Field of Research, in: Journal of Cleaner Production, Vol. 59, No. 1, 2013, pp. 5-21.

Haller, A./Durchschein, C. (2016): Entwicklung und Ausgestaltung der Prüfung von nach GRI-Normen erstellen Nachhaltigkeitsberichten in Deutschland, in: Zeitschrift für internationale und kapitalmarktorientierte Rechnungslegung, Vol. 16, No. 4, 2016, pp. 188-196.

Haller, A./Link, M./Groß, T. (2017): The Term 'Non-financial Information' – A Semantic Analysis of a Key Feature of Current and Future Corporate Reporting, in: Accounting in Europe, Vol. 14, No. 3, 2017, pp. 407-429.

Haller, A./Schnabel, J./Koch, M. (2014): Behandlung nichtfinanzieller Leistungsindikatoren in der Unternehmensberichterstattung nichtkapitalmarktorientierter Konzerne, in: Der Betrieb, Vol. 67, No. 45, 2014, pp. 2541-2546.

Hammersley, M. (1992): What's Wrong with Ethnography – Methodological Explorations, New York 1992.

Hannen, S. (2017): Integrated Reporting – Useful for Investors?, Frankfurt am Main 2017.

Hanson, N. (1965): Patterns of Discovery – An Inquiry Into the Conceptual Foundations of Science, Cambridge 1965.

Hardi, P./Zdan, T. (1997): Assessing Sustainable Development – Principles in Practice, Winnipeg 1997.

Hartmann, C. (2006): Internationalisierung der Lageberichterstattung – Darstellung und Vergleich des deutschen Lageberichts und der US-amerikanischen MD&A, Marburg 2006.

Hauschildt, J. (2004): Innovationsmanagement, 3rd edition, München 2004.

Hauschildt, J./Chakrabarti, A. (1988): Arbeitsteilung im Innovationsmanagement, in: Zeitschrift für Führung + Organisation, Vol. 57, No. 6, 1988, pp. 378-388.

Hauschildt, J./Chakrabarti, A. (1999): Arbeitsteilung im Innovationsmanagement, in: Hauschildt, J./Gemünden, H. G. (eds.), Promotoren, 2nd edition, Wiesbaden 1999, pp. 67-88.

Hauschildt, J./Kirchmann, E. (1999): Zur Existenz und Effizienz von Prozeßpromotoren, in: Hauschildt, J./Gemünden, H. G. (eds.), Promotoren, 2nd edition, Wiesbaden 1999, pp. 91-107.

Hauschildt, J./Kirchmann, E. (2001): Teamwork for Innovation – the 'Troika' of Promotors, in: R&D Management, Vol. 31, No. 1, 2001, pp. 41-49.

Hauschildt, J./Schewe, G. (1997): Gatekeeper und Promotoren – Schlüsselpersonen in Innovationsprozessen in statischer und dynamischer Perspektive, in: Die Betriebswirtschaft, Vol. 57, No. 1, 1997, pp. 506-616.

Hauschildt, J./Schewe, G. (2000): Gatekeeper and Process Promotor – Key Persons in Agile and Innovative Organizations, in: International Journal of Agile Management Systems, Vol. 2, No. 2, 2000, pp. 96-103.

Havelock, R. (1973): The Change Agent's Guide to Innovation in Education, 2nd edition, Englewood Cliffs 1973.

Haynes, K. (2017): Reflexivity in Accounting Research, in: Hoque, Z./Parker, L. D./Covaleski, M. A./Haynes, K. (eds.), The Routledge Companion to Qualitative Accounting Research Methods, London 2017, pp. 284-297.

Helfferich, C. (2011): Die Qualität qualitativer Daten – Manual für die Durchführung qualitativer Interviews, 4th edition, Wiesbaden 2011.

Hennrichs, J./Pöschke, M. (2017): Die Pflicht des Aufsichtsrats zur Prüfung des „CSR-Bericht", in: Neue Zeitschrift für Gesellschaftsrecht, Vol. 20, No. 4, 2017, pp. 121-127.

Herriott, R./Firestone, W. (1983): Multisite Qualitative Policy Research – Optimizing Description and Generalizability, in: American Educational Research Association, Vol. 12, No. 2, 1983, pp. 14-19.

High-Level Expert Group on Sustainable Finance (HLEG) (2018): Financing a Sustainable European Economy, URL: https://ec.europa.eu/info/sites/info/files/180131-sustainable-finance-final-report_en.pdf (13.03.2019).

Hillmer, H.-J. (2014): Integrated Reporting mit neuen Herausforderungen für Rechnungslegung und Controlling, in: Zeitschrift für internationale und kapitalmarktorientierte Rechnungslegung, Vol. 14, No. 7-8, 2014, pp. 394-398.

Hinze, A.-K. (2016): „Nichtfinanzielle Leistungsindikatoren" in der Berichterstattung, in: Die Wirtschaftsprüfung, Vol. 69, No. 21, 2016, pp. 1168-1173.

Hitzler, R. (1991): Dummheit als Methode – eine dramatologische Textinterpretation, in: Garz, D./Kraimer, K. (eds.), Qualitativ-empirische Sozialforschung – Konzepte, Methoden, Analysen, Opladen 1991, pp. 295-318.

Hitzler, R. (1994): Wissen und Wesen des Experten – ein Annäherungsversuch, in: Hitzler, R./Honer, A./Maeder, C. (eds.), Expertenwissen – die institutionalisierte Kompetenz zur Konstruktion von Wirklichkeit, Opladen 1994, pp. 13-30.

Holder-Webb, L./Cohen, J./Nath, L./Wood, D. (2009): The Supply of Corporate Social Responsibility Disclosures Among U.S. Firms, in: Journal of Business Ethics, Vol. 84, No. 4, 2009, pp. 497-527.

Holland, J. (1998): Private Disclosure and Financial Reporting, in: Accounting and Business Research, Vol. 28, No. 4, 1998, pp. 255-269.

Holland, L./Foo, Y. (2003): Differences in Environmental Reporting Practices in the UK and the US, in: The British Accounting Review, Vol. 35, No. 1, 2003, pp. 1-18.

Holstrum, G./Messier, W. (1982): A Review and Integration of Empirical Research on Materiality, in: Auditing: A Journal of Practice & Theory, Vol. 2, No. 1, 1982, pp. 45-63.

Holton, J. (2007): The Coding Process and its Challenges, in: Bryant, A./Charmaz, K. (eds.), The SAGE Handbook of Grounded Theory, Thousand Oaks 2007, pp. 265-289.

Hope, O.-K./Thomas, W./Vyas, D. (2013): Financial Reporting Quality of U.S. Private and Public Firms, in: The Accounting Review, Vol. 88, No. 5, 2013, pp. 1715-1742.

Hopf, C. (1978): Die Pseudo-Exploration – Überlegungen zur Technik qualitativer Interviews in der Sozialforschung, in: Zeitschrift für Soziologie, Vol. 7, No. 2, 1978, pp. 97-115.

Hopf, C./Hartwig, M. (2001): Liebe und Abhängigkeit, Weinheim 2001.

Hopf, C./Nevermann, K./Schmidt, I. (1985): Wie kamen die Nationalsozialisten an die Macht – Eine empirische Analyse von Deutungen im Unterricht, Frankfurt am Main 1985.

Hopf, C./Rieker, P./Sanden-Marcus, M./Schmidt, C. (1995): Familie und Rechtsextremismus – Familiale Sozialisation und rechtsextreme Orientierungen junger Männer, Weinheim 1995.

Horrigan, B. (2010): Corporate Social Responsibility in the 21st Century – Debates, Models and Practices Across Government, Law and Business, Cheltenham 2010.

Höschen, N./Vu, A. (2008): Möglichkeiten und Herausforderungen der Prüfung von Nachhaltigkeitsberichten, in: Die Wirtschaftsprüfung, Vol. 61, No. 9, 2008, pp. 378-387.

Howell, J./Shea, C./Higgins, C. (2005): Champions of Product Innovations, in: Journal of Business Venturing, Vol. 20, No. 5, 2005, pp. 641-661.

Hsu, C.-W./Lee, W.-H./Chao, W.-C. (2013): Materiality Analysis Model in Sustainability Reporting, in: Journal of Cleaner Production, Vol. 57, No. 1, 2013, pp. 142-151.

Huber, G./Power, D. (1985): Retrospective Reports of Strategic-Levels Managers, in: Strategic Management Journal, Vol. 6, No. 2, 1985, pp. 171-180.

Husillos, J./González, C./Álvarez, M. (2011): The Emergence of Triple Bottom Line Reporting in Spain, in: Spanish Journal of Finance and Accounting, Vol. 40, April-June issue, 2011, pp. 195-219.

I

Institut der Wirtschaftsprüfer (IDW) (2017): WP-Handbuch 2017 – Wirtschaftsprüfung und Rechnungslegung, 15th edition, Düsseldorf 2017.

International Auditing and Assurance Standards Board (IAASB) (2016): Handbook of International Quality Control, Auditing, Review, Other Assurance, and Related Services Pronouncements, New York 2016.

International Federation of Accountants (IFAC) (2013): International Good Practice Guidance – Principles for Effective Reporting Processes, URL: https://www.ifac.org/system/files/publications/files/Principles-for-Effective-Business-Reporting-Processes.pdf (13.03.2019).

International Federation of Accountants (IFAC) (2018): Business Reporting, URL: https://www.ifac.org/global-knowledge-gateway/business-reporting?overview (13.03.2019).

International Integrated Reporting Council (IIRC) (2013): The International <IR> Framework, URL: http://integratedreporting.org/wp-content/uploads/2015/03/13-12-08-THE-INTERNATIONAL-IR-FRAMEWORK-2-1.pdf (13.03.2019).

International Integrated Reporting Council (IIRC)/International Federation of Accountants (IFAC) (2015): Materiality in <IR> – Guidance for the preparation of integrated reports, URL: https://integratedreporting.org/wp-content/uploads/2015/11/1315_MaterialityinIR_Doc_4a_Interactive.pdf (13.03.2019).

Irvine, A./Drew, P./Sainsbury, R. (2010): Mode Effects in Qualitative Interviews – A Comparison of Semi-structured Face-to-Face and Telephone Interviews using Conversation Analysis, York 2010.

Ittner, C./Larcker, D. (2001): Assessing Empirical Research in Managerial Accounting, in: Journal of Accounting and Economics, Vol. 32, No. 1-3, 2001, pp. 349-410.

Ittner, C./Larcker, D. (2009): Extending the Boundaries – Nonfinancial Performance Measures, in: Chapman, C. S./Hopwood, A. G./Shields, M. D. (eds.), Handbook of Management Accounting Research, Amsterdam et al. 2009, pp. 1235-1251.

Ittner, C./Larcker, D./Randall, T. (2003): Performance Implications of Strategic Performance Measurement in Financial Services Firms, in: Accounting, Organizations and Society, Vol. 28, No. 7-8, 2003, pp. 715-741.

J

Jäger, P. (1974): Probleme und Möglichkeiten einer mit sozialen Kosten und Nutzen erweiterten Erfolgswürdigung öffentlicher Betriebe des Personen-Nahverkehrs, München 1974.

Johnson, B. (1997): Examining the Validity Structure of Qualitative Research, in: Education, Vol. 118, No. 2, 1997, pp. 282-292.

Jones, P./Comfort, D./Hillier, D. (2016): Managing Materiality – A Preliminary Examination of the Adoption of the New GRI G4 Guidelines on Materiality within the Business community, in: Journal of Public Affairs, Vol. 16, No. 3, 2016, pp. 222-230.

K

Kaiser, R. (2014): Qualitative Experteninterviews – Konzeptionelle Grundlagen und praktische Durchführung, Wiesbaden 2014.

Kajüter, P. (2004): Der Lagebericht als Instrument einer kapitalmarktorientierten Rechnungslegung, in: Der Betrieb, Vol. 57, No. 5, 2004, pp. 197-203.

Kajüter, P. (2013): Aktuelle Entwicklungen in der Unternehmensberichterstattung – Konzernlagebericht nach DRS 20, Management Commentary, Integrated Reporting, in: Freidank, C.-C./Velte, P. (eds.), Unternehmenssteuerung im Umbruch, Berlin 2013, pp. 119-153.

Kajüter, P. (2016): Neuerungen in der Lageberichterstattung nach dem Referentenentwurf des CSR-Richtlinie-Umsetzungsgesetzes, in: Zeitschrift für internationale und kapitalmarktorientierte Rechnungslegung, Vol. 16, No. 5, 2016, pp. 230-238.

Kajüter, P. (2017): Nichtfinanzielle Berichterstattung nach dem CSR-Richtlinie-Umsetzungsgesetz, in: Der Betrieb, Vol. 70, No. 12, 2017, pp. 617-624.

Kajüter, P. (2019a): §§ 289, 289a-f, in: Küting, P./Weber, C.-P. (eds.), Handbuch der Rechnungslegung – Einzelabschluss, Stuttgart 2019.

Kajüter, P. (2019b): IFRS und Controlling, in: Baetge, J./Wollmert, P./Kirsch, H.-J./Oser, P./Bischof, S. (eds.), Rechnungslegung nach IFRS – Kommentar auf der Grundlage des deutschen Bilanzrechts, Stuttgart 2019, pp. 1-34.

Kajüter, P./Bachert, K./Blaesing, D./Kleinmanns, H. (2010): Die DRS zur Lageberichterstattung auf dem Prüfstand, in: Der Betrieb, Vol. 63, No. 9, 2010, pp. 457-465.

Kajüter, P./Nienhaus, M./Nienaber, M. (2017): Prüfung des Lageberichts – Empirische Befunde einer explorativen Studie, in: Die Wirtschaftsprüfung, Vol. 70, No. 14, 2017, pp. 801-809.

Kajüter, P./Wirth, M. (2018): Praxis der nichtfinanziellen Berichterstattung nach dem CSR-RUG – Empirische Befunde für die DAX-Unternehmen, in: Der Betrieb, Vol. 71, No. 27-28, 2018, pp. 1605-1612.

Kaplan, R./Norton, D. (1996): The Balanced Scorecard – Translating Strategy into Action, Boston 1996.

Kaspersen, M./Johansen, T. (2016): Changing Social and Environmental Reporting Systems, in: Journal of Business Ethics, Vol. 135, No. 4, 2016, pp. 731-749.

Kaufmann, J.-C. (2015): Das verstehende Interview – Theorie und Praxis, 2nd edition, Konstanz et al. 2015.

Keeble, J./Topiol, S./Berkeley, S. (2003): Using Indicators to Measure Sustainability Performance at a Corporate and Project Level, in: Journal of Business Ethics, Vol. 44, No. 2, 2003, pp. 149-158.

Kelle, U. (2017): Computergestützte Analyse qualitativer Daten, in: Flick, U./Kardorff, E./Steinke, I. (eds.), Qualitative Forschung – Ein Handbuch, 12th edition, Reinbek 2017, pp. 485-501.

Kelle, U./Kluge, S. (2010): Vom Einzelfall zum Typus – Fallvergleich und Fallkontrastierung in der qualitativen Sozialforschung, 2nd edition, Wiesbaden 2010.

Kelle, U./Kluge, S./Prein, G. (1993): Strategien der Geltungssicherung in der qualitativen Sozialforschung – zur Validitätsproblematik im interpretativen Paradigma, URL: https://www.ssoar.info/ssoar/handle/document/1426 (13.03.2019).

Kenno, S./McCracken, S./Salterio, S. (2017): Financial Reporting Qualitative Interview Based Research – A Primer with an Illustrative Example, in: Behavioral Research in Accounting, Vol. 29, No. 1, 2017, pp. 77-102.

King, G./Keohane, R./Verba, S. (1994): Designing Social Inquiry – Scientific Inference in Qualitative Research, Princeton 1994.

Kirk, J./Miller, M. (1986): Reliability and Validity in Qualitative Research, Beverly Hills et al. 1986.

Kirsch, H. (2018): Weglassen nachteiliger Angaben in der nichtfinanziellen (Konzern-)Erklärung, in: Deutsche Steuer-Zeitung, Vol. 106, No. 7, 2018, pp. 231-237.

Kirsch, H.-J./Huter, M. (2017): Die Prüfung der nicht-finanziellen Erklärung, in: Die Wirtschaftsprüfung, Vol. 70, No. 17, 2017, pp. 1017-1024.

Kirsch, H.-J./Köhrmann, H./Huter, M. (2018): B 510 Inhalt des Lageberichts, in: Böcking, H.-J./Castan, E./Heymann, G./Pfitzer, N./Scheffler, E. (eds.), Beck'sches Handbuch der Rechnungslegung, München 2018, pp. 1-82.

Kluge, N./Sick, S. (2016): Geheimwirtschaft bei Transparenz zum gesellschaftlichen Engagement? Zum Kreis der vom CSR-Richtlinie-Umsetzungsgesetz potentiell betroffenen Unternehmen, Düsseldorf 2016.

Knauer, T./Wömpener, A. (2011): Management Forecast Regulation and Practice in Germany – Firm and Auditor Perspectives, in: Accounting in Europe, Vol. 8, No. 2, 2011, pp. 185-209.

Koch, R. (1994): Betriebliches Berichtswesen als Informations- und Steuerungsinstrument, Frankfurt am Main et al. 1994.

Kolb, S./Neubeck, G./Dreizler, A. (2016): Der Lagebericht – Grundsätze, Kommentierungen, Beispiele, Praxishinweise, 2nd edition, Bonn 2016.

Kolb, S./Plömpel, M. (2017): Prüfung von Systemen im Rahmen von IDW EPS 350, in: Die Wirtschaftsprüfung, Vol. 70, No. 13, 2017, pp. 739-745.

Kornberger, M./Justesen, L./Mouritsen, J. (2011): "When you make manager, we put a big mountain in front of you", in: Accounting, Organizations and Society, Vol. 36, No. 8, 2011, pp. 514-533.

Kornmeier, M. (2007): Wissenschaftstheorie und wissenschaftliches Arbeiten – Eine Einführung für Wirtschaftswissenschaftler, Heidelberg 2007.

KPMG (2017): The Road Ahead – The KPMG Survey of Corporate Responsibility Reporting 2017, URL: https://assets.kpmg.com/content/dam/kpmg/xx/pdf/2017/10/kpmg-survey-of-corporate-responsibility-reporting-2017.pdf (13.03.2019).

Krippendorf, K. (1980): Content Analysis – An Introduction to its Methodology, Beverly Hills et al. 1980.

Kromrey, H./Roose, J./Strübing, J. (2016): Empirische Sozialforschung, 13th edition, Konstanz et al. 2016.

Kropff, B. (1980): Der Lagebericht nach geltendem und künftigem Recht, in: Betriebswirtschaftliche Prüfung und Praxis, Vol. 32, No. 6, 1980, pp. 514-532.

Kruse, J. (2015): Qualitative Interviewforschung – Ein integrativer Ansatz, 2nd edition, Weinheim et al. 2015.

Küchler, M. (1983): „Qualitative" Sozialforschung – Ein neuer Königsweg?, in: Garz, D./Kraimer, K. (eds.), Brauchen wir andere Forschungsmethoden? – Beiträge zur Diskussion interpretativer Verfahren, Frankfurt am Main 1983, pp. 9-30.

Kuckartz, U. (2010): Einführung in die computergestützte Analyse qualitativer Daten, 3rd edition, Wiesbaden 2010.

Kuckartz, U. (2018): Qualitative Inhaltsanalyse – Methoden, Praxis, Computerunterstützung, 4th edition, Weinheim 2018.

Küpper, H.-U./Friedl, G./Hofmann, C./Hofmann, Y./Pedell, B. (2013): Controlling – Konzeption, Aufgaben, Instrumente, 6th edition, Stuttgart 2013.

L

Labbé, M./Stein, H.-J. (2007): Nachhaltigkeitsberichte als Instrument der Unternehmenskommunikation, in: Der Betrieb, Vol. 60, No. 49, 2007, pp. 2661-2667.

Lachnit, L. (1979): Systemorientierte Jahresabschlußanalyse – Weiterentwicklung der externen Jahresabschlußanalyse mit Kennzahlensystemen, EDV und mathematisch-statistischen Methoden, Wiesbaden 1979.

Lackmann, J./Stich, M. (2013): Nicht-finanzielle Leistungsindikatoren und Aspekte der Nachhaltigkeit bei der Anwendung von DRS 20, in: Zeitschrift für internationale und kapitalmarktorientierte Rechnungslegung, Vol. 13, No. 5, 2013, pp. 236-242.

Lai, A./Melloni, G./Stacchezzini, R. (2017): What Does Materiality Mean to Integrated Reporting Preparers? An Empirical Exploration, in: Meditari Accounting Research, Vol. 25, No. 4, 2017, pp. 533-552.

Laine, M. (2009): Ensuring Legitimacy through Rhetorical Changes?, in: Accounting, Auditing & Accountability Journal, Vol. 22, No. 7, 2009, pp. 1029-1054.

Lamnek, S./Krell, C. (2016): Qualitative Sozialforschung, 6th edition, Weinheim 2016.

Lander, M./Koene, B./Linssen, S. (2013): Committed to Professionalism, in: Accounting, Organizations and Society, Vol. 38, No. 2, 2013, pp. 130-148.

Lanfermann, G. (2018): Künftige Ausrichtung der EU-Unternehmensberichterstattung – Gesetzgebungspaket zu Sustainable Finance und „Fitness Check", in: Betriebs-Berater, Vol. 73, No. 29, 2018, pp. 1643-1647.

Lange, K. (2004): Berichterstattung in Lagebericht und Konzernlagebericht nach dem geplanten Bilanzrechtsreformgesetz, in: Zeitschrift für Wirtschaftsrecht, Vol. 25, No. 21, 2004, pp. 981-987.

Larrinaga-González, C./Bebbington, J. (2001): Accounting Change or Institutional Appropriation?, in: Critical Perspectives on Accounting, Vol. 12, No. 3, 2001, pp. 269-292.

Larrinaga-González, C. (2007): Sustainability Reporting – Insights from Neoinstitutional Theory, in: Unerman, J./Bebbington, J./O'Dwyer, B. (eds.), Sustainability Accounting and Accountability, London 2007, pp. 150-167.

Larrinaga-González, C./Carrasco-Fenech, F./Caro-González, F./Correa-Ruíz, C./Páez-Sandubete, J. (2001): The Role of Environmental Accounting in Organizational Change, in: Accounting, Auditing & Accountability Journal, Vol. 14, No. 2, 2001, pp. 213-239.

Lee, T./Hutchison, P. (2005): The Decision to Disclose Environmental Information, in: Advances in Accounting, Vol. 21, No. 1, 2005, pp. 83-111.

Leffson, U. (1987): Die Grundsätze ordnungsmäßiger Buchführung, 7th edition, Düsseldorf 1987.

Li, J./Pike, R./Haniffa, R. (2008): Intellectual Capital Disclosure and Corporate Governance Structure in UK Firms, in: Accounting and Business Research, Vol. 38, No. 2, 2008, pp. 137-159.

Lienert, G./Raatz, U. (1998): Testaufbau und Testanalyse, 6th edition, Weinheim 1998.

Lillis, A. (2006): Reliability and Validity in Field Study Research, in: Hoque, Z. (ed.), Methodological Issues in Accounting Research, London 2006, pp. 461-475.

Lincoln, Y./Guba, E. (1985): Naturalistic Inquiry, Newbury Park 1985.

Lindesmith, A. (1968): Addiction and Opiates, Chicago 1968.

Lingnau, V. (1995): Kritischer Rationalismus und Betriebswirtschaftslehre, in: Wirtschaftswissenschaftliches Studium, Vol. 24, No. 3, 1995, pp. 124-129.

Llewellyn, S. (1994): Managing the Boundary, in: Accounting, Auditing & Accountability Journal, Vol. 7, No. 4, 1994, pp. 4-23.

Locke, K. (2001): Grounded Theory in Management Research, London 2001.

Loew, T./Ankele, K./Braun, S./Clausen, J. (2004): Bedeutung der internationalen CSR-Diskussion für Nachhaltigkeit und die sich daraus ergebenden Anforderungen an Unternehmen mit Fokus Berichterstattung, Münster et al. 2004.

Lorenzen, P. (1974): Konstruktive Wissenschaftstheorie, Frankfurt am Main 1974.

Lovins, A./Lovins, L./Hawken, P. (1999): A Road Map for Natural Capitalism, in: Harvard Business Review, Vol. 77, No. 3, 1999, pp. 145-158.

Lozano, R./Huisingh, D. (2011): Inter-linking Issues and Dimensions in Sustainability Reporting, in: Journal of Cleaner Production, Vol. 19, No. 2-3, 2011, pp. 99-107.

Luft, J. (2009): Nonfinancial Information and Accounting, in: Accounting Horizons, Vol. 23, No. 3, 2009, pp. 307-325.

Lukka, K./Kasanen, E. (1995): The Problem of Generalizability – Anecdotes and Evidence in Accounting Research, in: Accounting, Auditing & Accountability Journal, Vol. 8, No. 5, 1995, pp. 71-90.

M

Maas, K./Schaltegger, S./Crutzen, N. (2016): Integrating Corporate Sustainability Assessment, Management Accounting, Control, and Reporting, in: Journal of Cleaner Production, Vol. 136, Part A, 2016, pp. 237-248.

Manetti, G. (2011): The Quality of Stakeholder Engagement in Sustainability Reporting, in: Corporate Social Responsibility and Environmental Management, Vol. 18, No. 2, 2011, pp. 110-122.

March, J./Simon, H. (1958): Organizations, New York 1958.

Maxwell, J. (2013): Qualitative Research Design, 3rd edition, Thousand Oaks et al. 2013.

Mayring, P. (2010): Design, in: Mey, G./Mruck, K. (eds.), Handbuch Qualitative Forschung in der Psychologie, Wiesbaden 2010, pp. 225-237.

Mayring, P. (2015): Qualitative Inhaltsanalyse – Grundlagen und Techniken, 12th edition, Weinheim 2015.

Mayring, P. (2016): Einführung in die qualitative Sozialforschung – Eine Anleitung zu qualitativem Denken, 6th edition, Weinheim et al. 2016.

Mayring, P. (2017): Qualitative Inhaltsanalyse, in: Flick, U./Kardorff, E./Steinke, I. (eds.), Qualitative Forschung – Ein Handbuch, 12th edition, Reinbek 2017, pp. 468-474.

Merchant, K./Van der Stede, W. (2006): Field-Based Research in Accounting – Accomplishments and Prospects, in: Behavioral Research in Accounting, Vol. 18, No. 1, 2006, pp. 117-134.

Merkens, H. (1997): Stichproben bei qualitativen Studien, in: Friebertshäuser, B./Prengel, A. (eds.), Handbuch Qualitative Forschungsmethoden in der Erziehungswissenschaft, Weinheim et al. 1997, pp. 97-106.

Merschdorf, M. (2012): Der Management Approach in der IFRS-Rechnungslegung – Implikationen für Unternehmen und Investoren, Frankfurt am Main 2012.

Messier, W./Martinov-Bennie, N./Eilifsen, A. (2005): A Review and Integration of Empirical Research on Materiality – Two Decades Later, in: Auditing: A Journal of Practice & Theory, Vol. 24, No. 2, 2005, pp. 153-187.

Messner, M./Moll, J./Strömsten, T. (2017): Credibility and authenticity in qualitative accounting research, in: Hoque, Z./Parker, L. D./Covaleski, M. A./Haynes, K. (eds.), The Routledge Companion to Qualitative Accounting Research Methods, London 2017, pp. 432-443.

Meuser, M./Nagel, U. (1991): ExpertInneninterviews – vielfach erprobt, wenig bedacht – ein Beitrag zur qualitativen Methodendiskussion, in: Garz, D./Kraimer, K. (eds.), Qualitativ-empirische Sozialforschung – Konzepte, Methoden, Analysen, Opladen 1991, pp. 441-471.

Meuser, M./Nagel, U. (2009): The Expert Interview and Changes in Knowledge Production, in: Bogner, A./Littig, B./Menz, W. (eds.), Interviewing Experts, Houndmills et al. 2009, pp. 17-42.

Meyer, J./Rowan, B. (1977): Institutionalized Organizations, in: The American Journal of Sociology, Vol. 83, No. 2, 1977, pp. 340-363.

Miles, M./Huberman, A./Saldaña, J. (2014): Qualitative Data Analysis – A Methods Sourcebook, 3rd edition, Los Angeles et al. 2014.

Mio, C./Venturelli, A./Leopizzi, R. (2015): Management by Objectives and Corporate Social Responsibility Disclosure, in: Accounting, Auditing & Accountability Journal, Vol. 28, No. 3, 2015, pp. 325-364.

Mishler, E. (1990): Validation in Inquiry-Guided Research, in: Harvard Educational Review, Vol. 60, No. 4, 1990, pp. 415-443.

Mock, S. (2017): Die Leitlinien der Europäischen Kommission zur CSR-Berichterstattung, in: Der Betrieb, Vol. 70, No. 37, 2017, pp. 2144-2147.

Moers, F. (2005): Discretion and Bias in Performance Evaluation, in: Accounting, Organizations and Society, Vol. 30, No. 1, 2005, pp. 67-80.

Monciardini, D. (2016): The 'Coalition of the Unlikely' Driving the EU Regulatory Process of Non-Financial Reporting, in: Social and Environmental Accountability Journal, Vol. 36, No. 1, 2016, pp. 76-89.

Montagna, P. (1968): Professionalization and Bureaucratization in Large Professional Organizations, in: American Journal of Sociology, Vol. 74, No. 2, 1968, pp. 138-145.

Müller, S./Stawinoga, M. (2013): Grundsachverhalte einer integrierten Nachhaltigkeitsberichterstattung im Lagebericht, in: Zeitschrift für Internationale Rechnungslegung, Vol. 8, No. 3, 2013, pp. 117-121.

Munda, G. (2005): "Measuring Sustainability", in: Environment, Development and Sustainability, Vol. 7, No. 1, 2005, pp. 117-134.

N

Nagar, V./Rajan, M. (2001): The Revenue Implications of Financial and Operational Measures of Product Quality, in: The Accounting Review, Vol. 76, No. 4, 2001, pp. 495-513.

Naumann, K.-P./Schmidt, M. (2015): Integrierte Berichterstattung aus der Perspektive der Abschlussprüfung, in: Freidank, C.-C./Müller, S./Velte, P. (eds.), Handbuch Integrated Reporting, Berlin 2015, pp. 388-419.

Nikolaeva, R./Bicho, M. (2011): The Role of Institutional and Reputational Factors in the Voluntary Adoption of Corporate Social Responsibility reporting standards, in: Journal of the Academy of Marketing Science, Vol. 39, No. 1, 2011, pp. 136-157.

Noll, D./Weygandt, J. (1997): Business Reporting – What Comes Next?, in: Journal of Accountancy, Vol. 183, No. 2, 1997, pp. 59-62.

Noy, C. (2008): Sampling Knowledge – The Hermeneutics of Snowball Sampling in Qualitative Research, in: International Journal of Social Research Methodology, Vol. 11, No. 4, 2008, pp. 327-344.

Noyes, J./Popay, J./Pearson, A./Hannes, K./Booth, A. (2008): Qualitative Research and Cochrane Reviews, in: Green, S./Higgins, J. (eds.), Cochrane Handbook for Systematic Reviews of Interventions, Chichester et al. 2008, pp. 571-592.

O

O'Dwyer, B. (2002): Managerial Perceptions of Corporate Social Disclosure, in: Accounting, Auditing & Accountability Journal, Vol. 15, No. 3, 2002, pp. 406-436.

O'Dwyer, B. (2003): Conceptions of Corporate Social Responsibility – The Nature of Managerial Capture, in: Accounting, Auditing & Accountability Journal, Vol. 16, No. 4, 2003, pp. 523-557.

O'Dwyer, B. (2005): Stakeholder Democracy – Challenges and Contributions from Social Accounting, in: Business Ethics: A European Review, Vol. 14, No. 1, 2005, pp. 28-41.

O'Dwyer, B. (2011): The Case of Sustainability Assurance – Constructing a New Assurance Service, in: Contemporary Accounting Research, Vol. 28, No. 4, 2011, pp. 1230-1266.

Oliveira, L./Lima Rodrigues, L./Craig, R. (2010): Intellectual Capital Reporting in Sustainability Reports, in: Journal of Intellectual Capital, Vol. 11, No. 4, 2010, pp. 575-594.

Orens, R./Lybaert, N. (2010): Determinants of Sell-side Financial Analysts' Use of Nonfinancial Information, in: Accounting and Business Research, Vol. 40, No. 1, 2010, pp. 39-53.

Organ, D./Greene, C. (1981): The Effects of Formalization on Professional Involvement – A Compensatory Process Approach, in: Administrative Science Quarterly, Vol. 26, No. 2, 1981, pp. 237-252.

Osann, M. (2010): Freiwillige Berichterstattung über immaterielle Ressourcen – Ein deskriptiv-explikatives Mehrebenenmodell, Lohmar 2010.

Ossadnik, W. (1993): Wesentlichkeit als Bestimmungsfaktor für Angabepflichten in Jahresabschluß und Lagebericht, in: Betriebs-Berater, Vol. 10, No. 25, 1993, pp. 1763-1766.

Oswald, H. (2010): Was heißt qualitativ forschen?, in: Friebertshäuser, B./Langer, A./Prengel, A. (eds.), Handbuch Qualitative Forschungsmethoden in der Erziehungswissenschaft, 3rd edition, Weinheim, Basel 2010, pp. 183-201.

Owen, D./Swift, T./Humphrey, C./Bowerman, M. (2000): The New Social Audits – Accountability, Managerial Capture or the Agenda of Social Champions?, in: European Accounting Review, Vol. 9, No. 1, 2000, pp. 81-98.

P

Panitz, K./Touré, A. (2015): Aufbau- und ablauforganisatorische Aspekte des Integrated Reporting, in: Freidank, C.-C./Müller, S./Velte, P. (eds.), Handbuch Integrated Reporting, Berlin 2015, pp. 125-149.

Panitz, K./Waschkowitz (2010): Reportingprozesse optimieren – Praxislösungen für ein effizientes Rechnungswesen, Stuttgart 2010.

Park, J./Brorson, T. (2005): Experiences of and Views on Third-Party Assurance of Corporate Environmental and Sustainability Reports, in: Journal of Cleaner Production, Vol. 13, No. 10-11, 2005, pp. 1095-1106.

Parmenter, D. (2010): Key Performance Indicators – Developing, Implementing, and Using Winning KPIs, 1st edition, Hoboken 2010.

Patten, D. (2002): The Relation between Environmental Performance and Environmental Disclosure – A Research Note, in: Accounting, Organizations and Society, Vol. 27, No. 8, 2002, pp. 763-773.

Pedell, B./Sautter, J./Tappe, K. (2014): Kennzahleneinsatz in der Nachhaltigkeitsberichterstattung, in: Zeitschrift für internationale und kapitalmarktorientierte Rechnungslegung, Vol. 14, No. 11, 2014, pp. 539-547.

Perrini, F./Tencati, A. (2006): Sustainability and Stakeholder Management, in: Business Strategy and the Environment, Vol. 15, No. 5, 2006, pp. 296-308.

Pfadenhauer, M. (2009): At Eye Level – The Expert Interview – a Talk between Expert and Quasi-expert, in: Bogner, A./Littig, B./Menz, W. (eds.), Interviewing Experts, Houndmills et al. 2009, pp. 81-97.

Picot, A. (1977): Betriebswirtschaftliche Umweltbeziehungen und Umweltinformationen, Berlin 1977.

Poland, B. (1995): Transcription Quality as an Aspect of Rigor in Qualitative Research, in: Qualitative Inquiry, Vol. 1, No. 3, 1995, pp. 290-310.

Popper, K. (2005): Logik der Forschung, 11th edition, Tübingen 2005.

Power, M. (2003): Evaluating the Audit Explosion, in: Law & Policy, Vol. 25, No. 3, 2003, pp. 185-202.

Prado-Lorenzo, J.-M./Gallego-Alvarez, I./Garcia-Sanchez, I. (2009): Stakeholder Engagement and Corporate Social Responsibility Reporting, in: Corporate Social Responsibility and Environmental Management, Vol. 16, No. 2, 2009, pp. 94-107.

Pulczynski, J. (1991): Interorganisationales Innovationsmanagement – Eine kritische Analyse des Forschungsprojektes GROWIAN, Kiel 1991.

R

Raffée, H. (1974): Grundprobleme der Betriebswirtschaftslehre – Betriebswirtschaftslehre im Grundstudium der Wirtschaftswissenschaft, Göttingen 1974.

Ragin, C. (1992): "Casing" and the Process of Social Inquiry, in: Ragin, C. C./Becker, H. S. (eds.), What is a Case? Exploring the Foundations of Social Inquiry, Cambridge 1992, pp. 217-226.

Rahaman, A./Lawrence, S./Roper, J. (2004): Social and Environmental Reporting at the VRA, in: Critical Perspectives on Accounting, Vol. 15, No. 1, 2004, pp. 35-56.

Ramanathan, K. (1976): Toward a Theory of Corporate Social Accounting, in: The Accounting Review, Vol. 51, No. 3, 1976, pp. 516-528.

Rauhut, J. (2012): Lageberichterstattung aus Unternehmenssicht, in: Baetge, J./Kirsch, H.-J. (eds.), Zukunft der Unternehmensberichterstattung, Düsseldorf 2012, pp. 35-53.

Rauschenberg, F. (2014): Die Prüfung nichtfinanzieller Informationen im Konzernlagebericht vor dem Hintergrund der regulatorischen Änderungen und der Haftung des Wirtschaftsprüfers, in: Der Konzern, Vol. 12, No. 9, 2014, pp. 319-328.

Reichertz, J. (2009): Die Konjunktur der qualitativen Sozialforschung und Konjunkturen innerhalb der qualitativen Sozialforschung, in: Forum: Qualitative Sozialforschung, Vol. 10, No. 3, 2009, Art. 29.

Reichertz, J. (2017): Abduktion, Deduktion und Induktion in der qualitativen Forschung, in: Flick, U./Kardorff, E./Steinke, I. (eds.), Qualitative Forschung – Ein Handbuch, 12th edition, Reinbek 2017, pp. 276-286.

Richardson, L./St. Pierre, E. (2018): Writing – A Method of Inquiry, in: Denzin, N. K./Lincoln, Y. S. (eds.), The SAGE Handbook of Qualitative Research, 5th edition, Thousand Oaks et al. 2018, pp. 818-838.

Richter, N./Johne, A./König, C. (2017): Umsetzung der CSR-Richtlinie in nationales Recht, in: Die Wirtschaftsprüfung, Vol. 70, No. 10, 2017, pp. 566-572.

Rimmelspacher, D./Schäfer, N./Schönberger, M. (2017): Das CSR-Richtlinie-Umsetzungsgesetz, in: Zeitschrift für internationale und kapitalmarktorientierte Rechnungslegung, Vol. 17, No. 5, 2017, pp. 225-232.

Robb, S./Single, L./Zarzeski, M. (2001): Nonfinancial Disclosures across Anglo-American Countries, in: Journal of International Accounting, Auditing and Taxation, Vol. 10, No. 1, 2001, pp. 71-83.

Roberts, E./Fusfeld, A. (1988): Critical Functions – Needed Roles in the Innovation Process, in: Katz, R. (ed.), Managing Professionals in Innovative Organizations, Cambridge 1988, pp. 101-120.

Roberts, R. (1992): Determinants of Corporate Social Responsibility Disclosure, in: Accounting, Organizations and Society, Vol. 17, No. 6, 1992, pp. 595-612.

Rodriguez, A./Cotran, H./Stewart, L. (2017): Evaluating the Effectiveness of Sustainability Disclosure – Findings from a Recent SASB Study, in: Journal of Applied Corporate Finance, Vol. 29, No. 2, 2017, pp. 100-108.

Roos, J./Roos, G./Dragonetti, N./Edvinsson, L. (1998): Intellectual Capital – Navigating the New Business Landscape, Houndmills et al. 1998.

Rost, K./Hölzle, K./Gemünden, H.-G. (2007): Promotors or Champions? Pros and Cons of Role Specialisation for Economic Process, in: Schmalenbach Business Review, Vol. 59, No. 4, 2007, pp. 340-363.

Rothwell, R./Freeman, C./Horlsey, A./Jervis, V.T.P./Robertson, A./Townsend, J. (1974): SAPPHO Updated – Project SAPPHO Phase II, in: Research Policy, Vol. 3, No. 3, 1974, pp. 258-291.

Rouse, R. (2013): SEC Leadership Continues to Evolve, in: Journal of Corporate Accounting & Finance, Vol. 25, No. 1, 2013, pp. 89-94.

Ruhnke, K./Schmidt, M. (2017): Veröffentlichungs- und Prüfungspflichten im Zusammenhang mit der Erklärung zur Unternehmensführung und der nichtfinanziellen Erklärung, in: Der Betrieb, Vol. 70, No. 44, 2017, pp. 2557-2563.

S

Schaefer, P./Schröder, N. (2015): Auswirkungen des DRS 20 auf die Berichterstattung nichtfinanzieller Leistungsindikatoren in den Lageberichten der DAX30-Unternehmen, in: Zeitschrift für internationale und kapitalmarktorientierte Rechnungslegung, Vol. 15, No. 2, 2015, pp. 95-107.

Schaltegger, S./Bennett, M./Burritt, R. (2006): Sustainability Accounting and Reporting – Development, Linkages and Reflection. An Introduction, in: Schaltegger, S./Bennett, M./Burritt, R. (eds.), Sustainability Accounting and Reporting, Dordrecht 2006, pp. 1-34.

Schaltegger, S./Herzig, C./Kleiber, O./Klinke, T./Müller, J. (2007): Nachhaltigkeitsmanagement in Unternehmen – Von der Idee zur Praxis – Managementansätze zur Umsetzung von Corporate Social Responsibility und Corporate Sustainability, Berlin et al. 2007.

Schatzmann, L./Strauss, A. (1973): Field Research – Strategies for a Natural Sociology, Englewood Cliffs 1973.

Scheffler, E. (1999): Der Deutsche Standardisierungsrat – Struktur, Aufgaben und Kompetenzen, in: Betriebswirtschaftliche Forschung und Praxis, Vol. 51, No. 4, 1999, pp. 407-417.

Scherer, A./Marti, E. (2019): Wissenschaftstheorie der Organisationstheorie, in: Kieser, A./Ebers, M. (eds.), Organisationstheorien, 8th edition, Stuttgart 2019, pp. 15-42.

Schewe, G./Tietmeyer, J./Bodenstein, D. (2009): Prozesssteuerung über Key Performance Indicators, Chair of Business Administration – Organization, Personnel and Innovation Working Paper No. 64, Münster 2009.

Schmidt, M. (2012): Möglichkeiten und Grenzen einer integrierten Finanz- und Nachhaltigkeitsberichterstattung, Düsseldorf 2012.

Schmotz, T./Schmidt, R. (2017): Nichtfinanzielle Berichtspflichten in der Finanzberichterstattung, in: Der Betrieb, Vol. 70, No. 49, 2017, pp. 2877-2884.

Schnell, R./Hill, P./Esser, E. (2018): Methoden der empirischen Sozialforschung, 11th edition, Berlin et al. 2018.

Schramm, P. (2012): Corporate Social Responsibility (CSR) und Risikomanagement: Vorschlag eines ganzheitlichen praxisnahen CSR-basierten Risikomanagementsystems, Hamburg 2012.

Schweitzer, M. (1978): Wissenschaftsziele und Auffassungen in der Betriebswirtschaftslehre – Eine Einführung, in: Schweitzer, M. (ed.), Auffassungen und Wissenschaftsziele der Betriebswirtschaftslehre, Darmstadt 1978, pp. 1-14.

Searcy, C./Buslovich, R. (2014): Corporate Perspectives on the Development and Use of Sustainability Reports, in: Journal of Business Ethics, Vol. 121, No. 2, 2014, pp. 149-169.

Searcy, C./Karapetrovic, S./McCartney, D. (2005): Designing Sustainable Development Indicators, in: Measuring Business Excellence, Vol. 9, No. 2, 2005, pp. 33-41.

Searcy, C./Karapetrovic, S./McCartney, D. (2009): Designing Corporate Sustainable Development Indicators, in: Environmental Quality Management, Vol. 19, No. 1, 2009, pp. 31-42.

Searcy, C./McCartney, D./Karapetrovic, S. (2008): Identifying Priorities for Action in Corporate Sustainable Development Indicator Programs, in: Business Strategy and the Environment, Vol. 17, No. 2, 2008, pp. 137-148.

Seidler, H. (2018): Nicht inhaltlich zu prüfende lageberichtstypische Angaben (IDW PS 350 n.F.) – ausgewählte Fragen aus Sicht der Abschlussprüfung, in: Betriebs-Berater, Vol. 73, No. 19, 2018, pp. 1067-1071.

Selchert, F./Erhardt, M./Fuhr, A./Greinert, M. (2000): Prüfung des Lageberichts – einschließlich Konzernlagebericht nach deutschem und internationalem Recht, Bielefeld 2000.

Shepard, H. (1967): Innovation-Resisting and Innovation-Producing Organizations, in: The Journal of Business, Vol. 40, No. 4, 1967, pp. 470-477.

Shockley, R. (1981): Perceptions of Auditors' Independence – An Empirical Analysis, in: The Accounting Review, Vol. 56, No. 4, 1981, pp. 785-800.

Siggelkow, N. (2007): Persuasion with Case Studies, in: Academy of Management Journal, Vol. 50, No. 1, 2007, pp. 20-24.

Simon, H. (1976): Administrative Behavior – A Study of Decision-Making Processes in Administrative Organization, 3rd edition, New York 1976.

Simon, H. (1979): Rational Decision Making in Business Organizations, in: American Economic Review, Vol. 69, No. 4, 1979, pp. 493-513.

Simons, R. (1995): Levers of Control – How Managers Use Innovative Control Systems to Drive Strategic Renewal, Boston 1995.

Smith, J. (1984): The Problem of Criteria for Judging Interpretive Inquiry, in: Educational Evaluation and Policy Analysis, Vol. 6, No. 4, 1984, pp. 379-391.

Smith, S./van der Heijden, H. (2017): Analysts' Evaluation of KPI Usefulness, Standardisation and Assurance, in: Journal of Applied Accounting Research, Vol. 18, No. 1, 2017, pp. 63-86.

Solomon, J./Edgley, C. (2008): The Abandoned Mandatory OFR, in: Social Responsibility Journal, Vol. 4, No. 3, 2008, pp. 324-348.

Sopp, K./Baumüller, J. (2017): Die Leitlinien der EU-Kommission für die Berichterstattung über nichtfinanzielle Informationen – Orientierungshilfe ohne Orientierung, in: Zeitschrift für Internationale Rechnungslegung, Vol. 12, No. 9, 2017, pp. 377-383.

Spanheimer, J. (2000): Spezifische Problemfelder des gesetzlichen Standardisierungsauftrages an den DSR gemäß § 342 Abs. 1 Nr. 1 HGB, in: Die Wirtschaftsprüfung, Vol. 53, No. 20, 2000, pp. 997-1007.

Spence, C. (2007): Social and Environmental Reporting and Hegemonic Discourse, in: Accounting, Auditing & Accountability Journal, Vol. 20, No. 6, 2007, pp. 855-882.

Spence, L./Lozano, J. (2000): Communicating about Ethics with Small Firms – Experiences from the U.K. and Spain, in: Journal of Business Ethics, Vol. 27, No. 1-2, 2000, pp. 43-53.

Spence, L./Rinaldi, L. (2014): Governmentality in Accounting and Accountability – A Case Study of Embedding Sustainability in a Supply Chain, in: Accounting, Organizations and Society, Vol. 39, No. 6, 2014, pp. 433-452.

Spicer, B. (1978): Market Risk, Accounting Data and Companies' Pollution Control Records, in: Journal of Business Finance & Accounting, Vol. 5, No. 1, 1978, pp. 67-83.

Spradley, J. (2011): The Ethnographic Interview, Belmont 2011.

Stawinoga, M./Velte, P. (2015): CSR Management and Reporting between Voluntary Bonding and Legal Regulation, in: Problems and Perspectives in Management, Vol. 13, No. 2, 2015, pp. 36-50.

Steinke, I. (1999): Kriterien qualitativer Forschung – Ansätze zur Bewertung qualitativ-empirischer Sozialforschung, Weinheim et al. 1999.

Steinke, I. (2017): Gütekriterien qualitativer Forschung, in: Flick, U./Kardorff, E./Steinke, I. (eds.), Qualitative Forschung – Ein Handbuch, 12th edition, Reinbek 2017, pp. 319-331.

Stoecker, R. (1991): Evaluating and Rethinking the Case Study, in: The Sociological Review, Vol. 39, No. 1, 1991, pp. 88-112.

Stojanović-Blab, M./Blab, D. (2017): Nachhaltigkeitsberichterstattung anhand der GRI Standards, in: Zeitschrift für internationale und kapitalmarktorientierte Rechnungslegung, Vol. 17, No. 7-8, 2017, pp. 307-316.

Stolowy, H./Paugam, L. (2018): The Expansion of Non-financial Reporting, in: Accounting and Business Research, Vol. 48, No. 5, 2018, pp. 525-548.

Strauss, A./Corbin, J. (1996): Grounded Theory – Grundlagen Qualitativer Sozialforschung, Weinheim 1996.

Strübing, J. (2002): Zum Konzept der Herstellung und Sicherung von Qualität in grounded theory-basierten Forschungsarbeiten, in: Kölner Zeitschrift für Soziologie und Sozialpsychologie, Vol. 54, No. 2, 2002, pp. 318-342.

Sustainability Accounting Standards Board (SASB) (2017): SASB Industry Standards – A Field Guide, URL: https://www.sasb.org/wp-content/uploads/2018/09/SASB_FieldGuide-web-080817.pdf (13.03.2019).

T

Tarca, A./Street, D./Aerts, W. (2011): Factors affecting MD&A disclosures by SEC registrants, in: Journal of International Accounting, Auditing and Taxation, Vol. 20, No. 1, 2011, pp. 45-59.

Theisen, M. (2007): Information und Berichterstattung des Aufsichtsrats, 4th edition, Stuttgart 2007.

Thiele, P./Schulze, M./Briem, C. (2015): Umsetzung eines Integrated Reporting – Wie sind die bestehenden Organisationsstrukturen anzupassen?, in: Controller Magazin, Vol. 40, No. 6, 2015, pp. 66-69.

Thomson, I./Bebbington, J. (2005): Social and Environmental Reporting in the UK, in: Critical Perspectives on Accounting, Vol. 16, No. 5, 2005, pp. 507-533.

Tilt, C. (2006): Linking Environmental Activity and Environmental Disclosure in an Organisational Change Framework, in: Journal of Accounting & Organizational Change, Vol. 2, No. 1, 2006, pp. 4-24.

Trinczek, R. (1995): Experteninterviews mit Managern – Methodische und methodologische Hintergründe, in: Brinkmann, C./Deeke, A./Völkel, B. (eds.), Experteninterviews in der Arbeitsmarktforschung, Nürnberg 1995, pp. 59-68.

Trinczek, R. (2009): Wie befrage ich Manager? Methodische und methodologische Aspekte des Experteninterviews als qualitativer Methode empirischer Sozialforschung, in: Bogner, A./Littig, B./Menz, W. (eds.), Experteninterviews – Theorien, Methoden, Anwendungsfelder, 3rd edition, Wiesbaden 2009, pp. 225-238.

Tsai, W. (2002): Social Structure of "Coopetition" Within a Multiunit Organization – Coordination, Competition, and Intraorganizational Knowledge Sharing, in: Organization Science, Vol. 13, No. 2, 2002, pp. 179-190.

U

United Nations Environment Programme (UNEP)/KPMG Advisory N.V./Global Reporting Initiative (GRI)/Unit for Corporate Governance in Africa (2010): Carrots and Sticks – Promoting Transparency and Sustainability, URL: https://www.globalreporting.org/resourcelibrary/Carrots-And-Sticks-Promoting-Transparency-And-Sustainbability.pdf (13.03.2019).

Utterback, J. (1971): The Process of Innovation – A Study of the Origination and Development of Ideas for New Scientific Instruments, in: IEEE Transactions on Engineering Management, Vol. EM-18, No. 4, 1971, pp. 124-131.

V

Van der Stede, W./Chow, C./Lin, T. (2006): Strategy, Choice of Performance Measures, and Performance, in: Behavioral Research in Accounting, Vol. 18, No. 1, 2006, pp. 185-205.

Velte, P./Stawinoga, M. (2016): Prüfung von Nachhaltigkeitsberichten, in: Der Konzern, Vol. 14, No. 1, 2016, pp. 13-19.

Vogel, B. (1995): „Wenn der Eisberg zu schmelzen beginnt …" – Einige Reflexionen über den Stellenwert und die Probleme des Experteninterviews in der Praxis der empirischen Sozialforschung, in: Brinkmann, C./Deeke, A./Völkel, B. (eds.), Experteninterviews in der Arbeitsmarktforschung, Nürnberg 1995, pp. 73-84.

W

Walley, N./Whitehead, B. (1994): It's not easy beeing green, in: Harvard Business Review, Vol. 72, No. 3, 1994, pp. 46-52.

Wallman, S. (1995): The Future of Accounting and Disclosure in an Evolving World – The Need for Dramatic Change, in: Accounting Horizons, Vol. 9, No. 3, 1995, pp. 81-91.

Walter, A. (1998): Der Beziehungspromotor – Ein personaler Gestaltungsansatz für erfolgreiches Relationship Marketing, Wiesbaden 1998.

Walton, J. (1992): Making the Theoretical Case, in: Ragin, C. C./Becker, H. S. (eds.), What is a Case? Exploring the Foundations of Social Inquiry, Cambridge 1992, pp. 121-137.

Weber, J. (1983): Zielorientiertes Rechnungswesen öffentlicher Betriebe, Baden-Baden 1983.

Weber, J./Schäffer, U. (2016): Einführung in das Controlling, 15th edition, Stuttgart 2016.

West, B./Kreuter, F./Jaenichen, U. (2013): "Interviewer" Effects in Face-to-Face Surveys, in: Journal of Official Statistics, Vol. 29, No. 2, 2013, pp. 277-297.

Westermann, U./Merten, T./Grelewitz, I./Gebauer, J. (2009): Status und Tendenzen der Nachhaltigkeitsberichterstattung deutscher KMU, URL: https://www.ioew.de/fileadmin/user_upload/BILDER_und_Downloaddateien/Publikationen/2011/I%C3%96W-future-Ranking_2011_KMU_01.pdf (13.03.2019).

White, A. (2010): The Five Capitals of Integrated Reporting – Toward a Holistic Architecture for Corporate Disclosure, in: Eccles, R. G./Cheng, B./Saltzman, D. (E.) (eds.), The Landscape of Integrated Reporting, Cambridge 2010, pp. 29-32.

Wiechers, K. (2000): Neue Anforderungen bei der Aufstellung und Prüfung des Lageberichts gemäß KonTraG, in: Unternehmenssteuerung und Bilanzen, Vol. 2, No. 3, 2000, pp. 130-136.

Winkeljohann, N./Schäfer, N. (2018): § 289b, in: Grottel, B./Schmidt, S./Schubert, W. J./Winkeljohann, N. (eds.), Beck'scher Bilanz-Kommentar – Handels- und Steuerbilanz §§ 238 bis 339, 342 bis 342e HGB, 11th edition, München 2018, pp. 1522-1533.

Witte, E. (1972): Field Research on Complex Decision-Making Processes – The Phase Theorem, in: International Studies of Management & Organization, Vol. 2, No. 2, 1972, pp. 156-182.

Witte, E. (1973): Organisation für Innovationsentscheidungen – Das Promotoren-Modell, Göttingen 1973.

Witte, E. (1977): Power and Innovation, in: International Studies of Management & Organization, Vol. 7, No. 1, 1977, pp. 47-70.

Witte, E. (1988a): Innovationsfähige Organisation, in: Witte, E./Hauschildt, J./Grün, O. (eds.), Innovative Entscheidungsprozesse, Tübingen 1988, pp. 144-161.

Witte, E. (1988b): Phasen-Theorem und Organisation komplexer Entscheidungsverläufe, in: Witte, E./Hauschildt, J./Grün, O. (eds.), Innovative Entscheidungsprozesse, Tübingen 1988, pp. 202-226.

Wolf, K. (2005): Neuerungen im (Konzern-)Lagebericht durch das Bilanzrechtsreformgesetz (BilReG) – Anforderungen und ihre praktische Umsetzung, in: Deutsches Steuerrecht, Vol. 43, No. 10, 2005, pp. 438-455.

World Commission on Environment and Development (WCED) (1987): Our Common Future – Report of the World Commission on Environment and Development, Oxford 1987.

Wrona, T. (2005): Die Fallstudienanalyse als wissenschaftliche Forschungsmethode, ESCP-EAP Working Paper No. 10, Berlin 2005.

Wrona, T. (2006): Fortschritts- und Gütekriterien im Rahmen qualitativer Sozialforschung, in: Zelewski, S./Akca, N. (eds.), Fortschritt in den Wirtschaftswissenschaften – Wissenschaftstheoretische Grundlagen und exemplarische Anwendung, Wiesbaden 2006, pp. 189-216.

Wrona, T./Gunnesch, M. (2016): The One who Sees More is More Right – How Theory Enhances the 'Repertoire to Interpret' in Qualitative Case Study Research, in: Journal of Business Economics, Vol. 86, No. 7, 2016, pp. 723-749.

Wyatt, A. (2008): What Financial and Non-financial Information on Intangibles is Value-relevant? A Review of the Evidence, in: Accounting and Business Research, Vol. 38, No. 3, 2008, pp. 217-256.

Wysocki, K. (1981): Sozialbilanzen – Inhalt und Formen gesellschaftsbezogener Berichterstattung, Stuttgart 1981.

Y

Yin, R. (2012): Applications of Case Study Research, 3rd edition, Thousand Oaks et al. 2012.

Yin, R. (2018): Case Study Research and Applications – Design and Methods, 6th edition, Thousand Oaks et al. 2018.

Yin, R./Davis, D. (2007): Adding New Dimensions to Case Study Evaluations – The Case of Evaluating Comprehensive Reforms, in: Julnes, G./Rog, D. J. (eds.), Informing Federal Policies on Evaluation Methodology, San Fransisco 2007, pp. 75-93.

Z

Zwirner, C./Boecker, C./Busch, J. (2016): IDW EPS 350 – neue Berufsgrundsätze zur Prüfung des Lageberichts, in: Unternehmenssteuerung und Bilanzen, Vol. 18, No. 1, 2016, pp. 411-417.

List of cited laws, regulations, standards and guidelines

Laws and regulations

4th EU-Directive	Fourth Council Directive 78/660/EEC of 25 July, 1978 based on the Article 54 (3) (g) of the Treaty on the annual accounts of certain types of companies.
7th EU-Directive	Seventh Council Directive 83/349/EEC of 13 June, 1983 based on the Article 54 (3) (g) of the Treaty on Consolidated Accounts.
Accounting directive	Directive 2013/34/EU of the European Parliament and of the Council of 26 June, 2013 on the annual financial statements, consolidated financial statements and related reports of certain types of undertakings, amending Directive 2006/43/EC of the European Parliament and of the Council and repealing Council Directives 78/660/EEC and 83/349/EEC
AktG	German Corporation Act as of 6 September, 1965 (BGBl. I p. 1089). Last amended by Article 5 Amendment Act dated 10 May 2016 (BGBl. I p. 1142).
BilReG	Act on the introduction of International Accounting Standards and the protection of the quality of audits (German Accounting Law Reform Act, Bilanzrechtsreformgesetz (BilReG)) of 4 December, 2004.
BiRiLiG	Act implementing the Fourth, Seventh and Eighth Directives of the European Council for the coordination of company law (Accounting Directives Act, Bilanzrichtlinien-Gesetz (BiRiLiG)) of 19 December, 1985.
BT-Drucksache 10/317	Draft law to implement the Fourth Directive of the Council of the European Communities on the coordination of company law (Accounting Directive) with explanatory memorandum – Bundestag printed matter 10/317 of 26 August, 1983.
BT-Drucksache 15/3419	Draft law for the introduction of International Accounting Standards and the protection of the quality of audits (German Accounting Law Reform Act, Bilanzrechtsreformgesetz (BilReG)) – Bundestag printed matter 15/3419 of 24 June, 2004.

BT-Drucksache 18/9982	Draft law to strengthen the nonfinancial reporting of companies in their management and group management reports (CSR directive implementation act, CSR-Richtlinieumsetzungsgesetz (CSR-RUG)) – Bundestag printed matter 18/9982 of 17 October, 2016.
CSR directive	Directive 2014/95/EU of the European Parliament and of the Council of 22 October, 2014 amending Directive 2013/34/EU (accounting directive) as regards disclosure of non-financial and diversity information by certain large undertakings and groups.
CSR-RUG	Act to strengthen the nonfinancial reporting of companies in their management and group management reports (CSR Directive Implementation Act, CSR-Richtlinieumsetzungsgesetz (CSR-RUG)) of 10 March, 2017.
HGB	German Commercial Code (Handelsgesetzbuch, HGB) of 10 May, 1897, RGBl. 1897, pp. 219-436, last amended by law on 10 July, 2018, BGbl. I, p. 1102.
Modernization Directive	Directive 2003/51/EC of the European Parliament and Council of 18 June, 2003 amending Directives 78/660/EEC, 83/349/EEC, 86/635/EEC and 91/674/EEC on the annual and consolidated accounts of certain types of companies, banks and other financial institutions and insurance undertakings.
SEC-Release 33-6835	Securities and Exchange Commission (SEC) Release 33-6835 "SEC Interpretation: Management's Discussion and Analysis of Financial Condition and Results of Operations; Certain Investment Company Disclosures", of 18 May, 1989.

Standards and guidelines

AA1000AS	AccountAbility 1000 Assurance Standard 2008, URL: https://www.accountability.org/wp-content/uploads/2016/10/AA1000AS_english.pdf (13.03.2019).
GAAS 5	German Amendment Accounting Standard No. 5 (GAAS 5) (Deutscher Rechnungslegungs Änderungsstandard (DRÄS) Nr. 5), adopted by the Accounting Standards Committee of Germany (ASCG) on 5 January, 2010, published by the Federal Ministry of Justice (FMJ) on 18 February, 2010.

GAS 5	German Accounting Standard No. 5 (GAS 5) "Risk Reporting", adopted by the Accounting Standards Committee of Germany (ASCG) on 3 April, 2001, published by the Federal Ministry of Justice (FMJ) on 29 May, 2001. Last revised by the ASCG on 5 January, 2010, published by the FMJ on 18 February, 2010. Replaced by GAS 20 on 4 December, 2012.
GAS 15	German Accounting Standard No. 15 (GAS 15) "Management Reporting", adopted by the Accounting Standards Committee of Germany (ASCG) on 7 December, 2004, published by the Federal Ministry of Justice (FMJ) on 26 February, 2005. Last revised by the ASCG on 5 January, 2010, published by the FMJ on 18 February, 2010. Replaced by GAS 20 on 4 December, 2012.
GAS 20	German Accounting Standard No. 20 (GAS 20) "Group Management Report", adopted by the Accounting Standards Committee of Germany (ASCG) on 2 November, 2012, published by the Federal Ministry of Justice (FMJ) on 4 December, 2012. Last revised by the ASCG on 22 September 2017, published by the Federal Ministry of Justice and Consumer Protection on 4 December, 2017.
GRI G4	G4 "Sustainability Reporting Guidelines", issued by the Global Reporting Initiative (GRI), Amsterdam 2015, URL: https://www.globalreporting.org/resource library/G4-Package.zip (13.03.2019).
GRI Standards 101	Global Reporting Initiative (GRI) Standards 101 "Foundation", issued by the Global Reporting Initiative (GRI), Amsterdam 2016, URL: https://www.globalreporting.org/standards/gri-standards-download-center/ (13.03.2019).
GRI Standards 102	Global Reporting Initiative (GRI) Standards 102 "General Disclosures", issued by the Global Reporting Initiative (GRI), Amsterdam 2016, URL: https://www.globalreporting.org/standards/gri-standards-download-center/ (13.03.2019).

GRI Standards 103	Global Reporting Initiative (GRI) Standards 103 "Management Approach", issued by the Global Reporting Initiative (GRI) Amsterdam, 2016, URL: https://www.globalreporting.org/standards/gri-standards-download-center/ (13.03.2019).
IAS 1	International Accounting Standard (IAS) 1 "Presentation of Financial Statements", issued by the International Accounting Standards Board (IASB), London, 2018.
IDW EPS 350	Entwurf einer Neufassung des Institut der Wirtschaftsprüfer in Deutschland e.V. (IDW) Prüfungsstandards: Prüfung des Lageberichts im Rahmen der Abschlussprüfung (IDW PS 350 n.F.), issued by the main committee on 6 September, 2006, changes as a result of the Accounting Law Modernization Act issued by the main committee on 9 September, 2009. Draft for a revised version prepared by the work group "Management report assurance", issued by the main committee on 13 January, 2016.
IDW PS 350 n. F.	Institut der Wirtschaftsprüfer in Deutschland e.V. (IDW) Prüfungsstandard: Prüfung des Lageberichts im Rahmen der Abschlussprüfung (IDW PS 350 n.F.), issued by the main committee on 6 September, 2006, changes as a result of the Accounting Law Modernization Act issued by the main committee on 9 September, 2009. Revised version issued by the main committee on 12 December, 2017.
IDW PS 821	Institut der Wirtschaftsprüfer in Deutschland e.V. (IDW) Prüfungsstandard 821: Grundsätze ordnungsmäßiger Prüfung oder prüferischer Durchsicht von Berichten im Bereich der Nachhaltigkeit (IDW PS 821), issued by the main committee on 6 September, 2006.
ISAE 3000 (Revised)	International Standard on Assurance Engagements (ISAE) 3000 (Revised): Assurance Engagements Other than Audits or Reviews of Historical Financial Information (ISAE 3000 (Revised)), published by the International Auditing and Assurance Standards Board (IAASB) on 9 December, 2013.

Münsteraner Schriften zur Internationalen Unternehmensrechnung

Herausgegeben von Peter Kajüter

Band 1 Daniela Barth: Prognoseberichterstattung. Praxis, Determinanten und Kapitalmarktwirkungen bei deutschen börsennotierten Unternehmen. 2009.

Band 2 Tobias Dickmann: Controllingintegration nach M&A-Transaktionen. Eine empirische Analyse. 2010.

Band 3 Simon Esser: Produktorientiertes Kostenmanagement in der chemischen Industrie. Eine empirische Analyse. 2011.

Band 4 Christian Reisloh: Influence of National Culture on IFRS Practice. An Empirical Study in France, Germany and the United Kingdom. 2011.

Band 5 Matthias Moeschler: Cost Accounting in Germany and Japan. A Comparative Analysis. 2012.

Band 6 Martin Merschdorf: Der Management Approach in der IFRS-Rechnungslegung. Implikationen für Unternehmen und Investoren. 2012.

Band 7 Kristian Bachert: Fair Value Accounting. Implications for Users of Financial Statements. 2012.

Band 8 Daniel Blaesing: Nachhaltigkeitsberichterstattung in Deutschland und den USA. Berichtspraxis, Determinanten und Eigenkapitalkostenwirkungen. 2013.

Band 9 Christina Voets: Kulturelle Einflüsse auf die Anwendung des Impairment-Tests nach IAS 36. Eine experimentelle Untersuchung in Asien und Europa. 2013.

Band 10 Thomas Poplat: Foreign Investments in BRIC Countries. Empirical Evidence from Multinational Corporations. 2014.

Band 11 Moritz Schröder: Cost Accounting in Anglophone Subsidiaries. Empirical Evidence from Germany. 2014.

Band 12 Maximilian Saucke: Full IFRS and IFRS for SMEs Adoption by Private Firms. Empirical Evidence on Country Level. 2015.

Band 13 Martin Nienhaus: Segment Reporting under IFRS 8. Reporting Practice and Economic Consequences. 2015.

Band 14 Gregor Hagemann: Financial Reporting Quality in Emerging Economies. Empirical Evidence from Brazil and South Africa. 2017.

Band 15 Stefan Hannen: Integrated Reporting. Useful for investors? 2017.

Band 16 Alexander Schulz: Cost Accounting in German Multinational Companies. An Empirical Analysis. 2018.

Band 17 Daniela Peters: Synergy and Goodwill Controlling. Empirical Evidence on Determinants and Acquisition Performance. 2019.

Band 18 Matthias Nienaber: Preparation Processes of Nonfinancial KPIs for Management Reports. Empirical Evidence on Process Design and Determinants. 2020.

www.ingramcontent.com/pod-product-compliance
Ingram Content Group UK Ltd.
Pitfield, Milton Keynes, MK11 3LW, UK
UKHW020834290926
15470UKWH00004B/1334

9 783631 802793